A TASTE FOR WRITING
COMPOSITION FOR CULINARIANS

VIVIAN C. CADBURY

A TASTE FOR WRITING
COMPOSITION FOR CULINARIANS

SECOND EDITION

VIVIAN C. CADBURY

ASSOCIATE PROFESSOR
THE CULINARY INSTITUTE OF AMERICA

CENGAGE
Learning®

Australia · Brazil · Japan · Korea · Mexico · Singapore · Spain · United Kingdom · United States

CENGAGE
Learning·

A Taste for Writing: Composition for Culinarians, Second Edition
by Vivian C. Cadbury

Senior Vice President, GM Skills & Product Planning: Dawn Gerrain

Senior Product Manager: Jim Gish

Senior Director, Development: Marah Bellegarde

Senior Product Development Manager: Larry Main

Senior Content Developer: Anne Orgren

Product Assistant: Sarah Timm-Barker

Marketing Manager: Scott Chrysler

Senior Production Director: Wendy Troeger

Production Manager: Mark Bernard

Senior Content Project Manager: Glenn Castle

Senior Art Director: Bethany Casey

Media Developer: Debbie Bordeaux

Cover image(s): Fork and Knife image: ©iStockPhoto.com/linearcurves

Typography: Copyright © 2015 Cengage Learning®.

For product information and technology assistance, contact us at
Cengage Learning Customer & Sales Support, 1-800-354-9706

For permission to use material from this text or product, submit all requests online at **www.cengage.com/permissions**. Further permissions questions can be e-mailed to **permissionrequest@cengage.com**

Library of Congress Control Number: 2013956752

ISBN-13: 978-1-1332-7791-0

Cengage Learning
200 First Stamford Place, 4th Floor
Stamford, CT 06902
USA

Cengage Learning is a leading provider of customized learning solutions with office locations around the globe, including Singapore, the United Kingdom, Australia, Mexico, Brazil, and Japan. Locate your local office at: **www.cengage.com/global**

Cengage Learning products are represented in Canada by Nelson Education, Ltd.

To learn more about Cengage Learning, visit **www.cengage.com** Purchase any of our products at your local college store or at our preferred online store **www.cengagebrain.com**

Printed in the United States of America
1 2 3 4 5 6 7 17 16 15 14

CONTENTS

APPENDICES

PREFACE

A Taste for Writing offers comprehensive coverage of topics in composition and grammar with a special interest in the analogy between writing and cooking. Imagine that you are going to cook potatoes, say a particularly elegant dish of creamy whipped mashed potatoes. Perhaps a few glistening rivulets of butter slip down the white slope of potato. When you slide your fork in, you leave an imprint, a ridge, like the crest of a meringue. You know there is no resemblance between the raw potatoes you begin with and that creamy swirl of goodness, yet you don't experience a moment of anxiety. Your focus is on a series of familiar steps rather than on what those steps are expected to produce. You have learned to have confidence in the *process*.

This book looks at writing from a similar perspective. Although you know that you need to end up with an essay or letter or report, you also know that it doesn't happen all at once; there are steps to go through and transformations that must take place. You may begin the process with a brainstormed list of ideas or a page of freewriting that bears no resemblance to the finished piece of writing, just as the unwashed raw potato bears no resemblance to a mound of creamy whipped mashed potatoes on a beautiful china plate. Then, through a series of physical and chemical transformations, both the raw potatoes and the raw ideas are "cooked" to perfection.

The culinary connection extends into the book's visual components as well. Many of the photographs and illustrations have food-related subjects, from chefs at work in the kitchen to front-of-the-house staff seating and serving their guests to the delicious food items themselves. The photographs include scenes from such popular films as *Ratatouille* and *Julie & Julia*, while the illustrations capture moments from *Kitchen Confidential* and *Chocolat*. In another interesting connection, the drawings were created by Rafael Hernandez, a working chef who's also a working cartoonist.

The photographs and illustrations also support another of the book's motifs—the value of storytelling. These images include stills from such favorites as *Harry Potter and the Sorcerer's Stone*, *The Blind Side*, and *The Hunger Games*, as well as from the television miniseries *Band of Brothers* and the original *Star Trek*. The illustrations represent such magical stories as *The Wizard of Oz* and *Star Wars*; literary classics like Chaucer's *Canterbury Tales*, Shakespeare's *Hamlet*, Hemingway's "A Clean, Well-Lighted Place," and Edgar Allan Poe's "The Raven"; and newer works like *Terminator 2: Judgment Day* and *The Girl with the Dragon Tattoo*.

This book encourages its audience to develop a taste for reading as well as for writing. Selections from the work of both student and professional writers, which exemplify points of composition in each chapter, are often food-related, from dining on Flying

Squirrel Noodles in Thailand and Bacalao in Alaska to cooking snails for a classical French chef and tasting chocolates for an English teacher, from the smell of coffee to the first taste of vichyssoise to a gargantuan mouthful of sandwich. Herman Melville offers a savory chowder from *Moby-Dick*, while Winnie-the-Pooh's A. A. Milne discourses on the glories of celery. "Tortillas," by artist, poet, and community leader José Antonio Burciaga, is a special gift, while five poems depict the ordinary activities of catching a fish, digging potatoes, picking blackberries, baking bread, and drinking a Coke in vivid and evocative detail.

As a classroom text, *A Taste for Writing* provides material for lecture and discussion and for independent reading, as well as activities, readings, and written assignments designed to help students understand concepts and practice skills. Instructors may follow the order of chapters as presented or devise a sequence that better suits their needs. For example, some chapters may be more appropriate as reference material, while others may be omitted altogether, according to the purpose and scope of the course. The instructor's manual offers a fuller discussion of these options and of ways to raise or lower the level of difficulty of the exercises and assignments. *A Taste for Writing* can be used in a high school or college course or as a reference book. Ultimately, it's meant for anyone who likes food and wants (or needs) to write.

NEW TO THE SECOND EDITION

The second edition of *A Taste for Writing* has been reorganized into three comprehensive units: Process, Patterns, and Presentation. The first unit breaks down the process of writing into more detail, including new chapters on developing ideas; planning your writing; working with paragraphs; reading various kinds of texts, including your own; and improving sentence fluency. The second unit begins with another new chapter, Finding Your Voice, while the chapters on persuasion and analysis have been extensively rewritten. The third unit gathers chapters on grammar and punctuation, with attention paid to clarifying the explanations and updating the exercises and illustrations.

New samples of both student and professional writing have been interwoven throughout the text of the second edition, with full-length essays at the end of the first seventeen chapters in a section called A Taste for Reading. The menu of inviting selections includes essays by seasoned food writers like John Thorne, Irena Chalmers, Tim Hayward, Monica Bhide, and Dara Moskowitz Grumdahl, as well as poems by award-winners Elizabeth Bishop, Martín Espada, Seamus Heaney, Yusef Komunyakaa, and Sharon Olds. The owners of the Canal House share a recipe for warm savoy cabbage salad, while a doctor weighs in on the intriguing similarities between chefs and surgeons. New samples of student writing, as well as favorites from the first edition, recount personal food experiences, argue for a sustainable approach to offal, and engage readers in literary analysis.

As part of the freshly updated design, the seventy new color photographs and fifty custom-drawn black-and-white illustrations give the book an appealing, modern look, while at the same time illustrating the concepts of the text. The vibrant color-coding of the chapter elements makes it easy to find exercises, review material, reading selections, and ideas for writing.

New teaching and learning resources—including a text-specific CourseMate website and an instructor companion website with revised instructor's manual, test bank, and lecture presentations—are available to support the second edition.

ORGANIZATION OF THE BOOK

PROCESS: CHAPTERS 1–9

The first nine chapters examine the processes of reading and writing in detail. Chapter 1, "Cooking Up Communication," summarizes the relationship between the writer, reader, purpose, text, and context using the famous "make my day" diner scene from Clint Eastwood's *Sudden Impact*. Chapter 2 offers a "recipe" for reading, including reading to revise your own writing. Chapter 3 reviews the writing process (often a messy affair, like peeling potatoes) and addresses what many writers find most difficult—getting started. Chapter 4 reviews different methods of developing ideas sometimes called "rhetorical modes." Chapters 5 and 6 offer guidance about planning and revising your writing, with special attention to paragraphs and transitions. Chapter 7 examines the framework of writing, the introduction and conclusion. Chapter 8 provides explanations and exercises on improving sentence fluency, while Chapter 9 looks at revising individual words.

PATTERNS: CHAPTERS 10–19

This unit begins with a chapter new to the second edition, "Finding Your Voice," which helps readers analyze the components of a writer's "voice," develop their own voices, and appreciate the role of voice in a personal essay. The remaining chapters expand on the modes or ways of developing an idea introduced in Chapter 4: narration (11), description (12), compare and contrast (13), process (14), and exemplification, definition, and cause and effect (15). Chapter 16 discusses strategies for persuasive writing, including accessible approaches to the Aristotelian concepts of *logos*, *ethos*, and *pathos*. Chapter 17 addresses skills needed to write about literature, including performing a close reading, planning a critical analysis essay, and using textual evidence.

Chapters 18 and 19 provide an introduction to research principles and methods, from finding and evaluating sources (18) to incorporating their information appropriately in your own writing (19). Chapter 19 also provides updated information about MLA (7th edition) and APA (6th edition) formats. A full-length annotated student research paper in MLA format appears in Appendix D.

PRESENTATION: CHAPTERS 20–31

This unit covers basic grammar and punctuation with a view toward improving editing and proofreading skills. Chapter 20 reviews the parts of speech, while Chapter 21 addresses basic sentence structure. The next three chapters examine common grammatical issues: sentence fragments (22), run-on sentences and comma splices (23), and subject–verb agreement (24). Chapter 25 explores additional aspects of verbs, one of the more complex parts of speech, followed by chapters on pronouns (26) and modifiers (27). Chapter 28 lays out the principles of parallel structure.

The final three chapters address aspects of proofreading, that is, checking the correctness of the spelling and punctuation. Chapter 29 outlines the importance of and process of proofreading, as well as providing information on spelling and commonly misused words. Chapters 30 and 31 review punctuation, with emphasis on the complexities of the comma.

APPENDICES

The four appendices include Spelling of Selected Culinary Terms, Commonly Misused Words, and an Annotated Research Paper. New to this edition, Types of Writing offers advice on composition in a variety of genres, including the basics of business writing.

SPECIAL FEATURES

CHAPTER EXERCISES AND ACTIVITIES

Each chapter features exercises designed to help students practice the concepts and skills presented in the text and concludes with a summary of its main points, Recipe for Review. The exercises may be used for group or individual work, in or out of class. Most of the exercises in Units 1 and 2 are found at the end of the chapter so as not to disrupt the flow of ideas. In Unit 3 the exercises are sprinkled through the text of each chapter in order that readers may practice each individual skill immediately. Unit 3 chapters also include a comprehensive quiz.

Units 1 and 2 (Process and Patterns) include full-length essays and poems at the end of each chapter under the heading A Taste for Reading. Questions about the reading follow each piece, while teaching ideas and additional questions and exercises about the reading are included in the instructor's manual. These two units also include Ideas for Writing, lists of topics connected to the chapter content that can be assigned as journal entries or polished into essays.

PROFESSIONAL AND STUDENT WRITING SAMPLES

Readers of the first edition of A Taste for Writing asked for additional models of professional writing, included here both as full-length, free-standing pieces and as shorter samples within the text. (See New to the Second Edition earlier in the Preface.) Both professional and student writing is featured in A Taste for Reading at the end of Chapters 1–17, and each of these pieces is followed by questions about the reading that promote comprehension and reinforce chapter content.

The book's student writing comes from young men and women who attended the Culinary Institute of America between 2001 and 2013. These writers did not intend their essays for publication but were simply completing a class assignment. Some essays were written over a period of days or weeks, while others were composed in a testing situation within a time limit of ninety minutes. While I have edited the essays slightly, I do not present them as "perfect" but rather as "tasty": they are included to exemplify a particular point of composition, such as using sensory details or tying the conclusion to the introduction, and especially to model open and engaging communication.

I have also used student writing as the basis for some of the grammar chapter quizzes. Students will correct the grammar and word usage of texts written by their peers rather than by a teacher. In order to provide this more genuine, inviting environment for practice, I received permission from the writers to introduce specific types of errors—sentence fragments, for example—into their texts. I owe a special thank you to these students for allowing me to do so!

SUPPLEMENTARY MATERIALS

CourseMate CULINARY COURSEMATE

Culinary CourseMate is available with this text and includes

- an interactive eBook, with highlighting, note-taking, and search capabilities
- interactive learning tools, including quizzes, flashcards, games, and additional exercises.

CourseMate

Go to cengagebrain.com to access these resources, and look for this icon to find resources related to this text in Culinary CourseMate.

INSTRUCTOR COMPANION WEBSITE

The instructor companion website for this text, available at login.cengage.com, contains a revised instructor's manual, test bank, and lecture slides.

The instructor's manual explains the philosophy behind this textbook and offers both general suggestions for teaching and specific hints and supplemental activities for each chapter. In addition, the manual provides options for a course syllabus and outlines methods of assessing students' achievement on individual papers and progress in the course. The manual describes approaches to journal writing and peer review, while appendices contain reproducible handouts related to revision and editing.

The manual then provides an overview of each chapter, noting especially any successes or challenges this author has encountered in teaching the material. Ideas for classroom activities include questions for discussion, often based on readings from this book or on specific film clips; topics for supplementary reading and research; and suggestions for group activities, including the use of manipulatives. Finally, the manual offers useful notes on the figures in the text, as well as answer keys for and comments on the chapter exercises.

ACKNOWLEDGEMENTS

In reflecting on all who helped make this book possible, I think first of my own early teachers: Florence Stein at the William H. Ray School in Chicago, Dick Mullen and David Bourns at Oakwood Friends School in Poughkeepsie, and from the University of Illinois at Chicago, Moreen Jordan, Dan Lindley, Mary Carruthers, and Gloria G. Fromm. I also want to acknowledge my students, who have taught me a great deal about teaching and writing over the years, and especially those at the Culinary Institute of America, many of whom generously contributed their work here.

I am enormously appreciative of the support of present and former colleagues at the Culinary Institute of America, including John Ahern, Bonnie Bogush, Leigha Butler, Anthony Chando, Raimundo Gaby, Anne Henry, Richard Horvath, Vincenzo Lauria, Claire Mathey, Amanda Vladick, Adam Williams, and Stephen Wilson. A special acknowledgement is owed to Marjorie Livingston, who suggested the title *A Taste for Writing*, and to Tim Ryan, who proposed the term *Culinarians*. I am indebted to Sharon Zraly, Kathy Merget, and Denise Bauer for their initial encouragement and to Sue Cussen, Nathalie Fischer, and Bruce Hillenbrand for their guidance with the first edition.

I am profoundly grateful to those at Cengage Learning who believed in *A Taste for Writing*, particularly Jim Gish, Sandy Clark, and Kristin McNary. Many, many thanks are due to Nicole Calisi and Anne Orgren, my patient project managers, to Alexandra Ricciardi for her invaluable assistance with permissions, and to Bethany Casey, whose design brought the book to life, as well as to Glenn Castle, Sarah Timm, and the rest of the Cengage team.

The marvelous illustrations were created for this edition by Rafael Hernandez, and I'm delighted with the playful energy they bring to the text. Rafael was born in Puerto Rico, raised half there, half in the Bronx, and has been drawing since early childhood. A digital art hobbyist and freelance artist, he is also a culinary graduate and professional cook. Rafael lives in Ohio with his wife Sarah and their two children.

For permission to reprint their wonderful essays and poems, I gratefully acknowledge the following: "A Question of Taste: It's Not Easy Accepting Who Gets to Lick the Spoon" by Monica Bhide. Copyright © 2005 by Monica Bhide. Used by permission of the author. Excerpt from *Kitchen Confidential: Adventures in the Culinary Underbelly* by Anthony Bourdain. Copyright © 2000 by Anthony Bourdain. Reprinted by permission of Bloomsbury USA. "Tortillas" by José Antonio Burciaga. Originally titled "I Remember Masa" and published in *Weedee Peepo*, 1988. Courtesy of University of

Texas – Pan American Press. "The Fish" from THE COMPLETE POEMS 1927–1979 by Elizabeth Bishop. Copyright © 1979, 1983 by Alice Helen Methfessel. Reprinted by permission of Farrar, Straus and Giroux, LLC. Introduction to *Food Jobs: 150 Great Jobs for Culinary Students, Career Changers and Food Lovers* by Irena Chalmers. Copyright © 2008 by Irena Chalmers. Used by permission of the author. "Everyone's a Critic" by Ike DeLorenzo. Published in *The Boston Globe*, June 2, 2010. Used by permission of the author. "Beyond Clogs, and White Coats" by Karen M. Devon, MD. Originally published as "The chef and surgeon have much in common" at *KevinMD.com*, November 2, 2012. Used by permission of the author. "Coca-Cola and Coco Frio" from CITY OF COUGHING AND DEAD RADIATORS by Martín Espada. Copyright © 1993 by Martín Espada. Used by permission of W. W. Norton & Company, Inc. Excerpts from Maxine Hairston's "Not All Errors Are Created Equal" from *College English* 43.8 (1981): 794-806. Copyright 1981 by the National Council of Teachers of English. Reprinted with permission. "Too Much of a Mouthful" by Tim Hayward. Copyright Guardian News & Media Ltd 2009. Used by permission. "Digging" from OPENED GROUND: SELECTED POEMS 1966–1996 by Seamus Heaney. Copyright © 1998 by Seamus Heaney. Reprinted by permission of Farrar, Straus and Giroux, LLC, and of Faber and Faber Ltd. "Warm Savoy Cabbage Salad" from *Canal House Cooking, Volume No. 5* by Christopher Hirsheimer & Melissa Hamilton. Copyright © 2010 by Christopher Hirsheimer & Melissa Hamilton. Used by permission. "Blackberries" from *Pleasure Dome: New and Selected Poems* © 2001 by Yusef Komunyakaa. Reprinted by permission of Wesleyan University Press. "How to Address Obesity in a Fat-Phobic Society" by Courtney E. Martin. Used by permission of the author. "Smell the Coffee" by Dara Moskowitz Grumdahl. First published in *City Pages*, a Voice Media Group publication, October 27, 1999. Used by permission. "Bread" from THE DEAD & THE LIVING by Sharon Olds, copyright © 1977 by Sharon Olds. Used by permission of Alfred A. Knopf, an imprint of the Knopf Doubleday Publishing Group, a division of Random House LLC. All rights reserved. "The Cadence of Great Writing" by Sean Savoie. Used by permission of the author. "One Knife, One Pot" from POT ON THE FIRE: FURTHER CONFESSIONS OF A RENEGADE COOK by John Thorne. Copyright © 1999, 2000 by John Thorne. This version as originally printed in Gourmet magazine. Reprinted by permission of North Point Press, a division of Farrar, Straus and Giroux, LLC. I am also indebted to Sara Bogush, Phillip Lopate, Kate Posey, Dr. Christos Vasilikiotis, and the Greenpeace Environmental Trust for permission to quote from their work.

In writing the second edition, I have once again been blessed by the support and encouragement of friends and family, particularly my mother's. Thank you!

Vivian C. Cadbury
August 2013

The author and Cengage Learning would like to thank the following reviewers:

For the second edition: Michele Bush, Western Maricopa Education Center, Glendale, Arizona; Grady Noland, Louisiana Culinary Institute, Baton Rouge; David Blackmon, Chicago Public Schools; and Richard Horvath, The Culinary Institute of America, Hyde Park, NY.

For the first edition: Michael F. Courteau, The Art Institutes International Minnesota (Minneapolis); Jo Nell Farrar, San Jacinto College Central, Pasadena, TX; Stephen C. Fernald, Lake Tahoe Community College, South Lake Tahoe, CA; Richard Horvath, The Culinary Institute of America, Hyde Park, NY; Nancy McGee, Macomb Community College, Warren, MI; John Miller, The Art Institute of New York City, New York, NY; James W. Paul II, MS, CCE, FMP, University of Nebraska at Kearney; Laima Rastenis, Cooking and Hospitality Institute of Chicago; Wayne Smith, Mesa State College, Grand Junction, CO; Lance Sparks, Lane Community College, Eugene, OR; Jorge de la Torre, Johnson & Wales University, Denver, CO; and Sharon Zraly, The Culinary Institute of America, Hyde Park, NY.

ABOUT THE AUTHOR

Vivian C. Cadbury has over twenty years' experience as an instructor at both the high school and college levels. In 2001 she began teaching at the Culinary Institute of America, where—not surprisingly—her students shared an intense passion for food. What *was* surprising were the rich connections between cooking and writing: finding the freshest raw ideas and cooking them up into an essay, seasoning with the right words and "plating" with punctuation. Exploring these connections, both literally and metaphorically, proved effective in the classroom and led to the writing of this book, first published in 2007.

In addition, the author has presented at national conferences, including the Conference on College Composition and Communication (2004, 2007, 2011), the National Association for Developmental Education (2008), and the Association for Career and Technical Education (2012). In 2008 the author's poster presentation on *A Taste for Writing* won the People's Choice Award at the Food Educators' Network International (FENI) Annual Summit. At the 2009 FENI Summit, she conducted a half-day workshop on teaching writing, led a roundtable discussion on improving study skills, and was one of six panelists addressing current trends in culinary education.

Professor Cadbury earned a bachelor's degree in English from the University of Illinois at Chicago (UIC) and completed the requirements for certification in grades 7–12. During her student teaching at Lane Technical High School in Chicago, she was interviewed with her class on Studs Terkel's radio program, which can be heard over the Internet at *Studs Terkel: Conversations with America.* As a graduate student at UIC, she specialized in the teaching of English and composition before completing her master's degree in English literature. She also studied for two years at Oxford University in England.

INTRODUCTION: RECIPE FOR WRITING

Food has never been more popular in the United States than now in the twenty-first century, and neither has food writing. The number of students in culinary programs continues to grow, along with the country's appetite for cookbooks and restaurant reviews, articles on nutrition or sustainability, and stories about satisfying hungers both physical and emotional.

Written communication is addressed to a particular audience for a particular purpose and, to be effective, is written in a style appropriate to both. In this way it can be compared to preparing and serving food. Particular eaters have particular purposes for eating, for example, to fill up, to get a healthy diet, to celebrate a special occasion. Various types of restaurants are designed to serve these purposes: the fast food restaurant, the family-style diner, the fine dining establishment. Writing, too, takes various forms, such as stories, letters, and essays. Further, just as we sometimes cook just for ourselves, we sometimes write for ourselves alone—perhaps in a journal, perhaps in a letter we didn't intend to mail.

> Writing is a therapy. It's a way to take things out of your system. Watching those thoughts come out of your brain and onto a piece of paper is like taking a shower and feeling all the dirt wash away. Once I was really mad at someone who had hurt me badly, so I grabbed a piece of paper and a pen and started writing, nothing grammatically correct, just swearing on a blank sheet. When I finished, I went to the kitchen, turned the stove on, and set the paper on fire to let it burn. I felt so good afterwards without having to talk to anyone. Writing is great therapy.
>
> —**Gerardo Vela Meza**, student writer

Writing is also a way of thinking. Writing doesn't just *record* our thoughts—it actually stimulates *new* ideas and insights.

> "Writing is thinking" means to me that we go through a whole thinking process as we write about something. If we pick any topic we want to extend our thinking about, we should just start writing about it. We can find ourselves with whole new ideas about it when we are done writing. Writing can take us places we don't expect to go. If we are having a

hard time thinking about something, we should start writing about it. As we write, we can encounter our most deep and hidden thoughts about the topic. We can realize things we never thought out brains held.

—**Idan Bitton**, student writer

Writing can reflect and develop our thoughts, and it can communicate those thoughts to others. Writing can also be a form of therapy or entertainment. But it isn't easy. Although we may have plenty of ideas, we can't always get them down on paper. Sometimes we have no ideas at all and stare helplessly at a blank sheet, unable to write a single word. In this book we will look at techniques intended to help with these very problems—how to find out what we think and how to write it clearly. Our skills will improve with experience and coaching, and ideally our self-assurance will grow as well. In the following journal excerpt, a student notes a change in her attitude.

Looking back to my past classes, I never enjoyed writing because I thought I could never hear my own voice. But now with all this practice, I am able to write a paper on whatever subject with confidence and pride. I know how to proofread it and what errors I am looking for, and I can correct them without doubting myself.

—**Astrid Sierra**, student writer

It looks like this cook has developed a taste
for writing.

"I could never hear my own voice," she writes. No wonder she had no taste for writing! With practice, however, she begins to feel "confidence and pride" in her papers, just as she has felt confidence and pride in her cooking.

This textbook was designed for culinarians, for those who take pride in the kitchen and its processes. And, surprisingly, the process of cooking has some intriguing parallels with the process of writing.[1] Both cooking and writing take certain ingredients and turn them into something new. Both can be messy at times, with pots and potato peels piling up in the sink, or reams of rough drafts littering the desk. One culinary student had this to say about the similarities between writing and cooking:

> These similarities include the need to pay acute attention to detail, the certainty that only hard work will result in assured success, the need to train, study, practice, and do research, and the importance of being able to work under pressure. Other somewhat more subtle similarities exist: both pursuits involve simplicity of tools and equipment, both rely on a foundation of tradition passed along through literature, and both are vitally dependent on criticism. . . . To be successful, the professional cook and the professional writer must acknowledge [their rich] traditions while striving to be creative, thereby standing out in similarly competitive fields of endeavor.
>
> —**Robert A. Hannon**, student writer

This book asks its readers to "train, study, [and] practice" and to be open, thoughtful, and creative in putting their ideas on paper. I am very proud of the students who have done just that, some of whose writing appears in these pages. Whether or not these culinarians enjoyed the composition process, they learned to appreciate its difficulties and, usually, its rewards. They developed a taste for writing.

SAVORY · GARLICKY · NUT...
FRUITY · GINGERY · LEMONY · CHOCOLA...
TART · SALTY · LEMONY · TART · JUICY · SAVO...
BRINY · SALTY · FRUITY · TART · JUICY · GINGERY · GA...
BITTER · FRUITY · SUGARY · TANGY · ...ALTY
HONEYED · BITTER · ...CKISH · ...OOMY · SUGARY · TANGY
...KY · HONEYED

UNIT 1
PROCESS

CHAPTER 1
COOKING UP COMMUNICATION

By the end of this chapter, you should begin to . . .

- think about what makes communication effective;
- recognize the parts of communication and the impact of time and place in shaping it;
- identify one or more purposes for writing;
- explore the relationship between speaking and writing; and
- think about what makes writing effective.

Communication is about sharing your thoughts and feelings with someone else, trying to move an idea from your brain into another's. Writing is one type of communication, but it is not the only kind, nor is it necessarily the most effective kind for every situation. *Effective* communication requires taking into account the audience, time and place, and purpose for communicating, and choosing a method accordingly. Depending on these factors, we might choose to communicate in one or more of the following ways: pictures, diagrams, body language, facial expressions, painting, sculpture, music, speech, writing, or, in some cases, food.

A CUP OF COFFEE

A dramatic example of the need to communicate effectively occurs in *Sudden Impact*, the fourth film in the series about Dirty Harry Callahan, the outspoken, rule-bending San Francisco detective played by Clint Eastwood. A judge has just reprimanded Harry for searching a car without a proper warrant, and the case has been dismissed. Filled with indignation, Harry heads for his favorite diner to get a cup of coffee. He's looking down at his newspaper as he enters the diner and doesn't notice the uneasy expressions on the faces of the waitress, the cook, and some of the customers—though we in the audience see them. As he remains absorbed in the paper, the waitress, Loretta, puts the coffee cup on the counter and begins to pour in sugar from the glass jar. She pours and she pours, all the time glancing nervously up at Harry and then around the diner.

Figure 1.1 Loretta sends a message through the cup of coffee.

On and on she pours, while the audience begins to chuckle and Harry remains oblivious (Figure 1.1). Finally she stops, and Harry takes the cup and walks out the door. Still reading the paper, he takes a few steps, sips the coffee—and spits it out. He looks back at the door of the café, and someone inside turns the "Open" sign to "Closed."

As it turns out, there is a robbery in progress in the diner, and Harry has gone in and out again without noticing a thing. But the coffee gets his attention. Without saying a word, and without attracting the attention of the three men holding the customers at gunpoint, Loretta has communicated very effectively. Harry understands the message and returns to the diner to stop the robbery. And when Harry stares down the barrel of the gun, the suspect understands that Harry will shoot. He doesn't even need to hear the famous lines. The expression on Clint Eastwood's face speaks more clearly than his verbal command. The coffee wasn't telepathic, but people are clever and effective communicators without words.

Communication can literally be a matter of life and death. Had Loretta not been able to communicate successfully with Callahan, the scene in the diner would have ended differently—with a robbery, certainly, and perhaps with the loss of civilian lives. Let's consider *why* Loretta's communication was successful. She had a purpose for communicating, one that she cared about, and she knew something about her audience. She was also aware of the time, that is, the urgent need to get her message across immediately, and of the place, the diner. So she chose a *form* of communication (filling up his coffee with sugar) that she knew would tell Callahan that something was wrong. Because she knew her audience, she was able to manipulate his expectation (that his coffee would be unsweetened) to get her message across. At the same time, she was able to evade the notice of the robbers, who would be unlikely to suspect that she was using sugar to communicate with the cop. If anything, they would expect her to say something or to write something, if she dared at all to disobey their orders. By not speaking or writing to Callahan, she communicated (falsely) to the robbers that she was following their instructions.

Although in this book we will be concerned with words rather than coffee, we'll need the same ingredients for successful communication: a "speaker," someone with something to say; an audience; and a message or "text" that is shaped by the writer's understanding of its purpose and context (that is, time and place).

MAPPING OUT COMMUNICATION

Loretta was able to save lives that day at the diner because she knew whom she was dealing with, and she chose a method of communication that fit the audience, as well as the time and place. Different audiences will have different backgrounds, needs, and interests. Understanding the audience—and shaping the message to meet its expectations—is an essential ingredient of effective communication. Would your succulent filet mignon be a success with a vegetarian? Would your scrumptious white chocolate macadamia nut cookies be a treat for someone with a nut allergy?

We already know a lot about differences between audiences. When you were growing up, weren't there some friends or family members who were more likely to give you money for ice cream, while others could be counted on to listen sympathetically to your complaint about a teacher at school? Discovering how to "work" an audience to achieve your purpose—acquiring the ice cream, or the sympathetic ear—is an important step in developing your communication skills.

Think about the attention a restaurant pays to its audience. Entrepreneurs try to predict who would be interested in and able to afford to eat at their new venue, and they often do very complete studies of the demographics of the target area. Managers of existing restaurants must also be very aware of their audience—without customers, the restaurant will not survive. In order to meet the expectations of different audiences, managers will make different decisions about the food and service they provide. Let's look at two examples.

Imagine that the first restaurant is a successful yet humble family diner in a suburban setting, while the second is an ambitious, high-end establishment located in a major city. Now suppose each restaurant offered a pasta and cheese entrée. Would the menu descriptions be similar? It's unlikely. The customers at the diner expect basic food items, solid and familiar, with a homemade feel, items like a Classic Mac & Cheese. We often see family names in diner menu descriptions: Grandma's Chocolate Chip Cookies, Uncle Bob's BBQ Ribs. Customers at the trendy urban restaurant, on the other hand, expect more details in their menu descriptions, including specific ingredients that are out of the ordinary, such as Quattro Formaggio Macaroni: Fontina, mild cheddar, mozzarella, and smoked gouda sauce over house-made pasta. There's no right or wrong here—just effective communication with two different audiences.

Sometimes when we're writing, we forget about the audience altogether. Out of sight, out of mind, they say. Yet in the same way that restaurants try to meet the expectations of their customers with their menu descriptions, writers are wise to think carefully about who their readers might be and to anticipate what their readers will expect from them. In terms of content, for example, we want to provide details and examples that will make sense to our particular readers, and we want to use a style or level of formality that is appropriate for the audience and for the occasion. If we're writing an email to a good friend, we unconsciously use a vocabulary she can understand, and we probably don't have to be as careful about grammar and punctuation as we would be in writing an essay for English class. A cell phone text might make use of specialized acronyms, such as BTW or TTYL, that would be understood by one audience (friends) but not another (grandparents). College professors and business professionals, on the other hand, expect that we will use the conventions of standard written English in terms of word choice, grammar, and punctuation.

The effectiveness of communication also depends upon the choice of "text" or method. Sometimes a look is most effective—has your mother ever glared at you when you tracked mud onto her freshly mopped kitchen floor? At other times a conversation works best, for example, when explaining why you didn't do your homework. In terms of written communication, we also have choices. Shall we send a text or an email? Put a letter in the United States mail? Write an essay or a report?

Finally, communication takes place most effectively if it is suited to the time and place, that is, the situation or context. Have you ever tried to say something and been hushed with a "This isn't the time" or "This isn't the place"? If you wanted to have a serious conversation about your career plans with a friend or mentor, you probably wouldn't choose to bring it up in the middle of the Super Bowl or five minutes before you had to leave the meeting. Instead, you would wait until both of you had time to talk and were in a place that was private and quiet enough.

The complex parts of communication are sometimes presented as a triangle illustrating the relationship between the speaker (writer), the message (text), and the audience (reader). Because these three parts are so closely interrelated, they are often depicted as the points of a triangle.

In *Sudden Impact*, for example, the "speaker" (Loretta) sent a message (sugar in the coffee) to an audience (police detective Harry Callahan). The triangle shape indicates that each part is influenced by the other two. Remember also that Loretta's decisions about *how* and *when* to communicate were influenced by the time and place, and by a secondary audience (the robbers) for whom she had quite a different message ("I'm not telling the cop anything"). Sometimes these additional factors—the context—appear on a line circling the triangle. Finally, the idea or purpose behind the communication can be placed in the center of the triangle.

Figure 1.2 Mapping Out Communication

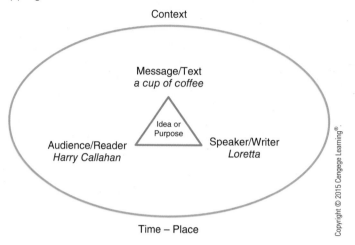

WRITING WITH A PURPOSE

We've said that communication of any kind generally means moving an idea from our brain to someone else's brain. However, *why* we share our thoughts—that is, the **purpose** of our communication—varies widely. In writing an email to a friend, for example, our purpose may be to make dinner plans, or to ask a favor, or to share a funny story. Or we may write letters with the purpose of carrying out business, such as applying for a job or a scholarship. Sometimes our writing is entirely personal, for example, a journal entry or a poem. Writing is also part of many school assignments and as such reflects the *teacher's* purpose: to expand students' knowledge through research, deepen their thinking through analysis, and/or improve their written communication skills through practice.

The various reasons we might have to share our thoughts and feelings are often placed into one or more of the following three categories: to inform, to persuade, to entertain. Of course, your purpose is usually quite specific, for example, to write an informative essay on the Bill of Rights for a history class or to convince your credit card company to waive the late payment fee this month or to liven up a boring vocabulary assignment with outrageous sentences. Are you trying to pass on information about how to lower the fat content of a particular dish by submitting an article for publication in a magazine? Do you want your boss to put your new dish on the menu, or are you trying to persuade your instructor to give you an extension on a deadline? Are you just trying to tell a funny story?

As you plan a new piece of writing, you will begin to shape it depending on your purpose and how you might best achieve that purpose with a particular audience at a particular time and place. Purpose is important because our reason for writing will influence our choices about content, organization, vocabulary, grammar, and punctuation. If your story is about a narrow escape with a hot saucepan, for example, your essay might have the purpose of informing your readers about safety as well as entertaining them with your antics in the kitchen. If your readers have restaurant experience, you might spice up your prose with a little culinary slang: "I was weeded that night!" If not, your tone might be more serious: "Second-degree burns require immediate medical attention."

Let's try another topic: foraging for chanterelle mushrooms. *MykoWeb* ("California Fungi") offers straightforward information about chanterelles and also about how to distinguish the true ones from the "false":

> This much sought-after edible is recognized by a fleshy, yellow, vase-shaped, fruiting body, wavy margin, and shallow, ridge-like gills that are conspicuously decurrent. . . . Collectors should be aware that other yellow mushrooms are occasionally mistaken for the chanterelle, notably *Hygrophoropsis aurantiaca* (false chanterelle) . . . a less fleshy, buff to orangish, probably edible species that grows on rotting wood or wood chips.

The tone (or attitude) is factual, and the vocabulary is specialized. Sometimes there is an additional reason for giving factual information, for example, to prevent accidental poisoning. In the following excerpt, the Missouri Department of Conservation lays out its purpose at the beginning:

> The purpose of this article is twofold: to help you identify a number of safe, edible wild mushrooms while avoiding mushroom poisoning, and to introduce you to the gentle sport of mushroom hunting, which among other things is a fine excuse to walk in the woods.

The article goes on to provide descriptive details that distinguish the two mushrooms. The tone is also factual, but here providing information has a higher purpose: to help readers recognize danger and persuade them to avoid it. The element of persuasion is present in the second purpose as well—to encourage the reader to participate in "the gentle sport of mushroom hunting."

A third example is pure entertainment. We don't have enough information to identify the toxic "false chanterelle," nor

Chanterelles in the Woods

© FotografFF/ShutterStock.com

does the author attempt to persuade us that mushrooms are too dangerous to eat. But the rich description and humorous, conversational tone of Michael Pollan's *The Omnivore's Dilemma* (285–286) make this passage tasty:

Hiking in the Berkeley Hills one afternoon in January I noticed a narrow shady path dropping off the main trail into the woods, and I followed it down into a grove of big oaks and bay laurel trees. I'd read that chanterelles came up this time of year around old live oak trees, so I kept an eye out. The only place I'd seen a chanterelle before was over pasta or in the market, but I knew I was looking for a yellowish-orange and thickly built trumpet. I scanned the leaf litter around a couple of oaks but saw nothing. Just when I'd given up and turned to head back, however, I noticed a bright, yolky glimmer of something pushing up the carpet of leaves not two feet from where I'd just stepped. I brushed away the leaves and there it was, this big, fleshy, vase-shaped mushroom that I was dead certain had to be a chanterelle.

Or was it?

How certain was that?

I took the mushroom home, brushed off the soil, and put it on a plate, then pulled out my field guides to see if I could confirm the identification. Everything matched up: the color, the faint apricot smell, the asymmetrical trumpet shape on top, the underside etched in a shallow pattern of "false" gills. I felt fairly confident. But confident enough to eat it? Not quite. The field guide mentioned something called a "false chanterelle" that had slightly "thinner" gills. Uh oh. Thinner, thicker: These were relative terms; how could I tell if the gills I was looking at were thin or thick ones? Compared to what? My mother's mycophobic warnings rang in my ears. I couldn't trust my eyes. I couldn't quite trust the field guide. So whom could I trust? Angel! But that meant driving my lone mushroom across the bridge to San Francisco, which seemed excessive. My desire to sauté and eat my first-found chanterelle squabbled with my doubts about it, slender as they were. But by now I had passed the point of being able to enjoy this putative chanterelle without anxiety, so I threw it out.

I didn't realize it at the time, but I had impaled myself that afternoon on the horns of the omnivore's dilemma.

As we look back over these three passages, we notice differences in choice of detail and vocabulary that reflect the different purposes of the authors. The first passage, an informative one, uses a specific, objective, even technical vocabulary: *false chanterelle, distinguishing factors, uniform [color], hue, graded.* The second piece uses words related to its purpose: *purpose, twofold, avoiding, introduce, fine excuse.* The third, a more literary, first-person narrative, uses a richly descriptive, often metaphorical vocabulary: *a yellowish-orange and thickly built trumpet; I scanned the leaf litter; a bright, yolky glimmer of something pushing up the carpet of leaves.* An effective writer will choose details, vocabulary, and point of view (among other factors) that reflect the purpose, audience, and context of the task.

SPEECH AND WRITING

Speech, like **writing**, is a form of **verbal communication**. Both of them use words, but, in addition to the words that are exchanged, speech also makes use of **nonverbal communication**. As we're talking, we can watch the facial expressions, hand gestures, and body language of the audience and make any necessary adjustments to improve communication. Similarly, the audience can watch us as we speak and can interpret the accompanying nonverbal cues as well as the words themselves. Some people find talking much easier than writing because of this nonverbal support.

When it comes to writing, however, it's as if a brick wall has been erected between the reader and the writer (Figure 1.3). The writer has an idea in her head that she wishes to share. She writes a text that puts this idea into words, then passes it on to the reader. In most cases there is no direct contact between the two, no opportunity to ask questions or check comprehension. Therefore, the writer must make a pretty good guess about what the reader already knows about the subject, what questions the reader might wish to ask, what vocabulary will be most clearly understood, what style will be most appropriate. The writer must use aspects of the text itself, including punctuation, to convey the nuances of meaning that might be expressed through nonverbal methods during a face-to-face or even a telephone conversation. Since writing doesn't allow for

Figure 1.3 Speech vs. Writing

When we're speaking, we can use nonverbal cues as well as words.

When we're writing, it's as if a brick wall separates us from the reader.

questions or corrections and must work without the assistance of body language and facial expressions, it needs to be very clear, specific, and complete.

That's not to say that what we know about speech won't help with our writing. On the contrary, that knowledge is vital. We'll use speech at the beginning of a writing assignment when we brainstorm, and we'll use it when we proofread at the end. We'll use the rhythm and vocabulary of our spoken "voice" to begin shaping our *writer's* voice. And we'll use our insights about how conversation works to make important decisions about how to reach and persuade our readers.

In ancient Greece, the philosopher Plato believed that speech was closer to the truth than writing because the speaker was "present." Written language offered only the "appearance" of truth. In fact, Plato believed that writing would lead to a "dumbing down" of his society because people would rely on the written word instead of on the "truer" words of speech. Yet the situation may not be that simple. In the scene from *Sudden Impact,* Loretta and Callahan were both physically present when she poured the sugar. Yet Callahan wasn't paying attention; in some sense he was "absent." It wasn't until he'd left the diner and actually tasted the coffee that the communication took place. Callahan was able to "read" the truth in its unexpected sweetness. Loretta was "present" in the sugary "text."

While Plato viewed the world in binary terms—truth versus appearance, presence versus absence, speech versus writing—some contemporary philosophers see these relationships as more complicated. Is the speaker necessarily more present or more effective than the writer? Can we not feel the presence of the writer through a letter or text or tweet? Do the words of a song sometimes seem to be speaking directly to us through the iPod? Looking at it another way, have we not been in the same room with someone who clearly was not present, not really paying attention, not speaking the truth?

Perhaps speech and writing are more similar than different. Both are forms of language that attempt to embody our thoughts, to achieve a particular purpose. Their success depends on a complex combination of factors, as we saw in Loretta's case: the speaker's character or trustworthiness, her knowledge of the audience, the skill with which she is able to shape the message, and her understanding of the fuller context, the time and place. In any particular situation, we'll try to choose the most effective form of communication.

WHAT MAKES WRITING EFFECTIVE?

Sometimes student writers may think their job is to write "what the teacher wants." And perhaps there is some truth in that. Students usually do have the goal of getting a decent grade, and teachers do have somewhat different ideas of what constitutes a "good" essay. However, if writers don't put their real thoughts and feelings into the essay, readers just won't be that interested. Teachers are somewhat of a captive audience; they have to read every writing assignment. But in the outside world—the world of cover letters and résumés, restaurant reviews and cookbooks—readers may lose interest if writers don't make a connection with them.

We all know people who are great storytellers—people with an eye for detail, a sense of humor, a unique voice, and the ability to keep us enthralled from beginning to end. We seek these people out and buy them a cup of coffee just to hear their latest story. On the other hand, we also know people who are so vague or boring or negative that we walk quickly in the opposite direction when we see them coming. The same is true of writing. There is some writing that we enjoy thoroughly, that is vivid and detailed, funny or suspenseful. There is other writing that strikes us as dull, pretentious, wordy, insincere—and we just put the book down.

Every piece of writing begins with a need to communicate, that is, with a purpose. Every piece of writing should take into account the background and experience of the audience, as well as the time and place of the communication. Between the writer and the reader is the message, the text, and this message must be "cooked" so that it becomes both tasty and digestible. Effective writing always suggests effective communication. It requires making good decisions about the reader. What would have happened in *Sudden Impact* if Harry Callahan had sipped the coffee immediately? What if the robbers had noticed the excess of sugar? As it turned out, Loretta did know both her audiences and communicated effectively with both.

So, what makes good writing? The answer is, some of the same things that make good cooking: fresh ingredients, specialized skills, and a passion to reach the audience. Our purpose in this book is to find the freshest ingredients for our writing, the freshest ideas, examples, descriptions; to acquire particular skills, such as brainstorming, revising, editing; and to connect our own interests and passions to the content of any given writing assignment, creating texts that effectively communicate what's on our minds.

A TASTE FOR READING

In this chapter from the early pages of Moby-Dick, *the narrator (Ishmael) and his new friend, the cannibal Queequeg (see photo on p. 504), arrive in Nantucket on their way to meeting up with Captain Ahab and setting off in pursuit of the great white whale.*

****

Chowder
from Moby-Dick, or The White Whale by Herman Melville

It was quite late in the evening when the little Moss came snugly to anchor, and Queequeg and I went ashore; so we could attend to no business that day, at least none but a supper and a bed. The landlord of the Spouter-Inn had recommended us to his cousin Hosea Hussey of the Try Pots[a], whom he asserted to be the proprietor of one of the best kept hotels in all Nantucket, and moreover he had assured us that cousin Hosea, as he called him, was famous for his chowders. In sort[b], he plainly hinted that we could not possibly do better than try pot-luck at the Try Pots. But the directions he had given us about keeping a yellow warehouse on our starboard hand till we opened a white church to the larboard, and then keeping that on the larboard hand till we made a corner three points to the starboard, and that done, then ask the first man we met where the place was: these crooked directions of his very much puzzled us at first, especially as, at the outset, Queequeg insisted that the yellow warehouse—our first point of departure—must be left on the larboard hand, whereas I had understood Peter Coffin to say it was on the starboard. However, by dint of beating about a little in the dark, and now and then knocking up a peaceable inhabitant to inquire the way, we at last came to something which there was no mistaking.

Two enormous wooden pots painted black, and suspended by asses' ears[c], swung from the cross-trees of an old top-mast, planted in front of an old doorway. The horns of the cross-trees were sawed off on the other side, so that this old top-mast looked not a little like a gallows. Perhaps I was over sensitive to such impressions at the time, but I could not help staring at this gallows with a vague misgiving. A sort of crick was in my neck as I gazed up to the two remaining horns; yes, *two* of them, one for Queequeg, and one for me. It's ominous, thinks I. A Coffin my Innkeeper upon landing in my first whaling port[d]; tombstones staring at me in the whalemen's chapel; and here a gallows! and a pair of prodigious black pots too! Are these last throwing out oblique hints touching Tophet[e]?

I was called from these reflections by the sight of a freckled woman with yellow hair and a yellow gown, standing in the porch of the inn, under a dull red lamp swinging there, that looked much like an injured eye, and carrying on a brisk scolding with a man in a purple woolen shirt.

"Get along with ye," said she to the man, "or I'll be combing ye!"

"Come on, Queequeg," said I, "all right. There's Mrs. Hussey."

And so it turned out; Mr. Hosea Hussey being from home, but leaving Mrs. Hussey entirely competent to attend to all his affairs. Upon making known our desires for a supper and a bed, Mrs. Hussey, postponing further scolding for the present, ushered us into a little room, and seating us at a table spread with the relics of a recently concluded repast, turned round to us and said—"Clam or Cod?"

"What's that about Cods, ma'am?" said I, with much politeness.

"Clam or Cod?" she repeated.

"A clam for supper? a cold clam; is *that* what you mean, Mrs. Hussey?" says I; "but that's rather a cold and clammy reception in the winter time, ain't it, Mrs. Hussey?"

---

[a]The name of the inn, from the pots used to "try," or boil, the whale blubber
[b]Most likely "In short"
[c]The handles of the pot
[d]The landlord the Spouter-Inn was named Coffin.
[e]An allusion to hell

But being in a great hurry to resume scolding the man in the purple shirt, who was waiting for it in the entry, and seeming to hear nothing but the word "clam," Mrs. Hussey hurried towards an open door leading to the kitchen, and bawling out "clam for two," disappeared.

"Queequeg," said I, "do you think that we can make out a supper for us both on one clam?"

However, a warm savory steam from the kitchen served to belie the apparently cheerless prospect before us. But when that smoking chowder came in, the mystery was delightfully explained. Oh, sweet friends! hearken[f] to me. It was made of small juicy clams, scarcely bigger than hazel nuts, mixed with pounded ship biscuit, and salted pork cut up into little flakes; the whole enriched with butter, and plentifully seasoned with pepper and salt. Our appetites being sharpened by the frosty voyage, and in particular, Queequeg seeing his favorite fishing food before him, and the chowder being surpassingly excellent, we despatched it with great expedition: when leaning back a moment and bethinking me of Hrs. Hussey's clam and cod announcement, I thought I would try a little experiment. Stepping to the kitchen door, I uttered the word "cod" with great emphasis, and resumed my seat. In a few moments the savory steam came forth again, but with a different flavour, and in good time a fine cod-chowder was placed before us.

We resumed business; and while plying our spoons in the bowl, thinks I to myself, I wonder now if this here has any effect on the head? What's that stultifying saying about chowder-headed people? "But look, Queequeg, ain't that a live eel in your bowl? Where's your harpoon?"

Fishiest of all fishy places was the Try Pots, which well deserved its name; for the pots there were always boiling chowders. Chowder for breakfast, and chowder for dinner, and chowder for supper, till you began to look for fish-bones coming through your clothes. The area before the house was paved with clam-shells. Mrs. Hussey wore a polished necklace of codfish vertebrae; and Hosea Hussey had his account books bound in superior old shark-skin. There was a fishy flavour to the milk, too, which I could not at all account for, till one morning happening to take a stroll along the beach among some fishermen's boats, I saw Hosea's brindled cow feeding on some fish remnants, and marching along the sand with each foot in a cod's decapitated head, looking very slip-shod, I assure ye.

Supper concluded, we received a lamp, and directions from Mrs. Hussey concerning the nearest way to bed; but, as Queequeg was about to precede me up the stairs, the lady reached forth her arm, and demanded his harpoon; she allowed no harpoon in her chambers. "Why not?" said I; "every true whaleman sleeps with his harpoon—but why not!" "Because it's dangerous," says she. "Ever since young Stiggs coming from that unfort'nt v'y'ge of his, when he was gone four years and a half, with only three barrels of *ile*, was found dead in my first floor back, with his harpoon in his side; ever since

---

[f]Listen

then I allow no boarders to take such dangerous weapons in their rooms at night. So, Mr. Queequeg" (for she had learned his name), "I will just take this here iron, and keep it for you till morning. But the chowder; clam or cod to-morrow for breakfast, men?"

"Both," says I; "and let's have a couple of smoked herring by way of variety."

ABOUT THE READING

- Describe the different types of communication in "Chowder."
- At what point does communication break down? Why? What nonverbal communication reassures the hungry travelers that their dinner won't be a disaster?
- Define the following words: *starboard, larboard, gallows, prodigious, repast, stultifying.* What does "despatched it with great expedition" mean?
- Written over 150 years ago, *Moby-Dick* has a context and some vocabulary we may not be familiar with. How might this affect the book's ability to communicate with contemporary readers? How did it affect you?

Santi Sinrapanurak is a culinary arts major at the Culinary Institute of America. In this journal entry, he reflects on the ups and downs of a hiking trip in northern Thailand.

****

Flying Squirrel Noodles
by Santi Sinrapanurak

It seemed as if we had been walking for fifteen hours at that point, when in actuality we probably had only gotten two hours into our second day of trekking. The combination of humidity and exhaustion was starting to show its effects on our entire group, but I especially was showing the obvious signs of physical exertion. While everyone else had a genteel amount of sweat peppered to their brow, I was so thoroughly soaked from perspiration that you would have thought I had just walked under a waterfall. Not to mention, the poor choice of footwear had also became a burden as *both* my feet had become swollen and infected from the continuous bombardment of monsoon-like weather conditions on two of the three days of our Northern trek.

As I tried to hasten my climbing speed, I thought to myself, "How did I think that this was a good idea for a vacation?" I heard the leader of our pair of guides call out from far ahead, and I remember the moment of panic when I was able to figure out what exactly he had said. Nuut, one of our guides, had shouted that the only way to ascend to base camp, as well as to that day's only true meal, was to cross an incredibly rocky riverbed, and the only way to do so was to literally swing over it with a vine. At first I thought that this must be some ill-timed sense of humor during the more difficult part of the trek, but as I soon discovered, he was as serious as my foot infection.

We finally were winding down our day's route as we reached the infamous river. In truth, the actual swinging across the riverbed was not as intimidating as it had sounded earlier in the day. I, of course, still managed to hop skip my way through the bramble of jagged rocks that protruded from the water and blocked the path to that day's only meal. As everyone started to wind down and dry off their clothes, we prepared to encircle the campfire that our two guides had set up for us. There is something to be said about physically pushing oneself to the limit in an unfamiliar and mountainous jungle environment in monsoon season, and the specific hunger that follows that particular experience. That is why, after the day I had endured, I expected something not only substantial, but exceedingly appetizing as well. However, as soon as I had seen our navigational duo skewer a flying squirrel, skull first, onto a gnarled stick they had found to the side of the campfire, my hopes were nearly obliterated. And to add insult onto injury, the guides quickly tossed about a half a dozen instant packages of dried Japanese ramen noodles into a pot of pre-simmered water from the river I had just mangled my ankles in. Squirrel meat is both gamey and bitter, so limp yellow noodles, as an accompaniment, do not bring out any hidden attributes to this particular protein.

Needless to say, the time spent in Northern Thailand trekking with a friend would accompany, if not haunt, my future experiences with camping trips. To this day, I harbor no nostalgia for bland instant ramen noodles and fire-roasted flying squirrel meat.

ABOUT THE READING

- What words or phrases particularly strike you? Why?
- Who is the intended audience? What is the purpose of the piece?
- Did the flying squirrel noodles communicate anything to the author? Explain.
- Describe two or three examples—real or imagined—of food used for communication.

RECIPE FOR REVIEW

A CUP OF COFFEE

Communication means sharing thoughts, feelings, and ideas. Verbal communication, like writing and speaking, uses words, while nonverbal communication does not.

MAPPING OUT COMMUNICATION

The three parts of communication are the speaker (or writer), the audience (reader), and the message (written text), all of which are impacted by the time and place. This complex relationship is often diagrammed as a triangle set within a circle or oval (see Figure 1.2).

WRITING WITH A PURPOSE

Writing is said to have one or more of the following general purposes: to inform, entertain, and/or persuade. The purpose of a given writing task will likely be quite specific.

SPEECH AND WRITING

While speakers can also use nonverbal communication, writers must rely on their words alone to achieve their purpose. Yet what we know intuitively about speech can help us become more effective writers.

WHAT MAKES WRITING EFFECTIVE?

Good writing consists of "fresh" ideas that are clearly organized and expressed through well-chosen words and fluently constructed sentences. It has a consistent, individual voice and uses the grammar and mechanics appropriate for the purpose and the audience.

CHAPTER EXERCISES

1. *A Cup of Coffee*—How can or does food communicate?
2. *Mapping Out Communication*—Briefly describe three separate restaurants of different types. What do the customers at each restaurant expect from their food? Now, write three different menu descriptions for a ground meat item, each one designed for a particular purpose.
3. *Writing with a Purpose*—What is one of your favorite childhood dishes? Write a paragraph in which you simply inform the reader about the dish. Next, write a paragraph in which your primary purpose is to entertain rather than inform. Finally, write a paragraph in which you attempt to persuade the reader to try this dish. What differences do you notice between the three paragraphs in terms of details and word choice? Explain.
4. Explain the expression "on the horns of a dilemma." Then explain Michael Pollan's title *The Omnivore's Dilemma*.
5. *Speech and Writing*—Write a set of instructions for blowing a bubble or tying a shoe. Read the instructions to the person next to you. Are they effective? What would you change? How would these instructions have been different if you had been speaking instead of writing?
6. What makes a good dish (of food)? List as many characteristics as you can. Then list as many characteristics of a good piece of writing as you can think of. Compare the two lists. Are there any similarities? Explain.
7. *"Talking with Your Fingers"*—Read John McWhorter's essay "Talking with Your Fingers" (*The New York Times*, April 23, 2012). Do you agree that texting is a new form of communication? Why or why not?

Captain James T. Kirk (left) and Mr. Spock from the original *Star Trek* series, 1966. Captain Kirk holds a "communicator," often cited as the inspiration for today's cell phones.

NBC/Photofest © NBC

IDEAS FOR WRITING

1. Write an essay or paragraph in which you discuss the differences between writing and speaking. Is one easier for you than the other? Explain.
2. Who is a person you think of as an effective communicator? What makes him or her effective? Write an essay or paragraph in which you explain your answer.
3. Write a short story about a person who uses only food to communicate. Use concrete, vivid, sensory details. Explore how other people might react and what problems might arise.
4. What are the advantages and disadvantages of texting as a form of communication? When (if ever) do you choose to send a text rather than make a phone call? Why?

CHAPTER 2
RECIPE FOR READING

By the end of this chapter, you should begin to . . .

* apply the steps of the reading process to a variety of texts;
* distinguish between different purposes for reading and use appropriate, effective strategies for each;
* incorporate "writing to read" strategies in your reading; and
* use effective reading strategies as part of your revision process.

Writing and reading are as closely and inevitably connected as cooking and eating. Just as the end goal in cooking is for someone to eat the food, the end goal in writing is for someone to read the words—whether the writing is a text message, business letter, poem, or academic essay. For most cooks, eating—or *tasting*—is a part of the cooking process itself.[a] Similarly, for effective writers, *reading* is part of the writing process. Writers must read their own work as they revise it, and they must be *good* readers. Unless they can see what their words *actually* say, they won't be able to judge whether the words accurately reflect what they *want* to say. Further, just as good cooks may taste other people's dishes as part of developing their cooking skills, good writers will "taste" other people's writing to get new ideas or to "educate their palates."

Reading is also like listening, and good reading is like good listening. Good listeners will first try to understand what the other person is saying before jumping in with their own comments. Poor listeners, on the other hand, are always thinking about what they are going to say next and in doing so are likely to miss the other person's point altogether. As readers, we should focus on what the actual words say. Read them aloud. Listen to them. Once we've understood the reading, once we've *tasted* all the flavors in a particular dish, then we can evaluate and respond.

Texts come in many different forms, just as foods do, and we have different reasons for reading (or eating) them. (The word "texts" here refers to any piece of writing, not just the message sent from your cell phone.) We don't eat all foods in the same way or for the same purpose. Would you wolf down a chocolate bar the same way you would savor an expensive dessert? No, nor would you read a text message from a friend in the same way you'd read an article about molecular gastronomy or a sonnet by Shakespeare.

---

[a]See Chapter 12 for a description of cooking *without* tasting!

In this chapter we'll look at strategies for "tasting" different types of texts. If we're reading only for entertainment ("snacking"), we can skim through and ignore nutritional value. However, when we're concerned with more focused, high-stakes types of reading, such as reading for information or ideas ("balanced meals"), we need to take the time to "chew" the text carefully. The following series of steps can help us to read more effectively, that is, to improve our "digestion."

Warner Bros./Photofest

In *The Blind Side*, Michael Oher and S. J. Tuohy are absorbed in listening to Leigh Anne read the children's classic *The Story of Ferdinand*.

THE READING PROCESS

Before you even begin to read, it's helpful to get an idea of the size and scope of the reading. What is the text about, and how long is it? (We do the same with meals—how long does it take to eat a dinner of EasyMac versus a Thanksgiving feast?) If it is a chapter in a textbook, skim through the pages and note the headings. These will give you important clues about the main points covered in the reading.

As you're scanning the chapter, it's also helpful to ask yourself what you already know about that topic. It's easier to understand and remember new information if you have a sense of where it fits in with the knowledge you have now. For example, if you're assigned to read a chapter about foodborne illness, you might think about what you already know about bacteria such as *E. coli* and about cross-contamination, and then ask yourself how the reading will expand on your knowledge. It's as if you're creating a framework for the new information. Then, as you read, you place the new bits of knowledge inside the frame you've already created.

Scanning the chapter will also give you a sense of how much time you'll need to read it carefully. The more you already know about the topic, the less time it may take you to add new information to your mental framework. The less you know, the more time it will take to create and fill that mental framework.

After you have a framework for the new information, go ahead and read the chapter or article. Unlike reading for entertainment, reading for information usually means you don't just read straight through. Instead, you read sections of the text, then pause to make sure you understand what you've just read. If you don't understand, you should read it again, perhaps out loud. Chew it over. Depending on the purpose of your reading, you may want to make a note of any questions you have in order to ask them in class or try to find answers through research. Whatever the topic is, try to *visualize* what you're reading about. If you can imagine the ripening of a tomato or the whisking of a hollandaise sauce, you are more likely to enjoy your reading—and to understand and remember it.

As you read, it is useful to highlight important points and concepts in some way, whether in the text itself or on a separate page of notes. It's more effective to read the chapter once, stopping to understand and record what's important, than to read it through several times without really digesting or retaining the information. Think again about the comparison to eating: the faster you chew and swallow, the less likely you are to perceive and appreciate the flavor profile of a dish. You might even get indigestion! However, when you're focused on *tasting,* you may go very slowly, stopping to inhale the aromas, holding the chocolate or wine in your mouth in order to experience each flavor note completely. Further, chewing each bite carefully improves digestion.

One way to highlight important points is literally with a hi-liter, a brightly colored marker. Highlighting is fun, a smooth slip along the paper. Don't highlight too much, though, or you won't be able to find those important points easily. Instead, highlight just the main idea, key terms, and significant supporting details. Look at the example in Figure 2.1.

Figure 2.1   Highlighting Important Points in the Text

That set of rules for preparing food we call a cuisine, for example, specifies combinations of foods and flavors that on examination do a great deal to mediate the omnivore's dilemma. The dangers of eating raw fish, for example, are minimized by consuming it with wasabi, a potent antimicrobial. Similarly, the strong spices characteristic of many cuisines in the tropics, where food is quick to spoil, have antibacterial properties. The meso-American practice of cooking corn with lime and serving it with beans, like the Asian practice of fermenting soy and serving it with rice, turns out to render these plant species much more nutritious than they otherwise would be. When not fermented, soy contains an antitrypsin factor than blocks the absorption of protein, rendering the bean indigestible; unless the corn is cooked with an alkali like lime its niacin is unavailable, leading to the nutritional deficiency called pellagra.

—Michael Pollan, *The Omnivore's Dilemma,* p. 296

If you need more detailed notes, or if you want to be able to erase your notes, try marking up the text with a pencil. Your notes might include any or all of the following: main ideas, supporting points, questions, vocabulary. Compare the notes in Figure 2.2 taken on a portion of the same passage from *The Omnivore's Dilemma.* If you use a good system

Figure 2.2   Detailed Penciled Notes

advantage –
it's more nutritious

The meso-American practice of cooking corn with lime and serving it with beans, like the Asian practice of fermenting soy and serving it with rice, turns out to render these

Like natto?

plant species much more nutritious than they otherwise would be. When not fermented,

definition

soy contains an antitrypsin factor than blocks the absorption of protein, rendering the

Scientific
explanation

bean indigestible; unless the corn is cooked with an alkali like lime its niacin is unavailable, leading to the nutritional deficiency called pellagra.

not enough
niacin

of note-taking, you don't have to keep re-reading the chapter; you simply refresh your memory by looking over your notes. Some people find it more effective to take notes on a separate sheet of paper. These notes can range from quite formal outlines to simple lists of the points you want to remember.

Michael Pollan, An Omnivore's Dilemma, p. 296

I. Benefits of cuisine, that is, specific food pairings
   A. Killing microbes – wasabi with raw fish
   B. Killing bacteria – tropical spices
   C. Enhancing nutritional value – lime with corn and beans, fermented soy with rice

In addition to taking notes of some kind, it can be useful to check your comprehension of the reading by summarizing sections of the text (through writing or speaking) and connecting them to what you already know. Look at the following summary of the paragraph:

Many traditional cuisines use food combinations that protect their "eaters" from foodborne illness and enhance the nutritional value of the ingredients.

If your understanding of the text is limited by an unfamiliar word or reference, try to figure out its meaning from the **context**, that is, from the other words and sentences around it. However, that isn't always possible. Because misunderstanding a word can prevent you from grasping something essential about the passage, it might be more effective to look up words and jot down the definitions in the margins of the text or on your separate page of notes. You don't want to go down the wrong path and have to retrace your steps later. If you need to learn vocabulary words or facts, making flashcards is an extraordinarily effective activity.

Another way of learning and reviewing material from the text is to create your own charts and diagrams or to explain in your own words a chart or diagram from the text. Each time you turn words into pictures or pictures into words, you use both hemispheres of the brain—literally "broadening" your understanding of the text. If you're reading a political or philosophical text, for example, make a chart that compares and contrasts the views of one writer with those of another or with your own. Or, if you're looking at an illustration of the human circulatory system, try explaining it in words. Respond creatively to a text, perhaps by recording your impressions in a journal or writing an imaginary letter to the author. The more "work" you do with a text, the more thoroughly you will understand and remember it.

The steps in the reading process will vary, of course, depending on your purpose in reading, your previous knowledge of the topic, and the difficulty of the text. Let's look at some of the different types of reading you might have to do.

READING FOR INFORMATION

Reading for information is what we do with such texts as news articles, recipes, or textbooks. We're looking for facts and processes, and—depending on how much we already know—we can often skim through, looking for the new facts and details we need and placing them within the framework we've already developed. It might be that we need very specific information, such as the year in which the potato arrived in Europe, and we will simply scan the chapter in search of that detail. If the information is unfamiliar, however, we'll have to read more carefully, and probably take notes on the new terms or steps in a recipe. If the reading is part of a course, you'll need to make sure you learn and remember the new information. You'll probably want to make a separate set of notes for easy review, as well as flashcards if you need to learn specific information like dates, formulas, or vocabulary.

Reading for information is an important skill in the kitchen.

You will also want to be certain that you're reading a reliable source. If the text has been assigned by your instructor, chances are that it has already been vetted. However, not everything we might read contains accurate information. Just because something has been published does not mean it is true. You will want to make some kind of assessment of the credibility or authority of the reading. Ask yourself if the author seems to be knowledgeable and if the publisher or online source is reputable. Test the new information against what you already know. Ask yourself *why* the author is writing this particular text and for what audience. (For a more detailed discussion of evaluating the accuracy of your information, see Chapter 18.)

Reading for information is foundational in our school work and in much of our professional lives. Therefore, the more effective we are at harvesting and digesting information from the text, the better. Dig in to the reading about potatoes in Exercise 2.1.

Exercise 2.1 | Reading for Information

Read the following passage from Harold McGee's *On Food and Cooking* (first edition, 191–192) and note important details. Be sure to look up the meaning of any unfamiliar words.

The potato, a relative of tobacco and the tomato, is indigenous to Central and South America, from the southern United States to the tip of Chile. It was cultivated more than 4000 years ago in mountainous areas, up to 15,000 feet, where corn cannot grow, and was a staple food of the Incas. The name comes from a Caribbean Indian word for the *sweet* potato, *batata*. Spanish explorers brought the plant to Europe around 1570, and England and Ireland had it by about 1610 and immediately accepted it as an important food crop. Because it was hardy and easy to grow, the potato was inexpensive and the poor were its principal consumers. . . . The potato came to the United States as a food crop indirectly, via Ireland, in 1719; the first large area of cultivation was near Londonderry, New Hampshire. It quickly became established on all continents, in temperate, subtropical, and tropical climates, and is now the most important vegetable in the world, excluding only the tropical lowlands, where manioc, another large tuber (tapioca is made from its starch) is more easily grown.

Answer the following questions:
1. How old is the potato?
2. What does *indigenous* mean?
3. Who were the Incas?
4. Why were poor people more likely to eat potatoes?
5. How and when was the potato introduced to the United States?

In addition to answering questions about the reading, thinking creatively about the information can help us to understand and remember it. Try the activities in Exercise 2.2 using the same paragraph from McGee.

Exercise 2.2 | Activities to Increase Comprehension

1. In one or two sentences, summarize the paragraph from McGee in Exercise 2.1.
2. Describe a scene in which an American family in 1719 is cooking with potatoes for the first time.
3. Create a timeline of the potato's travels.
4. Draw a map of the potato's travels, labeling the appropriate areas and dates.

READING FOR IDEAS

In addition to reading for information, we may also read for *ideas*; that is, we may read in order to understand a concept and perhaps to apply it to a new situation. Like certain foods, some kinds of written materials are harder to "digest" than others. A book about psychology or economics, for example, will most likely require more time and effort to read than a restaurant or movie review. You may need to read the text several times—perhaps read it out loud to *hear* as well as see the words—and to stop and think carefully about what the author means. Let's look at an example.

In *A Whole New Mind: Moving from the Information Age to the Conceptual Age*, Daniel H. Pink discusses the types of skills needed for success in a changing world. First, he defines two ways of thinking, L-Directed and R-Directed:

> Call the first approach *L-Directed Thinking*. It is a form of thinking and an attitude to life that is characteristic of the left hemisphere of the brain—sequential, literal, functional, textual, and analytical. Ascendant in the Information Age, exemplified by computer programmers, prized by hardheaded organizations, and emphasized in schools, this approach is directed *by* left-brain attributes, *toward* left-brain results. Call the other approach *R-Directed Thinking*. It is a form of thinking and an attitude to life that is characteristic of the right hemisphere of the brain—simultaneous, metaphorical, aesthetic, contextual, and synthetic. Underemphasized in the Information Age, exemplified by creators and caregivers, shortchanged by organizations, and neglected in schools, this approach is directed *by* right-brain attributes, *toward* right-brain results. (26)

Pink then argues that *both* types of thinking are essential for success in the Conceptual Age; that is, a "whole" mind is needed. He goes on to define six of these combined skills, including design. "Design," he explains, "is a classic whole-minded aptitude, "a combination of *utility* [L-Directed Thinking] and *significance* [R-Directed Thinking]" (70). Examples help to make his point clear. From cars and TVs to vegetable brushes and toasters, he writes, the aesthetic appeal or significance of an item is as important to its success in the Conceptual Age as its performance.

Examples are very useful in giving the reader a better handle on an idea. They're a way of re-reading or re-thinking the material. Imagining your own examples or applications can also be helpful. In your experience, for instance, how do the two sides of design play out in a restaurant's dining room or on its menu? Do you choose your kitchen knives and pots based on their utility or on their beauty, or both?

Finally, to check your comprehension, it is useful to paraphrase or summarize the author's idea in your own words.

Exercise 2.3 | Paraphrasing or Summarizing the Reading

Explain L-Directed and R-Directed Thinking in your own words. Then explain how "design" uses both kinds of thinking.

Exercise 2.4 | Finding Your Own Examples

Think about two purchases you've made recently. What role did the "design" of each item play in your decision to buy it over its competitor?

As in all kinds of reading, when you read for ideas you will begin by looking at the facts of the text, the surface details, but you will then want to look *beneath* the surface of the text or "between the lines" and draw conclusions about what is *not* written. For example, ask yourself, What is the author's purpose in writing this particular text? (In a conversation, you might ask yourself, Why is he telling me this?) What assumptions does the author seem to make about the reader's knowledge about the topic and about his political, ethical, or religious beliefs? As we consider another example, the concluding paragraph from José Antonio Burciaga's essay "Tortillas" (Courtesy of University of Texas-Pan American Press), let's look first at the surface details and then at what may lie beneath them.

> Then there is *tortilla* art. Various Chicano artists throughout the Southwest have, when short of materials or just in a whimsical mood, used a dry *tortilla* as a small, round canvas. And a few years back, at the height of the Chicano movement, a priest in Arizona got into trouble with the Church after he was discovered celebrating mass using a *tortilla* as the host. All of which goes to show that while the *tortilla* may be a lowly corn cake, when the necessity arises, it can reach unexpected distinction.

The main idea is that *tortillas* have sometimes been used as art rather than food, and the paragraph offers the two examples of "a small, round canvas" and "the host" in the celebration of mass. We'll want to be sure we understand the surface details, such as the meaning of "whimsical" and the reference to the "Chicano movement." We may want to examine Burciaga's *tone* or attitude in the last sentence and think about whether or not *he* was offended by this use of the *tortilla,* and whether he expects the reader to be.

Exercise 2.5 | Reading for Ideas

Re-read the paragraph from "Tortillas" and answer the following questions:

1. What is the effect of Burciaga telling us that the event (the priest getting into trouble) occurred "at the height of the Chicano movement"?
2. Look up information on Burciaga's life. How does this add to your understanding of the paragraph? Why?

READING LITERATURE

The process of reading a story, poem, or other literary work is similar to the other types of reading we've discussed in that we begin with the surface details, the characters and events, the time and place. We look for the main idea in each paragraph, and we'll also want to look for any implied meaning, assumptions, or contradictions. We may need to look up unfamiliar words or references. We may also want to use such outside

The Harry Potter books continue to engage readers of all ages.

clues as information about the author and the historical context, mythology, psychoanalytic theory, or other fields of study to enrich our understanding of the work. Reading literature differs most perhaps in the degree to which we become engaged with the material. As we read a story, for example, we often empathize with the characters and try to make predictions about what will happen to them. We may discover that the story has connections with our own lives and with other works.

Current research in neuroscience supports the idea that we make strong connections with the stories we read.[2] Apparently when we see a word for a smell (like "coffee") or a texture (like "velvet"), our brains light up in the same areas we'd use when actually smelling or touching something. When we read about a movement of the arm or leg, such as kicking a soccer ball, our brains light up in the same areas we'd use when performing that action ourselves. Further, reading about human interactions in a story can help us develop our social skills as if we were living through the experiences along with the characters. Think back to the reading from *Moby-Dick* in Chapter 1: inhaling the "warm savory steam" of the chowder, chewing the "small juicy clams." Perhaps we imagined ourselves "plying our spoons in the bowl" as Ishmael and Queequeg did.

Look now at the following paragraph, excerpted from Sarah Vowell's essay "Shooting Dad" (17–18), about a father and daughter who disagree on almost everything.

Our house was partitioned off into territories. While the kitchen and the living room were well within the DMZ, the respective work spaces governed by my father and me were jealously guarded totalitarian states in which each of us declared ourselves dictator. Dad's shop was a messy disaster area, a labyrinth of lathes. Its walls were hung with the mounted antlers of deer he'd bagged, forming a makeshift museum of death. The available flat surfaces were buried under a million scraps of paper on which he sketched his mechanical inventions in blue ballpoint pen. And the floor, carpeted with spiky metal shavings, was a tetanus shot waiting to happen. My domain was the cramped, cold space known as the music room. It was also a messy disaster area, an obstacle course of musical instruments—piano, trumpet, baritone horn, valve trombone, various percussion doodads (bells!), and recorders. A framed portrait of the French composer Claude Debussy was nailed to the wall. The available flat surfaces were buried under piles of staff paper, on which I penciled in the pompous orchestra music [that] I started writing in junior high.

The main idea of this paragraph is clearly stated in the first sentence: "Our house was partitioned off into territories." Author Sarah Vowell then develops this idea through comparing and contrasting the "territories" that belong to her father and herself. Her father, a gunsmith, has a work space filled with tools and ingredients related to his craft, while her space reflects her interest in music. Read the paragraph carefully, checking your understanding of the vocabulary and references.

Exercise 2.6 | Reading Surface Details

Answer the following questions from your reading of the excerpt from "Shooting Dad":

1. What is "the DMZ"?
2. What's a "lathe"? What does a "labyrinth of lathes" look like?
3. Why is the floor "a tetanus shot waiting to happen"?
4. What does "pompous" mean?

If you thought "pompous" meant "excellent" or "romantic," say, rather than "self-important" or "pretentious," you might miss an important clue about the narrator. Sometimes we get tired of looking up new words, but it usually pays off.

Once you're clear about the details, read the paragraph again and try to make sense of what those details tell us about the story and its characters. For example, we might ask what the term "DMZ" or "demilitarized zone" suggests about the relationship between the author and her father. Or we might wonder what the choice of Debussy suggests about the narrator's interests and personality. To answer these questions more fully, of course, we would need to read the entire essay. These are just examples of the *kinds* of questions that help us to look beneath the surface of a literary text.

Reading literature is also different from reading a news story and other types of texts in that the structure of the sentences and the choice of the words themselves are central to the meaning and impact of the work. Notice that although their interests seem diametrically opposed (guns and music), both father and daughter have work spaces described as "a messy disaster area." Also, in each work space "the available flat surfaces were buried under . . . paper." These parallel phrases reveal to the careful reader that there is a similarity between father and daughter. We might reach the same conclusion by visualizing the items mentioned in the paragraph. There are long, hollow metal objects (guns and trumpets) in each work space; therefore father and daughter have something in common.

A special aspect of reading literature is observing and analyzing the use of figurative language, such as metaphor, personification, alliteration, and onomatopoeia. In Vowell's paragraph, we can find the following examples of alliteration, that is, repetition of the initial consonant: "a labyrinth of lathes" (repeated initial *l*'s) and "makeshift museum" (repeated initial *m*'s). Notice how the repetition of sounds draws attention to the passage, adds interest to the text, and suggests a playfulness in the narrator's attitude. (For more on figurative language, see Chapters 12 and 17.)

Finally, in reading literature—as in all types of reading (and listening)—we need to distinguish between what the text actually says and what thoughts we might have about the same topic. Otherwise we might misunderstand the text because we jump too quickly to an "interpretation." Suppose a reader who was opposed to hunting saw the line about "the mounted antlers of deer he'd bagged" and jumped to the conclusion that the father was brutal and unsympathetic, completely missing *Vowell's* clues about her father's personality. While it is natural for us to bring our own experiences into our reading, we also need to be very clear about the difference between our thoughts and the author's actual words. We should always return to the evidence of the text and check our interpretations against it.

READING TO REVISE

In order to be effective writers, we also need to be effective readers of our own work. We have to learn how to read what is actually written on the page rather than get lost in what we were thinking about as we were writing. We have to step away from the work somehow and try to look at it objectively, as if we hadn't written it ourselves. Try to let some time pass before revising—ideally a day or more. If you don't have that much time, however, at least get up and move around, get a drink of water, before looking at what you've just written. At that point you are more likely to read your work effectively.

Just as you might take notes on a textbook chapter, you may find it helpful to take notes on your own writing. Mark passages that are especially good (positive reinforcement works well), that need more information, or that should be revised or deleted. Pencil in ideas. Highlight words or phrases that need revision. If the order of sentences or paragraphs seems off, try re-reading in a different sequence; then make a note of your preference. Be sure to record your reactions *as you read;* you don't want to take the chance of forgetting some important insights.

Another way to increase your effectiveness as the reader of your own work is to read it *aloud,* whether to yourself or others. Reading aloud to a real audience, whether a class or just one person, can dramatically increase your sense of who your readers might be and whether or not your writing is communicating effectively with them. Sometimes you can literally see on their faces whether or not you're getting the reaction you're aiming for—like watching your customers taste the dish you've prepared for them. You may hear that a transition is missing, or that you need to begin a new paragraph. You will also have a reaction yourself: "Yes, it sounds good" or "No, it's not right."

In addition to helping you think about content and organization, reading aloud can help you adjust the rhythm and flow of each sentence. Think about it—reading aloud uses the mouth and tongue just as eating does. By reading aloud we literally feel and taste the words. Sometimes they taste good. They're easy to say, and the sound of them is pleasing. At other times, however, they leave a bad taste, whether because they're confusing, boring, or awkwardly phrased. When you come across such a sentence, try several different alternatives and read each of them out loud. Then choose the most delicious one!

Let's look at an example. Suppose you'd written the following sentence. Read it out loud.

> In Sarah's case the father and daughter seem fine with each other maybe not super close but who knows maybe they shared some interest that they found out later they had in common.

After reading the sentence out loud, we hear that it needs to be shorter, smoother, less repetitive. (It's quite motivating to *hear* the problem. Weak writing is easier to ignore when we just scan over it with our eyes.) Consider this alternative to that clunky sentence:

> Although Sarah and her father aren't particularly close, they seem fine with each other. Maybe one day they'll discover some common interests.

Reading aloud is also useful in proofreading, as it both slows you down and makes you more aware of your audience. It can be helpful to place a sheet of colorful paper on your text to hold your focus on each line. (See also Chapter 29.)

Revision can be frustrating because we just don't want to read our work anymore. We just want the assignment to be over with! However, thoughtful reading and rewriting can dramatically increase the effectiveness of a piece of writing. Taste, and re-season.

A TASTE FOR READING

Elizabeth Bishop has been called one of the most important American poets of the twentieth century, winning the Pulitzer Prize in 1938 and the National Book Award in 1967. Her poetry is known for its precise representations of the physical world and its underlying themes of struggle, grief, and longing.

****

The Fish
by Elizabeth Bishop

I caught a tremendous fish
and held him beside the boat
half out of water, with my hook
fast in a corner of his mouth.
He didn't fight.
He hadn't fought at all.
He hung a grunting weight,
battered and venerable

and homely. Here and there
his brown skin hung in strips
like ancient wallpaper,
and its pattern of darker brown
was like wallpaper:
shapes like full-blown roses
stained and lost through age.
He was speckled with barnacles,
fine rosettes of lime,
and infested
with tiny white sea-lice,
and underneath two or three
rags of green weed hung down.
While his gills were breathing in
the terrible oxygen
—the frightening gills,
fresh and crisp with blood,
that can cut so badly—
I thought of the coarse white flesh
packed in like feathers,
the big bones and the little bones,
the dramatic reds and blacks
of his shiny entrails,
and the pink swim-bladder
like a big peony.
I looked into his eyes
which were far larger than mine
but shallower, and yellowed,
the irises backed and packed
with tarnished tinfoil
seen through the lenses
of old scratched isinglass.
They shifted a little, but not
to return my stare.
—It was more like the tipping

of an object toward the light.
I admired his sullen face,
the mechanism of his jaw,
and then I saw
that from his lower lip
—if you could call it a lip—
grim, wet, and weaponlike,
hung five old pieces of fish-line,
or four and a wire leader
with the swivel still attached,
with all their five big hooks
grown firmly in his mouth.
A green line, frayed at the end
where he broke it, two heavier lines,
and a fine black thread
still crimped from the strain and snap
when it broke and he got away.
Like medals with their ribbons
frayed and wavering,
a five-haired beard of wisdom
trailing from his aching jaw.
I stared and stared
and victory filled up
the little rented boat,
from the pool of bilge
where oil had spread a rainbow
around the rusted engine
to the bailer rusted orange,
the sun-cracked thwarts,
the oarlocks on their strings,
the gunnels—until everything
was rainbow, rainbow, rainbow!
And I let the fish go.

ABOUT THE READING

- What happens in the poem?
- What words and phrases describe the fish?
- How does the narrator feel about the fish? How do you know?
- Why do you think the narrator lets the fish go? What lines in the poem support your answer?

Grant Rainiere Young was born and raised in the Philippines. He is studying culinary arts in the United States.

****

Bitter Dinners
by Grant Rainiere Young

Food can be one of the most pleasurable things that everyone experiences. Its purpose is not only to nourish us. The happiness food brings to the people who are savoring it exceeds this primal reason. On every occasion, I see food as a component that binds the people who are enjoying it. When families and friends gather, food can uplift the company. Even between strangers, food can ignite a joyful encounter. Yet, in the case of two stories I have read, food made an opposite impression on the characters. The memories of the past bring together the stories of the narrators from "Fish Cheeks" and "Killing Dinner." Between their families and the writers themselves, conflicts with their family arise on the occasions they remember, which all revolve around food. In "Fish Cheeks," it is the traditional Chinese dinner. In "Killing Dinner," it is the slaughtering of the chicken. Because of the events that happened in each story, I have seen that the characters' relationship with food changed.

In my understanding from the stories, these unfortunate events came from the characters' choices in their lives that were not in total accordance with who they were and what their family expected them to be. In "Fish Cheeks," when Amy knew that her crush, an American named Robert, was coming for Christmas dinner, she cried because she was afraid that he might dislike the Chinese customs of her family. Her tears were a manifestation of her worries that not being an American by ethnicity was not acceptable to her potential lover. Being overly caught up with her qualms, she mumbled, "What would Robert think of our shabby Chinese Christmas? What would he think of our noisy Chinese relatives who lacked proper American manners? What terrible disappointment would he feel upon seeing not a roasted turkey and sweet potatoes but Chinese food?" (116) It appeared to me that she was not proud to be Chinese. On a stronger point, it seemed she even would want to change herself into being white. She stated, "For Christmas I prayed for . . . a slim new American nose" (116). Having grown up in and been exposed to a culture that was not her own might have enveloped her true identity. This could explain her scorn for her family's food and dining traditions.

On the other hand, in "Killing Dinner," Gabrielle Hamilton talked about a father who was angry at his daughter. Even before she failed to kill the chicken efficiently, I believe that her father was already unhappy with her being a seventeen-year-old high school dropout who was living with him. She stated, "That fall, I spent a lot of time sitting outside on the log pile at dusk smoking hand-rolled cigarettes in my canvas jacket, watching the garden decay and thinking about death and the inherent beauty of the cycle of life" (71). This might have increased the aggravation in her relationship with her father, who might not have approved of her apparent idleness in life. I believe that her father only did what he did to discipline his daughter. Her mastery in butchering various types of meats came later. She boasted, "I have butchered two-hundred-and-twenty pound sides of beef, . . . carved tongues out of the heads of goats, . . . boned the saddle and legs of rabbits, which even skinned, look exactly like bunnies" (71). However, this confidence didn't start out in a pleasant beginning.

Because of these scornful and unhappy feelings, the characters' reaction toward an enjoyable occasion turned out to be bitter. The food that was the center of their stories caused them suffering and embarrassment. On the night of the Christmas dinner, the fourteen-year-old Amy Tan was in absolute despair. Around the dinner table, every person had caused her so much misery because she thought that their actions were not acceptable to the person she wanted to like her and perhaps also to herself. She mentioned, "Dinner threw me deeper into despair. My relatives licked the ends of their chopsticks and reached across the table, dipping them into the dozen or so plates of food" (117). When the main dish of steamed fish was brought out, she was terrified. Robert's grimace when he saw the whole fish added to her misery. She was very ashamed. She said, "I wanted to disappear" (117).

In the same way Amy dreaded the fish cheeks, killing a chicken horrified Gabrielle when she unsuccessfully hit it in the neck multiple times. Although it might have started with Gabrielle confident, the dull hatchet her father gave her caused the chicken to suffer. This revolted her father. In her story she said, "My dad was animated with disgust at his dropout daughter—so morose and unfeminine." With this, she also suffered. She stated, "I kept coming down on the bird's throat—which was now broken but still issuing terrible clucks—stroke after miserable stroke, until I finally got its head off. I was blubbering though clenched teeth" (72). She carried the guilt of disappointing her father throughout the meal. When they had the bird at the dinner table, she thought to herself, "I'm not sure you should sit across from each other and eat the roasted bird in resentful silence, either, but we did that too, and the meat was disagreeably tough" (73). She could have smoothly killed the chicken with pride. At first, she had felt honoured. "I said it was important to confront the death of the animal you had the privilege of eating, that it was cowardly to buy cellophane-wrapped packages of boneless, skinless breasts at the grocery store" (72). Because of her actions, her father may have tried to teach her a lesson of responsibility. In his own way of discipline, he intentionally gave her that dull hatchet.

In both stories, the main characters felt negatively toward the food that was supposed to be enjoyed. Amy felt shame about her family's food traditions. Instead of devouring her favourite dish of fish cheeks, her adverse thoughts about losing Robert because of her customs hampered what could have been a wonderful meal. For Gabrielle, her botched slaughtering of the chicken made her father angry. It was not directly because of how the food tasted, but the consequence of their actions was to make their experience with food unpleasant. However, this change in perception about a certain food or occasion around food was transient. Even though the food might have caused conflicts and suffering between the characters, I could still see that these events also provided them enlightenment. It made Amy proud of her culture when she understood that her family was only trying to bring her back to her roots. At the end of the miserable night, her mother gave her a miniskirt because she knew Amy wanted to be American. But her mother reminded Amy, "But inside you must always be Chinese. You must be proud you are different. Your only shame is to have shame" (117). After many years, Amy realized that her actions on that Christmas Eve were pointless. With Gabrielle, that unfortunate event might have driven her to becoming a successful chef. Her passion for meat, butchering, preparing and cooking it, could have stemmed from her debacle with the bird. I could see that her struggle opened her eyes to accept that she needed to become more responsible. Yes, there might be instances, like what happened in the stories, when food could be a source of unhappiness. But, in the end, food will always give people a smile in their faces.

Works Cited

Hamilton, Gabrielle. "Killing Dinner." *Best Food Writing 2005.* Ed. Holly Hughes. New York: Marlowe, 2005. 71–73. Print.

Tan, Amy. "Fish Cheeks." *The Bedford Reader.* 11th ed. Ed. X. J. Kennedy, Dorothy M. Kennedy, and Jane E. Aaron. Boston: Bedford/St. Martin's, 2012. 116–117. Print.

ABOUT THE READING

- What makes the two dinner experiences "bitter"?
- In what ways are Amy's and Gabrielle's conflicts with their families similar? In what ways are they different?
- Do you think the author learned anything about his own or others' real lives by reading these stories? Did you? Explain.
- Read the two stories for yourself. What aromas, textures, and actions do you find?

RECIPE FOR REVIEW

THE READING PROCESS

1. Look over the "ingredients," that is, the text to be read, to find out what it's about. Scan the pages, looking for clues in headings and illustrations. Think about what you might already know about the topic, and prepare a framework on which to "hang" new information.
2. Read the text, pausing to check you've understood it. Look up unfamiliar words or unclear references.
3. Record important information by highlighting or taking notes on main ideas and key terms, noting questions, and/or summarizing in your own words.
4. Depending on your purpose for reading, you may wish to create a more formal set of notes and/or summaries, as well as flashcards for key terms and concepts. Writing a response to the author and talking to classmates about the reading can also be very helpful.

READING FOR INFORMATION

1. Summarize main points.
2. Take notes on key facts, dates, formulas, ingredients, vocabulary.
3. Be sure the source is reliable.

READING FOR IDEAS

1. As always, check reliability.
2. You may need to read more slowly to understand ideas, or read a passage more than once. Stop and think about what the author is saying. Can you put the author's thoughts into your own words? Can you think of other examples?
3. Look beneath the surface of the text for clues to the author's purpose and assumptions. Think about how that affects your understanding of the author's meaning and reliability.
4. You may want to consider evidence *outside* the text as well, such as biographical information about the author, the historical context of the work, and other works on the same topic.
5. Be sure to distinguish the thoughts conveyed in the text from the thoughts you already have about the topic.

© CLS Design/ShutterStock.com

Reading about movements of the arms or legs stimulates the parts of the brain we'd use to perform those actions ourselves.

READING LITERATURE

1. Reading literature can engage us both emotionally and intellectually as we make connections with the text. Further, reading about movements of the arms or legs stimulates the parts of the brain we'd use to perform those actions ourselves.
2. Be prepared to read a story or poem several times. First, read for the "facts." Who's there? What's happening?
3. Next, use these facts or surface details to make sense of the story, the characters, and/or ideas in the text.
4. Pay attention to the language itself, including sentence structure, word choice, and figurative language.
5. You may want to consider such outside clues as biographical information, historical context, psychoanalytic theory, or mythology in interpreting a literary text.
6. The experience and knowledge that the reader brings to literature is very important. However, you need to be careful to distinguish between the thoughts conveyed in the text and the thoughts you already have about the topic.
7. See also Chapter 17.

READING TO REVISE

1. Just as you might take notes on a text you're reading, read your own writing carefully and take notes on potential revisions to content, organization, and word choice.
2. Be careful to focus on what you've actually written; don't get distracted by what you think you've written.
3. Reading aloud can be extremely effective, particularly reading aloud to an audience or having someone else read your work to you.

IDEAS FOR WRITING

1. Imagine that you were living on a farm in Ireland around 1610 when the potato first arrived. Write a dialogue between yourself and a neighboring farmer in which you discuss the strange new vegetable.
2. Choose a food you know well, like potatoes or rice. Then, using Burciaga's "Tortillas" as a rough model, write an essay in which you define the food and describe its various uses.
3. Describe the ways in which you are similar to and different from a family member.
4. Tell the story of a food experience you've had, such as catching a fish or butchering a chicken, or eating a "bitter dinner."

CHAPTER 3
GETTING STARTED WITH THE WRITING PROCESS

By the end of this chapter, you should begin to . . .

* get an overview of the writing process;
* create a framework for a writing assignment, including purpose, audience, and scope;
* get started with freewriting and other brainstorming techniques;
* work effectively with the tools of writing; and
* use strategies to deal with procrastination, if necessary.

Imagine that you are going to cook potatoes, say a particularly elegant dish of creamy whipped mashed potatoes. Perhaps a few glistening rivulets of butter slip down the white slope of potato. When you slide your fork in, you leave an imprint, a ridge, like the crest of a meringue. It sounds lovely. You know there is no resemblance between the raw potatoes you begin with and that creamy swirl of goodness, yet you don't experience a moment of anxiety. Your focus is on a series of familiar steps rather than on what those steps are expected to produce. You have learned to have confidence in the *process.*

Let's look at writing in the same way. Although you know that you need to end up with an essay or letter or report, you also know that it doesn't happen all at once; there are steps to go through and transformations that must take place. You may begin the process with a brainstormed list of ideas or a page of freewriting that bears no resemblance to the finished piece of writing, just as the unwashed raw potato bears no resemblance to a mound of creamy whipped mashed potatoes on a beautiful china plate. Then, through a series of physical and chemical transformations, both the raw potatoes and the raw ideas are "cooked" to perfection!

Although it is the end product of writing that is consumed (through reading), writing is all about the *process.* Just like cooks, writers begin with raw ingredients, cook and season them, and plate them attractively. Just like cooking, writing can take a shorter or a longer time, and can even be quite messy. Yet experienced cooks and writers walk confidently into the kitchen (or sit down confidently at the desk) and know where to

Like peeling potatoes, brainstorming ideas can be fun, creative, and messy.

begin. When we understand the process, whatever it is, we can approach it with assurance and can focus on improving the quality of the end product. We have a place to start and specific techniques to follow, especially if things are not going smoothly.

Writing is quite complicated, in fact. There are so many different types of writing (see Appendix C) and so many different types of writers and so many different types of readers that it can seem overwhelming. Again, a comparison with cooking may be helpful. Clearly, there are many different types of foods and cooking methods and meals and eaters, so we must keep in mind that the "process" we use must be flexible. The messiness of the process often comes as a surprise. Perhaps we imagined ourselves dropping rounded tablespoons of words onto a pristine sheet of paper as if we were dropping spoonfuls of chocolate chip cookie dough onto a baking sheet. However, the writing process is not exactly like a recipe for cookies. We don't always have to follow the same steps in the same order. In fact, there's no guarantee that following the steps will produce an essay the first time. It's not like knowing the cookies will be done after ten minutes in a 350°F oven.

At the heart of the writing process is the writing itself, the writing and the rewriting—that is, the "cooking" of ideas. There are steps before, during, and after the writing (and cooking) that help to enhance the end product. These steps are variable. They may or may not be performed, or they may be performed in different orders for different assignments. We'll be looking at all the possible steps, and practicing them, so that when you are confronted with academic or professional writing tasks, you will have a range of strategies to rely on.

THE STEPS OF THE WRITING PROCESS

Both the writing process and the cooking process must be flexible in order to be successful with very different assignments. For example, making grilled cheese sandwiches for lunch is quite a different task from making lasagna or from making a three-course dinner in which half the recipes must be started the day before. Sometimes the preparation of the raw ingredients is extensive, sometimes not. Sometimes the cooking itself takes hours, sometimes only minutes. Sometimes you're cooking for two, sometimes for two hundred. Nevertheless, there is a certain general outline of steps in each process that can be easily adapted to specific dishes or papers.

The Cooking Process

1. **Plan** the menu and timeline according to purpose, audience, and scope of task
2. **Get started** by listing and obtaining raw ingredients and equipment
3. **Prep** the raw ingredients
4. **Mise en place**: assemble the necessary equipment
5. **Cook** the food by an appropriate method
6. **Taste** the food, and **re-season** as needed
7. **Plate** the food, and **clean up**

Let's see how the process plays out with a couple of examples. First, the grilled cheese sandwich. Not much planning or preparation is involved. Once we have the idea, it's the work of a moment to assemble the ingredients, butter the bread, and heat up the frying pan before we begin cooking. In the case of lasagna, more planning is required. Do we have all the ingredients? What is the timeline? More prep is also required—boiling the pasta, cooking and draining the meat, getting out the cheese and sauce (which you may have made yourself—another part of prep), and assembling the lasagna. The process will be even more complex for that three-course meal requiring some items prepared days in advance.

A parallel outline of steps makes up the writing process:

The Writing Process

1. **Plan** the writing task according to its purpose, audience, and scope
2. **Get started** with outlining/brainstorming/research
3. **Develop** ideas and details through brainstorming and/or research (prep)
4. **Outline** the sequence of ideas (mise en place)
5. Compose (cook) a **rough draft**
6. **Revise** the focus, content/details, organization, and word choice (taste and re-season)
7. **Edit** grammar and usage; **proofread** spelling and punctuation (plate and clean up)

For example, if you were writing an email to a colleague about setting a meeting date, the planning, developing, and outlining of your ideas might flow smoothly into a draft. With a few quick edits, the email is ready to send. In contrast, if you were assigned a four-page paper comparing *The Hunger Games* with Shirley Jackson's post–World War II story "The Lottery," you would want to read the instructions carefully, as well as both texts. Before beginning to write a draft, you might do a good deal of brainstorming, and several revisions might be necessary to develop your ideas fully and express them clearly. Finally, if you were writing a report on the threats and opportunities posed by other restaurants in the area, you might spend days or weeks in research before starting on a draft.

Success in both cooking and writing depends on an understanding of the process, a certain mental preparedness and agility, and sufficient time to "cook" the product, whether that product is a meal or an essay.

> Mental *mise en place* is key. When you're cutting or at the stove, you need to be able to multitask effectively if you want to last in a professional kitchen for more than five minutes. You need to do what takes the longest first, be able to keep things hot, time everything correctly, remember all the steps and be able to work with multiple components. . . . When writing you also need to be organized. Introduction gets the ball rolling and grabs hold of the reader. That's like reading a menu—brings you all in. Next the body is the real execution, just like preparation and cooking. Finally the conclusion, it's a wrap up of all your hard work. That is the main dish, the end result.
>
> —**Marc Magro**, student writer

INITIAL PLANNING

Whether we're cooking or writing, we're usually going to design a particular kind of meal (or text) for a particular kind of customer (or reader) at a particular time and place, and we'll make a plan based on those "particulars." Our menu planning will proceed differently depending on whether we're going to prepare a breakfast buffet in a hotel for 100 people, or an à la carte dinner at a small upscale restaurant, or a sandwich lunch for our family. Similarly, in creating the initial framework for a piece of writing, we will want to consider its audience and purpose.

For example, if you were sending a cover letter and résumé to a job prospect, you would want to organize it both to meet the expectations of the audience and to stand out in the crowd. Or if you were writing a letter to the administration of your school or workplace about changing a policy, you would want to organize your argument to appeal to that particular audience with its own needs and expectations. If you were writing a paper for a college class, you would want to read the instructions carefully regarding genre and length as well as content in order to plan the essay efficiently.

This kind of planning, and the adjustments in approach that result from it, are not new to us. Whenever we speak, we make those same types of decisions (at least, ideally—there are times we may speak *before* we think!). We speak to our grandmother at Thanksgiving dinner about our career plans in a different way than we speak to our close friends while driving to a movie on Friday night about a relationship problem. We can use our knowledge and instincts about communication strategies as we begin to plan each new writing task.

One of the first questions is about **purpose**. If you have directions of any kind, read them carefully at this point. Is your main purpose to inform, entertain, or persuade, or some combination of the three? More specifically, are you planning a research paper on molecular gastronomy, entertaining your peers with a funny restaurant review for the school newspaper, trying to land a catering job, or writing an essay about *Moby-Dick?*

Think also about the anticipated **audience**. Is it professional, academic, or personal? Is it someone you know, like your boss or teacher, or is it a stranger? Does the audience have specialized knowledge about your topic, or will you need to add background material and explanations? An awareness of their audience's expectations is crucial for both writers and cooks, as this culinary student explains in the following paragraph.

> Both writing and cooking allow you to get a feel for your reader or customer. If you're writing for a romance novel, you're not going to have very many jokes or pictures. If you were writing a children's story, you wouldn't make the reading very difficult. It is just the same with cooking. You don't go to an Italian restaurant and start cooking Japanese food; moreover, you wouldn't cook a roasted tenderloin for a vegetarian.
>
> —**Joseph Pierro**, student writer

Within each type or genre of writing, even the simple fact of length will affect your planning process. Suppose you have an assignment for school such as the following:

> Write and revise a short personal narrative. As the basis of your story, choose a food-related incident from your own experience that you remember well and that involved some significant conflict or choice, or that revealed something important to you. The final draft should be 2–3 typed pages and is due in two weeks.

The instructions give you some important planning information. You know that you have two weeks to complete the task and that the finished product must be at least two typed pages in length. You know that the paper asks for a narrative of your own firsthand experience so that no outside research is required. In terms of initial planning, you know that you need to set aside time to remember and write down details about the experience; to organize those details into paragraphs, and to organize those paragraphs into a coherent flow; and to revise, edit, and proofread so that you can hand the paper in on the due date. If the instructions were for a longer paper, you would need to make additional time to develop and polish your ideas. If outside sources were required (see Chapters 18 and 19), you would need to plan time to find, evaluate, read, and take notes on the material; to incorporate the ideas into your own thinking and perhaps to use quotes in your paper; and to create parenthetical citations and a Works Cited page.

As you find answers to these questions about purpose, audience, and scope, you can begin to think about the major parts of the essay or other writing task and perhaps to make an initial and quite general organizational plan. You might pencil in a list, or create a more formal **outline** with levels (I, II, III), or draw a flow chart, like designing the flow of service. If you work better with hands-on strategies, try jotting down ideas on index cards or sticky notes, then physically moving them around to experience different arrangements of your main points. Your goal here is to get a workable plan—nothing carved in stone by any means—but a plan that will allow you to move forward with building the essay.

Depending on your personality and perhaps on how busy you are, you may wish to write down a timeline for this writing task. For some writers, this detailed planning is crucial to their eventual success. Others are able to manage the timeline in their heads. What's important is to know your own strengths and challenges, and to plan accordingly. Be sure to allow room for unexpected delays or problems. As in the kitchen, flexibility is key. Whether the stove suddenly stops working or you've run out of potatoes, whether you spill coffee on your laptop or run out of ink for the printer, it's wise to have a bit of a time cushion before the due date! (See Chapter 5 for more ideas about timelines and other preparations.)

GETTING STARTED WITH FREEWRITING

Whenever I ask students what the most difficult part of writing is, the most common response is "getting started." A scene from the film *Finding Forrester* illustrates this difficulty and offers a useful strategy. The film is about a successful older writer named Forrester and a talented high school student named Jamal, whose teacher is highly critical of his writing. As the two men become acquainted, they begin to help each other. At one point, Forrester places two typewriters on a table, sits down, and quickly types a page of script. Of course, Jamal wants to produce something really impressive and is consequently unable to type a single letter. He tries to explain that he's just getting ready to write, but Forrester shakes his head. He shows Jamal the page he dashed off in ten seconds. The message is "just do it."

Forrester encourages Jamal to **brainstorm**, to free himself from the fear of criticism, from the limitations of the sequence-oriented and analytical right brain. Brainstorming is the job of the more creative, emotional left brain—the "heart." In this first stage of writing, we search for a connection, for something we're passionate about, and let that passion drive our words onto the page. Once we get a rough draft down on paper, we develop and polish it during revision, which is a job for the right brain.

Meanwhile time passes, and Jamal sits helplessly staring at the blank page. The sun is setting and the room darkens, but Jamal doesn't move. "Writer's block" has paralyzed his fingers. Then Forrester has an idea. He brings out a copy of one of his old stories and tells Jamal to begin copying it. As the movement of his fingers helps him relax, Jamal can tap into the passion of the right brain and write down his own words.

Forrester (left) encourages Jamal to brainstorm, to free himself from the fear of criticism, to find his own words.

The image of Jamal frozen in front of the typewriter in the fading light is an excellent illustration of the value of brainstorming. Jamal is so worried that the very first word he writes won't be perfect that he is unable to move. The solution Forrester offers is **freewriting**, that is, writing a certain number of pages, or writing for a certain length of time, without giving a thought to the shape or quality of the final product, or to grammar, spelling, and punctuation. The idea is simply to unlock the words and let them spill out onto the page. Later on, some of these words might be useful for the first draft. However, even if no interesting ideas or details are revealed in this exercise, the freewriting has the effect of stimulating the brain, like heating up the oven.

Let's see how this might work. Imagine we have been writing the narrative mentioned earlier. We sit down to get started, but we can't think of a single idea or even a single word to write down. We need to peel the potato. We need to pick up a pencil, or open a laptop, and just start writing. Here we go:

> So freewriting supposedly it helps in getting started I need to write about an experience with food well of course I have thousands of those but it's also supposed to have taught me something or what not but I can't think of anything that specific right now but yet I have to keep writing so what shall I pick what's been really dramatic about food oh maybe that time with the snails ugh

This is probably the kind of freewriting that Forrester pounded out on his typewriter to Jamal's amazement, a kind of stream-of-consciousness that clears away clutter in the brain and often leads to the germ of an idea. Here it's *snails*. It's as if we were making stock and periodically skimming the fat off the top. Freewriting can be done relative to *time*—that is, "write steadily for five minutes"—or to *space*—"fill up a page of notebook paper." Freewriting is useful at other points in the writing process as well. Whenever you need new material, or whenever you get stuck, freewriting can help.

MORE STRATEGIES FOR GETTING STARTED

Freewriting doesn't work for every person or for every situation. Therefore it's helpful to experiment with different types of brainstorming to get an idea of what works best for you. Furthermore, you might not always use the same type of brainstorming each time. If one technique seems to lose steam, try another—and another. Second, brainstorming doesn't happen only at the beginning. At any point during the writing process, it may be helpful to stop for a moment and reenter this very free and creative phase of writing. Suppose you're well into revision, the fourth step of the writing process, and the paper is fine except for a rather dull introduction. This would be an excellent time for some freewriting, or for bouncing ideas off another person. If your potato dish is selling out fast, you're going to go right back to the sink and start peeling.

Here are some additional ideas for getting started, or for brainstorming at any point in the writing process.

LISTING

Another effective way to brainstorm is to make a list. Back to the snails, for example, we might jot down all the details we remember about that dramatic experience. While we won't be as "free" to write just anything as we were in freewriting, we must not slow ourselves down by trying to evaluate the quality of these details. Remember, we don't always use the whole potato in the end. We're still in a messy, creative phase where we're just trying to keep the words flowing. Here's a list of details about the day of the snails:

Day 4	French chef
fig and hollandaise sauce	disgusting
couldn't swallow	staring at me
Culinary Olympics	someone came through the door
small bites	sound of snails
Wednesday	day of torture

As we look back over this list, the specific food items seem quite promising, for example, the *fig and hollandaise sauce*. The energy of *disgusting* and *day of torture* sounds quite promising as well. Some details might turn out to be irrelevant, such as the fact that the incident occurred on a Wednesday.

WEBBING

A third way of getting some ideas down on paper is often called webbing or clustering. Figure 3.1 shows a web about *chocolate*. Or we might put *snails* at the center of the web to start us off. Then in a series of branches circling around that detail we might write *fig and hollandaise sauce, ran out of kitchen, lesson learned*. If we extended each branch, *fig and hollandaise sauce* might lead us to *disgusting* and *couldn't swallow*, while *lesson learned*

Figure 3.1 An Example of Webbing

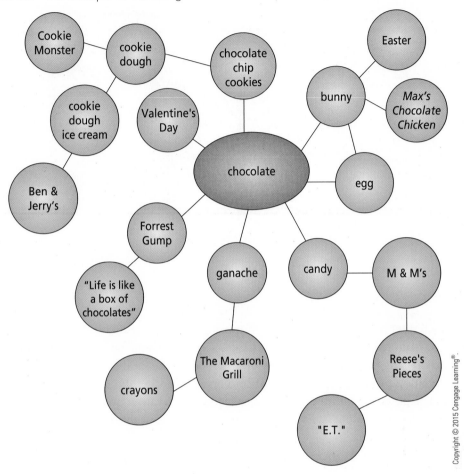

Copyright © 2015 Cengage Learning®

might lead to *take small bites.* For many students, this method of brainstorming can be more attractive and effective than the more traditional outline using Roman numerals.

PICTURES/CHARTS/GRAPHS

Sometimes drawing can be an effective method of freeing up your ideas. For example, you might try to get a better handle on the characters in Ernest Hemingway's "A Clean, Well-Lighted Place" by drawing them (Figure 3.2). Diagrams or charts can also get your thoughts moving (Figure 3.3). Again, if you choose to brainstorm like this, work freely and do not judge the usefulness or quality of each picture. That comes later.

TALKING

A very effective method of brainstorming—though not one that is appropriate to every *classroom* situation—is talking with someone about the topic. As we began to

Figure 3.2 Hemingway's "A Clean, Well-Lighted Place"

see in Chapter 1, speech can play an important role at various points in the writing process, from asking questions about the assignment and brainstorming about the topic to revising the rhythm and flow of sentences in the final draft. In this early phase of the writing process, the stimulus of conversation and of the sound of the words, as well as the potential for helpful feedback, can lead us rather quickly to some interesting ideas and vivid details. Even talking to yourself—out loud—can be helpful!

BROWSING THE WEB

Finding out what other people have written about your topic can help you get started, and browsing the Web is an easy way to find some of that writing. However, you must be careful to evaluate the reliability of anything you read, and you must be sure not to *copy* what you read into your own writing without properly citing it. (See Chapters 18 and 19 for more information.)

THE TOOLS OF WRITING

Remember Forrester's advice to Jamal? When we begin the first complete draft of a paper, we need to write it with our hearts. It's not that the topic itself has to be an emotional one. But we do need to feel a *connection* with it and let the words spill out freely.

As you prepare to write this first draft, be sure you have the kind of work space or environment that helps you concentrate. Some people need absolute quiet, while others like to play music—from Bach to Bob Marley to Beyoncé—and still others like the chaos

Figure 3.3 Brainstorming with a Flow Chart

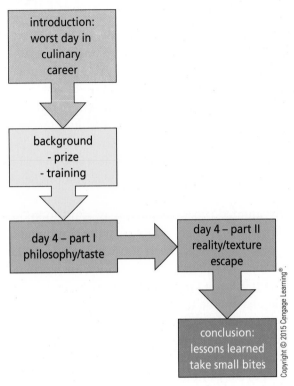

of a kitchen table in the midst of family activity or the friendly sounds and smells of a coffee shop. If you have not already determined which environments are helpful to you, do some experimenting.

You also need to find the right "tools." Sometimes this may be determined by the assignment. If you have an in-class writing activity or exam, for instance, you probably cannot use your computer and listen to Aretha Franklin on the headphones. Assuming you have options, however, try whether a pencil feels better than a pen, or whether typing helps your thoughts flow more freely. I find that I like to freewrite on the laptop but outline with a pencil. Typing seems to open up my ideas, while the slight resistance of the graphite on the paper helps me concentrate on organization. Each person will have a unique combination of materials and environment that makes writing a little easier.

A word about digital writing—back up your work! Writing on a laptop or other device with word processing is fast and easy. However, there are some pitfalls we want to be aware of. Save your drafts, including at least one of them on paper, in case you lose everything on the laptop. Back up your work on a flash drive or other external storage device. To reduce ink, you can print drafts of your papers in a special draft mode. Print drafts on the back of recycled paper.

Finally, understand the limitations of your tools, and make the best use of those that are available, as Loretta did with the sugar!

WHAT TO DO ABOUT PROCRASTINATION

"I'm a procrastinator," students will tell me, often with an expression that says "I have an incurable disease." Well, I'm a procrastinator, too. Sometimes procrastination doesn't cause much of a problem. If I put off making dinner and go to a movie instead, I can probably just serve sandwiches that night and cook the chicken the next day. But if I keep putting off the chicken, it will go bad. And if I keep putting off changing the oil in my car, the car will go bad. And if I wait until the last minute to write a paper, the paper might not have time to get good.

Procrastination has been studied from a number of different angles. If you're interested, there is plenty to read about it from scientists and philosophers, as well as from humorists!

Psychologically minded procrastinators may want to know *why* they procrastinate. For example, is it that you just don't like to write? Putting it off feels good because you're not writing—and it may even mean you just don't do the task. Perhaps you hate writing so much that the consequences of not writing are worth it. Or maybe you don't mind writing the first draft, but you hate looking at it again. Yet if you wait until the last minute, you won't have time for revision.

Others may procrastinate because they're afraid of doing poorly on the assignment. If you can forget about it entirely, you may think, then you won't be afraid. But leaving the work until the last minute doesn't make sense. Instead, plan to include time to visit your instructor or the campus writing center or a friend who can help.

Sometimes becoming aware of the *way* we procrastinate can help us identify and change the behavior. The Writing Center at the University of North Carolina offers the following possibilities:

How do you procrastinate?

- Try to ignore the task, hoping against hope that it will go away?
- Over- or underestimate the degree of difficulty of the task?
- Minimize the impact that your performance now may have on your future?
- Substitute something important for something really important? (For example, cleaning your room instead of writing your paper.)
- Let a short break become a long one, or an evening in which you do no work at all? (For example, claiming that you are going to watch TV for ½ hour, then watching it all night.)
- Focus on one part of the task at the expense of the rest? (For example, keep working on the introduction while putting off writing the body and conclusion.)
- Spend too much time researching or choosing a topic.

Perhaps if we understand a little more about our behavior, we can be more effective in changing it.

"I'm a procrastinator."

So that's great—but what are some immediate, concrete, doable strategies that we can attempt as soon as we notice we're procrastinating? Try these.

- **Peel the potato.** You may find that freewriting is a very effective way of overcoming procrastination. Just get something down on paper! After all, words *are* what you're looking for, so you'll feel productive. And once you have something down, you can begin to add or delete without the same feeling of blockage.
- **Be realistic about the amount of time you need.** Being an optimist is usually a good thing—until it interferes with being a realist. You may underestimate the amount of time you need to complete a writing project and find yourself working desperately fast as the deadline approaches. While you may get the work done, it might have been better quality work had you allowed more time, and you might have been more comfortable.
- **Don't try to do everything at once.** Break the assignment into smaller chunks— do the reading one week, for example, and during the next week do a small amount each day—write an outline one day, the introduction the next, and so on. Revise in the third week, and type up the Works Cited page.
- **Begin wherever you can.** If you feel nervous about writing the introduction, just jump right in and start writing in the middle. Brainstorm. Don't judge yourself. Just get something on paper.
- **Take the pressure off.** If you're paralyzed by the thought of how important this assignment is and how awful it will be if you don't do a good job, change your

mindset with an internal conversation. Yes, you might tell yourself, this is an important assignment—but the world won't end if I don't get an A.

- **OR—put the pressure on!** Long before the actual deadline for the paper, set your own deadlines. Reward yourself if you meet them.

Remember that much of what we do is habit. If you look closely at how and why you procrastinate, and if you keep experimenting with different strategies to control it, you may find yourself able to change this uncomfortable and unproductive habit.

LET'S GET STARTED

Beginning a writing project is often difficult. Perhaps our initial focus is too much on the end product rather than on the process. Like Jamal, we might become paralyzed by the pressure to perform. Even without anxiety, we still might be "at a loss for words," unable to "think" of anything to say. Freewriting and the other brainstorming techniques described in this chapter are powerful tools for smashing "writer's block" and getting started.

Many students find that focusing on the steps of the process rather than trying to jump to the end product helps them work more effectively and write a better paper. You don't want to serve a Thanksgiving turkey that's underdone or an essay that's underdeveloped.

A TASTE FOR READING

Daniela Moreira Camia is from Argentina. She currently attends culinary school in the United States.

****

Day 4: Snails
by Daniela Moreira Camia

How do you manage to pretend that you like a high-scale dish that a 70-year-old famous master chef cooks for you? Well, apparently I'm an award-winning escape artist, and I found a way to disappear from the incredible kitchen that I was in. It was the worst day in my culinary career.

I was attending school, taking professional cooking classes. I used to travel two hours every day to get to school and stayed in class for eight to ten hours. Of course, as "Miss High Achiever" I was doing all I could do to be the best and learn as much as I could, and that is how I got chosen as a competitor in the Culinary Olympics that year. I trained for four months, day and night, not stopping, thinking about food 24 hours a day, being under pressure most of the time and learning from the best chefs in my city.

I won the first place that year; it was kind of a big deal in the school, not just because I won, but for the prize. I was going to be trained by a master chef in French cuisine.

A month later the training began. Day 1: French sauces. Day 2: duck. Day 3: foie gras. Day 4: snails (I wasn't looking forward to that day). And last, day 5, desserts. What you really have to know about a French chef is that if he doesn't live in your country, chances are that he is not very good at your language. And that was exactly what happened. I didn't understand a word of what he was saying. I couldn't even understand his handwriting. It was like reading symbols. Anyway, I kind of understood what was going on while he was cooking, but when he spoke to me I just nodded and pretended that I was getting all the information he was giving me.

Day 4 came—as I remember it, "the day of torture." I didn't even know that there were so many different kinds of snails. I never thought of eating one, just the simple image of that day that I have on my mind makes me sick. As a good future chef, I was ready to eat everything, no matter what. My philosophy was that

"As a good future chef, I was ready to eat everything, no matter what."

I had to try everything to learn, to understand what is out there, what are people eating. But one thing I never learned is that if you are tasting food, you just have to "taste," that means small bites, don't put the whole thing in your mouth if you don't know how it is going to taste. That day, the chef taught me how to cook snails, and we made different French dishes. I remember one very clearly: snail stuffed with fig and hollandaise sauce, in other words, "disgusting." Just hearing the sound that your mouth makes when you are eating snails is horrible. That nasty noise comes in my head every time I hear the word snail, and let's just not even talk about the texture that those creatures have.

I put the whole thing in my mouth; it probably wasn't that big, but for me it was like putting a big old shoe in my mouth. I couldn't swallow, tears started running out of my eyes, I couldn't spit it out, how was I going to do that in front of the chef? He was watching me closely to see how I was reacting, waiting for me to tell him how good that little nasty thing was. It was the end of my life. There was no escape. I knew it—I was going to have to swallow that thing, and probably vomit all over the place.

The chef started staring at me, waiting for me to say something, and that was the point when I stopped breathing. I wasn't going to throw up in front of him. He was a "famous French Chef"—you just don't do that. It was the end of my career. I was never going to be a chef if I couldn't even eat that classic French dish. What was I going to do? The only solution was to change careers. I remember my mind going so fast, having all kinds of crazy thoughts, until somebody opened the kitchen door, right on time to save my life. I don't even know who it was and what he was doing in there, but what I remember is how I noticed that the chef wasn't paying attention to me, so I ran. I ran as fast as I could. I don't remember ever running so fast in my entire life. The bathroom was the best place in the world for me that day, and I will be always thankful to the lady who realized what was about to happen and moved out of the way, letting me go first.

I am not sure if the chef found out what happened that day. He didn't mention anything, and of course I didn't either. I was very glad he didn't ask me if I liked the class. I was glad it was over. I didn't learn much in those lessons; between the chef's thick accent and his handwriting, I probably got just a quarter of the information. But I did learn an important lesson: I don't need to like snails or French cuisine to be a chef. And when I am tasting new things, I have to remember to be smart in the way I put food in my mouth.

ABOUT THE READING

- Who do you think the intended audience of this piece is? Why?
- The author gives a good deal of information about herself before she gets to day 4 in the kitchen. How does this background enrich the central story of the snails?
- What details or images are particularly effective?
- How does the author build suspense?

RECIPE FOR REVIEW

STEPS OF THE WRITING PROCESS

1. **Planning**: Identify the purpose, audience, and scope (length, time frame, etc.) of the writing assignment.
2. **Getting started**: Freewrite, make lists, create webs or charts, draw pictures, talk to classmates, do research, do experiments.
3. **Developing ideas**: Ask and answer questions about your topic's characters, events, descriptive details, relation to other topics, process, examples, causes and effects.
4. **Organizing ideas**: Put main points in order; use a list, outline, or diagram.
5. **Drafting**: Write a rough draft, focus on the main idea, get the whole thing on paper, ignore spelling and grammar.

6. **Revising**: Read the essay with new eyes. Is the main idea clear? Is it developed with sufficient details and examples? Is it logically organized? Does the introduction focus on the subject and get the reader's attention? Does the conclusion highlight the main idea?

7. **Editing and proofreading**: Check grammar and word usage, spelling, and punctuation.

CHAPTER EXERCISES

1. *Freewriting*—Like Forrester and Jamal, write or type a single page—without stopping and without "thinking"—on the following topic: Tell the story of an especially funny, frightening, or embarrassing experience in your life.

2. *Listing*——Brainstorm a list of details about the people, places, and things in the story you began in Exercise 1.

3. *Webbing/Clustering*—Choose a topic, such as *chicken* or *noodles*, and write it in the center of a circle. Then fill in the branches with ideas and details you associate with that central word. Work quickly, and do not judge the value of your choices; you're just peeling the potato here.

4. *Outlining*—Look at your brainstorming work from Exercises 1 and 2. Where should that story begin in order to be clear to a reader who doesn't know you? Where should it end? Briefly outline the main events of the story, that is, the main parts of the essay, in an informal list, formal outline, flow chart, or whatever format is helpful to you.

IDEAS FOR WRITING

1. Write a paragraph in which you explain your own writing process and assess its effectiveness.

2. Describe your ideal workspace for writing tasks. At what time of the day are you most creative? most careful with details? Do you prefer to write by hand or on a computer?

3. Take time now to write the first draft of your story about a funny or frightening experience in your life. Find the right environment, assemble your writing materials, and start writing. Don't think about the end product, and don't worry about the grammar, spelling, and punctuation. You're just cooking the potato, remember; it's not ready for plating.

4. Do you procrastinate? If so, in what situations and in what ways? Does it bother you? If it does, how might you change that habit?

CHAPTER 4
DEVELOPING YOUR IDEAS

By the end of this chapter, you should begin to . . .

- develop a topic or idea by asking and answering questions in the following categories: narration, description, comparison, process, definition, example, classification, causation, and analysis;
- develop a topic or idea by asking and answering questions about your likes and dislikes, what you don't understand, what's funny, what's a metaphor for your topic, and what your readers want or need to know; and
- begin to think about how these methods of developing ideas may become part of a finished piece of writing.

When we compared the initial phase of the writing process to "peeling the potato," it sounded pretty simple. Yet getting started on a piece of writing can actually be quite difficult. In this chapter, we'll talk in more detail about how to find and develop ideas about a topic. We talked earlier about the parallels between writing and cooking. The concept of developing ideas in writing or speaking is parallel to that of finding and preparing the ingredients of a dish. You're dealing both with ingredients, that is, with the ideas and details of your writing, and with the method you use to prepare them, that is, the way in which you explore and organize those ideas and details.

It's all driven by questions. How many times have you asked yourself, or someone else, What's for dinner? Perhaps the answer is, I have a chicken in the fridge, and then the questions start to move faster. How shall we cook the chicken? What shall we season it with? What sides shall we have? What shall we have for dessert? Do we have anything for a starter? As these questions are answered, an outline of the meal emerges, a timeline is created, the ingredients are gathered, and the preparations begin.

Developing a topic for writing can also be driven by questions: What happened? Where did it happen? When did it happen? Why did it happen? The rhythm of question and answer not only creates a process for brainstorming useful details and examples, but it also gives a forward movement to your writing, an energy and flow that leads you from one thought to the next, from one detail to the next, just as one delicious bite leads to the desire for another one. Think about the energy in the game of Twenty Questions: one question leads to the next as you narrow down the fields of "animal, vegetable, or mineral" to the specific item. Or what about the suspense inherent in a courtroom drama as the lawyers *develop* the idea of guilt or innocence in the minds of the jury members? Somehow you'd like to get that energy of speech into your thinking and writing. Remember that this phase of writing—brainstorming—is free, creative, experimental, and often messy. If you find yourself resisting, perhaps try to think of it as a game. Find the fun in it.

Let's go back to dinner for a moment. Suppose we've got some potatoes on hand. The question follows: How shall we prepare them? Shall we bake them, mash them, fry them, roast them in the oven with the chicken, or make potatoes au gratin? Similarly, if we have to *write* about potatoes, we ask ourselves how to develop that topic. Shall we tell a story about potatoes, or describe their appearance, or compare different varieties?

Methods of cooking and writing

Process	Ingredient	Method
Cooking	potato	baked, mashed, fried, oven roasted, au gratin
Writing	potato	story, description, process, comparison, example

Suppose we chose a different topic, like *tortillas*. What is your first memory of tortillas? What other stories do you know about tortillas? How would you describe tortillas? How do you make tortillas? How would you define *tortilla*? What kinds of tortillas are there? In this very free first phase of the writing process, let the questions lead you, whether along one line or in many different directions.

As you ask and answer questions about a topic, remember that the ideas and details that emerge through this brainstorming can be captured in a variety of ways, as we saw in Chapter 3. Sometimes freewriting works best, just writing or typing whatever comes to your mind in response to a particular question. These questions can also be answered in lists or webs or in other types of charts and graphs, for example, Venn diagrams. Finally, talking about the topic with other people, if possible, can be an extremely effective way of finding new ideas and testing them immediately with an audience.

NARRATION—WHAT HAPPENED?

One of the most natural ways of thinking about and developing an idea is to tell a **story**. Storytelling, or **narration**, means recounting *what happened*, reporting a series of events. A story can be very short (like a six-word tweet) or very long, like the 700 pages of *Moby-Dick* or the 1200 pages of *War and Peace*. A story can also be part of another type of writing, such as a magazine or news article, research paper or report, restaurant review, or cookbook. Stories and recipes go well together, for example, in Shoba Narayan's

One of the interwoven love stories in *Monsoon Wedding* is that of the housemaid Alice and the wedding planner P. K. Dubey.

Monsoon Diary: A Memoir with Recipes and Laura Esquivel's *Like Water for Chocolate: A Novel in Monthly Installments with Recipes, Romances, and Herb Remedies.*

In the following brief excerpt from "Salt Cod, Alaska" (see Chapter 11), the writer records events (I spit the spoonful into the bowl) and dialogue ("Come on, Bobby, it is very good for you") from the past in order to explain a moment in the present.

> Unfortunately, Bebe had an excellent memory, and a few days before my departure back to Seattle, he appeared with a foul bowl of Bacalao. "Come on, Bobby, it is very good for you," he said. Tentative, I lifted a tiny spoonful to my mouth and tasted it. A potent saltiness filled my mouth, followed by a rank fishiness. The flavor was more concentrated and far more disagreeable than the smell. I spit the spoonful into the bowl, and, as Bebe howled with amusement, I ran down the narrow wooden hallway of the dormitory, grabbed my tooth brush, and scrubbed frantically.
>
> —**Robert A. Hannon**, student writer

The writer also provides descriptive details: the spoonful was tiny; the hallway was narrow and wooden; the Bacalao had a rank fishiness. The idea in a story is developed through details about what happened and what was said, and often about what things looked and tasted like.

Whenever we read a story or watch a movie, we automatically begin asking and answering such questions as the following:

- What is the story about?
- Where does it take place?
- Who are the characters?
- What do the characters want?
- Is there a problem they're trying to solve? What's getting in their way?
- How will it end?

Sometimes we'll actually hear someone in the movie theater speaking these questions out loud. This can be annoying, yes, but we're probably asking the same questions ourselves. One question will lead to an answer, which will lead to another question, and so on. Perhaps you have a friend who's not the best storyteller, and you have to prompt him or her with a series of questions: Wait a minute, who said that? Why? What did she want? Whether we're telling the story of something that actually happened or a story that we've created, it's important to imagine the questions a reader would ask so that we can provide the answers.

DESCRIPTION—WHAT DOES IT LOOK LIKE?

Another basic method of developing an idea is through **description.** A person or place is mentioned in the course of a story or process, and we ask, What does it look like? As we'll see in Chapter 12, effective description uses all the five senses, creating for the reader a vivid experience. Our questions continue: What does it look like? What does it sound and feel like? What does it smell and taste like? In the following example, the answer to an essay question in writing class, the writer describes the "harsh environment" of war in Iraq by answering such questions. Note that the idea of the paragraph is contained in the first sentence, which is the most common and often a very effective placement for it.

> The Hurt Locker takes place in a harsh environment. There is little to no grass, only dry, cracked dirt and sand. The sand is rough beneath your foot and it crunches as you walk. As the wind blows, gusting across the flat, arid land, the sand billows up in massive clouds that can block your vision and sting your skin. The sun beats down on the ground, heating up the air. Every breath is dry, a gulp of pure heat with not a drop of humidity to dull the warmth. It feels like taking a bite of the sun. All around are the sounds of people talking, vendors at stalls hawking their goods, children running and laughing, cars puttering down the crowded streets. The center of the town hangs heavy with the smells of food cooking; rich, earthy spices mingled with citrus and fruit. The sun filters down through the buildings to tinge the air golden yellow. Further outside of the town, the sand piles up in dunes. Buildings are left abandoned and crumbling, and the wind blows the tiny grains of sand up against solitary, freestanding walls in drifts taller than you can reach. Here and there grow scrubby bushes, providing only enough shade for the smallest creature to hide under and get a reprieve from the sun.
>
> —**Molly-Iris Alpern**, student writer

It can be helpful to imagine that your audience has not seen or tasted what you're writing about. Look for details that will help readers share your experience.

COMPARISON: WHAT ARE THE SIMILARITIES AND DIFFERENCES?

Comparing one item to another, often with the goal of choosing between them, is one of our most basic thought processes. **Comparison**, or **compare and contrast**, can be used just in the brainstorming phase as a way to get started, or it can become the method of development of one or more paragraphs within an essay, or it can become the controlling method for an entire paper or book (which is explored more fully in Chapter 13). Charts and graphs can be particularly helpful in brainstorming similarities and differences.

Comparison is one of the most common ingredients of professional writing. For example, suppose you were writing a proposal for investors about a new restaurant you'd like to open. You would want to find similarities between your concept and existing successful restaurants, while at the same time highlighting the differences that would make your restaurant unique. We might ask questions like the following:

- What other restaurants are in the same neighborhood?
- Given the age, income, ethnicity, and other characteristics of potential customers, what other restaurants would attract the same customers, and what new customers might your restaurant cater to?
- How will your menu offerings, pricing, and service be similar to and different from those of local competitors?

In the following example, students have asked themselves these and other questions in order to identify the "opportunities" and "threats" offered to their proposed restaurant, Braizen, by one of their local competitors.

Opportunities

Menu Options: Braizen will be able to take advantage of the lack of options on the menu at this restaurant. We will be offering a variety of different braised proteins and greens as well as daily specials. Our menu will provide the consumer a higher level of food with the same sense of convenience, portability, and speed.

Portion Size: The items on our menu will be provided at a portion size, which will satiate and appease our consumers at a single serving. Crif Dogs' items are often seen as just a snack between meals, and multiple items must be purchased for the customer to be satiated.

Threats

Popularity: Crif Dogs has become a very popular brand, well known to many people especially between the ages of 18 to 35. Besides the popularity of the menu itself, the restaurant offers branded apparel including shirts, hats, and other novelty type items with the Crif Dogs logo and packaging.

Delivery: The fact that this restaurant delivers to local customers could easily make it a threat to our business. Customers that do not have transportation or the ability to drive will often choose a restaurant that delivers over one that doesn't.

Variety: While their main staple is the bacon-wrapped hot dog, Crif Dogs does provide the consumer with a variety of toppings and sauces to mix and match between. If that is too overwhelming, they have preselected specialties with enough variety to satiate even the pickiest consumer.

—**James Shum, David Murray**, and **Jason Hsu**, student writers

Sometimes we develop an idea through asking how two items are *similar,* even though they may appear to have little in common, for example, writing and cooking. In Chapter 3, we looked in some detail at those similarities, particularly in terms of process. We might also develop a topic through focusing on the *differences* between two or more items that are essentially similar, like peaches and apricots. While both are stone fruits often used in baking, the differences in flavor and texture should be evaluated in order to make the best decision about ingredients.

> When using peaches and apricots in baking, you should treat them as differently as you would apples and oranges since they will contribute different components to the product. If you want a bolder flavor, use the peach and add some sliced almonds and vanilla to enhance it. If you want a subtler flavor, use the apricot. Adding some fresh ginger will play up its "green" components and make for an interesting complexity of flavors. Think of its velvety feel and how that will affect the overall consistency of the dish. A pudding or ice cream would show off the apricot's creamy texture.

—**Elizabeth Best**, student writer

We can imagine such a paragraph in a cookbook.

Comparison lies at the heart of much academic writing as well. You might be asked to write a paper comparing Shakespeare's *Macbeth* with the 2005 film version in the collection *Shakespeare Retold,* in which Macbeth is a restaurant chef who murders his boss. Which elements of Shakespeare's story were retained in the "retold" version? Which elements were changed? You could probably list or graph many answers to each question. Most likely, though, the comparison is not the end goal of such a writing assignment. Instructors might ask you to evaluate the effect of these changes; simply listing the changes would not be sufficient. As you will see in Chapter 13, the major risk in comparison is that it won't go much past the brainstorming stage. There should be some meaning or purpose to the comparison, or some conclusion to be drawn.

PROCESS—HOW DO YOU DO THAT?
HOW DOES IT WORK?

One of the most important ways to develop ideas for those in the food industry is **process**. Whether you're writing a recipe, a restaurant review, or a standard operating procedure for your kitchen (such as a HAACP plan), it is crucial to identify the necessary equipment and ingredients, and the correct sequence of steps, in order to perform the process correctly. The addition of pertinent explanations and cautions makes the instructions even more effective. You might begin with questions like the following:

- What ingredients and equipment are needed?
- Are there special restrictions on time and place?
- Do you need specialized knowledge or training?
- What is the sequence of steps in the process? Is the order flexible at all?
- If you've performed the process yourself, what personal experience of your own might be helpful to your readers?
- What might go wrong? How might you prevent and/or fix these problems?

Processes involving food preparation generally answer these questions. Transcribed from a well-worn index card in my grandmother's collection, the following recipe comes from the Steer family, who were farming in northeastern Ohio in the early 1900s. They raised cows and chickens, and kept horses for all the jobs later performed by tractors and automobiles. On a hot, sunny day during the haying season, ice-cold blackberry vinegar was often carried out to the workers in the fields. Haying is sweaty, dusty work for both horses and humans. When you saw a child come from the farmhouse carrying a jug, it was a welcome signal to stop work briefly, give the horses some water, and enjoy a cup of blackberry vinegar. Blackberries[a] were plentiful on the farm, and this drink—made every year—was an especially refreshing one. It has a lovely dark color and, like lemonade, a taste both sharp and sweet.

Blackberry Vinegar

Put 5 pts blackberries in stone jar & cover with vinegar & let stand for 24 hrs. Squeeze the juice out & put 5 more pts into juice & let stand 24 hrs again. Strain out all juice. For every cup of juice, add ¾ cup sugar. Bring to boil, skim & seal. ¼ cup juice to ¾ water when ready to use.

Incorporated within the instructions are the ingredients (the blackberries and vinegar, and later the sugar and water) and equipment (the stone jar). The sequence of steps is clear, though no explanations were apparently deemed necessary. However, there is one caution. At the bottom of the card is a penciled note from the 1950s that reads: Too much vinegar.

---

[a]For more about blackberries, see the poem by Yusef Komunyakaa on page 159.

As you're brainstorming about a process, it can be helpful to remember the times when you've performed it yourself or seen it performed. Think also about your probable readers, what they already know and how to explain new ingredients and procedures. Try to use specific words that help the reader see what's happening. Vivid description can help your reader understand (and enjoy) the process, while some of the necessary explanations and cautions can be put in the form of stories. See Chapter 14 for more details on writing about a process.

DEFINITION—WHAT IS IT?

Sometimes we might begin to develop a topic or idea by getting a clear **definition**. We'll often look something up in a dictionary or in Wikipedia. Then brainstorm by expanding on it—What does it look like? What is it made of? Where can you find it? What does it do? What is it used for? Note how Harold McGee explores the definition of a potato in the following excerpt from the revised edition of *On Food and Cooking: The Science and Lore of the Kitchen:*

> The potato is a tuber, the tip of an underground stem that swells with stored starch and water and bears primordial buds, the "eyes," that generate the stem and roots of a new plant. It is sometimes a little sweet, with a slight but characteristic bitterness, and has a mild earthy flavor. (302)

As always, the potato provides a fairly straightforward example Compare. José Antonio Burciaga's essay at the end of this chapter, in which the author devotes pages to defining a *tortilla*. You might find yourself defining more abstract topics, such as *happiness, justice,* or *marriage*; or specialized professional terms, such as *stem cell, molecular gastronomy,* or *onomatopoeia*; or slang terms such as *bagging, weeded,* or *chick flick*. Definition can play an important role in argument and is discussed in more detail in Chapters 15 and 16.

EXEMPLIFICATION—CAN YOU GIVE ME AN EXAMPLE?

Like stories and descriptions, **examples** are ways of thinking that we use automatically in speech and that transfer effectively to writing. Examples are common in many types of writing, *for example,* textbooks and reports. Examples make an idea concrete; they put a picture in the reader's mind. We use examples to illustrate or explain a point or sometimes to "prove" one. Often a general statement is best illustrated through a specific example. In the journal entry that follows, the writer uses three different examples to illustrate his points about revenge and justice.

> Revenge is a dark and twisting path, one that changes people, and affects them and the lives of those around them more than seemingly

In his grief over his mother's death, Anakin Skywalker turns to thoughts of revenge, thoughts that will eventually lead him to become Darth Vader.

possible. Justice, however, is the opposite, a straight and narrow path that leads to a clean slate. We see opportunities and examples of the choice we have between the two roads all the time in our everyday lives, in movies, in books, in the news. . . . [In] "Star Wars," Anakin's mother gets killed by the Sand People. Instead of doing the right thing, and seeking out justice for the crime committed, [Anakin] turns to revenge, killing the Sand People. This act then leads to more acts of revenge and hatred, all the while eating away at him until nothing is left but his evil, revenge-twisted soul, known to the galaxy as Darth Vader. In the book "The Hunger Games," the protagonist, Katniss, gets sucked into this death match that occurs every year, put on by the government of her world. Upon winning the Game, she doesn't gloat, she uses her newfound press power to seek out justice rather than revenge for the crimes committed. I guess the main point is why take more lives, or create more anguish to get back at someone? In the end, it would make you just as bad as them. Finally, we see a conjunction of the two, in the book series "Harry Potter."

—**Timothy Fisher**, student writer

As with all types of writing, it's important to think about what your audience knows. If they don't know the examples you use, you may not be able to communicate as effectively as you would like.

CLASSIFICATION—WHAT KINDS ARE THERE?

We often need to narrow or broaden a topic, and looking at different kinds or categories can be a helpful start. What kinds of restaurants are there, for example, and what are the characteristics and subcategories of each kind? This sorting can be done by any number of different principles. You could sort restaurants by size, location, price, or cuisine. If you were categorizing movies, you might look at comedy, drama, romance, thriller, action, science fiction, documentary, blockbuster, indie. Within each category there might be additional types. **Classification** can be an excellent way to get both a broad overview of a topic and to begin to narrow down your particular interest.

Classification is often used in thinking and learning about food. In the revised edition of *On Food and Cooking*, Harold McGee discusses two kinds of potato:

> There are two general cooking categories of potato, called the "mealy" and the "waxy" for their textures when cooked. Mealy types (russets, blue and purple varieties, Russian and banana fingerlings) concentrate more dry starch in their cells, so they're denser than waxy types. When cooked, the cells tend to swell and separate from each other, producing a fine, dry, fluffy texture that works well in fried potatoes and in baked and mashed potatoes, which are moistened with butter or cream. In waxy types (true new potatoes and common U.S. red- and white-skinned varieties), neighboring cells cohere even when cooked, which gives them a solid, dense, moist texture, and holds them together in intact pieces for gratins, potato cakes, and salads. (302–303)

Classification is an excellent way to organize your thoughts about many different topics. Using visual representations such as charts or boxes may help you "see" things with a fresh perspective.

Classifying Potatoes

Type of Potato	Varieties	Characteristics	Uses
mealy	russets, blue and purple varieties, Russian and banana fingerlings	fine, dry, fluffy texture when cooked	in fried, baked, and mashed potatoes
waxy	true new potatoes and common U.S. red- and white-skinned varieties	solid, dense, moist texture when cooked	in gratins, potato cakes, and salads

CAUSATION—WHY DID IT HAPPEN? WHAT ARE THE CONSEQUENCES?

Cause and effect, or **causation**, is one of the methods of thinking that we often use in argument, and we may need to conduct more or less extensive research to be certain of our answers. It can also be an effective way of opening up and developing an idea. For example, one of the current hot topics is the growing number of children who are overweight. What do you think might have caused this? Inactivity? The increase in fast food restaurants? Sugary drinks? Processed foods? Changes in the environment or in the water supply?

Cause and effect might also lead us to think about recipes and cooking. Why did one variation on a recipe turn out better than another? What caused the hollandaise sauce to break? Thinking again about the potato—one of its most popular uses in the United States is the French fry. In the following passage from the first edition of *On Food and Cooking*, Harold McGee explains why the two-stage method of cooking leads to the perfect result.

> Several authoritative cookbooks concur in the view that in order to obtain the best French-fried potatoes, one should subject the potato strips to two cooking periods, first at a low temperature, around 325° F, and then at a higher one, perhaps 370° F (163° and 188° C). This odd-sounding technique does make sense. In frying foods, we aim both to cook them through and to brown the surface sufficiently to produce the characteristic fried flavor. But too high a frying temperature will brown the surface before the interior is cooked, while too low a temperature will take a long time and result in the absorption of more oil and perhaps in an overcooked interior. In the two-stage method, the first serves to cook the potato through without browning the surface: the typical direction is to fry the potatoes until limp, which is to say until the starch granules have gelatinized. We then let the strips cool to room temperature. By the second treatment, the potato strips have been precooked and covered with a film of gelatinized starch, which slows any further oil absorption. The second frying can then be done at a high temperature and stopped as soon as the outside is browned. (175–176)

Note that the ideas in this passage are also developed through process analysis.

Another part of causation is looking at the consequences of an action, whether that is substituting applesauce for sugar in a cake recipe or passing a law banning cigarette smoking in restaurants. What differences would we find in the consistency and flavor of the cake? What would happen to restaurant business if smoking were banned? Try to think of many possible causes or effects in order to get a broad perspective.

ANALYSIS—WHAT ARE ITS PARTS?

When you analyze a topic or an idea, you break it down into its component parts and examine how it's put together in order to learn something about the whole. In brainstorming, **analysis** encourages you to "break down" assumptions and stereotypes, to push beyond what you have thought about the topic until now and discover other ways to look at and feel about it. You might begin by asking how someone else looks at it—someone older, younger, of a different gender or race, or even a different species. Many excellent stories and films have analyzed human society from the perspective of animals (from Kafka's six-foot cockroach to *The Planet of the Apes*) or aliens (from *E.T.* to *District 9*).

In *The Omnivore's Dilemma*, Michael Pollan confronts "the ethics of eating animals" and analyzes meat-eating from multiple points of view. He looks at many different human perspectives, often opposing ones, and tries to see things from the animals' side as well: "There's a schizoid quality to our relationship with animals today in which sentiment and brutality exist side by side. Half the dogs in America will receive Christmas presents this year, yet few of us ever pause to consider the life of the pig—an animal easily as intelligent as a dog—that becomes the Christmas ham" (306). This whole section of his book is driven by questions, one leading to the next: "Why should we treat animals any more ethically than they treat one another?" Yet "Do you really want to base your moral code on the natural order?" (309–310). Yet again, "Wouldn't life in the wild be worse for these creatures?" Do animals think? Do they suffer? Do their lives have meaning independent of humans? (See Chapter 16 for Pollan's argument on the ethics of eating animals.)

Analysis is very important in the business world. In the following excerpt, the students who earlier compared their proposed restaurant Braizen with a competitor now analyze the competitor's strengths.

> *Unique*: Every aspect of Crif Dogs sets it apart from the other restaurant in the area, the décor, attire of the staff, the method of ordering and the focus on such a popular American food item are all relevant to why this competitor stands out. The area where your order is taken is comprised of dim lights, poster covered walls, vintage arcade games and grunge style music. Simply walking into this location is an experience all on its own.
>
> *Convenient*: Hot dogs have always been known as a convenience friendly food and Crif Dogs takes advantage of their popularity. The opportunity to walk into a restaurant, order a hot dog with your favorite toppings and walk back outside, is an experience that every young, busy NYC resident has desired at one point or another.
>
> *Hours of Operation:* This restaurant offers later than average hours and will be able to take advantage of crowds looking for food at all hours of the day and night.
>
> *Variety*: This restaurant has been extremely creative and innovative with ways to garnish a hot dog and make it interesting. With each location offering a list of at least 26 topping combinations, one can only assume that a wide variety of customers will be satisfied with their meal.
>
> —**James Shum, David Murray,** and **Jason Hsu,** student writers

With a clear picture of the competition, entrepreneurs can find the most likely opportunities for success.

Analysis is also used in literature classes, where assignments to *analyze* or *explain how or why* are common. How does the author use imagery to enhance the reader's experience? Just what is that experience anyway? Why does the author choose one image over another? Why does the author choose to end with the scariest image of all? In the following excerpt, a student analyzes how specific images give readers an emotional and sensory experience "deeper than words printed on paper."

When Maxine Hong Kingston [in "No Name Woman"] introduced the idea of her aunt trying to impress the men by paying special attention to her looks, she used some specific details that enhanced the telling of the story. "Once my aunt found a freckle on her chin, at a spot that the almanac said predestined her for unhappiness. She dug it out with a hot needle and washed the wound with peroxide." The combination of words allows the reader to feel the burn of the peroxide on their own skin and with that natural connection, the reader can dive deeper into the text. The detail showed the reader how serious the aunt was about maintaining her beauty so that the men were attracted to her.

Amit Majmudar uses sensory details in his poem ["Rites to Allay the Dead"] by making the reader feel the ghost as if it was right next to them. "They'll try to billow through their onetime sleeves . . . and whistle you near through the shuddering leaves." The feeling of cool breeze creates goose bumps on the reader's arms as a result of this combination of words. The way that words are creatively used creates an effect; and rather than just reading the text, the reader will be able to feel something that is deeper than words printed on paper.

—**Heather Roebbeke**, student writer

When you have a complicated or controversial topic, don't accept assumptions, traditions, slogans, or advertisements without question. Break them down into their component parts. Ask *why* and *how.* Like Dorothy in *The Wizard of Oz,* look behind the curtain. See if it's a real wizard.

MORE QUESTIONS

The types of questions described in this chapter are often referred to as **rhetorical modes** and can be very effective in developing your ideas. However, other questions can energize your brainstorming and help in refining your particular topic. You might, for example, jump in with a list of likes and dislikes. What do you like about this topic, whether it's stem cell research, the latest CD by Mumford & Sons, or a new recipe for *gnocchi*? What *don't* you like about it? Complaining can be fun as well as productive.

Another line of questions might start with words, concepts, or processes that you don't understand. Or perhaps you see immediately that you need more information. Searching the Internet can kick off a brainstorming session quite effectively—just be careful not to copy information without proper citation (see Chapter 19).

For a different approach, ask yourself what's funny about your topic. Even if the answers don't end up in your research paper or business letter, you may find some great ideas, and enjoy yourself along the way. Another creative strategy is to think up metaphors and similes for your topic. If your topic were a vegetable, what would it be? If your

Develop your ideas with a sense of humor: If you were a vegetable,
which would you be, and why?

topic had to do with sports, would it be a baseball glove, a basketball hoop, or a hat trick? This kind of playful question and answer can generate pages of good ideas.

Asking questions about your potential audience may also be helpful in developing your ideas. As you begin a new piece of writing or start revising a draft, ask yourself what *this* reader needs or wants to know about your topic. Will this reader be open to what you're writing? If not, how might you tempt him to reconsider? Your ultimate goal is to use the ideas, details, and vocabulary that will achieve your particular purpose with a particular audience at a particular time and place.

THE NEXT STEP

The various methods for developing a topic or idea that we've been talking about may turn out to be useful only for brainstorming, or they may play an important role in the planning and organization of the final piece of writing. Sometimes the entire assignment will be written in only one of these methods, for example, a short story (narration) or a recipe (process). Sometimes the actual directions for a writing assignment will contain the method—describe this, compare that. Most likely, however, a piece of writing will be "cooked" using several methods. A good story will often have description in it, and process may use narration and description. Let's think of a piece of writing like a dish. On a single plate you might have a slice of pork (roasted), a scoop of mashed potatoes (boiled), and a colorful selection of peppers (grilled). Sometimes even a single component of the dish has required several different methods of cooking. A serving of lasagna, for example, may have been prepared with boiling, frying, and baking. In the end, the methods of developing an idea (rhetorical modes) are as simple or as complex and flexible as the varieties of cooking methods and plate composition.

José Antonio Burciaga was born in El Paso, Texas, in 1940. After serving in the United States Air Force, Burciaga worked as a graphic illustrator and in 1974 began writing newspaper articles, short stories, and poems. "Tortillas" was published in 1988. Burciaga was also a painter, particularly of mural art, including the "Last Supper of Chicano Herves" at Casa Zapata, a dormitory at Stanford University in which half the students were Chicanos. As both an artist and an activist, Burciaga exposed discrimination and worked for social justice until his death in 1996.

****

Tortillas
by José Antonio Burciaga

My earliest memory of *tortillas* is my *Mamá* telling me not to play with them. I had bitten eyeholes in one and was wearing it as a mask at the dinner table.

As a child, I also used *tortillas* as hand warmers on cold days, and my family claims that I owe my career as an artist to my early experiments with *tortillas*. According to them, my clowning around helped me develop a strong artistic foundation. I'm not so sure, though. Sometimes I wore a *tortilla* on my head, like a *yarmulke,* and yet I never had any great urge to convert from Catholicism to Judaism. But who knows? They may be right.

For Mexicans over the centuries, the *tortilla* has served as the spoon and the fork, the plate and the napkin. *Tortillas* originated before the Mayan civilizations, perhaps predating Europe's wheat bread. According to Mayan mythology, the great god Quetzalcoatl, realizing that the red ants knew the secret of using maize as food, transformed himself into a black ant, infiltrated the colony of red ants, and absconded with a grain of corn. (Is it any wonder that to this day, black ants and red ants do not get along?) Quetzalcoatl then put maize on the lips of the first man and woman, Oxomoco and Cipactonal, so that they would become strong. Maize festivals are still celebrated by many Indian cultures of the Americas.

When I was growing up in El Paso, *tortillas* were part of my daily life. I used to visit a *tortilla* factory in an ancient adobe building near the open *mercado* in Ciudad Juárez. As I approached, I could hear the rhythmic slapping of the *masa* as the skilled vendors outside the factory formed it into balls and patted them into perfectly round corn cakes between the palms of their hands. The wonderful aroma and the speed with which the women counted so many dozens of *tortillas* out of warm wicker baskets still linger in my mind. Watching them at work convinced me that the most handsome and *deliciosas tortillas* are handmade. Although machines are faster, they can never adequately replace generation-to-generation experience. There's no place in the factory assembly line for the tender slaps that give each *tortilla* character. The best thing that can be said about mass-producing *tortillas* is that it makes it possible for many people to enjoy them.

In the *mercado* where my mother shopped, we frequently bought *toquitos de nopalitos,* small tacos filled with diced cactus, onions, tomatoes, and *jalapeños.* Our friend Don Toribio showed us how to make delicious, crunchy *taquitos* with dried, salted pumpkin seeds. When you had no money for the filling, a poor man's *taco* could be made by placing a warm *tortilla* on the left palm, applying a sprinkle of salt, then rolling the *tortilla* up quickly with the fingertips of the right hand. My own kids put peanut butter and jelly on *tortillas*, which I think is truly bicultural. And speaking of fast foods for kids, nothing beats a *quesadilla*, a *tortilla* grilled-cheese sandwich.

Depending on what you intend to use them for, *tortillas* may be made in various ways. Even a run-of-the-mill *tortilla* is more than a flat corn cake. A skillfully cooked home-made *tortilla* has a bottom and a top; the top skin forms a pocket in which you put the filling that folds your *tortilla* into a taco. Paper-thin *tortillas* are used specifically for *flautas*, a type of taco that is filled, rolled, and then fried until crisp. The name *flauta* means *flute*, which probably refers to the Mayan bamboo flute; however, the only sound that comes from an edible *flauta* is a delicious crunch that is music

Old Spanish Market

to the palate. In México *flautas* are sometimes made as long as two feet and then cut into manageable segments. The opposite of *flautas* is *gorditas*, meaning *little fat ones*. These are very thick small *tortillas*.

The versatility of *tortillas* and corn does not end here. Besides being tasty and nourishing, they have spiritual and artistic qualities as well. The Tarahumara Indians of Chihuahua, for example, concocted a corn-based beer called *tesgüino*, which their descendants still make today. And everyone has read about the woman in New Mexico who was cooking her husband a *tortilla* one morning when the image of Jesus Christ miraculously appeared on it. Before they knew what was happening, the man's breakfast had become a local shrine.

Then there is *tortilla* art. Various Chicano artists throughout the Southwest have, when short of materials or just in a whimsical mood, used a dry *tortilla* as a small, round canvas. And a few years back, at the height of the Chicano movement, a priest in Arizona got into trouble with the Church after he was discovered celebrating mass using a *tortilla* as the host. All of which only goes to show that while the *tortilla* may be a lowly corn cake, when the necessity arises, it can reach unexpected distinction.

ABOUT THE READING

- What stories does Burciaga tell in this essay? How do they help to define *tortillas*?
- How are *tortillas* used other than for food?
- Create an outline of the essay. For each paragraph, explain the method he used to develop his central topic, *tortillas*.
- Define the following words: *yarmulke, maize, absconded, adobe, concocted, whimsical.*

RECIPE FOR REVIEW

METHODS OF DEVELOPMENT

Asking and answering questions is an effective strategy for developing your topic or idea. Study the common methods of development in Figure 4.1.

Figure 4.1   Methods of Development

Method of Development	Sample Questions
Narration (Chapter 11)	What happened? Where did it happen? Who did it happen to?
Description (Chapter 12)	What did it look like? sound, smell, taste, feel like?
Comparison (Chapter 13)	How is A similar to and/or different from B?
Process (Chapter 14)	How do you do that?
Definition (Chapter 16)	What is it? What does it do?
Exemplification (Chapter 15)	Can you give me an example?
Classification (Chapter 15)	To what group(s) does it belong?
Causation (Chapters 15 and 16)	What caused this? What are the effects/consequences?
Analysis (Chapter 17)	What are its parts?

Additional methods of development include questions about your likes and dislikes, what you don't understand, what's funny, what's a metaphor for your topic, and what your readers want or need to know.

THE NEXT STEP

These methods of development may move beyond brainstorming to become part of the finished piece of writing. Sometimes a whole piece may be developed by a single method, but most often several methods are used.

CHAPTER EXERCISES

Read each of the following six paragraphs. Then decide whether the primary method of development is that of narration, description, example, comparison, process, or causation. Write the method on the line provided.

1. _____

    When there is no wind, the lakes are still. All the surrounding landscape reflects off the water and continues on throughout the sky as if it were a great mirror. At night the light from the moon shines on the water and reflects laser beam-like light in all directions.

    —**Nicolas J. Goergen**, student writer

2. _____

    I don't know why I felt this burning passion for fried chicken fingers. I guess I love the flavor that fried chicken provides. That nice crunchy outer layer of flour or batter mixed with perfectly cooked chicken would always hit the spot! I also think that I was afraid of all the different choices that menus had. I had no idea what anything was, or what was in it. Since I was between four and five then, I did not want to take any chances. I did not want any of those tricky vegetables to end up on my plate.

    —**Thomas Monahan**, student writer

3. _____

    When Torcila, our neighbor, saw us at the window, we said *"Hola becina,"* and she let us in. *Tom and Jerry* was on, making us laugh. Not realizing the time, we were sitting for more than an hour. The door was knocked again and again. It was my mother. The first thing she said to us was *"Buenos tardes caballeros, ya esta el almuersa"* (Good afternoon, gentlemen. Is lunch ready yet?). We ran out of the room like rabbits when they see a dog.

    —**René S. León**, student writer

4. _____

    Instead of addressing the problem [of obesity] themselves, Americans often try to place the blame on the fast food corporations for making them fat. While this issue is obviously not the fault of chefs all over the country, there are alternatives that they could popularize to help keep our nation healthy. An example of this is Fast Good, a chain that sells healthful, non-genetically modified food that is available just as quickly as pulling through the McDonald's drive-thru.

    —**Justine A. Franz**, student writer

5. _____

After the chicken pieces are fried, they are put into a deep baking dish and smothered with heavy cream, garlic, and mushrooms. To loosen the sauce, chicken broth is added, and the dish is baked for an hour. My mouth is watering just writing about it! After that hour, the sauce should be boiling. Serve it hot so the chicken stays moist and delicious.

—**Vincent Amato**, student writer

6. _____

Both of the officers flip their points of view about African-Americans during the movie [*Crash*]. The one that started off being good and did not think of any racism turns out to be someone that shoots a black person. The one that starts out as a racist person and insults African-Americans comes to realize that it does not matter what race you are; everyone is equal [in a burning car].

—**Matthew Rutter**, student writer

IDEAS FOR WRITING

1. Develop a list of things you like and dislike about one of the following topics: school, dating, cities, vacations.
2. Choose a topic, and think up three metaphors or similes for it. (For example, writing is like cooking.) Then develop the best metaphor in a page or two of freewriting.
3. Create a classification system for a topic like restaurants, movies, families, or friends. Write a definition for each category, and give examples.
4. Choose a favorite food, and brainstorm ideas about it using five of the methods described in this chapter.

CHAPTER 5
PLANNING AND REVISING YOUR WRITING

After reading this chapter, you should begin to...

- plan an initial draft of a writing assignment by developing a central idea or thesis and supporting points;
- use a variety of strategies to organize your ideas into an essay or other type of writing;
- develop, revise, or delete the content of your writing as needed to clarify your ideas; and
- revise the organizational plan of your writing as needed to improve its shape and movement.

When we're planning an essay, we sometimes begin a draft simply as a continuation of **freewriting**; at other times, we'll construct a rather detailed outline *before* we begin to write. Or we can use a cycle of writing and outlining, writing and outlining. Think about how you might plan a meal. Perhaps you have certain ingredients already and design a menu around them; on the other hand, perhaps you have an idea for a menu and obtain the ingredients to support it. Often you'll have *some* items on hand, get an idea for the menu, and then head to the store to buy the rest of the ingredients.

In the previous chapter, we considered strategies for developing ideas, and sometimes that type of brainstorming leads directly to a first draft. For other assignments, we may need to spend time planning before we begin to write the draft. In this chapter, we'll look first at finding and refining a central idea, then move to planning and revising the content and organization of a piece of writing. You may wish to move back and forth between this chapter and the previous one as you work through your ideas for any particular assignment. Writing can be a very flexible, at times even circular, process.

FINDING THE CENTRAL IDEA

There are many different types of writing, some of which don't place the same importance on a **central idea**, or **thesis statement**. A story, for example, typically doesn't have a thesis, and a business letter also has somewhat different expectations. But academic papers tend to focus on and develop a central idea. Sometimes we have an idea in mind before we even begin to write, or perhaps it emerges clearly during some initial freewriting. At other times we have to work harder to find it.

We spoke in the last chapter about how asking questions could drive our search for information and ideas, as well as the organization of the finished paper. A question works to guide us as we explore or define an issue—and it can work well as a framework in which to present our ideas to the reader. Among those questions we've asked, there may be one that seems more interesting or important to us than the others. In answering that question, we will have a statement of our central idea.

Let's look at an example. Suppose you read Tim O'Brien's short story "The Man I Killed" (a chapter from his book *The Things They Carried*) and were especially struck by his use of repetition. You decide to write about that, and you begin looking for your central idea. Perhaps you ask yourself these questions: What types of things does he repeat? How many times? What effect does that have? Now suppose you're most interested in the last question, What effect does the repetition have? Once you answer that, you have your central idea.

Note that the central idea is more specific than the topic. While the topic is often expressed as a short phrase, the statement of the central idea is usually a complete sentence. Compare the following two items:

Topic   Repetition in "The Man I Killed"

Thesis   In "The Man I Killed," the effect of Tim O'Brien's deceptively simple technique of repetition is to create a realistic experience for readers.

We also need to construct a statement that is not *too broad* for the assignment. Compare the next two sentences:

Too Broad   O'Brien uses imagery in "The Man I Killed" to make a better story.

Better   O'Brien uses graphic images of "the man [he] killed" to force the reader to share his reaction.

The central idea doesn't have to be controversial or emotional, but it should be something that can be proved—such as a proposition or a **claim**—rather than a fact or observation.

Fact   O'Brien repeats images like the "star-shaped hole" numerous times in the "The Man I Killed."

Thesis   The repetition of images like the "star-shaped hole" re-creates for the reader the narrator's psychological state following the killing.

The statement of your central idea is like a promise you make to your readers about what you're going to tell them, and it may also provide a map of your paper, a guide to the sequence of ideas. Consider the following example:

> In "The Man I Killed," O'Brien re-creates the narrator's psychological state for the reader through the repetition of graphic images of the Vietnamese soldier's body (both horrific and tender) and of beautiful images of the forest setting.

If this is the central idea, then we'd expect the paper at some point to define "the narrator's psychological state" and to describe the various repeating images. A full statement of the central idea can also help us begin to organize the paper. Typically, the points listed in the thesis statement will be addressed in the same order in the body of the paper—in our example, horrific images of the dead man's wounds, then almost tender images of what's left undamaged, followed by beautiful images of nature. Notice how easily a simple organizational plan can be constructed from the statement of the central idea:

- Introduction—state or prepare for central idea
- Repetition of horrific images
- Repetition of tender images
- Repetition of nature images
- Effect of repetition—re-creates narrator's psychological state
- Conclusion—highlight central idea

The statement of the central idea focuses the paper. Every paragraph should tie back to it, develop it, illustrate it, support it. (See Figure 5.1.) If you find that a

Figure 5.1 Finding the Central Idea

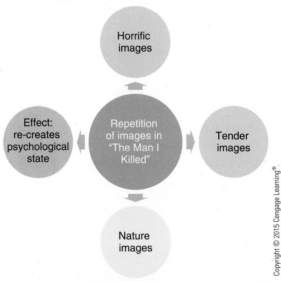

paragraph does *not* relate to the central idea, either you must delete it, or you must rewrite your thesis to include it. For example, another powerful element of "The Man I Killed" is the background the narrator imagines for the Vietnamese soldier. However, because these imagined details create a different effect than that of the observed details (the horrific, tender, and natural images), they do not belong with this particular central idea.

Finally, one of the most important things to remember about your central idea is that it can be revised! As you write, you will continue to think about your topic, and it may be that your ideas will change.

DESIGNING THE FLOOR PLAN

Essays, and most other pieces of writing, are organized generally into three parts: the introduction, the body, and the conclusion. Beyond that, there are no hard and fast rules about how to arrange your ideas, no single formula that must be followed. For each paper, you're looking for a sequence that fits the content. Given the particular purpose and audience, what is the best way to organize your ideas?

Let's think about the types of organization that are involved in serving a restaurant meal. First, as in telling a story, there's an order of events, a movement through time, both in the kitchen and the dining room. In the kitchen, food preparation has begun before the customer arrives and continues until cleanup at the end of the night. In the dining room, customers are seated, offered drinks and appetizers, served their main course and often dessert, and finally given the check. Second, as in a description, both the kitchen and the dining room are organized in terms of space so that meals can be prepared and customers served in the most efficient way. The very word "line" suggests an ordering of activity in a particular space. Similarly, the organization of an essay is driven both by movement (the reader moves through time to read it) and by space (the look of the paragraphs on the page, the shape of the outline).[3]

If you were designing the layout of the kitchen in a restaurant, you would want to make sure that there was space for each function or station, and that workers could move as needed from one station to the next. Each station also should be designed to carry out its narrow task in the most effective way—worktop, equipment, storage space all carefully planned. This kind of planning is also necessary for your essay to ensure that each idea is fully developed and that your readers can move smoothly and effectively from one idea to the next.

For example, information might be arranged in **chronological order,** that is, according to the order of events: first this happened, then that happened, and now this. Stories or narratives generally follow this pattern (see Chapter 11). Sometimes an entire paper will be organized chronologically, sometimes just a paragraph or two. Suppose you have participated in a chocolate tasting, for example, and

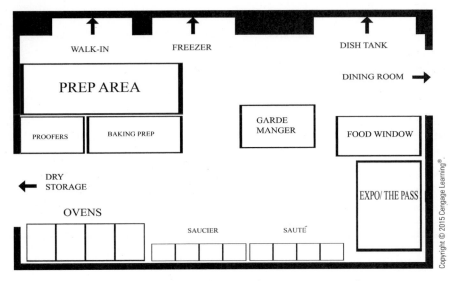

The floor plan of this kitchen outlines its shape in space and suggests the flow of movement within that space.

have chosen to write it up in a straightforward chronological order, driven by questions such as the following: What did I think of the first chocolate? What did I think of the second? Which one did I like the best? You might outline the paper as follows:

- How we tasted the chocolates (introduction)
- First chocolate—aroma, flavor, texture
- Second chocolate—aroma, flavor, texture
- Third chocolate—aroma, flavor, texture
- Preferred chocolate (conclusion)

Another pattern of organization has to do with the physical layout, the **spatial order.** This pattern often works well with a description. For example, in describing the features of the kitchen or dining room in a prospective restaurant, the writer might clearly indicate where each item is located in relation to others—to the left or right, above or beneath.

> Now because the kitchen was so small, it needed to be very organized, and everything needed to be in its place. A three-part sink lined one whole wall of the kitchen, with containers and storage units placed neatly on a shelf above. On the opposite wall there were two refrigerators, one walk-in with food stored for the whole week, and a regular fridge with items that were used throughout the day. In between the two were more shelves with extra bags, boxes, and fortune cookies. Along the back of the entire length of the kitchen were four huge woks

where all dishes were prepared. Next to the woks were a fryer, a small prep table, and a rice cooker that got extremely warm. Two feet back away from the woks was another small prep table, as well as a rack with every vegetable we needed and a flip fridge with all the pork, beef, and chicken.

—**Matthew K. Greene**, student writer

Perhaps one of the most common and valuable ways to think about the overall organization of the paper is about the order of importance, or the **emphatic order.** In explaining a set of reasons, for example, or a cluster of effects, we might choose to begin with the most important point. Or, we might choose to emphasize the most important point by placing it at the end of the paragraph or essay. Let's look at an example. Suppose you are arguing to potential investors that the restaurant you'd like to open will be successful for three reasons. Which of them will you begin with? Perhaps you believe the most important point is that a similar restaurant in the same neighborhood has just closed, even though it was very successful, and therefore has left a gap that you can fill. You may want to lead with that most important point, especially because you suspect that not all of your investors will even read your entire proposal. Your organizational plan might look like this:

Emphatic Order—Most Important to Least Important
I believe this new restaurant will be successful because
- a similar restaurant in the same neighborhood just closed, leaving a gap
- I've run other restaurants successfully
- I've hired one of the best chefs in town

In other cases, however, you might decide it would be more effective to *build up* to the most important point. Perhaps you're writing a paper about the many benefits of drinking enough water each day. Although all the benefits are significant, emphasizing the last group gives a sharper focus and adds more energy to the points you're making. Your organizational plan might look like this:

Emphatic Order—Least Important to Most Important
If you drink enough water, you will
- look better (staying hydrated can improve health and appearance of skin and help you lose weight)
- feel better (even minor dehydration can have a negative effect on your mood and brain function)
- and, most important, *be* better (water helps digestion, reduces congestion, and lowers the risk of breast and colon cancer)

Papers can also be organized through the methods of developing ideas outlined in Chapter 4, such as **compare and contrast** (see also Chapter 13). For example, a different student writing about the chocolate tasting might choose to emphasize the differences between them. What did the chocolates look like? How could one describe the aromas?

What did they taste like? Which one did I like the best? This series of questions might lead to the following organizational plan:

- Introduction—reason for comparing three chocolates
- Appearance of each chocolate
- Aroma
- Flavor & texture
- Conclusion—preferred chocolate

A recipe, of course, will be organized according to the sequence of steps in the **process** (see Chapter 14), while another writing assignment might follow a **causal chain** (see Chapter 15).

Quite often, a paper is organized through a combination of methods. For example, in the student essay "When Life Gives You Lemons," reprinted at the end of Chapter 14, the author's task for her writing course was to tell the story of a significant moment in her life. The central event—making a lemon meringue pie at the age of ten—occupies paragraphs 2 through 9 of the eleven paragraphs in the essay. Beginning as a straightforward narrative, the paper moves into a process narrative for paragraphs 4 through 7, then back to narrative again. To complete the organizational plan, the author frames the story (paragraphs 1 and 10) with a current event, making pie crust. The concluding paragraph (11) analyzes the effect of the central story on the writer's "palate" and "soul."

Let's look at another example. Remember that the same types of questions that drove the development of your ideas can drive the organization of your writing. A student at the chocolate tasting, Luis Bustamante (whose full essay appears on pages 89–90), developed this topic in a number of different ways: description, analysis, and narrative. What was this chocolate like? he asked himself. How did I feel about it? What did it remind me of? What memories do I have of chocolate, and how is it used in my native Mexican cuisine? What was the purpose of the tasting? What effect did this experience have? The way these questions develop might provide a working outline for the essay:

- Description of chocolate
- Analysis of experience
- Previous history with chocolate
- Chocolate in Mexican cuisine
- Purpose/effect of tasting

There is no one-size-fits-all recipe for building an essay. What we want to keep in mind is our audience. What sequence of ideas (paragraphs) will be most effective in conveying our meaning to the reader? Do we want to build to the most important point? Or, as in a cover letter or restaurant review, do we want to put the most important, most persuasive details first?

MORE THOUGHTS ON PLANNING

Among the striking similarities between writing and cooking is the need for planning, as a culinary student notes in the following journal excerpt:

> I realized the way you prepare for [culinary] class is very similar to the way you prepare to write a paper. One must plan, think things through, look at presentation, and be organized. The day before class, I plan what I need to do the next day, what I'll need, times when things need to be done, and so on. Writing is very similar. To write a paper, you must brainstorm what you want to write about, your thoughts must be organized, and there should be a flow throughout the paper. It takes time and mental energy to do this successfully, just as in kitchen classes.

> —**Courtney Lebedz**, student writer

Constructing an accurate timeline from purchasing and preparing the ingredients to cooking and serving the meal is a valuable, even essential skill in the kitchen.

Not all planning is directly linear, though. Sometimes our brainstorming produces a wide assortment of ideas and details that must be sorted into categories before any sequence can be determined. For example, Temple Grandin, a scientist and professor at Colorado State University, autism activist, and consultant to the beef industry, has said that she thinks in pictures rather than words (Figure 5.2). She forms ideas by sorting these pictures into categories and by making connections or associations between them. Then she uses words to describe the result.

The planning process for any given piece of writing may vary with each assignment. It may be that we have a relatively clear idea of the topics we want to cover and can begin with

Figure 5.2 Temple Grandin has said that she thinks primarily in pictures and then describes the pictures in words. Actress Claire Danes (below) portrayed Temple Grandin in a critically acclaimed biographical film in 2010.

HBO/Photofest © HBO

an outline or flow chart of the overall organization, as in the previous examples. We build the essay step by step: identify the order and topics of the paragraphs, then write them. However, sometimes we'll begin a writing task with lots of freewriting in order to get a clearer sense of our thoughts. This might be the case with anything from the cover letter for a job application to an essay on the image of the diner in various literary works. Very often we'll move back and forth from a loose outline of the organization to freewriting individual paragraphs. Then we'll cut up the paragraphs and literally move them around and read them in different orders to get a sense of what flows naturally, what proceeds most logically for the reader. We'll keep writing and sorting, writing and sorting, until the shape is right.

Individual personalities will also play a role in planning. Some writers work best with a series of freewrites that are gradually reshaped. Once you've written a good amount of material, you can begin to re-read and explore the ideas you've generated. Then you sort through it, read and write a little bit, *taste* it. Perhaps there are only one or two useful sentences in a page of freewriting. Take these, and begin a new round of brainstorming. Ask yourself which ideas seem the most interesting and worth pursuing. Consider whether there is anything that should come out. Sketch out a rough order for your points—write it out. Or put ideas on index cards and move them around. Read them in different orders. Have blank cards handy to catch additional ideas or supporting details.

Other writers prefer to outline their ideas first. The classic outline—Roman numerals and capital letters—works for some. Others find that a formal outline is more helpful once they've generated some material. Perhaps a more linear type of outline would be better, or a flow chart. Perhaps try a graphic or diagrammatic approach, as if you're designing a cake, or laying out a plate presentation, or setting a table. Look at it. If it makes sense, write it out and see. If it doesn't make sense, move things around.

Outlining the flow of ideas in "Two Wives" (pp. 233–234)

1 *Introduction*: I found differences between the two wives, Celeste and Annabeth.

2 While Celeste's distrust of her husband destroyed her family, Annabeth's belief in her husband kept her family firmly together.

3 Celeste and Annabeth were both housewives, but they had a different belief about their husbands.

4 Secondly, I was able to see a difference between the two women's abilities to protect their families.

5 Finally, the two women's appearances indicated how they were different.

6 Conclusion: By those three points, I saw how different the two wives were (loyalty, protection, appearance).

Be bold. While the computer has many advantages for writers, it does not allow you to see all the bits of your thinking laid out on the table or on a bulletin board.

Writing is a flexible process; you're often thinking new thoughts as you're writing a draft, and some of them may require re-thinking the whole organization. But that's a good thing, too—planning doesn't mean you're stuck with it, so there's no need to feel stressed. Try something. Mix up the batter. Put the sauce on the stove. Apply the heat of the writing process, and see what happens.

TASTE AND RE-SEASON

The most unpredictable part of the writing process is **revision**. Revision is difficult because we must change gears. While we were brainstorming, outlining, and writing the rough draft, we allowed ourselves a great deal of freedom. We wrote from the heart, and we intentionally refrained from evaluating our work. But during revision we need to step back and take a cool, critical attitude. We need to read the paper now as if it belonged to someone else. Most important, we need to be ready to get rid of words, sentences, paragraphs, even entire drafts that don't work, and this is difficult because we often become very attached to the words we've produced with such effort!

Let's think about cookies for a moment. Suppose we weren't paying attention and added a cup of salt instead of sugar to a batch of chocolate chip cookies. Could we fix those cookies? Could we sprinkle sugar on top and serve them to the customer? No. In this case, as with some rough drafts, we have to throw the cookies out and start again. That is, we'll have to revise. Revision is so important and so complex that we will talk about it again in several of the chapters that follow, but let's look at some of the basics here.

Once we have a complete first draft, we begin a more "serious," analytical phase, evaluating the flavor and adjusting the seasoning. The initial revision may be quite complex because we're looking at two large, crucial aspects of the paper: the content and the organization. First, we re-read the essay as if we're seeing it for the first time. Once again, the process is driven by questions. We ask, Is it the right story or topic? Is the main point clear? Are there enough supporting details? Should parts of the essay be eliminated because they are repetitive or irrelevant? It's often helpful to read the essay aloud, or to have someone else read the paper aloud. Errors that we might miss when just looking for them on the page become brutally clear when we *hear* them.

A second major area we want to look at as we begin to revise is the organization, including the order of sentences and paragraphs, the effectiveness of the introduction and conclusion, and the presence of appropriate transitions (see Chapters 6–7). Sometimes the writing is in such good shape at the end of the first draft that revision will be mostly a matter of adding details or replacing words. However, sometimes the first draft just doesn't work at all. This is why revision is the least predictable step of the writing process. One paper might be done in two drafts; others may take four or more. We should understand that the number of drafts is not a measure of our skill or of the quality of the end product.

REVISING THE ORGANIZATIONAL PLAN

As we begin looking at complete drafts, we'll want to check frequently whether there is an inner logic to the sequence of ideas. We've probably all had the experience of listening to a poor storyteller who jumps so randomly from one event or character to another that we get completely lost. That mustn't be the case with our own writing. We have to think of the reader, what she knows and how to lead her through our thinking in the clearest way possible.

When the floor plan is a good one, workers flow smoothly from one station to the next.

When you're evaluating the flow of service through a restaurant, you will look for any breaks or delays; similarly, as you read through your essay draft, feel for any unexpected jumps or unwanted repetition in the sequence of ideas. This can be a moment where an outside reader is particularly helpful. At some point, writers will start reading what's in their minds rather than seeing clearly what they've actually put on the page.

Perhaps after writing a rough draft following the outline in the previous section, Luis decides to revise the order of ideas as follows:

- Purpose of tasting (introduction)
- Previous history with chocolate
- Chocolate in Mexican cuisine
- Description of chocolate
- Analysis/effect of experience (conclusion)

In his revised plan, Luis begins with the purpose of the chocolate tasting and ends with an analysis of the tasting's effect (see Figure 5.3). The organization now has a smoother, more tightly constructed feel.

Figure 5.3 Comparing the Organizational Plans

First-Draft Plan	Revised Plan
Description of chocolates	Purpose of tasting (introduction)
Analysis of experience	Previous history with chocolate
Previous history with chocolate	Chocolate in Mexican cuisine
Chocolate in Mexican cuisine	Description of chocolate
Purpose/effect of tasting	Analysis/effect of experience (conclusion)

Satisfied with this revised plan, Luis writes the essay printed at the end of this chapter. Later, he writes in his journal:

> Writing is not as easy as many people think; at least for me it has always been really hard to express my point of view in a paper. Writing my first essay for this class was difficult for me because I constantly erased or modified what I was writing, trying to make it perfect from the beginning. However, I have learned that a good essay takes time and writing a rough draft is a good option for spotting mistakes and catching the main idea. When I learned it was okay to have mistakes, everything turned out to be simpler.

—**Luis Bustamante**, student writer

Sometimes the kind of revision we do is quite straightforward—to switch the order of two or three paragraphs, as Luis did, or beef up the introduction. However, sometimes the paper seems choppy and rough, and we're not quite sure why. That's a good time to be bold—cut the paper up!

Although **cut and paste** is most well known nowadays as a function of the word processor, the old-fashioned method is still extraordinarily effective. When an essay's organization seems rocky or unclear, get a second copy of your draft and a pair of scissors. Then cut the copy up into individual sentences, groups of sentences, or paragraphs. You want to put similar ideas together, regardless of their original form. Once you've cut up the essay, physically move the pieces around and read them in different orders. This exercise forces you to "think outside the paper," literally. One of the most powerful roadblocks to good writing is a premature, rigid attachment to the first draft. And one of the most effective tools for removing such a roadblock is a pair of scissors!

Once you've cut the paper up into meaningful chunks, where each slip contains one idea, spread them out and give them a fresh look. Shuffle the slips around, and test the logic of the new order by reading through the ideas again. Although word processing is a terrific invention and makes it easy to revise, it also makes it difficult to see the whole paper at a single glance, the way you can if you lay out the individual paper pages on a table or floor.

In addition to being less flexible than paper, the cut-and-paste function on the computer is more dangerous. If we're not careful to save both electronic and paper copies before beginning to cut and paste, we may inadvertently lose chunks of text. When you cut and paste on the computer, make it a point to preserve all the notes and ideas from the original by holding on to some of the slips of paper or by making notes on the new copy, typing them in a different color or writing them in pencil. Until you're certain the paper is finished, save your drafts in separate files on the computer, and occasionally print them, just in case the electronic copies are lost.

A TASTE FOR READING

In this essay, student writer Luis Bustamante connects his childhood in Mexico with a chocolate tasting in the United States.

****

A Piece of Mexico in Everyone's Mouth
by Luis Bustamante

Yesterday morning was a little bit different from the rest of the days I've had here in school because my writing class teacher had planned a chocolate tasting for us. The main reason why she did it was to show us in a more active way the importance of making a description using all senses.

Even though I'm from Mexico and chocolate had its origin there, I've never considered myself a chocolate fan. This may be because since I was a little child I'd rather eat a fruit than eat candies, chocolates included. As time went by, I learned that chocolates were not my thing and that I could easily stay without having one for months. Although I did not like chocolates as much as other people did and I did not need to buy them, chocolates were always present in my life because my mom often used them in the kitchen.

My mom has always been a great cook; she never had any formal education in Culinary Arts or Baking and Pastry, but she does have a delicate palate, which is what every diner thanks her for. Sometimes she'd get chocolate to bake cakes, breads and cookies or to prepare savory dishes. In Mexico, people use chocolate in a different way than they do here in the United States. Chocolate is used as an important ingredient in more complex dishes like Mole Poblano, where unsweetened chocolate is melted and combined

"I learned that chocolates were not my thing."

with dried ancho, mulato, pasilla and chipotle chilies, tomatoes, raisins, parsley, onions, garlic, brown sugar, sesame seeds, cinnamon, cloves, peanuts, anise seeds, and chicken stock. Then everything is ground until a rich thick sauce is obtained. No wonder why Mole, a Nahuati word pronounced MOH-lay, means "concoction or mixture."

I am not used to chocolates just by themselves because that is not how we use them in my country. But if I had to choose one from yesterday's tasting, I would pick the very last one, which was a Nirvana Belgian Spicy Aztec Bar. This chocolate has a smooth varnished look on the outside; its color is an appealing deep dark brown that invites [you] to taste it. Once [it is] broken, you can notice that it has white dusty specks that look like almonds. This Belgian chocolate has a combination of aromas that go from soft hints of vanilla, cinnamon, and almonds to stronger ones like nutmeg and spices, while a strong rich cocoa butter aroma closes this wonderful combination.

The moment you put the chocolate in your mouth and rest [it] there for a few seconds, your tongue can feel how this chocolate suffers a transformation; the nearly unbreakable chocolate starts to slowly melt inside the mouth, letting you feel each and every one of its elements. The little white specks play an important role because they are "texture changes." In the beginning, [the] chocolate was rigid and smooth, but as seconds passed the little almond specks merged, turning it into a grainy texture. In the end, if I had to describe the flavor, I'd say it was a perfect rainbow; it started smooth, but as soon as it melted, it became more intense. I noticed its complexity, the salty and nutty taste came out, and a big spicy/smoky note created the perfect climax for this chocolate. After such a perfect harmony of elements, it became less intense; however, it took a couple of minutes to have it completely gone from my palate.

The chocolate tasting ended, and I was amazed how intricate chocolate could be. I started to understand why people spend good money on it; it is not about having that chocolate taste, but to experiment and turn on the senses bite after bite. Now I am curious about this product and chances are that before this week ends, I may take a visit to the library to learn more about it. Who knows? I may begin to like it and sometime in the future cook Mexican dishes with some of these wonderful European chocolates.

ABOUT THE READING

- What's different about the way chocolate is used in Mexico?
- How did the writer's attitude toward chocolate change? Why did it change?
- Is the description of the Spicy Aztec Bar effective? Can you imagine the way it looks and tastes? Explain.
- Define *nirvana*. Is this an effective name for a chocolate brand? Explain.

RECIPE FOR REVIEW

FINDING THE CENTRAL IDEA

1. The **central idea** (often called the thesis or thesis statement) states the main point you want to make, the **claim** you want to prove. As you ask and answer questions about your topic, you may find your central idea by answering the most important question.
2. The central idea is not the same as the topic. While a topic may be a word or phrase, the central idea is usually expressed as a complete sentence. The central idea is not a fact; it's a proposition or an idea that must be argued.
3. The statement of the central idea may map the organization of the essay. Every paragraph should support it.
4. The thesis may evolve as you continue to write and revise your ideas.

DESIGNING THE FLOOR PLAN

1. Your essay may be designed in **chronological**, **spatial**, or **emphatic order**; in one of the methods discussed in Chapter 4, such as process or compare/contrast; or in a mixture of such methods.
2. The planning process will vary according to a particular writing task and the preference of the writer. An assignment might grow easily from initial freewriting, or be meticulously outlined early in the process, or develop from a combination of drafting and outlining.

TASTE AND RE-SEASON

1. Check the focus of your writing. Does the thesis still fit? Does each paragraph relate to and support it?
2. Is there material that needs greater development? Is there material that doesn't fit and should be deleted?

REVISING THE ORGANIZATIONAL PLAN

1. Check your draft for a logical sequence of ideas within each paragraph and over the essay as a whole.
2. List or outline the main ideas; try rearranging them to get a clearer sequence.
3. Try cutting and pasting with scissors and tape. Obtain a fresh copy of your draft (photocopied or printed). Cut up the draft by sentences, groups of sentences, or paragraphs. Physically rearrange the "ideas" into a clearer sequence.
4. Rewrite the essay in the new sequence, adding or revising sentences and transitional expressions as needed.

CHAPTER EXERCISES

1. *Finding the Central Idea.* Look at three or four of the pieces in A Taste for Reading. Find a statement of the central idea, or, if it is only implied rather than stated, write such a statement yourself.

2. *Designing the Floor Plan.* Think about the way you typically write a paper. At what point do you reflect specifically about the organization? Do you write down an outline or map? Have you ever tried cutting and pasting with actual scissors and tape?

3. *Analyzing the Floor Plan.* Read Molly-Iris Alpern's essay in Chapter 14, thinking specifically about the organizational plan. Why do you think she chose to start in the present rather than when she was a child? How would the essay feel different if she had begun her essay with the childhood incident, that is, if she'd used a strictly chronological order?

4. *Revising the Organizational Plan.* Look back at the first draft and revised organizational plans (Figure 5.2). Which plan do you think is more effective? Why?

IDEAS FOR WRITING

1. Write a brief essay in which you describe the restaurant, bakery, or café you'd like to open. Explain the flow of service in the front and back of the house.

2. Choose a food item you're somewhat ambivalent about. Then plan and revise a short essay about that food: Find your central idea, design a floor plan, taste, and re-season.

3. Look back at José Antonio Burciaga's "Tortillas" in Chapter 4, and discuss the *order* of the paragraphs. Why did Burciaga choose this particular order, do you think? What happens if you move the paragraphs around?

4. Explain the unusual organizational principle(s) behind a particular film, for example, *Pulp Fiction* or *Memento*.

CHAPTER 6
WORKING WITH PARAGRAPHS AND TRANSITIONS

By the end of this chapter, you should begin to . . .

- explain the form and function of a paragraph;
- evaluate and revise paragraphs to improve unity, development, impact, and sequence; and
- improve coherence and flow through the use of transitional expressions and repetition.

The paragraph is as important to a letter or essay as the plate is to a meal or as each station is to the restaurant kitchen. It's like the pot in which we cook our ideas. Yet for many writers, working with paragraphs is one of the most challenging aspects of the writing process, from arranging their order in the piece as a whole to maintaining their internal unity and coherence. When essays go off the rails, it's often because we've lost control of our paragraphs.

While the preceding chapter focused on the overall planning and revision of the essay, this chapter works with individual paragraphs. As you write and revise an essay, letter, or report, you will probably move continually from the overall organization and flow of the piece to the organization and flow of individual paragraphs. Within a paragraph, you will evaluate both the sequence of the sentences and the flow and correctness of each individual sentence.

WHAT IS A PARAGRAPH?

A **paragraph** is a series of sentences that develops a single idea. Paragraphs share many of the ingredients of an essay: a main idea, supporting details, and transitions that move the reader from one idea to the next. In addition to developing its own topic, each paragraph must also relate directly to the central idea of the paper. Paragraphs are the "building blocks" of an essay, letter, or report. They must be strong enough to "support" each other and smooth enough to fit seamlessly with the other blocks (Figure 6.1).

Figure 6.1 "Plating" an Essay

Each paragraph in Luis Bustamante's "A Piece of Mexico in Everyone's Mouth" relates to the central idea (chocolate tasting) and to the paragraphs before and after.

1 Purpose of chocolate tasting

6 Chocolate tasting ended. Now I am curious...

2 I'm not a fan of chocolate

A Piece of Mexico: Chocolate Tasting

5 This chocolate had complex flavor & texture

3 People use chocolate differently in Mexico

4 I'd choose the Spicy Aztec Bar

Copyright © 2015 Cengage Learning®

Let's think of the essay as a plate of food. First, each individual food item (paragraph) is unified and well cooked, like a perfectly grilled steak. Second, each item fits smoothly with the other items on the plate—the baked potato with butter and sour cream, the deep green broccoli trees, just soft enough for the fork to slide in. In the same way, although it is part of a larger "plate" or essay, each paragraph should be individually cooked and seasoned (Figure 6.2).

The concept of cooking or developing an idea is crucial for effective writing, and the paragraph is the unit in which we do that. The paragraph outlines an idea and provides details that "support" it, that is, tell a story about it, or provide examples of it, or describe it. The *type* of details that are added, that is, the method by which the topic of the paragraph is developed, can sometimes be classified by so-called rhetorical mode, such as narration, comparison, or process. In some ways, each paragraph is like the answer to a question, so that the essay is like answers to a series of questions. The development of the main idea from question to question and the energy created by the reader's search for answers give a sense of movement to the essay.

We may have been told to think of the paragraph in terms of a specific range, such as five to seven sentences. More helpful perhaps are two other measures—whether you're still working on the same topic, and how much space the paragraph takes up on the page. Let's look at this latter measure first. Paragraphs break up the text, so that the reader's eyes are more comfortable. A certain amount of white space is restful. Also, since the paragraphs indicate a change in topic, the physical space created by indenting the first line of the paragraph helps the reader make the mental shift to a new topic.

Some types of writing have shorter or longer paragraphs than others. A newspaper article, for example, tends to have very short paragraphs, sometimes only a sentence in length. A business letter's paragraphs will most likely be shorter than an essay's. The paragraphs in this textbook may be shorter than the paragraphs in a book about philosophy. As with almost everything about the writing process, how you use paragraphs comes back to what will make your communication most effective.

Figure 6.2 Like the paragraphs in a well-written essay, these dumplings are individually shaped and cooked, touch on the central idea (the bowl of soy sauce), and lie smoothly next to one another.

© Elena Elisseeva/www.Shutterstock.com

EVALUATING AND REVISING YOUR PARAGRAPHS

As you revise a piece of writing, you will want to pay particular attention to each paragraph. Ask yourself the following questions:

- What is the unifying idea or topic sentence of each paragraph? Should you start a new paragraph? Combine two short ones?
- Is the idea in the paragraph sufficiently developed (through narrative, description, comparison, process, or combination thereof)? Or is there too much detail? Irrelevant detail? Repeated detail?
- Where will that topic sentence have the most impact? At the beginning or the end? In the middle? Left unstated?
- What is the best/smoothest/most logical order of sentences within the paragraph? Chart the sequence of ideas to see if they make sense, flow smoothly.
- Is it clear how each sentence is connected to the one before and after?
- Is each sentence successful?

DEVELOPING A SINGLE IDEA

As you read through the essay, it can be helpful to outline the main ideas as you have written them, just to double check that they flow smoothly and logically. This can also be a clue as to whether you have too much information or too little in any particular paragraph. Both are common problems.

We've said that each paragraph is about one idea. If you find that you're moving to a new idea, begin a new paragraph. For example, suppose you're exploring a topic through comparison and contrast. Depending on the size of the paragraph, it may help readers to follow your train of thought more clearly if you begin a new paragraph when you get to the contrasting features. Or perhaps the idea is so complex that it requires several examples to explain. In that case, it may be wise to begin a new paragraph with a fresh example to help the reader re-focus. Finally, the paragraph may just take up too much space on the page and make the reader feel a bit overwhelmed. It's as if the steak and potato have filled the whole plate so that the vegetable—though still part of the entrée—is served on a small side plate. There are really no hard and fast rules about this. Just be sensitive to the appearance of the paragraphs on the page as well as to their unity in terms of topic.

Once you're certain that you have a single idea in your paragraph, check that it has enough information for your readers to learn what you want them to learn. Have you answered the questions they might ask? Chapter 4 offers a number of ways you might develop the idea of a paragraph, including the following:

- Give one or more examples
- Tell a story
- Add descriptive details
- Define terms
- Compare and/or contrast; use an analogy
- Explain a process
- Find supporting facts, statistics, quotes
- Look at causes and effects, reasons for and consequences of
- Provide a timeline

You can develop paragraphs from two opposite directions. First, you might use freewriting to draft the paper, then gradually start to notice where new paragraphs should begin, for example, when you start a new idea or when the paragraph becomes too long. Second, you might begin the draft with very specific plans as to what each paragraph will contain. You may even combine these approaches as you revise each successive version of the paper. As you're reading through a draft, you will look at the way the paragraphs are set up on the page. You will also listen to the content and flow of the paragraphs and the sentences within them. You will have to move backwards and forwards, re-reading the entire paper each time you make a change in the sequence or makeup of its paragraphs. One change may have a significant ripple effect on the rest of the draft. Imagine that an essay is like a plate. If you need to change the type of protein, you may need to change the starch and vegetable as well.

SHAPING THE IMPACT OF A PARAGRAPH

The "shape" of a paragraph has to do with the placement of its single idea, sometimes called the **topic sentence**. (Not every paragraph will have one sentence that summarizes the main idea, however. The idea might be implied rather than stated explicitly.) If the paragraph begins with the idea, followed by the details, it might be said to have the shape of a triangle. The top point or apex represents the single idea, which then expands to the base as more supporting details are added. The following paragraph about preparing for culinary class follows this shape, and perhaps most paragraphs may be said to do so.

I realized the way you prepare for culinary class is very similar to the way you prepare to write a paper. You must plan, think things through, look at presentation, and be organized. The day before class, I plan what I need to do the next day, what I'll need, times when things need to be done, and so on. Writing is very similar. To write a paper, you must brainstorm what you want to write about, your thoughts must be organized, and there should be a flow throughout the paper. It takes time and mental energy to do this successfully, just as in kitchen classes.

—**Courtney Lebedz**, student writer

It makes sense to start a paragraph with the main idea. We know that first impressions are important, and, in fact, research shows that what we hear first makes the strongest impact.

Another fairly common shape for paragraphs, especially for introductions, is an upside-down triangle. This type of paragraph begins with a breadth of detail and narrows down to the main point. The following example is taken from an essay about the film *Mystic River*.

Three childhood friends, Jimmy, Dave, and Sean, grew up in a small and shabby village in Boston. They used to spend their time playing hockey. One day, David was kidnapped by two strange men. A few days later, David escaped successfully from them. But their happy time in childhood ended. They didn't keep in touch with each other. Twenty-five years later, those three guys met again by a tragedy: Jimmy's daughter was killed. In that time, David's wife Celeste suspected her husband had killed Jimmy's daughter. As Jimmy pursued the question of the accident, Celeste confessed to Jimmy what she thought. Jimmy burned with revengeful thoughts and killed David, but it turned out David was not the murderer. Jimmy told his wife, Annabeth, everything that happened to him. When she heard about David, she might have been shocked. But she wasn't agitated. She showed her husband her strong loyalty for him. **While Celeste's distrust of her husband destroyed her family, Annabeth's belief in her husband kept her family firmly together.**

—**Soyang Myung**, student writer

While research suggests that we remember best what we hear first, it also suggests that we remember what we hear last almost as well. As writers, we'll think about what we want to emphasize in a particular paragraph—detail or idea—and shape the paragraph accordingly.

Now it might be that we'd like to highlight the main idea by placing it both at the beginning and at the end of the paragraph, as in this example:

> **Writing is a therapy**. It's a way to take things out of your system. Watching those thoughts come out of your brain and onto a piece of paper is like taking a shower and feeling all the dirt wash away. Once I was really mad at someone who had hurt me badly, so I grabbed a piece of paper and a pen and started writing, nothing grammatically correct, just swearing on a blank sheet. When I finished, I went to the kitchen, turned the stove on, and set the paper on fire to let it burn. I felt so good afterwards without having to talk to anyone. **Writing is great therapy**.
>
> —**Gerardo Vela Meza**, student writer

The paragraph begins with a simple statement of the topic: "Writing is a therapy." It then expands on that statement, offers a simile, and ends with a powerful restatement: "Writing is *great* therapy."

The next example begins with a statement of the topic (a picture of a cook's life) and develops it with specific, lively details.

> **Let me paint a picture of the life of a full-time cook**. You wake up early and don't go to bed until at least 2 a.m. You work 13 to 14 hour days, on your feet for at least 95% of that time. Let's not forget the 100 degree kitchen in which you are sweating out of every pore of your body. You work weekends, holidays and have no night life. In a really busy part of the year, you will not see the light of day. You arrive before the sun is up and leave long after it's down. The people who live this life know all about it. They see the young gung-ho culinary students who saw Alton Brown on TV and decided they wanted to be chefs as young fools who have no idea what they are getting themselves into. It's a high stress job. People move quick, they work with fire and knives all day, plus the chef is yelling at you to get food out because the dining room is packed. The young misled culinarians will be in the trenches taking grenades. **This world attracts a very special breed. Not everyone can do it.**
>
> —**Marc Magro**, student writer

After painting the picture of the life of a full-time cook, the writer goes further to form an idea about the topic: "This world attracts a very special breed." The paragraph's shape catches the reader's attention in the first sentence, maintains it with a series of lively details, and then states the conclusion that might already be forming in the reader's mind: "Not everyone can do it."

"Let me paint a picture of the life of a full-time cook."

Perhaps the least common placement of the main idea is somewhere in the middle of the paragraph. We might begin with some details, lead the reader to a statement of the idea, then finish the paragraph with another example. Look at the following paragraph:

I am not used to chocolates just by themselves because that is not how we use them in my country. But if I had to choose one from yesterday's tasting, **I would pick the very last one, which was a Nirvana Belgian Spicy Aztec Bar.** This chocolate has a smooth varnished look on the outside; its color is an appealing deep dark brown that invites [you] to taste it. Once [it is] broken, you can notice that it has white dusty specks that look like almonds; this Belgian chocolate has a combination of aromas that go from soft hints of vanilla, cinnamon and almonds to stronger ones like nutmeg and spices, while a strong rich cocoa butter aroma closes this wonderful combination.

—**Luis Bustamante**, student writer

The writer begins by reminding us of his previous chocolate background, but his main point is contained in the next sentence: I would pick the very last one, which was a Nirvana Belgian Spicy Aztec Bar. The rest of the paragraph describes that delicious treat.

If these shapes seem confusing and unnatural, by all means ignore them! You certainly don't have to see a shape in order to write an effective paragraph. This is just one possible way of thinking about how to present your main idea, how to emphasize what you want to emphasize, how to lead the reader along the path of your thinking.

IMPROVING SEQUENCE AND FLOW

The paragraph exists in *time* as well as in space. The order of the sentences within each paragraph, as well as the order of paragraphs throughout the essay, should help make your points clear to the reader. One way to get a sense of whether the organization is working is to ask someone else to read it. If he doesn't follow your ideas, try to find out at what point the organization seems to break down. If no obliging reader is at hand, you'll have to check the paper yourself. Jot down the topic of each sentence. It can be helpful to number them, as in the following example, or to highlight similar topics in a particular color. Then ask yourself whether this sequence of ideas seems logical, clear, and effective.

The Meat Room (Rough Draft)

(1) When walking around the meat room, one gets a sense of history, from the walls riddled with names to the knowledge that is sealed inside, waiting to be grasped and wielded like a sword. (2) All the knowledge that is held in the dark and damp of the meat cellar—from the understanding of the equipment or the selections of deli meats to the cuts of meat themselves—it all comes together under one roof. (3) There was the smell; it was the scent of life and death. (4) Even though the air was tainted with the scent of blood, it symbolized all the people who would live off the lives of the animals who had given theirs. (5) It almost provided a sense of reverence. (6) From the moment I stepped on the elevator, I got this feeling in the pit of my stomach—and it wasn't hunger. (7) It was a sense of life and death. (8) First it was the elevator, all the names. (9) It showed the past lives of the handful of people who had had the chance to experience the school. (10) So much culture on that wall—for the first time since I had arrived, I felt at home. (11) And the beauty of it is that this gem is not hoarded like Grandma's bundt cake recipe but passed down the generations, perpetually growing with time. (12) It is undying, not only eternal but reborn with each new student that has come to feast on the wisdom and wealth of information that the meat room has to offer.

Some of the sentences clearly belong together, but the paragraph doesn't seem to flow smoothly. The sentence groupings can be listed as follows:

1	intro—knowledge waiting in meat room
2	various kinds of knowledge
3–5	smell of blood—both life and death
6–10	elevator—sense of history, belonging
11	knowledge of the meat room is passed to others
12	conclusion—knowledge is essentially eternal

In the revised version of "The Meat Room" that follows, the author introduces the idea of knowledge in the first sentence and chooses a chronological pattern of organization, moving next to the elevator, his first contact with the meat room. Then comes the smell, which—again according to the original sequence of events—became apparent only as the author began his descent in the elevator. Finally, the types and significance of the knowledge found in the meat room are explored, and the piece ends with the thought that knowledge is eternal. As you read the revised paragraph, think about whether, and why, this new organization is more effective.

The Meat Room (Revised Organization)

When walking around the meat room, one gets a sense of history, from the walls riddled with names to the knowledge that is sealed inside, waiting to be grasped and wielded like a sword. From the moment I stepped onto the elevator, I got this feeling in the pit of my stomach—and it wasn't hunger. It was a sense of life and death. First it was the elevator, all the names. It showed the past lives of the handful of people who had had the chance to experience the school. So much culture on that wall—for the first time since I had arrived, I felt at home. Then there was the smell; it was the scent of life and death. Even though the air was tainted with the scent of blood, it symbolized all the people who would live off the lives of the animals who had given theirs. It almost provided a sense of reverence. Finally, all the knowledge that is held in the dark and damp of the meat cellar—from the understanding of the equipment to the selections of deli meats to the cuts of meat themselves—it all comes together under one roof. And the beauty of it is that this gem is not hoarded like Grandma's bundt cake recipe but passed down the generations, perpetually growing with time. It is undying, not only eternal but reborn with each new student that has come to feast on the wisdom and wealth of information that the meat room has to offer.

—**Jesse Dowling**, student writer

Note that several transitional expressions have been added or revised to tie the paragraph together in the new sequence, for example, "then" and "finally."

Let's look at another example, this one from an early draft of Luis Bustamante's "A Piece of Mexico in Everyone's Mouth" (see Chapter 5 for the full essay):

My mom has always been a great cook; she never had any formal education in Culinary Arts or Baking and Pastry, but she does have a delicate palate, which is what every diner thanks her for. Sometimes she'd get chocolate to bake cakes, breads and cookies or to prepare Mexican dishes like Mole Poblano. In Mexico, people use chocolate in a different way than they do here in the United States. Chocolate is used as an important ingredient in more complex dishes like Mole Poblano, where unsweetened chocolate is melted and combined with dried ancho, mulato, pasilla and chipotle chilies, tomatoes, raisins, parsley, onions, garlic, brown sugar, sesame seeds, cinnamon, cloves, peanuts, anise seeds, and chicken stock. Then everything is ground until a rick thick sauce is obtained. No wonder why Mole, a Nahuati word pronounced MOH-lay, means "concoction or mixture."

In many instances, the repetition of words and phrases can effectively tie a paragraph together. However, in the previous paragraph, the repetition of *Mexican* and *In Mexico* on the same line is a bit jarring, while the two mentions of *Mole Poblano* make the reader feel as if the paragraph is doubling back on itself. What if the writer simply eliminated the repetition?

> My mom has always been a great cook; she never had any formal education in Culinary Arts or Baking and Pastry, but she does have a delicate palate, which is what every diner thanks her for. Sometimes she'd get chocolate to bake cakes, breads and cookies or to prepare savory dishes. In Mexico, people use chocolate in a different way than they do here in the United States. Chocolate is used as an important ingredient in more complex dishes like Mole Poblano, where unsweetened chocolate is melted and combined with dried ancho, mulato, pasilla and chipotle chilies, tomatoes, raisins, parsley, onions, garlic, brown sugar, sesame seeds, cinnamon, cloves, peanuts, anise seeds, and chicken stock. Then everything is ground until a rick thick sauce is obtained. No wonder why Mole, a Nahuati word pronounced MOH-lay, means "concoction or mixture."
>
> —**Luis Bustamante**, student writer

Now the paragraph flows more smoothly from his mother's cooking skill to her use of chocolate in *savory* dishes, which leads to the different use of chocolate *in Mexico*. The *Mole Poblano* then appears naturally as an example of this different, savory use of chocolate.

It's often through revising and rewriting that your best thinking emerges. If possible, let time pass before you re-read and revise the rough draft. You don't need to remain committed to your first ideas, nor should you cling to the text of your first draft. Let your mind continue to range freely over the topic. Pursue interesting lines of thought. Look for better details and examples. And don't hesitate to experiment with completely different organizational plans.

TRANSITIONAL EXPRESSIONS

Transitional expressions help in communication by showing how your ideas are connected in terms of time, space, similarity or difference, and so on. Think Transit Authority. A transition is like a bus. The reader hops in and is driven to the appropriate destination. Like a passenger on the bus, the reader doesn't have to do the work of walking, nor does he run the risk of getting lost. He's delivered right to the door of the next idea (see Figure 6.3).

Figure 6.3 In "A Piece of Mexico," the repetition of the word *mom* carries the readers smoothly from one paragraph to the next.

Transitions have another important similarity to the public transportation system: When they're working, we don't even notice them. But when they're *not* working, or when they're missing altogether, we're left frustrated and fuming.

Transitional expressions are words and phrases that show the reader where and how to move from one idea to the next. For example, transitions such as *first, next,* or *after the water boils* might be included in a recipe to make clear the order in which the steps are to be performed. Transitions might also show a cause-and-effect relationship between ideas, such as *consequently, therefore,* or *as a result.*

While inexperienced writers often miss the importance of transitions, readers find an absent transition as obvious as a missing fork; they find the wrong transition as jarring as a piece of shell in the egg salad. Think about a restaurant meal. Perhaps you've begun with a cup of soup, a hearty pumpkin seasoned with nutmeg and ginger. You're eagerly anticipating the next course—a tender filet mignon with béarnaise sauce—but the wait extends to thirty, forty minutes. When it finally arrives, the steak is delicious, but the *transition* between the two courses has created a problem. Or think about the role of transitions in songs, perhaps in Queen's "Bohemian Rhapsody." A jump in tempo, a guitar riff, or a change in key can signal a new idea or a new mood. Similarly, expressions such as *suddenly* or *on the other hand* or *the next thing that happened* are used in writing to mark the beginning of a new idea or a new mood and to explain *how* the new idea is related to the old.

Movies and television can also give us some information about the importance of transitions. On a talk show, for example, the transition to a commercial is signaled very clearly. Often the host will turn to the camera and say, "We'll be right back." Sometimes the transition is heightened by the camera zooming out. Only then does the series of commercials begin. Television shows may actually be written to accommodate commercial breaks. Perhaps there is a dramatic pause, a close-up on a tearstained face, as in a soap opera. Or perhaps, as in many television movies of the 1980s, the action builds toward a climax, pauses on the brink, and—cut to commercial. All of these devices work; that is, they let the audience know a shift is coming from the story to a scene outside it. In contrast, some contemporary shows do not have a clear transition from story to commercial, whether this is because the writers don't like to insert an unnatural pause or because the advertisers don't want to give the audience a chance to change channels. Whatever the reason for it, the lack of transition can cause a painful jolt.

This is why film editors exist—to make the transition from one scene to the next comfortable and clear. A fadeout/fade-in is smooth and pleasant, while a cut from the telephone in one house to the telephone in another house seems logical. The fact remains that transitions are themselves an ingredient of any story or essay, and what we do with them has a profound effect on the audience's understanding of and response to what we've written.

TYPES OF TRANSITIONS

Transitional expressions explain how ideas are related in a number of ways. Some transitions have to do with **time**, for example, when an event takes place or when one event occurs in relation to another. You've used many transitions relating to time, especially when telling a story. Consider this example:

> One day I step into the walk-in and notice a primal cut of beef that still has the head on it. **As soon as** I see this, the gears in my mind shake the dust off and start to turn.
>
> —**Brendan Cowley**, student writer

The phrase "as soon as" indicates that the gear-turning occurred immediately after the writer saw the primal cut. Other transitions have to do with **space**, as in this example:

> A three-part sink lined one whole side wall of the kitchen, with containers and storage units placed neatly on a shelf above. **On the opposite wall** there were two refrigerators, one walk-in with food stored for the whole week, and a regular fridge with items that were used throughout the day.
>
> —**Matthew K. Greene**, student writer

Some common transitions **introduce an example** that illustrates a concept or fact. The phrase "the best example" in the following sentence connects the idea of "a politically engaged chef" with a specific personality:

> **The best example** of a politically engaged chef is Alice Waters of Chez Panisse. Her movement to foster the farm–restaurant connection, as well as her programs to provide school lunches and teach children the concept of sustainable agriculture, illustrates the political potential of chefs in America today.
>
> —**Payson S. Cushman**, student writer

A final category of transitions concerns **moving from one item to a dissimilar one**, as in the following paragraph:

> The texture of the peach is very juicy. The juices run down the hands and face as you bite into it. It is sticky, reminiscent of a sorbet. **In contrast,** the apricot is noticeably drier. It has a very creamy feel in the mouth. I like to **compare** it with custard, because of the rich, full mouthfeel.
>
> —**Elizabeth Best**, student writer

Study the list of common transitional expressions in Figure 6.4.

REVISING TRANSITIONS

When transitions are missing from a piece of writing, we see more clearly the important role they play. Read the following paragraph:

> Celeste and Annabeth were housewives. They had a different belief about their husbands. Celeste had a distrust. Annabeth had a strong loyalty for her husband. Celeste's husband David came home with a bloody T-shirt. She was embarrassed. It was discovered that Annabeth's daughter had been murdered. Celeste began to suspect her husband was the killer. She made a mistake. She confessed to Jimmy (Annabeth's husband) what she thought without any objective evidence. In the case of Annabeth, she heard that her husband had killed David. She was not agitated. She was stunned. She remained firm. She consoled her husband. That showed us that their beliefs about their husbands were contrary to each other.

Figure 6.4 Common Transitional Expressions

Type of Transition	Examples
time	after, before, currently, during, meanwhile, now, once, since, then, until
space	above, around, below, here, next to, on the other side, there
examples	for example, for instance
comparison/similarity	both, in the same way, likewise, similarly
contrast/difference	although, but, however, in contrast, on the other hand, yet
sequence	first, second, third, next
cause and effect	accordingly, as a result, because, consequently, for this reason, therefore
addition or emphasis	also, in addition, besides, further, in other words, moreover

Without transitions, the reader has to stop and struggle a bit to follow the *connections* between ideas. It can be done, but it uses up precious time and patience on the reader's part. It's like having the customer cook his own dinner at a restaurant. Now read the same paragraph with the original transitional expressions restored (in bold type):

> Celeste and Annabeth were **both** housewives, **but** they had a different belief about their husbands. **While** Celeste had a distrust, Annabeth had a strong loyalty for her husband. **For instance, when** Celeste's husband David came home with a bloody T-shirt, she was embarrassed. **The next day, when** it was discovered that Annabeth's daughter had been murdered, Celeste began to suspect her husband was the killer. She made a mistake. She confessed to Jimmy (Annabeth's husband) what she thought without any objective evidence. **On the other hand**, in the case of Annabeth, she heard that her husband had killed David. She was not agitated. **Even though** she was stunned, she remained firm; **furthermore**, she consoled her husband. That showed us that their beliefs about their husbands were contrary to each other.
>
> —**Soyang Myung**, student writer

Note how the transitions lead the reader smoothly from one idea to the next and tie the whole paragraph together. Further, the transitions add rhythm and variety to the sound of the sentences.

As useful as transitions are, there are times when they are overused or, more often, when the same one is repeated so frequently that it has the effect of clouding rather than illuminating the connections between ideas. Three of the worst offenders are *and, so,* and *then.* Read the following paragraph:

> Celeste and Annabeth were both housewives, **and** they had a different belief about their husbands. **So** Celeste had a distrust, **and** Annabeth had a strong loyalty for her husband. **So** Celeste's husband David came home with a bloody T-shirt, **and** she was embarrassed. **So** the next day it was discovered that Annabeth's daughter had been murdered, **so then** Celeste began to suspect her husband was the killer, **and** she made a mistake. She confessed to Jimmy (Annabeth's husband) what she thought without any objective evidence. **So** in the case of Annabeth, she heard that her husband had killed David. She was not agitated. She was stunned. **Then** she remained firm, **and** she consoled her husband **so** that showed us that their beliefs about their husbands were contrary to each other.

When we compare this version to the original paragraph reprinted earlier, we find that the simple and repetitive *so*'s and *and*'s lack the meaningful connections provided by *while, for instance,* or *even though.*

UNIFYING AN ESSAY WITH TRANSITIONS AND REPETITION

Transitions play a similar role in full-length essays. They show connections *between* paragraphs, as well as within them, and they keep the reader focused on the central idea of the writing. Figure 6.5 shows the flow of ideas in "A Piece of Mexico in Everyone's Mouth."

The repetition of key words and phrases is another way that writers connect ideas and tie their paragraphs together. For example, in "A Piece of Mexico in Everyone's Mouth," the second paragraph ends with this clause: "Chocolates were always present in my life because my mom often used them in the kitchen." An indent indicates visually that we're moving to the third paragraph, but the repetition of the word *mom* keeps us moving smoothly: "My mom has always been a great cook."

When you're editing the final draft of your essay, read it carefully to judge whether you have the correct balance of transitions: enough to make the essay clear, smooth, and unified, but not so many as to make the writing seem stilted and artificial. You don't need to hit the reader over the head with "In conclusion"; instead, find a more specific way to let him know this is the last paragraph, for example, "The chocolate tasting ended."

Figure 6.5 Unifying an Essay through Repetition

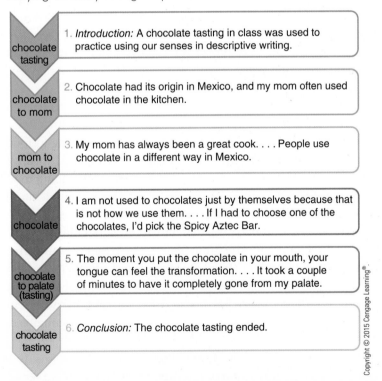

1. *Introduction:* A chocolate tasting in class was used to practice using our senses in descriptive writing. — chocolate tasting

2. Chocolate had its origin in Mexico, and my mom often used chocolate in the kitchen. — chocolate to mom

3. My mom has always been a great cook. . . . People use chocolate in a different way in Mexico. — mom to chocolate

4. I am not used to chocolates just by themselves because that is not how we use them. . . . If I had to choose one of the chocolates, I'd pick the Spicy Aztec Bar. — chocolate

5. The moment you put the chocolate in your mouth, your tongue can feel the transformation. . . . It took a couple of minutes to have it completely gone from my palate. — chocolate to palate (tasting)

6. *Conclusion:* The chocolate tasting ended. — chocolate tasting

Dara Moskowitz Grumdahl's food writing has appeared in Gourmet, Saveur, *and* Bon Appétit, *as well as six editions of the* Best Food Writing in America *anthology. She has been nominated ten times for James Beard Awards, the Oscars of the food world, and has won five times.*

****

Smell the Coffee
by Dara Moskowitz Grumdahl

Everybody makes such a big stinking deal about curare. Oooh, it's such a deadly poisonous root, but people in South America figured out that they could eat it if they boiled it, pounded it, buried it, and then boiled it some more. Wow, that's so *crazy*—I mean, who were the recipe testers on the first versions? Haw-haw.

But get this: There's another tropical plant, an evergreen that grows high up in the mountains of Africa, and this evergreen makes a little berry that takes *seven* months to ripen, and there's barely any berry to it at all, it's mostly just two seeds that fit together into a ball, and around that there's a parchment membrane and some sticky pulp and then a tough outer skin. It's not an attractive fruit—as twigs are to zucchini, so are these meager nubs to peaches, passion fruit, papayas.

Still, people figured out that if they collected enough of these things and let them dry in the sun, and then worked them over with rocks and pulled the double-thick skins off, and finally collected about fifty of those seeds, and roasted them till they spilled smoke all over the place, and then they took the charred things, ground them up into a fine powder, and boiled that powder with water, it would yield a non-nutritive beverage, and everyone would want it. Go figure.

Now, somehow, I've managed to go to a bunch of coffee tastings, or "cuppings," as they're known in the trade, but I never managed to absorb what an amazing discovery coffee really is. For one thing, that tortuous route from wild thing to food makes you realize how much of our diet began as a quixotic experiment—I mean, I can't think of the last time I looked at something and said, "You know, I'm going to take that little tiny thing there and dry it, and really break my back trying to husk it, and then roast it, and then grind it up, boil it, and see if it's any good then." (For all I know, this would make the cassette tapes and paperbacks that line my shelves delicious.)

For another, remember the environmentalist refrain that we can't afford to destroy the rain forest because we don't know what treasures lurk within it: Thinking about coffee's origins, the only response can be: Jumping jahoozefats, yes! Get in there and taste it all! And finally, examining the twisty tale of coffee has an unnerving way of knitting together all of human history, from prehistoric nibbling in the mountains of Ethiopia to the double latte spilled on your mouse pad.

Ethiopian coffee is particularly close to those prehistoric origins: It grows on the same line of trees, in the same soil and much the same climate as it did tens of thousands of years ago. Most important, it is also processed the same way—the ripe fruit picked by hand, dried in the sun, and then painstakingly stripped down to the bean. In contrast, most South American coffees are processed by soaking the ripe fruits in water, which allows the outer layers to ferment off. This is a big deal in coffee circles, with some arguing that "wet processing" removes subtle flavor while others maintain that a dry process can allow the fruit to overripen and the beans to sour.

Nessim Bohbot, president of Alakef Coffee, a local roaster, says it's not simply a matter of which method is better or whether Ethiopian coffee is really superior to any other: "It is true that most of the time Ethiopian coffee has a very rich body," he explains. "But coffee is like wine—you like one for one reason, another for another reason. People like Ethiopian coffee for its profile and complexity, but even people who love a certain Costa Rican coffee might like an Ethiopian sometimes for a change."

That change is easy to come by: A quick run around Loring Park recently scared up three varieties of Ethiopian coffee. Dunn Bros. was selling a batch of big, whole, beautiful, and freshly roasted beans imported from the highlands near the Ethiopian city of Sidamo, for $9.15 a pound. Across the park, Starbucks offered another, darker-roasted Sidamo at $9.95 a pound. They also had a water-processed Lekempti, which despite the steep $13.65-a-pound price tag looked dismayingly bashed up and broken.

Back home I cupped all three coffees—a goofy process whereby you douse fresh-ground beans with boiling water, let them cool for a minute or two, break the crust of grounds that forms on top with a spoon, and slurp up the liquid making a lot of noise and endeavoring to spray the coffee over all the regions of your mouth at once. My first discovery was that all my finds made beautiful brews. The Dunn Bros. Sidamo was one of the fullest coffees I've ever had, the grassy, herbal top notes and bright acidity rounding out essential, strong bass notes. The Lekempti from Starbucks was a delicate, beautiful thing smelling faintly of lavender and finishing with a chocolatey fullness. The Starbucks Sidamo basically didn't stand up to the other two, though it might have done fine had I tested it against less noble beans.

Arabic Coffee Set

Having sealed my flavor adventures, the next thing I discovered was that I remain a lousy cupper: You're supposed to swish and spit, not swallow the coffee grounds and all, but, of course, I did, so I had to spend the rest of the night running circles round the chandelier and gibbering to the tune of "Tie a Yellow Ribbon."

Later in the week, mostly recovered, I made a pilgrimage to Addis Ababa, the bright little storefront of an Ethiopian restaurant situated across from Fairview-Riverside Hospital. This little place, which dishes up fresh, lively versions of Ethiopian stews for around $7 a meal, also serves an Ethiopian coffee that is truly a revelation. (The menu says the coffee service is only done weekdays, but the staff assures me it can be had anytime; one $5.95 order is enough for one or two people.)

The adventure begins with your server roasting a handful of beans in a small pot with a long handle and a screen bottom; at one point the server brings them to your table, shaking the pot so the beans make a skittering noise like maracas and gray smoke spills out like a waterfall. The server then disappears into the kitchen, giving you time to contemplate that people around the world prepared coffee in a similar contraption until the early twentieth century: If Wild Bill Hickok or Charles Dickens drank coffee, it was roasted like this.

The coffee eventually returns to your table on a tray that holds two small espresso-sized cups, a pitcher of sugar, a beautiful, black, round-bottomed earthenware pot resting in a straw base, and, most dramatic, an hourglass-shaped stand of glowing incense. It's a terribly impressive display: In the billowing cloud of smoke, coffee seems magical the way it must have been back when the first cups were brewed and people dreamed up the story of the dancing goats. (Legend has it that the effect of caffeine was discovered when a goatherd found his charges hippity-hopping around a particular tree. He figured out they had munched the berries, soon he did the same, and a few millennia later there I was, circling the chandelier.)

The Addis Ababa coffee tastes mainly big and smoky, and a few herbal notes may or may not be detectable—it's hard to taste anything when your nose is full of incense. I tried filling my cup up with sugar, and the doubly potent brew made me feel awfully exotic, even more so since *Xena, Warrior Princess* was playing on the TV in the corner. After a lot of sipping and sniffing, I emerged back on the streets quick-hearted and bright-eyed, a little goat-like, and maybe a little less attractive to bugs.

See, it turns out that one of science's best guesses as to the role of caffeine is that it's nature's own Deep Woods Off!, keeping insects from devouring the otherwise tasty beans. But nature's best-laid plans went awry: What bugs found distasteful commuters found highly desirable, and the rest is history.

—First published in City Pages, a Voice Media Group publication

ABOUT THE READING

- Outline the essay by summarizing the main idea of each paragraph. Does the essay have a unifying idea? Explain.
- Choose five of the paragraphs and explain how each is developed.

- What types of transitions does the author use both within and between paragraphs? Give specific examples.
- How would you describe the tone of the essay, that is, the author's attitude toward the topic and the audience? Point to specific words and phrases that illustrate your answer.

RECIPE FOR REVIEW

WHAT IS A PARAGRAPH?

1. A paragraph is a series of sentences that develops a single idea through various modes, such as narration, description, compare and contrast, process, and cause and effect.
2. Each paragraph should clearly relate to the central idea of the essay and to the paragraphs before and after it.

EVALUATING AND REVISING YOUR PARAGRAPHS

1. As you revise a piece of writing, pay attention to each paragraph. Ask yourself the questions listed on p. 93.
2. Each paragraph should develop a single topic or idea.
3. The paragraph's single idea is most often contained within the first sentence, though sometimes it is in the last. Occasionally the idea occurs in the middle of the paragraph or is implied rather than stated directly.
4. The sequence of sentences within a paragraph should flow smoothly and logically.

TRANSITIONAL EXPRESSIONS

1. Transitional expressions are words and phrases used to show the connection between ideas, both within and between paragraphs.
2. Transitions may be related to time, space, examples, comparison and contrast, sequence, cause and effect, and emphasis. See Figure 6.3.

CHAPTER EXERCISES

1. *Revising a Paragraph*—Read and revise the following paragraph, both in terms of the sequence of sentences and the structure of each sentence. Ask yourself the questions listed earlier in the chapter.

> *Finding Forrester* is set in the heart of the Bronx in New York, a city which has been recognized for its poverty, racial discrimination, and dangerous streets. The reason this specific city was more essential in telling the story is because not many people would think that a creative genius from a single parent family would emerge from the depths

of a hard-knock life, and become one of the greatest writers ever known. The Bronx has always had a reputation of being a bad place to be to those who know absolutely nothing about the city. When we take a look at the beginning of the film, the director shows several clips of the city's lifestyle depicting the setting perfectly. A boy rapping in the streets, the rundown basketball court that Jamal and his friends play in, the graffiti stained buildings, the people who occupy the city, and the deprivation that surrounds everything that lives within its walls create the ideal visual for the audience to get a feel of what the movie will be about.

2. *Adding Transitions to a Paragraph*—Rewrite the following paragraph, adding at least five transitional expressions to make connections clear and tie the paragraph together.

> The restaurant was in a medium-sized building with two floors and fits one hundred people. The feel of the restaurant was warm and exciting. The dining room had beautiful pictures on the walls and vibrant colors of green and orange on the ceiling. I walked in. I felt as though I was in Mexico. Music of Spanish guitars was playing throughout the building. It was a loud restaurant due to all of the customers. I was able to make conversation with the other patrons.

3. *Transitions across the Essay*—Explain the transitions from paragraph to paragraph in one of the other pieces in the A Taste for Reading sections at the end of Chapters 1–17.

4. *Using Repetition*—Choose a speech (try www.americanrhetoric.com), such as Martin Luther King's "I Have a Dream," and analyze its use of repetition.

IDEAS FOR WRITING

1. Choose a food or drink, and develop your ideas and memories about it in a series of loosely connected paragraphs. Include research, if you wish. Do you find you have an underlying central idea? Explain.

2. Why does Dara Moskowitz Grumdahl call her essay "Smell the Coffee"? What popular saying does it refer to? Is it an effective title? Explain.

3. Write a short paper, using one of the following food sayings as inspiration:
   - You should eat to live; not live to eat. (Socrates)
   - Eat breakfast like a king, lunch like a prince, and dinner like a pauper. (Adele Davis)
   - The more you eat, the less flavor; the less you eat, the more flavor. (Chinese Proverb)
   - Tell me what you eat, I'll tell you who you are. (Jean Anthelme Brillat-Savarin)

4. After watching *The Cutting Edge: The Magic of Movie Editing*, a 2004 documentary, discuss the parallels with writing.

CHAPTER 7
WRITING INTRODUCTIONS AND CONCLUSIONS

By the end of this chapter, you should begin to . . .

- write an introduction that presents the paper's topic and engages the reader's interest;
- rewrite the introduction, once you have a complete draft, to sharpen its focus and tie it more closely to the conclusion;
- write a conclusion that highlights the paper's central idea and perhaps mirrors the introduction in some way; and
- choose an appropriate, effective title, when necessary.

Two of the most important paragraphs in a piece of writing are the introduction and the conclusion. You only have one chance to make a first impression, whether it's at the beginning of an essay, a job interview, or a first date. In fact, research has shown that what is said first is most likely to be remembered by readers. What is said last is the next most likely to be remembered. Therefore conclusions are also extremely important—the handshake after the interview, the tentative kiss at the end of the first date, the last scene of a movie, the final paragraph of an essay.

The **introduction** to an essay is like the first scent to catch your attention as you step into a restaurant. The aroma may invite you in—or you may decide to dine elsewhere! Now, if you're reviewing the restaurant, you'll probably stay even if your first impression is not promising. Similarly, your instructor will read your essay whether or not the introduction is inviting. In most cases, however, customers and readers are free to try another venue if the first impression is poor. Therefore we want to make that first impression a good one, whether it's an enticing aroma or a captivating introduction.

Now, imagine that the customers have finished eating. We want to ensure that they leave the restaurant with a good impression and that they pass that good impression on to their friends. In the concluding moments of the meal, we want to remind the customers that we delivered on our initial promise—that they enjoyed the experience. By offering coffee and dessert, we encourage them to take the time to think back over the meal and decide if it's worth the price on the check. Likewise, the **conclusion** of an essay is a chance for us to highlight our main point and show the reader that we kept the promise made in the introduction. For both cooks and writers, introductions and conclusions play important roles and present unique challenges.

SHAPING THE INTRODUCTION

The introduction is the first transition in a piece of writing: it draws the reader from the outside into the world of the writer's ideas. In the same way, delicious aromas emanating from the kitchen tempt customers to step into the restaurant. Imagine the rapturous expression on the faces of hungry diners as their noses follow the trail of a fabulous fragrance. The introduction has a second important task as well: to tell the reader what the writing is about. Once customers have stepped inside the restaurant—drawn by those delicious aromas—they may then glance over the menu to get a sense of what the restaurant is "about."

In addition to getting the reader interested, the introduction usually states the topic of the essay and gives important background information. Like a funnel or an

Imagine the rapturous expression on the faces of hungry diners as their noses follow the trail of a fabulous fragrance.

upside-down triangle (see Chapter 6, as well as Figure 7.1 on page 120), the introduction opens wide to draw the reader in with a statement that is broadly appealing or a story that is uniquely interesting. With each new sentence, the introduction narrows its focus until it concludes with the specific subject of the essay. Look at the following example:

> As a child, everyone has a dish that he or she loves so much it becomes an essential to survive. It's usually "fun" food, like French fries and chicken fingers, which can be picked up and eaten at any time. Yet every once in a while, a child comes along that enjoys eating entrées and side dishes other than the usual simple deep-fried meals. My favorite childhood dish was my grandmother's red cabbage.
>
> —**Kenneth Zask**, student writer

The introduction begins with the general statement that "everyone" has a much loved favorite food. The second sentence outlines typical childhood preferences. The third lets us know that something different is coming. The fourth sentence narrows the focus to the writer's favorite dish—"my grandmother's red cabbage." In this way, the paragraph funnels the reader into the body of the essay, which will focus on that cabbage.

Here's another example of an introduction that **moves from the general to the specific:**

> We often seem to hold on to our past. We carry it on our shoulders, using it as an excuse, a hideaway, or as a compass for our future. Beating ourselves up for the past has become second nature to us. I should have. I would have. I wish I had. Although there's nothing that can change the

Corn on the cob may be this child's favorite dish!

past, by leaving our past behind we can now focus on the future, which can be the new foundation of our lives. In *The Shipping News,* the Quoyle family had trouble letting go of a past that hindered their growth. But they eventually learned that the past was merely a stepping stone. They learned that life still goes on.

—**Gerald Houston**, student writer

Again, the introduction begins with a general statement—"we often seem to hold on to the past"—explains it, and ends with a specific focus. It is the Quoyle family who is holding on to "a past that hindered their growth."

In addition to narrowing the focus of an essay, the introduction may also **map out the main points**, as in this example:

Today nearly everybody goes to college. It is almost a must-have for every job. The people that do go to college see that it is very different from high school. There have been many differences I have seen, but the three that stand out the most are the amount and difficulty of the work, the responsibility of getting up on my own, and the friends I have made.

—**James Virus**, student writer

The last line of this introduction makes clear that the next three sections of the essay will discuss the difficulty of college work, the responsibility of caring for oneself, and the making of new friends. This introduction offers a very specific promise to the reader in terms of both content and organization, and you may find such a road map to be an effective component of many academic essays.

While some introductions begin with a general statement, others **start with specific details or examples**, such as the following:

With the Food Network, TLC, Bravo, Travel Channel, and Cooking Channel all over television sets, we are constantly surrounded by images of food. Food and cooking shows are becoming increasingly popular in America and the rest of the world. There are the "demo shows" like *Everyday Italian*, the "competition shows" like *Iron Chef*, the "show and tell" *Man vs. Food,* and the "reality shows" like *Cake Boss.* It has gotten to the point where we have almost every style of TV show, just about food! The shows are great exposure for our industry, but they also paint an image of us that is sugar coated.

—**Samuel Beard**, student writer

Another effective type of introduction uses a **specific image or quotation** that relates to the topic of the essay. Movies, of course, are all about the image. The first scene of *The Matrix*, for example, displays lines of mysterious symbols unfolding across a computer screen. Initially uncertain what this image might mean, the viewer comes to understand that it represents the inner world of the Matrix, the computer software that has relegated human beings to the status of batteries. Movies can also make good use of words. For example, *About a Boy* begins with a game show question about John Donne's quote, "No man is an island." Throughout the film, one of the main characters continually refers to this quote and refines his interpretation of it.

Sometimes the introduction **tells a short story or anecdote** that is related to the body of the essay. For example, the film *Miss Congeniality* begins on a playground in New Jersey where a tough little girl defends a boy from a bully. The boy doesn't appreciate her, however, and as she impulsively punches him in the nose, the title of the film drops ironically across her face: Miss Congeniality. Twenty years later, the little girl has grown up to become an FBI agent, and the movie continues to explore her twin impulses to protect—and to punch. The story of the little girl and the bully has both caught our attention and laid the groundwork for the film's main ideas.

Many students like to begin an essay with a **question to the reader,** such as "When was the last time you went on a picnic?" or "Do you like to snowboard?" There are some risks involved with this type of opening, however. First, the question often requires such a simple answer—perhaps "last summer" or simply "yes"—that the reader may not be intrigued enough to continue reading. Second, the reader may be more interested in the *writer*'s point of view and thus not welcome a shift toward her own. In the end, this type of question may ring false since the reader's response cannot really be shared with the writer.

With that said, it is also true that some questions can make thought-provoking and effective introductions to your topic. A good question will be intriguing and open-ended, often beginning with *How* or *Why*, arousing the reader's curiosity, and requiring a more complex and thoughtful answer. "*How* would you create a truly unusual and impressive picnic menu?" or "*Why* might someone prefer snowboarding to skiing?" (Note that questions do not always need the personal *you*.) The example that follows is from an essay about the movie *Tortilla Soup*.

> What is a tortilla soup? As I'm not familiar with Mexican food, except for some representative dishes such as fajita, burrito and quesadilla, "tortilla soup" was a big question mark in my mind. My curiosity about the title first caught my interest; then I fell into the movie, which had such attractive and fruitful cooking scenes from the beginning to the end. The introductory cooking procedures were the most impressive scenes to me because they were powerful and vivid descriptions of Mexican food.
>
> —**Na Yeon Kim**, student writer

A related type of introduction presents a **problem to be solved**, such as how to improve weak study habits or how to make a cheesecake with as little fat as possible. In the following introduction to an essay, the writer explores ways in which chefs can help with food-related problems. The paragraph begins with the idea that "every occupation entails some sort of civil duties" and leads to a focus on those problems it might be a chef's duty to address.

> Every occupation entails some sort of civil duties. Some of these duties are quite obvious, such as a soldier's duty to defend his or her own country; however, other jobs include dealing with less obvious societal issues. Ordinary people may not think that chefs have much to do with society other than feeding the general public, but there are more responsibilities in being a chef that meet the eye. Food-related problems are rapidly increasing world-wide, and who better to help conquer these issues, such as obesity, eating disorders, and world hunger, than people who have a strong passion for and understanding of food.
>
> —**Justine A. Frantz**, student writer

Finally, an introduction may engage the reader through a vivid **sense of the author's personality**. For two excellent examples of this, read the first paragraphs of Dara Moskowitz Grumdahl's "Smell the Coffee" (Chapter 6) and John Thorne's "One Knife, One Pot" (Chapter 8).

Although introductions can take many different forms, they share a desire to catch the reader's attention and move her toward the subject of the paper.

WRITING AND REWRITING THE INTRODUCTION

Since the introduction is the first part of the essay, it may seem reasonable that it should be the first part we write, and that it should be all clean and tidy before we address the next part of the essay, the body. In fact, though, the opposite is often true. Although we might be tempted to work on the introduction extensively before straightening out the body of the essay, the introduction may be the last part of the essay to reach its final form. It makes sense that once we have found exactly where we're going, we can more effectively write an introduction that points the reader in that direction.

In writing the first draft of the essay, it is important not to get stuck on the introduction. Either breeze through it just to get something down, or, if you're really stumped, jump over the introduction completely for the moment and write whatever part of the essay you can. If you labor too long over one part of the first draft, you may use up precious time. Once you have something written, even if it seems weak, you'll be able to rewrite and reorganize. If you can't get anything down for an introduction, it works better to move on to another part of the essay, at least temporarily. Once you're satisfied with the body of the paper, go back and experiment with some of the different kinds of introductions discussed earlier. The chances are good that you'll find one that works.

Look at this rough draft of an introduction to a personal essay:

> I remember that one moment that changed my life. The day began like so many others before it. This one, however, was somewhat needful after juggling work and school all week.
>
> —**Charles A. Dunn**, student writer

The paragraph introduces the topic—the moment that changed the writer's life—but not much else beyond the stress suggested by "juggling." The moment itself is quite dramatic, with serious and far-reaching consequences. After exploring the story, the writer revised his introduction as follows:

> I vividly remember the moment that changed my once mischievous life. It was two days before Christmas, so the atmosphere was cheerful. This day, however, ended up somber.
>
> —**Charles A. Dunn**, student writer

In the first sentence, the addition of three words brings a vitality and charm to this revised introduction. The memory is "vivid" and the writer "once mischievous." This new paragraph also sets the time of year at "two days before Christmas" and builds some suspense. Why, the reader wonders, did the "cheerful" day end up "somber"? That's the hook.

WRITING AN EFFECTIVE CONCLUSION

As we have said before, the conclusion is like the coffee and dessert that follow the meal. It does not contain the majority of the words and information needed to make the essay's point; that is, the role of the body paragraphs. Instead, the conclusion provides time and space for the reader to think about what has been said by summarizing or highlighting the main idea. If the introduction promised to inform the reader about different varieties of apples, for example, the conclusion would review that information, reminding the reader that the promise had been kept.

Let's look at some examples of concluding paragraphs. This first one **summarizes the main points** of the essay:

> Sean Devine showed me his honesty by rejecting the invitation to the bar from a female officer. He showed his professionalism by not allowing his personal problems with Lauren to interfere with his job. He showed his calm and detached personality when he announced that the body in a hole in the park was his friend's daughter. He knew how to handle himself, and that is the thing that makes him my favorite character.
>
> —**René S. León**, student writer

Often the conclusion will **highlight the most important point** or share a deeper insight into the topic. In the conclusion to "Beyond Clogs and White Coats," Dr. Karen Devon reflects on the most "vital" part of her day as a surgeon and the "most subtle, yet significant parallel" between chefs and doctors:

> Perhaps most vital in my day is the feeling that I contribute to some fundamental need. Of health, shelter, and food, the last may be most essential. Medical students learn a standard algorithm for writing orders where, 'Diet' comes first—ahead of 'activities' and 'vital signs.' The first 'restaurants', in 18th century France, were designed to 'restore' the health of those who were ill rather than entertain the bourgeoisie. And a surgeon's job can revolve around restoring patients' ability to chew, swallow, use the gut, and nourish the body. Luckily, not everyone needs an operation; but we must all eat! We yearn to feed and be fed, as we begin and frequently end life through this shared act, often ritualized and joyful. The personal satisfaction gained out of arousing emotion through our interactions may be the most subtle, yet significant parallel between the chef and I. It is a privilege that bonds us much more than our clogs and white coats.

Another type of conclusion **offers a solution to the problem** described in the paper. In the following example, the writer sums up the main point of the movie *Crash*, in which prejudice creates serious problems for the characters.

> All these cases reflect a natural quality of human beings. Prejudice, selfishness and disenfranchisement make us lose our sense of judgment. Prejudice produces rage, and rage gives birth to tragedy. If nobody stops it, this vicious cycle goes on and on. This story goes beyond the people in the movie; they are us. We are victims as long as we operate out of prejudice, selfishness and disenfranchisement. As the movie shows, those with one-track minds do not help us to live together. In the end, I came to know that love is the only thing to reduce the crashes and help us to live together in harmony.

> —**Mee-kyoung Kim**, student writer

In addition to highlighting the idea that "prejudice, selfishness and disenfranchisement make us lose our sense of judgment," the conclusion suggests an approach to ending that "vicious cycle": "love is the only thing to reduce the crashes."

Conclusions very often **explain why the topic is important** or **emphasize the importance of a particular point** in the essay, as in the following example "A Piece of Mexico" (see Chapter 5 for the complete essay):

> The chocolate tasting ended, and I was amazed how intricate chocolate could be. I started to understand why people spend good money on it; it is not about having that chocolate taste but to experiment and turn on the

senses bite after bite. Now I am curious about this product and chances are that before this week ends, I may take a visit to the library to learn more about it. Who knows? I may begin to like it and sometime in the future cook Mexican dishes with some of these wonderful European chocolates.

—**Luis Bustamante**, student writer

Sometimes the last page of a book or the last scene of a movie suddenly changes direction and **ends in a completely unexpected way.** Remember the famous twist in *The Sixth Sense?* It took most viewers completely by surprise. The twist was particularly successful, but it had more than shock value. It made sense of the plot, and it explained the "haunting" mood of the film. Twists can be effective in essays as well, especially when combined with a sense of humor, as in this example:

Although I would be alone on the island, I wouldn't miss my complicated life. In fact, I would relish the solitude provided by the island. With a regular food supply of the mix plates, Mom's sweet potato pies, and the sunflower seeds, I could stay indefinitely—ironically becoming the only person to get fat while stranded on a desert island.

—**Cheyenne Simpkins**, student writer

Many writers peter out when it's time to write the conclusion; they're simply exhausted! Don't give up, though. While the first impression made by the introduction is important, the conclusion provides an opportunity to leave a *lasting* one.

TYING THE INTRODUCTION AND CONCLUSION TOGETHER

The conclusion in some way returns to the place where the essay began—but with a new perspective. Think first about the table in a fine restaurant. We sit down looking at the immaculate tablecloth, the perfectly arranged silver, the spotless glasses. When we reach the end of the main course, the crumbs have been swept away, glasses have been refilled, and the table has been set for dessert. We're back to the place where we began, with a difference. Our stomachs are quietly full, our taste buds satiated. We have a glow of content as we anticipate the final summing up of the meal—coffee, brandy, dessert, cheese plate. As we begin that last course, we do so with the knowledge of what has gone before and with an awareness that the experience is coming to an end.

Think about the movie *Saving Private Ryan.* In the opening scene, an old man is looking out over a cemetery. Then the film flashes back fifty years to D-Day, the sixth of June, and tells the story of a three-day search through Normandy for a young soldier whose brothers have all been killed. The movie ends by flashing forward to the same place it began—the same old man looking at the same cemetery—but now the audience knows who he is and what it took to get him to this point,

Figure 7.1 The Three Parts of an Essay

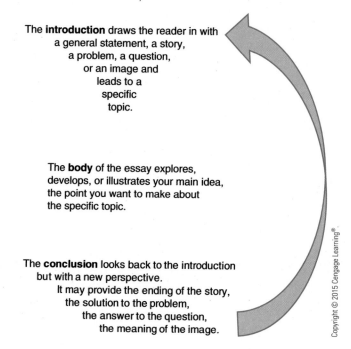

The **introduction** draws the reader in with
a general statement, a story,
a problem, a question,
or an image and
leads to a
specific
topic.

The **body** of the essay explores,
develops, or illustrates your main idea,
the point you want to make about
the specific topic.

The **conclusion** looks back to the introduction
but with a new perspective.
It may provide the ending of the story,
the solution to the problem,
the answer to the question,
the meaning of the image.

alive, surrounded by his family, and remembering with emotion the sacrifice of those who saved him.

In the same way, the end of the essay looks back toward the beginning, performing a graceful arc within the reader's imagination. Conclusions are often especially effective when they clearly reflect some material in the introduction. Do not simply repeat the thesis statement, however! If the introduction told a story, let the conclusion allude to it. If the paper began with a quotation, it's nice to include or continue it, or in some way refer to it again. A question in the first paragraph might be answered in the last, or a problem introduced in the beginning might be solved in the end. There are no hard and fast rules; just remember that the reader will be pleased to be reminded of where she has come from when she gets to the end of your paper.

In this first example, the introduction propels the reader into the action of a "scorching hot" kitchen in the middle of service. The second-person point of view and the present tense increase the sense of excitement.

The clock strikes six, and your first ticket hits the board. There is an eerie silence until the sound of cold raw fish hitting a scorching hot grill fills the kitchen. Suddenly the kitchen fills with light as the sauté station also receives the first tickets for the night. When you arrived at three, the kitchen was a cool 80°. Now only ten minutes into service, it feels as though the restaurant stands on top of the sun. At a scorching 110°, the kitchen's on fire, but in this case it's a good thing. Some people call me a crazy fool, but I on the other hand like to look at myself as a passionate artist. The sauté pan and the grill are my tools, and here is how I use them.

—**Anthony Guarino**, student writer

The conclusion looks back to the introduction and mirrors the same information—time, sound, temperature—as well as hitting the main idea at the very end.

It's one in the morning, and you've just burned your last ticket. The silence sweeps the kitchen again. The sauté station is cool. Everyone has started to clean up, thinking "Thank god, it's over"—not because they don't love it, just because now they get the sweet rewards. "Good job, guys, we turned them over three times." Grilling and sautéing make everything so fast that time flies, but yet the sense of accomplishment is still so immense. This is why these are my favorite tools.

—**Anthony Guarino**, student writer

As the tickets hit the board and the fish hits the pan, this cook savors the heat and urgency of the dinner rush.

Sometimes the conclusion gently **twists the image created in the introduction.** In this next example, the health concerns raised at the beginning of the essay vanish in a smile at the end.

Introduction

When I was a child, I was slender because I did not eat a lot of food, and my mother worried about my health. I looked like a weak girl, compared with my sisters. I weighed just 19 kilograms [about 42 lbs.] when I was in second grade. Therefore, my mother wanted me to eat a lot of food to gain more weight. She tried to find my favorite dish to make me eat a lot. Finally, she found that I loved her Tom-Yum noodles. . . .

Conclusion

If I had not had my mother's Tom-Yum noodles, I could not grow up to be a fat girl like today!

—**Kanyalanee Jirattigalachote**, student writer

The Conclusion Mirrors the Introduction . . .

	Introduction	Conclusion
Time	the clock strikes six	it's one in the morning
Sound	there is an eerie silence until the sound of cold raw fish hitting a scorching hot grill	the silence sweeps the kitchen again
Temp	the kitchen's on fire	the sauté station is cool

Main Idea
The sauté pan and the grill are my favorite tools.

The conclusion can **resolve the question or problem** raised in the introduction, as in the following example:

Introduction

We are constantly presented with choices and decisions in life. As seen time and time again, every action has a reaction, so every move we make must have a reason behind it. The difference between getting revenge and seeking justice is a large one, and each will produce a very different outcome. In the movie *Mystic River,* for example, Jimmy and Dave are both affected by revenge, and the third friend, Sean, is affected by justice.

Conclusion

In the end, it seems revenge gets Jimmy and Dave nowhere. Dave ends up dead, and Jimmy ends up mourning his dead daughter, killing his friend, and being hunted for that murder by another friend. It appears that Sean, the man of law, the man of justice, is the only one with a happy ending. His wife comes back to him with their daughter, a family reunited. The only way he obtains this, however, is by putting his personal relations aside, doing the hard thing, taking the high road. He seeks justice rather than revenge, and is rewarded with happiness.

—**Timothy Fisher**, student writer

Finally, the conclusion can **drive home the emotional impact** of a topic, as in the following example:

Introduction

When I was eight years old, my parents got divorced. My sister and I chose to live with our father and only visit our mother. In the meantime my father had to instantly change from being not only Dad but "Mr. Mom." He then had to take on the roles of both parents in the house. He had to wash clothes, clean, raise my sister and me, and worst of all, cook. He didn't know how to cook much, but every Tuesday he knew how to make the best macaroni and cheese. I will always remember this dish and its meaning. It's not always how you cook it; it might just be who you're eating it with that makes it tasty. . . .

Conclusion

Despite the fact that my dad really couldn't make much of anything, he knew how to make the most memorable meal. He did it all by himself, without help from anyone. This made him grow without my mother, yet my sister and I grew by eating a simple meal with three people that loved each other, instead of four that didn't.

—**Tammi Bertram Gonzalez**, student writer

The conclusion of an essay or a meal asks the audience a question: Was it worth it? At a restaurant, the value is partly financial since the customers are presented with a check. As they look over the figures, they will have a reaction, perhaps a sense of satisfaction that the meal was worth the money. An essay's conclusion also asks the audience to evaluate the experience. Do we nod our heads in understanding? Or shake them in frustration? Was the essay worth the time it took to read? By looking back at the introduction, the conclusion strengthens our sense that the whole paper hangs together—a very satisfying feeling.

Movies are especially well designed to create that satisfaction through the use of recurring images and musical themes. *Mystic River,* for example, begins with a view of the Boston neighborhood along the river's edge in which the main characters grow up. Two hours later, after telling a complicated story of abuse and revenge, the movie returns to the river. And now the river has a symbolic meaning in keeping with its name—it is into the river that the bodies of two murdered men are thrown. Like the River Styx in Greek mythology, the Mystic River lies between life and death. In the last scene, the simple piano tune heard first at the start of the film begins again. The camera moves closer to the water, skimming for a moment along the surface, then plunges beneath it into darkness.

CHOOSING A TITLE

The **title** of an essay or story is like a shortened form of an introduction: With just a brief word or phrase, a good title can draw readers from the outside into the world of your ideas. The title usually refers to the topic of the paper and is designed to attract the reader's attention, often with a play on words or a vivid image. The title of the movie *Tortilla Soup,* for example, places the focus immediately on food, in fact, on Mexican food, as does the very first scene. Tortilla soup is also on the menu at a climactic dinner. By the end, tortilla soup represents the resolution of the movie's familial and cultural conflicts.

Single words often make effective titles, particularly when the word is part of the essay's main idea. Look at the following title and introductory paragraph:

Lost

Dreams, goals, or aspirations are something one strives to achieve throughout life. This is about my dream as a young man of nineteen and how I came to the realization that I would not be able to attain my dream without sacrificing the life I wanted. Few people who have met me after June 2003 know that I have not always aspired to be a chef. As long as I can remember, I wanted to a Navy SEAL, "the best of the best" on the front lines fighting for my country.

—**Roth Perelman**, student writer

As the essay continues, we learn that the writer's dream of a career with the SEALs was "lost" because of an injury. The title foreshadows the essay's main point.

Titles are important in the business world as well. In the following paragraph, the authors explain the reasoning behind their choice of "Braizen" as the name of their proposed restaurant:

The name of a restaurant has a deep and resounding impact. It must define who you are, what it is you represent, your ideals and philosophical intentions, all while being short, concise, and pleasant to the ear and eyes.

In the end, we looked at two words which summed up everything we were doing: *brazen* and *braising*. While we are a braising-centralized restaurant, we are also doing something that has yet to be done in this neighborhood. In that sense, brazen seemed to fit our actions and decisions perfectly. Together, we have *Braizen*, a quick to say and easy to remember word which embodies our mission statement in its entirety.

—**James Shum, David Murray,** and **Jason Hsu**, student writers

In the next example, the title combines an image with a little word play:

Garlic: The Sprouting of My Career

When I was young, I would love watching my mother cook. My job was to help get her ingredients for the family meal she was about to prepare. I was too young at the time to reach into the cupboard, so she would lift me up and I would grab the ingredients she needed. One day when I was helping my mother in our kitchen, she lifted me up and told me to reach for the garlic. I found a bulb of garlic and grabbed it, but to my surprise I saw another one that had started to sprout!

—**Winston G. Caesar**, student writer

The author's interest in food and cooking "sprouted" along with the garlic bulb.

The best titles may become a symbol for the audience's experience of the story. The movie *Crash*, for example, reveals the origin of its title in the very first scene. By the end of the film, however, the word *crash* has been enriched by the audience's deepening understanding of the original quote. After the film is over, the title acts as a reminder both of the central *image* of the film—the car crash—and of the impact of its poignant stories on the viewer.

A TASTE FOR READING

Ike DeLorenzo writes about food and culture for the Boston Globe *and other publications. He edits The Ideas Section, a blog on food, technology, and language.*

****

Everyone's a Critic
by Ike DeLorenzo

Restaurant dining has new bookends. The experience often begins and ends with the Web. Before you go out, you find a good place to eat; after you dine, you post a review. Millions of diners are now civilian critics, letting Chowhound, Yelp, Citysearch, and others in on their recent meals.

The domain of criticism was once the preserve of magazines and newspapers. This year has seen a flurry of activity for restaurant review sites, and for some new approaches to public critiques. Two big players—the biggest actually—want in on the action. Last week, Facebook began mailing door stickers to restaurants asking diners to "like" (there's no "dislike") and comment about restaurants with Facebook pages. Google recently launched Google Place Pages, also with door stickers, which allow diners with smartphones to point the camera at a bar code and instantly display a comments page. All of this is enough to make restaurateurs worry about every single diner.

In the same way that travelers use various Web sites to find evaluations of hotels, diners are now turning to online food sites for advice on where to eat. As staggeringly fast as participation in food and restaurant Web sites has grown, so has the attention being paid to amateur critics. Comments and ratings from any one diner may, of course, be biased or even false. Many Internet pundits believe in something called "the wisdom of the crowd." The theory is that with many people commenting, you eventually get to the truth about a restaurant. As the public posts about the food, the service, the ambience, the bearnaise, the baguettes, a fuller and more accurate picture is supposed to evolve. The amateurs are not going away, which restaurateurs once might have hoped, and they are making chefs nervous.

Yelp, a social networking site where users post their own reviews, in March had 31 million unique visitors, up from 20 million a month last year. Since Yelp launched in 2004, 10 million reviews, mostly for restaurants, have been written. Similar sites also show strong growth. But because they hope to profit from what is submitted, these sites have goals that may be at odds with the restaurants, and even with the commenters. Yelp and its aspirants are in the business of making money by brokering information.

But there are suggestions—well, allegations even—that the natural ratings that should result are being manipulated. Kathleen Richards, a reporter for The East Bay Express in Oakland, Calif., wrote a widely circulated story last year about Yelp's advertising and editorial practices. According to Richards, Yelp sales representatives would routinely cold-call Bay Area restaurants asking that they agree to a yearly contract to advertise on Yelp ($299 per month and up). Part of the pitch involved promises to remove bad Yelp reviews or move them off the main page. Richards also presented evidence that, in some cases, bad reviews had been written by the Yelp sales representatives themselves to force a sale. Failing to agree meant prominent bad reviews.

On its blog (and elsewhere), Yelp CEO Jeremy Stoppleman forcefully denied these claims throughout the year, maintaining that Yelp only offered restaurants a chance to "feature" a review of its choice, and that any removals were done by "automatic filters" designed to detect fraudulent posts (from, say, friends, relatives, or known adversaries of the establishment). At the same time, more restaurants and other businesses, now from around the country, came forward claiming they had received similar solicitations from Yelp sales reps. To say the food blogs have been abuzz is an understatement.

The situation culminated in a dozen businesses, mostly restaurants, filing a federal class-action lawsuit against Yelp in February, a year after the story broke. The strongly worded suit accuses the company of "extortion." Last month, in a bitter blog post, Stoppleman announced some changes. Restaurants can no longer select a "sponsored review" to appear prominently on the top of its Yelp page, and reviews suppressed for any reason are now available on a separate, though somewhat obscure, "filtered reviews" area of the page.

Grover Taylor, owner of Eat at Jumbo's in Somerville, says his ratings dropped sharply last year when he declined to advertise on the site. "They called every week, telling me I needed to pay $500 a month to advertise. When I said no, a lot of one-star reviews started appearing on top. And then the phone would ring. Hi, this is Art from Yelp. We can make them disappear." Taylor says the calls slowed and changed tone when he told the Yelp agent he was joining the class-action suit. "Art stopped calling. A new guy from Yelp is calling now."

Individual restaurants now spend a lot of time handling existing reviews. "It basically eats many hours, on a weekly basis, going through Yelp and trying to address all the posts," says Peter Rait, owner of Beacon Hill Bistro in Boston. Like many Boston restaurateurs, Rait has engaged an outside company to help his staff understand and react to Yelpers on the site itself. Rait thinks continuing the conversation with customers after they leave his restaurant can be a distraction. "I'm a little bit old school. We take care of each customer who comes in. We want to concentrate on quality while the diner is here, not somehow creating the perception of quality afterward."

But Erica Pilene, general manager of Finale Park Plaza, embraces the challenge. "We are constantly monitoring Yelp to see how we are doing. When we see a comment—say a server was being rude—I'll take the server aside and say, we need to talk about this. It makes you more on top of your game than you ever have been. The feedback doesn't go away, you can't erase it, and everyone can see it."

Since Yelp and Citysearch are stand-alone services, it's easier for people who want to game the system to sign up for many accounts with various e-mails, cast many votes, and create a suspiciously large number of positive (or negative) ratings. In these cases, the sites have conflicting motivations: more accounts make for impressive numbers, fake accounts create false ratings. Now that Yelp has been forced to abandon removing and shifting reviews, setting the bar for other sites, it also may be forced to be more aggressive in rooting out counterfeit opinions.

A partner, such as Google or Facebook, who has a better handle on account-holders' identities, could help moderate reviewer vitriol and reduce duplicate reviews. For them, ad hoc and additional accounts are easy to detect (no Facebook friends, no messages in their gmail box), and so they may have an advantage. In 2009, Google made overtures to purchase Yelp for a reported $500 million. Google was ultimately spurned, perhaps now driving Yelp into the arms of Facebook. Recent partnerships between Yelp and Facebook, and coy statements by their CEOs, have industry insiders speculating about a purchase.

But why is Yelp so valuable? The reason is simple. Tweets and status posts about what you ate this afternoon have limited shelf life. Thoughtful posts on a restaurant, accompanied by a star-rating, have lasting worth, and aggregate value as others weigh in. Whichever company owns this data then owns the Web gateway many people turn to for information. And tying your tastes to your identity is the holy grail of Internet marketing. Leave a long review of an Italian restaurant and you are bound to get spam from an Italian food importer.

Neither 200-pound gorilla is standing still. Google and Facebook both are trying to get existing users to review restaurants. Google's large restaurant sticker dwarfs other Web site stickers already on the door, and has its next-generation technology angle.

Sites like Yelp and Citysearch will be hard to defeat. Both have elevated those frequent contributors who are heavily "liked" (in the social networking sense) to a status akin to a traditional restaurant critic. Yelp calls them the "Elite Squad," and Citysearch calls them "Dictators." In both cases, they are presented as those users who are the authoritative tastemakers for a given city, their reviews are most prominently featured, and they are invited by the site to special events in their local cities. Only the online names of these users are known to the two companies, which is a lot of influence to delegate to people you know little about. The practice helps sites compete with traditional media by creating cheap (as in unpaid) experts.

Some restaurateurs and staff who do not have a favorable view of these sites spoke to me under condition of anonymity. "There's sometimes a faceless nastiness on the sites," says one. "People will sometimes attack chefs personally in a way that's baseless and cruel." A well-known restaurateur who refused to put a Google sticker on his door says, "They collect personal information and sell it. Why should I help? They can manufacture popularity with these sites, but it can go the other way."

Talented civilian reviewers who outgrow review sites are creating alternatives. Successful writers on Chowhound and eGullet (a popular bulletin board for food discussions) have gone on to create compelling food and restaurant blogs. In this area, there's North Shore Dish (www.northshoredish.com), Eat Boutique (www. eatboutique. com), The Boston Foodie (www.thebostonfoodie.blogspot.com), Fork It Over, Boston (www.forkitoverboston.blogspot.com), and Table Critic (www.tablecritic.com).

Placid amid a storm of Internet recommendations, restaurateur Rait puts it this way: "They might tell me to make hamburgers for dinner, and we could sell a lot of hamburgers. But that's not the experience we want to offer."

Still, his diners are newly accessorizing the table setting: fork on the left, knife on the right, iPhone top center. It's chew and review, toast and post.

ABOUT THE READING

- Have you read "civilian" reviews before trying a new restaurant? Have you posted your own review afterwards? Explain.
- Explain the theory about "the wisdom of the crowd" discussed in the third paragraph. Do you agree? Why or why not?
- How have restaurant owners reacted to the increasing number of civilian reviews? How would you react? Why?
- Explain the following: "Tying your tastes to your identity is the holy grail of Internet marketing."

RECIPE FOR REVIEW

INTRODUCTIONS

1. The purpose of the **introduction** is to catch the reader's attention and explain the subject of the paper. The introduction may also map out the main supporting points.
2. Although it appears first in your papers, the introduction is often the last part to be written. Only when you know exactly where you're going in the body of the essay can you guide the reader in the right direction.

3. Introductions may use general statements that narrow to a specific focus; tell a short story that is related to the body of the essay; begin with a quotation, a question, an interesting fact, or a strong opinion; or outline a problem to be solved.

CONCLUSIONS

1. The purpose of the **conclusion** is to highlight the main idea of the essay and to let the reader know that this is the last paragraph.
2. Sometimes the conclusion, like the introduction, cannot be written until several revisions have helped you think through the topic. At other times, the conclusion may be the first part of the essay you're sure of.
3. The conclusion may raise a question or add information about the main idea, answer a question, or outline a solution to a problem raised in the introduction.
4. The conclusion often reflects some aspect of the introduction, such as a story, image, quote, or allusion.

TITLES

1. **Titles** should relate to the topic of your essay and catch the reader's attention.
2. A good title will emphasize a particularly important or exciting point about your paper.

© Bill Perry/www.Shutterstock.com

Just as this river reflects the arc of the bridge above it, the conclusion of an essay often reflects some aspect of the introduction.

CHAPTER EXERCISES

1. *Comparing Introductions*—Pick a topic, such as your favorite food or the idea that success is 10% talent and 90% hard work, and write an introduction that moves from the general to the specific. Then write another introduction to the same topic in which you tell a short story. Does one of the introductions seem more successful than the other? Explain.

2. *Rewriting the Introduction*—Pick one of the sample introductions in the first section of this chapter and rewrite it in a different way. For example, if the introduction told a story, rewrite it as a question or a problem. Then discuss the result.

3. *Tying the Introduction and Conclusion Together*—Choose one of the sample introductions earlier in this chapter. Think about what the body of that essay might say. Then write a concluding paragraph that ties it all together.

4. Which of the selections in A Taste for Reading (at the end of Chapters 1–17) has the most effective introduction, in your opinion? Why? Which has the most effective conclusion? Explain your answers.

5. How are the introduction and conclusion of "Digging" (Chapter 17) tied together? What idea or theme is emphasized by this connection? What makes the title effective?

6. *Choosing a Title*—Make a list of five movie (or book or television series) titles that seem especially catchy and appropriate. Then make another list of titles that seem especially dull or off target. Choose one of the good titles and explain why it is effective. Then choose one of the poor titles, explain why it is ineffective, and think of two better alternatives for it.

7. *Naming an Essay*—Write a title for the untitled story by Brendan Cowley in Chapter 11, p. 187. Explain your choice.

IDEAS FOR WRITING

1. Choose a movie (or book) that you're especially fond of. Describe the first scene. Is it effective in drawing you in? Explain. Then look at the last scene. Is it effective? Does it echo the introduction in some way?

2. Choose a restaurant in which you've eaten recently, and describe your first impression.

3. Evaluate the effectiveness of the title, introduction, and conclusion of "Everyone's a Critic" or one of the other readings in this book.

4. Write a brief essay in which you describe the restaurant, bakery, or café you'd like to open. Choose a name for the property and defend the name's effectiveness.

CHAPTER 8
IMPROVING SENTENCE FLUENCY

By the end of this chapter, you should begin to . . .

- analyze sentence variety in your own and others' writing;
- create variety by changing the pattern and length of your sentences;
- vary the beginnings or "starters" of your sentences;
- combine short, simple sentences to create compound, complex, and compound-complex sentences; and
- use sentence patterns to construct and/or emphasize meaning.

What is the chef's most important tool? The knife, perhaps? The pot? For the writer, one of the most important tools is the sentence. The sentence is the basic unit through which we express a thought, by which we begin to shape and *cook* our ideas. The more skillfully we construct our sentences, the more clearly we can communicate our ideas.

The concept of *skill* is often captured by the word *fluency*, that is, doing a good job with a certain ease and flow. The word is often applied to language skills. You may hear people describe themselves as "fluent" in a foreign language, for example, by which they mean that without much effort they can speak so as to be understood by others. *Sentence* fluency has to do with writing sentences that are clear in meaning but also appealing and varied in style.

June Casagrande agrees that the sentence is the writer's most important tool, and she begins her book *It Was the* Best *of Sentences, It Was the* Worst *of Sentences: A Writer's Guide to Crafting Killer Sentences* as follows:

> *This sentence rocks.* It's concise. It's powerful. It knows what it wants to say, and it says it in clear, bold terms.
>
> But upon quickly or slowly reading a sentence such as this, in which the writer quite clearly is wanting to make a point regarding various issues pertaining to general written communication, it suddenly becomes more than clear that this is a sentence whose aspirations of rocking have been handily eclipsed in favor of the act of sucking.

The long sentence that makes up the second paragraph is difficult to follow—it's wordy, convoluted, pretentious—but, of course, that is the very point that Casagrande intends to make! If we're trying to avoid writing such clunky sentences, we must pay close attention to their words and rhythms.

Food writer John Thorne is renowned for his beautifully crafted sentences. Here's a sampling from his essay "One Knife, One Pot," the full text of which appears at the end of this chapter:

The knife is one of a cook's most important tools.

> I fell into cooking as many do: by necessity. I was nineteen, a college dropout, living alone in a dirt-cheap fifth-floor walk-up on New York's Lower East Side. I had no experience, no kitchen equipment, no money, but none of that mattered, because I had no palate then, either. Everything I made tasted good to me because everything I made was an adventure. At that time, frozen corn and frozen peas were five boxes to the dollar; a pound of hamburger was even less. So, until I discovered rice, a weekday meal was simply a box of the one cooked with a fifth of a pound of the other, and I ate it feeling amazed at what a clever fellow I was.

Read these sentences aloud; they are engaging, dexterous, and fluent. For instance, when Thorne repeats a word or structure in a sentence, it is in order to achieve a certain effect. The *no*'s in the following example build to the funny *no palate:* "I had no experience, no kitchen equipment, no money, but none of that mattered, because I had no palate then, either." In the next example, he repeats the phrase *everything I made,* and we relish the repetition along with his youthful sense of adventure: "Everything I made tasted good to me because everything I made was an adventure." In this chapter, we'll look more closely at how to develop our own fluency with the sentence.

ANALYZING SENTENCE VARIETY

"Variety," wrote eighteenth-century poet William Cowper, is "the very spice of life." If every food tasted the same, if we ate the same dinner every night, we'd literally lose much of life's flavor. Similarly, if every sentence had the same pattern, readers would soon become bored. Effective writers use a variety of sentence patterns to keep their readers interested. Look at the following example:

(1) It started in the library. (2) Almost every weekend my father, sister, and I would take a drive down to our local library and spend the afternoon browsing the stacks and thumbing pages. (3) For some reason, this day I couldn't find anything that held my attention. (4) I must've been around ten years old and stuck between the children's books and the young adult novels. (5) Looking for something to keep me occupied, I wandered down through the tall cases of books. (6) I passed through the reference books, the short stories, passed through the home improvement section, and glanced at the foreign fiction. (7) Just before I gave up all hope, I found myself surrounded by my favorite genre of books, one I didn't even know existed at the library. (8) I had stumbled into the cookbook section.

—**Molly-Iris Alpern,** student writer

Look at the first sentence: *It started in the library.* It's short (5 words) and direct (no introductory words or phrases like *However* or *Ten years ago*). The first two words call upon the reader's memory of other similar beginnings where the "it" that started the sentence was something important. The pattern is simple:

(1) subject + verb + phrase

The next sentence is dramatically different: *Almost every weekend my father, sister, and I would take a drive down to our local library and spend the afternoon browsing the stacks and thumbing pages.* This second sentence is 27 words long and contains an introduction, two verbs, and an additional phrase. The pattern here is the following:

(2) intro + subject + verb + phrase + second verb + phrase

Both are technically "simple" sentences, but the length, rhythm, and imagery are completely different.

Let's look now at the third sentence in the paragraph: *For some reason, this day I couldn't find anything that held my attention.* Like the previous sentence, this one begins with introductory material, but there the similarity ends. This sentence is half the length (13 words) and, while the longer one was still a "simple" sentence, this one is "complex" because it contains a dependent clause, that is, a "sentence" that can't stand alone.

(3) intro + subject + verb + dependent clause

The fourth sentence is slightly longer (18 words), but again is a "simple" one and, for the first time in this paragraph, begins directly with "I." Sentence #5 is a similar length (16 words), but it has a different pattern: **intro + subject + verb + phrase**.

It might become tedious to discuss each sentence separately, but it's worth taking a little more time to review the different types of sentence variety that this paragraph contains. Study the breakdown on sentence variety in Figure 8.1.

Figure 8.1 Sentence Variety in a Paragraph

Sentence #	Sentence Type	Length (words)	Sentence Pattern
1	simple	5	subject + verb + phrase
2	simple	27	intro + subject + verb + phrase + verb + phrase
3	complex	13	intro + subject + verb + dependent clause
4	simple	18	subject + verb + phrase + verb + phrase
5	simple	16	intro + subject + verb + phrase
6	simple	21	subject + verb + phrase + verb + phrase + verb + phrase
7	complex	26	introductory dependent clause + subject + verb + phrase + dependent clause
8	simple	7	subject + verb + phrase

In this paragraph, 75% of the sentences are simple, while 25% are complex; 25% of the sentences are under ten words, 37.5% are between ten and twenty, and 37.5% are longer than twenty words. In terms of pattern, half of the sentences have some kind of introduction, while half do not. Three of the eight sentences have more than one verb.

Exercise 8.1 | Analyzing Sentence Variety

Make a chart of the sentences in the following paragraph according to length and pattern. Is there enough variety? Explain.

(1) Revenge is a dark and twisting path, one that changes people, and affects them and the lives of those around them more than seemingly possible. (2) Justice, however, is the opposite, a straight and narrow path that leads to a clean slate. (3) We see opportunities and examples of the choice we have between the two roads all the time in our everyday lives, in movies, in books, in the news. (4) It's a constant decision-making process that affects all of us, all the time. (5) As seen in the movie series *Star Wars*, Anakin's mother gets killed by the Sand People. (6) Instead of doing the right thing, and seeking out justice for the crime committed, he instead turns to revenge, killing the Sand People. (7) This act then leads to more acts of revenge and hatred, all the while eating away at him until nothing is left but his evil, revenge-twisted soul, known to the galaxy as Darth Vader.

—Timothy Fisher, student writer

While it isn't necessary to analyze all of your sentences in this way, it may be useful or at least interesting to do so now and then, particularly if you notice yourself getting stuck in the same patterns over and over. Try Exercise 8.1.

CHANGING THE PATTERN

If you find yourself looking at a paragraph of very similar sentences, an effective way of creating variety is to change some of the patterns. If all the sentences begin right with the subject, mix things up, and have some of them begin with a lead-in or starter. Put some parts from the beginning or the end in the middle, or put some parts from the middle at the beginning or the end. If you have complex sentences, experiment with putting the main clause first, or the dependent clause first. Look at the differences in the following sentences created by changing the order of the words:

1. The chef in the immaculate white jacket tosses the pizza dough into the air and nods at the watching guests.
2. With a nod to the watching guests, the chef in the immaculate white jacket tosses the pizza dough into the air.
3. The chef in the immaculate white jacket, with a nod to the watching guests, tosses the pizza dough into the air.

Notice also how these changes affect the way readers will hear the sentences, whether aloud or in their imaginations. The first one moves swiftly to the end; the second has a single pause about one-third through; and the third has a real change in rhythm and pitch, as the reader lowers and softens his voice for the middle section. In this respect, a sentence is like a musical phrase.

Here are some more examples of varying the pattern of a sentence by rearranging the words. Notice that none of the words are actually changed. The variation comes through putting the main and dependent clauses (like the main and side dishes on a buffet table) in different places.

1. The talented young chef was offered a position on the Food Network after he competed on the television show *Chopped*.
2. After he competed on the television show *Chopped*, the talented young chef was offered a position on the Food Network.
3. The talented young chef, after he competed on the television show *Chopped*, was offered a position on the Food Network.

The first sentence begins with the main clause and emphasizes the job offer. It reads smoothly and swiftly from beginning to end. By placing the subordinate clause first, the second sentence highlights the possible *reason* for the job offer, the chef's role as a contestant on *Chopped*. It has a different rhythm—a pause in the middle—and a more varied pitch to it as the reader's voice rises and falls. The third also highlights the reason for the job offer, while offering a different pattern of rise and fall in the reader's voice.

Exercise 8.2 | Changing the Pattern

Write two variations of the following sentence by changing the pattern or order. Then describe the emphasis and "music" of each of the three.

1. The Cairn terrier is intelligent and courageous, with a tendency to believe it is bigger than its small body and an irrepressible instinct to chase anything that flees.

2. _____

3. _____

In *The Wizard of Oz*, Toto is the quintessential Cairn terrier— intelligent, courageous, and irrepressible.

We can also write different sentence patterns by adding details that rename, identify, or describe one or more nouns. These words or phrases are placed next to the noun they describe and are usually separated from it by commas. Variety can be created by placing the phrase before or after the noun. In the following examples, the phrase is added in the middle of the sentence, at the end, and at the beginning.

Rename: The chocolate, Madagascar's Hottest Secret, was made in Madagascar.
Identify: The chocolate was made in Madagascar, an island off the eastern coast of Africa.
Describe: Spiced with cinnamon and sakay pepper, the chocolate was made in Madagascar.

Sometimes we find additional details through brainstorming or research. At other times, we notice that we've written two or three simple sentences with all the information we need, but find that the sentences have a boring sound. By merging these shorter sentences into one (see Combining Sentences later in the chapter), we can create more varied and interesting patterns.

VARYING THE STARTER

We said the subject of a sentence is most often at or near the beginning. However, the beginning of the sentence is one of the places where we want to introduce some variety, whether by adding one word (*However*), a phrase (*Spiced with cinnamon and sakay pepper*), or an entire clause (*After he competed on the television show* Chopped*). This is the same kind of variety we might look for in a week of dinners. Would you choose to have a bowl of soup before *every* meal? More likely, you would mix it up, perhaps soup one night, a plate of melon and prosciutto the next, or a shrimp cocktail, and on some nights no starter at all. In the earlier paragraph about the trip to the library, we found that half the sentences had starters while the other half did not. There is no prescription for this; it's a matter of personal style and taste (see Chapter 10). Good writers, though, are aware of how they begin their sentences.

Starters often contain some kind of transitional information (see Chapter 6) that shows how the sentence is connected to the one before it. In the previous paragraph, for example, the word "However" indicates that the sentence *contrasts* with the one before it. In the previous sentence, the phrase "for example" indicates that the sentence provides an *example* of the general statement that preceded it. Starters might contain additional detail about the subject of the sentence:

Spiced with cinnamon and sakay pepper, the chocolate was made in Madagascar.

They might provide information about the time or place of the sentence:

In 1961, Julia Child published her first book, *Mastering the Art of French Cooking*.

Alternating between Paris and Brooklyn, *Julie & Julia* tells the story of two very different home cooks whose lives intertwined.

Another way to add variety is to begin the sentence with a dependent clause.

After he competed on the television show *Chopped*, the talented young chef was offered a position on the Food Network.

Perhaps the two most important pieces of advice are the following:

- DO add *some* variety to the beginnings of your sentences. Without variety, your sentences will eventually bore your readers. What if the terrific paragraph about the library had been written like this:

    It started in the library. It happened almost every weekend. My father, sister, and I would take a drive down to our local library. We would spend the afternoon browsing the stacks and thumbing pages. I couldn't find anything on this day that held my attention. I must've been around ten years old. I was stuck between the children's books and the young adult novels.

- DON'T use the *same* beginning more than once in a paragraph, although it's easy to fall into that habit. Maybe you have a great-sounding beginning, like *As,* but after a couple of repetitions, the reader sees *only* the repetition and misses your point.

    As I looked at the screen, I was horrified to see that the game was now tied. As I anxiously watched the pitcher's face, I realized he was nervous as well. As he released the ball, a tense silence fell upon the stadium. Then as the bat connected, the silence was broken by shouts of hope and dismay.

> **Exercise 8.3 | Varying the Starter**
>
> Rewrite the last paragraph using a variety of patterns, with and without starters, and with different kinds of starters.

COMBINING SENTENCES

Another way of varying the patterns of your sentences is to combine two or more shorter sentences into one longer one. This can be done in a number of different ways. Look at this series of short sentences:

Julia Child was one of the most influential figures in the culinary world. She published *Mastering the Art of French Cooking* in 1961. It was her first book. It was an immediate critical and financial success.

By taking descriptive words and phrases from the other sentences, we can create an interesting pattern for the middle one.

In 1961, Julia Child, one of the most influential figures in the food industry, published her first book, *Mastering the Art of French Cooking,* an immediate critical and financial success.

This is still a **simple sentence**, that is, it contains only one subject–verb pair or independent clause. Another combining option is to join two simple sentences with one of the coordinating conjunctions, *for, and, nor, but, or, yet, so* (see also Chapter 23), as in these examples:

The chocolate contained cinnamon and sakay pepper. The chocolate was made in Madagascar.

The chocolate contained cinnamon and sakay pepper, and it was made in Madagascar.

The sentence might have an even nicer flow, however, if we made the second half into an introductory phrase.

Actress Meryl Streep captures
Julia Child's spirit
in *Julie & Julia*.

Made in Madagascar, the chocolate contained cinnamon and sakay pepper.

When we combine two simple sentences, we call the result a **compound sentence**. Here's another example.

The iced coffee looked delicious. It tasted flat and stale.

The iced coffee looked delicious, **but** it tasted flat and stale.

Notice that by joining the two shorter sentences with *but,* we give a smoother rhythm to the writing and also tell the reader *how* those two ideas are related. They *contrast.*

When we join two sentences with one of the *coordinating* conjunctions, they both remain independent, equally important. However, if we join two sentences with one of the *subordinating* conjunctions, they are no longer equal. One *depends* on the other. This is called a **complex sentence**. Look at this example:

The iced coffee looked delicious. It tasted flat and stale.

Although the iced coffee looked delicious, it tasted flat and stale.

The way we combined these two sentences shows that the *taste* of the coffee is more important than its appearance because the coffee's delicious look is now described in a dependent clause. Joining sentences in this way also affects the rhythm and melody of the writing. Read the two lines aloud, and listen to the difference in their "music" and flow.

In this next example, the two sentences we worked with earlier are joined through a **relative clause**, a type of dependent clause that uses a relative pronoun (such as *who, which,* or *that*) to "relate" to a noun or pronoun earlier in the sentence (see also Chapter 22).

The chocolate contained cinnamon and sakay pepper. The chocolate was made in Madagascar.

The chocolate, which was made in Madagascar, contained sakay pepper and cinnamon.

By subordinating the sentence about the chocolate's origin, we indicate that it is less important than the chocolate's ingredients. We also change the rhythm and pitch of the sentences. The clause *which was made in Madagascar* would most likely be spoken in a softer tone of voice, like an aside to the audience during a play. Sentences with one independent clause and one (or more) relative clause(s) are also **complex**.

Finally, we may choose to join two or three shorter sentences in a series of connected independent and dependent clauses called a **compound-complex sentence**, as in this example:

> The tiny roadside diner sold iced coffee. The iced coffee looked delicious. It tasted flat and stale.

> The tiny roadside diner sold iced coffee, but, while the iced coffee looked delicious, it tasted flat and stale.

Note that commas must follow any independent clause, as well as any dependent clause that *begins* a sentence.

The four sentence types are summarized in Figure 8.2. However, the names of these sentences are far less important than your ability to create variety and interest through sentence combining.

Figure 8.2 The Four Sentence Types

Sentence Type	Example
simple	The tiny roadside diner sold iced coffee. The iced coffee looked delicious. It tasted flat and stale.
compound	The iced coffee looked delicious, but it tasted flat and stale.
complex	Although the iced coffee looked delicious, it tasted flat and stale.
compound-complex	The tiny roadside diner sold iced coffee, but, although it looked delicious, it tasted flat and stale.

Exercise 8.4 | Combining Sentences

Rewrite each set of three shorter sentences into one longer, more musical sentence. Be sure to include all the detail.

1. Cardamom is a plant in the ginger family. Cooks use the dried, unripe fruit of the plant. Cardamom is used in pastries, curries, and coffees.

   _____

   _____

2. *The Girl with the Dragon Tattoo* was written by Stieg Larsson. It was published in Swedish in 2005. It was published in English in 2008. Larsson died in 2004.

   _____

   _____

MUSIC, MEANING, AND MEMORY

The exercises in rearranging sentences that we've been working with may seem a bit mechanical at times. Perhaps it's like playing scales on a piano in order to strengthen the fingers. The exercises may not be much fun, but they prepare us for more "musical" work. Sentences can be "musical" too. They have rhythm and sometimes rhyme, a rise and fall to the voice, a cadence that can flow smoothly or be interrupted by a pause. In "The Cadence of Great Writing," Sean Savoie discusses the importance of cadence, or rhythm:

The Girl with the Dragon Tattoo

> In writing, as in most all forms of art (and even life itself), rhythm plays a crucial role. I do not say this simply because I have played drums for 31 years, but rather because it is increasingly evident as I develop my own skills in various art forms. Painting has rhythm; the human eye dances around a painting repeatedly returning to the reds and yellows, the longest wave lengths. The longer and shorter scenes in films predictably create a reaction in an audience. Tempo is king. Perfect timing in movement guarantees the most effective result in martial arts. The active and resting cycles of human life likewise have a profound influence on human health and longevity. In short, movement is at the core of life and expression. Call it "cadence". . . .
>
> Movement in writing is felt in both the smaller and larger units, the smaller units being sentences and the larger ones being paragraphs (or chapters in longer works). Masterful authors have a keen sense and control of long and short cadence when composing literary works. This, once again, is exactly the same sensitivity that a master musician has when composing music. Very long sentences, if not broken up into smaller segments, can be boring if used too often. Similarly, short sentences can make the reading "choppy" so that it does not move well. Paying attention to the length of an expressed idea is the first step to attaining better control over the influence your writing has on the reader. An interesting combination of long and short sentences produces a more engaging rhythm.

One way to test the cadence of a written work is to read it out loud. When reading aloud, a person must synchronize reading with breathing. When I read an excellent book, I read very slowly and savor the movement and voice of the author. That's right. The voice of a narrator is in my head and pulls me deeply into the story. Imagine, for example, how a paragraph would sound if it were played on a saxophone. Yes, this is a bit abstract, but sax players must always consider phrasing in order to know when they should breathe. When reading aloud, the essence of the phrasing becomes far more obvious. Being a drummer, it took me years to learn how to make my drum set breathe like a wind instrument, but it is extremely effective. Try to imagine an essay as a living animal with its own temperament and biology; for an essay to really speak to a person it must have breath.

In addition to creating memorable sentences through their sounds, we can construct sentences that highlight or enhance our points through the order of the words and the use of subordinate clauses. Readers tend to pay more attention to what comes first or last in the sentence—the first and last impressions. In fact, we use this same inclination in organizing our paragraphs and essays as well. Do we move from most important to least important, that is, put the word or phrase (idea) we want to highlight at the *beginning* of the sentence? Or, do we build from least important to most important, that is, make the reader feel the suspense building to the final words? Our goal in improving our sentence fluency is to write sentences that sound good, make sense, and live on in our readers' memory.

A TASTE FOR READING

John Thorne is a most fluent and memorable food writer, the best in the country according to Leo Lerman of Gourmet *magazine. His books include* Serious Pig: An American Cook in Search of His Roots *and* Pot on the Fire: Further Confessions of a Renegade Cook *(with Matt Lewis Thorne).*

****

One Knife, One Pot
by John Thorne

Cooks, at least serious cooks, can be divided roughly into two groups: pot cooks and knife cooks. Of course, each sort uses both implements; it is a matter of which serves as the lodestone of their kitchen, the piece of cookware that, in case of a fire, they would rescue first. There is no doubt that I would save my knives. Not only am I a knife cook, but it wasn't until I found the right knife that I became any sort of cook at all.

I fell into cooking as many do: by necessity. I was nineteen, a college dropout, living alone in a dirt-cheap fifth-floor walk-up on New York's Lower East Side. I had no experience, no kitchen equipment, no money, but none of that mattered, because I had no palate then, either. Everything I made tasted good to me because everything I made was an adventure. At that time, frozen corn and frozen peas were five boxes to the dollar; a pound of hamburger was even less. So, until I discovered rice, a weekday meal was simply a box of the one cooked with a fifth of a pound of the other, and I ate it feeling amazed at what a clever fellow I was.

But even if I didn't know what to think about what I ate, I had definite opinions about the kitchen equipment I cooked it with. Most of my tiny collection had been bought at a store on East Fourteenth Street. It was different from other junk stores only in that everything it sold was brand-new—instant junk. My single kitchen knife was far from sharp, but, even worse, it *felt* dull, as if it had been made to look like a knife rather than to be one. It was little better than a toy—and so were the cheap pans that warped at once if put empty on the flame and scorched anything, even soup, if you weren't careful.

This upset me. I had an adolescent's volatile sensitivity to anything that threatened my *amour-propre*. Aspiring to become a novelist, I knew I needed a decent, solid typewriter, and I had sacrificed everything to get one. Then, when it was stolen from my apartment a week later, I found a way to buy another, and discovered that sacrifice could pull even more out of me than I knew I had to give. Now I yearned almost as much for two things more: one good knife and one good pot.

This was in the early 1960s, and at that time there was a cook's store on the Avenue of the Americas near Twenty-first Street called Bazar Français. I had come across it on one of my rambles, and I could tell it was the right sort of place as soon as I walked in the door. The store itself was austere and slightly scary; the customers and the equipment they were examining looked serious and professional.

I began to browse, with trepidation. The smallest copper pot cost more than I earned in a week, working as I did then in the mail room of a steamship line. The kitchen utensils—the spatulas, ladles, skimmers—were made for pots and pans whose dimensions seemed larger than life. I couldn't have put one in any pot or pan I owned without causing it to tumble off the stove.

Then I came to the knives. Of course, there were many of these that were also beyond the timid reach of my wallet. But this didn't matter. Almost at once I saw a knife that I both desired intensely and could easily afford. Although there was no mark on it that said so, the store claimed it was made in France. If it was, it was certainly not at the top of the manufacturer's line. No knife could have been more utilitarian: It had a blade and a handle, and that was all. I don't remember exactly what it cost, but I know that the price was less than ten dollars.

This knife, three decades later, sits beside me on the desk as I write. It is made of carbon steel, with a full tang—the metal extending the entire length of the knife, with the two halves of the wooden handle clamped to it with brass rivets. Not in shape, size, or hauteur would it ever be confused with a chef's knife: It makes no statement whatsoever about the taste or expertise of the person who uses it. It is simply a tool, and all it says is "I cut."

That, it proved, was enough. The synonyms for *cut* in my thesaurus smack, almost all, of the rough and violent—"gash," "pierce," "slash," "cleave," "sever," "rip," "lacerate"—but with this knife the experience became eerily sensuous. The blade slid through a piece of meat almost as if it were cutting butter, and the slithery ease of it had a giddy edginess: One slip, and it would as easily slide into me. No matter how many times you've done it before, picking up a razor-sharp knife puts the nerves on alert, and practice teaches you to feel rather than cut your way around gristle and bone.

In other words, that knife brought the act of cooking to life. I don't doubt that a skilled cook can prepare good meals with the crummiest of kitchenware, because I have done this myself. But after the challenge has been met, there is no real pleasure in doing so. Cheap stuff is never neutral; it constantly drags at your self-respect by demeaning the job at hand. Only if you start a life of cooking knowing that dead weight can you truly appreciate the feeling of release, even joy, when you finally lay hands on your first good knife, your first good pot.

Eventually, I retired that first knife. The same metal that could be honed sharp enough to shave with also stained the moment it touched a tomato, rusted if not dried immediately, and gave any onion it sliced the faint taste of metal. When knives made of a new high-carbon stainless steel appeared on the market, with blades that could be kept sharp by regular honing and that were far less vulnerable to everyday use, I searched one out and put the older knife away. However, while I may have been done with it, it was hardly done with me. That first good knife had become a partner as much as a possession. With it close by, I knew I could make myself at home in any kitchen. Were it to disappear, I would feel like a stranger on my own.

The road to my first good pot turned out to be a much longer one. To begin with, pots are far more complicated than knives. Even when they are tucked away in a cupboard, their presence looms in the kitchen the way a knife's never does. A pot is the kitchen itself made small. After all, it is inside the pot that the actual cooking takes place.

Consequently, it is the pot—really, the set of pots—that is the kitchen's pride. The more self-aware the cook, the more those pots take center stage, not hidden in kitchen cabinets but hung proudly from open racks—sturdy, gleaming, clean. And, let's admit it, expensive. Acquired as wedding presents, they are often less participants in the cook's first fumbling efforts than silent, slightly intimidating witnesses. Spouses are easy to please; the cook's real task is to live up to a set of All-Clad or Calphalon.

As a teenager, one of my household chores had been to wash the dinner dishes, a task that always culminated in the ritual cleaning of the pans. My mother's pride and joy was a set of stainless-steel, copper-bottomed cookware, and there was no escaping the kitchen until these pots sparkled . . . a process that began with steel wool, went on to copper polish, and ended with the nervous rush to get each one dry and put away before its bottom was stained with a single water spot.

I wanted no such bullying presence in my free-and-easy bachelor's kitchen. In fact, the first pan I acquired, a small cast-iron frying pan, was in appearance and temperament the very antithesis of "house-proud." It entered my apartment greasy inside and rust-stained without, looking as surly as a junkyard dog. I cleaned it up a bit and taught it how to do a few basic tricks—the skillet equivalents of "sit" and "beg"—and tried to give it as few chances to bite me as I could.

Still, we got along all right. I found that I felt at ease with the lesser breeds of cookware: other, larger, equally grumpy cast-iron skillets, a cheap aluminum pasta pot, an unmatching assortment of saucepans made of thin steel and coated with cream-colored or blue-speckled enamel.

The truth is, I had a lot of growing up to do before I understood what good pots are all about. Knives are easy to understand. They are about cutting the Gordian knot. They offer immediate gratification, the opportunity to make decisions first and live with the consequences later. The sharper the knife, the quicker that choice is made. Pots, on the other hand, are about patience, about resolving things through mediation, taking the time to get something just right. The better a pot, the less it can be hurried.

I might never have learned this had I not, in my forties, finally gotten married. At this point in our lives, the problem was not one of quickly acquiring a *batterie de cuisine* but one of merging two very different ones. Since my wife, Matt, owned pots and pans of a much higher quality than my own, I was quite content to get rid of almost all of mine. In return, I was introduced to what would become, for me, *the* pot: a solid, stainless-steel, four-quart Italian-made saucepan with a thick aluminum plate welded to its base.

As with the knife, it was love at first sight, perhaps because the pot's serious cookware look was tempered by a pair of jug ears—two oversize steel handles—that gave it a gawky sweetness. More than that, though, its particular proportions drew me to it. I just loved to feed that pot. Our ideal cooking vessel must surely be shaped in some mysterious way to fit our appetite, and this one was a perfect measure to mine.

Like the knife, it asserted a simple, unintimidating confidence that somehow was transferred to me. By tolerating my capricious kitchen ways—refusing, say, to let a risotto scorch merely because my attention had lapsed at a crucial moment or to boil a cut of beef into shoe leather because I had forgotten to check how the temperature was holding—it got me to tolerate them more myself and, thus, to stop letting them get in my way.

It was also a delight to use. The heavy bottom not only made hot spots a thing of the past, it absorbed and then radiated heat in a way that made tasks like searing meat or browning onions seem rewarding rather than tedious, especially since the results were so compellingly delicious. Matt and I suddenly found ourselves eating chowder or cioppino, some curry or another, butterbean soup, or hoppin' John almost every night—dishes that seemed conceived for no other purpose than for me to take the pot through its paces. And so it was that this knife cook finally found his pot and discovered that, with it, his kitchen was complete.

ABOUT THE READING

- Define the following words: *lodestone, volatile,* amour-propre, *austere, trepidation, surly, Gordian knot,* batterie de cuisine, *capricious.*
- What differences does the author find between a knife and a pot? Use specific quotes and details from the text to support your answer.
- Read the essay aloud, and mark sentences that particularly strike you. How would you describe them? What do they suggest about the narrator's attitude and personality?
- How does the author's discovery of the right kitchen tools contribute to his development as a cook and mirror his growth as a person?

RECIPE FOR REVIEW

ANALYZING SENTENCE VARIETY

Sentence fluency has to do with writing sentences that are clear in meaning and varied in style. Fluent writers tend to use sentences of different lengths and patterns. Analyze your own sentences periodically, perhaps as you're editing a final draft.

CHANGING THE PATTERN

Putting the subject or main idea of your sentences in different places (beginning, middle, end) adds variety to the pattern. By choosing the placement carefully, you can also highlight your most important points. Use the structure of the sentence to create as well as reflect meaning.

VARYING THE STARTER

A simple and effective way to add variety to your sentences is to vary the way you start them.

COMBINING SENTENCES

Another effective way of adding variety is to combine several shorter sentences into a single, more complex and interesting sentence. Be sure to use the structure of the new sentence to highlight the most important point or detail.

MUSIC, MEANING, AND MEMORY

The sound or "music" of a sentence can help construct and clarify its meaning, as well as preserve it in the reader's memory.

IDEAS FOR WRITING

1. Choose one of your favorite books or stories, and read a good number of its sentences. Are they "fluent"? Are they memorable? Explain.
2. Look back at some of your own writing. Identify two or three of your most fluent and memorable sentences, and explain what makes them especially effective.
3. Re-read Sean Savoie's "The Cadence of Great Writing" on pp. 141–142. In what ways are sentences like music? Provide specific examples, if you can.
4. In what ways are sentences like knives and pots? Be specific.

CHAPTER 9
REVISING WORD CHOICE

By the end of this chapter, you should begin to . . .

* choose an effective word for the purpose and audience of the writing;
* revise words with both denotation and connotation in mind;
* eliminate unnecessary words;
* revise slang and jargon as needed; and
* avoid clichés and sexist language.

As we evaluate the structure and flow of individual sentences (Chapter 8), we begin to "taste" the accuracy and effectiveness of individual words. The search for the right word is like the search for the right seasoning. Experimenting with different words and flavors is both constructive and entertaining, and one small decision can change an ordinary sentence or dish into an extraordinary one. Look at the following sentence, from an essay about making lemon meringue pie (read the full story in Chapter 14):

> I held the edges of the quick-cooling aluminum foil and carefully lifted it up, but a few errant beans shimmied loose and clattered to the floor.
>
> —**Molly-Iris Alpern,** student writer

The dried beans have been used to hold the aluminum foil around the edge of the crust, and a few of them are *errant*, that is, *adventurous* or *mischievous*. What a delicious bit of flavor this adds to the sentence! Furthermore, the beans didn't just *slip and fall* to the floor. No—first they *shimmied* loose—not *shook* or *wobbled*—which again has an intentional, fun-loving appeal. Perhaps they were practicing their dance moves for the weekend. Then the bean *clattered* to the floor, almost with a suggestion of *chattering* about their adventures.

Choosing the right word is also about expressing your personality. Sometimes students misinterpret the purpose of a writing course as somehow to subtract their personality from their writing. I believe the reverse is true: A writing course should make your written communication more effective in expressing both your thoughts and your personality. Choosing the best word is about choosing what suits the purpose and audience of your communication; it's about using words efficiently and not wasting the reader's time with extra ones; and it's about experimenting with words in a fresh and interesting way rather than trotting out tired old clichés like "it was cooked to perfection" or "it melted in my mouth" or "it was divinely decadent."

CHOOSING THE RIGHT WORD

Much of word choice is about style and personality as much as correctness. In both speaking and writing, the words we use—along with the types of sentences, topics, tone, or punctuation—make up our distinctive "voice" (see also Chapter 10). We learned in Chapter 2 that reading about smells, textures, or actions causes our brains to light up as if we were actually smelling the smells, feeling the textures, and performing the actions. So we want to be as precise and vivid as we can in choosing our words. We'll look more closely at descriptive words in Chapter 12, but here let's take a look at one of the central words in every sentence—the verb.

Verbs don't have to involve action. In some instances we might choose a linking verb such as *is* or *was*. If we're using an action verb, though, let's pick the right one.

> The house was packed, traditional Lebanese music was **playing**, and all
> of my relatives were trying to talk over the noise, which made it even louder!

The sentence is perfectly clear, but in "tasting" it a few days later, the writer decided that *blasting* added a delicious spice.

> The house was packed, traditional Lebanese music was **blasting**, and all
> of my relatives were trying to talk over the noise, which made it even louder!
>
> —**Monica Hannoush,** student writer

Blasting is much louder than *playing.* Look at the next example:

> The warm pita bread that I **topped** with hummus and olive oil was pure
> satisfaction.

> The warm pita bread that I **smothered** with hummus and olive oil was pure
> satisfaction.
>
> —**Monica Hannoush,** student writer

Here the writer pumped up the volume by replacing the neutral *topped* with the more dramatic *smothered.* Let's look at an example by a different writer:

> I saw one student trying very hard to remove excess fat from a pork
> tenderloin while another tried to tie up a strip loin of beef.

Although this sentence is clear and correct, look what happens when another word is substituted for *tried* in the second line.

I saw one student trying very hard to remove excess fat from a pork tenderloin while another **battled** to tie up a strip loin of beef.

—**Nelson Tsai,** student writer

Using a strong verb such as *battled* adds important information, creates a sharp mental picture, and invigorates the text.

CONNOTATION AND DENOTATION

How do we find these delicious words? The thesaurus is a very useful tool, whether you find it on your computer, through your smart phone, or in a book. For example, the girl in the photo (Figure 9.1) is biting into an apple. If we look up *bite,* we find such synonyms as *chew, chomp, crunch, gnaw, masticate, munch, nibble,* and *nip.* So, is she *munching on* the apple? *Nibbling? Gnawing?* How do we decide? Although the words all mean "bite," they differ in the kind of bite. At this point the dictionary will help us choose the word that fits our purpose. *Munching* sounds energetic and loud; *nibbling* suggests tiny, gentle bites; while *gnawing* makes me think of a rat, or even a zombie.

Looking for the best word can be fun, and with a thesaurus right there on the computer, it's easy to find all kinds of synonyms. Yet this search can also seem rather daunting, especially because English has nearly a million words to choose from! Was that steak you had last week *tender, juicy,* or absolutely *scrumptious?* Were you *astounded, flabbergasted,* or simply *surprised?* Would you describe yourself as *obstinate, resolute,* or merely *stubborn?*

Figure 9.1 Is she munching on the apple? Nibbling? Gnawing?

© Inga Marchuk/www.shutterstock.com

If you check your computer's thesaurus under *stubborn,* you are likely to find quite a few alternatives: *obdurate, dogged, pig-headed, mulish, inflexible, willful,* and *intractable.* You'll find even more synonyms in a print thesaurus. The following words are also synonyms for *stubborn,* but with more positive associations: *persistent, resolute, unwavering, steadfast.*

The similarities and differences we see here have to do with a word's denotation and connotation. The **denotation** of a word is a simple definition. The italicized words that follow *stubborn* in the previous paragraph have the same denotation. However, they do not share the same **connotation**, the feelings or associations that make a word seem positive or negative, or simply neutral. *Obstinate,* for example, suggests that the stubbornness in unreasonable; it has a negative connotation. In contrast, *resolute* suggests that the stubbornness is brave, that someone is holding fast to a principle or a position even when it's dangerous to do so. It has a positive connotation. Or think about the difference between *fragrance* and *stench. Fragrance* sounds positively delicious, like the odor of a freshly baked pie or an expensive perfume, while *stench* would more likely be used for dirty socks or rotting meat.

As you revise your writing, it is good to experiment with new words. Use the thesaurus to find interesting alternatives. However, it's wise to then look them up in the dictionary to confirm that *both* the denotation and connotation fit your purpose. We don't want to confuse or offend our audience with a poor word choice. For example, you wouldn't make a good impression on a date's family by exclaiming over the "stench" coming from the kitchen! Try to select words whose connotations communicate your intended meaning accurately and effectively.

ELIMINATING UNNECESSARY WORDS

As we've said many times, when you're writing a rough draft, you're not thinking critically about exactly *how* you're expressing the ideas; you're just trying to get them down on paper. The idea of eliminating extra words need not even cross your mind until the revision process begins.

Why are extra words a problem? If your meaning is clear, what does it matter whether you used ten words or a hundred? Those one hundred words may easily contain repetitious or unnecessary phrases. Once these have been removed, your writing will be more efficient. Let's think about the service at a restaurant. The same meal could be served after ten minutes—or thirty. Which do you think the customer would prefer? In making your writing as concise and pointed as possible, especially in business letters and reports, you're respecting the reader's time. Perhaps in turn the reader will respect your point of view.

As you revise, omit words that are simply unnecessary. For example, the following wordy sentence can easily be cut in half:

At this point in time, due to the fact that I am sleepy, I will proceed to get ready for bed. [*wordy*]

I'm sleepy now, so I'll get ready for bed. [*concise*]

In *A River Runs Through It*, the narrator's father had him write something, then shorten it by half, then shorten it by half again. This is good practice, and perhaps young Norman Maclean learned a skill that he used as a professional writer. Yet the lesson was uncomfortable at times. After he made the second cut—and waited tensely for the verdict—his father told him to throw the paper away. Although frustrated, the boy did as he was told, including spending the afternoon in the Montana wilderness practicing fly-fishing.

Just like fly-fishing and potato-peeling, editing skills improve with practice. Look over some of your writing and determine if you tend to use extra words. If so, consider making the types of revisions suggested in Figure 9.2.

Wordiness is also caused by repeating the same term or by using synonymous terms.

> Blake is a student at the local community college where he is the best student in his Economics class at college. *[wordy]*

This sentence repeats the word *student* unnecessarily. Note how a little revision eliminates an entire clause:

> Blake is the best student in his Economics class at the local community college. *[better]*

Here's an example of a sentence brimming with synonymous and redundant words:

> The color of the new tile was a very unique purple shade. *[wordy]*

Figure 9.2 Revising Wordy Expressions

Wordy	Concise
In my opinion, I think	I think
They proceeded to go	They went
Due to the fact that For the reason that Because of the fact that	Because
At the present time At this point in time	Now
In the event that	If
In the neighborhood of	About
In spite of the fact that	Although

Copyright © 2015 Cengage Learning®

Color and *shade* are so close in meaning that it makes sense to eliminate one. Further, *purple* actually *is* a color, so we don't need *color* or *shade*. Finally, can anything be *very* unique, since by definition *unique* means "one of a kind"?

> The new tile was a unique purple. *[concise]*

Just as we revise our sentences to make them concise, we revise our paragraphs to avoid unnecessary or repeated sentences. While the repetition of key terms can be used effectively to unify an essay, wordiness is awkward and distracting. Read the following rough draft:

> Revenge is one of the most common human emotions. To some, revenge provides closure that regular actions don't provide. When you look up revenge in the dictionary, you will notice the definition says "to inflict punishment in return for injury or insult." In the movie *Mystic River,* revenge plays a large part in the story. In fact, the whole driving force behind the movie is revenge. Two out of the three main characters' whole purpose in the movie is revenge. The most obvious one will have to be Jimmy Markham, whose revenge was the cause of his daughter's death. But he is not the only one seeking revenge throughout the movie. David Boyle is seeking revenge toward his childhood monsters.
>
> —**Nicholas Quintero,** student writer

The paragraph contains good ideas but is encumbered with unnecessary and repetitive phrases. With a bit of revision, the writing becomes more clear and concise:

> Revenge, one of the most common human emotions, is the driving force behind the movie *Mystic River.* For two out of the three main characters,

revenge provides closure. The most obvious is Jimmy Markham, whose search for revenge was the cause of his daughter's death. But he is not the only one. David Boyle is seeking revenge toward his childhood monsters.

—**Nicholas Quintero,** student writer

If you find your rough drafts are wordy, don't despair. That's what revision is for. Don't forget that with the rough draft we're still peeling the potato, and we don't always use the peels.

REVISING SLANG, JARGON, CLICHÉS, AND SEXIST LANGUAGE

In order to communicate effectively with your audience, you must use words that the audience understands. Sometimes communication is blocked because we're essentially speaking a different language. For instance, it would be difficult to persuade a restaurant customer to order a particular item if the two of you didn't speak the same language or if you used such specialized technical terms that your customer didn't know what you meant. Further, it would be difficult to impress a customer with your chicken and peanuts stir fry if she had a peanut allergy. We want to use ingredients of food and of language that our audience will both understand and appreciate. In general, therefore, we want to avoid slang, jargon, clichés, and sexist language.

REVISING SLANG EXPRESSIONS

The word **slang** refers to words or phrases that have become popular within a certain group of people—teenagers, for example, or computer programmers, or restaurant workers—but that may not be recognized by all readers. Would the following terms be clearly understood by all audiences?

I've got to hunker down and swot for that wicked hard test.

Probably many readers would need the following translation:

I need to get to work and study for that very hard test.

Readers of different generations, even when they share the same profession, may not always share the same slang. You're probably familiar with some American diner slang from the middle of the last century, phrases such as *Adam and Eve on a raft* for two poached eggs on toast. In fact, some diner slang has entered the general vocabulary, such as *a cup of joe* for "coffee" or *86'd* for "sold out." Yet would all food service workers today understand the following slang expressions? (Translations can be found at the end of the chapter.)

a. shingle with a shimmy and a shake
b. bossy in a bowl

The customer explains his order in this scene from *Fragments*. Will it be "Adam and Eve on a raft" or a simple "cup o' Joe"?

c. Mike and Ike

d. dog and maggot

e. customer will take a chance

Slang expressions can be especially difficult for non-native speakers. One international student was horrified to hear passersby talking about "da bomb" on a Los Angeles street. In this post-9/11 world, she immediately thought of a terrorist attack. Imagine her surprise and relief when an American friend explained that the passersby had simply been praising the attractiveness of the girl walking ahead of them! In any successful communication, we want to avoid using words that might be unclear or confusing to our readers. Therefore, as you revise your rough drafts, consider your audience, and replace slang expressions with vivid, concise, but more formal language.

AVOIDING JARGON

Another type of vocabulary that can be hard for some readers to understand is **jargon**, the technical words specific to particular jobs, professions, or specialties. If your readers aren't familiar with a particular job, they may have difficulty understanding its specialized vocabulary. Even when writing for people in the same profession, it is often best to use direct and ordinary language rather than to rely too heavily on jargon. Again, think about your audience. If you must use a technical term, if it's the only word for what you need to say, go ahead and use it, but define if for the reader. Figure 9.3 lists examples of jargon from a variety of fields.

Writers will sometimes use jargon intentionally to establish an atmosphere or a character. On *CSI*, for example, there's a lot of talk about *DBs*, *DOAs*, and *vics*. In works of fiction, these abbreviated expression are appropriate; in an academic essay or a piece of writing for a general audience, however, you would most likely spell out "dead body," "dead on arrival," and "victim." Like slang expressions, jargon also may move into the general vocabulary. For example, we have "front-runner" from horse racing and "touch base" from baseball. Jargon can easily become clichéd—so common as to lose most of its meaning. In the worst cases, jargon is used to impress or intimidate readers, or to avoid an unwelcome truth. It's like an artificial smile rather than a warm handshake. The corporate world, for example, is fond of inflated language like "strategic relationships," "core competencies," and "benchmarking." Despite their impressive appearance, the precise meaning of such terms is not always clear. Like a pungent spice, jargon should be used with care.

Related to this kind of jargon is a type of word choice called **euphemism**, a watered-down term used supposedly to spare the reader's feelings when uncomfortable topics like death or sex must be discussed. And, indeed, many people prefer to say someone "passed away" rather than "died" or to say "went to bed" rather than "had sexual intercourse." Yet euphemism all too easily may become a tool of *mis*communication. Think about the term "downsizing." It doesn't sound too threatening, maybe Grandma moving from the big, old house in which she raised five children to a condo in North Carolina. However, it really means *firing*—it's about people losing their jobs and perhaps the ability to own any kind of home at all. This emphasis on what sounds "positive" rather than on what will accurately represent the facts is especially evident in the language of business, politics, and the military. The truth is best told in plain and simple language.

Figure 9.3 Examples of Jargon

Specialty	Examples of Jargon
computer programming	Boolean operators HTML TCP/IP protocol
medicine	normal sinus rhythm sedimentation rate tension pneumothorax
wine	sommelier quaffer legs
culinary arts	AP weight salamander persillade
business	strategic relationships core competencies benchmarking

AVOIDING CLICHÉS

In the introduction to this chapter, we singled out the expressions "cooked to perfection" and "melted in my mouth" as **clichés** that are less effective in our writing than fresh, clear, and specific language. Although we often assume that clichés are easily understood by our readers, they may actually be both tedious and confusing. Study the following example:

The steak was cooked to perfection.

What does that phrase really mean? To you, "cooked to perfection" may mean bleeding onto the plate. To your dinner companion, it may mean so well done it would make a thud instead of a splooshy splat if you dropped it on the floor. The following sentence is more specific:

Grilled over a fragrant wood fire, the steak had a slightly crisp outside and a tender, deep pink inside.

You can often recognize a cliché by its fill-in-the-blank nature. Complete these expressions:

Hungry as a _____

Quiet as a _____

Last but not _____

What does it *mean* to be hungry as a horse? And why not hungry as a hamster? Or a hippopotamus? Try to find a fresh description that your readers will be sure to understand.

Hungry as a _____

horse? hamster? howler monkey?

hyena? hippopotamus? hammerhead shark?

Copyright © 2015 Cengage Learning®

Suppose you wanted to describe a loyal friend *without* using a cliché. Instead of saying "Karen is a loyal friend: she stood by me *through thick and thin*," you could give a specific, real-life example. "Karen is a loyal friend; she called me every night for two weeks after my boyfriend and I broke up." As with all your writing, be clear and direct. In general, avoid clichés. Would you rather serve store-bought muffins or freshly baked homemade ones?

Of course, "rules are made to be broken." Sometimes writers will intentionally use a cliché and develop it in unexpected or powerful ways. For example, in *Silver Linings Playbook*, the main character turns the cliché of a "silver lining" into a strategy to rebuild his life. Sometimes the store-bought muffins are just right.

REVISING SEXIST LANGUAGE

Sexist language, though clear enough, is not generally acceptable in formal written communication. It may alienate the portion of your audience that has been left out. While in the past it was conventional to use *he* to refer to both men and women, writers now prefer to use *he or she*, or to use neutral plural forms such as *they* or *people*. In a longer work, such as this textbook, half of the chapters may use the pronoun *he* while the other half will use *she*. Traditional titles such as *chairman* can be rewritten neutrally as *chairperson* or, more simply, *chair*. Often the gender-specific suffix *–man* can be replaced by the neutral *–er: firefighter, police officer, worker.* Don't assume you know a person's sex just because you know his or her job description. Remember that men, like Ben Stiller's character in *Meet the Parents,* can be nurses, too.

Although slang, jargon, clichés, and sexist language are inappropriate in academic writing, they can be effective in other types. Word choice reflects background and personality; thus, slang, jargon, clichés, and sexist language can be used in fiction to reveal something important about a character. In journalism, too, vivid slang expressions can make good quotes:

> "I was totally in the weeds last night, but Chef just told me to man up,"
> said one of the restaurant's line cooks.

As always, the purpose and audience of a piece of writing determine what type of vocabulary is most effective.

A TASTE FOR READING

Yusef Komunyakaa was born in Bogalusa, Louisiana. His poems about his Southern childhood and about his experience in Vietnam, where he served as a correspondent in the United States Army, often address complex moral issues. Komunyakaa won the Pulitzer Prize for Poetry in 1994.

****

Blackberries
by Yusef Komunyakaa

They left my hands like a printer's
Or thief's before a police blotter
& pulled me into early morning's
Terrestrial sweetness, so thick
The damp ground was consecrated
Where they fell among a garland of thorns.

Although I could smell old lime-covered
History, at ten I'd still hold out my hands
& berries fell into them. Eating from one
& filling a half gallon with the other,
I ate the mythology & dreamt
Of pies and cobbler,[a] almost

---

[a] deep-dish fruit pie topped with rich biscuit crust

Needful as forgiveness. My bird dog Spot

Eyed blue jays & thrashers.[b] The mud frogs

In rich blackness, hid from daylight.

An hour later, beside City Limits Road

I balanced a gleaming can in each hand,

Limboed between worlds, repeating *one dollar.*

The big blue car made me sweat.

Wintertime crawled out of the windows.

When I leaned closer I saw the boy

& girl my age, in the wide back seat

Smirking, & it was then I remembered my fingers

Burning with thorns among berries too ripe to touch.

ABOUT THE READING

- What happens in the poem? What does "they" refer to in the first two lines? What are the "two worlds"? What happens in the last stanza?
- Explain "Wintertime crawled out of the windows." Why do you think the author chose the word *crawled* rather than *blew* or *leaked?*
- What are some other words for *smirking?* What do we learn about the story from this particular word choice?
- How do the ampersands (&) affect the look and feel of the poem? It might be helpful to replace the ampersands with *and,* then study the differences.

Tim Hayward is a British writer and food expert whose essays have appeared in the Financial Times, Guardian, Observer Food Monthly, *and* Saveur. *He is also a regular presenter and panelist on BBC Radio 4. His book* Food DIY: How to Make Your Own Everything *was published in 2013.*

****

Too Much of a Mouthful
by Tim Hayward

I'm a pretty big bloke: big body, big appetites and a great big mouth. I'm also keen on street food. I like to pick up my lunch and launch into it with a vulgar gusto involving as much of the upper body as possible. I've been this way ever since I first blossomed from an underfed, etiolated teenager into the man of substance I became.

---

[b]a kind of bird, related to the mockingbird

But these days I'm beginning to feel less comfortable. Not with the size of my body . . . oh dear God, no . . . my problem is with the size of the food.

Last week I walked past a fashionable butcher's in Knightsbridge. It was approaching lunchtime and, as I paused to browse a display of offal, I noticed a section of the counter serving sandwiches. These weren't, you understand, those depressing triangular plastic pods containing bread-wool, mayonnaise and a thin stratum of morose charcuterie; these were the kind of sandwiches an earl would duel to call his own. Each contained a good 250g of prime cooked meats, tomatoes that screamed flavour and a healthy sub-canopy of foliage, all encased in a hunk of fresh-cooked baguette the thickness of a human thigh.

That, I thought, looks like lunch, and in moments we were united. Like long-separated lovers, we hurried to a nearby park bench to indulge and it was there, to my abiding shame, that my body failed me. Try as I might, I couldn't get the bloody thing into my mouth. I tried nibbling at the sides, only for my teeth to skid off the armoured crust—I must have looked like a rat gnawing a torpedo. I tried it end-on, stretching my mouth to its fullest but, without the extensible jaw of an anaconda there was simply no physical way I could get any kind of dental purchase on the thing.

I was damned if I was going to sit in full public view, picking my lunch apart like some irritable-bowelled receptionist and so I hacked at it with a clasp-knife, swearing cathartically until passers-by began to stare. Finally, with half the sandwich consumed, a small but bloody gash in my right thigh and a jaw that felt like I'd been chewing a tyre, I wrapped the other half neatly and handed it to a nearby panhandler. If he didn't want to eat the thing he could probably hollow it out and sleep in it.

Why? Why this mad arms race to create ever more stupendously gargantuan foods?

Since man first found a dead mammoth and decided it might do for tea, human food preparation has been as much about managing size as managing heat. It's not cooking that turns a cow into a steak, a sheep into mutton or a pig into pork chops: it's the cutting, the act of reducing it to a manageable and eatable size.

The greatest triumphs of our culinary development as a species, from Odysseus's lamb kebabs, through Catherine di Medici's ravioli to the chicken McNugget have involved the reduction of ingredients into bite-sized chunks. Japanese cuisine, arguably the most refined and advanced on the planet, is so committed to delivering food that's easy to pop in the mouth that they don't use knives in the dining room.

There are places, of course, where big food makes sense. Some of the sandwiches at the legendary Carnegie Deli in New York feature around a pound of charcuterie—but there the excess is the whole point. You're not supposed to eat it all . . . even the most dedicated fresser is supposed to be stunned by it, take it apart, reassemble it into manageable sections and ask for a doggy bag.

Perhaps the most irritating manifestation of oversized food is the 'gourmet' burger. Say what you like about a compressed mince patty in a cotton-wool bun but at least it squashes down nice and thin and fits in the hole at the bottom of your face.

A near spherical lump of char-grilled, traceable, organic, grass-fed Wagyu in a hand-finished, artisanal, ancient-grain mini-loaf might make your mouth water but it won't go past your teeth—not without completely non-ironic deconstruction—ideally with a power saw.

Perhaps the best illustration of the phenomenon comes from Comptoir Gascon, the 'fast' manifestation of one of London's most exciting French restaurants. They serve a gourmet duck burger—rare, pink and pristine, topped with a creamy slice of foie gras and served in a fresh crisp brioche roll with a friable, razor-edged crust that makes any kind of assault from the human mouth a technical impossibility. Am I missing the point? Am I overlooking the chef's exquisite jeu d'esprit in the meal's intellectual narrative? A culinary torture: perfection so tantalisingly close yet enclosed by a baked cage of chastity. They might as well wrap it in an eight-inch ball of barbed wire.

But it's been today's lunch that's been the last straw. I bought a beautiful, hand-raised pie. You know the kind of thing: rich meaty filling in a robust pastry crust, designed to be eaten by simple rustics in a short break from threshing. But now I can't simply eat it: I have to plan how I'm going to get into it. Preliminary reconnaissance has revealed a line of weakness in the lower crust which might reward attrition. But if I go in from that angle—like Luke Skywalker seeking the vulnerabilities on the underside of the Death Star—I'm going to end up with gravy running down my neck.

Any cook worthy his Maldon salt, be he three star chef, sandwich slinger or piemaker, will have thought long and hard about every aspect of a dish he's created. By the time he's given it a final wipe with the rag and sent it out to delight me he will have used all of his knowledge, skill, experience and training to ensure that it is properly sourced and prepped; perfectly cooked, seasoned, rested and sauced. Is it really too much to ask then, that it should also fit in my mouth?

ABOUT THE READING

- Tim Hayward uses a number of characteristic British words (as well as the British spelling of *flavour* and *armoured*) in this essay, for example, *bloke, keen,* and *panhandler*. What would be a typical American synonym for each word? How does this choice affect the "flavor" of the text?
- Define the following: *etioliated, morose, fresser, pristine, friable, jeu d'esprit, robust, attrition*. Now use them in sentences of your own.
- List five phrases or sentences that catch your attention, and explain why.
- In the last paragraph, Hayward uses the pronoun *he* to refer to "any chef." Do you take that to mean only male chefs, or is Hayward using *he* to mean cooks of both genders? Is it an issue? Explain. Rewrite the paragraph in inclusive language, and evaluate the change.

RECIPE FOR REVIEW

CHOOSING THE RIGHT WORD

1. Choose words that fit the rhetorical situation: formal or informal, professional or academic, personal or objective.
2. Don't overlook the importance of the verb. The right choice can create a vivid picture and add energy to your writing.

CONNOTATION AND DENOTATION

1. The **denotation** of a word is its basic definition.
2. The **connotation** includes the feelings or associations that make a word seem positive or negative, or simply neutral. Be sure that a word's connotation does not unintentionally confuse or offend your readers.

ELIMINATING UNNECESSARY WORDS

1. Refer to Figure 9.2 for ideas on avoiding or revising common wordy expressions.
2. As you revise, eliminate unnecessary or repeated words and phrases.

REVISING SLANG, JARGON, CLICHÉS, AND SEXIST LANGUAGE

1. **Slang** refers to the informal words and phrases used by a relatively small group of people.
2. **Jargon** refers to the specialized terms used by people in a particular job, as well as to any wordy or pretentious language designed more to manipulate than to communicate.
3. A **cliché** is a phrase that has been used so often that it has lost both precision and interest.
4. **Sexist language** refers to expressions that inappropriately specify one gender when both should be included.
5. As you revise your writing, replace slang, jargon, clichés, and sexist language with clear, vivid, and appropriate words and phrases.

TRANSLATION OF DINER SLANG

a. shingle with a shimmy and shake[4] = buttered toast with jam
b. bossy in a bowl = beef stew
c. Mike and Ike = salt and pepper shakers
d. dog and maggot = crackers and cheese
e. customer will take a chance = hash

CHAPTER EXERCISES

1. *Choosing the Right Word*—Look up five synonyms for *walk* and put them in the following sentence: Ron and Harry _____ across the street. Then describe the different pictures created by the different verbs.

2. *Denotation and Connotation*—Look up the following words in a dictionary: *inflexible, obstinate, persistent, pigheaded, resolute.* Explain the different connotations of each word. Then, on a separate sheet of paper, rewrite each sentence, inserting the appropriate word.

    a. The boy was _____ in his refusal to go to bed despite being tired.

    b. The activists were _____ in continuing their peaceful protest, even when threatened with arrest.

    c. The dedicated student was _____ in finishing her homework.

    d. In *Cool Hand Luke*, the _____ title character is determined to eat fifty eggs, even though it nearly kills him.

    e. If you're lucky, your instructor will not be entirely _____ about due dates.

3. *More Practice with Connotation*—Choose an adjective like *fat, thin, young,* or *old,* and look up ten synonyms in a thesaurus. Then look up the definition of each synonym in a dictionary. Finally, use each word in a sentence that illustrates its connotation as well as its denotation.

4. *Eliminating Unnecessary Words*—Rewrite the following sentences in more concise language.

    a. In my opinion, I think that it is difficult and hard to achieve a fluffy texture in a soufflé.

    b. After the movie was over, we proceeded to go to the coffee shop for coffee after the movie.

    c. Doreen served the punch in Styrofoam cups because of the fact that her glass cups and ceramic mugs were still packed away in boxes and stored in the attic.

    d. The lively and energetic dog, who was a terrier, raced very quickly across the road in pursuit of a squirrel.

    e. In today's society, there is a lot of technology that people use every day on a daily basis.

5. *Revising Slang Expressions*—Rewrite the following sentences to avoid using slang expressions.

    a. Carrie was jonesing for a cig.

    b. We had to give her props on the bling.

    c. Hey, dude, I need to borrow the porcelain.

    d. The amputated foot in *Saw* made the audience want to hurt.

    e. Girl, your tude is a real buzzkill.

6. *Avoiding Jargon*—Rewrite the following sentences in clear, ordinary English. You may wish to consult a dictionary.[5]
   a. The powder hound went off piste and ended up in the blood wagon.
   b. The department implemented a new initiative designed to enhance investment in human capital.
   c. Roger that. ETA ten minutes.
   d. Jack described the wine as complex and supple with a long finish.
   e. Derek received the following flame: Check the FAQ or RTFM.
7. *Avoiding Clichés*—Rewrite the following sentences, replacing any clichés with fresh, specific language.
   a. That awesome chocolate just melted in my mouth.
   b. The line cook remained as cool as a cucumber throughout the dinner rush.
   c. That old restaurant is going down the tubes.
   d. We had to postpone the picnic—it was raining cats and dogs.
   e. Jerry thought his new job would be better, but it was just out of the frying pan and into the fire.
8. *Revising Sexist Language*—Rewrite the following sentences to eliminate sexist or gender-specific language.
   a. Each student needs to bring his book to mathematics class tomorrow.
   b. The discovery of penicillin was a benefit to all mankind.
   c. Every man should have the right to vote in his own country.
   d. She was the chairman of the Academic Standards Committee.
   e. Each new chef carves his initials on his knives.
9. *Analyzing Word Choice*—Select one of the pieces in A Taste for Writing at the end of Chapters 1–17, and examine the author's choice of words. Does he or she use slang, jargon, euphemisms, or clichés? Explain, citing specific examples. Describe the effect of these word choices.

IDEAS FOR WRITING

1. In what types of writing is slang or jargon appropriate? Use specific examples to illustrate your point.
2. Visit the website *Weasel Words* (www.weaselwords.com.au), being careful to add the *au* to the URL (otherwise you may end up on a site about ferrets). Why does the author believe jargon is dangerous? Do you agree? Explain.
3. Jargon can also be fun, however. How about "seagull manager" and "blamestorming"? Google "corporate jargon" on the Internet, and see what you can find. Then write a short paper about the fun side of jargon, using plenty of specific examples.
4. Take a well-known cliché, such as "that's the icing on the cake" or "I'm happy as a clam," and write a story or essay in which you use the saying in a literal or unexpected way. See, for example, "Smell the Coffee" (Chapter 6) and "When Life Gives You Lemons" (Chapter 14).

SAVORY · GARLICKY · NUT... · FRUITY · GINGERY · LEMONY · CHOCOLA... · SAVO... · TART · SALTY · GINGERY · LEMONY · TART · JUICY · GINGERY · G... · CHOCOLATE · BRINY · TART · SALTY · FRUITY · TART · SUGARY · SALTY · TANGY · BITTER · ...OOMY · HONEYED · ...CKISH

UNIT 2
PATTERNS

CHAPTER 10
FINDING YOUR VOICE

By the end of this chapter, you should begin to . . .

- identify the various components of voice;
- analyze the voices of other writers;
- develop your own voice through various strategies;
- use punctuation to "write" your voice; and
- appreciate the role of voice in the personal essay.

We probably have an instinctive feeling about what "voice" might mean in writing, even if we haven't thought much about it. We hear it in others, and in ourselves—or we *miss* hearing it.

> Looking back to my past classes, I never enjoyed writing because I thought I could never hear my own voice. But now with all this practice, I am able to write a paper on whatever subject with confidence and pride.
>
> —**Astrid Sierra**, student writer

In these few lines, Astrid gets right to the heart of this chapter: "I never enjoyed writing because I thought I could never hear my own voice." Voice is one of the crucial ingredients to good writing, sometimes described as its "flavor." If we think for a moment about the various components of flavor, we begin to see how complex—and essential—the concept of "voice" is.

THE WRITER'S VOICE

When we think about the distinctive voice of a friend, we mean the *sound* of the voice, the pitch, the monotone or lilt of it, the accent, the volume, the cadence (for example, the distinctive rhythms of Morgan Freeman's or Clint Eastwood's speech). We also mean the choice of words—some people pepper their speech with slang (or culinary images), while others choose a more formal vocabulary. Some speak in short bursts (Walken), while others move smoothly through long and relatively complicated sentences. Some use a loud voice, others a soft. All of these characteristics together make up a speaker's unique "voice." What then do we mean by a *writer*'s voice?

When communication works—whether it's a look, a song, a dish, or a story—it's often because we feel the person is speaking directly to us. We sense the distinctive personality behind the words, the melody, the food. I've seen students look at a picture of a dish and identify it instantly as from The French Laundry. And can't you recognize distinctive bands and singers, even if you don't particularly like them?

A writer's **voice** consists of a combination of features, including the attitude toward the topic, the choice of details that develop the topic, the choice of vocabulary, and the rhythm of the sentences. Here's the voice of Katniss Everdeen as we first "hear" it in *The Hunger Games* by Suzanne Collins (pp. 3–4):

> When I wake up, the other side of the bed is cold. My fingers stretch out, seeking Prim's warmth but finding only the rough canvas cover of the mattress. She must have had bad dreams and climbed in with our mother. Of course, she did. This is the day of the reaping.
>
> I prop myself up on one elbow. There's enough light in the bedroom to see them. My little sister, Prim, curled up on her side, cocooned in my mother's body, their cheeks pressed together. In sleep, my mother looks younger, still worn but not so beaten-down. Prim's face is as fresh as a raindrop, as lovely as the primrose for which she was named. My mother was very beautiful once, too. Or so they tell me.
>
> Sitting at Prim's knees, guarding her, is the world's ugliest cat. Mashed-in nose, half of one ear missing, eyes the color of rotting squash. Prim named him Buttercup, insisting that his muddy yellow coat matched the bright flower. He hates me. Or at least distrusts me. Even though it was years ago, I think he still remembers how I tried to drown him in a bucket when Prim brought him home. Scrawny kitten, belly swollen with worms, crawling with fleas. The last thing I needed was another mouth to feed. But Prim begged so hard, cried even, I had to let him stay. It turned out okay. My mother got rid of the vermin and he's a born mouser. Even catches the occasional rat. Sometimes, when I clean a kill, I feed Buttercup the entrails. He has stopped hissing at me.
>
> Entrails. No hissing. This is the closest we will ever come to love.

What do we notice about Katniss's voice? The sentences are relatively short, direct, sometimes not even sentences but fragments. The words are vivid but simple words from Old English like *bed* and *bucket*, *dream* and *drown*, *fingers* and *fleas*, *hissing* and *swollen*. *Hunger* and *games* are themselves derived from Old English, as are *day* and *reaping*. (See Figure 10.1.)

The impression created by these Old English words is one of strength, no nonsense, maybe anger at times, or a sense of urgency. The "world's ugliest cat" comes in

Figure 10.1   The Etymology of *The Hunger Games*

Origin	Words Used by Katniss
Old English	bed, bucket, cheek, cold, day, dream, drown, elbow, feed, fingers, fleas, fresh, game, hate, hissing, home, hunger, kill, love, mashed, mouse, mouth, raindrop, rat, reaping, rotting, swollen, ugliest, wake, yellow
Americanism	scrawny (from Norwegian), squash (from Narragansett)
Latin	beautiful, cocoon, entrails, flower, vermin

for a barrage of Old English criticism. Katniss is no pushover, no sentimental ooh-er and ahh-er. She's definitely unsentimental, businesslike. The closest she will come to love with the cat is to toss him a snack of squirrel guts. Even before we know her age and her situation, we hear both the stress and the strength in her voice.

There's something about the idea of *voice* that suggests power, personal knowledge, and conviction. Voice is about asserting yourself; often it's about trying to change things. On this day of the "reaping," when the names of a boy and girl will be drawn at random and the two children sent off to fight to the death in the Hunger Games, Katniss uses her voice—simple, direct—to take power by volunteering to fight in her younger sister's place (p. 22).

> "Prim!" The strangled cry comes out of my throat, and my muscles begin to move again. "Prim!" I don't need to shove through the crowd. The other kids make way immediately allowing me a straight path to the stage. I reach her just as she is about to mount the steps. With one sweep of my arm, I push her behind me.
>
> "I volunteer!" I gasp. "I volunteer as tribute!"

"I volunteer as tribute!"

Lionsgate/Photofest ©Lionsgate Photographer: Murray Close

Until this point Katniss has tried to stay out of public view, preferring to hunt unseen in the wilderness outside District 12. But her instinct to protect the vulnerable is overpowering, and she uses her voice to enter the arena of this particular Hunger Games and, later, of revolution.

LISTENING TO OTHER VOICES

We first learn to speak by listening to others. Similarly, we can learn a lot about writing by "listening" to other writers' texts. Let's look at some examples, noticing such features as sentence length and variety, vocabulary, figurative language, distinctive turns of phrase, energy and flow, as well as larger elements related to topic and attitude.

Anthony Bourdain's voice is well known both on the Food Network and from his many books. Let's read this excerpt from *Kitchen Confidential* (pp. 9–10):

My first indication that food was something other than a substance one stuffed in one's face when hungry—like filling up at a gas station—came after fourth grade in elementary school. It was on a family vacation to Europe, on the *Queen Mary*, in the cabin-class dining room. There's a picture somewhere: my mother in her Jackie O sunglasses, my younger brother and I in our painfully cute cruisewear, boarding the big Cunard ocean liner, all of us excited about our first transatlantic voyage, our first trip to my father's ancestral homeland, France.

It was the soup.

It was *cold*.

This was something of a discovery for a curious fourth-grader whose entire experience of soup to this point had consisted of Campbell's cream of tomato and chicken noodle. I'd eaten in restaurants before, sure, but this was the first food I really noticed. It was the first food I enjoyed and, more important, remembered enjoying. I asked our patient British waiter what this delightfully cool, tasty liquid was.

"I remember everything . . . the rich, creamy taste of leek and potato; the pleasurable shock, the surprise that it was cold."

"Vichyssoise," came the reply, a word that to this day—even though it's now a tired old warhorse of a menu selection and one I've prepared thousands of times—still has a magical ring to it. I remember everything about the experience: the way our waiter ladled it from a silver tureen into my bowl; the crunch of tiny chopped chives he spooned on as garnish; the rich, creamy taste of leek and potato; the pleasurable shock, the surprise that it was cold.

I don't remember much else about the passage across the Atlantic. I saw *Boeing Boeing* with Jerry Lewis and Tony Curtis in the *Queen*'s movie theater, and a Bardot flick. The old liner shuddered and groaned and vibrated terribly the whole way—barnacles on the hull was the official explanation—and from New York to Cherbourg, it was like riding atop a giant lawnmower. My brother and I quickly became bored and spent much of our time in the "Teen Lounge," listening to "House of the Rising Sun" on the jukebox, or watching the water slosh around like a contained tidal wave in the below-deck saltwater pool.

But that cold soup stayed with me. It resonated, waking me up, making me aware of my tongue and, in some way, preparing me for future events.

As we might expect from a world traveler, Bourdain draws words from multiple origins (Figure 10.2). But notice that he relies most heavily on multisyllabic words derived from Latin, from his book titles *Kitchen Confidential* and *A Cook's Tour* to his description of his fourth-grade self as *excited* and *curious*. His tasting of the *vichyssoise*, though, comes appropriately from Old French: *enjoyed, soup, garnish, shock, surprise*. At the end of the passage, Bourdain uses the vigor of Old English (*waking, aware, tongue*) to spice up the Latin (*resonated, preparing, future, events*).

Figure 10.2 The Etymology of *Kitchen Confidential*

Origin	Words Used by Bourdain
Latin	confidential, cook, curious, events, excited, experience, face, family, future, indication, kitchen, noticed, pleasurable, preparing, resonated, substance, tour, vacation
Old/Middle French	enjoyed, garnish, shock, soup, stuffed, surprise, taste
Old English	aware, cold, hungry, leek, tongue, waking
Greek	magical
Taino[a]	potato (through Spanish)

[a]Primary language of the Caribbean islands

Bourdain's sentence structure has a fluid, conversational feel—educated but informal. He has a fondness for the em dash. His tone is urbane, slightly mocking at times. He likes the "pleasurable shock" of the *vichyssoise,* and, as he exposes secrets of the "culinary underbelly," we can infer that he likes to shock the reader, too. Unlike Katniss, he's not out to change the world but rather to enjoy it and to share that enjoyment with us.

FINDING YOUR OWN VOICE

An excellent way to begin hearing your voice in writing is actually to write as if you are speaking. You can do this literally—record your spoken thoughts, then transcribe them onto paper. Or, you can just start writing but with a clear sense of hearing your own voice as you go. Sometimes you can speak out loud and write what you say. Of course, you must not worry about grammar and spelling during this type of writing. You must simply focus on listening to and transcribing your words as you would speak them. At a later point, you may edit these transcripts, depending on what the final product requires.

Reading your work out loud, or listening to someone else read it, can help you find your own distinctive writer's voice. Listen to the text. Hear it. Does it sound like you? Do you like it? If a sentence is hard to listen to, it may not be easy to read either.

It can be very helpful to imagine a specific audience, an individual or a group— perhaps your grandma, best friend, or a stranger sitting next to you on the train— and write or "talk" to this specific audience. This strategy is also valuable in creating the overall design of a particular piece—what does your audience want or need to know, what do they already know? Maybe think of a familiar face, or visualize a new one. What would you say if you were sitting at a coffee shop with this person? What words come naturally? Perhaps try writing your first draft as a letter. Even if you keep only a few fresh phrases, the exercise may help you identify key elements of your voice.

I find that the more students write informally, the more likely they are to develop an authentic and engaging voice in their formal writing projects. Keeping a journal is an excellent way to get that extra writing in, whether you simply freewrite about your day or whether you have certain questions or themes to address. Artists of all kinds use journal-writing to maintain a flow of creativity. Try other kinds of writing as well. Write (and read) stories, poems, screenplays, letters, recipes, tweets, and personal essays.

Voice has a lot to do with attitude. Experiment with different moods and tones in your writing. For example, describe an event in a happy mood; then describe the same event in an angry or disappointed mood. Find the rhythms that seem natural when you read aloud, and find the punctuation marks that create or reflect these rhythms (see the next section, "Writing" Your Voice).

Talking or writing about something we know well—in contrast to struggling to write an important business letter or difficult school paper—is more likely to take place in our own voice. Practice writing about your life, memories, plans, problems you're working through, dreams for the future. Use what you know and what you care about to bring out your true voice.

Our voice won't be exactly the same in everything we write, of course, just as it isn't exactly the same in every spoken context. Across the spectrum of our voice, we have more and less formal sentences and word choices, in addition to lighter and more serious topics and attitudes. When speaking, we automatically choose the "voice" that fits the occasion. The same is true of writing. From a variety of options, we choose a particular voice to fit the content, audience, and purpose of our writing.

"WRITING" YOUR VOICE

On the page, voice is conveyed through more than the words. It's the punctuation that tells the audience how to read the words, when to pause, when to stop, when to raise or lower the volume, when to whisper. Listen to the difference as you read the following sentences aloud:

Hi Peter, how are you?
Hi—Peter. How *are* you?

The first sentence flows along smoothly—no particular subtext, no hidden tension there. In the second sentence, however, the em dash after the greeting creates a significant pause, as if the speaker initially couldn't remember Peter's name. The period brings the reader to a full stop, a pause, maybe an awkward one. Meanwhile the italicized *are* may suggest an insincerity on the speaker's part. Punctuation also has a *visual* effect. A paragraph peppered with semicolons looks serious, perhaps even pretentious, while a series of dashes looks more informal, lively, "dashing."

Of course, we generally think of punctuation in terms of rules. What is the correct way to use a semicolon? When do we need a comma? Yet, as writer Pico Iyer writes in "In Praise of the Humble Comma," punctuation is about more than rules: "By establishing the relations between words, punctuation establishes the relations between people using words." In speaking, we use many nonverbal cues to create closeness to or distance from our audience. In writing, punctuation performs that role. Iyer continues:

> [Punctuation] scores the music in our minds, gets our thoughts moving to the rhythm of our hearts. Punctuation is the notation in the sheet music of our words, telling us when to rest, or when to raise our voices; it acknowledges that the meaning of our discourse [lies] in the pauses, the pacing, and

the phrasing. Punctuation is the way one bats one's eyes, lowers one's voice, or blushes demurely. Punctuation adjusts the tone and color and volume till the feeling comes into perfect focus. . . .

Punctuation, in short, gives us the human voice.

Because punctuation changes the way we hear words, it changes the way we hear the writer's voice.

THE PERSONAL ESSAY

Outside of fiction, nowhere is the writer's voice more important and distinctive than in the personal essay. The word *essay*, which comes from a French word meaning "to try," was used at the end of the sixteenth century by Michel de Montaigne to describe the writing in which he mixed ideas with personal anecdotes and perspectives. An essay "tries" to explain an idea, and a personal essay does so in the writer's own voice. A personal essay is not like a research paper, though it may involve research.

A personal essay is not quite like a story either, though it may tell one. Although the personal essay often includes or even centers on a story, the main focus is the writer's response to and interpretation of that story.

In a personal essay, the writer often seems to be conversing with readers, creating an informal, confidential tone. In his preface to *The Art of the Personal Essay*, Phillip Lopate writes:

> The hallmark of the personal essay is its intimacy. The writer seems to be speaking directly into your ear, confiding everything from gossip to wisdom. Through sharing thoughts, memories, desires, complaints, and whimsies, the personal essayist sets up a relationship with the reader, a dialogue—a friendship, if you will, based on identification, understanding, testiness, and companionship. (xxiii)

The author of a personal essay often seems to be trying to figure something out. Why was this event significant? Why do I believe what I believe? The personal essay can be a way of shaping the writer's experience, of creating meaning from it. This is not to say that the topic of a personal essay must always be serious and philosophical. It can

In a personal essay, the writer often seems to be conversing with readers, creating an intimate tone, and honestly trying to figure something out.

be about anything the writer wants, though ideally it will also be about a topic that readers will connect with. It might be about an "important" topic, or an ordinary one. It might be funny or angry or inspiring.

A writer known for her skill with the personal essay is M. F. K. Fisher. In the passage quoted here, from the Foreword to *The Gastronomical Me* (p. 353), she explains why she chose to write about food:

> People ask me: Why do you write about food, and eating and drinking? Why don't you write about the struggle for power and security, and about love, the way others do?
>
> They ask it accusingly, as if I were somehow gross, unfaithful to the honor of my craft.
>
> The easiest answer is to say that, like most other humans, I am hungry. But there is more than that. It seems to me that our three basic needs, for food and security and love, are so mixed and mingled and entwined that we cannot straightly think of one without the others. So it happens that when I write of hunger, I am really writing about love and the hunger for it, and warmth and the love of it, and the hunger for it . . . and then the warmth and richness and fine reality of hunger satisfied . . . and it is all one.
>
> I tell about myself, and how I ate bread on a lasting hillside, or drank red wine in a room now blown to bits, and it happens without my willing it that I am telling too about the people with me then, and their other deeper needs for love and happiness.
>
> There is food in the bowl, and more often than not, because of what honesty I have, there is nourishment in the heart, to feed the wilder, more insistent hungers. We must eat. If, in the face of that dread fact, we can find other nourishment, and tolerance and compassion for it, we'll be no less full of human dignity.
>
> There is a communion of more than our bodies when bread is broken and wine drunk. And that is my answer, when people ask me: Why do you write about hunger, and not wars or love?

We can see immediately from the title, *The Gastronomical Me,* that Fisher's subject is a personal one. In this excerpt, in fact, the Foreword (a kind of introduction) to the book, she dives right in to an explanation—almost a justification, perhaps—of the topic of her works, food. Perhaps for some readers, food seemed too ordinary or even too "gross" a topic for a literary essay. But Fisher argues that the hunger she writes about is more than the hunger for food: "So it happens that when I write about hunger, I am really writing about love and the hunger for it, and warmth and the love of it and the hunger for it." In writing about her unique, specific encounters with food, she appeals to a universal hunger for shared experiences.

On a lighter note, Fisher's essay "Love and Death Among the Molluscs" (p. 125) combines scientific content with a musing tone that would be out of place in a research paper.

> An oyster leads a dreadful but exciting life. . . . [I]f he should survive the arrows of his own outrageous fortune. . . . , the years afterwards are full of stress, passion, and danger.

With a delicious humor, Fisher wonders about the mollusc's gender and admires his—and her—fertility. Reading this essay is about enjoying Fisher's individual voice and her skill with the language, our interest piqued by the "stress, passion, and danger" faced by the tasty oyster. As she concludes the essay (p. 128), Fisher's tone becomes more philosophical, and we enjoy that, too.

> Life is hard. . . . An oyster's life is worse. She lives motionless, sound-less, her own cold ugly shape her only dissipation, and if she escapes the menace of duck-slipper-mussel-Black-Drum-leech-sponge-borer-starfish, it is for man to eat, because of man's own hunger.

Personal essays are as different as the individuals who write them. Yet the very specific and unusual experiences of the author become for the reader somehow accessible, touching on shared, universal experiences of struggle and defeat, strength and hope.

A TASTE FOR READING

Jackie Parker is a poet and writer who teaches writing workshops nationwide as a vehicle for well-being. She has developed courses for UCLA's Arts and Healing program and USC's Department of Work and Family, as well as stress-reduction programs for businesses in New York, New Jersey, and Los Angeles. Parker's novel Our Lady of Infidelity *will be published by Arcade in 2014.*

****

The Music of Language
by Jackie Parker

I had been asked to teach a writing workshop for a group of women and their teenage daughters who lived within blocks of each other in Alhambra, California, a city of 80,000 eight miles from downtown Los Angeles. Alhambra is the birthplace of the painter Norman Rockwell whose scenes of everyday American life graced the covers of the Saturday Evening Post magazine for forty years. Many of these women were first generation Americans: Mexican, Filipino, Korean, who by any standards had achieved a great deal. One had begun selling hotdogs at Dodger games. She now owned several properties, another was a nursing supervisor in a large hospital, another a social worker with a Master's Degree in family counseling. They had worked and studied their way to impressive positions, bought homes, raised families, lived in a manner far exceeding their parents' dreams for them.

But it seemed that they were having trouble getting along with their teenage daughters, and one of the women, who was enrolled in a workshop of mine, thought that by writing together they would find a way to create meaningful connections and a basis for understanding each other as women. The daughters, who had known each other since they were toddlers, had agreed to give it a try.

As I sat down in the comfortable living room and looked around at the fourteen of them—I was apprehensive and yet excited to see what would happen in the next two hours. The truth was I had no idea what I was going to ask them to write about, and no idea whether this group would end in disaster or triumph. I rarely prepare a topic before meeting a group, feeling out the needs of the people in the room by listening to what they write in the first exercise: a five minute freewriting that elicits results I still don't understand after fifteen years of doing this work. People open up to aspects of themselves that are moving and deep and true, as if those truths are standing behind a door waiting to be invited into the room. But would teen-age girls risk writing their truths with their mothers right there? Would their mothers risk revealing themselves to their girls?

I had asked everyone to leave their phones and connective devices in another room and one of the girls said she felt really strange. Even stranger when we began simply by sitting in quiet together, breathing in silence for five minutes. A few of the girls laughed nervously. Some of them squirmed. I held the quiet like a cloak, spreading it out over the fidgets and giggles as they settled in. Sometimes just five minutes of silence in a room can shift moods and connect us to the inner life that we hunger for and often fear, but that we must work consciously to give to ourselves these days because so much that is rich waits for us there.

Just before the writing began one of the women asked if she could write in her native language. "Of course," I said, off handedly. "Write in whatever language feels right for you." She was the first person to read that day. "I know you won't understand what I'm saying but I had to write this," she began.

I had never heard Filipino spoken at such length. And no one but her daughter could follow the story. And yet, as she read, haltingly at first, and then musically, her words rising into a rhythm and meaning we could sense but not quite know, something happened to us all. I looked around the room and there were tears in the eyes of many of the women and girls. Simply hearing the language had moved us. Was it possible that we had gleaned their meaning as well? "Could you read it again?" everyone urged once she had finished. How beautiful was her first language. It was a privilege to listen, we all agreed. A privilege just to hear. Then she translated her story to us. "It's a letter to my mother," she said. "I'm apologizing to her. She had wanted me to become a doctor, but I failed. I failed her. All I was able to do was become a nurse. I have never spoken these words to anyone. I don't even think I have ever really let myself feel them."

Her daughter got up from her chair and embraced her. The tissues were passed around the room. We heard many deep and wise stories that day, in Spanish and Korean, in English, as well. It was a day of profound connection on many levels, far exceeding my goals for the group. It was a day that changed my teaching. Now wherever I go I remind people that they may write in any language they choose. And roomfuls of people are graced with the music of languages they might never have heard. And if not the language, then the stories that arise from the experiences that are held in the quintessential American experience: our immigrant selves. There are 92 languages spoken in the City of Los Angeles. One day, I want to have heard stories in them all.

ABOUT THE READING

- What was unexpected about the event Parker describes? How does she re-create the experience for the reader?
- For the workshop participants, in what ways was listening to the story like listening to music?
- What effects does the quoted speech have on your reading of the essay? How would the piece have been different without it?
- What makes this piece more of a personal essay than a story?

A. A. Milne (1882–1956) was an English writer now best known for his stories about Winnie-the-Pooh and for the children's poems collected in When We Were Very Young *and* Now We Are Six. *"A Word for Autumn" was published in 1919 in a book of essays entitled* Not That It Matters.

****

A Word for Autumn
by A. A. Milne

Last night the waiter put the celery on with the cheese, and I knew that summer was indeed dead. Other signs of autumn there may be—the reddening leaf, the chill in the early-morning air, the misty evenings—but none of these comes home to me so truly. There may be cool mornings in July; in a year of drought the leaves may change before their time; it is only with the first celery that summer is over.

I knew all along that it would not last. Even in April I was saying that winter would soon be here. Yet somehow it had begun to seem possible lately that a miracle might happen, that summer might drift on and on through the months—a final upheaval to crown a wonderful year. The celery settled that. Last night with the celery autumn came into its own.

There is a crispness about celery that is of the essence of October. It is as fresh and clean as a rainy day after a spell of heat. It crackles pleasantly in the mouth. Moreover it is excellent, I am told, for the complexion. One is always hearing of things which are good for the complexion, but there is no doubt that celery stands high on the list. After the burns and freckles of summer one is in need of something. How good that celery should be there at one's elbow.

A week ago—("A little more cheese, waiter")—a week ago I grieved for the dying summer. I wondered how I could possibly bear the waiting—the eight long months till May. In vain to comfort myself with the thought that I could get through more work in the winter undistracted by thoughts of cricket grounds and country houses. In vain, equally, to tell myself that I could stay in bed later in the mornings. Even the thought of after-breakfast pipes in front of the fire left me cold. But now, suddenly, I am reconciled to autumn. I see quite clearly that all good things must come to an end. The summer has been splendid, but it has lasted long enough. This morning I welcomed the chill in the air; this morning I viewed the falling leaves with cheerfulness; and this morning I said to myself, "Why, of course, I'll have celery for lunch." ("More bread, waiter.")

"Season of mists and mellow fruitfulness," said Keats,[b] not actually picking out celery in so many words, but plainly including it in the general blessings of the autumn. Yet what an opportunity he missed by not concentrating on that precious root. Apples, grapes, nuts, and vegetable marrows[c] he mentions specially—and how poor a selection! For apples and grapes are not typical of any month, so ubiquitous are they, vegetable marrows are vegetables *pour rire*[d] and have no place in any serious consideration of the seasons, while as for nuts, have we not a national song which asserts distinctly, "Here we go gathering nuts in May"? Season of mists and mellow celery, then let it be. A pat of butter underneath the bough, a wedge of cheese, a loaf of bread and—Thou.

How delicate are the tender shoots unfolded layer by layer. Of what a whiteness is the last baby one of all, of what a sweetness his flavour. It is well that this should be the last rite of the meal—*finis coronat opus*[e]—so that we may go straight on to the business of the pipe. Celery demands a pipe rather than a cigar, and it can be eaten better in an inn or a London tavern than in the home. Yes, and it should be eaten alone, for it is the only food which one really wants to hear oneself eat. Besides, in company one may have to consider the wants of others. Celery is not a thing to share with any man. Alone in your country inn you may call for the celery; but if you are wise you will see that no other traveller wanders into the room. Take warning from one who has learnt a lesson. One day I lunched alone at an inn, finishing with cheese and celery. Another traveller came in and lunched too. We did not speak—I was busy with my celery. From the other end of the table he reached across for the cheese. That was all right! it was the public cheese. But he also reached across for the celery—my private celery for which I owed. Foolishly—you know how one does—I had left the sweetest and crispest shoots till the last, tantalizing myself pleasantly with the thought of them. Horror! to see them snatched from me by a stranger. He realized later what he had done and apologized, but of what good is an apology in such circumstances? Yet at least the tragedy was not without its value. Now one remembers to lock the door.

[b]Nineteenth-century English poet
[c]Summer squash
[d]Not serious
[e]Latin: The end crowns the work.

Yes, I can face the winter with calm. I suppose I had forgotten what it was really like. I had been thinking of the winter as a horrid wet, dreary time fit only for professional football. Now I can see other things—crisp and sparkling days, long pleasant evenings, cheery fires. Good work shall be done this winter. Life shall be lived well. The end of the summer is not the end of the world. Here's to October—and, waiter, some more celery.

ABOUT THE READING

- What does the author like about celery? Why? Do you think he's serious?
- Describe the author's voice, including such elements as word choice, figurative language, repetition, and the use of parentheses.
- How does the author develop his topic? Summarize the main idea of each paragraph; then explain the organizational plan.
- Who is "Thou" at the end of the fifth paragraph? "A loaf of bread, and thou" is an allusion to the *Rubaiyat of Omar Khayyam*. After reading about the *Rubaiyat* and/or some verses from it, describe the effect of the allusion in Milne's essay.

Like his uncles in the following story, James Broome is a member of the Grand Traverse Band of Ottawa and Chippewa Indians in Peshawbestown, Michigan. He is currently studying at the Culinary Institute of America.

****

The Vietnam War and What It Cost
by James Broome

The Vietnam War was probably the most expensive war we Americans have ever seen, whether the costs be financial, physical, or emotional. We don't really have to look far to find a story of this war. There is evidence everywhere. Aging vets are all around us, buying groceries, building our homes, policing our streets, and even teaching here at the Culinary Institute of America. Each of them with their own stories and accounts of a war that went on too long. In fact, many of them say it was over before it started. Did we win this war that our country and countless families sacrificed so much for? Ask a veteran of this war, and he will tell you. With bravery and a sense of duty, soldiers traveled to a foreign land and put it all on the line for our freedom. Some went willingly and some without a choice, but all for the greater good of this country. The draft took so many of our youth and put them in harm's way, forcing them to do things a lot of them grew up knowing as a sin, murder.

Like many other draftees, my uncle Bill Chippewa was very young. He received his notice of draft and began to prepare for war. Not liking the idea of his brother going alone, my uncle Ernest Chippewa volunteered as well, and together they went to Vietnam. Assigned as paratroopers, they had a swift training; then it was on to battle. Between the two of them, they successfully completed hundreds of jumps into enemy territory. They fought in many battles and were exposed to the worst of human nature, yet somehow they both survived. Facing a threat they had never known before, they stuck together and fought bravely until the day came that they were sent home. Unfortunately, they were not necessarily given the best welcome. Like many others coming home from the war, they were booed, pelted with fruits and vegetables. Some were even struck by stones. Not the best memory for them, I'm sure, but they carried on, making their way to Florida where my grandmother lived at the time, and found work picking oranges.

Like my uncles, the narrators of "Facing It" by Yusef Komunyakaa and "The Man I Killed" by Tim O'Brien experienced things most never will. The reality of "kill or be killed" was all around them, and with each passing day, the war took a little more of them. In the poem "Facing It," the narrator gives the reader a sense of emotion as he gazes upon the wall of names,[f] remembering friends lost and left behind in Vietnam. A real feeling of shame and regret is expressed through his words. He states that he "half-expect[ed] to see [hi]s own in letters like smoke" amongst the endless names of fallen warriors. He then explains the memories that rush through his mind as he "touch[es] the name Andrew Johnson." He describes "the booby trap's white flash," obviously implying the last sight his friend would ever see. As he reminds us where we are by scribing the sights at the wall, "a red bird's wings cutting across [his] stare," "a white vet's image float[ing ever] closer," we feel his internal panic. The white vet's "pale eyes look through [his]." A vet that has "lost his right arm" now looks into his transparent soul; they feel each other's pain. They never really stopped serving their country, as his last few lines show his need to protect the names.

We often take for granted the toll war has on people's lives. Most came back never to be the same, yearning for the innocence they once possessed. I have heard many stories of the Vietnam War, and not one of them had a happy ending. Deeds done left these brave soldiers almost crippled with regret and shame, as demonstrated in the story "The Man I Killed." The repetitive nature of his account shows the almost demonizing feeling that comes from taking a human life. The crisp details show his focus on the kill, as well as his profound respect for life and his inability to successfully process what has happened. His questions about the victim's circumstances before his demise plague the author to the point of obsession. Pondering the man's possible career or school aspirations, and even whether or not he's married or engaged, shows the author's deep regret for ending a life that was just beginning. Due to observations of his victim's appearance, such as "his long shapely fingers," the eyebrows "thin and arched like a woman's," and the small, "almost dainty" frame of his body, the author makes assumptions which show the obsessive, irrational thoughts that entered his mind. Details such as "his jaw was in his throat," the "star-shaped hole" where his eye had been, a torn earlobe, the fact that his nose was undamaged, and even the minor environmental memories further portray the narrator's hurting soul. Even with his comrade's congratulating him on a

---

[f]The names are listed on the Vietnam Veterans Memorial in Washington, D.C.

successful kill, he still remains in a state of shock throughout the whole piece, reflecting over and over on every aspect of the dead body he created.

While trying to grasp the kind of despair these warriors endure, I can't help but try and put myself in their shoes. To wake up every day and go to sleep every night tormented by the past is no kind of life, yet we have forced fellow humans into that very situation time and time again. Granted some volunteer, but even they are changed and hurt the same way. Patriotism is powerful, the feeling of duty, the feeling of pride. They all had it, my uncles, both authors, and all vets from any war really. Both of my Vietnam vet uncles made it home, but both later died from Agent Orange[g] poisoning that was compliments of the war. Hearing their stories of failed parachutes and tight quarters under heavy fire really stuck with me. They were warriors that sacrificed for the greater good, they told themselves, all the while tormented by post-traumatic stress disorder and recurring flashbacks that sometimes woke them up screaming in terror. I lost my uncles to that war before I was ever born, and I had to watch them both slowly die from inside out. They had to live with a constant feeling of guilt, regret, and sorrow for what they had to do, along with the endless memories good and bad, of lost friends and fellow warriors during the war effort in Vietnam. I was 12 when my uncle Bill passed and 31 when my uncle Ernie joined him; they were, and are still, true American heroes.

A few months ago I received a call to let me know that my cousin Joe (Ernie's son) had died. After the loss of his father he drank himself to death. The day my uncle Bill got notified that he was chosen for the draft was a lot like throwing a stone in the water. The initial splash was huge, but the waves kept coming and coming. Although it seems at times that the waves have subsided, suddenly we are all reminded that the effects of this war are still very much a part of my family's lives, as I'm sure is the case with most other war veterans' families. Again I reflect upon the real costs of war.

Through these soldiers' eyes, we are given a glimpse of war in a raw and unfamiliar way. We are left with no choice but to transport [ourselves] there, feel what they felt, and face questions that, to say the least, are troubling and worrisome. They were expendable; at least the government deemed them so. My uncles, the eldest of five boys and six sisters, were expendable. So many people were deemed expendable.

All songs sound creepy when slowed down enough, maybe none more than "Grand Ole Flag" the day you bury your uncle who died from Agent Orange poisoning from the Vietnam War, but hey, maybe it's just me. To this day I get the shivers when thinking of what they had to endure, and they did it for us, all of us. Maybe Jimmy Hendrix was able to capture the feeling when he wrote "Purple Haze"; my uncles would play it over and over. "Is it tomorrow or just the end of time" or "Excuse me while I kiss the sky"—powerful words for some soldiers. As they danced with death (kissing the sky) or questioned their mortality (end of time), they are the few that can answer the question. What does the war really cost? Everything.

---

[g]Agent Orange was one of several chemical mixtures used by the United States military to remove vegetative groundcover. Exposure to Agent Orange is believed to have caused cancer and other serious health problems.

- Describe the author's voice. In which paragraph(s) do you "hear" it most clearly? Explain.
- In addition to a distinctive voice, which elements of the personal essay in Recipe for Review do you find in this piece?
- Describe the evidence or perspectives the author uses to develop his topic, including the two very different songs mentioned in the last paragraph.
- Have you, or your family or friends, served in the armed forces? If so, how would you assess the "cost" of the experience?

RECIPE FOR REVIEW

THE WRITER'S VOICE

A writer's personality is revealed by a combination of features, including the choice of and attitude toward the topic, the choice of details that develop the topic, the choice of vocabulary, and the structure and rhythm of the sentences. Punctuation plays a significant role in shaping the way readers "hear" the writer's voice.

LISTENING TO OTHER VOICES

Develop your understanding of voice by reading ("listening to") the texts of a variety of skilled writers.

FINDING YOUR OWN VOICE

To find your writer's voice,

- "listen" to the voices of other writers;
- begin your draft by writing as you speak; you can edit as necessary later on;
- read your writing aloud—does it sound like you?
- think of a specific audience, and write for that audience;
- try writing your first draft as a letter;
- stay in practice by keeping a journal;
- experiment with different moods and rhythms in your writing; and
- choose topics you know and care about.

THE PERSONAL ESSAY

Elements of the personal essay include the following:

- a distinctive voice;
- a sense of intimacy between writer and reader;

- the feeling that the writer is trying to figure something out;
- an air of honesty, often vulnerability;
- a story that is specific but has some universal interest or application; and
- a focus ultimately on the author's way of thinking, rather than on the story itself.

CHAPTER EXERCISES

1. *Describing Voice*—Read one of the pieces in A Taste for Reading at the end of Chapters 1–17, and describe the author's voice.
2. *Comparing Sentences*—Analyze the sentence structures (as we did in Chapter 8) contained in a paragraph from each of the four writers quoted in this chapter.
3. *Comparing Voices*—Choose two or three pieces in this book, and compare and contrast all the elements of voice.
4. *Analyzing Voices*—Choose a speech on www.americanrhetoric.com and analyze the elements of its voice.
5. *Experimenting with Voice*—Describe a vivid memory from your childhood as if you were talking about it today. Then describe it as if you were that age again. What changes did you make in your word choice and sentence structure? Why?
6. *Writing Your Voice*—Describe the effects of the following punctuation marks and style conventions: comma, semicolon, period, exclamation point, question mark, em dash, parentheses, italics, all capitals.
7. *Analyzing the Role of Punctuation*—Go back to the four paragraphs you compared in Exercise 2. What role does punctuation play in creating the different voices?

IDEAS FOR WRITING

1. Describe your own or a friend's speaking voice. What do the various elements reveal about the personality and values of the speaker?
2. In what ways is punctuating a sentence like setting lyrics to music or putting clothes on a body? Can you think of other analogies?
3. Describe an event that took an unexpected turn or that became unexpectedly important.
4. Write a personal essay about one of the following topics:
   - Describe a grandparent or other family member whom you admire.
   - Describe a risk you have taken or a challenge you have faced. What happened?
   - Describe an event or decision that haunts you.
   - Tell the story of your most frightening or embarrassing experience.

CHAPTER 11
TELLING A STORY

By the end of this chapter, you should begin to . . .

- identify the basic ingredients of a story;
- understand the value of stories in different writing contexts;
- write and revise a story to fit your purpose, paying attention to the series of events, use of detail, and point of view;
- organize your story effectively; and
- recognize the potential of stories for personal growth.

Stories make up a significant part of our conversations, our writing, even our thinking, whether we tell about a series of events or the development of an idea. Much of our conversation with family and friends involves giving an account of "what happened today." We're hungry for stories, from books and tweets read by millions to movies and Facebook posts seen around the world. Storytelling can also be an important part of the writing *process.* When you first approach a piece of writing, it's often helpful to begin as if you're telling a story to a friend. The impulse is so natural that it can frequently move us past any hesitation or blockage we might have in writing an "essay." Sometimes a story becomes part of the essay. In fact, cognitive scientists suggest that storytelling is fundamental to the way the brain operates, to the way it processes and creates meaning out of the data it gathers. Stories are the organs through which we "taste" our lives.

A TASTE FOR CALCULUS

The 1988 film *Stand and Deliver* tells the true story of math teacher Jaime Escalante, whose hard work and dedication helped his students from a "low-performing" high school in East Los Angeles exceed the low academic expectations set for them both by outsiders and by the students themselves. Escalante used innovative classroom techniques to awaken their math sense, including donning the cap of a short-order cook and cutting up an apple so that students could "taste" fractions. Part of Escalante's success was due to the time he spent with students *outside* the classroom. Although young Angel is gifted in mathematics, he's initially reluctant to pursue it because it's not

In *Stand and Deliver*, math teacher Jaime Escalante (right) uses the warmth and intimacy of his kitchen to encourage Angel to study.

cool. But Escalante is persistent, and wisely uses the warmth and intimacy of his own kitchen to build the mutual respect and trust that inspires Angel to commit himself to learning.

Like many good stories, *Stand and Deliver* is full of plot twists and complicated characters. Once Angel and the other students begin to focus on math, Escalante is impressed with their abilities and decides to teach them calculus. He asks them to attend summer school in a boiling classroom, to ignore the lure of gang life and avoid the risk of pregnancy, to overcome their own fear—and society's expectation—that they will fail. Then in the middle of it all, he suffers a serious heart attack. When the students finally take the AP Calculus exam and score mostly 4s and 5s, the story twists again as they're accused of cheating on the test and have to gear up to retake it.

Through the story, we in the audience can "taste" the daily life and culture of these characters. We can feel the slow emergence of hope as they begin to believe in themselves. Any of us with math anxiety might catch a glimpse of a world where math is manageable. Stories can lead us into places we're ignorant of or perhaps reluctant to visit. Stories can shock or soothe, inspire or disgust. They are powerful tools for the writer.

THE INGREDIENTS OF A STORY

A story answers the question *What happened?* Many of our sentences in early childhood reflect the impulse to answer that question: I fell down, or I saw a big dog. When we tell a story to someone in person, we have an idea about who that person is, what that audience is like, and therefore how much background information we need to provide and what "style" or vocabulary will be most appropriate. The audience can also ask for more information. With a written story, however, we don't always know much about the audience, our readers, and we must think carefully about what they need to know in order to understand the events we're about to describe. Don't assume that the audience knows anything about you or any other aspect of the story. Thus, while one important ingredient of a story is the events that happen, another is the background information or context that makes those events clear and meaningful. The story of *Stand and Deliver*, for example, would have an entirely different effect if set in a wealthy white suburb.

In telling a story, you will probably want to explain who the **characters** are, where the story takes place (**setting**), and what happens (**plot**). As we saw in Chapter 4, it's often helpful to develop ideas through asking and answering questions. See Figure 11.1.

Figure 11.1 The Ingredients of a Story

The Characters

Who are the characters in the story?
How are they related?
How old are they?
What are they like? What do they want?
Furthermore, who is *telling* the story? Is it one of the characters speaking in the first person? Or is it someone outside the story using the third person?

The Setting

Where and when does the story take place?
What does the area look like?
Does the setting explain or illustrate something about the story? If it plays an important role, be sure to describe the setting more carefully.
Could this story take place in another setting?

The Plot

What happens in the story?
What's the central idea, often a problem or conflict? What additional complications or twists appear throughout the story? How is the problem resolved?
Will you tell the story chronologically, that is, from beginning to end, or will you move around in time? If so, what advantage does that have for the reader?
Will you tell the story in the past, present, or future tense?

The Point

Why do the events happen? Why is *this* story important? Stories may *suggest or imply* a reason for the events, as well as explain why the events are important.

Let's look at an example.

Back in the late 1970s, my grandparents bought and remodeled a pub in Farmington, Michigan. Our long-time day manager has been a fiery Irishwoman named Carol. She and I get along just fine, but occasionally we like to play pranks on each other. Usually they're nothing serious, but this time I might have gone too far!

One day I step into the walk-in and notice a primal cut of beef that still has the head on it. As soon as I see this, the gears in my mind shake the dust off and start to turn. My plan is complete. This will be the prank to end all pranks. The pure horror of it will send shivers down even the bravest men's spines.

After breaking down the primal, I remove the head and stick it upside down in the freezer. Twelve hours should congeal the blood into a thick pudding. The plan is to put the head in the beer cooler. The beer cooler is Carol's cooler, and she gets mad if anyone messes with it. Every day around 8:00 a.m. she goes down and takes inventory. I put the head upright on a sheet tray on top of a keg. I open the mouth and pull out the tongue so that it is flopping around like a wet noodle. The trap is set; it's a waiting game now.

Exactly at eight o'clock the next morning she comes downstairs and walks into the cooler. I'm standing behind the line waiting to hear a blood curdling scream, but there is only silence. I peek around the line into the cooler, and I see Carol standing there, face to face with this bloody cow head. It couldn't be more perfect. The blood has started to thaw, so it is dripping out of every orifice it can find. I can see this red jelly-like substance coming out its ears, nose, eyes, mouth, and the severed section of its neck.

Finally Carol snaps out of her trance. I see this twisted face come over her, as if someone has poked her with a hot skillet, and she runs out of the kitchen. After she leaves, I go take a closer look. There is blood everywhere. It's all over the keg and all over the floor, and it's seeping out into the main kitchen area.

It takes me about an hour to clean up all the mess. Then I go upstairs to gloat. I find out that Carol was so disturbed by the sight of the cow head that she got sick in the bathroom and went home. Upon hearing that, I realize that maybe I've gone a little too far. Unfortunately, that is the end of the pranks.

—**Brendan Cowley**, student writer

The first paragraph of the story introduces us to the two main characters: the narrator and Carol. We find out that the narrator's family has owned a pub in Michigan for some thirty years and that Carol has been employed there for a long time. We learn that Carol is "fiery," although she gets along well with the narrator, and that they like to play pranks on each other. This first paragraph also zeroes in on the problem: "This time I might have gone too far."

The chain of events is clear; we know what happened and when. After explaining the background of the story in the first paragraph, the writer follows the events in simple **chronological order**—that is, in the order in which they occurred—and uses a number of **transitional expressions** to assist in keeping the sequence clear, such as "after breaking down the primal," "exactly at 8 o'clock," and "then I go upstairs." Not all stories are told in sequence, of course. Such films as *Pulp Fiction* and *Memento* demonstrate that stories can move backward, forward, almost sideways, and still be clear to the audience.

In telling about the "primal" prank, the writer includes another important ingredient of a good story: details. Not only do we *know* what happened, but we can also *see* it, from preparing the bloody cow head to watching its effect on Carol. The details are particularly gruesome and effective: "I put the head upright on a sheet tray on top of a keg. I open the mouth and pull out the tongue so that it is flopping around like a wet noodle. The trap is set." The image of the noodle is an especially nice touch! And how about this gruesome image: "The blood has started to thaw, so it is dripping out of every orifice it can find. I can see this red jelly-like substance coming out its ears, nose, eyes, mouth, and the severed section of its neck." The description of Carol's reaction also contains effective details: "I see this twisted face come over her, as if someone has poked her with a hot skillet, and she runs out of the kitchen."

Brendan fills his story with excitement and anticipation. How does he do this? First, he prepares us even in the very first paragraph for something unusual: "This time I might have gone too far." The anticipation is heightened in the second paragraph with these provocative statements: "This will be the prank to end all pranks. The pure horror of it will send shivers down even the bravest men's spines." The suspense is maintained by the rhythm of the story. We don't get to the punch line too quickly; we dwell on the horrific details, down to "waiting to hear a bloodcurdling scream." Finally, like the narrator, we "peek around the line into the cooler" and "see Carol standing there, face to face with this bloody cow head." Good timing is a terrific bonus in storytelling. Without actually stopping—as we might do in telling the story to a live audience—the

"I see Carol standing there, face to face with this bloody cow head."

writer uses sentences that continue to give some information but at the same time create pauses in the action. "It couldn't be more perfect," he writes, before we actually get to the climactic moment:

> It couldn't be more perfect. The blood has started to thaw, so it is dripping out of every orifice it can find. I can see this red jelly-like substance coming out its ears, nose, eyes, mouth, and the severed sections of its neck.

The use of the first person, *I*, and the present tense also contribute to the immediacy and drama of the story. Look what happens with a change to the *third* person and the *past* tense:

> Finally Carol snapped out of her trance. Brendan saw this twisted face come over her, as if someone had poked her with a hot skillet, and she ran out of the kitchen. After she left, Brendan went to take a closer look. There was blood everywhere. It was all over the keg and all over the floor, and it was seeping out into the main kitchen area.

It's still detailed and exciting, but it's finished. The blood isn't "all over" the kitchen floor *right now*.

As the narrative comes to a close, the writer tells us what happened to Carol: "She got sick in the bathroom and went home." Further, "that is the end of the pranks." The reader likes to know what happened at the end of a story. Think of movies like *Remember the Titans* and *Apollo 13*, in which lines of text just before the closing credits tell us in a nutshell what happened to the characters we've become attached to. Did Jim Lovell ever make it to the moon? we wonder. The film tells us he did not. The audience also likes to know why the story is important. For example, the primal cut prank is significant because it's the one that axed the series, while at the end of *Remember the Titans*, we learn that the movie was based on the true story of a turning point for race relations in Virginia.

THE IMPORTANCE OF STORIES

Stories are fun. Entertainment. Escape. And that last word seems to have a negative connotation, especially in the Puritanical stream that still flows through American culture. We should be working all the time, productive all the time, cry the Puritans. If it feels good, it must be bad. And stories do feel good. Yet they have more "serious" uses.

Storytelling is one of the six abilities that Daniel Pink identifies in *A Whole New Mind: Why Right Brainers Will Rule the Future* as essential for job success in the twenty-first century, what he calls the Conceptual Age. Prior to this, in the so-called Information Age, we needed people whose job was to master the new technology and find information. However, information is now so easily retrieved that what we need is people who can put it into context, interpret it, explain what it means. That, says Pink, is the job of Story.

He describes companies whose success relies on the effective use and interpretation of stories. For example,

> Xerox—recognizing that its repair personnel learned to fix machines by trading stories rather than by reading manuals—has collected its stories into a database called Eureka that *Fortune* estimates is worth $100 million to the company. In addition, several ventures have emerged to help existing companies harvest their internal stories. One such firm is StoryQuest, based in suburban Chicago. It dispatches interviewers to a company, records the stories of that company's employees, and then produces a CD that uses these personal narratives to yield broader insights about the company's culture and mission. In the United Kingdom . . . clients read and act Shakespeare's plays to elicit lessons in leadership and corporate governance. (106)

Stories are also effective marketing tools. In looking at colleges, for example, you may find that admission materials often include stories about past and current students. Angie's List compiles stories—good or bad—about specific companies to help readers make an informed choice among them. Lawyers know that putting the "facts" of the case into a compelling, credible *narrative* is a powerful persuasive strategy. And marketing research suggests that viewers are more likely to remember a television commercial that tells a story than one that simply describes the product.

Why are stories so useful? They are part of the way human beings think, how we process and remember information and experiences. Pink explains:

> Stories are easier to remember [than facts]—because in many ways stories are *how* we remember. "Narrative imagining—story—is the fundamental instrument of thought," writes cognitive scientist Mark Turner in his book *The Literary Mind.* "Rational capacities depend on it. It is our chief means of looking into the future, of predicting, of planning, and of explaining. . . . Most of our experience, our knowledge and our thinking is organized as stories." (99)

Because of the way they are embedded in our brains, stories are often used in quite serious contexts. The story of a particular individual can highlight a general problem, increase understanding, and motivate action. The actor Michael J. Fox, for instance, has used his story in working on behalf of those suffering from Parkinson's disease.

Stories can also be a part of the way we heal. For example, Pink describes a new program at Columbia University Medical School, where Dr. Rita Charon "is attempting to place story at the heart of diagnosis and healing. . . . [A]ll second-year medical students take a seminar in narrative medicine in addition to their hardcore science classes" (110, 111). Pink quotes Dr. Howard Brody, a family practice physician:

Stories—that's how people make sense of what's happening to them when they get sick. They tell stories about themselves. Our ability as doctors to treat and heal is bound up in our ability to accurately perceive a patient's story. If you can't do that, you're working with your hands tied behind your back. (110)

Vietnam veteran and author Tim O'Brien explores stories' potential for healing the writer. Although his conclusions are ambiguous, he notes in *The Things They Carried* (213): "But this too is true: stories can save us." Healing, both physical and psychological, is the theme of two of the stories in this chapter, "My Father" and "The Story of a Moment."

WRITING AND REVISING A STORY

Although this book is not about writing fiction or poetry or screenplays, many other types of writing, including academic and business writing, often contain narrative elements. For example, Lynne Truss's popular guide to punctuation, *Eats, Shoots & Leaves*, illustrates the importance of the comma with a funny story about a panda's visit to a café. Or think about how often a restaurant review includes the *story* of the meal—setting, characters, plot—as well as a description of the food. Stories appear frequently in other kinds of food writing as well. M. F. K. Fisher, for example, weaves her own narrative through her essays about food. In the excerpt from *Kitchen Confidential* in Chapter 10, Anthony Bourdain tells the story of his first meaningful experience with taste. Even a very short story can add significant interest, emotion, and information.

Whether long or short, the story you need to write can be explored with the same basic questions listed in Figure 11.1. In your brainstorming, think about the purpose of the story and what specific moment or insight you want to highlight. Ask yourself what readers need to know in order to see the story as you do, and what they want to know just because they're curious.

Sometimes the elements of a story—the setting, characters, and events—are so clear in our minds that jumping directly into writing can be as effective as brainstorming. Perhaps a cross between freewriting and drafting works well. You may wish to write to yourself—or you may wish to imagine yourself telling the story to a friend over a cup of coffee. At some point, of course, you will need to identify the particular audience of your story and ensure that your readers have the information they need.

As you're writing, try to relive or imagine the story as vividly as possible. Use descriptive details to help the reader see and hear what's going on. As with all initial drafts, don't stop and edit yourself critically. See the story in your mind as you write it on the page. Perhaps you can imagine an expressive audience, telling you with a look when more information or explanation is required. It's easy to assume that the reader knows what you know, but that may not be the case. Instead, you must learn to think outside your own skull. Figure out who your audience is, and anticipate what background information will help that audience understand the story you want to tell.

A SERIES OF EVENTS

A story is a series of events. Whatever sequence you choose for a particular series, your audience needs to know what that sequence is, that is, the order in which those events occur. Thus, it is important that the verbs in a story reflect the order in which things happen by sticking consistently to one **tense**, whether it be past, present, or future. If an action occurs out of the main sequence, however, the verb must indicate that, too. For example, in the story about the primal cut prank, most of the verbs are in the **present tense**, and the sequence of events unfolds in that time frame. The very first sentence, though, is in the **past tense** because it indicates a time some twenty-five years earlier. Another variation occurs in the last paragraph: "I find out that Carol was so disturbed by the sight of the cow head that she got sick in the bathroom and went home." *Find* is in the present tense since it is part of the main character's sequence of events. However, *was, got,* and *went* are in the past tense because those things happened *before* the narrator found out about them.

DETAILS

When you're telling a story, you want to give the reader enough detail—but not too much. Use details to create pictures, smells, and tastes in the reader's mind. Even the smallest details can make a difference. For example, what picture do you get in the following sentence: *I ate some fruit.* Not much of an image here, right? What about the next sentence?

> I ate a Fuji apple, thinly sliced and arranged in concentric circles on a dark blue plate.

Now we *see* the fruit.

Details often provide essential information on character and setting, and keep the reader focused on what is important. Don't use details simply to fill space or because you want to toss in some big words. Keep details specific and relevant.

Finally, be sure your reader understands the point of the story, its beating heart. You may state it directly—"This will be the prank to end all pranks"—or you may choose to let an image convey your point, as in the following story.

My Father

My dad has always been a serious person. He doesn't laugh or smile too often. He also doesn't show very much emotion to his friends and family. I've never seen my father crying, angry, stressed, or even confused about something. My father would show his affection to my brothers and me by slapping us behind the head. It was his way of saying, How was your day? or Everything will be all right, I am here for you. I remember one time when I asked my father for a hug, he just looked at me with a crooked eye, gave me a slap on the back, and went on his way. I always did wonder why he was like that, but he would never tell me.

I thought that I would never see my father show some emotion, until one day I woke up screaming with pain in my stomach. My parents rushed me to the hospital, and the doctor found out that my appendix had to be removed. So the next day, the day of my surgery, the doctor made a mistake and cut my stomach wrong, and they could not close my wound. About three hours later, they finally sealed the wound, and I was asleep in my hospital room. That night I woke up crying because of all the pain. The nurse gave me some pills to calm me down, but the pain was too strong. The doctor had to come down into my room, reopen my wound, and reseal it while I was awake.

A day later I slightly woke up. It was about four in the morning, and I saw my father over me dripping tears. My father was praying to God, telling God not to take his only big boy, that he would rather take his own life to let me live. After a few minutes, my father wiped the tears off his face. He bent over and, not knowing I was awake, he whispered something in my ear that will always stay with me. Then he gave me a blessing and a kiss on the forehead, and left the room before my family came.

Months later, after I had fully recovered and everything was back to normal, I thought about the night when I saw my father emotional. I asked him what had happened that night. He did what he always did—looked at me with that crooked eye, gave me a slap behind my head, and went on his way. But right before he got into his car he turned around and gave me the biggest smile he's ever given anyone.

—**Moises Ortega**, student writer

By the time we've reached the end of the story, we understand all the power and delight of that smile. Having laid the groundwork in the earlier paragraphs—"He doesn't laugh or smile too often"—the writer wisely lets the final picture speak for itself. The writer also withholds some information from us: "He whispered something in my ear that will always stay with me." Like the concluding image of the smile, this undefined "something" adds a delicacy to the story that is both sophisticated in its technique and touching in its effect.

As it happens, the final draft of this story is very close to the first one. It is clearly a moment that the author has thought about. Perhaps it is a story he's told on other occasions. There were nevertheless some interesting revisions. First, the original draft contained a sentence about the author's mother: "My mother, on the other hand, is a very emotional person, but that's another story." Even as he was writing the words, he realized that they belonged somewhere else, perhaps in a different story. Second, where the original reads simply "he just looked at me," the final draft adds "he just looked at me with a crooked eye." That tiny detail hints at something behind the father's look, for example, an impulse to express his feelings.

Another change is as simple as one word. Where the first draft says "I saw my father over me *shedding* tears," the final reads, "I saw my father over me *dripping* tears." The second choice is less common and somehow more poignant. The tears are not noisy, yet they cannot be stopped. Finally, a small change to the concluding paragraph has the effect of tying the story together with the repetition of a phrase. In the first draft, when asked what happened that night, the father "looked at me weird." In the final version, however, the father "looked at me with that crooked eye," a phrase that recalls the effective image from the second paragraph and prepares us for the final picture, as the crooked eye is unraveled by a big smile.

POINT OF VIEW

Choosing an effective **point of view** for your story is important. The story about the primal cut is told from the point of view of a narrator who uses the first person (*I*) and is also a participant in the action. It has the effect of implicating the reader in Carol's distress—maybe it's the end of the pranks for us as well as Brendan. Another story in the first person is *The Hunger Games*. We have complete access to *Katniss's* thoughts, but not to the thoughts of others. We have to interpret what she sees in light of our own experience. It's a *limited* point of view. Stories are often written in the third person as

In the last scene of *About a Boy*, the two lonely "boys" celebrate Christmas with their new friends.

well, and if that's the case, the author must choose whether to enter the minds of one or more characters, or simply to narrate the events.

A pair of first-person points of view is used effectively in the movie *About a Boy*, based on the novel by Nick Hornby. The story unfolds initially from two entirely different perspectives, that of Will, a 38-year-old bachelor, and that of Marcus, the 12-year-old son of a struggling single "mum." Not only do we see the events through their eyes (figuratively speaking—it's not a first-person shooter), but we hear the thoughts in their heads, often with hilarious results. When Will, for example, is following the ambulance containing Marcus's unconscious mother, his voice-over reveals that although he's aware of the seriousness of the situation, he's really pumped to be racing in pursuit of the siren and flashing lights. In the final scene of the film, Marcus has the last word—he's happy that the two lonely "boys" have "backup" at last.

Occasionally, a story is told in the second person, which creates an interesting and unusual texture in the story, as in this example:

> The nut cooler when you open the door has three sides filled with stainless steel shelves containing boxes and clear bins filled with nuts. Pecans, pistachios, cashews, walnuts, even sunflower seeds are stacked all the way to a grown man's head. You can hear the sound of the nuts being poured into bags. If an almond sliver happens to land in your mouth, the thin, crisp sliver with its tan skin greets your taste buds with a rich nutty flavor.
>
> —**Caitlin Crowley**, student writer

I especially enjoy the author's sly observation "If an almond sliver *happens* to land in your mouth," as if the nuts have a life of their own. The second person works well here, and, more important, it is used consistently throughout the essay. Whichever point of view you choose, stay with it, and focus on the pronouns. Do not switch back and forth between *I* and *you*, for example (see also Chapter 26).

> I was walking down the crowded city street when **you** saw one of those hot dog stands in a cart. [*unnecessary shift from I to you*]
>
> I was walking down the crowded city street when **I** saw one of those hot dog stands in a cart. [*consistent use of I*]

Note that just because you've taken a first-person point of view doesn't mean you won't have to use the pronouns *he, she,* or *they* when speaking about other characters in your story. And if you've chosen the unconventional second-person point of view, you might also need to use some third-person pronouns. The most likely "error" in point of view is an unnecessary and distracting jump to *you* in the middle of a story about *I* or *she.*

ORGANIZING YOUR STORY

Time is a somewhat elusive concept for human beings. Although we measure it in scientifically accurate minutes and hours, we often *experience* it as moving at different speeds. Time can "stand still" as we slip in the kitchen and realize the tray of china we're carrying is going to crash onto the floor, or it can speed by when we're hoping to delay taking a test. The way we tell a story can reflect that. It doesn't make for a good story if we narrate the events too evenly, minute by minute, without any sense of building to a climax. In his story of the primal cut, for example, Brendan Cowley gives us a blow-by-blow account, but only of important events so that the action *rises* toward the climactic discovery of the bloody head.

One part of organizing your story is selecting the important events to tell and the important details to describe. Another part of organization, though, has to do with the *chronology* or sequence of events. You could decide to tell the story in strict chronological order, that is, from beginning to end. Many stories are told this way. Or, you might choose to start **in medias res**, in the middle of things, as the ancient Greek poet Homer did. When telling the story of the Trojan War in the *Iliad*, he began in the ninth year of the ten-year conflict. Or you might frame the story as a **flashback**, as Steven Spielberg does in *Saving Private Ryan.* We start out looking at an emotional man in uniform in a cemetery in 1994, then flash back fifty years to the series of events that led to the "saving" of Private Ryan, then flash forward again to the cemetery, this time with a full awareness of what this moment means to Ryan.

In the story "Salt Cod, Alaska," student writer Robert Hannon essentially tells *two* stories, one embedded within the other like a flashback. (Read the full story on p. 199.) The narrative begins with a recent meal in his culinary school, a meal he'd have to write about for his class in gastronomy.

> The appetizer was Brandade de Morue, which sounded exotic and intriguing in French. Then I read the translation, and the words "salt cod" splashed through me like the frigid Alaskan ocean in the state where I'd first tasted it.

The writer pauses a moment on the threshold of the memory, which is not a happy one. Here, then, is the problem—he is presented with that very dish in a situation that will make it impossible for him to decline it. As he stares at the menu, he shares the story of Bebe, his roommate in a fish factory one summer in Alaska, and of Bebe's salt cod, which the writer vowed "never to taste" again.

What are the advantages of embedding one story within the other? Why not go chronologically—tell the story about Bebe's *bacalao,* then the Brandade de Morue? By setting the earlier story within the later one, we've raised the stakes. It doesn't matter that Rob didn't like the *bacalao* when he tried it in Alaska—what matters is that he's now in a situation where he *must* eat it again.

Organizing "Salt Cod, Alaska"

"Setting" the Scene
at the Culinary Institute of America
eagerly anticipating an experience
of haute cuisine

Outlining the Problem
small mauve menu reveals a dish to
which the writer has a strong aversion:
salt cod
but he has to write an essay about it
for a gastronomy course

Memory
the source of the problem
Bebe and his Bacalao
it smelled like rotting fish

I lifted a tiny spoonful
a potent saltiness filled my mouth
I spit out the fish and frantically brushed my teeth
Bebe howled with amusement
I vowed never to taste salt cod again

Climax
a single delicate cod cake

Problem Solved
despite my previous experience
I really enjoyed the salt cod
Bebe would never believe it

TAKING A RISK

Every day I encourage students to be open and genuine in their writing, to write about what's important to them, to take risks. It isn't always easy. To reveal our thoughts may make us feel vulnerable, while to relive our pain may seem intolerable. No one has impressed me more with her courage in this respect than Lori Vrazel, a student who, when asked to write about a moment that had changed her life, allowed herself to revisit a moment of terrible pain, to remember the smallest details, to press forward and continue writing and rewriting until the story felt complete.

The Story of a Moment

I'll never forget that cool autumn evening that changed my life forever. It was a beautiful fall sunset with the sun's crimson glow illuminating the sky and the crisp southern winds whipping past. As I walked into my house, I found it busy with activity. However, as the phone rang, everyone grew quiet. My mother began to speak with a smiling face, but that faded away. An unsettling silence was all that was left from the commotion of before. My family members gathered around the kitchen table with looks of woe across their faces. Suddenly, we noticed our mother's eyes had filled with tears which began to fall like sparkling rain drops. Then she muttered, "Aaron. He's been in a car accident. He's not responding." That was all she could manage to say, and a flood of emotion engulfed my family.

The emotions that I saw from my family members on this day were unlike any that I had ever seen from them before or since. My sister began to despair and tears formed in her eyes. This was the first time that I had ever seen her so vulnerable. My brother began to pace back and forth out of anxiety. However, I could not build up enough strength within me to even move, so I just sat down and watched the others.

Just as the sun finished setting and happiness disappeared, Dad arrived. I found my father's display of emotion to be the most unsettling. He simply rushed around gathering clothes for his journey to the hospital. I could tell that he was trying to stay strong, but his heart's pain got the better of him, especially when he was about to get into his car to leave. As my father stood near the narrow doorway to the dark carport, his eyes filled with tears and he told me, "Lori. Don't worry. I'll bring him home to us." Then my mother and he swiftly got into the car and drove away.

Seeing my father cry made everything seem real to me, and I finally reacted. I got up from the large round kitchen table and walked outside, ignoring all of the sorrow within the house. I needed to be alone, and I was alone outside in the garden. Everything was dark and dreary as I wandered over to the white bench swing that was covered with flowers. It was here that I realized that everything was going to be different. I realized how abruptly life is taken, and with this understanding I found myself wanting to change. I sat down and quickly said a prayer asking God to please let Aaron live. Suddenly, a warm moist tear ran down my cheek, and it was soon followed by what seemed to be millions more.

There were no words that could describe the pain inside of us, and there was nothing that we could do to change the day's events. I had never seen my family as helpless as they were the day the news of Aaron arrived at our home. Life as I knew it changed. I no longer thought of it as a solid structure that was almost impossible to break. The only thing left for me to do was to take Aaron's death and mold it into a positive force. I wanted to make him and me proud. So I gathered up all of my dreams and hopes for the future and leaped into life with him by side.

—**Lori Vrazel Kallinikos**, student writer

This story has stayed with me for years. And the best thing about it is that it's helped Lori to remember and honor her brother, "to take Aaron's death and mold it into a positive force." This is the real power of stories—to make sense of our experience. It is the power to heal.

A TASTE FOR READING

Robert A. Hannon wrote this story while a student at the Culinary Institute of America.

****

Salt Cod, Alaska
by Robert A. Hannon

I strode into Alumni Hall, the main dining room at the Culinary Institute of America, eagerly anticipating our "stage meal," which was served to us in the haute cuisine style. We were served this meal daily during the first three weeks of our curriculum. Haute cuisine is a French concept based upon culinary principles and methods that the school (as well as the French!) considers the fundamental building blocks of fine cooking and dining.

I glanced at the small mauve menu, which described the three courses we were to be served. I was slightly anxious, because the meal would be consumed with the knowledge that I'd be writing about it for a gastronomy assignment. The appetizer was Brandade de Morue, which sounded exotic and intriguing in French. Then I read the translation, and the words "salt cod" splashed through me like the frigid Alaskan ocean in the state where I'd first tasted it. Instantly, in this haute cuisine setting (fine French food served by skilled cooks to discerning gourmands on tables bedecked with crystal, linen, and perfectly placed silverware), I was overwhelmed by memories of my friend Bebe and my college summer working in a salmon processing plant in Kodiak, Alaska. I felt a tinge of irritation as well. I didn't like salt cod, based on my summer experience with Bebe, and yet here I was staring at salt cod, when there were so many more desirable, less mundane items to cook and serve.

Bebe was my roommate in the salmon plant, where we worked up to twenty hours a day gutting salmon on a slime line. We became friends, enjoying fishing for Coho (Silver) salmon in Kodiak Sound, hiking the emerald grassy hills, and exploring what little night life existed in Kodiak. Only one thing about Bebe was bothersome: his Philippine Bacalao, the salt cod that he cooked in a rice cooker in our room every morning. He'd always offer it to me, and I'd always decline. It smelled like the rotting Chum salmon that we'd encounter on our fishing excursions. I did promise Bebe I'd try it, though as the summer progressed and he ate his accursed Bacalao every morning, I found myself fervently hoping he'd forget my vow.

Unfortunately, Bebe had an excellent memory, and a few days before my departure back to Seattle, he appeared with a foul bowl of Bacalao. "Come on, Bobby, it is very good for you," he said. Tentative, I lifted a tiny spoonful to my mouth and tasted it. A potent saltiness filled my mouth, followed by a rank fishiness. The flavor was

© Julie Flavin Photography/www.Shutterstock.com

"The words 'salt cod' splashed through me like the frigid Alaskan ocean."

more concentrated and far more disagreeable than the smell. I spit the spoonful into the bowl, and, as Bebe howled with amusement, I ran down the narrow wooden hallway of the dormitory, grabbed my tooth brush, and scrubbed frantically. Despite my efforts, the taste persisted through the day. I brushed my teeth, and washed my face and lips continuously, like an innocent Lady Macbeth. Finally the taste subsided, and I made a solemn vow never to taste salt cod again.

Yet here was salt cod on the menu, and I really had no choice but to sample it: we were on stage, and I needed to write about it for an assignment. When the dish arrived, I sniffed nervously, but could detect no fishy odor. The dish itself was visually appealing, a colorful arrangement of complementary colors and designs. A single delicate cod cake, golden brown and perfectly round, rested atop a salad of micro greens. The light and dark greens were commingled with cubes of red and yellow peppers. The dish was encircled with an almost fluorescent lime-green parsley dressing. The cake crackled between my teeth as I bit into it. The flavor was clean and sweet, tinted with garlic, and was only slightly salty. The micro greens added an appealing bitterness and were a piquant counter-balance to the cod. The sour tang of the dressing cleansed my palate.

Despite my previous experience with salt cod, I really enjoyed the dish, and finished the entire plate. I'm sure Bebe would never believe that I could enjoy salt cod, but then he's probably never eaten Brandade de Morue. I doubt he'd like it, though; I'm quite sure he'd find it insipid and egregiously lacking in flavor.

—**Robert A. Hannon**, student writer

ABOUT THE READING

- What is the central problem in the story? Is it resolved? Explain.
- What details or images do you find particularly striking? What do they add to the story's development of character or theme?
- Outline the organization of the story. Why does the writer choose to frame one story within the other? How would the story be different if told in strictly chronological order?
- Describe the writer's "voice" in the story.

RECIPE FOR REVIEW

THE INGREDIENTS OF A STORY

A story answers the question *What happened?* Key ingredients include characters, setting, and plot. Stories are often enriched with vivid descriptive details, a complex problem for the characters, suspense, surprising twists and turns in the plot, and some deeper meaning.

THE IMPORTANCE OF STORIES

Cognitive scientists believe we process and remember information and experiences through stories. Stories can entertain, inform, and heal.

WRITING AND REVISING A STORY

- Determine the series of events you want to use, and which you want to emphasize. Use the same tense (past or present) for events in sequence. Use the appropriate tense for those events that might be out of that sequence (see also Chapter 25).
- Use details to emphasize what is important and to create a picture for the reader. Include only important details—but include enough of them.
- While point of view is a complex aspect of storytelling that you may wish to explore further, the most basic need is to choose a point of view (first, second, or third person) that suits your purpose. Then use pronouns consistently to fit that point of view (see also Chapter 26).

ORGANIZING YOUR STORY

You might choose a straightforward chronological order for your story, or you might begin *in medias res* (in the middle of things). Your central story might be framed as a flashback, as in *Saving Private Ryan*. Or you may choose to weave back and forth between different times, as in *Into the Wild*.

CHAPTER EXERCISES

1. *Ingredients of a Story*—What was your favorite story as a child? Briefly describe its ingredients by answering the questions in Figure 11.1. Then explain why it was your favorite.
2. *The Importance of Stories*—Find two or three examples of stories used in a serious, nonliterary context, and describe their effect.
3. *Using Stories in Your Writing*—Find a restaurant review that contains a story. What is the setting? Who are the characters? What are the main events?
4. José Antonio Burciaga tells quite a few small stories in his essay "Tortillas" (Chapter 4). List as many as you can find. Then choose one and explain how it is used in the essay.
5. *Consistent Tense*—Read the following paragraph (adapted from an essay by Caitlin Crowley) and put all the verbs in the past and then the present tense. Which do you prefer? Why?

> As you walk along, you found the rough brown potato sacks, the cold plastic wrap of lettuce, and the damp cardboard. One box is holding leeks, long rubbery shocks of white and green. Next to them were the mustard greens, with their small, thin, deep green, frilly leaves that are still glistening with water. As you pick off a piece and chew a leaf, you experienced a hot mustard taste in your mouth, but only for a second.

6. *Analyzing the Ingredients of a Story*—Who are the characters in the story "My Father"? What do we know about them? We aren't told where or when the story takes place—does it matter? Explain. What is the problem in the story? How is it resolved?
7. *Describing an Experience with Food*—Do you have any food aversions; that is, is there any food that you strongly dislike? Write a paragraph in which you describe the food in vivid detail. Make the reader dislike it, too. Now write another paragraph in which you imagine that you've had a new experience with the food and have come to enjoy it. Make the reader enjoy it, too.

IDEAS FOR WRITING

1. Tell a story about a friend, family member, or yourself that illustrates something important about that person.
2. Tell the story of the worst or funniest experience you've ever had at work or school, or eating in a restaurant.
3. Tell the story of an argument you had recently with a friend or family member— from your point of view. Then, rewrite the story from *the other person's* point of view. What did you learn about the incident?
4. Does it make a difference whether a story is "true" or not? Explain, using specific examples.

CHAPTER 12
WORKING WITH DESCRIPTIVE DETAILS

By the end of this chapter, you should begin to . . .

- use vivid sensory details to improve descriptions;
- write effective descriptions of food;
- identify specific rather than general descriptive terms;
- create a particular impression through organizing your description effectively; and
- flavor your descriptions with figurative language.

Good storytellers provide details about how things look, sound, smell, taste, and feel. They are sensual. Our response to a good storyteller might be, "Oh yes, I *see* that. I *see* what you mean." Good cooks are also highly sensual. They offer us a plate of peppers, vibrant red, yellow, orange, and green. We hear the crisp fragments of a potato chip break between our teeth; we feel the rubbery skin of apple give way to a burst of juice. The more we can use vivid descriptive details in our writing, the more our readers will understand and enjoy it. In fact, as you might imagine, **description** is an especially important part of writing in the hospitality industry, from menus and restaurant reviews to proposals for prospective investors.

Descriptive details that evoke the five senses are especially effective. If we wrote "that meat was amazing," we would actually communicate very little. But what about "the cube of tenderloin had a crispy brown outer layer with inner stripes of light brown and finally pink"? There is no need to use fancy or dramatic language; often a simple, almost scientific, vocabulary is more effective. You're trying to create a picture for the reader, not knock him out with your big words.

Description can also suffer from a reliance on old, tired words and phrases. Were you "hungry as a horse" when you entered the restaurant? Did the dish "melt in your mouth"? When someone first said these things, they would have seemed new and fresh. However, these expressions are now used so often by so many people that they have become **clichés** (see Chapter 9). If everyone fills in the blanks with the same word (for example, cool as a cucumber), the phrase is so old that it can't really tell us anything new.

SENSORY DETAILS

The five senses—sight, smell, taste, touch, and hearing—provide outstanding descriptive details. We don't need to use every one of the senses for every description, and we don't need to go overboard, but a well-chosen phrase about a texture or an aroma can pull the reader immediately into the world of our thoughts. "The new desert uniforms were stiff and scratchy," writes Dale Andrews about his deployment to Kuwait, while Luis Bustamante describes a Belgian chocolate's "soft hints of vanilla, cinnamon and almonds" and "strong, rich cocoa butter aroma." Research indicates that just reading about textures and scents activates the part of the brain we'd use if we were *really* touching and smelling.[6] Of course, noises and tastes are also important. Listen to the dinner rush in the following sentence:

> The clock strikes six, and your first ticket hits the board. There is an eerie silence until the sound of cold raw fish hitting a scorching hot grill fills the kitchen.
>
> —**Anthony Guarino**, student writer

Interestingly, Americans seem to rely most often on their sense of sight.[7] When asked to describe an experience, they may concentrate on what they *saw*. Yet the other four senses are also at work, receiving data and sending it to the brain for analysis. And one of these others may be far more effective in communicating your thought or feeling than sight is. The sense of smell, for example, can bring back a memory with extraordinary speed and intensity—the aroma of your mother's spaghetti sauce transports you to the dinner table of your childhood, or the unmistakable scent of a certain aftershave propels you into the ardent embrace of an old boyfriend.

In the kitchen we're immersed in all five senses. But which do we rely on most heavily during the cooking process? For many people, it's the sense of taste—but not for everyone. Monica Bhide, a "food writer by night," visited Chef Jonathan Krinn in his restaurant in Washington, D.C. Bhide relates that Krinn's interest is in French-American food, her own in Indian. While making a sauce, Krinn shocked Bhide by tasting a spoonful of the liquid. "Don't you know you're not allowed to taste while you cook?"

But Krinn is shocked in his turn. If you didn't taste the sauce, "How would you know when to season?"

Unlike most of us, Bhide learned to cook not by taste but by "sight, smell, sound and texture." Her father taught her to listen to the sound of roasting spices: "coriander whimpers, cumin smolders, mustard sizzles and cinnamon roars." He taught her to watch the colors as the spices cooked and to notice the smells. "Roast, sizzle, temper, broil, boil, bake, simmer, sauté, fry—we had to do it all by watching and listening." The reason lies in the Hindu culture. "The first offering of the food was for the gods. If you tasted while you cooked, it made the food impure." (Read the full story at the end of this chapter.)

Collage of Indian Spices

When you think about description, try not to rely on a single sense. Remember that senses other than sight can be extremely effective in evoking the experience of a particular scene.

EAT YOUR WORDS

Although they are filled with sensory experiences, food items are some of the most difficult things in the world to describe. Try to approach a food as if for the first time. Look at it with new eyes. Savor the tastes and smells and textures. Use specific, sensory words. Avoid clichés. Taste your words as carefully as you taste the foods they describe.

As you read this first example, notice that the writer uses clear, straightforward language to create a vivid picture.

I looked to my left to find the strawberries piled high in their crates,
their plump, intense red bodies spotted with black seeds like freckles,
tapering down to a rounded bottom, topped with a leafy green halo,
ripe and delicious, ready to be eaten.

—**Roth Perelman**, student writer

This writer seems to have eaten first with his eyes! Texture—the mouthfeel—is also an important part of our experience with food. In this next example, the writer reminisces about his favorite childhood dish.

> My aunt would spread the peanut butter on the toast right after it came out of the toaster, so it was melted when she brought it to me. I can still remember the warm silkiness of the peanut butter as it hit my mouth.
>
> —**Dylan Chace**, student writer

Feel the difference between the *silkiness* Dylan describes and an ordinary *smoothness*.

The sense of smell is crucial to a full enjoyment of food descriptions. Consider the following evocative portrayal of aromas:

> The aroma of the peach is very complex, with many notes intertwining in the nostrils. You can pick up a floral note, almost like a honeysuckle. Next you may pick up a sweet, almost musky scent. Perhaps the strongest aroma is honey. It smells like a very rich, wild honey, like that of the wild clover. Almond is present with the underlying aroma of vanilla. A faint scent of nutmeg can be sensed, lingering for a second.
>
> —**Elizabeth Best**, student writer

The sense of smell is also essential to the perception of *flavor*. Although we can perceive the five basic tastes—salty, sweet, sour, bitter, and umami (Figure 12.1)—with our tongues alone, we need our noses to sense the full range of flavor. Have you ever noticed that your appreciation for the flavors of food and drink is significantly diminished during a head cold? Experiment. Hold your nose and breathe through your mouth. Then eat something. Now let go of your nose and try another bite. That's the difference between *taste* and *flavor*. See Figure 12.2 for more ideas for describing flavors and aromas.

Figure 12.1 The Five Tastes

sweet   sour   salty

bitter   umami

Figure 12.2 Words for Flavors and Aromas

tasty, flavorful, palatable, savory
hot, spicy, peppery, tart, sour, bitter, salty, gingery
pungent like Dijon mustard, curry, jalapeño, fiery
pungent like onion, garlicky, cayenne
mild, bland, tasteless
sour, acerbic, acrid, tart, vinegary, green
aromatic, fragrant, perfumed
incense, musky, potpourri, flowery
sweet, sugary, honeyed, candied, syrupy, caramel
smoky, mushroomy
fruity, apples, oranges, lemony, banana, raspberry
nutty, chocolaty, mint, tarragon, basil, rosemary, thyme

SPECIFIC DETAILS

When writing a description, try to avoid both vague or general words as well as difficult or fancy words. Instead, give the reader specific details—whole scenes can be conjured by a car's make and model or by the name of a candy bar.

I sat in the front seat of an old Dodge Ram pickup truck and nibbled on a Snickers bar.

When you know the name of a specific item, use it. One caution, however—don't use the name just to use it. Be sure it fits the need of your description and doesn't distract or irritate the reader.

Compare the following two descriptions, the first using the passionate but very vague expression "awesome," the second using simple but specific words.

The chocolate ice cream was awesome.

I slipped the rich chocolatey spoonful between my lips, tasting the dark velvet, the bright ice.

That ice cream probably *was* "great." But don't *tell* the reader that; *show* him. In general, try to avoid the all-purpose, somewhat vague terms listed in Figure 12.3. Instead, use specific details to show the reader what you see and hear and taste so that it is the *reader* who exclaims, "Oh, that's beautiful" or "That sounds amazing."

CREATING AN IMPRESSION

In describing a space, it is important to help the reader *see* the relationships between the various objects. Writers do this by using specific descriptive details

Figure 12.3 Words to Avoid

amazing

awesome

awful

bad

beautiful

good

great

horrible

marvelous

terrible

wonderful

perfect

connected with spatial transitions. These words and phrases explain where one thing is in relation to another. In the following example, a description of a professional kitchen, the transitional expressions are printed in bold type.

> Because the kitchen was so small, it needed to be very organized, and everything needed to be in its place. A three-part sink lined **one whole side wall** of the kitchen, with containers and storage units placed neatly on a shelf **above**. **On the opposite wall** there were two refrigerators, one walk-in with food stored for the whole week, and a regular fridge with items that were used throughout the day. **In between the two** were more shelves with extra bags, boxes, and fortune cookies. **Along the back of the entire length of the kitchen** were four huge woks where all dishes were prepared. **Next to the woks** were a fryer, a small prep table, and a rice cooker that got extremely warm. **Two feet back, away from the woks**, was another small prep table, as well as a rack with every vegetable we needed and a flip fridge with all the pork, beef, and chicken.
>
> —**Matthew K. Greene**, student writer

Notice how the details and the words that connect them build a clear, well-organized mental picture of Rice Kitchen.

In this next example, the writer begins the paragraph with a simple statement of the impression she intends to create: the "harsh environment."

> *The Hurt Locker* takes place in a harsh environment. There is little to no grass, only dry, cracked dirt and sand. The sand is rough beneath your foot and it crunches as you walk. As the wind blows, gusting across the flat, arid land, the sand billows up in massive clouds that can block your vision and sting your skin. The sun beats down on the ground, heating up the air. Every breath is dry, a gulp of pure heat with not a drop of humidity to dull the warmth. It feels like taking a bite of the sun. All around are the sounds of people talking, vendors at stalls hawking their goods, children running and laughing, cars puttering down the crowded streets. The center

of the town hangs heavy with the smells of food cooking; rich, earthy spices mingled with citrus and fruit. The sun filters down through the buildings to tinge the air golden yellow. Further outside of the town, the sand piles up in dunes. Buildings are left abandoned and crumbling, and the wind blows the tiny grains of sand up against solitary, freestanding walls in drifts taller than you can reach. Here and there grow scrubby bushes, providing only enough shade for the smallest creature to hide under and get a reprieve from the sun.

—**Molly-Iris Alpern**, student writer

The author puts us right in the middle of this "harsh environment" and describes what is literally under our feet. The sand looks "dry" and "cracked," it feels "rough," and it "crunches" as you walk. The picture is not a static one. The "wind blows" and the "sand billows up in massive clouds that can block your vision and sting your skin." Then we hear sounds, vendors hawking their goods, children laughing, cars puttering. We're in the "center of town" that "hangs heavy" with smells. Then the description moves "further outside the town," where "sand piles up" and "buildings are left abandoned and crumbling." Notice this movement: you look down, then sideways, then up to the sun. You look and feel, hear and smell, moving outward from the center of the town. The sensory details combine with this sense of motion to create an exceptionally vivid impression for the reader.

In another military story, the writer uses descriptive details effectively to share his impressions about deployment:

Deployment

It was the last day of February. I was standing outside in formation. I was a sergeant in the 101st Airborne Division at Fort Campbell, Kentucky. This would be one of our last briefs before deploying to Kuwait. It was cool out. Morning had begun to fade away. It was starting to get warmer, and the fog had started to dissipate. I was tired. We were all tired, but we were all very wide awake.

I can remember some of the details so vividly. The new desert uniforms were stiff and scratchy. I could smell many different things—all the new equipment and the booze from a couple of the guys next to me. My mind faded in and out during the briefing. I really don't remember what it was about. I had only slept for about an hour the night before. The whole unit had to be in early this morning. There had been a lot to do. The process had to be followed, weapon issues, casualty cards to fill out, and troops to inspect. The list went on.

The brief ended. Some of the soldiers went inside the gym to visit with their families. Some of them stayed outside fixing their rucksacks and smoking cigarettes. Fear was heavy in the air. I saw it in everyone's eyes. The wives that were there tried to be strong. Most of them were crying and hugging their husbands.

We had only one more hour until we would go to the flight line. This would be the last time some of us would ever see our families. The older soldiers knew how dangerous this deployment would be, but they were supportive of the younger ones' fear.

It was time to leave. I hugged my girlfriend tight and promised that I would do my best to come back in one piece. Then all of us soldiers got on the bus. As I found my seat and felt the bus creep forward, the fear of what would be gripped me like a giant hand.

To this day it still makes me shudder when I think about that moment in time. There were scarier things yet to come, but that memory is the most vivid. I think it is because we are afraid of what will happen and what we don't know.

—**Dale Andrews**, student writer

The style is clear and direct, with a military precision. The details tell the story: the 101st Airborne Division, deployment to Kuwait, stiff and scratchy desert uniforms, rucksacks, cigarettes, tears. Only near the end does emotion grip the narrator—and the reader—like a giant hand.

USING FIGURATIVE LANGUAGE

Your descriptive writing can often be spiced up with **figurative language**, a group of methods by which you compare one item with another to create pictures or explore ideas. A **simile** makes the comparison directly with the use of *like* or *as*. Feelings can often be effectively described through similes. When Dale Andrews was deployed, fear gripped him "like a giant hand." Imagine it, a hand so big it can wrap right around you and squeeze, stopping your breath for a moment. That's what fear feels like. Or, on a lighter note, Elizabeth Best found the aroma of the peach was "like a very rich, wild honey." Smells are tough to describe; almost always we end up comparing them to *another* smell.

Pictures are sometimes easier to create with a simile. In this passage, the *mole* looks "like a volcano":

At the end it's a plate looking like a volcano hot and steamy just erupted red sauce all over the chicken running down like a river streaming so delightful and when I put it in my mouth it just melts the taste buds all over.

—**Randy Gonzalez**, student writer

In addition to the picture painted by the simile, notice how the structure of the sentence itself reflects the image; it streams over the page like the red sauce!

Let's look at some of the similes professional writer Tim Hayward uses in "Too Much of a Mouthful" (Chapter 9's A Taste for Reading). He and his sandwich met "like long-separated lovers." In trying to bite through the thick baguette, he "must have looked like a rat gnawing a torpedo." And perhaps my favorite, describing his attempt to penetrate a "robust" meat pie:

> Preliminary reconnaissance has revealed a line of weakness in the lower crust which might reward attrition. But if I go in from that angle—like Luke Skywalker seeking the vulnerabilities on the underside of the Death Star—I'm going to end up with gravy running down my neck.

Notice also the **allusion** in this description to the well-known *Star Wars* franchise. Such references to stories and people, as well as to places and things, that readers will most likely understand add another layer to the language.

While a simile makes the comparison of items explicit, sometimes we imply the comparison by simply stating that one thing is another; that is, we use a **metaphor**. In the next passage, a kitchen is compared to the fires of hell through the term *inferno* and the allusion to Lucifer:

> The kitchen was a cardboard box inferno that employed three line cooks and a chef. I truly believe Lucifer himself would have asked for a glass of water there from time to time. The only movement on the line was a pivot from the steam table to twelve spider-webbed burners that roared full blast, singeing anything that dared to come close to them.

—**Nathan E. Bearfield**, student writer

Notice also how the writer uses the word "spider-webbed" both to describe the burners' appearance and to suggest a sinister personality. They're alive and malevolent, "singeing anything that dared to come close to them." Nice.

Personification, that is, attributing human thoughts and feelings to inanimate objects, works particularly well with metaphor. In another of Tim Hayward's sandwiches, the tomatoes "screamed" flavor. In Monica Bhide's "A Question of Taste," the onions "sing" and the tomatoes "marry."

Using figurative language can bring a new dimension to our *thinking* as well as to our writing. We have done something similar throughout this book in exploring cooking as a metaphor for writing: peeling the potato, seasoning and plating the dish.

The kitchen was a cardboard box inferno.

A TASTE FOR READING

Sharon Olds is known for her intensely personal, at times graphic poetry, which is often an intimate portrayal of family life. The Dead and the Living *(1984), from which "Bread" is taken, is one of contemporary poetry's best-sellers. Olds received the Pulitzer Prize in 2013 for* Stag's Leap, *a chronicle of her divorce.*

****

Bread
by Sharon Olds

When my daughter makes bread, a cloud of flour
hangs in the air like pollen. She sifts and
sifts again, the salt and sugar
close as the grain of her skin. She heats the
water to body temperature
with the sausage lard, fragrant as her scalp
the day before hair-wash, and works them together on a
floured board. Her broad palms
bend the paste toward her and the heel of her hand
presses it away, until the dough
begins to snap, glossy and elastic as the
torso bending over it,
this ten-year-old girl, random specks of
yeast in her flesh beginning to heat,
her volume doubling every month now, but still
raw and hard. She slaps the dough and it
crackles under her palm, sleek and
ferocious and still leashed, like her body, no
breasts rising like bubbles of air toward the
surface of the loaf. She greases the pan, she is
shaped, glazed, and at any moment goes
into the oven, to turn to that porous
warm substance, and then under the
knife to be sliced for the having, the tasting, and the
giving of life.

ABOUT THE READING

- What happens in the poem?
- What details or images do you find particularly striking? Why?
- Explain the relationship between the bread and the girl.
- List the similes in the poem, and evaluate their effectiveness in terms of the poem's story and themes.

Monica Bhide is an engineer turned food writer whose work has been published in Food & Wine, The New York Times, Bon Appétit, *and* Saveur. *Her latest cookbook is* Modern Spice: Inspired Indian Recipes for the Contemporary Kitchen.

****

A Question of Taste: It's Not Easy Accepting Who Gets to Lick the Spoon
by Monica Bhide

It started out as a perfectly normal workday. A food writer by night, I was working at a consulting firm, out of my lonely cubicle, on the seventh floor of a suburban D.C. office. I worked alone, since most of my teammates were all over the United States, part of what is called a virtual team. It sounds glamorous but translates into being very lonely at work. So imagine my surprise when the receptionist called me to say I had a visitor. I could hear her giggling on the other end of the phone. "Who is it?" I demanded to know. "Well," she hesitated, "it's a gentleman in a chef's uniform and he has a picture of you holding your cookbook. Says it's from The Washington Post."

A chef here in my office? With my picture in hand, no less. If you live long enough you see everything, my grandmother used to say, and sure enough here it was—a chef asking for a novice writer at an HR consulting firm.

And there he was, a young man in uniform, chef's hat and all. He extended his hand toward me, saying, "Hi, I am Jonathan Krinn and I have just opened a new restaurant downstairs in this building. It's called 2941. My mother saw the article about you in the newspaper and told me to check you out. She thought we might enjoy meeting each other."

Those were his exact words. I thought his mother was matchmaking. It must have shown on my face. "Since you write books and I cook," he quickly added.

I wasn't sure how to react. He invited me to his kitchen, to learn more about him and his cooking. And I agreed, reluctantly, not knowing what would be expected of me.

We set a date and he left.

I took the day of our meeting off from work and arrived armed with nothing more than anxiety, for now I had Googled him and knew who he was. What on earth would we talk about, I wondered.

The interior of the restaurant looked like a new bride: perfectly adorned, a bit coy and yet very inviting. He met me at the door and led me into the kitchen. It was huge, almost as big as the restaurant. I was in awe of all the gadgets. As we chatted, a chemistry began to develop. His passion was French American food and mine was Indian, so vastly different, and yet the soul behind them was the same.

He muttered something about showing me how to make a perfect sauce. I was completely ill at ease, my knowledge of French stopped at "*oui*," and he was talking a mile a minute about ingredients and techniques. We were standing over the pot. And then it happened, that bewildering incident.

He took a spoon, dipped it in the sauce and then proceeded to . . . dare I say, lick it. I was stunned. Completely horrified and stunned. He offered me some and I shook my head. "Are you okay?" he inquired.

I stuttered, "You tasted the sauce. . . . How could you do that? Don't you know you are not allowed to taste while you cook?"

Now it was his turn to look stunned. "I have never heard of that," he said. "How would you know when to season?"

When you least expect it, culture shows up. I had learned to cook by sight, smell, sound and texture. In our kitchen we were not allowed to taste.

My father would teach me to roast spices and learn that coriander whimpers, cumin smolders, mustard sizzles and cinnamon roars. I learned to cook by sight as the colors of the spices turned and then by smell—sweet, earthy, heady, sharp if they are roasting correctly, or the unforgiving acrid smells if they burn.

My mother taught me to make curries by hearing how onions sing in oil, from a slight sizzle to a glorious harmony as they get perfectly caramelized. I learned to watch the tomatoes marry the onions. The sign the union was complete and ready for spices to be added was when the oil separated from the mixture.

Roast, sizzle, temper, broil, boil, bake, simmer, sauté, fry—we had to do it all by watching and listening.

The reason, I was told many years later, was that in our house the first offering of the food was for the gods. If you tasted while you cooked, it made the food impure. My grandmother would carefully take the first piece of bread she cooked each night, place it on a plate along with a helping of all the other vegetables and lentils, and set it aside before the meal for the family was served. After we all ate, she would go outside and set the plate in front of the cows that used to hang around our neighborhood. Cows are considered sacred in the Hindu religion and feeding them is said to be akin to feeding God.

Jonathan listened carefully to my story and nodded. Then he held the spoon to me and said, "Here, taste it. There are no cows in D.C."

ABOUT THE READING

- Explain the major difference between the two cooks in the story and the reason for that difference.
- Why do you think the story ends with Krinn's statement "There are no cows in D.C."?
- Describe the author's attitude toward food and cooking. What descriptive details from the story support your interpretation?
- Do you use senses other than taste when you are cooking? Explain.

RECIPE FOR REVIEW

SENSORY DETAILS

1. Use data from the five senses to describe what you see, hear, smell, taste, and touch.
2. Try using different senses to find a fresh description.
3. Avoid clichés.

EAT YOUR WORDS

Flavors and aromas can be particularly difficult to describe. Too often we may fall back on tired old clichés. If you like to write about food, begin assembling a personal thesaurus of fresh and vivid words for smells, tastes, and textures.

SPECIFIC DETAILS

1. Avoid vague or general words like *wonderful* or *amazing*.
2. When you know the name, use it: *Ryan Gosling, Butterfingers, Vidalia onions.*

USING FIGURATIVE LANGUAGE

1. A **simile** compares two items using *like* or *as,* for example, the *mole* looks "like a volcano."
2. A **metaphor** implies the comparison by stating that one thing *is* another: "our family is a plate full of ingredients."

Flavors can be difficult to describe. Taste each bite—and each adjective—carefully.

CHAPTER EXERCISES

1. *Enjoying Description*—Find a story or article you've enjoyed and look carefully for descriptive passages. Copy one of them onto a sheet of notebook paper. What drew you to this particular passage? Does it contain details from the five senses? Does it "paint a picture"? Explain.

2. *Describing a Lemon*—First, take out a sheet of paper and describe a lemon in two to three sentences. Next, get a real lemon—but don't look at it! Close your eyes, and get to know the lemon using the other four senses.[8] Take several minutes to do this. Finally, put the lemon aside (don't look at it!), and write a description of that particular lemon. How does this description differ from your first one?

3. *Writing Descriptions of Food*—Select a food item such as a piece of fruit or a hearty soup. Carefully study the appearance, aroma, texture, sound (as you eat it), and flavor of the food. Make notes at each step. Review the selection of words for flavors and aromas in Figure 12.2. Then write a paragraph in which you describe the food with vivid sensory details.

4. *Flavor Wheels*—Look on the Internet for *flavor wheels* or *aroma wheels*.[9] What new descriptive words did you discover? Write a paragraph in which you use five or ten of these words.

5. *Using Specific Details*—Rewrite the following general descriptions to include specific details. The idea is to *show* the reader what you're feeling so that the reader says, "Oh, that's beautiful" or "That sounds amazing."
   a. The sunset was beautiful.
   b. I heard a terrible sound.
   c. The kitchen smelled great.
   d. _____ (fill in the blank) was a awful movie.
   e. _____ (fill in the blank) is an amazing song.

6. *Creating an Impression*—Describe a space you have worked in, the layout, the sounds and smells. Use specific sensory details that help the reader see and hear (and smell and taste, perhaps) what you did in that space.

7. *Describing Emotions*—Find a dozen or more words for feelings, such an *angry, frightened, overjoyed*. Then write a paragraph in which you describe one of these feelings without using any of the feeling words. Show, don't tell.

8. *Using Figures of Speech*—Fill in the blanks in the following comparisons. Then choose one, and expand the idea into a descriptive paragraph.
   a. The _____ smelled like a _____.
   b. The _____ looked like a _____.
   c. The _____ sounded like a _____.
   d. The _____ tasted like a _____.
   e. The _____ felt like a _____.

IDEAS FOR WRITING

1. Describe with vivid, specific details a dish that you have eaten recently. Consider its appearance, aroma, flavor, and texture. You might also describe your feelings about the dish.

2. Think about a specific place and the feeling it evokes in you. Perhaps a treehouse makes you feel peaceful, or a busy city street makes you feel excited. Write a description of this place that shows the feeling—but don't name it. Does it work?

3. Describe in detail the face of a person you and your friends know well. If you read the description to friends, do they recognize the person?

4. Look up some of the other figures of speech, such as *alliteration* and *hyperbole,* in addition to the ones explained in this chapter. Then describe an ordinary household item or food using at least five of these figures. Which one makes the most successful description? Why?

CHAPTER 13
COMPARE AND CONTRAST

By the end of this chapter, you should begin to ...

- explore the similarities and differences between items through a variety of brainstorming techniques;
- develop a compare and contrast writing assignment with specific, relevant details and examples;
- discover and explain the implications of the comparison; and
- organize a compare and contrast topic in block or alternating format.

Imagine that you are at the farmer's market, squeezing and sniffing the different varieties of apples. How will you decide which one to buy? You will probably begin by *comparing* the varieties in terms of appearance, flavor, and texture. You will think about how you plan to use the apple and how much each variety costs. Some types may be organically grown; others may not. Will you go with a familiar Golden Delicious or try a less common variety, such as Mutsu or Elstar? As a result of your study of the similarities and differences between the varieties, you will be better equipped to choose among them.

Or perhaps you need to buy a car. There are many aspects to that decision, including cost, size, maintenance, and mileage. Perhaps you'd like to try one of the new hybrids. Will you rent or lease? And what about the color? Particularly with such an expensive purchase, it is very useful to break down the similarities and differences among the options so that you can make a wise decision.

Weighing the pros and cons can have even more far-reaching consequences in the decisions you make about your career.

I had always thought I wanted to be a neurosurgeon. When I was in high school, I only took classes that would help me achieve that dream. I took Anatomy and Physiology, AP Biology, Issues in Science, which was a college-level course, and even Physics. I loved all of the classes, and I thought I was in the right lane because I did well in the classes and loved them too. I thought it was a win-win situation. I had found what I love.

I am the type of person that loves to challenge herself, so on top of all the classes that I was taking during the week I signed up for Saturday classes at my school. The class was called "Culinary," and it was the most sought-after class. My first day there was lovely. I loved the class, and everything came naturally to me. After I took that class in the second semester of my junior year, I made the big decision to become a pastry chef.

—**Elizabeth Duker**, student writer

Although her family was not initially in favor of this choice, Elizabeth changed their minds and entered culinary school. Nor are the two careers as dissimilar as we might think. Read the piece at the end of this chapter about chefs and surgeons.

Compare and contrast is a useful way of brainstorming details, exploring ideas, and organizing a piece of writing.

BIG NIGHT

Many, many stories and films—as well as important life decisions—are developed through comparison and contrast. For example, the story of *Big Night* grows out of the differences between two brothers who own a small Italian restaurant.

Secondo perceives food as money, a way to sustain a high end lifestyle that also happens to be beautiful and delicious. Primo perceives food as art, a sacred tradition and celebration, which may also provide enough money to live a minimalistic lifestyle. They share the idea that the food being created is special, but they differ in regard to the priority of money over art.

—**Megan Brown**, student writer

This isn't just a philosophical difference: it has consequences in the brothers' lives that threaten both their livelihood and their relationship.

Primo is stubborn in his dedication to perfecting classic Italian food. Secondo agrees that the food is art and should be appreciated. Primo would rather sacrifice financial gain and remain true to traditions than compromise the quality to satisfy the potential clientele. Throughout the movie various scenarios display the positive reactions of people tasting Primo's food, but they also emphasize that these encounters do not generate any revenue.

—**Megan Brown**, student writer

Despite their differences, the brothers find in the end that it is their similarities—like the eggs Secondo cooks—that bind them more tightly:

> The omelet scene is very quiet; all you hear is the cracking, mixing, and cooking of the eggs and the clang of the plates. Primo and Secondo make peace and forgive each other over a simple breakfast of eggs and bread.
>
> **—Jessie Kuznitz**, student writer

DEVELOPING A COMPARISON

We know the saying, "You can't compare apples and oranges." But we *can* and probably *should* compare different varieties of apples when we are trying to choose the best one for our needs. For example, suppose we are choosing between Red Delicious and Granny Smith apples. They are similar in that they are readily available throughout the year, can be eaten fresh or used in cooking, and are about the same price per pound. How would we choose between them, then? By looking at the *differences*.

> While the Granny Smith apple is round and smooth with a bright green color, the Red Delicious is oval in shape with bumps on one end and a dark red hue. The Granny Smith is crisp in texture with a tartness to its flavor. In contrast, the Red Delicious has a mealy feel and a sweet taste.

Notice that we want to examine the same characteristics of each apple—appearance, texture, flavor. It would not be helpful to say something like, "While the Granny Smith apple is round and smooth with a bright green color, the Red Delicious has a mealy feel and a sweet taste." A meaningful comparison studies the same points of each item.

The first task in developing a comparison is to decide on your focus. If you are choosing between varieties of apple, the focus is clear. The items have a basis of comparison already—they are all apples—and brainstorming their differences in terms of flavor, cost, and other factors is likely to be quite straightforward. Similarly, the two brothers in *Big Night* have a clear basis for comparison: they're from the same family and own the same restaurant. Yet the differences between them are causing conflict and putting the restaurant's

A shopper chooses among varieties of apples.

Figure 13.1 Art vs. Money in *Big Night*

	Primo	Secondo
Job	Executive chef Back of house	Host Front of house
Goal	Creative success	Financial success
Beliefs	Food is art. The tradition behind the food is more important than money or what the customer wants.	Food is money. The customer is always right because that attitude makes money.
Personality	Shy	Outgoing and social

future in jeopardy. To get a handle on these differences, we can fill in a table or grid like the one in Figure 13.1. Creating such a chart can remind us of the importance of *balancing* the time we give to each item we're comparing. If we had all kinds of details about Primo, but only one or two about Secondo, for example, we would immediately see that in the chart and take steps to fix it. If we couldn't find the balance on any one characteristic, it might be that we would omit that characteristic altogether, or mention it as an outlier.

Sometimes you will have to choose between similar items, as in the examples of the apples and the brothers. At other times, you might decide to compare your item with another, perhaps more familiar one, in order to increase the reader's understanding. For example, in order to explain a papaya to someone who has never tasted one, you might talk about the texture of the more familiar peach or the acidic bite of an orange. This type of comparison is called an **analogy** and can be used to great effect in persuasive writing. See Exploring Similarities at the end of this chapter, as well as Chapter 16.

In developing this kind of topic, you may find that a list works more smoothly than a table. You're looking initially for meaningful similarities, so you'll only need one column. In preparing an argument about lowering the drinking age, for example, you might list other types of activities that involve using good judgment (don't drink and drive) at a young age, such as buying cigarettes, enlisting in the armed forces, or voting for the President of the United States.

ADDING DETAILS

As with all of our writing, it is the details that make the ideas real and fresh. For example, one August my class tasted peaches and apricots, both stone fruits, locally grown and dead ripe. We made a chart (see Figure 13.2), similar to the one for *Big Night,* and carefully recorded our observations about their appearance, aroma, flavor, and texture.

Figure 13.2 A Tasting of Local Apricots and Peaches. Both are stone fruits, related to almond.

	Apricot	Peach
Aroma	honey pumpkin	floral/honeysuckle fresh mountain air
Texture	drier	creamier
Flavor	earthy sweet/tart wilder floral citrus spicy (nutmeg) nutty melon	bright sweeter tamer richer, not quite as lean nutty (pecan, close to skin)

In the passages that follow, notice how the student writers use the descriptive details to bring the comparison to life.

> The outward appearance of the peach displays brilliant reds, oranges, and yellows that resemble the sky at sunset. The appearance of the peach seems to beckon those who view it to come over to take a closer look. . . . The apricot does not possess all of the vibrant colors of the peach but instead delivers one outstanding color of its own. The apricot looks like the sun as it rises in the morning.
>
> —**Lori Vrazel Kallinikos**, student writer

In this passage, the writer uses a contrasting image to highlight the difference in color: the peach "resemble[s] the sky at sunset" while the apricot "looks like the sun as it rises in the morning." It would have been far less effective to use two *different* images here; for example, the peach "resemble[s] the sky at sunset" while the apricot looks like a fresh egg yolk. Of course the sunset doesn't look like a yolk. But the sky at one moment might be effectively contrasted with the sky at another.

The next writer contrasts the aroma of the peach with that of the apricot:

> The aroma of the peach is very complex, with many notes intertwining in the nostrils. You can pick up a floral note, almost like a honeysuckle. Next you may pick up a sweet, almost musky scent. Perhaps the strongest aroma is honey. It smells like a very rich, wild honey, like that of the wild clover. Almond is present with the underlying aroma of vanilla. A faint scent of nutmeg can be sensed, lingering for a second. However, the aroma of the apricot is deeper, reminiscent of a hay field. The apricot also smelled "greener" than the peach and lighter. It did not smell as rich and full-bodied as the peach.
>
> —**Elizabeth Best**, student writer

This writer does an excellent job of exploring the aromas—we sense her genuine effort to communicate her experience despite the fact that smells and tastes may be two of the most difficult things to describe. She also uses an effective transition, "however," to move from the peach to the apricot, and she continues to make the contrast clear with phrases such as "greener than the peach" and not "as rich and full-bodied."

> The texture of the peach is very juicy. The juices run down the hands and face as you bite into it. It is sticky, reminiscent of a sorbet. In contrast, the apricot is noticeably drier. It has a very creamy feel in the mouth. I like to compare it with custard, because of the rich, full mouthfeel.
>
> —**Elizabeth Best**, student writer

This passage offers several fresh and vivid descriptions of the fruits' textures: the juices "run down the hands and face," the peach is "sticky" like a "sorbet." The comparison to the two desserts—sorbet and custard—works well. Again, it would not be as effective (or palatable) to relate the peach's texture to that of a sorbet but the apricot's to cold cream! Notice also the use of the transition "in contrast." Other effective transitions that show contrast are *although, but, however, instead of, on the other hand,* and *unlike.*

Details are also important in illustrating the tension between creative and financial success in *Big Night*.

> Secondo knows that you have to make what people want in order to make any profit at all, even if you do not agree with what it is. For instance, risotto is a starch and should not be served with pasta which is also a starch. Yet if a customer asks for risotto with a side of pasta, you have to make it. You cannot just tell them, "Oh, we do not do that, food does not work like that." If the customer wants it and will pay for it, then they should receive it. Primo does not want to decrease the quality of his products because to lose quality would be to give up on everything he stands for. Secondo does not understand this until the very end of the movie. In earlier parts, Secondo tries to change the menu options and allow for lesser quality produce to be bought, which Primo does not approve of. Close to the last scene, during the fight between Primo and Secondo on the beach, Primo explains to Secondo that food is all he has and without it he is nothing. At the end of this scene Secondo finally understands Primo's bond with food.
>
> —**Jessie Kuznitz**, student writer

The specific details about the risotto, the produce, and the scene on the beach help readers see more clearly what's at stake in the conflict between the brothers.

DIGGING DEEPER

While it's usually quite easy to generate lists of similarities and differences, we must be certain we've got a good basis for comparison and that we take time to dig beneath surface details to find the *significance* of the comparison. *Why* did we compare the items? What did we learn? What does it all *mean?* In our peach and apricot tasting, the meaning was fairly practical: How might we use each of the two fruits?

> When using peaches and apricots in baking, you should treat them as differently as you would apples and oranges since they will contribute different components to the product. If you want a bolder flavor, use the peach and add some sliced almonds and vanilla to enhance it. If you want a subtler flavor, use the apricot. Adding some fresh ginger will play up its "green" components and make for an interesting complexity of flavors. Think of its velvety feel and how that will affect the overall consistency of the dish. A pudding or ice cream would show off the apricot's creamy texture.
>
> —**Elizabeth Best**, student writer

Note how the writer has moved beyond the measurements taken in the classroom, the measurements of aroma, texture, and flavor, in order to explore the *uses* of the two stone fruits. With these observations, her knowledge of baking and pastry, and her imagination, the writer has found the *meaning* of the comparison, and it is this search for meaning that is sometimes neglected or omitted in a compare and contrast paper. The point of compare and contrast is to *explore* the idea, widely, deeply. Don't settle even for a simple decision such as "I like the peach better," or "I like the apricot better." Ask questions about *why* or *how*, as in the following example:

> Although Primo may have too little focus on being paid for the food he makes, Secondo may also be entirely too focused on money and may lack passion for the art. Primo and Secondo's dueling opinions are reflective of the nature of the food service industry. There are always ways to make money with food; the question becomes "What part of you are you willing to sacrifice to be financially successful?"
>
> —**Megan Brown**, student writer

Secondo (left) contrasts his focus on business with his brother Primo's devotion to tradition.

At the heart of this comparison lies a difficult question about personal values and their financial consequences, a question that the writer ultimately leaves to us to answer.

In this paragraph from an essay comparing the main characters in the film *Mystic River*, the author digs into the reasons behind their different fates:

> In the end, it seems revenge gets Jimmy and Dave nowhere. Dave ends up dead, and Jimmy ends up mourning his dead daughter, killing his friend, and being hunted for that murder by another friend. It appears that Sean, the man of law, the man of justice, is the only one with a happy ending. His wife comes back to him with their daughter, a family reunited. The only way he obtains this, however, is by putting his personal relations aside, doing the hard thing, taking the high road. He seeks justice rather than revenge, and is rewarded with happiness.
>
> —**Timothy Fisher**, student writer

It is through pursuing revenge that Jimmy loses his daughter and any hope of redemption. In contrast, because Sean consistently pursues justice, his family and thus his hope for the future are restored to him.

Now, looking at similarities between different items often has a different purpose. You're usually not making a choice, but instead trying to explain an unfamiliar concept to the reader. Thus you may wish to leave the similarities on the surface, as with the comparisons between the papaya and the orange. In some persuasive contexts, you'll want to touch only lightly on similarities because the inevitable differences may not work in your favor (see the discussion of analogy in Chapter 16). But digging deeper into surprising similarities can sometimes yield as profound a question about personal values as our exploration of creative versus financial success in *Big Night*.

Karen Devon is a surgeon and a professor at the University of Toronto. In an article reprinted at the end of this chapter, she explores the many surprising similarities between chefs and surgeons, from their "clogs and white coats" to their long apprenticeships and obsession with cleanliness. Practitioners of both traditionally male-dominated specialties view their time in the kitchen or operating room as a carefully choreographed performance sport. Devon continues to dig deeper into these connections, concluding that "[t]he personal satisfaction gained out of arousing emotion through our interactions may be the most subtle, yet significant parallel between the chef and I. It is a privilege that bonds us much more than our clogs and white coats."

ORGANIZING THE COMPARE AND CONTRAST ESSAY

As in all your writing, the ideas you discover in a compare and contrast essay may end up organizing themselves, for example, in time, space, importance. There may be special challenges, however, in terms of helping the reader keep track of which item you're talking about. Is it the peach that has the touch of nutmeg, or the apricot? One way to keep the ideas clear is to build the essay around the comparison itself. Two such structures are often taught, the first of which involves writing all about one of the items you're comparing, then all about the other. For example, some students who had tasted the peaches and apricots wrote all about the peach first—the aroma, texture, and flavor, say—and then all about the apricot—again, the aroma, texture, and flavor. This type of organization is sometimes called a **block format** (Figure 13.3). Other students focused on the characteristics of each fruit one by one, writing about the aroma of the peach and the apricot, the texture of the peach and the apricot, and the flavor of the peach and the apricot. This might be called an **alternating format** or **point-by-point format** (Figure 13.4).

Remember our paragraph about the apples? It was structured in this second method, alternating. We focused on the three characteristics—appearance, texture, and flavor—and noted the differences between the apples:

> While the Granny Smith apple is round and smooth with a bright green color, the Red Delicious is oval in shape with bumps on one end and a dark red hue. The Granny Smith is crisp in texture with a tartness to its flavor. In contrast, the Red Delicious has a mealy feel and a sweet taste.

The same information might be structured differently, following the *block* format.

> The Granny Smith apple is round and smooth with a bright green color. It is crisp in texture with a tartness to its flavor. In contrast, the Red Delicious is oval in shape with bumps on one end and a dark red hue. It has a mealy feel and a sweet taste.

In general, use the block format when you have only two items to compare and you are interested in their overall similarities or differences. Use the alternating format when you have more than two items to compare or when you have a longer paper, so that readers don't forget the points you made about the first item five pages earlier. The alternating format also works better for a closer analysis of individual points of comparison.

BLOCK FORMAT: COOKIE TASTING

In this example of block format, student Casey Mondry reviews two cookies and decides on a preference. The block format works well, as he gives a vivid description of each cookie from appearance to mouthfeel.

Cookie Tasting

During writing class today we tasted two cookies from the same bakery, the mudslide and the chocolate chip. I thought that the look of both was appealing and told a lot about how they would taste. Although I liked both, I found that I preferred one to the other as an everyday treat.

Figure 13.3 Block Format: Granny Smith vs. Red Delicious Apples

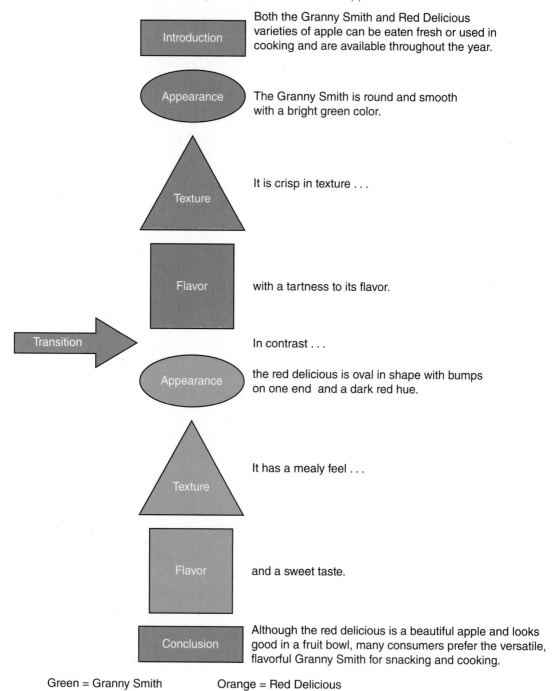

Introduction — Both the Granny Smith and Red Delicious varieties of apple can be eaten fresh or used in cooking and are available throughout the year.

Appearance — The Granny Smith is round and smooth with a bright green color.

Texture — It is crisp in texture . . .

Flavor — with a tartness to its flavor.

Transition — In contrast . . .

Appearance — the red delicious is oval in shape with bumps on one end and a dark red hue.

Texture — It has a mealy feel . . .

Flavor — and a sweet taste.

Conclusion — Although the red delicious is a beautiful apple and looks good in a fruit bowl, many consumers prefer the versatile, flavorful Granny Smith for snacking and cooking.

Green = Granny Smith   Orange = Red Delicious

Figure 13.4 Alternating Format: Granny Smith vs. Red Delicious Apples

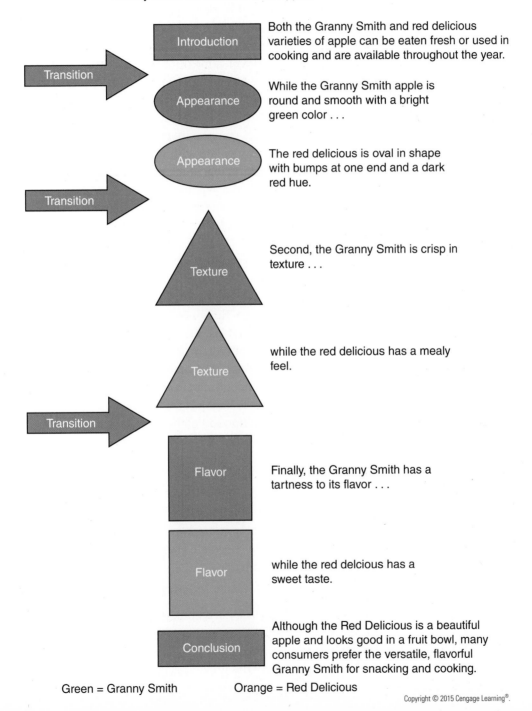

Organizing a Compare/Contrast Paper
"Granny Smith vs. Red Delicious Apples"

Transition → **Introduction** — Both the Granny Smith and red delicious varieties of apple can be eaten fresh or used in cooking and are available throughout the year.

Appearance — While the Granny Smith apple is round and smooth with a bright green color . . .

Appearance — The red delicious is oval in shape with bumps at one end and a dark red hue.

Transition →

Texture — Second, the Granny Smith is crisp in texture . . .

Texture — while the red delicious has a mealy feel.

Transition →

Flavor — Finally, the Granny Smith has a tartness to its flavor . . .

Flavor — while the red delcious has a sweet taste.

Conclusion — Although the Red Delicious is a beautiful apple and looks good in a fruit bowl, many consumers prefer the versatile, flavorful Granny Smith for snacking and cooking.

Green = Granny Smith   Orange = Red Delicious

The mudslide had a very rich dark brown color with earthquake-type cracks and the tips of a few nuts peeking out. When I split the cookie in half, some irregularly shaped, dime-sized crumbs broke off. The inside was dense with areas that looked gooey, and there were whole walnuts that gave a light tan contrast to the rich dark brown color. The density and color made the cookie look heavy or rich. When I bit into the mudslide, the rich bittersweet chocolate flavor came out very quickly. Parts of the cookie were moist and creamy like ganache and contrasted wonderfully with the drier, crisper outer edges. I enjoyed the way the walnut complemented the lingering dark chocolate flavor, although this cookie was too heavy for my taste. While its complexity went very well with my coffee, it was difficult to cleanse my palate with water, due to the mudslide's rich after taste and the gooey parts that stuck in my teeth.

The chocolate chip cookie, on the other hand, was more my type, having a nice golden brown outside that was lighter in the center and darker at the rim. The top was smooth with specks of the chocolate chips poking through. The bottom was porous and looked like it would be perfect for soaking up milk, one of my favorite ways to eat a chocolate chip cookie. However, I chose to have water; that way I could eat the cookie plain and evaluate it without intrusions. Breaking into the cookie, I could tell it was going to be dry because of how it crumbled. The inside looked aerated or fluffy and lightly tan. When I took my first bite, I didn't get a chocolate chip but instead tasted the rest of the cookie. I found the cookie somewhat sugary, with a light flavor of molasses from the brown sugar and a little saltiness. The cookie crumbled and dissolved in my mouth if I let it sit on my tongue long enough, and in doing so a hint of vanilla came out. I thought it was very nice to have just a few milky sweet chocolate chips in it. I find chocolate overwhelms most of the other flavors in cookies, perhaps because its flavor stays longer. I also enjoyed the finish of the cookie. It was clean and didn't stay too long. That way when the next bite came it was just about like re-tasting the entire cookie.

With both cookies, the look fit the taste well. The light golden brown and sparse chocolate chips in the chocolate chip cookie suited its subtle but somewhat chocolate taste. The rich color and complex texture of the mudslide also matched its flavor. I like the chocolate chip for its subtlety, and I didn't care for the overpowering mudslide.

—**Casey Mondry**, student writer

The block format allows the reader to experience each cookie fully. Each body paragraph is packed with specific details, from the "earthquake-type cracks" to the "irregularly shaped, dime-sized crumbs." In addition, each paragraph concludes with an assessment of the eating experience, from "the gooey parts stuck in my teeth" to "when the next bite came it was just about like re-tasting the entire cookie."

ALTERNATING FORMAT: TWO WIVES

A compare and contrast essay can also be structured through a focus on each separate point of comparison. In the paper that follows, the writer compares two wives in the film *Mystic River* and uses the alternating format to highlight their differences in terms of loyalty to their husbands, ability to protect their families, and appearance at the end of the film.

Two Wives

The story in *Mystic River* unfolded calmly like a river flowing in gentle waves. In this largely silent movie, I saw how important the housewife was in the family. Also, I found differences between the two wives, Celeste and Annabeth.

Three childhood friends, Jimmy, Dave, and Sean, grew up in a small and shabby village in Boston. They used to spend their time playing hockey. One day, David was kidnapped by two strange men. A few days later, David escaped successfully from them. But their happy time in childhood ended. They didn't keep in touch with each other. Twenty-five years later, those three guys met again by a tragedy: Jimmy's daughter was killed. In that time, David's wife Celeste suspected her husband had killed Jimmy's daughter. As Jimmy pursued the question of the accident, Celeste confessed to Jimmy what she thought. Jimmy burned with revengeful thoughts and killed David, but it turned out David was not the murderer. Jimmy told his wife, Annabeth, everything that happened to him. When she heard about David, she might have been shocked. But she wasn't agitated. She showed her husband her strong loyalty for him. While Celeste's distrust of her husband destroyed her family, Annabeth's belief in her husband kept her family firmly together.

"While Celeste's (right) distrust of her husband destroyed her family, Annabeth's belief in her husband kept her family firmly together."

Celeste and Annabeth were both housewives, but they had a different belief about their husbands. While Celeste had a distrust,

Annabeth had a strong loyalty for her husband. For instance, when Celeste's husband David came home with a bloody T-shirt, she was embarrassed. The next day, when it was discovered that Annabeth's daughter had been murdered, Celeste began to suspect her husband was the killer. She made a mistake. She confessed to Jimmy (Annabeth's husband) what she thought without any objective evidence. On the other hand, in the case of Annabeth, when she heard that her husband had killed David, she was not agitated. Even though she was stunned, she remained firm; furthermore, she consoled her husband. That showed us that their beliefs about their husbands were contrary to each other.

Secondly, I was able to see a difference between the two women's abilities to protect their families. Celeste lied about the truth to Jimmy. That meant that she was an egoist and didn't take care of her husband and her family, including her son. She just wanted to protect herself from David. In the long run, her irresponsible conduct destroyed her family. Because of her hasty judgment, her son Michael would live under a fatherless family, and she would live with a guilty conscience. On the other side, Annabeth tried to protect her family from tragedy. As she said "Your father is a king," she encouraged her husband and made her family hold fast. While Celeste exposed her family's problem, Annabeth concealed hers.

Finally, the two women's appearances indicated how they were different. In the movie, Celeste looked sad and full of doubt. Her face was filled with worries and clouded with anxiety. But Annabeth had a fair and a brilliant look. In the parade at the end of the movie, that was distinguished clearly. After the end of the murder case, Celeste avoided the eyes of other people, such as Annabeth and Jimmy, while Annabeth was looking at Celeste as if nothing had happened.

By those three points, I saw how different the two wives were. They were different with regard to their loyalty to their husbands, their ability to protect their families, and their appearance in life. Through seeing this movie, I realized how important the housewife's role and her belief about her husband are because those things could affect not only individuals but also the entire family.

—**Soyang Myung**, student writer

The introductory paragraph lets us know that the items being compared are two wives, Celeste and Annabeth. In the next paragraph, the writer summarizes the main story line and shows how it impacts these women in terms of their belief in their husbands, their ability to protect their families, and their appearance by the end of the film. The writer then addresses these points one by one, evaluating their implications for Celeste and Annabeth. By going from one point to the next, the contrast is emphasized more heavily than it would be in a block format.

In the end, the essay touches on the importance of this examination: "I realized how important the housewife's role and her belief about her husband are because those things could affect not only individuals but also the entire family." After you've discovered and assessed the differences between items, try to push toward some realization or conclusion. What is the significance of your study? What did you learn? What are the implications for future action?

EXPLORING SIMILARITIES

As we noted earlier, a compare and contrast essay might also examine the similarities between two or more items that are clearly different. This text, for example, explores the surprising and often instructive similarities between the clearly different processes of cooking and writing. Let's look again at the following paragraph about these processes, which we first saw in the introduction:

> These similarities include the need to pay acute attention to detail, the certainty that only hard work will result in assured success, the need to train, study, practice, and do research, and the importance of being able to work under pressure. Other somewhat more subtle similarities exist: both pursuits involve simplicity of tools and equipment, both rely on a foundation of tradition passed along through literature, and both are vitally dependent on criticism. . . . To be successful, the professional cook and the professional writer must acknowledge [their rich] traditions while striving to be creative, thereby standing out in similarly competitive fields of endeavor.
>
> —**Robert A. Hannon**, student writer

Note how the first sentence points out that these two items—writing and cooking—are so different that we wouldn't ordinarily think of comparing them. Only a "closer examination" reveals the similarities, which culminate with the role of creativity in a successful career in either field. The paragraph also uses effective transitions such as *both* and *similarly*. Other transitions that show similarities include the following: *also, in the same way, just, like, likewise,* and *neither.*

Whether you choose to look for similarities or differences or both, remember to organize your points clearly and look for the more interesting observations and inferences that lie beneath the surface.

Called "the Latino poet of his generation," Martín Espada has published more than fifteen books as a poet, editor, essayist, and translator, and is the recipient of numerous awards. Much of his work addresses issues of social justice, particularly for immigrants and the working class.

****

Coca-Cola and Coco Frío
by Martín Espada

On his first visit to Puerto Rico,
island of family folklore,
the fat boy wandered
from table to table
with his mouth open.
At every table, some great-aunt
would steer him with cool spotted hands
to a glass of Coca-Cola.
One even sang to him, in all the English
she could remember, a Coca-Cola jingle
from the forties. He drank obediently, though
he was bored with this potion, familiar
from soda fountains in Brooklyn.

Then at a roadside stand off the beach, the fat boy
opened his mouth to coco frío, a coconut
chilled, then scalped by a machete
so that a straw could inhale the clear milk.
The boy tilted the green shell overhead
and drooled coconut milk down his chin;
suddenly, Puerto Rico was not Coca-Cola
or Brooklyn, and neither was he.

For years afterward, the boy marveled at an island
where the people drank Coca-Cola
and sang jingles from World War II
in a language they did not speak,
while so many coconuts in the trees
sagged heavy with milk, swollen
and unsuckled.

ABOUT THE READING

- What is the story in this poem? What happens?
- Describe the differences between the two drinks in the first and second stanzas. What other differences do you notice?
- Explain the last two lines of the second stanza.
- What questions remain in the boy's mind after his trip to Puerto Rico?

Dr. Karen Devon is Assistant Professor of Surgery at the University of Toronto. She writes about food, travel, photography, fashion, and people, with a side of endocrine surgery and ethics. Follow her on Twitter @specialkdmd.

****

Beyond Clogs and White Coats
by Karen Devon, MD

From the moment I first stepped into a restaurant kitchen, it felt like home; even though for the past eight years my real home has been an operating room, as I am a surgeon.

Though many on the outside may not realize it, the chef and the surgeon have much in common. Both profess modest beginnings. Cooks were slaves and surgeons were barbers. Those who did the cutting were not even considered physicians. While I needed to go through the cultural ritual of medical school, lectures and books did not make me a doctor.

The learning of surgery, like that of chefery, is an apprenticeship, the quality of which is highly dependent on those that train you. For both professions, learning comes through the difficult and repetitive daily grind of working intimately with peers and mentors. As I rotated from team to team, and am gradually awarded more responsibility, small rewards turn terrible weeks into triumphs. Some quit. Some continue. And there is always someone there to push you forward, sometimes not in the most pleasant or enlightened manner. Some of the best in the culinary world are often the most tyrannical, and in them I hear echoe[d] the tone of my surgical residency. "What this operation needs is five of me and none of you."

The worlds of the chef and the surgeon attract brilliant personalities that when not destroying you can turn you

"The chef and the surgeon have much in common."

into a master. Until I shook the hand of a sweaty line cook, I thought that my colleagues and I were the only ones who endured such a labile initiation into the joy of serving others. I watched with star-struck excitement as highly efficient teams exchanged assaults and high praises under immense time-pressures and sleep deprivation. We awoke early, complained, stayed late, complained, came in sick, complained, skipped holidays with family, complained, and buried our social lives in coffee and alcohol. We share other serious job hazards as well. I have ignored cuts, burns, and strains of all sorts for fear of falling behind.

"Outsiders" merely notice the end-result, but we see cooking and operating as performance sports. I still remind new medical students of three essential rules: "eat when you can, sit when you can, and sleep when you can." Both settings are carefully choreographed. It's why operating rooms were called theatres and I always covet the seat by an open kitchen. At work, I am constantly watched, criticized or applauded by colleagues, interns, and higher-ups, who can also be confused for friends. Mistakes are taken seriously. We dissect them at length so as not to repeat them, and discuss things in private so reputations are not tarnished. Every so often a mistake is a discovery, a recipe for success. Certain individuals have innate talents—indefinable qualities that call them to the table. If you make it, as I have, you become part of an elite group.

While my operating room is female run, if you peek into the average one you will see male prowess still prevailing. Kitchens too are boys clubs, with a few female champions. I sometimes like to dream I'm a bit of a Julia Child.

Having now experienced a kitchen's inner workings, I think I possess the necessary attributes to be a chef. I am good with my hands; contact lenses give me 20/20 vision; and I use my sense of smell all too often during surgery. My knowledge of anatomy is invaluable—aiding in the necessary dissection of the thymus for making sweet breads.

I also suffer from several essential compulsions. In surgery, "scrubbing in" is an age-old, hand-washing ritual. The chef's mutual intense dislike for Salmonella and E.Coli is what makes kitchens shimmer like operating rooms.

Cleanliness is part of the obsession with perfection. In some professions, competence is sufficient, but a steak ordered medium simply could not be served medium-rare. And perfect surgery is in the preparation. An operating room's instrument-set evokes images of the waiter's marking tray, and pre-operative briefings mimic those performed before serving meals.

What's more, chefs and surgeons respect artistry in a way that transcends common sense. A dish doesn't have to please the eye, to appease the palette. Similarly, I know that stitches don't necessarily need to align in order to heal, but I seem to instinctively require that things appear beautiful. Like with my food, I don't choose style over function, but the perfect combination is magical.

A career combining art and science makes for a fulfilling life of trial, and occasionally error, on the quest for a key ingredient: consistency. Other people are the subjects of our experimentation. Every detail—from the host or nurse who greets you, to the light, sound and temperature in the room—affects one's experience. Thus I understand the heavy feeling that comes not only from large frequent meals, but also from shouldering that responsibility.

We face ethical dilemmas regarding finite resources. Zealous debates on farming mirror those on health care and both contribute large slices of our economy. Research and innovation push limits but new technology does not reliably correlate with quality. Devices are great if results improve, but when I need to solve a problem, I tend to return to the basics. Likewise, I know that my favorite truffle pasta can only be delicately hand crafted.

Perhaps most vital in my day is the feeling that I contribute to some fundamental need. Of health, shelter, and food, the last may be most essential. Medical students learn a standard algorithm for writing orders where 'Diet' comes first—ahead of 'activities' and 'vital signs.' The first 'restaurants', in 18th century France, were designed to 'restore' the health of those who were ill rather than entertain the bourgeoisie. And a surgeon's job can revolve around restoring patients' ability to chew, swallow, use the gut, and nourish the body. Luckily, not everyone needs an operation; but we must all eat! We yearn to feed and be fed, as we begin and frequently end life through this shared act, often ritualized and joyful. The personal satisfaction gained out of arousing emotion through our interactions may be the most subtle, yet significant parallel between the chef and I. It is a privilege that bonds us much more than our clogs and white coats.

ABOUT THE READING

- Despite their obvious differences, the professions of chef and surgeon have some important similarities. List them.
- Which similarities does the author find most important? Do you agree? Explain.
- Which details or examples seemed most effective in illustrating the surprising similarities between chefs and surgeons?
- List the transitional words and phrases used in the piece. Do you think the author should have used more of them? Explain.

RECIPE FOR REVIEW

DEVELOPING A COMPARISON

- Choose *similar* items and explore the *differences* between them (for example, two types of chocolate cookies), or choose two *dissimilar* items and explore the *similarities* between them (for example, writing and cooking).
- Brainstorm through freewriting, lists, charts, graphs, diagrams.
- Use details and examples to support, explain, or illustrate similarities and differences. Be sure that you have parallel, balanced information for all items.
- Be clear what the purpose of your comparison is. What are you trying to highlight? What did you learn through comparing and contrasting?

ORGANIZING THE COMPARISON

- Organize the paper either by writing all about one of the items and then all about the other (block format), or by focusing on one characteristic at a time (alternating format). See Figures 13.3 and 13.4.
- Use appropriate transitions to clarify for the reader which item you are referring to in each sentence or passage. See Figure 13.5.

Figure 13.5 Transitions for Compare and Contrast Writing

To indicate similarities between items	To indicate differences between items
also, both, in the same way, just as, like, likewise, neither, similarly	although, but, however, in contrast, instead of, on the other hand, unlike

CHAPTER EXERCISES

1. *Developing a Comparison*—First, choose two or three somewhat similar items to compare. They might be varieties of a fruit or vegetable (such as Gala and Braeburn apples), methods of cooking (steaming and grilling), characters in a movie (Luke Skywalker and Han Solo), or characters in different movies (Luke Skywalker and Frodo Baggins). Or you might choose two kinds of music or two musical artists. Second, make a chart of the differences between the items you're comparing. Finally, put this information into sentences.

2. *Adding Details*—Take ten minutes and brainstorm about the topic you chose in Exercise 1. Try to include specific events, sensory details, and examples that will explain the differences with greater impact. Put this information into a paragraph or short essay.

3. *Tasting the Difference*—Conduct a tasting in class of two or more varieties of fresh fruit, cookies, chocolate, cheese, or whatever food you choose. Determine the characteristics to be compared (for example, aromas, flavor, texture) and use a chart to record your observations. In small groups or as individuals, put the information into a paragraph or short essay. Look for fresh, vivid descriptive details and for the meaning behind the comparison.

4. *Digging Deeper*—Read over your writing from Exercise 2 or Exercise 3. What have you learned? Why is the comparison interesting or important? How can this information be used? Write a paragraph about your thoughts.

5. *Organizing the Comparison*—Look back at your writing from Exercise 2 or Exercise 3. Rewrite it in two ways, block and alternating format. Which do you prefer? Why?
6. *Choosing a Format*—Rearrange the cookie tasting essay included earlier in this chapter in an alternating format. What differences do you notice in the new organization? Which do you prefer? Why?
7. *Exploring Similarities*—In what real-life situations would you focus on the similarities of two apparently dissimilar items?
8. Use an analogy other than cooking to explain what you know about the writing process.

IDEAS FOR WRITING

1. Explore the similarities and differences between two or three poems on the same subject, for example, "Digging" by Seamus Heaney (see p. 300) and "Banking Potatoes" by Yusef Komunyakaa (in his *Pleasure Dome: New and Collected Poems*); or between "Blackberries" by Yusef Komunyakaa (see p. 157), "Blackberry-Picking" by Seamus Heaney (from his *Death of a Naturalist*), and "Blackberry Eating" by Galway Kinnell (from his *Three Books*).
2. Compare and contrast the food traditions of two cultures or families with which you are familiar. Use specific examples and details. Explore the sources and effects of these traditions.
3. Examine two professions, perhaps two that you yourself are interested in, and outline the similarities and differences. Would you choose one over the other? Could the two be combined in some way? (See the excerpt from Irena Chalmers' *Food Jobs* in Chapter 15.)
4. Experiment in the kitchen with two methods of cooking the same food (for example, steaming or grilling vegetables) or with varying the ingredients in a recipe (for example, sweetening muffins with sugar or fruit juice). Write an essay explaining what you did and what you learned. Include vivid sensory details.

CHAPTER 14
PROCESS—ANALYSIS, NARRATIVE, RECIPE

By the end of this chapter, you should begin to . . .

- define three types of writing about a process: process analysis, process narrative, and instructions or recipes;
- identify the audience and purpose, and adjust details and vocabulary accordingly;
- identify the ingredients and equipment necessary to perform a process, and break the process down into a sequence of steps;
- provide helpful explanations and appropriate cautions; and,
- when appropriate, add stories, context, language, etc., that give the writing personality.

Explaining how to do something—giving directions—is a task that we've probably performed at work, school, and home. Perhaps you've taught a child to tie his shoes or make scrambled eggs. Or perhaps you've explained the layout of the kitchen to a new co-worker. In a face-to-face interaction, you can see at each moment whether your directions are being understood and followed correctly. You can make adjustments as you go. "No," you say to the little boy, "make the loop this way," or "See, the eggs are ready." In writing, though, as we've said before, we do not have the opportunity to supervise the process directly, and we must put all the necessary information in the text.

TYPES OF WRITING ABOUT A PROCESS

Writing about a process falls generally into three types: **process analysis**, in which you explain how something is done; **process narrative**, in which you tell how you (or someone else) did something; and **instructions** or recipes, in which you give directions on how to do something. All writing about a process includes a list of ingredients and equipment, an outline of the necessary steps in the correct sequence, and appropriate explanations and cautions. All writing about a process should use the vocabulary and level of detail appropriate to the audience and purpose of each piece. Process analyses and process narratives are written in essay format with an introduction and a conclusion. Their purpose is to help the audience understand the process but not necessarily

Even with a recipe, some processes are difficult to master—especially for the Three Stooges!

Columbia Pictures/Photofest © Columbia Pictures

perform it. The sentences are not commands like "fold the egg whites into the batter" but statements: "The egg whites are then folded into the batter." The following paragraph is from a process analysis.

> To make hollandaise, finely chopped shallots, white wine and cracked black peppercorns are reduced until they are almost dry; then they are mixed with a little water and added to a bowl. Next, egg yolks are added and heated over a pot of steaming water and whisked until their temperature reaches about 145° Fahrenheit. At this point the eggs will have roughly tripled in volume and will fall off the whisk in long strands. If the eggs are undercooked, they will fall off the whisk like water, and if they are overcooked, they will curdle in the metal bowl, evidenced by small semi-solid chunks of soon-to-be-cooked eggs.

> —**Robert A. Hannon**, student writer

One difference between a process analysis like this one and a process narrative is that the analysis is written in the third person (*he* or *she, one,* etc.) or in the passive voice (as in the preceding paragraph), while the process narrative is often written in the first person (*I*). The analysis is also more likely to be in the present tense, while the narrative may be in the past tense.

A recipe is a set of instructions or directions for completing a process. Like a process analysis and a process narrative, a recipe lays out ingredients, defines procedures, moves forward in strict sequence, uses appropriate transitional expressions, and offers guideposts—ways to know if things are proceeding correctly. Unlike an analysis or narrative, however, and unlike an essay, a recipe does not consist of a series of paragraphs that are made up of statements. Instead, a recipe is a list of *commands* whose subject is the reader, "you." Its purpose is to help readers perform the process themselves. Notice how the student paragraph about making hollandaise sauce might be rewritten in recipe format:

Ingredients

finely chopped shallots

white wine

cracked black peppercorns

water

egg yolks

Reduce shallots, wine, and peppercorns until almost dry. Mix with a little water and place in bowl. Add egg yolks and, whisking continuously, heat over pot of steaming water until mixture reaches 145° Fahrenheit. At this point eggs have tripled in volume and will fall off whisk in long strands.

Since a recipe's purpose is to prepare the reader to reproduce the process, it will specify the amount of each ingredient. An essay need not do so. Further, in a recipe we may

Types of Writing about a Process

	Process Analysis	Process Narrative	Recipes/Instructions
Purpose	to explain how a particular process works	to tell the story of how someone performed a particular process	to instruct the reader how to perform the process
Format	essay format	essay format	list of ingredients and steps
Point of View	third person: **Shallots** *are reduced.*	first person: *I reduced the shallots.*	second person: *(You) Reduce the shallots.*
Verb Tense	present or past: *Shallots **are** reduced. Shallots **were** reduced.*	past or present: *I **reduced** the shallots. I **reduce** the shallots.*	[not applicable].
Mood: statement (indicative mood) v. command (imperative mood)	statement: *Shallots are reduced.*	statement: *I reduced the shallots.*	command: *Reduce the shallots.*
Ingredients	part of explanation	part of story	listed at the beginning
Sequence of steps	correct sequence	correct sequence	correct sequence

dispense with articles (*the* or *a*) before nouns, and sometimes with pronouns as well (we can write "place in bowl" rather than "place it in a bowl"), while in an essay we use formal sentences, complete with articles and pronouns. Consider the differences between recipe and essay formats in the following examples:

Recipe   Add egg yolks and, whisking continuously, heat over pot of steaming water until mixture reaches 145° Fahrenheit.

Essay   I added the egg yolks and, whisking continuously, heated them over a pot of steaming water until the mixture reached a temperature of 145° Fahrenheit.

Recipes are one of the most common applications of writing about a process, but instructions are important in all types of jobs, schools, and home settings. Process analyses can be found in textbooks and in such writing tasks as the proposal for a new restaurant, which analyzes the flow (or process) of service. Finally, process narratives make excellent essays and stories.

KNOW YOUR AUDIENCE

One of the most important aspects of writing about a process is understanding who your audience is and what terms and processes they already know. In the hollandaise paragraph, for example, would every audience understand how to "reduce" shallots, wine, and peppercorns? Probably not. Yet most would know how to "whisk" egg yolks. In writing for an audience of experienced cooks, you might explain the steps in less detail and feel free to use specialized culinary terms such as *mirepoix* or *en papillote*. For a general audience, however, you will want to define these terms or else explain the procedure without using them.

You must also decide how far to break down the process. As you write any given step, you are likely to assume that the reader already has a certain amount of knowledge or experience. In describing how to make scrambled eggs, for example, do you need to be as specific as "First, take the eggs out of the refrigerator"? That sounds funny, but the principle is an important one. In another essay, you might write "First, I saddled the horse." But does your audience know how to saddle a horse? Do you need to break down that part of the process further?

First I lifted the saddle, making sure the stirrups were tucked up into their leathers so that they didn't swing against the horse's

Has the horse been saddled correctly?

belly and frighten him. Then I laid the saddle gently on his back, slightly up on his withers, and slid it into place. In this way his coat would lie smoothly under the saddle.

And if you write with this level of detail, do you need to define *pommel* and *withers*? Or is this *too much* detail? You can only answer these questions when you have a specific audience and purpose in mind. For example, for general readers, you need to define your terms. However, unless you are preparing them to saddle a horse themselves, you may not need to break the process down into small steps.

INGREDIENTS AND STEPS

All writing about process includes some information about the ingredients and equipment used. In a set of directions like a recipe, the ingredients are often listed first so that the reader can assemble them in one place, so that he can prepare his *mise en place.* Remember the hollandaise recipe we looked at earlier, or turn to the recipe for Warm Savoy Cabbage Salad on page 249. Sometimes additional information is provided about the ingredients. In *Joy of Cooking,* for example, Irma Rombauer prefaces a recipe for Baked Potatoes with the following:

> The best baked potatoes are flaky when served—so start with mature baking types like Idahos. Although new potatoes can be used and will need only about half as much baking time, they will never have the desired quality. The present rage for wrapping potatoes in foil inhibits flakiness, because too much moisture is retained. In fact, to draw moisture out of bakers, they are often placed on a bed of rock salt. (319)

In a process analysis or narrative, the necessary ingredients or equipment may be discussed in an early paragraph, as they would be in a recipe, or they may be mentioned only at the point at which they are brought into play. In the next example, a process narrative, the equipment and ingredients are mentioned in the order of their appearance in the process.

> The recipe began with one can of Campbell's tomato soup. The circular lid was quickly taken off. The juicy, royal-deep red contents of the can were meticulously scraped into a small pot sitting on the stove. Following the soup contents, one can of cool, crisp water was stirred in. As the tomato soup began to simmer on the stove top, the rice was almost done cooking. After a few minutes, my mother added a cup of steaming hot, fluffy, long-grain rice to the pot. I could smell the lovely aromas of tomato soup. My lips tingled: I was dying to taste it.

—**Jahnna Howell**, student writer

Descriptive words spice up a process narrative, as in the previous example, and can be quite useful in cookbooks. For example, they can help us check that we have the right equipment—for omelets, Rombauer uses "a skillet with a long handle and a 5-inch base flaring gently to a 7-inch top"—and that we are handling the ingredients properly. Rombauer continues:

> The success of all these so-called omelets demands that the pan and the fat be hot enough to bind the base of the egg at once so as to hold the softer egg above, but not so hot as to toughen the base before the rest of the egg cooks.
>
> Eggs, therefore, and any food incorporated with them, must be at least 70° before being put into the pan. More omelet failures are due to eggs being used direct from the refrigerator than to any other cause. There is always, too, the problem of salting. As salt tends to toughen the egg structure, it should, in general, be added to the fillings or garnishes you choose to fold into the omelet. (226).

In the following process analysis, students explain the flow of service—that is, the steps in the process—in a PR Fact Sheet and Market Survey for their proposed new restaurant. The ingredients? Their friendly and highly trained staff.

Flow of Service

Once a patron steps in and to the counter, he or she will be greeted by the cashier in a cheerful and polite manner and offered help. If the consumer has never been there before, the cashier will give them a ten-second summary of the establishment. Whenever possible, the daily special will be pushed.

The order will be placed by a cashier who will input the order into the POS system and ask for the customers' name. If a beverage is ordered, it will be provided on the spot. The customers will be asked to step over to their left (right of the cashier) to wait for their order. If there is a long line, the cashier would begin to take orders in a slower fashion to allow for the kitchen to catch up. They might bide their time by fulfilling drink requests or taking orders slightly slower, but not enough to upset the patrons.

The ticket machine will print out the orders to the back, near the pass window. The Executive/Sous chef will read the order and plate the order as requested from a steam tray set below the window. As the amount of food being hot-held begins to decrease, the chef will call out to the commis to reheat some of the protein, greens, and starch on the stove or oven. Once heated to the appropriate temperature for the appropriate amount of time, the dishes will be brought over to the steam tables.

Once the food has been checked to be of the proper quality and plated, it will be sent out through the window where the food runner/cashier will call out the name of the patron to retrieve their food.

As pots and pans are being used and trays being sent back, the porters will wash them, dry them and place them back to their appropriate locations.

During slower services, the chefs and commis will prep for the next day's service.

Whenever there are no patrons by the counter, it will be wiped clean and the top organized.

—**James Shum, David Murray, and Jason Hsu**, student writers

The correct sequencing of the steps in a process, combined with enough detail for the audience to understand them, creates an effective process analysis and, here, a persuasive proposal.

The sequence of steps, whether incorporated into paragraphs within an essay or listed by number in a set of directions, is typically the focus when you're writing about a process. In a set of directions, the steps follow the ingredients and are listed as commands, as we saw in the earlier example about making hollandaise sauce. While the placement of the ingredients and the level of detail will vary depending on the audience and purpose of your writing, in all cases you will be careful to put the steps of the process in the correct sequence.

EXPLANATIONS AND CAUTIONS

When you are writing about a process, it is often helpful to include explanations and cautions. Particularly when you are writing a set of directions that you expect the reader to carry out, it is helpful for him to understand the reason for particular steps and to be warned of things that might go wrong. In describing how he prepares his sauté station, the writer in this next example explains why he holds items in "a nearby cooler":

I fill the sauce bins and hold the rest in a nearby cooler, along with the cream and cheese, for easy access when I run low. This helps because I don't have to go all the way to the walk-in during a rush.

—**David Filippini**, student writer

Here's an example from an essay about preparing breakfast for four:

On another stove top burner, heat a non-stick 12-inch sauté pan. The flame should not top medium. At this time locate some paper towels. They will help to absorb the fat when draining the bacon, thus making it less greasy. With a circular motion, move the hash browns in a counter clockwise motion to release them from the pan. At about this time—and do not attempt if stuck—flip the hash browns.

—**Nathan E. Bearfield**, student writer

Another writer includes this important caution:

> Don't forget to cover with the pot lid while cooking. . . . The rib meat has to be soft enough to come off from the bone when people bite it. That's the key point of this food. If the meat does not come off from the bone, it cannot be Galbe.
>
> —**Euijin Kim**, student writer

When directions involve potential dangers like fire or electrocution, it is essential to caution the reader about them and explain how to avoid them. Further, for safety's sake, such warnings should come at the beginning of the set of instructions as well as immediately before the dangerous step itself.

Sometimes a particular process allows variations on the steps or ingredients, as in this process narrative:

> When I would make Dulce de Leche, I would put the whole can [of evaporated milk] in the pressure-cooker. I learned from experience that the longer someone lets it cook, the darker and more bitter it becomes. I would let it cook for about 45 minutes to get a deep brown appearance and slowly open it after waiting 30 minutes for it to cool a bit. The reason I do this step is because if you open it while it is still hot, a long stream of hot and sticky caramel will come shooting out. After opening the can, I was told to add whatever I wanted, but to make sure I didn't add anything that would mix flavors. My mother used to add walnuts, but I just add a couple of teaspoons of pure vanilla extract. Without [that], the caramel would taste bitter.
>
> —**Simon M. Imas**, student writer

As you think through the steps of a process you are writing about, be sure to consider what might go wrong and how to prevent it. If you are writing about a process you know well, try to remember what it was like when you first performed it. What mistakes did you make? How do you avoid making them now?

PROCESS AND PERSONALITY

Writing about a process can be especially successful when the author's personality seems to emerge through the text. Editor Judith Jones, who discovered Julia Child's *Mastering the Art of French Cooking,* believed Child's engaging voice would make the book a bestseller in the United States. Jones's instinct was correct: The book and its author became a huge success. A quick search of the Internet yields pages of quotes that illustrate Julia Child's jovial, conversational tone and deliciously wicked sense of humor.

> "It's so beautifully arranged on the plate—you know someone's fingers have been all over it."

"Always remember: If you're alone in the kitchen and you drop the lamb, you can always just pick it up. Who's going to know?"

As we saw in Chapter 10, "voice" consists of all the decisions the writer makes about what details to include, how to organize the ideas, how to shape each sentence and choose each word. Irma Rombauer's *Joy of Cooking* is also written in a distinctive, often humorous, voice. About Fudge Pie, for example, Rombauer notes that it is a "crustless pie or cake unexcelled in its delicious and devastatingly rich quality. But do not let a little devastation deter you" (656). In the next example, notice the quirky use of "snug" to describe a "phrase" and the funny story about an inexperienced cook in this recipe for simple Baked Potatoes:

This little girl rolls out the dough with care.

We have always liked the snug phrase "baked in their jackets" to describe this process. But we are told that at least one young cook, after encountering it, called a home economist at the local utility company and complained that her grocer was unable to supply her with potato-jackets! (319)

Background information about the author's culture, such as that "[m]ost Koreans believe that food tastes better when it cooks with touch of hands" (**Jina Chun**, student writer), enriches a description of technique. Some cookbook writers discuss the historical context of their recipes, as Richard J. Hooker does in *The Book of Chowder:*

Until modern times a stark simplicity characterized the meals on Nantucket Island. A visitor there in the late eighteenth century described the diet of a large family as consisting mainly of clams, oysters, and Indian corn bread. (53)

For more about chowder, see the excerpt from *Moby-Dick* reprinted on pages 13–16.

Writing about process is also enlivened by a good story, whether about the nameless "young cook" in the earlier *Joy of Cooking* excerpt or the personal family connection in the following paragraph:

> My mom used to let me help her cook Chicken Supreme every time she made it. This might be the reason it is one of my favorites. Each time she tells me the story of her and her mother doing the same thing when she was a child. My mother would help my grandmother cook this same dish.
>
> —**Vincent Amato**, student writer

Books like Shoba Narayan's *Monsoon Diary: A Memoir with Recipes* and Laura Esquivel's *Like Water for Chocolate: A Novel in Monthly Installments with Recipes, Romances, and Herb Remedies* interweave stories and recipes, while process narratives like Molly-Iris Alpern's "When Life Gives You Lemons" (in this chapter's A Taste for Reading) seamlessly blend them.

Good writing about a process clearly outlines the necessary ingredients and the proper sequence of steps. Great writing explains the reasoning behind the steps, offers tips to judge how the process is going, and warns of possible problems. Best-selling writing offers a personal connection with an engaging author—the secret to the continued success of certain classic cookbooks.

A TASTE FOR READING

Christopher Hirsheimer and Melissa Hamilton, both formerly at Saveur, *describe themselves as "home cooks writing about home cooking for other home cooks." In 2006 they launched their own food magazine called* Canal House Cooking. *The following recipe is from Volume 5, which collects some of their favorites.*

****

WARM SAVOY CABBAGE SALAD
from *Canal House Cooking*
serves 8

This warm salad is a classic of the Alsace region. Even if it seems slightly weird to mix Japanese with Alsatian, we prefer the rice wine vinegar's slightly sweet mellow flavor to traditional white wine vinegar's sharp bite. This dish is a delicious counterpoint to rich meats like goose or ham.

8 pieces thick-sliced bacon, sliced into thin pieces
1 cup rice wine vinegar
1 apple, peeled, cored, and chopped

1 savoy cabbage, cored, leaves julienned
Salt and pepper

Fry the bacon in a large heavy pot, stirring from time to time over medium heat until it is crisp and brown, about 20 minutes. Keep the heat low so the fat doesn't burn and take on an unpleasant taste. Lift the bacon from the pot with a slotted spatula and drain on paper towels.

Pour the vinegar into the pot with the bacon fat and cook for a minute over medium heat. Add the apples and cabbage, and season with salt and pepper. Cook until wilted and tender, about 30 minutes. Taste and adjust seasoning (don't hold back on the pepper, this dish benefits from its spicy bite). Transfer to a serving bowl and sprinkle with the bacon. Serve warm or at room temperature.

ABOUT THE READING

- What do we learn about this recipe from the introductory paragraph?
- The list of ingredients includes some processes as well. Explain.
- What equipment is required?
- What explanations and cautions do the authors provide?

In this process narrative, student writer Molly-Iris Alpern engages her readers with fluent sentences, vivid word choice, and the story of an important childhood achievement.

****

When Life Gives You Lemons
by Molly-Iris Alpern

My hands moved deftly and almost without thinking. The fork swept through the dry mixture, spinning up mini dust storms that settled down into fluffy piles. As I laughed and joked with my mother, I cut in tiny pats of cold butter with two knives and sprinkled ice water on the top to bring it all together. I shook some flour onto a pastry board handed down from my great-grandmother and rolled the dough into a neat circle. As I rolled out the dough, the smooth wood board wobbled and clattered. I flipped the neat circle of soft dough effortlessly into the pie plate, slipped a whisper-thin sheet of aluminum foil under long grains of rice, and slid the whole thing into the oven. As the crust slowly turned golden under the heat, I thought back to the first time I had gone through these motions.

It started in the library. Almost every weekend my father, sister, and I would take a drive down to our local library and spend the afternoon browsing the stacks and thumbing pages. For some reason, this day I couldn't find anything that held my attention. I must've been around ten years old and stuck between the children's books and the young adult novels. Looking for something to keep me occupied, I wandered down through the tall cases of books. I passed through the reference books, the short stories, passed through the home improvement section, and glanced at the foreign fiction. Just before I gave up all hope, I found myself surrounded by my favorite genre of books, one I didn't even know existed at the library. I had stumbled into the cookbook section.

I sat down on the carpet amid a sea of cookbooks that had caught my eye. Slowly and methodically, I went through every page, every picture, and every recipe in each book. One of the last books I picked up was a book full of dessert recipes and mouth-watering pictures. I could almost feel my teeth aching as I looked at the sugar-sweet dishes. All of the desserts looked delicious, but that afternoon one in particular called out to me—a recipe for lemon meringue pie. The picture showed a slice removed from the pie, and I was intrigued by the creamy, vibrant lemon curd topped by the toasted meringue. I closed the book and tucked it beneath my arm to bring home.

"I set to work turning the clear, gelatinous egg whites into a fluffy, soft, pure white meringue."

On the way home, my dad stopped at the store and we got a bag stretched taut from the weight and bulk of a dozen lemons, a paper egg carton full of brown speckled eggs, and two full pounds of unsalted butter. At my house my grandmother was there, and my mother had friends over to play bridge, but I was determined to ignore the chaos around me and make the pie. As the oven heated up, I studied the recipe carefully and gathered everything I would need. My grandmother helped me cut the butter into the flour for the crust and roll it out into a circle. We carefully wound it around the rolling pin that had once belonged to her and laid it down into the glass pie plate. On top of that I put a layer of crinkled aluminum foil, then poured in dried beans to weight it down. I slid the pie plate into the oven and set the timer.

While the crust blind-baked, I set to making the lemon curd. Using a glass citrus juicer from my great aunt, I spun the lemon halves until every drop of juice had been released from the firm, puckered skin. On the side of a glass bowl I cracked eggs and let the viscous whites slip between my fingers into a small bowl for later. In another bowl I collected the yolks and the lemon juice, dropped in a few pats of butter, and a healthy scoop of sugar. On the stove there was a small pot of water bubbling and I placed the glass bowl over it, letting the steam slowly heat the simple ingredients and turn them into a rich, thick, complex custard. As I stirred, I watched my spoon make patterns in the creamy lemon curd.

After taking the pot off the heat, I got two pot holders and carefully took the crust out of the oven and set it down on a rack to cool. I held the edges of the quick-cooling aluminum foil and carefully lifted it up, but a few errant beans shimmied loose and clattered to the floor. The edges of the crust were light brown and crisp, the bottom pale and dry to the touch. I impatiently waited for it to cool before spooning the rich, buttery lemon curd into the bottom of the shell. Back into the oven it went as I made the meringue.

I took the slithery, liquid-firm egg whites and sprinkled sugar onto the top, lugged our archaic hand mixer out of the bottom drawer, and set to work turning the clear, gelatinous egg whites into a fluffy, soft, pure white meringue. My arm ached as I mixed for what felt like an hour but finally the whites stood up in stiff peaks. The pie was out of the oven and cooled, and I piled the meringue on top of the creamy custard. Using a spoon, I spiked the meringue up so the little tips would brown under the heat of the broiler. I slid the pie back under the heat, excited and full of anticipation.

My mother and grandmother had been helping me all night, and they were just as excited as I was. As I watched the meringue turn cream colored, then tan, then a rich golden brown, I couldn't wait for it to be finished. Finally I pulled it out and tried to be patient, but the excitement won out. I cut a thick slice and lifted it out of the plate. The side view was even better than the one in the book—the crust was a crisp, flaky base, the lemon curd was glossy and thick, and the meringue was pure white tipped by toasted brown. As I took a bite, the tart lemon hit me first—sweet and tart at the same time, creamy and cool. The meringue came next, almost like a cloud on my tongue. The crust was buttery and firm, so flaky it almost melted on my tongue.

After eating another piece of the pie, I helped my mom clean the kitchen. Worn out from my long hours in the kitchen, I headed up to bed. Before I went upstairs, I turned around and said to my mother, "Mom, I'm so happy. Do you know why? Because today, I made my first pie crust." With that, I turned around and went to bed.

The calendar pages flipped forward and I pulled the finished apple pie out of the oven. As I did, I reminded my mom about my first experiences with the mysterious pie crust, the delicious lemon curd, and the fluffy meringue. As we sat at the table, eating the spiced apple pie with a lattice top, we laughed at my first attempts nearly eight years before. It may have taken hours and been a disorganized mess, but I still look back on it fondly.

The experience of taking raw ingredients, things so basic and familiar, and turning them into a true food was a new concept in my mind. My whole life had been full of culinary experimentation with less-than-successful results. For the first time, I could almost taste the result of the dish, and I could nearly feel the different textures on my tongue. It marked a change for me, a point where I realized I wanted to expand my knowledge and follow recipes, learn what others before me already knew and take what I could from it. It gave me a taste of pastry art and was one of my first successful baking projects, satisfying to my palate and my soul.

ABOUT THE READING

- Is "When Life Gives You Lemons" a process narrative or a process analysis? Explain.
- What does the title refer to? Do you think it's a good title for this piece? Why or why not?
- Describe the organization of the piece, paragraph by paragraph.
- What descriptive details do you find particularly effective? Use specific examples, and explain what you like about them.

RECIPE FOR REVIEW

TYPES OF WRITING ABOUT A PROCESS

1. **Process analysis** explains how something is done.
2. **Process narrative** tells how you did something.
3. **Instructions or recipes** give directions on how to do something.
4. Essay versus recipe format:
   - Process analyses and process narratives are written in essay format. They have an introduction and a conclusion, and sentences are written in the indicative mood (that is, *not* a command).
   - Recipes are different in that they usually begin immediately with a list of ingredients. The steps themselves may be listed or appear in small "paragraphs," but they are not in essay format. The steps are written in the imperative mood (that is, as commands).

RECIPE FOR WRITING ABOUT A PROCESS

- *Know Your Audience:* Use the vocabulary and level of detail appropriate to the audience and purpose of each piece.
- *Ingredients and Steps:* List and define the ingredients and equipment. Decide how much detail to include about each step, and check that the steps are in the correct order. Consider adding an explanation of the reasoning behind two or three of the steps.
- *Explanations and Cautions:* Try to anticipate what problems might arise in the process, such as the hash browns getting stuck or the pot not being tightly covered.
- *Process and Personality:* Consider adding background information about the process or a discussion of what you've learned through the process and why it's important to you. In other words, add a touch of personality.

CHAPTER EXERCISES

1. *Types of Process Writing*—Rewrite the process analysis on hollandaise sauce on p. 241 as a process narrative. Use the first person and the past tense.
2. *Know Your Audience*—Choose a process you are familiar with from home, school, or work, and write a short process analysis for a general audience. Your purpose is to help the audience understand the process but not necessarily perform it.
3. *Ingredients and Steps*—Add a separate list of ingredients and steps to your process analysis from Exercise 2. Check that the steps are in the correct sequence.
4. *Explanations and Cautions*—Add an explanation of the reasoning behind two or three of the steps you listed in Exercise 3. Then try to anticipate what problems might arise in the process, such as the hash browns getting stuck or the pot not being tightly covered. Add this information to the process analysis.
5. *Process and Personality*—Add some background information about the process you've been working with in Exercises 2–4. Conclude the piece with a discussion of what you may have learned through the process or why it's important to you. In other words, add a touch of personality.
6. *Recipes*—Choose an old family recipe, and find out all you can about it. Is there a story behind it? If possible, prepare the dish yourself. Then write the recipe (and story, if available), including a list of ingredients and the sequence of steps. Add any helpful explanations or cautions you can.

IDEAS FOR WRITING

1. Choose a process that you are familiar with from home, school, or work (perhaps how to change the oil in your car, or how to make chocolate chip cookies), and write a complete set of instructions (recipe) for a general audience. Think carefully about what terms to use, which ones to define, and how far to break the process down.
2. Write a "How To" article, perhaps on a humorous topic.
3. In what ways is the writing process outlined in Chapter 3 like a recipe? How is it different from a recipe?
4. Explain the differences between the processes of cooking and baking.

CHAPTER 15
EXAMPLE, DEFINITION, CAUSE AND EFFECT

By the end of this chapter, you should begin to . . .

- use specific, relevant examples to develop and illustrate your ideas;
- use definition to develop and clarify your ideas; and
- use cause and effect to clarify, explain, and organize your ideas.

This chapter offers a combination platter: three additional methods of developing and illustrating your ideas, from examples and definitions to cause and effect. These methods or modes of development are like methods of cooking: will you boil, bake, or braise? Or is some combination of cooking methods the best way to achieve the desired result? We may develop our ideas through different methods within the same essay just as we may use several different cooking methods to prepare a single dish.

WORKING WITH EXAMPLES

There's nothing like a good **example** to make communication more effective. "Brush your teeth at least twice a day to prevent health problems," says the dentist. This general advice may not make much of an impact, though, unless we're offered some concrete examples. "Poor dental hygiene may cause bad breath, tooth decay, gum disease, and inflamed arteries." That's much clearer, isn't it? And it's much more effective as advice.

"If you improve your written communication skills," your instructor intones, "you can have a successful career as a food writer." Sure, you reply, but what *is* food writing? Your instructor responds with a list of examples: "There are many different kinds of food writing, for example, recipes and cookbooks, menu descriptions, restaurant reviews, scientific articles, and textbooks."

Examples are frequently used with other methods of development. In the following paragraph, the writer classifies food and cooking shows as demo, competition, show and tell, or reality. Then he gives an example of each category.

Top Chef is another popular cooking competition.

> With the Food Network, TLC, Bravo, Travel Channel, and Cooking Channel all over television sets, we are constantly surrounded by all of this exposure to food. Food and cooking shows are becoming increasingly popular in America and the rest of the world. There are the "demo shows" like *Everyday Italian*, the "competition shows" like *Iron Chef*, the "show and tell" *Man vs. Food,* and the "reality shows" like *Cake Boss.* It has gotten to the point where we have almost every style of TV show, just about food! The shows are great exposure for our industry, but they also paint an image of us that is sugar coated.

—**Samuel Beard**, student writer

Like telling a story, using an example is a way of developing ideas that we use automatically when speaking and that transfers effectively to writing. Examples make an idea concrete; they put a picture in the reader's mind. We use examples to illustrate or explain a point and sometimes to prove one.

USING SPECIFIC EXAMPLES

Examples often come to mind as the most natural way of explaining oneself. "What do you mean by that?" we might ask. "Give me an example." Examples are especially useful in explaining concepts or points of view that might be unfamiliar to the reader. In the following passage, the writer uses specific examples to explain the relationship in his childhood between his state of mind and the sauce he chose for dipping his chicken fingers.

> There were so many sauces to choose from, depending on my mood. If I was happy, it would be the sweet and sour. If I was angry and resentful, it had to be honey mustard. And, of course, there were those "I don't know" moods when I would get BBQ sauce.

—**Thomas Monahan**, student writer

Examples can give shape to the idea in your mind. They can create an image that illustrates the point. Often a general statement is best illustrated through a specific example, as in the following paragraph about the movie *Chocolat:*

> The most interesting scene in the movie is when Vianne asks people to spin the dish and then tells what kinds of sweets best suit each person. For example, there is a young boy who is interested in the dark arts. When Vianne spins the dish, he sees a skull. Vianne recommends to him a dark chocolate. She sees through people's souls and makes the best chocolates for them. Soon, people begin to discover the mouth-melting effects of her wonderful treat.
>
> —**Jina Chun**, student writer

The little boy's dark chocolate helps us understand the general statement that Vianne "tells what kinds of sweets best suit each person." And it is especially important that we do understand this since it is "the most interesting scene" for the writer.

Examples can also be used to win the reader over to one's point of view, especially when the reader is likely to resist. In stating that writing and cooking have similarities, for instance, the next writer invites the audience to appreciate this point by offering specific examples from each field:

> Both writing and cooking allow you to get a feel for your reader or customer. If you're writing for a romance novel, you're not going to have very many jokes or pictures. If you were writing a children's story, you

Chocolatier Vianne tells what kinds of sweets best suit each person.

wouldn't make the reading very difficult. It is just the same with cooking. You don't go to an Italian restaurant and start cooking Japanese food; moreover, you wouldn't cook a roasted tenderloin for a vegetarian.

—**Joseph Pierro**, student writer

Romance novel writing is one "cuisine" in the realm of fiction, just as Italian and Japanese cooking are cuisines in the world of food. The writer uses this analogy to illustrate one of the similarities between writing and cooking: that it's important to address the needs and expectations of your audience. For example, "You wouldn't cook a roasted tenderloin for a vegetarian." The examples are parallel and precise.

USING RELEVANT EXAMPLES

In much of our writing, there is an element of "proof." We want the reader to understand that our ideas are important and reasonable, even if she doesn't actually agree with them. Examples can be of critical importance here. By choosing an example that relates to the main idea, we can be more persuasive. An off-topic example, on the other hand, tends to cast doubt on our main idea. Suppose we tried to insist that knives are a useful survival tool because so many different types are manufactured. Is the number of types really relevant to the knife's usefulness? Probably not. But see how the examples in this paragraph *are* relevant:

The knife can be used for both hunting and building on the island. For instance, I can use the knife to sharpen a straight stick to use as a spear. The spear can be used to catch fish in the water or to stab unsuspecting birds or other small animals. With the knife I can cut my way through thick vegetation. I can also cut down large leaves and branches to build a shelter. The shelter will keep me safe from wild animals and bad weather. The knife will be necessary for my survival.

—**Nicholas Castellano**, student writer

The knife is useful, we discover, because it helps provide food and shelter, assistance that is unrelated to the variety of knives available in camping stores. We *see* the uses of the knife from the sharpened stick with its sudden "stab" to the shelter of leaves and branches. When the paragraph wraps up with the firm statement "The knife will be necessary for my survival," we can readily agree. The examples have been so specific and relevant that the final sentence seems simply to state the obvious.

Good examples can boost your credibility and persuade your readers. Too few examples or poorly chosen examples can weaken the effectiveness of your writing.

WORKING WITH DEFINITIONS

Because of our desire to communicate effectively with our readers, we may need to define any special terms we use. If you're writing a cookbook for a general audience, for example, you may need to define such technical culinary terms as *mirepoix* or *bain marie*. Often a **definition** may be a simple synonym, as in the following example:

> The opening scene eerily foreshadows, or predicts, the final events of the story.

Or we may follow a new term with a phrase that defines it:

> Chris developed an interest in algebraic topology, which involves mapping complex spaces.

At other times the definition may require a full paragraph. For example, in an essay about Dave Boyle's character in the film *Mystic River,* we might want to write a paragraph explaining the basic characteristics of post-traumatic stress disorder. In this excerpt from *How Music Works,* author John Powell briefly defines *arpeggio* as a "chord played as a stream of its individual notes" but then develops his explanation further:

> Arpeggios add a layer of complexity and subtlety to music because you can choose exactly which notes from the chord will coincide with particular notes in the tune and also add a rhythm to the arpeggio pattern. (112)

Note Powell's use of causation: Arpeggios create a certain effect *because.* Powell also makes good use of examples, noting that arpeggios are common not only in classical but also in rock music, for instance, at the beginning of Led Zeppelin's "Stairway to Heaven" and the Eagles' "Hotel California." (112–113)

A definition can also center around a process, like this one from Harold McGee's *On Food and Cooking* (revised edition):

> [F]ill the water-based liquid with droplets of oil, which are much more massive and slow-moving than individual molecules of

Research may be required to develop accurate definitions.

water, impede their motion, and so create a thick and creamy consistency in the mixture as a whole. Such a dispersion of one liquid in another is called an *emulsion*. (625)

In *Setting the Table*, successful restaurateur Danny Meyer explains his understanding of *hospitality* through compare and contrast:

Understanding the distinction between service and hospitality has been at the foundation of our success. Service is the technical delivery of a product. Hospitality is how the delivery of that product makes its recipient *feel*. Service is a *monologue*—we decide how we want to do things and set our own standards for service. Hospitality, on the other hand, is a *dialogue*. To be on a guest's side requires listening to that person with every sense, and following up with a thoughtful, gracious, appropriate response. It takes both great service and great hospitality to rise to the top. (65)

In the following paragraph, Harold McGee defines *allspice* with a combination of description, classification, comparison, and process:

Allspice is the brown, medium-sized dried berry [description] of a tree of the New World tropics. *Pimenta dioica* is a member of the myrtle family and a relative of the clove. [classification] Allspice took its modern name in the 17th century because it was thought to combine the aromas of several spices, and today it's often described as tasting like a mellow combination of clove, cinnamon, and nutmeg. It is indeed rich in clove's eugenol and related phenolic volatiles, with fresh, sweet, and woody notes (but no cinnamon volatiles) [comparison]. . . . The berries are picked when green and at the height of flavor, briefly fermented in heaps, "sweated" in bags to accelerate their drying and browning, then sun-dried for five to six days (or machine-dried). [process] Allspice finds notable use in pickling fish, meats, and vegetables, as well as in pie seasonings. (423)

It might also be that an essay will itself be an **extended definition**, which focuses the entire paper on defining a complex term such as *success, marriage,* or *tortillas*. In an extended definition, you may use several different additional methods of development. See "Tortillas," for example, in Chapter 4.

A final caution about definitions: Before using one, be certain that it's really necessary for your particular audience. We often look up terms in order to confirm their definitions for ourselves. Then it's an almost irresistible impulse to begin our paper with "Justice means" or "Irony is defined as." However, it's unlikely that your readers will benefit from the dictionary definition of *justice* or *irony*. Certainly your instructor will not, if your audience is an academic one. It would be better to let the examples and discussion in your paper reveal the meaning of these terms. Or, if a quick definition is necessary, it's a good idea to write it in your own words.

WORKING WITH CAUSE AND EFFECT

Culinary students know all about cause and effect. When you beat the eggs, they froth up. When you add yeast, the dough rises. When you heat the water in the double boiler, the chocolate melts. The heat is the cause; the melting is the effect. Studies of cause and effect go beyond the kitchen, of course. Historians write about the causes of World War II while engineers study the causes of a bridge's collapse. Economists warn us about the effects of a stock market crash while legislators review the effects of a change in the drinking age.

Narration, or storytelling, shows *what* happened. Process analysis tells *how* it happened. **Cause and effect** explains *why* it happened. Like narration, process analysis, and the other rhetorical modes, cause and effect may be central to the subject and organization of a particular essay, or it may be confined to a single paragraph within a larger piece. Like definition, cause and effect can play a major role in persuasive writing.

ANALYZING CAUSES

An essay or paragraph often focuses on the various causes of a single event. What were the causes of World War II? Why did that bridge collapse? What caused the hollandaise sauce to break? The passage that follows offers a partial answer to that third question.

> A hollandaise sauce may break because the fat added to the yolks might have been too hot or too cold, the fat may have been added too fast, or the hollandaise was held at too high a temperature.
>
> —**Matthew Berkowski**, student writer

The temperature of the egg yolks is also important, as the next example makes clear.

> Egg yolks are added and heated over a pot of steaming water and whisked until their temperature reaches about 145° Fahrenheit. At this point the eggs will have roughly tripled in volume and will fall off the whisk in long strands. If the eggs are undercooked, they will fall off the whisk like water, and if they are overcooked, they will curdle in the metal bowl, evidenced by small semi-solid chunks of soon-to-be-cooked eggs.
>
> —**Robert A. Hannon**, student writer

Note that the writer describes the precise effects of undercooking and overcooking the eggs: the eggs will "fall off the whisk like water" or form "small semi-solid chunks." These details paint a vivid picture of the doomed hollandaise! Further, these causes and effects seem reasonable; we could test them by trying the hollandaise ourselves. Although there are times when we might not be sure what caused an event and so want to suggest causes that haven't been proved, it is best to avoid proposing *unreasonable* causes (such as the hollandaise broke because the chef wasn't wearing a side apron) or *simplistic* causes (the hollandaise broke because something went wrong).

Causes are often explained or presented in relation to time. In the previous example, the causes of the broken hollandaise are *immediate* and occur a very short time before the event. Sometimes causes can be *remote,* that is, farther away in time. In the case of the hollandaise, the remote cause might have been that the chef did not get a good night's sleep and so forgot to warm the butter appropriately. Though part of the chain of events, the chef's poor sleep is not as close to the broken hollandaise as the cold butter.

A second way to think about causes (or effects) is in terms of importance or strength, that is, to identify the *main* or most important and powerful cause of an event versus the *contributing* or less important and powerful causes. While the chef's poor sleep *contributed* to the problem with the hollandaise, the *main* cause of the broken emulsion was the cold butter.

Analyzing Causes: Why did the sauce break?

Analyzing causes in terms of . . .		
time	immediate cause	the butter was added too quickly
	remote cause	the chef did not get a good night's sleep
importance	main cause	the butter was too cold
	contributing cause	the cooler's thermometer malfunctioned

ANALYZING EFFECTS

While some topics focus on causes, others focus on *effects*. They answer the question "What happened *as a result?*" This example describes the effects of a character's "irresponsible conduct" in the film *Mystic River*:

> Celeste lied about the truth to Jimmy. That meant that she was an egoist and didn't take care of her husband and her family, including her son. She just wanted to protect herself from David. In the long run, her irresponsible conduct destroyed her family. Because of her hasty judgment, her son Michael would live under a fatherless family, and she would live with a guilty conscience.
>
> —**Soyang Myung**, student writer

The event or *condition* here is Celeste's failure to take care of her family, her "irresponsible conduct," which results in her husband's death, her son's grief, and her own despairing guilt.

CAUSAL CHAINS

We often recognize the presence of a *series* of causes and effects, that is, a **causal chain**, in which one consequence is the cause of another, which in turn causes another. In *Mystic River*, Dave's childhood trauma caused him to act strangely, which attracted the attention of the detectives investigating a murder twenty-five years later. Yet because he fears becoming a pedophile himself, as a result of his early experience, he refuses to tell anyone what really happened. Since he doesn't tell the truth, the victim's father assumes he is guilty and kills him in revenge. And since Dave is dead, his son Mike is now doomed to repeat Dave's own sad, fatherless youth.

The broken hollandaise can also be part of a causal chain. Suppose the cook has a toothache that causes her to lose sleep, which in turn causes her to hold the hollandaise at too high a temperature. The high temperature causes the sauce to break moments after it is served to the customer, causing the customer to complain to the server, who in turn complains to the cook. Now three people have had a bad day!

ORGANIZING A CAUSE AND EFFECT ESSAY

In organizing a cause and effect essay, you may wish to begin with the cause (or effect) nearest in time and continue in chronological order. The writer of the following paragraph introduces the topic—the drama of a broken hollandaise—and outlines three causes.

Oil and Water Don't Mix, or Do They?

Just imagine you're at a very fine dining establishment; the garçon comes with your eggs benedict, and you notice that the hollandaise is broken. Broken hollandaise is not only visually demeaning to the customer, but it doesn't please the palate either. The chef should have recognized that the hollandaise was broken. But maybe the hollandaise broke on the way from the kitchen to the table. A hollandaise sauce might break because the fat added to the yolks might have been too hot or too cold, the fat may have been added too fast, or the hollandaise was held at too high of a temperature.

—**Matthew Berkowski**, student writer

A problem may first arise with the *mise en place*. Is the fat too hot or too cold? A little later on in the process, the problem might be caused by the method: has the fat been added too quickly? Finally, the sauce might break *after* it's made if it is held at too high a temperature.

As the writer develops and explains each of these causes, he uses clear transitional sentences to keep the reader on track:

In order for a hollandaise sauce not to break, the fat that is added to the egg yolk concoction cannot be too hot or too cold.

Causal Chain

The cook's toothache
causes her to lose sleep

which causes her to hold the sauce
at too high a temperature

which causes the sauce to break
before it reaches the customer

which causes the customer to complain
to the server, who complains
to the cook . . .

and all three have a bad day.

Another reason that the hollandaise may break is that the fat might have been added too quickly.

Finally, hollandaise may break because it was stored at too high or too low of a temperature.

Words like *reason* and *because* are useful transitions in a cause and effect essay. The writer also mentions an alternative to the tricky handmade emulsion:

There is another method of making hollandaise that doesn't result in a sore arm or having to bother someone. Having a second person helping you makes this sauce produce pretty darn fast.

The writer concludes, however, that "making the hollandaise by yourself takes a little longer, but it strengthens your skills." He distinguishes between the more remote but important effect of improved skill and the immediate, practical result of a helping hand.

DEVELOPING AN ESSAY WITH CAUSE AND EFFECT

Like the other rhetorical modes, cause and effect is a way of thinking about or developing our ideas. It is likely to be only one of several modes used in writing an essay, just as braising may be only one of several cooking methods used in putting together a plate. In the following essay, the writer analyzes the evolution of her philosophy about food and cooking, a complex series of causes and effects. As you read, notice the various types of causes and effects but also the other methods by which ideas are developed.

My Mother's Kimchee

My mother has a genius for making Kimchee, which is the famous and representative Korean dish served at almost every Korean meal. Though the recipe of Kimchee is common for every Korean, there are huge differences between each Kimchee according to the person who makes it. My mother's Kimchee is well known as fabulous among the close neighbors. Kimchee is made of fermented vegetables—such as cabbage or turnips—that are mixed with chili powder, some fish sauces, minced garlic, a little bit of granulated sugar, and various Korean seasonings. The Kimchee is pickled before being stored in tightly sealed pots or jars to ferment. In this process of fermentation, the Kimchee gets a unique taste that is spicy, pungent and sour, and a crispy texture. Especially the spicy and pungent flavor is aroused by chili powder.

In November—the season in which Kimchee is most often prepared—Koreans lay up large stocks of Kimchee for winter, because it is hard to find fresh vegetables then. People want to make Kimchee together with my mother because they want to get the delicious Kimchee—the important commodity for their loving family. Preparing and making Kimchee with several close neighbors together is such a major event. While preparing all the ingredients and sharing my mom's hidden recipe, each of the neighbors often notices that the secret of my mom's Kimchee is not that much different from their own, so they catch a little surprise. The essential point of making a dish is not that far away from the dish's general process, which almost everyone knows. Just a small additive touch and some switches within the process make differences. For example, my mother uses several different kinds of chili powders together, not selecting only one kind of chili powder. The mixing of the hottest one and the mild but sweet chili powder boost the flavor of Kimchee in a sophisticated way, and the result is different.

My mother also spends more time to find fresh ingredients. The red pepper for chili powder is famous in Chunyang, a southern area of Korea. She visits there in person and buys it for year-round use, though it takes four hours to get there. When I was young, I felt that she was too obsessive, even though she could make a delectable Kimchee. However, I have changed my attitude toward admiring my mother as I became a woman. Her efforts and passion to give a delicious dish to her family must have been accumulating in my mind, and now I see that making and completing a dish need a person's spiritual faith. I received inspiration from what she did; to live as a chef is a wonderful way of being absorbed in ingredients. I could create a totally different dish with them, and then I could give pleasure to people. I am more enthusiastic about the cooking process than about just eating a dish that is made by others and served. I especially like to think what I will cook for family or friends, what vegetable would be good for this season; then I imagine how the taste will be, what kinds of food would be appealing to them, and so on. I believe caring about people and preparing food are strongly linked to each other, and both of them create the thing we always crave, "love."

Like my mother who made an effort to look for better ingredients, the basic philosophy that I keep in mind as a prospective chef is to put love into my dishes. As the generations have changed and people's living patterns developed, food is not only providing nutrients but is also another method to work off people's frustration. Thus the custom of eating and sharing nice food has been developed through human history. Since I decided to be a chef, I feel that I am charged with a sense of duty as if I have become a therapist who gives a mental peace to people who need treatment. Sharing my food will be a prescription (recipe) for people who have a lack of fullness from their lives.

—**Hyun Ah Seong**, student writer

The first sentence states the central idea—"My mother has a genius for making Kimchee"—and the introductory paragraph goes on to describe the ingredients of this popular Korean dish. Cooking, as we've said, is all about cause and effect, and the writer notes that the process of fermentation affects the flavor and texture of the vegetables: "Especially the spicy and pungent flavor is aroused by chili powder."

The writer then explores both the causes of her mother's "genius for making Kimchee" and its effects on her as a child and as an adult. Words like *because* and *result* emphasize the relationship between cause and effect.

> The mixing of the hottest one and the mild but sweet chili powder boosts the flavor of Kimchee in a sophisticated way, and the result is different.

The writer also identifies a more *remote* cause than the mixing of the chili powders: "My mother also spends more time to find fresh ingredients." She travels four hours to find a certain pepper, for example. As a girl, the writer found this "too obsessive." Only later did she realize that her mother's "efforts and passion to give a delicious dish to her family must have been accumulating in my mind." The result is a philosophy of cooking:

> Like my mother who made an effort to look for better ingredients, the basic philosophy that I keep in mind as a prospective chef is to put love into my dishes.

Perhaps the most important cause of her mother's genius for Kimchee is the love she puts into it.

When we think about cause and effect, we are asking *Why?* We are tapping into one of the human being's most important traits: curiosity. In exploring ideas through questions about causes and effects, as Hyun Ah does, we may discover something about ourselves.

A TASTE FOR READING

Irena Chalmers has written over forty books and contributed regularly to such publications as The New York Times, Food & Wine, Gastronomica, Food Arts, *and* Nation's Restaurant News. *Check out her food blog at www.foodjobsbook.com.*

****

Introduction to *Food Jobs: 150 Great Jobs for Culinary Students, Career Changers and Food Lovers*
by Irena Chalmers

I get an enormous amount of satisfaction and pleasure from teaching at the Culinary Institute of America. At the first meeting of my professional-food-writing class, I ask the students to tell me something about themselves that will surprise me. I know they are all attending the school because they love to cook and are passionate about food. I also know not all of them will choose to become professional chefs upon graduation. So what else do they *love* to do?

Recently, a rather grumpy-looking girl folded her arms and glared at me. In response to what she clearly thought was a dumb question, she answered, "I *love* to go shopping." Everyone laughed, but I thought this was a really useful piece of information.

I told her about a former colleague at Windows on the World who is a tabletop consultant. She scours manufacturers' showrooms for the latest designs of china, glassware, and distinctive serving plates for several upscale restaurants. My student now does the same thing. She works part-time as a tabletop counselor and is also a prop stylist for a food photographer. She too goes shopping every day. When a chef wants a tagine, mandolin, or any other specialized piece of equipment, she knows exactly what it is and can lay her hands on it immediately. She found her *bliss*—her perfect food job.

Another student arrived early to class carrying the *Wall Street Journal.* After graduation, he joined an investment banking firm that paid his way to become a financial analyst specializing in food companies. He combined his culinary knowledge with his interest in finance and embarked on a career for which he was uniquely qualified.

A student in the culinary program responded to my question by saying, "I want to be a rock star." I couldn't help him become a great musician, but instead I suggested he find a job as a personal chef for his favorite rock group. He did. When he cooks something good for them to eat, they sometimes let him play with them. He found himself a really cool job; he had the courage to offer his food knowledge and the leader of the band was happy to give him a seat on the bus.

A Korean culinary student whose English-speaking ability did not quite match his exemplary cooking skills found work as a private chef at the Korean Embassy in Washington, D.C. The diplomats were delighted to have "home-cooked" food prepared by someone who spoke their language.

These are examples of using your knowledge, experience, and passion to find your perfect food job. None of these students, or many others I have met, knew these jobs existed. And if they had, they wouldn't know where to begin to apply for such positions. Even experienced food professionals are largely unaware of the dazzling range of career paths that will enable them to find work that is interesting, challenging, and fulfilling.

You may not know that there's an ice-cream company that employs a full-time taster. You may not know how to become a tea or coffee taster or an account executive promoting beef, pork, peaches, pears, or other commodities. You may be unaware that the United States Postal Service employed a chef to provide meals for the cycling team that it sponsored. *American Idol* engages a personal chef to feed the secluded finalists. An experienced cook may earn eighty thousand dollars a year—tax-free—working on a luxury yacht cruising the Greek islands. Chefs work at NASA developing food for astronauts. A food lover with no formal training may find success as a restaurant critic if he possesses a vibrant palate and can write well.

There is always plenty of work to be found in restaurants, but food lovers could explore other opportunities and think about becoming a private chef for a movie star, a sports hero, or a television anchor. Have you thought about a career as a literary agent, cheese-shop owner, food-travel writer, bartender, artisanal bread baker, wedding-cake designer, food photographer, recipe tester, food-trends researcher, radio interviewer, publicist, bed-and-breakfast owner, cooking-school teacher, media trainer, or any one of literally hundreds of other ways to earn a living in the food world?

Whether you are interested in science or supermarkets, in engineering, accounting, human relations, or flower arranging for fancy parties, in cookbook reviewing or judging cooking contests, there is a job in the food field for you. Or you can dream up something that has never been done and make it happen.

ABOUT THE READING

- What do *you* love to do? Can you imagine a dream job that combines several of your interests? Explain.
- Do you think the examples are specific and relevant? Explain. Why do you suppose the author offers more than one or two examples?
- Outline the *order* of the examples, and explain its effect.
- How does the author define—or *redefine*—"food job"?

RECIPE FOR REVIEW

WORKING WITH EXAMPLES

Examples are events, stories, facts, or other specific information that is used to illustrate, explain, or prove a general point.

- Examples should be specific and relevant. Ask yourself whether the example really proves your point.
- Consider also how many examples you need. Too few will leave the reader unconvinced; too many will leave her overwhelmed or bored.

WORKING WITH DEFINITIONS

You may use **definition** to explain single words or complex concepts.

- Examples and analogies can help clarify a definition.
- Definition is often part of persuasive writing (see Chapter 16).
- The definition of a complex or controversial term may be **extended** through an entire essay.

WORKING WITH CAUSE AND EFFECT

Cause and effect explores a topic by asking *why* something happened or *why* something is the way it is (**causes**) or by asking what the *results* or *consequences* of a particular event are (**effects**). Essays may focus on causes only, effects only, or a combination of the two. Causation is often part of persuasive writing (see Chapter 16).

- Causes and effects can be organized in terms of *time* (immediate and remote) and *importance* (main and contributing). Causes and effects sometimes form a sequence in which one event hinges on the next to form a **causal chain.**
- *Cautions:* You should be able to prove that two events are connected; don't mistake one event being followed by another for one event *causing* another. Be sure your causes or effects are not unreasonable or oversimplified.

CHAPTER EXERCISES

1. *Finding Specific Examples*—What does it mean to be a good friend, a good cook, or a good student? Brainstorm a list of examples that illustrate your ideas. Be sure they are vivid and specific.
2. *Finding Relevant Examples*—Look back at your brainstorming from Exercise 1. Which of the examples seems the most relevant? Why? Try to find two more relevant examples that might help the reader to understand your point.
3. *Examining Definition*—Describe how definition is used in "Tortillas" (Chapter 4) or one of the other selections in A Taste for Reading.
4. *Writing Definitions*—Choose three of the vocabulary words from this chapter's A Taste for Reading, and rewrite the definition in your own words. Add an example of how the word could be used in a sentence.
5. *Identifying Main and Contributing Causes*—Think about one of your good friends (or a favorite movie, actor, food, or restaurant). List all the reasons you can think of that you like this person, for example, a kind personality, wise advice, sense of humor, loyalty, similar interests, or other reasons. Now, among those reasons, which one is the most important or powerful? Why?
6. *Analyzing Effects*—Choose an event or situation that you are familiar with, and analyze its effects. For example, if you overslept, were you then late for work or school? Which effect is the most important? Why?

IDEAS FOR WRITING

1. Choose one of the following topics, and use specific examples to develop your answer: How would you be different if you were five years old? Eighty years old? A different race? A different gender? A different species?
2. What is a problem in the food service industry? Write a paragraph or essay in which you explore specific examples of the problem.
3. Write an essay-length extended definition of *success, marriage,* or *good food.*

4. Think of a food you particularly like or particularly dislike. Brainstorm the reasons why, including more and less important reasons, past and present reasons. Perhaps taste the food as you brainstorm to increase the number of sensory details in your writing.

5. Pick a topic in cooking or baking, such as why emulsions form or why bread rises. Do a little research into the science behind the event, perhaps by reading the relevant section from *On Food and Cooking: The Science and Lore of the Kitchen* by Harold McGee. Organize the cause or causes in terms of importance or time, and write the essay.

6. Choose a topic from contemporary culture, such as Why are reality television shows so popular? or What effect did *Super Size Me* have on McDonald's and on American culture as a whole? You may wish to research the topic (see Chapter 18). Then answer the question in an essay, citing any sources appropriately both within the text and on the Works Cited page (see Chapter 19).

CHAPTER 16
PERSUASIVE WRITING

By the end of this chapter, you should begin to . . .

- identify three types of persuasive writing: blame, values, and choice;
- use evidence and reasoning effectively (*logos*);
- present yourself as fair-minded, reasonable, and knowledgeable (*ethos*);
- understand when and how to appeal to the audience's emotions (*pathos*);
- shape your argument based on your understanding of its context (*kairos*);
- anticipate and refute opposing views; and
- organize a persuasive essay effectively.

Persuasive writing is about changing your readers' opinions or encouraging them to take action. It's about making your case. The skills of persuasive writing (and speaking) apply to all aspects of our lives, from school essays and college applications to business letters, résumés, legal briefs, and menus. In a sense, all of our writing is persuasive, as we hope the reader will understand, appreciate, accept, and perhaps agree with our words.

The word *persuasion* is sometimes used interchangeably with the word *argument*, and either one may conjure up strong images and feelings. A first definition of *argument* often suggests a disagreement that becomes heated and may leave behind bitter and angry feelings if it includes personal attacks or degenerates into *contradiction* ("yes, it is!"—"no, it isn't!"). Or *argument* may call up the image of a formal *debate*, with an idea of winning and losing. For some students, debate sounds exciting; for other, it sounds like a fight. In either case, debate is not the same as the kind of argument we'll be writing and reading about here.

In this chapter we'll be using **argument** in a less combative sense to mean a series of connected statements or claims that are supported by evidence and used to prove a point. For example, lawyers in the courtroom will "argue" that their client is innocent because an alibi or other evidence proves it. It is in this sense that argument is a form of "persuasive" writing. We're trying to prove a point or to convince someone to agree with us.

Now the word *persuasion* can also have a negative connotation, often as a sinister understatement. "If you won't talk, I will have to *persuade* you," says the bad guy, and he doesn't mean by using logic! We might imagine a knife clutched in his hand or a goon

Intimidation vs. Persuasion

lurking in the shadows. In this chapter, however, we will think of persuasive writing as respecting the readers' intelligence and free will while using various strategies (including argument) to encourage them to agree with us. In order to be successful, we'll need to consider the background and attitude of the audience and what types of evidence or logic may be persuasive; to present ourselves as reasonable and knowledgeable individuals; and, when it seems effective, to appeal to the readers' sympathies.

TYPES OF ARGUMENT

Persuasive strategies are useful in a thousand different settings, from the living room to the office to the professional kitchen, whenever you want someone to agree with you or to do something for you. Trying to persuade people is different from just giving information, though you may want to include information as part of your argument. Think about the differences between a straight news story and an editorial. While the news story restricts itself to informing the public, to presenting the facts of the story without a particular bias, the editorial presents an opinion and seeks to enlist the agreement of the reader. Suppose there's an outbreak of *E. coli*, which is eventually traced to bags of spinach. A news story might give details of the investigation and an update on the victims' health; the news story is about *informing* the reader. On the other hand, an editorial on this same topic might express an *opinion* about whether the government is doing enough to ensure the safety of our food supply. It might try to *persuade* readers to take specific action, such as boycotting certain brands or writing to their legislators.

Much of what is still taught about persuasive writing and speaking comes from the Greek philosopher Aristotle, who lived over 2,300 years ago. Aristotle identified three uses of persuasion: to assign blame, to determine value, and to propose a course of action or a choice. In the case of the *E. coli* outbreak, one set of arguments might concern who is at fault (blame). Another set of arguments might look at the overall picture: Are corporate profits worth more than public safety (value)? Finally, one might argue that there should be stricter laws about food safety or stricter enforcement of existing laws (choice).

ASSIGNING BLAME

Blame is what happens in a courtroom. An action occurred in the past, and the various attorneys attempt to persuade the judge and jury that a particular person or group is responsible for that action. Evidence is put forward by both sides. The verbs are all in the past tense: for example, "On the night of May 17, the defendant *was seen* in the vicinity of the crime." In a courtroom, the purpose of assigning blame is then to assign punishment. If the defendant is found guilty, he or she may be sentenced to pay a fine or to spend time in prison. In other contexts, the purpose of assigning blame might be to effect change. If a store's policy concerning the receipt of produce is proved to have led to accepting the contaminated lettuce, one might argue that the policy should be changed in order to prevent the problem's recurrence. Arguments about blame take place in the past tense and often rely on cause and effect to make their points.

While this type of argument certainly has its place, it can at times turn into an unproductive "blame game." You probably know this from personal experience. If someone borrowed your phone, for example, and deleted an important text or voice message, you could spend your energy "blaming" the other person, or you could take steps to recover the lost message and to ensure that such an accident would not happen again. The damage has been done, whether by accident or on purpose. The usefulness of assigning blame is limited.

DETERMINING VALUE

Arguments about value, about what is right or what is good, attempt to change the readers' beliefs or opinions. For example, you might try to persuade your audience that a particular variety of apple is the best kind for baking, or that a particular movie is the best war film ever. Such an argument describes the ideal specimen in a category, for instance, the perfect apple or the ultimate war movie. It then *evaluates* how close a specific example comes to this ideal. Is this particular apple a "good" one? Restaurant and movie reviews typically make this type of argument. Sometimes the reviews lead to a suggested course of action, such as that the reader visit the restaurant, while at other times the goal is simply to gain the agreement of the audience: "You're right, that *is* the best war movie ever." An *ethical* argument seeks to measure right and wrong against an accepted moral or ethical framework. For example, is it *wrong* for athletes to use steroids, or is it *right* to eat animals? Arguments about value typically use the present tense.

Now, it's actually quite difficult to change someone's opinion. Like arguments focused on blame, those about values can easily become heated and unproductive. Arguments about what is right or good are perhaps more useful in opening up discussion, in bouncing ideas off of other people and thus discovering more clearly what you yourself believe. These arguments might begin as questions: What are the pros and cons of eating meat?

PROPOSING A CHOICE

Arguments that support proposals about what to do in the future were Aristotle's favorite because they are often the most productive. Rather than getting caught up in the blame game or in an unwinnable debate about values, we can focus on moving forward, on offering readers a solution to a problem or a course of action designed to improve the quality of life. For example, passing a law about water purity in facilities that handle produce might reduce the chance of another outbreak of *E. coli.* In proposals, the verbs are likely to be in the future tense, and the argument often relies on cause and effect: "The effect of this proposed change will be a lower risk of foodborne illness."

In making this type of argument (choice), you may be less heated and contentious, less personal, and more likely to find common ground—an effective strategy in moving the reader to your position. If you want to borrow the family car to take a date to a late movie but you haven't had much experience driving at night, you might begin by finding such common ground with your parents as, "Of course, we all want me to be safe."

The following chart reviews arguments of blame, value, and choice:

Types of Argument

	Blame	Value	Choice
Question	Who is at fault?	What is more important?	How shall we solve the problem?
Purpose	to assign responsibility and, potentially, punishment	to establish what is good or what is right, to change someone's opinion	to propose a change or a specific course of action
Verb tense	past	present	future
Examples	The company failed to ensure the lettuce was properly picked and stored.	Public safety is more important than corporate profits.	Finding a more reliable water source and training workers more thoroughly will lower the risk of foodborne illness.

STRATEGIES FOR PERSUASIVE WRITING

Once you've established the type of argument you'd like to make, you can begin to assemble the most effective strategies to bring your readers over to your point of view. Three of these strategies have to do with the three parts of communication we first looked at in Chapter 1: the text, the writer, and the reader. Aristotle called them **logos**, which concerns the text; **ethos**, which concerns the writer; and **pathos**, which concerns the reader. You will decide if and how to use these depending on the situation, that is, the time and place of your argument—what Aristotle called **kairos**. Remember—persuasive writing is not the same as creative writing. The focus is less on expressing what's inside you and more on changing what's *outside* you, that is, your reader.

Let's think back to the scene from *Sudden Impact* described in Chapter 1. Loretta must communicate to Detective Callahan that robbers are hiding in the diner. Because she's working in a restaurant at gunpoint (*kairos*), she must use the tools at hand, namely the sugar in the coffee (*logos*). Because he has known her for ten years, Loretta has established her character (*ethos*) with him as a competent waitress, one who wouldn't accidentally pour a whole cup of sugar into his coffee. Because she has known Callahan for ten years, she is confident that once he understands the situation, he will feel pity (*pathos*) and be motivated to do something about the dangerous situation. And, in the end, Loretta's persuasive strategies are successful.

Strategies for Persuasive Writing

The Message
Logos
establish the truth with facts, statistics,
stories, reasoning

The Audience/Reader
Pathos
establish a connection
with the audience
through emotion

The Speaker/Writer
Ethos
establish yourself as
trustworthy, fair-minded,
knowledgeable

The Situation
Kairos
seize the opportune moment, the teachable moment
adapt your message to the time and place

LOGOS—LOOK FOR THE "TRUTH"

Logos, Greek for "word," has to do with the reasons for your opinion or proposal. It can often be seen as establishing the truth through the use of *logic* or reasoning, supported by evidence such as facts, statistics, and examples. As we mentioned earlier, this specialized kind of persuasion is sometimes called "argument," although in a broader sense the terms *argument* and *persuasion* are often used interchangeably. *Logos* is the strategy most often called for in an academic essay: to present information—the "truth"—and interpret it persuasively or to demonstrate an irrefutably logical conclusion. We have already encountered a number of these strategic approaches or rhetorical modes: definition, comparison, and causation. As with other types of writing, these modes can be used singly or in combination to make the best possible argument. In addition, writers may use evaluation and ethical arguments to persuade their readers.

The ARTS of Evidence

When we think about the arguments that take place in a courtroom, the need for evidence seems especially clear. Although the trustworthiness of the lawyer and the sympathy of the jury can play an important role in determining the verdict, at the center of the trial is the evidence, and all involved look to this evidence to establish the truth. Evidence—both your own and your opponents'—may be judged by the following criteria:

The ARTS of Evidence

Is the evidence . . .

- **Accurate:** Are you using current, reputable research or examples?
- **Relevant:** Does the evidence actually relate to the argument?
- **Typical:** Is the evidence typical? That is, are there more examples or studies like it? Or could it be an anomaly?
- **Sufficient:** Do you have enough evidence? Perhaps one good study or example is sufficient, but more evidence may be more persuasive.

Evidence is usually associated with logic or reasoning. The success of such reasoning depends on the validity of the initial assumption or generalization. For example, suppose you want your parents to buy you a car (up till this point you've been borrowing the family car or getting rides). You say, You should buy me a car because *all* my friends' parents have done it. First of all, is this accurate? No, only *two* of your friends were given a car by their parents. Second, even if the statement *were* accurate, would it make sense? Is it reasonable to do something simply because "everyone is doing it"? Of course not.

Problems with evidence: The initial statement—"all my friends' parents bought cars for them"—might be described as a "hasty generalization." Making a strong, sweeping statement such as "All fats are bad for you" might seem like a good way to impress your readers. But you are taking the risk of alienating them if they know something about the topic (some fats are *good* for you) or take offense at the simplicity of your thinking. Another thing that can turn readers off right away is if you make a generalization that doesn't apply to them. Suppose you write "Everyone enjoys a juicy grilled steak." If your reader is a vegetarian, then whatever you say next may be lost in his disagreement with your generalization.

We must also be careful that our statements actually move toward a conclusion. Instead of a series of connected statements that build to a proposition, circular reasoning just goes around in a circle. For example, "Parents buy their children cars because that's what parents do," or "That's my favorite because I like it the best." Finally, an argument that you should do something because "everyone else is doing it" raises so many questions ("Would you jump off a cliff if everyone else was doing it?") that it's unlikely to be effective.

The role of outside sources: Even when we know quite a bit about a topic already, it can be very effective to cite outside experts in support of our arguments. It's a way of building our own credibility (see the discussion of *ethos* later in this chapter). Suppose you'd taken a class in nutrition and learned that too much added sugar can cause heart problems. Most likely you'd include quotes from or links to reputable scientific studies or medical recommendations to add credibility to your points.

Problems with outside sources: You want to be sure, however, that the sources you're using are accurate. If you cite statistics or other information that is clearly biased or unreliable, you risk alienating your readers and blowing your chance to persuade them. For example, if your studies on the safety of cigarettes come from the tobacco industry, or from only one personal example—"I know someone who smoked a pack a day and lived to be 90"—your evidence may not be typical.

Logos Strategy: Definition

An argument based on a **definition** has two parts. First, we must establish the definition itself. What are the criteria that define a vegetable, for example? Second, we must prove that a particular case meets the accepted definition. Is pizza a vegetable? We would provide a definition of *vegetable,* then show how *pizza* does or does not meet it. The principle behind the argument is that things in the same defined category should be treated in the same way. If pizza can be defined as a vegetable, it should count as one on the public school lunch menu. If it can *not* be defined as a vegetable, public schools need to provide a side of broccoli.

You may remember those headlines a few years ago that Congress had declared pizza a vegetable. The story involves some big issues for the United States—the growing problem of childhood obesity and the role of the federal government in citizens' personal lives, for example, as well as the role of lobbyists in the federal government. The argument revolves around the definition of "vegetable." A headline such as "Pizza Is a Vegetable? Congress Defies Logic, Betrays Our Children" is certainly an

Two sisters enjoy making a vegetable pizza.

attention-grabber (Wartman). Later stories, however, redefined the controversy: "No, Congress did not declare pizza a vegetable" (Kliff). It was the tomato sauce that was being thus defined. "Tomato paste will continue to get outsized credit [as a vegetable], with one-eighth of a cup essentially counted as something four times larger." The definition was based on a comparison between the nutrients in one-eighth cup of tomato paste and one-half cup of apples:

> All told, the nutrition facts look really similar. Tomato paste does do a lot worse on sodium, but it also does much better in terms of calcium and potassium content. It also slightly edges out apples on dietary fiber, with a lower amount of sugar.

Comparisons can become an important and effective component of a definition. Of course, both tomatoes and apples are fruits, not vegetables, but that's another issue. And in the end there is perhaps no meaningful difference—the lobbyists need tomato sauce and/or pizza to be a vegetable simply in order to sell more of their food to public schools.

Defining—and redefining—your terms can be an effective strategy. So can redefining the terms of an *opponent's* argument. Much of the controversy surrounding abortion, for example, focuses on the definition of when life begins, or the definition of "human being" versus "embryo" or "fetus." In arguments about the death penalty, the definition of "cruel and unusual punishment" plays an important role for both sides. As you make your arguments, think about how defining and redefining your terms and your opponents' terms can work for you.

Problems with definition: "Defining" a complex issue as a simplistic *either/or* choice may bypass critical thinking by ignoring other alternatives and can seem like bullying. Sometimes the crux of the argument is the definition itself. In the pizza example, the very question "Is pizza a vegetable?" muddies rather than clarifies the issue. If you cannot agree on a definition, move on to another strategy.

Logos Strategy: Comparison or Analogy

Arguing by **analogy** involves looking for similarities and assuming that similar items should be treated in the same way. Analogies can be fun and lively, but the differences between the analogous items can potentially sabotage your argument in the end. Thus you might use an analogy in a limited way, perhaps to warm up the audience. Of course you will focus on the similarities that support your argument.

For example, you might argue that the age at which young adults can buy alcohol should be the same as that at which they can buy cigarettes because of similarities between smoking and drinking. The goal is to transfer the reader's beliefs/feelings/opinions/judgments about the old thing to the new thing you propose, and this can be very effective. You'll want to be careful about the analogy you choose, however. If your audience is as opposed to 18-year-olds buying tobacco as it is to 18-year-olds buying alcohol, an argument for lowering the drinking age will not be effective.

On the other hand, what if you argued for an analogy between the age at which you can order a drink and the age at which you can enlist in the armed forces? If an 18-year-old's brain is not developed enough to make a decision about drinking, then it's not developed enough to make a decision about joining the military. Or you might argue that teenagers should get a license to drink in the way they get a license to drive, with learner's permits, tests, and consequences administered by the state.

Examine these two sets of arguments from "Drinking Age ProCon.org" (©ProCon). The first argues that the drinking age should be 18.

> 18 is the age of adulthood in the United States, and adults should have the right to make their own decisions about alcohol consumption. Turning 18 entails receiving the rights and responsibilities of adulthood to vote, smoke cigarettes, serve on juries, get married, sign contracts, be prosecuted as adults, and join the military—which includes risking one's life.

The second argues that the drinking age should be 21.

> Many rights in the United States are conferred on citizens at age 21 or older. A person cannot legally purchase a handgun, gamble in a casino (in most states), or adopt a child until age 21, rent a car (for most companies) at age 25, or run for President until age 35. Drinking should be similarly restricted due to the responsibility required to self and others.

Arguments on both sides use analogy.

Problems with analogies: Analogies can make powerful arguments, but you must be sure that you don't end up thinking, or writing, that one part of the analogy is the *same* as the other. If you were making an argument to lower the legal drinking age to 18, the same as the legal age to buy cigarettes, you might rely partly on an analogy between the two situations: the age at which young people may purchase a potentially dangerous drug. However, the two drugs are not the same, and if you imply that they are, you may lose your readers' trust.

Logos Strategy: Causation

Many arguments use **cause and effect**. An argument about blame might focus on what caused an event or problem. For example, in the movie *Flight,* was the crash caused by mechanical failure or pilot error? An argument about choice might propose a solution that solves a problem or prevents undesirable consequences. See Chapter 15 for a more detailed discussion of cause and effect.

The debate over the drinking age also employs arguments about causation on both sides. Again from "Drinking Age ProCon.org" (©ProCon), here is a cause and effect argument in favor of lowering the drinking age:

> Allowing 18- to 20-year-olds to drink alcohol in regulated environments with supervision would decrease unsafe drinking activity. Prohibiting this age group from drinking in bars, restaurants, and other licensed locations causes them to drink in unsupervised places such as fraternity houses or house parties where they may be more prone to binge drinking and other unsafe behavior.

Another cause and effect argument works against lowering the drinking age.

> Lowering [the] MLDA [Minimum Legal Drinking Age] [from] 21 to 18 will irresponsibly allow a greater segment of the population to drink alcohol in bars and nightclubs, which are not safe environments. 76 percent of bars have sold alcohol to obviously intoxicated patrons, and about half of drivers arrested for driving while intoxicated (DWI) or killed as alcohol-involved drivers in traffic crashes did their drinking at licensed establishments.

Problems with causation: Don't confuse *chronology* with *causation.* When one event follows another, it does not necessarily mean that one event *caused* the other. For example, suppose you put on a red shirt and later that day scored 95% on an exam. Does this mean that putting on the red shirt *caused* you to do well? Unlikely, and it would weaken your credibility with your readers if you were to argue that it did. There might have been no relationship at all between the two events—a coincidence—or it might be that a third event caused you to choose the shirt and ace the text.

Nor does *correlation* equal causation. Correlation describes a relationship between two measurements. When one changes, so does the other, and in a predictable way. In 2012, for example, the *New England Journal of Medicine* published a story about the correlation between the amount of chocolate a country ate per person and the number of

Nobel Prize winners it produced.[10] Switzerland's citizens consumed the most chocolate and had the most winners; China's citizens consumed the least chocolate and had the fewest winners. So does this mean that eating chocolate *caused* people to win the Nobel Prize? That wasn't proven by the study. Correlation is not the same as causation.

Another problem with causation is making too big a slide from an event to some disastrous and not particularly likely effects—for example, if someone were to argue that allowing umpires to review a videotape of the play before calling a runner out at first base would destroy the game of baseball. This lack of true reasoning is called a "slippery slope." Exaggerating the effects of an event, action, or decision—"if I let you borrow the car today, you'll *always* want to borrow it"—is also an unreasonable and probably ineffective strategy. Read more about causation in Chapter 15.

ETHOS—MAKE THE READER TRUST YOU

While *logos* is about making the text as effective as possible, *ethos* is about you, the writer. *Ethos* is about presenting yourself as knowledgeable, fair-minded, and trustworthy. For Aristotle, this was the most important strategy.

Show You Are Knowledgeable

You want the reader to see you as an authority on the topic. You want to establish *credibility*—you're an expert, you have education or work experience, perhaps you're associated with a reputable organization, you have personal experience, you've witnessed something. Define or explain anything about your topic that might be unclear. You want to make it easy for readers to understand you, as well as to show them that you are an authority on the subject. The goal is to make them more willing to listen

In *Band of Brothers*, the ten-part miniseries about a company of the 101st Airborne Division in World War II, Lieutenant Winters establishes a powerful *ethos*. His men believe he is knowledgeable, fair-minded, and trustworthy.

HBO/Photofest © HBO

to you. If you're confused or unclear about what you think, you're unlikely to have a positive effect on your reader.

Using outside sources can help to establish your own authority. It shows you're smart enough to consider expert opinion, also from reasonable, reputable sources. For example, in his chapter on "The Ethics of Eating Animals," Michael Pollan cites (among others) moral philosopher and animal rights expert Peter Singer, philosopher and cognitive scientist Daniel Dennett, animal-handling expert Temple Grandin, and holistic farmer Joel Salatin.

Show You Are Fair-Minded

Taking a neutral position at first can be effective. You might pretend you're exploring the issues with the reader, even if you already have a firm position. Michael Pollan offers an excellent example of how to earn readers' trust by warning them of difficulties in the text and by putting himself in the readers' position:

> This is not something I'd recommend if you're determined to continue eating meat. *Animal Liberation,* comprised of equal parts philosophical argument and journalistic description, is one of those rare books that demands you either defend the way you live or change it. Because Singer is so skilled in argument, for many readers it is easier to change. . . . [W]ithin a few pages he had succeeded in throwing me and my meat eating . . . on the defensive. (307)

Pollan sets his argument in a steakhouse in which he is reading Peter Singer's *Animal Liberation.* He establishes a connection with readers likely to disagree with him (those of us who love steak) and walks us gently through Singer's argument, even warning us beforehand of the likely result: "*Animal Liberation* has converted countless thousands to vegetarianism."

> Singer's argument is disarmingly simple and, provided you accept its premises, difficult to refute. Take the premise of equality among people, which most of us readily accept. Yet what do we really mean by it? After all, people are not, as a matter of fact, equal at all—some are smarter than others, handsomer, more gifted, whatever. "Equality is a moral idea," Singer points out, "not an assertion of fact." The moral idea is that everyone's interests ought to receive equal consideration, regardless of "what they are like or what abilities they have." Fair enough; many philosophers have gone this far. But few have then taken the next logical step. "If possessing a higher degree of intelligence does not entitle one human to use another for his or her own ends, how can it entitle humans to exploit nonhumans for the same purpose?"

This is the nub of Singer's argument, and right away, here on page six, I began scribbling objections in the margin. *But humans differ from animals in morally significant ways.* Yes they do, Singer readily acknowledges, which is why we shouldn't treat pigs and children alike. Equal consideration of interests is not the same as equal treatment, he points out; children have an interest in being educated, pigs in rooting around in the dirt. But where their interests are the same, the principle of equality demands they receive the same consideration. And the one all-important interest humans share with pigs, as with all sentient creatures, is an interest in avoiding pain. (307–308)

As Pollan explains the "nub" of Singer's argument, he keeps us with him by raising our own objections: "right away, here on page six, I began scribbling objections in the margin" (308). Before the reader can be entirely turned off or fall into simple contradiction ("yes, it is!"—"no, it isn't!"), he validates our reaction and so gets us to read a little further. A good writer is open and truthful, but perhaps also a bit subtle!

Show You Are Trustworthy

How can you establish the trust and confidence that will encourage readers to take your points seriously? Think carefully about who your audience is, and use words that show you understand their values and concerns. Look for common ground. For example, if you're eighteen years old and you're trying to persuade an older audience to lower the drinking age, would it be helpful to begin by saying something like, "You old folks have forgotten what it's like to be young"? Or would it be more effective to say, "I know you're only thinking of our welfare"? Here you've established yourself as reasonable—concerned with safety, not partying.

In a business letter, demonstrate that you know what the recipient's concerns are and that you also care about them, whether you're writing to a potential employer or client, to a vendor, or to someone within your own company. Think of a résumé or a menu as an argument, in the same way a letter or proposal is.

For an academic essay assignment, read the directions carefully. The quickest way to lose credibility with your instructor is to demonstrate that you haven't taken the trouble to understand and follow the instructions. Know what you're talking about, but don't pretend to be an expert if you aren't one. Experiment with vocabulary, but don't try to sound like someone else. Pay attention to the small details as well: have you used the desired format, fonts, and headings? Have you used the appropriate style, for example, MLA, APA, or Chicago? Have you checked spelling and punctuation?

Your choice of words is critically important in an argument. If you're speaking to a group that already agrees with you (say, at a school pep rally or a political campaign fundraiser), you can use more highly charged words, even a kind of shorthand, and you may speak disparagingly of your opponents. But in a fair and open argument, use words that are neutral or at least not aggressive and insulting.

PATHOS—PUT THE READER IN A SYMPATHETIC FRAME OF MIND

While some writers frown upon the use of emotion in argument, it is clearly an effective persuasive tool when used appropriately. Even Aristotle recognized that emotion was valuable in moving an audience from agreement to action. Like the other aspects of argument—reasoning and character—it is dependent on the particular audience you're addressing. How to appeal to readers' emotions, even whether to use emotion at all, will depend on your understanding of the audience.

Remember that *pathos* usually refers to the emotion you draw forth in your audience. *You* are in general maintaining a more objective demeanor, or, if you show emotion, you give the impression that you are trying to control it. Tears that you're visibly holding back may be more effective than those running freely down your cheeks. If it's a topic you *are* emotional about, speak from the heart, simply, directly. Avoid fancy or forced language.

Sometimes you may try to rouse your readers' emotions to make your points more emphatic or memorable. If you sense that your audience is indifferent to the topic, shocking them with pity, even disgust, can pique their interest. Think of Swift's "A Modest Proposal," for example. In suggesting that Ireland's famine be alleviated by eating babies, Swift clearly was not serious. He was successful, though, in shocking his readers and making the topic one of national interest.

Emotion can also move readers from agreement to action. You've given the logical arguments and backed them up with facts and statistics, but a personal story makes people open their checkbooks. In *Thank You for Arguing,* Jay Heinrichs writes, "When you want to change someone's mood, tell a story" (81). This is the concept of the "poster child." It's one thing to say "children are starving all over the world." It's quite another to tell the story of one particular child and invite readers to help.

If your argument has to do with a very controversial topic, you may try to enlist the readers' sympathies with a personal story. If you suspect your readers strongly disagree with your position, you may want to do this gently, kind of sneak into it. Perhaps you'll tell a brief story of someone who's dealt with the controversial issue personally—abortion, stem cell research, capital punishment. With a more neutral audience, you might show your hand earlier. Humor can also be an effective way of reducing the tension that surrounds certain topics and making it easier for the reader to understand and accept your points.

Michael Pollan's discussion of eating animals combines an ethical argument with some uncomfortable truths about how animals are raised and slaughtered. His conclusion is powerful:

> The industrialization—and brutalization—of animals in America is a relatively new, evitable, and local phenomenon: No other country raises and slaughters its food animals quite as intensively or as brutally as we do. No other people in history has lived at quite so great a remove from the animals they eat. Were the walls of our meat industry to become transparent, literally or even figuratively, we would not long continue to raise, kill, and eat animals the way we do. Tail docking and sow crates and beak

clipping would disappear overnight, and the days of slaughtering four hundred head of cattle an hour would promptly come to an end—for who could stand the sight? Yes, meat would get more expensive. We'd probably eat a lot less of it, too, but maybe when we did eat animals we'd eat them with the consciousness, ceremony, and respect they deserve. (333)

What do you think? A rousing call to action? Or too emotional?

Problems with Using Emotion

Be careful with *pathos*. Some audiences are uncomfortable with or even offended by a display of emotion—or humor—and your argument may be lost. Readers may also resent feeling manipulated. You need to be subtle. You also need to be careful as to which emotions you seek to arouse. Pity and compassion may make readers sympathetic to your case, but they can go too far. If your readers are *overwhelmed* by the pain and suffering you describe, they won't be able to *think* about your argument, and that's not what we want. If you bully readers by playing on their fears and prejudices, you might make them do what you want, but it will not be as a result of the free and independent *thought* we're hoping for. If emotions like fear and hate are used without first earning the reader's trust and laying out your arguments in the open field of debate, *pathos* may become manipulative.

Persuasive writing is an ancient and respectable art. Yet if persuasive techniques discard the truth and discourage debate, they can become **propaganda**. Like editorials and advertisements, propaganda attempts to influence the beliefs and actions of its readers—not by free and open debate, however, but through the exploitation of symbols and the manipulation of emotions. Sometimes movies are criticized for being manipulative rather than truthful or realistic. Viewers clap and cheer as the music swells with triumph and the underdog sports team claws its way to a win. They sob along with the violins as a child succumbs to terminal illness. But are these reactions produced by genuine emotion or by clever manipulation?

A good piece of persuasive writing encourages its readers to explore a question for themselves as well as to agree. Propaganda, on the other hand, discourages that kind of independent thinking (see Figure 16.1). In the *Propaganda Critic,* Aaron

Figure 16.1 Debate vs. Propaganda

Debate	Propaganda
Appeals to reason/logic	Avoids reason/logic
Appeals to ethics	Ignores ethics
Appeals to emotion	Creates fear or manipulates emotion
Invokes pity or compassion	Ignites hate

Delwiche writes that "propagandists love short-cuts—particularly those which short-circuit rational thought. They encourage this by agitating emotions, by exploiting insecurities, by capitalizing on the ambiguity of language, and by bending the rules of logic." For example, an advertisement may seek to transfer an audience's respect for a certain symbol, such as a doctor's white coat, to a particular goal, such as the sale of toothpaste. While these techniques may be successful, it is best to avoid them in persuasive writing.

As with all aspects of your writing, your decision on how to approach the topic will depend on your understanding of the audience and on your individual style. Do your particular readers like "just the facts"? Are they especially sensitive to issues of right and wrong? Or can you sway them by stirring up powerful emotions?

KAIROS—SEIZE THE OPPORTUNITY

Let's think about a restaurant setting. You want to persuade your customers to purchase a meal, so you ensure that their first impression of your establishment fits their expectations. Now, these expectations won't be the same for every type of restaurant. If you have an old-fashioned diner, you will probably use paper napkins and you probably won't serve your bacon and eggs under a *cloche*. However, if you have an upscale French restaurant, you may want to meet customers' expectations of classic service and use the *cloche*—and you definitely *won't* set the table with paper napkins. Your servers in the old-fashioned diner might be warm and motherly, swift and accurate. In the French restaurant they might be elegant and politely distant, meeting a very different set of expectations. In other words, you must know your purpose and your audience, and design your restaurant accordingly.

Have you ever entered an argument, tried to persuade someone to do something, for example, and then realized that it was absolutely not the right time and place? If your best friend has just broken up with her boyfriend, is that the best time to convince her that "there are other fish in the sea"? If she's just lost her job, is that the best time to suggest trying the most expensive restaurant in town? Our persuasive strategies are more likely to be successful if we consider the entire **context** or setting, and understand how the particular time and place affect the particular audience we're addressing.

Let's look at a couple of examples. Say you want to borrow the family car for the evening. Would you choose to raise the question with your parents while they are stressing out over preparing their tax return? Or would you wait until they were relaxing over a dinner that you yourself had gone to the trouble of preparing? Or say you want to ask your teacher for an extension on an assignment. Would you interrupt the lesson, or would you wait until after class? We can see the effect of context in national arguments as well.

Your understanding of the purpose of your argument, the time and place, and the audience will determine how you present yourself and what strategies you use.

In the previous paragraph, notice how volunteering to make dinner establishes your character as mature, responsible, and cooperative—the very qualities you'd like to emphasize as entitling you to a share in the family car. In the second example, your success in getting the extension may depend on how many times you've asked for one in the past. If you've already established yourself as a dedicated student, your teacher may feel more inclined to grant your request than if your work is typically turned in late or incomplete.

We'll also want to think carefully about the context as we choose which persuasive strategies to try. With much informative writing, our concerns with the reader have to do mainly with how much information to include and what type of vocabulary (general or specialized, formal or slang) to use. With persuasive writing, however, we need to look more deeply into the minds of our readers and try to discern their beliefs and values. Such an understanding will help us construct arguments that will be most likely to influence them. We should be wary of focusing on arguments that seem persuasive to *us* and instead try to anticipate which arguments will be persuasive to a particular audience at a particular time and place.

To think more concretely about the types of decisions and changes you might make in a persuasive piece, let's look again at the drinking age. Should the drinking age be 18 or 21, or should it be abolished? Whatever position you take in your essay, imagine first that you are writing a letter to the editor of the student newspaper on a college campus. Second, imagine that you are writing a letter to local members of MADD (Mothers Against Drunk Driving). Finally, imagine that you are writing a letter to the owner of a local bar. How would you change your arguments and writing style to communicate most effectively with each particular audience? Is your purpose to raise awareness, stimulate debate, or move the audience to action? Does your audience share your views, oppose your views, or have yet to form an opinion? The answers to these questions will dramatically affect the content and style of your writing.

REFUTATION

Although some arguments can be successful addressing only one side, your paper will often be more persuasive if you are able to see all around the issue and understand what objections might be raised to your argument. Brainstorming is helpful, as well as conversations with others or extensive reading on the topic. Then you'll be able to anticipate and counter, refute or dismiss these objections. First, this makes a powerful appeal to *ethos* by establishing your character as fair-minded and knowledgeable. Second, it's a chance to find some common ground with your audience. Perhaps there's a *part* of the counterargument that you can support in some way. This strategy, concession, can be extremely effective. Third, when you include a **refutation** in your argument, you address the reader's possible objections with an immediate response.

Let's look again at Michael Pollan's strategy. Remember that he distances himself from the conclusion and puts himself in the reader's shoes (a clever *ethos*) by scribbling furiously in the margin when he disagrees with Singer's points. So *he* raises the objections to Singer's argument (with which he ultimately agrees) and points out how brilliantly Singer refutes them. The eighteenth-century philosopher Jeremy Bentham (another reputable outside source that Pollan cites) reasons thus:

> There are humans—infants, the severely retarded, the demented—whose mental function does not rise to the level of a chimpanzee. Even though these people cannot reciprocate our moral attentions (obey the golden rule, etc.) we nevertheless include them in the circle of our moral consideration. So on what basis do we exclude the chimpanzee?
>
> *Because he's a chimp,* I scribble furiously in the margin, *and they're human beings!* For Singer that's not good enough. To exclude the chimp from moral consideration simply because he's not human is no different than excluding the slave simply because he's not white. . . . Either we do not owe any justice to the severely retarded, [Singer] concludes, or we do owe it to animals with higher capabilities. (308–309)

Your strategies for refuting opposing arguments should also take the particular time and place and the particular audience into account. In most cases, suggesting that there are problems with the evidence used in opposing arguments is a good start. Just as the ARTS of evidence outlined earlier in this chapter can help you evaluate the evidence in your own arguments, they can also help you evaluate and refute the evidence in your opponents' arguments. Can you suggest that the evidence is not accurate, relevant, typical, or sufficient? Can you find evidence that outweighs or contradicts that of your opponents? If an opponent cites one study, you can discredit it, or cite a more creditable one, or cite a different pattern in numerous other studies. You might argue that the opponent's data are not complete or recent enough, or the authority is not reputable.

In the arguments earlier in the chapter about Congress declaring pizza a vegetable, one article focused on the comparable nutritive value of tomato paste and apples. We might concede that point, but go on to say that the real issue is whether we want schoolchildren eating frozen pizza with its high fat content and chemical additives. We argue that the evidence is not relevant or sufficient, and we cite a different study. If the argument relies on reasoning, you may refute it by finding logical flaws. Is the argument a hasty generalization or slippery slope? (See the previous section on *logos*.) Or you might challenge the *ethos*—is the opponent ignorant? Neither tomatoes nor apples are actually vegetables! Or is the opponent biased? Can you reasonably argue a new drug is safe if you work for the company that's selling it?

Arguments in favor of keeping the drinking age at 21 often rely on statistics that show a decrease in alcohol-related traffic fatalities after the age was raised from eighteen.

If you wished to challenge that evidence, you might note that it didn't take into account the increase in nontraffic fatalities in this same age group, as drinking went more underground and binge drinking became more widespread. If the common goal is to protect the safety of our young people, it seems that changing the drinking age didn't completely solve the problem. Now you have an opportunity to propose a *new* solution, perhaps a "license" to drink.

Successful refutation often takes the energy of your opponents' objections and defuses it by conceding a point or redefining the "nub" of the argument in a way that favors your perspective. Perhaps you challenge the opponents' assumptions; Singer apparently did a good job of this on Michael Pollan! Perhaps your best choice is to keep the focus on *choice*. Try to find common ground and move the discussion forward to a solution that meets everyone's needs. (See "Offal Wasteful" later in the chapter for a partial solution to Pollan's dilemma.)

ORGANIZING A PERSUASIVE ESSAY

A formal persuasive essay written for an American college course typically favors the appeal to reason and relies on certain types of evidence. Great emphasis is placed on supporting your opinion with facts and statistics that you have found in well-respected sources and that you have documented appropriately (see Chapters 18 and 19). This type of persuasive writing—the essay that takes a side and uses evidence to support it—is often organized in the following way:

1. Introduction—explain the issue, its importance, and your position on it
2. Persuasive statements or claims—make your case, starting with your strongest points and using evidence to support them
3. Refutation—outline one or more statements or claims *on the opposite side* and explain why they are inaccurate, unreasonable, unethical, or otherwise not persuasive
4. Conclusion—restate your argument and/or propose a solution

This organizational plan draws on some of the methodology of a compare and contrast essay. You are essentially contrasting the claims on different sides. Thus it can be often helpful to list the reasons for and against a position, as we listed differences between the appearance, texture, and flavor of two varieties of apples in Chapter 13.

Once you have assembled the evidence and decided on your position, you will need to organize your arguments in some type of logical sequence. You will often wish to emphasize the most important reason by placing it either first or last. The same is true when you are outlining the claims on the other side. As in all your writing, you must be the judge of what sequence best suits your purpose, your audience, and your point of view on the topic. Typically each body paragraph will state one reason or claim (either for or against), then develop it with evidence of some kind. If the paragraphs are mixed up—for example, two or three different points in a single paragraph—or if the overall order is illogical, you may lose the reader's attention.

Let's look at an example. Another controversy involving the food industry is the government ban on smoking in restaurants and bars. The following chart lays out arguments on both sides of this issue:

Brainstorming about the Smoking Ban

	Arguments in Favor of Ban	Arguments Opposed to Ban
A. Fact	Secondhand smoke is dangerous.	Smoke is not the only pollutant.
B. Emotion	People can't enjoy the flavor of their meal in a smoky environment.	Smokers will feel uncomfortably stressed if they can't light up.
C. Value	The safety of all patrons is more important than the pleasure of some.	All customers should be entitled to enjoy their favorite mealtime activities, whether smoking a cigarette or drinking a coffee.

If you were writing an essay on this topic, you would consider which is the most important or effective argument, given your purpose and audience. If you favored the ban and believed your audience most likely to value safety, then you might argue A, then C. If you thought your audience was more concerned with comfort, you might lead with B. In planning your refutation, you also want to identify the most important or effective counterargument or claim *for your particular audience* and then be sure to address it.

Beginning an argument with your strongest reason is most typical of academic or legal situations, but it isn't the only option. You could start off from a neutral position and offer an overview of the issue, only later zeroing in on your position. Or you might begin by taking the opposite side and disagreeing with it, as Michael Pollan does in "The Ethics of Eating Animals." This approach reverses the order of a typical academic essay, putting the refutation of the opposing argument first, followed by the reasons that support your argument. Depending on your audience and on the nature of the writing assignment, you may choose to end your essay with your most persuasive point. If you plan to appeal to your readers' emotions, you might do so right at the beginning to soften your readers up, or at the very end to drive home your position and/or inspire action.

In this essay, student writer Drew Jacobs offers a partial solution to Michael Pollan's dilemma about eating animals.

****

Offal Wasteful
by Drew Jacobs

Throughout history man has eaten animals, but in recent history in the United States people have begun consuming solely the flesh of the animal, leaving the innards and other variety meats to go to waste. The decision by many Americans that the innards and variety meats, also called offal, are inedible can be attributed to the fact that "most of us have lost touch with where our food comes from" (Ellis 238). In many other countries across the world, variety meats have been eaten as part of tradition for centuries and continue to be eaten in current times. If Americans returned to consuming the entire animal as we did prior to the turn of the twentieth century, we would be making giant strides toward increasing the sustainability of our country's livestock.

Even though Americans choose not to utilize the entire animal, a vast majority of the countries in the world do consume offal as part of everyday eating. In ancient times, the Chinese would consume thousands of duck tongues in a single sitting (Allen and Gin). In present day Mexico, menudo, a traditional soup made with tripe, or cow's stomach, ground dried chilies and hominy, is eaten at family gatherings and special occasions. In Puerto Rico, brain, which is blanched in stock then either fried or high-heat sautéed, is eaten amongst family members during times of celebration. In northeast Brazil, a traditional dish called buchada is eaten to utilize all of the innards of the goat native to the area. Haggis, which is similar to buchada, is a traditional Scottish dish in which a sheep stomach is stuffed with chopped heart, liver, lungs and kidneys; then the stomach is sewn shut and boiled for hours. In many European countries, the blood of the animal is kept at the time of slaughter and used to make blood sausage. In Mediterranean countries, such as Turkey, there is a traditional Easter dish called kokoretsi. This dish consists of variety meats from a lamb, such as the heart, liver, spleen, lungs and kidneys, which are wrapped with the lamb's caul fat, then the washed intestines of the same lamb and cooked on a spit over a coal fire. Kokoretsi serves as a great example of the utilization of the entire animal. However, in the United States, the use of offal faded as the industrial revolution collided with the agriculture industry.

In *The Great American Meat Book*, Merle Ellis writes about variety meats that "being the most perishable parts of the animal, they were traditionally eaten first, often at some great feast to celebrate the success of a hunt, or for dinner on the farm following hog-killin' time" (238). However, as the twentieth century progressed, Americans became more estranged from offal, which can be attributed to the rapid decline in the number of farmers.

In the early 1900s, more than 95 percent of Americans either raised livestock or grew produce and understood the importance of letting no part of the animal go to waste, but the American mentality changed as the century progressed and the number of Americans involved with agriculture declined to about two percent (Ellis). Americans became spoiled as farming progressed industrially because the beef sirloins, chicken breasts, pork loins, and various other typical cuts of the animal were readily available at every corner grocery store. The times when Americans consumed the entire animal were no more.

In the early 1900s, Americans lived a much more sustainable lifestyle, but out of necessity not by choice. The current-day movement to use more sustainable food sources is nothing more than a movement to return to the simpler agricultural processes. A large part of sustainability is the animal's welfare; therefore it is crucial that "animals are treated humanely and with respect" ("What Is Sustainable Agriculture?"). Where is the respect in allowing the innards of an animal to go to waste? As Fergus Henderson describes, "it would seem disingenuous to the animal not to make the most of the whole beast: there is a set of delights, textural and flavorsome, which lie beyond the fillet" (XIX). If every American were to eat variety meats for one meal a month, hundreds fewer animals would need to be slaughtered per year. If fewer animals were slaughtered per year, the movement away from factory farming would be less difficult because that type of farming is focused on maximizing the quantity of animals raised and slaughtered, not on using all of what each animal has to offer. Using the entire animal is usually a focus of the smaller farming operation because it is important to use everything in a business that traditionally has a small profit margin. The idea of letting nothing go to waste is simple, but because the average American doesn't understand offal it is shunted aside.

In *Innards and Other Variety Meats,* Jana Allen and Margaret Gin write that "not only are [variety meats] readily available, reasonably priced and highly nutritious, their uses are boundless" (5). The healthiest of the variety meats is the heart because it is the strongest muscle in any animal's body, therefore containing virtually no fat. Heart has a crisp tender texture and lacks any strong flavor or smell. Tongue, which is very similar in flavor to heart, becomes very tender due to its high fat content and must be braised, smoked or roasted for long periods of time so the fat completely breaks down. There are some variety meats that are unhealthy such as brain and sweetbreads, which is due to their extremely high fat content, but as Eric Slatkin explains, the finished product of sweetbreads is creamy due to their soft texture and is an excellent palette for bold flavors. Even though there are a few variety meats that are unhealthy, the large majority of offal is as healthy as or healthier than the typical cuts of meat.

During this movement towards sustainability in the United States, we have to think about both the positives and negatives of using variety meats as part of everyday cuisine. As the rest of the world has proven, offal poses no threat to the health of human beings, who have consumed it throughout history. Most variety meats also offer superior nutrition to the food that many Americans eat every day. As seen throughout this essay, the positives of using variety meats far outweigh the negatives, so why be wasteful? Next time you're looking to make a cheap meal, go out to the local butcher shop and ask for some beef heart or maybe even some sweetbreads.

Works Cited

Allen, Jana, and Margaret Gin. *Innards and Other Variety Meats.* San Francisco: 101 Productions; [distributed by Scribner, New York], 1974. Print.

Ellis, Merle. *The Great American Meat Book.* New York: Knopf, 1996. Print.

Henderson, Fergus, and Anthony Bourdain. *The Whole Beast: Nose to Tail Eating.* New York: HarperCollins, 2004. Print.

"Offal Good Eatin'." *Real Men Eat Green/Where Manliness Meets Greenliness.* 4 Nov. 2009. Web. 1 Mar. 2010.

Slatkin, Eric. "Brains, Intestines, Pizzle: It's What's for Dinner." *CHOW – Recipes, Cooking Tips, Resources, and Stories for People Who Love Food.* 16 Apr. 2007. Web. 9 Mar. 2010.

"What Is Sustainable Agriculture? – Introduction to Sustainability." *Sustainable Table.* Web. 3 Mar. 2010.

ABOUT THE READING

- What persuasive strategies does the author use? Provide specific examples, and evaluate their effectiveness.
- Does the author address and refute objections? Explain.
- Describe your own feelings about and any personal experience with offal. How does this background affect your reading of this essay?
- Compare the points raised in this essay with those summarized by Michael Pollan earlier in the chapter. Do they have any common ground?

Courtney E. Martin is the author of Perfect Girls, Starving Daughters: The Frightening New Normalcy of Hating Your Body. *You can read more about her work at www.courtneyemartin.com.*

****

How to Address Obesity in a Fat-Phobic Society
by Courtney E. Martin

A friend of mine—I'll call her Ellen—recently went to her regular medical clinic after realizing that she was newly suffering an old family problem: acid reflux. Her doctor was out on maternity leave, so she met with a replacement. Without asking Ellen any questions about her relationship to her weight (she is overweight and well aware of it), he launched into a robotic exposition about dieting.

Ellen explained to him that she worked out regularly and also did her best to eat healthy, but had a philosophical problem with turning food into the enemy. He simply retorted: "The only way you're going to lose weight is to the cut the carbs. So . . . cut the carbs."

"When he brought up my weight I wanted to have a real conversation with him, but instead he gave me his version of my 'problem'," Ellen said. "It made me really angry."

My friend's experience is not an anomaly. In fact, it is representative of a still unchanged attitude among too many medical doctors and nutritionists that fat people are problems to be solved; if they can just come up with the perfect equation, they figure, BMIs can be lowered and the supposed obesity epidemic eradicated.

This attitude shows up in doctor's offices where overweight and obese patients are often subjected to inquisition-like questioning. Yet they are rarely asked other, arguably more important questions: *What's your experience of your body? How is your quality of life? How do you feel about your weight?*

It also shows up in obesity intervention programs throughout the country, where a person's culture, class, education, or even genetics, are overlooked in the dogged pursuit to motivate what too many clinicians see as "lazy Americans" to lose pounds.

It's not as if we don't have the evidence that these factors—culture, class, education, genetics—matter. Yet another study just came out by University of Washington researchers who found gaping disparities in obesity rates among ZIP codes in the Seattle area. Every $100,000 in median home value for a ZIP code corresponded with a 2 percent drop in obesity.

Adam Drewnowski, director of the UW Center for Obesity Research, told the Seattle Post-Intelligencer, "If you have this mind-set that obesity has to do with the individual alone, then ZIP codes or areas really should not come into this. But they do, big-time."

This is not to say that individual behavior doesn't play a vital role in our country's obesity rate, but we too often neglect to think about the cultural and institutional influences on a person's behavior when it comes to eating and exercise.

You would never look at a working class, single mother driving a jalopy with three kids crawling around in the back and say, "Gees, what's her problem? Why can't she drive the Lexus hybrid like me?" You understand that she doesn't have the means, and furthermore, probably doesn't have the peer influence that would make it seem like a viable option.

Our judgmental, fat-phobic society seems even more ridiculous when you consider that there is a strong genetic component to weight. We now have ample scientific evidence suggesting that we are each born with a set point within which our metabolism will automatically adjust no matter how many calories we consume. It's like our working class mom could be dedicatedly saving up for that hybrid, but the money just keeps disappearing from her bank account.

Instead of vilifying fat people, this country needs to look long and hard at the roots of our obesity epidemic. While we can't change someone's genetics, we can work to change the institutional disparities that make maintaining a healthy weight difficult for people with less money. Encouraging supermarkets to open up in poor neighborhoods by adjusting zoning laws and creating tax-incentive programs is a start. More funding for public schools in low-income areas would translate into better quality food in the cafeterias and more nutrition and physical education.

In addition to addressing these classist systems, we need to do some soul searching about our own attitudes about fat. Until those of us who care about public health can truly separate the potential health risks of being overweight from our own internalized stigmas about fat, we won't be effective. We have to learn to distinguish between those who are satisfied with their current body size and those who want to lose weight, and then, learn to provide complex guidance that takes societal and genetic factors into account.

Those in the field of public health need to remember how motivation really works (hint: not by coercion or humiliation) and rethink how quality of life is measured when it comes to overweight patients. It is not the clinician's—often prejudiced, frequently rushed—point of view that matters most, but the individual's.

Dr. Janell Mensinger, the Director of the Clinical Research Unit at The Reading Hospital & Medical Center, also recommends shifting the goals of obesity intervention programs: "Focusing on health indicators such as blood pressure, cholesterol, blood sugar would serve to de-stigmatize obese individuals and help them engage in better eating habits and physical activity for the purpose of healthier living as opposed to simply being thinner. Although I see some programs shifting in this direction, I don't think they have gone far enough."

Mensinger adds, "We have to avoid promoting the dieting mentality! Encourage acceptance of all shapes and sizes while promoting the importance of physical activity and eating well for the purpose of living and feeling better, mentally and physically. The people that most successfully achieve this goal are those with an expertise in eating disorders as well as obesity. They know best what can happen if the message is misconstrued."

Whether you are a primary care provider, a nurse practitioner, a nutritionist, or a community health advocate, I urge you to treat your next patient like a living, breathing human being with complicated feelings, economic concerns, and cultural affiliations. Weight loss isn't the ultimate goal; economic equality, cultural diversity, wellness and happiness are.

ABOUT THE READING

- Define the following terms: *anomaly, BMI, eradicated, dogged, jalopy, coercion.*
- Why does the author criticize some healthcare providers' attitudes toward weight? How do the expressions "robotic exposition" and "inquisition-like questioning" illustrate her objections?
- According to the author, what factors contribute to Americans' problems with weight management? What kinds of evidence does she use to support her claims?
- How does the author appeal to the readers' emotions? Do you think this strategy is effective? Explain.

RECIPE FOR REVIEW

PERSUASIVE WRITING

Unlike simply informative writing, persuasive writing seeks to compel a response from the audience, whether it is sympathy, agreement, or action.

TYPES OF ARGUMENTS

- **Blame:** Arguments about blame take place in the past tense: The company failed to ensure the lettuce was properly picked and stored.
- **Values:** Arguments about values take place in the present tense: Public safety is more important than corporate profits.
- **Choice/Proposal:** Arguments that make a proposal take place in the future tense: Finding a more reliable water source and training workers more thoroughly will lower the risk of foodborne illness.

STRATEGIES FOR PERSUASIVE WRITING

- *Logos* uses reasoning, supported by facts and examples, to draw logical conclusions. The reader is invited to follow the logic and accept the conclusion. *Logos* relies on evidence or examples that are accurate, relevant, typical, and sufficient. Arguments may be developed through definition, analogy, causation, and evaluation.
- *Ethos* shows the reader that you are knowledgeable, fair-minded, and trustworthy.
- *Pathos* seeks to invoke pity or courage or hope, which in turn will move the reader to agreement and possibly action. Propaganda also seeks to compel a response but may use manipulation rather than the fair-minded appeals to reason, ethics, and emotion used by persuasive writing.

KAIROS—SEIZE THE OPPORTUNITY

The better you understand the context of your argument—the time and place, as well as the audience, purpose, and subject—the better you can make decisions about which persuasive strategies to use.

REFUTATION

Try to anticipate opposing arguments and then refute them (show they are inaccurate or irrelevant). Sometimes, however, conceding the validity of an opponent's argument can also be effective.

ORGANIZING A PERSUASIVE ESSAY

A formal persuasive essay written for an American college course typically favors the appeal to reason and often begins with the strongest reason or claim Alternatively, etc. Alternatively, persuasive writing can build to the strongest reason, sometimes beginning with a concession or refutation of opposing points.

CHAPTER EXERCISES

1. Watch a persuasive documentary like *Super Size Me* by Morgan Spurlock, and identify examples of appeals to reason, emotion, and ethics. Are the methods effective? Explain.
2. Read a movie or restaurant review, and identify examples of appeals to reason, emotion, and ethics. Are the methods effective? Explain.
3. Write your own movie or restaurant review.
4. The Food and Drug Administration has various rules and regulations that govern advertisements for food. Find some examples of these regulations, and do some research on how some advertisements try to bend them. For example, see Bonnie Liebman's article "Designed to Sell" in the *Nutrition Action Healthletter* (2006).
5. Research a bill that is about to come before the state or federal legislature. Brainstorm the arguments for and against the bill, and choose a side. Then write a letter to your senator or representative in which you persuade him or her to vote your way.
6. Read the editorial page of a newspaper and find two editorials or letters to the editor that interest you. What point does each try to make? How does each writer try to "prove" that point? Are their arguments successful? Explain.
7. Explore the similarities and differences between Aristotelian, Toulmin, and Rogerian argument.
8. Look up the definitions of one or more logical fallacies, and then explain them with your own words and examples.

IDEAS FOR WRITING

1. Describe an argument you've had in specific detail. What was the issue? What was at stake? How did it end?
2. Describe the "dream job" you'd like to have in two to five years. Then write a letter to the employer that would prove you're the best candidate.
3. What is a law you think should be changed or abolished? Why? Write a persuasive essay supporting your proposal.
4. Is advertising persuasion or propaganda? Include specific examples in your discussion.

CHAPTER 17
ANALYSIS—WRITING ABOUT LITERATURE

By the end of this chapter, you should begin to . . .

- perform a "close reading" of a literary text;
- use "writing to read" strategies;
- analyze a story or poem in terms of its theme, narrative voice, development of plot and character, figures of speech, and other elements;
- plan a critical analysis essay;
- incorporate textual evidence into your writing about literature; and
- troubleshoot problems that might arise when reading and writing about literature.

Creating a piece of art is one process—cooking, painting, performing, writing. Analyzing how and why the art creates a particular effect is another process. Part of the experience is just tasting: savoring a dish, looking at a painting, listening to a song, reading a poem. Then we add together all the details we perceive and begin to make sense of it. We may also sooner or later arrive at an evaluation of the work. Indeed, that may be our primary purpose. Taste this—do you like it or not? But when our purpose is to *analyze* the work, we try to understand and explain to others how and why the text or dish creates its effects or tastes as it does. It may not matter whether or not those effects are "good" or whether or not we "like" the taste.

Much of the process of writing about literature and other works of art is similar to the process of writing about anything else. There are some important differences, however, and it is these we will focus on in this chapter. Critical reading is an essential skill in writing about literature, and some knowledge of its component parts (plot, setting, character, imagery) is useful in conducting an analysis. Textual evidence, while often used in the same way as other kinds of evidence, has some unique features. Finally, we'll troubleshoot particular problems that might block some students as they read and write about literature.

CLOSE READING—TASTING THE TEXT

Our ability to write about literature depends upon our ability to read it. Whether or not we *enjoy* reading poems and stories, writing about them involves a different kind of reading—an attentive, analytical process called **close reading**. Not only are we paying attention to surface details, but we are looking at each sentence and each word, trying to undertand how the syntactical structures and word connotations influence our interpretation of the text. This is like a *tasting*. Imagine a wine expert gently swirling the liquid in the glass, inhaling its aroma, finally sipping, holding the wine in her mouth. She's performing a "close tasting".

Imagine a wine expert gently swirling the liquid in the glass, inhaling its aroma.

When we read literature, we'll most likely go over the text several times. The writing, especially in a poem, is denser than in a business letter (though we may also need to read between the lines of a business letter). We "taste" a story or poem (or painting or piece of music) as we might taste food—and let's imagine it's not just a sandwich that we gulp down on a ten-minute break, but a special dish at a family holiday or new restaurant. First, we just want to taste and feel, to perceive the aromas, flavors, and textures of the dish. Similarly, when we read a poem like the one that follows, we first listen to the words, then look them up in a dictionary if we don't know what they mean, and we try to imagine what is being described.

As always, potatoes are a natural starting point. Let's read the following poem, perhaps silently at first, noting any words we don't know or any line that particularly strikes—or confuses—us.

DIGGING
by Seamus Heaney

Between my finger and my thumb
The squat pen rests; snug as a gun.

Under my window, a clean rasping sound
When the spade sinks into gravelly ground:
My father, digging. I look down

Till his straining rump among the flowerbeds
Bends low, comes up twenty years away
Stooping in rhythm through potato drills
Where he was digging.

The coarse boot nestled on the lug, the shaft
Against the inside knee was levered firmly.
He rooted out tall tops, buried the bright edge deep
To scatter new potatoes that we picked,
Loving their cool hardness in our hands.

By God, the old man could handle a spade.
Just like his old man.

My grandfather could cut more turf in a day
Than any other man on Toner's bog.
Once I carried him milk in a bottle
Corked sloppily with paper. He straightened up
To drink it, then fell to right away

Nicking and slicing neatly, heaving sods
Over his shoulder, digging down and down
For the good turf. Digging.

The cold smell of potato mould, the squelch and slap
Of soggy peat, the curt cuts of an edge
Through living roots awaken in my head.
But I've no spade to follow men like them.

Between my finger and my thumb
The squat pen rests.
I'll dig with it.

First, consider the surface details. If you find any unfamiliar words or concepts—for example, "spade," "lug," "potato drill," or "peat"—look up the definitions. Then *listen* to the text, perhaps read it aloud yourself, perhaps find an audio of the author on the Internet. A popular montage of Seamus Heaney reciting "Digging" at various ages includes footage of a potato harvest and of cutting turf in a "bog."

Now begin to think about what the words tell you. What is happening at the beginning of the poem? The narrator is holding a pen in his hand. He looks out the window after hearing the "clean rasping sound" of a shovel ("spade") and sees his father, "digging . . . among the flowerbeds." The action is in the present tense, right in the moment. Yet as the narrator "look[s] down," his father's "straining rump . . . Bends low, comes up twenty years away." The narrator seems to remember what his father was doing two decades earlier: "Stooping in rhythm though potato drills / Where he was digging." The verb moves now to the past tense—he *was* digging.

Notice that Heaney sees the scene in clear detail—the boot is "coarse," the shaft of the spade is "levered firmly" against the knee, the children "lov[e] the cool hardness" of the new potatoes. The "we" here may be Seamus's younger siblings (he was the oldest of nine). It seems like he's remembering his childhood on the farm, helping to harvest the potatoes, admiring the skill and strength of his father.

A man rests on his spade during an afternoon of "digging" potatoes.

> By God, the old man could handle
>   a spade.
> Just like his old man.

With that last line, the narrator moves from memories of his father to memories of his grandfather, also digging, but this time it's "turf" instead of potatoes. Again, the older man's strength and skill inspire the boy's respect: "My grandfather could cut more turf in a day / Than any other man on Toner's bog." The narrator appears in this memory as well, carrying milk "in a bottle / Corked sloppily with paper." Can you see him, perhaps six years old, walking very carefully, staring intently at the bottle, willing it not to spill? In addition to his strength and skill, the grandfather has an impressive work ethic. He didn't take a real break, but drank the milk standing right there and "then fell to right away." Notice how the verbs in these stanzas about the poet's memories have been in the past tense.

In the penultimate stanza, the narrator comes back to the present as the vivid images of his past "awaken." He touches on all five of the senses in just two lines here: the temperature and aroma of the "potato mold," the sound of "soggy peat," the sight and feel of the "curt cuts through living roots." Then the narrator, whom perhaps we again see looking out of his window, reveals the pivotal insight:

> But I've no spade to follow men like them.

He hasn't the strength and skill that his father and grandfather have with the spade, or perhaps he hasn't the interest. What he does have is his "squat pen," and he concludes, "I'll dig with it." When we listen to Heaney read his poem, this last stanza is even clearer as he emphasizes *I'll* and *it*. In other words, he will work with a pen rather than a spade, and what's more, his work will be as admirable and fulfilling as that of his father and grandfather. There seems to be a bit of regret or disappointment in the poem, but at the end, the writer seems confident in his choice. There's a simple pride in the statement—I'll dig with it. And since Heaney went on to win the Nobel Prize for Literature in 1995, it's difficult to imagine that his family would not be extremely proud of him.

Our "tasting" of the text also involves noticing and thinking about more technical features of the poem. First, look at the different parts, the movement of the poem from the introductory title and first stanza to the concluding lines. A **stanza**, a group of lines in a poem, is very much like a paragraph. Through stanzas, the poet tells the reader that these lines belong together, expressing a single idea or creating a single image. In this poem we have the introduction of the topic, then of the setting and the character of his father (stanzas 1–2). In stanzas 3 and 4, we flash back twenty years and explore the narrator's memory of his father. The two lines of the 5th stanza provide a **transition** from the father to the grandfather, who is then described in stanzas 6 and 7. In stanza 8, the narrator returns to the present, acknowledging he must take a different path. The concluding lines echo the beginning, the first of them literally: "Between my finger and my thumb / The squat pen rests." But here the poet goes on with a new confidence—and the future tense—to assert his right to his own "digging."

I'll [I will] dig with it.

Heaney compares his work as a writer with the work of his father and grandfather on the farm. Any disappointment he or his family might have felt at his choice of career is assuaged (at least partially) by this comparison and by the fact that his poetry celebrates the family's life and traditions in loving detail.

WRITING TO READ

Through a close reading of the text, we can begin to peel away its layers and dig for what's beneath the surface or "between the lines." We can continue to explore these layers through various kinds of writing exercises. For example, a straightforward summary or explication of the piece can push us to put what we noticed about the text into our own words. It's as if we're cooking with the text. Writing down questions we have about the story, or definitions we've looked up, or references the author makes to other people, places, and events can open up new perspectives on the text and provide useful notes for later writing assignments. Through writing, we are able to read even more closely and effectively.

FOCUSED FREEWRITING

We've worked with freewriting in earlier chapters as a brainstorming technique, and it performs the same function here. The question or prompt might be quite open-ended, such as "What is your first reaction to the text?" Or it might be more factual, such as "Who is speaking to whom?" or "What do you think happened?" or "Where are we?" Sometimes the question can be more analytical, such as "Explain the connection between digging and writing in Seamus Heaney's 'Digging.'" Here's an example of freewriting in response to this last prompt:

> After reviewing Seamus Heaney's poem "Digging," I was able to sense that he was expressing a sort of sad reflection at the fact that he did not grow up to become a farmer. However, that does not mean that he was not proud of himself for being a poet, he stood by what he did but he couldn't help but feel distanced from his father and his father's father for not following in their footsteps and becoming a farmer himself. I felt that he expressed admiration to their profession but it is simply a field that was not meant for him. "I've no spade to follow men like them."
>
> The connection between digging and writing becomes evident towards the end of the poem. The line "the squat pen rests. I'll dig with it" concludes the poem. He watched his father with admiration as he dug the soil with his shovel and gave life to produce such as potatoes. He wrote about how his father and grandfather were hardworking men that gave themselves to their field. "My grandfather could cut more turf in a day than any other man on Toner's bog." Indicating the hard work these men have poured in. On the other hand, the poet is also a farmer in a sense. As his father dug the soil with his shovel, the poet dug paper with his pen. His father gave life to plants and fields while the poet gave life to poems and art. This concludes that even though he might have felt emotions of inferiority, he was still proud and accepting of what he did.
>
> —**Layla Saif**, student writer

It can also be helpful to write in a more creative or playful vein. What about composing a letter to the author, and even imagining what the author might write back to you?

> Dear Seamus, How do you feel about potatoes now? Has your family accepted your decision to be a poet?

Or we might write a dialogue between two of the characters in the piece (Heaney's father and grandfather, for example: What's going on with young Seamus?), or between two characters from different pieces. (See Figure 17.1 for additional ideas for freewriting.[11]) There are no right or wrong answers here—we're just exploring. We're also beginning to synthesize our ideas and put them into our *own* words, which is an important part of writing well and of avoiding plagiarism.

Figure 17.1   Writing to Read

What images particularly strike you? Why?
What line or paragraph is most important—to the text, the author, you?
What is the most important detail in the text? Why?
What is *missing* from the text?
If the text were the answer to a question, what would the question be?
If two of the characters met in a diner, what would they say to each other?

MAKING CONNECTIONS

Often our freewriting will be about connections we find between our own lives and the text, or about our personal reading of or response to it. Particularly when the text is a difficult one, we can gain confidence through this kind of connection, as a student does in the following journal entry:

> The poem "cutting greens" by Lucille Clifton is about the feeling the author gets when she cuts greens. Typically collards and kale are mentioned in this poem. Honestly, I like the poem. It is just something I can relate to. Greens is always something I can look forward to eating during the holidays. One thing that I disliked about the poem was that it was too short. I needed more information. There was a lot of visual imagery in the poem for such little information. The one question I have about the poem is "What did the author mean when she was talking about her hand?" She described a black cutting board, a black knife, and her hand. My assumption is that she was making a statement that she is African-American.
>
> Collard greens are a tradition in my family. The history of this type of vegetable goes back in time since slavery. When the slaves didn't have too much to eat, they ate whatever was edible. Collard greens is a very bitter food; it takes a lot of seasoning for it to become a delicious entrée or side dish. My mother wouldn't let me cook collards because she thought that I couldn't season them right. One day when I was cooking dinner, I snuck some frozen greens in a pot to cook. My mother came into the kitchen and saw the box on the counter. She asked me why I was cooking the greens when she told me not to. I told her that I wanted to make them and I knew she would like them. Sure enough, she tasted my greens, they were good she said, but they weren't better than hers. I can agree with her on that.
>
> —**Alicia Lacey**, student writer

In addition to making our own personal connections with a text, we can look for connections between texts. It's an easy way to get started. It's the compare-and-contrast thought process at work, a process we've been familiar with for years. For example, in preparing to write an essay on the themes of revenge and justice in *Mystic River,* a student might explore connections between *Mystic River, The Hunger Games, Star Wars,* and the Harry Potter series. Which characters in the various works pursued revenge and which sought justice? Whether the final writing assignment requires such connections or not, the freewriting we do about them can open up new insights, as well as push us to express ideas in our own words.

In the short piece that follows, the student writer explores connections between Edward Hopper's painting *Nighthawks* (1942), an episode from *The Twilight Zone* entitled "Will the Real Martian Please Stand Up?" (1961), and a scene from Clint Eastwood's *Sudden Impact* (1983). Divided by a span of forty years and differences in medium, the "texts" nevertheless share a common setting—a diner—and, as the writer will show, some common themes and symbols.

"Illusion, that's all. Just an Illusion."

Diners, so American, so familiar. A common meeting place, a fried egg, a safe haven. Most minds will conjure up images of metal edged plastic table tops, chrome fixtures and swiveling bar stools at just the word. It seems to make sense, then, that the concept of diners comes into play in many American cultural works. In just the short list up for consideration for this exercise, four of the pieces use a diner as a setting. This pattern should not be taken lightly, for as is usual, cultural fiction very closely mimics cultural reality.

As with most cultural symbols, it is not just this American nostalgia that the diner speaks to, but the American illusion. The tendency for denial, to smooth things over and pretend that everything is normal and satisfactory. When Clint Eastwood, who plays a police officer, walked into the diner for a cup of coffee in *Sudden Impact,* he was so lulled by the familiarity and comfort of the diner setting that he didn't even realize that it was being robbed. It was only when he noticed that his daily black coffee was full of sugar that it occurred to him something might be amiss. The use of coffee as a symbol also frequented the pieces we discussed. It's the drink of the American worker, and it symbolizes just that: the harried, fast-paced mindset so many of us have today. In *Sudden Impact,* it took the ruining of his coffee to slow Clint Eastwood's mind down enough for him to see past the illusion of safety in the diner.

Edward Hopper's 1942 painting *Nighthawks* also makes use of the symbolistic diner setting. The painting's diner is like a fishbowl, with large wrap-around windows and no visible doors, demonstrating how the painting's subjects are trapped within this illusion. Coffee machines are also visible in the diner, appearing as one of the only food products in the eatery, eerily showcasing the way the characters keep up their illusion. Because Edward Hopper depicted this sense of illusion so clearly by making the homey, American diner seem so eerie, this picture is an almost uncomfortable confrontation for the viewer.

Again, the diner as an illusion of safety and comfort recurs in *The Twilight Zone* episode "Will the Real Martian Please Stand Up?" Both the characters in the show and the viewers are so lulled into a false sense of security by the setting, with its warm, homey glow and friendly counterman, that they don't even realize the "businessman" and the counterman are in fact both aliens. And again, the use of the black coffee as a symbol surfaces before the big reveal, alluding to the fast-paced, absent-minded acceptance of the characters and viewers. The recurring symbols of the diner and the coffee seem a blatant warning of the dangers of this "American" mindset, warning their audiences not to become trapped by their own preconceptions. After all, as Ross says in *The Twilight Zone*, they're "just an illusion."

—**T. Marit Rubenstein**, student writer

The writer explores the common setting of the diner, what details stand out in each text, and she finds another connection—the cup of coffee. In the first text, *Sudden Impact,* the coffee is used as a warning, revealing that the diner's sense of comfort and safety is merely illusory. As the writer continues to look at connections between the three texts, she finds that they all seem to reveal this false sense of security. She begins to develop an idea based on the connections: "The recurring symbols of the diner and the coffee seem a blatant warning of the dangers of this 'American' mindset, warning their audiences not to become trapped by their own preoccupations."

Making connections: Imagine that Loretta from *Sudden Impact* and the countermen from *The Twilight Zone* and *Nighthawks* are speaking to one another and to us.

Making connections between texts may bring important features of one or more of them into clearer focus, as it did in Rubenstein's piece. If she were to go on to write a critical analysis of the topic, she would explain more fully how each text develops the diner setting as an illusion of safety, using many of the persuasive strategies we discussed in Chapter 16. Evidence would consist of details, descriptions, summaries, and quotes. Counterarguments or alternative interpretations would be outlined and refuted.

This kind of discovery process—making connections—is very much like the kind of surfing we often do on the Internet. We begin to read one page or post, and that makes us think of a question or another related story, and with a touch, or at most a brief search, we've moved on to another page. At the end of the process, we may have broadened our understanding of that first story, found a new perspective, or stumbled upon a new topic altogether.

ANALYZING THE TEXT

In an analytical paper, we look at one or more distinct parts or aspects of the text, for example, a particular character, or the way an author develops character; or the use of the sonnet form or rhyme scheme; or the role of imagery in a particular text. While we are breaking it down into its parts, our end goal is to achieve a deeper understanding of the whole. (It's kind of like prepping your ingredients before cooking them.) Sometimes students get frustrated with this process—the analysis seems to take the life out of the work. Yet analytical thinking has applications in almost any career—a proposal for a new restaurant, perhaps, which must *analyze* the costs, opportunities, and risks in order to make a case for the whole, that is, an investment in the property.[a]

After performing a close reading of the text, go back and make notes of the elements you want to analyze. Perhaps make lists or charts on a separate sheet of paper as well. See Figure 17.2, for example. As with other ways of thinking, analysis can be driven by questions. Who are the characters? Who is speaking, and to whom? Where does the story take place? What happens? What do we notice about the point of view, voice, imagery? Is there a conflict or problem, and is it resolved? Sometimes we turn the questions back on ourselves and analyze our response to the work and the reasons for it. Suppose you looked at Edward Hopper's famous painting *Nighthawks* and found yourself feeling oddly uncomfortable, a bit breathless. You might then ask what about the painting caused you to feel this way. What details about light and shape and color, details included and details omitted, led to your response? What is unclear or ambiguous?

With any text, it's useful to explore the connotations of the words, and their figurative potential. Consider Seamus Heaney's central metaphor, for example. How else could "digging" be used? Are the "living roots" in the peat bog, or the poet's brain, or both? With poetry especially, we'll want to consider the sound of the words.

---

[a] See the two excerpts from an analysis of a restaurant's competitors in Chapter 4, pp. 60–61, and Chapter 14, pp. 245–246.

Although Heaney uses **rhyme** in the poem, he doesn't use a rigid or traditional rhyme scheme. We have a slant or partial rhyme at the end of lines 1 and 2—*thumb* and *gun*—and a true rhyme of lines 3 and 4—*sound* and *ground*. The third line of this stanza ends with *down*, another slant rhyme. After looking at all the rhyme, we might ask ourselves what effect it has on our reading of the poem. Why might Heaney choose to use rhyme in this way? How does it work? If we can answer these questions, we may find a new perspective on or deeper understanding of the poem.

Any feature could be analyzed in this way, for example, **character**, **plot**, **setting**, **imagery**, **rhyme**, **symbolism**, or **irony**. Often we will analyze two or more works in terms of a shared element as, for example, in the earlier short piece that explored the illusion of a diner's safety in several different "texts." In addition to analyzing features within the text, we may choose to look outside it for further information and insights.

IDENTIFYING SOURCES

Sometimes we'll make connections between a literary text and its source. For example, Shakespeare often borrowed plots from earlier works, and many artists have used Shakespeare's plays as inspiration. The story of Romeo and Juliet was known in various formats before Shakespeare's play of the same name. We might write a paper in which we trace the influence of these sources on Shakespeare's text, or in which we look at how a more recent work used Shakespeare as a source. How many versions of *Romeo and Juliet* have you seen? The 1967 film directed by Franco Zeffirelli or the updated version starring Leonardo DiCaprio and Claire Danes? The musical interpretations *West Side Story* or *High School Musical? Gnomeo & Juliet in 3D?*

Members of the Puerto Rican gang, the Sharks, dance on location in New York City in 1961's *West Side Story*.

Exploring the connections between different versions of a story is often a direct and fruitful way to begin an analysis. Such a paper might develop briskly through a process of compare and contrast. Then, in asking which similarities and differences are important, and why, we may devise a potential topic for a critical analysis essay.

BIOGRAPHICAL AND HISTORICAL CONTEXT

Readers often like to know something about the **biographical background**, connecting details of the author's life with themes in his work. For example, how old is the narrator in "Digging" in this first scene at the window? The poem was published in 1966, when the poet was twenty-seven years old. The poem may have been written earlier, of course. Perhaps Heaney was on a visit home when these memories overcame him, memories of his father's prime and of his own childhood. "Digging" is one of Heaney's early poems; it's the first poem in his very first book, and we might argue that it introduces some of his most pervasive themes and techniques.

The **historical background** or context can also deepen our understanding of a writer's themes. Heaney, for example, was born in 1939 under the shadow of World War II and also lived through decades of the Irish "troubles." He may be alluding to these when he speaks of the pen lying in his hand "as snug as a gun." We might also think of the role the potato has played in Irish history and culture. The Irish Potato Famine of 1845–1852, known in Ireland as the Great Hunger, is familiar to most readers, and for Heaney would have been a reminder of the critical turning point in Irish history. In terms of **psychological background**, Heaney has written of the tension between his very quiet father and his very outspoken mother, a tension that contributed to his own inner conflict. At times the **scientific,** or perhaps agricultural, **background** can also be relevant. What's a potato drill? How was the turf used? The brief lines of the poem extend into more and more questions and answers, like the living roots themselves.

Critics and teachers differ on how much weight they give information outside of the text, whether it's biographical information on the author or personal connections with the reader. Read your instructions carefully, and always check your interpretations against the details of the text.

PLANNING A CRITICAL ANALYSIS ESSAY

A **critical analysis essay** is a form of persuasive writing. You will "argue" that your interpretation of a text is a reasonable one and you will produce specific, relevant evidence to support your interpretation. It's not about being "right," necessarily, but about being persuasive; and many of the same persuasive strategies we looked at in Chapter 16 will apply here. You must establish an authoritative, fair-minded character or *ethos* by demonstrating your knowledge of the text, presenting your argument in a reasonable tone, and considering alternative interpretations (that you refute).

The choice of topic is important. Once you've explored and analyzed the text in one or more ways, you can begin to focus on a particular question or problem it raises. This question or problem can have to do with many different aspects of the text, such as the ideas, characters, events, setting, narrative voice or point of view, imagery, figurative language, or structure. In asking and answering questions around this question or problem, you develop the **central idea** of your paper. (See also Chapter 5.) Here a student writer records the questioning that initially drove the development of his essay:

> As we read "Shooting an Elephant," "The Man I Killed," and "Killing Dinner" and I reflected on the similarities between them, I found myself curious as to why each of these authors focused so heavily on the violent, colorful aspects of the graphic scenes they were describing. Each of these authors was very young when the scenarios took place, late teens or early twenties, and I could not help but find that they were affected so deeply because of their immaturity and the extreme condition of violence they encountered. So I asked myself, how do the graphic, colorful depictions of violence and childlike shapes and references reflect the way our young authors were affected by and handled the events in the story?
> —**Andrew Novak,** student writer

Once you have a working question or problem for the paper, read through the text(s) again (or watch the movie, look at the painting) and begin to assemble and categorize your evidence. You've broken the text into its component parts; now you're going to put them back together. For example, if you were analyzing the use of childlike imagery in several texts, it might be useful to create a chart (see Figure 17.2).

Figure 17-2 Analysis of Images

Type of Image	Shooting an Elephant	The Man I Killed	Killing Dinner
childish images	grandmotherly air toad under a steamroller	star-shaped hole small blue flowers shaped like bells butterfly	pet beagle bunnies blubbering through clenched teeth
primary colors	pale pink throat blood like red velvet	red and yellow blue deep purplish black	blue enamel lobster pot yellow pool of light livery, bloody [red] jewels

What do you notice? Is there a pattern? Is one type used more often? The evidence you discover will lead you to some resolution of your initial question and then—organized and explained by you—will be used to persuade the reader to agree with your point of view.

Let's look at some more examples. In "Bitter Dinners," the writer analyzes how a "bitter" dinner experience affects the characters in two personal essays, "Fish Cheeks" and "Killing Dinner." The writer introduces his analysis as follows:

> Food can be one of the most pleasurable things that everyone experiences. Its purpose is not only to nourish us. The happiness food brings to the people who are savouring it exceeds this primal reason. On every occasion, I see food as a component that binds the people who are enjoying it. When families and friends gather, food can uplift the company. Even between strangers, food can ignite a joyful encounter. Yet, in the case of two stories I have read, food made an opposite impression on the characters. The memories of the past bring together the stories of the narrators from "Fish Cheeks" and "Killing Dinner." Between their families and the writers themselves, conflicts with their family arise on the occasions they remember which all revolve around food. In "Fish Cheeks," it is the traditional Chinese dinner. In "Killing Dinner," it is the slaughtering of the chicken. Because of the events that happened in each story, I have seen that the characters' relationship with food changed.
>
> —**Grant Rainiere Young**, student writer

The problem seems to revolve around why the characters' relationship with food changed to a "bitter" one.

In this third example, the writer has chosen a broader topic: the concept of *halftime*, as used in a television commercial during the Super Bowl and as applied to two literary texts.

> "Halftime" is a term that can be interpreted in so many ways. We hear this word, and our minds automatically drown themselves in sports images, but halftime can be anywhere, anytime. The objective of halftime is to allow the players to switch sides of the field to allow equal advantages or disadvantages; halftime also allows for a recap of the situation. During this period spectators get entertainment while the players lie in desperate thoughts of how the game will end. This time allows a silence in our minds where our thoughts try to organize themselves as we think of how to go about the next part. In "The Man I Killed" and "Shooting an Elephant," [Tim] and George face their own halftime as they think of how to go about the next step in their situations, facing the previous events and the possibilities of the future. With every decision comes a consequence, but it is impossible to foresee the future. Each decision is different from the next, and the outcome of one can change the fate of the entire game.
>
> —**Nicole Philipson**, student writer

See the complete text of Young's essay at the end of Chapter 2; Novak's and Philipson's essays are reprinted at the end of this chapter.

A critical analysis essay can be organized in a number of ways. You will choose the method that best suits your topic and the assignment. For example, Andrew Novak's "Blue Bells & Butterflies" devotes a body paragraph to analyzing the images in each of the three works he examines: "The Man I Killed," "Shooting an Elephant," and "Killing Dinner." In contrast, Grant Rainiere Young in "Bitter Dinners" moves back and forth between "Fish Cheeks" and "Killing Dinner" as he analyzes the narrators' familial relationships and the role of a particular dinner in revealing them. These outlines mirror the block and alternating formats described in Chapter 13 (see Figures 13.3 and 13.4). The organization of "It's Halftime, So Now What" is more complex. Philipson's piece might also be classified as a **personal essay**, with a looser organizational framework that highlights the writer's individual journey.

USING TEXTUAL EVIDENCE

The reader's own background, experience, interests, and abilities play a major role in her interpretation of a text. Often there is no right or wrong answer about a question of interpretation. However, we need to be able to support that interpretation with evidence from the text. We have to make an argument. If we say the images in the stories are child-like and innocent, we need to be able to point to a line or lines in the text itself that imply or exemplify it, for example, the butterflies and bluebells in "The Man I Killed" or the toad and the grandmother in "Shooting an Elephant." It is in our use of specific, relevant evidence that we show our knowledge of the text and the reasonableness of our interpretation.

This **textual evidence** will include **direct quotes** from the text—and you'll use more of these in a literary analysis than you would in a research paper. You're trying to convey a sense of the **voice** or "flavor" of the work here. On the other hand, you still want the majority of the writing to be in your words, and you want to be sure everything you quote is directly useful. Don't quote two sentences where one will do, or five words where three will do, and so on. Sometimes you may choose to summarize or paraphrase in your own words, rather than to quote directly. (See also Chapter 19.) In the following example, the writer "seasons" his words with phrases from the texts he's analyzing, here highlighted in yellow.

With the task at hand of shooting a once enraged but now calm elephant, Orwell reluctantly kills it, and we can see a similar use of colorful imagery and peaceful similes used to describe the violence. The elephant's "pale pink throat" and "the thick blood [that] welled out of him like red velvet" are some examples of this. While not as childish as O'Brien's images, we must look at the fact he too notices these colors (again with "red") and uses them to help describe his chaos. He also relies on youthful similes, such as perceiving a "grandmotherly air" about the creature, or being a "toad under a steamroller"—all images that remind us of our childhood—as his escape mechanism. I look at each of these images, and I start missing my grandmother and the toads I used to set up terrariums for as a child, and the big Tonka steamroller I had, and it makes sense to me why he would use these expressions as a way to ease his mind. He becomes a "hollow, posing dummy" and "turns tyrant," which shows me he too is naïve about death, presuming himself a tyrant for (only) killing a wild animal.

—**Andrew Novak**, student writer

The highlighting helps us see how Novak uses single words and short phrases to make his points, rather than feeling obliged to quote an entire sentence. Textual evidence may also include descriptions of structural or formal features, such as chronology, rhyme scheme, and even visual aspects of the text.

In analyzing other kinds of "texts," you'll look at different features, but the principle remains the same. If you're writing about a film, for example, your "textual" evidence will go beyond the words the characters say and include details of their actions, descriptions of their appearance and expressions, descriptions of the music and scenery, discussion of the film techniques. If you're writing about a painting, your evidence will include details of the colors and shapes, as well as the type of paint, canvas, use of brushstrokes, and other techniques specific to that medium. If you're writing about food or wine, your evidence will include details of flavor and texture, body and finish. In any case, both the development of your central idea and your presentation to the reader will rely on your close "reading" of the "textual" evidence. It's worth repeating that while your own perspective is an inevitable and essential part of this reading, you will still return to the "text" itself to support any particular interpretation. And, just as in other types of persuasive writing, it can be effective to look at alternative interpretations of the text and expose their weaknesses.

TROUBLESHOOTING

Writing about literature isn't that different from other types of writing, except in the attitudes and expectations we may bring to it. I find that students have varied responses to an assignment to read and write about a story or poem. For many, it is a familiar and manageable assignment; for others, it is completely unfamiliar, though they are willing to give it a try. For some students, however, it is an uncomfortable reminder of earlier unpleasant experiences of reading and writing about literature.

If you don't like to read . . .

- Try sampling a few paragraphs to see if there's any character or detail you can connect with. Try to see it in your mind's eye. If your attention wanders, go back and find that picture again.

- Be patient. Give it a chance. Often the story in a book unfolds more slowly than one in a movie. Think of a book more like a television series, like *Games of Thrones*. It takes months or years to tell the story.
- Perhaps find out something about the author. Something about the "real" story might spark your interest.
- Some people find that listening to music makes reading more enjoyable.

If reading is physically uncomfortable, or hurts your eyes . . .

- You may be sensitive to light. Although it's the most common combination, black print on a glossy white page may be the most difficult for you to read. If you can, read on blue paper or get a colored screen to cut off the glare.
- It might be helpful to see a doctor. Perhaps you need glasses or a different prescription.

If you feel you don't understand the reading . . .

- Read the text at least twice, first to get the general idea, then to perform a "close" reading.
- Try not to focus on getting the "right" answer, for example, about what something symbolizes or what something means. Listen carefully to what the text says, and use all your knowledge and experience to construct some sense of it.
- Don't worry if other people do seem to understand right away, although it can be intimidating when other students seem able to process a text and questions about it more quickly than we can. Remember that people have different abilities. Sometimes it's great to process things quickly, but many tasks require thinking carefully and deeply, and in the end insights grow with time.
- If poetry is particularly difficult, try to stick with the literal meaning. Who's talking? What's happening? Look for the story. *See* the images.

If you think the reading is a waste of time . . .

- Imagine that the writer has something to tell you. Listen for it.
- Try just being polite, as if you're at a family party and spending time with an ancient relative. Remember you probably have something in common; try to find out what that is.

If you don't know what to write about . . .

- Do a lot of brainstorming. Try the freewriting exercises in Figure 17.1. What interests you? What do you connect with? Develop a topic based on this connection.
- Talk to your instructor. Most likely she has lots of ideas and can help you choose one that interests you.

That last bit of advice is probably the most important: Talk to your instructor.

Nicole Philipson is from Mexico City and recently received a degree in culinary arts.

****

It's Halftime, So Now What?
by Nicole Philipson

"Halftime" is a term that can be interpreted in so many ways. We hear this word, and our minds automatically drown themselves in sports images, but halftime can be anywhere, anytime. The objective of halftime is to allow the players to switch sides of the field to allow equal advantages or disadvantages; halftime also allows for a recap of the situation. During this period spectators get entertainment while the players lie in desperate thoughts of how the game will end. This time allows a silence in our minds where our thoughts try to organize themselves as we think of how to go about the next part. In "The Man I Killed" and "Shooting an Elephant," Tim and George face their own halftime as they think of how to go about the next step in their situations, facing the previous events and the possibilities of the future. With every decision comes a consequence, but it is impossible to foresee the future. Each decision is different from the next, and the outcome of one can change the fate of the entire game.

Every year in America the Super Bowl event is anxiously awaited and not just because of the game. The Super Bowl ads are now also extremely anticipated. In 2012 a very powerful commercial was played by Chrysler, talking about halftime not in the game but in America. It speaks about the pause in American society: an economic pause, a political pause, and an employment pause. "People are out of work and they're hurting and they're all wondering what they're going to do to make a comeback and we're all scared because this isn't a game" (Chrysler). The strategy isn't working, and a re-evaluation must be done, but by whom? Civilians or our government? In every game there are rules that can't be changed, so even if we have the perfect game plan, if it doesn't comply with the law we cannot execute it. Despite what we would like to think, others constantly control the decisions we make. In the ad, Chrysler mentions the change people have to make by coming together to move forward, but this idea is off the table as soon as we consider the lack of power we actually have in making our own decisions; it's here where we see that freedom of action is truly an overstatement.

Citizens in a democratic environment are constantly reminded of their freedom of speech and action. In school the words "your actions have consequences, mister" come out of our teacher's mouth every now and then. This idea brings me to the thought, Are we really making our own decisions, or are we influenced through others to act a certain way? The actions and decisions of others dictate ours, ours dictate others, and so on, causing a never-ending cycle. In "Shooting an Elephant," George has a decision to make: kill the elephant, or let it live. In his own morality the right thing to do is to let it live until its keeper comes back and controls it, but the entertained crowd fogs his thinking and decision-making. This moment is George's halftime; while he deliberates, the crowd jeers in amusement. "They were watching me as they would watch a conjuror about to perform a trick" (666). At the end George gives in to the pressure and his hunger to impress, and shoots the elephant, causing it a deep and painful death. "I often wondered whether any of the others grasped that I had done it solely to avoid looking a fool" (669). George's regret over his actions is hidden between his words but is still very clear for the reader. Even though he had time to think his "moves" through, he still manages to do what he considers the wrong thing.

Tim in "The Man I Killed" also finds himself facing a pause during his actions, and a rather long one in comparison to the sense of urgency that runs through places like battlegrounds. The interesting thing about Tim's halftime point is that it happens after the action has already occurred; it's as if you make the pass and then go over the game plan that was supposed to take place. This is what I mean when I say that halftime can be anywhere and anytime; it is not precisely in the middle of a situation or before we make the final decision. Tim faces a complete "emptiness" in himself when he looks at the man he has just killed, thinking about who he might have been, what his actions have caused, and how to go on after this. "All you needed was time—some mental R&R," says Tim's friend Kiowa (124). Decisions facing life and death are always harder, and the consequences aren't as easy to get through. Taking time to process images or actions like this one is inevitable. "Take it slow. Just go wherever the spirit takes you," says Kiowa (120). This passage really reflects what halftime is about.

America, Tim, and George are all in silence: "It seems that [they've] lost their heart" somehow (Chrysler), drowning in their own thoughts and self battles. We have our own moral compass which guides our decisions; this compass is built through our life experiences, family values, our culture and our society; due to this we learn to make decisions and choose paths. We learn to build our game plans when we find ourselves in halftime, and we learn to prioritize. The problem is when we lose our morality and fall into someone else's. When George finds himself facing the elephant, he knows what should be done, but as soon as he notices the crowd and thinks about his already unpopular status around the Burmans, he chooses to go against his own will. That's when we lose the game.

We are constantly facing events that aren't fair. We are forced into situations and actions that cause regret in our life. We are drawn in by pressure and the expectation that lies on us. Are we still in control like we thought we were? Are these the consequences of *my* decisions? I don't think our voices can really be heard through the echo of the greater voices. So yes, it is time for us to re-think what we've been told. It is time for us to take a step back and reflect upon our choices. "We find a way through tough times and if we can't find a way, then we'll make one" (Chrysler). Take a halftime and earn your freedom through your peace of mind, because "our second half is about to begin."

Works Cited

Chrysler. "Halftime in America." Advertisement. 5 Feb. 2012. Television.

O'Brien, Tim. "The Man I Killed." *The Things They Carried.* 1990. New York: Mariner Books, 2009. 118–124. Print.

Orwell, George. "Shooting an Elephant." *The Bedford Reader.* 11th ed. Ed. X. J. Kennedy, Dorothy M. Kennedy, and Jane E. Aaron. Boston: Bedford/St. Martin's, 2012. 663–669. Print.

ABOUT THE READING

- What associations do *you* have with the concept of halftime?
- What questions does the writer ask to develop her central idea?
- What evidence does she use to support her interpretations? Is it persuasive?
- What does the writer mean by "take a halftime and earn your freedom through your peace of mind"?

A veteran of the United States Air Force, Andrew Novak currently studies at the Culinary Institute of America. His son was two years old when this essay was written.

****

Blue Bells & Butterflies
by Andrew Novak

As we read "The Man I Killed," "Shooting an Elephant," and "Killing Dinner" and reflected on the similarities between them, I found myself curious as to why each of these authors focused so heavily on the violent, colorful aspects of the graphic scenes they were describing. Each of these authors was very young when the scenarios took place, late teens or early twenties, and I could not help but find that they were affected so deeply because of their immaturity and the extreme condition of violence they encountered. So I asked myself, how do the graphic, colorful depictions of violence and childlike shapes and references reflect the way our young authors were affected by and handled the events in the story?

Looking at "The Man I Killed," it is easy for us to see how graphic the violence was for Tim O'Brien in the way that he presents it to us in his story. He is a young man, at war unwillingly, and the way he visualizes the brutality shows his immaturity and naivety about death. I personally believe that in times of overwhelming distress or discomfort we reach back to our childlike nature in trying to see colors and peaceful shapes and images. He presents us with colorful diversions such as "the star-shaped hole was red and yellow," "along the trail there were small blue flowers shaped like bells," and "the blood at the neck had gone to a deep purplish black" (O'Brien). Focusing on the shapes and images he uses, star-shaped holes and bells, I am reminded of my son playing with his wooden blocks, while flowers and butterflies remind me of a peaceful garden. One could argue that the colors, the simplest primary ones, are used because they are the base colors for everything and learned first during childhood. Because O'Brien witnessed the violence in its full reality we understand why—at such a young age and never exposed to such gruesome images—he tried to reach out and find these childlike colors and shapes to distract him. Being reminded by Kiowa several times that there was "nothing *anybody* could do" and to "stop staring" shows that it had truly captivated his attention. He focuses not only on the violence, but also on the distracting, colorful aspects of his victim and surroundings—as he points out the bell-shaped flowers and the butterfly on his victim's chin.

This was also the case in the story "Shooting an Elephant" where our author George Orwell writes colorful recollections of a violent event during his younger years. As we go through this story, we learn that a youthful Orwell, like O'Brien, was not in favor of the work he was doing. With the task at hand of shooting a once enraged but now calm elephant, Orwell reluctantly kills it, and we can see a similar use of colorful imagery and peaceful similes used to describe the violence. The elephant's "pale pink throat" and "the thick blood [that] welled out of him like red velvet" are some examples of this. While these are not as childish as O'Brien's images, Orwell too notices these colors (again with "red") and uses them to help describe his chaos. He also relies on youthful similes, such as perceiving a "grandmotherly air" about the creature, or being a "toad under a steamroller"—all images that remind us of our childhood—as his escape mechanism. I look at each of these images, and I start missing my grandmother and the toads I used to set up terrariums for as a child, and the big Tonka steamroller I had, and it makes sense to me why he would use these expressions as a way to ease his mind. He becomes a "hollow, posing dummy" and "turns tyrant," which shows me he too is naïve about death, presuming himself a tyrant for (only) killing a wild animal. Perhaps not as bothered by the elephant's death as Tim O'Brien is by that of the man he killed, these images stuck into Orwell's memory after all these years, telling us that he too used colors, shapes, and childlike images to distract from the violence that he caused. In his youth he is unable to handle the brutality of the death and "could not stand it any longer and went away," even as the villagers "stripped his body almost to the bones by the afternoon."

If we go a little further, we will see how yet another author uses similar colorful, childlike imagery in her story of youthful violence. Our seventeen-year-old author Gabrielle Hamilton finds herself in a similar bloody situation, though willingly through her family's work, where she is around "farm-like" violence on a daily basis. Immediately I saw the childlike references she makes to keep herself comfortable in such an environment when referring to the suckling pigs as the "same weight and size as a pet beagle" and the "rabbits, which, even when skinned, look exactly like bunnies." This imagery, through grim references to the slaughtered animals they represent, shows me that instead of seeing a dead pig, she sees a friendly beagle, or a bunny. When she decides to execute a chicken for the first time and it all goes awry, she ends up "blubbering through clenched teeth" at the traumatic experience, revealing her unfamiliarity with that level of violence. While it is still a very graphic depiction of the event, I noticed the colorful and youthful images are not used in the story until after the butchering fiasco, and not during. I point this out because after all these years she is still able to recall the images in their primary colors, not only because of how extreme the event was, but because her youthful mind sought them out when coping with the situation. She remembered the "dead brown leaves" that the "bloody and ragged" chicken fell over into. She remembers the exact "blue enamel lobster pot" that she boiled the chicken in and the "yellow pool of light" that she sat in while plucking it on the back steps. She also mentions evisceration yielding "livery, bloody jewels" that she "tossed out into the dark yard." Like O'Brien and Orwell, she describes the violence with colorful and child-like imagery in her attempt to escape the horrible way she is feeling.

In all three of these stories, the narrators suffered a traumatic experience that left life-long impressions on them. I think a combination of their age and their unfamiliarity with death presents them with a mental dilemma, and they seek relief from the violence through using simple colors and shapes to help lighten the intensity of their situation. While the authors still use adult, violent, descriptive images of their kill, they all were clearly affected to the point of using primary colors and childlike images to distract themselves from the settings they are in. Literally worlds apart, all three authors suffered similar experiences and give us the ability to see what they observed on those days, perhaps using these images as a way to help us empathize with them, or even as a deeper way of understanding the extreme sense of discomfort or pain of their stories. Regardless, as we conclude each story, we feel like we know exactly what they have seen, and we can relate to the use of their colorful and shapely images as their way to escape a traumatic experience.

Works Cited

Hamilton, Gabrielle. "Killing Dinner." *Best Food Writing 2005*. Ed. Holly Hughes. New York: Marlowe, 2005. 71–73. Print.

O'Brien, Tim. "The Man I Killed." *The Things They Carried*. 1990. New York: Mariner Books, 2009. 118–124. Print.

Orwell, George. "Shooting an Elephant." *The Bedford Reader*. 11th ed. Ed. X. J. Kennedy, Dorothy M. Kennedy, and Jane E. Aaron. Boston: Bedford/St. Martin's, 2012. 663–669. Print.

ABOUT THE READING

- What advantages does the writer find in discussing the three texts in this particular order, that is, "The Man I Killed," "Shooting an Elephant," and "Killing Dinner"? What advantages might be found in a different order?
- What transitional words and phrases does the writer use to move the essay from one point to the next?
- How does the writer use quotes from the three stories?
- Where does the writer use the evidence of his own experience? Is that evidence persuasive? Explain.

RECIPE FOR REVIEW

CLOSE READING

In preparing to write about literature, read carefully or "closely," identifying the denotation and connotation of words, looking up unfamiliar references and allusions. Then *listen* to text. Read it aloud, or listen to someone else read it aloud. You might find a recording of the author reading the work. Look at the surface details. What is happening? Who is involved?

WRITING TO READ

To broaden and deepen your perspective on the work, use writing to read strategies such as focused freewriting. See Figure 17.1 for ideas.

ANALYZING THE TEXT

Examine specific features or elements of the text, such as characterization, plot structure, setting, imagery, metaphor, symbolism, irony, and genre. Ask yourself how they contribute to the work as a whole. If warranted, consider the biographical, psychological, historical, and cultural contexts of the work. Look for connections between your own experience and the text, and between other texts, perhaps in other media (a poem with a painting, for example).

PLANNING A CRITICAL ANALYSIS ESSAY

- An analysis of a literary or other artistic "text" looks at how specific features or elements work to create certain effects.
- A critical analysis essay is like an argument. It attempts to persuade the reader that this interpretation is reasonable and well supported by evidence.
- A focused question or problem can drive the development of the essay.
- If you are writing for a class or for publication, be sure to read the instructions carefully.

USING TEXTUAL EVIDENCE

The "evidence" you present will be quotes, summaries, details, and descriptions from and of the "text," details that can be independently verified by the reader. Textual evidence should be specific and relevant. See also Chapter 16, p. 277.

TROUBLESHOOTING

Be patient. Take the pressure off. Read closely. Keep an open mind. Make connections. Talk to your instructor.

1. *Close Reading*—Choose a poem, and perform a close reading.
2. *Writing to Read*—After reading the poem, choose two of the writing to read strategies in Figure 17.1.
3. *Making Connections*—Choose three poems (or stories, films, etc.), and explore the connections between them in terms of one or more elements such as story, theme, structure, voice, and imagery. (For example, Seamus Heaney, Yusef Komunyakaa, and Galway Kinnell have written terrific poems about blackberries.)
4. *Biographical Context*—Read Seamus Heaney's Nobel Prize acceptance speech. What do you learn about his life and philosophy that offers a new perspective on "Digging"?
5. *Identifying Sources*—Compare a recent version of a Shakespearean play, for example, the BBC's *Macbeth* set in a professional kitchen (one of the four works in *Shakespeare Re-Told*, 2005), with Shakespeare's text.
6. *Analyzing a Cartoon*—Analyze the cartoon in Figure 17.3. Why is it funny?

Figure 17.3   Exercise 6—Analyzing a Cartoon

7. *Analyzing Irony*—Look up "friends of irony pictures" or "funny FAIL pictures and videos" on the Internet, and choose three or four images. Now explain what *irony* is, using as examples the pictures you chose.

8. *"Reading" a Plate*—Write a set of directions for "reading" a dish. Include such features as the appearance, aroma, texture, and flavor of the food; the quality of the ingredients; and the arrangement of items on the plate.

9. *"Reading" Music*—Do some reading on what happens in the brain when we listen to music. For example, dip into John Powell's *How Music Works* or Google a question like "Why does music give you chills?" Summarize your findings in a paragraph or two.

IDEAS FOR WRITING

1. What story or film kept you thinking about it days later? Why? Was it because of a particular character or a particular moment? Write an analysis of your response.

2. Write a critical analysis of a song, paying attention to elements of both the music and the lyrics and explaining how they work together to create a certain effect.

3. Write a restaurant review in which you analyze your experience and try to persuade the reader that your assessment is reasonable.

4. Another type of response to a text is a personal re-working, almost an imitation. Write your own version of "Digging," using the title and structure but substituting your own subject and theme.

CHAPTER 18
AN INTRODUCTION TO RESEARCH I—FINDING AND EVALUATING YOUR SOURCES

After reading this chapter, you should begin to . . .

- construct focused, effective research questions;
- identify appropriate sources of information in order to answer your questions;
- evaluate the reliability of books and articles;
- evaluate the reliability of Internet resources; and
- understand the role of good research techniques in boosting your credibility.

One of the most popular television series in recent years has been *CSI*, that is, *Crime Scene Investigation*. We love to watch Grissom pursue a theory of the crime with one of his gruesome experiments—the popsicle made of freshly ground beef, for example. We marvel at the increasing effectiveness of DNA testing. We applaud the team's attention to detail—mapping out the blood spatter, shining their little flashlights into every corner and under every sheet. Based on the high ratings of this show and its spinoffs, we should be a nation passionately devoted to research. Because that's what research is—investigation. Research is as cool as the CSIs and most of it can be done without crawling across the floor with a pair of tweezers!

Research simply means "look carefully" or "search again." You've probably already done quite a bit of research in the kitchen as you experimented with different ingredients and cooking methods. Does this cookie taste better with white chocolate or dark? What happens if I cook this sauce another three minutes? You have probably also looked at many, many recipes, sometimes using them exactly as they were written, sometimes altering them. You've most likely explored the quality and pricing of various food items at different supermarkets. When you write a research paper, you are doing this same type of activity.

Three aspects of the research paper are particularly challenging. The first is constructing a specific, thoughtful research question that can be addressed in the available space and time. The second is finding current, reliable, relevant information. The third, which is explored in Chapter 19, is adding that information to the knowledge you already have, mixing well, and cooking up a tasty and nutritious essay.

CSI's Dr. Raymond Langston (Laurence Fishburne) and Catherine Willows (Marg Helgenberger) arrive at a crime scene.

CONSTRUCTING A RESEARCH QUESTION

With unimaginable quantities of data literally at our fingertips, a research topic can easily become unmanageable. Therefore, like other types of writing, research papers and reports should have a specific, manageable focus. A research question that is clear, focused, specific, appropriately complex, and genuine will guide our search for information.

As with other writing tasks, the scope of the question will depend on the space and time available. Whether the assignment is for school or for work, or something you want to find out just for yourself, there is likely to be a length requirement (for example, eight to ten pages) and a deadline (for example, two weeks from today, or at the end of the semester, or on the first day of each quarter). It's unlikely that you can write a good ten-page paper in two days.

Good research questions will avoid simple *yes* or *no* answers. If you can answer your question with a quick Google search, so can your readers. Why would they be interested in your paper, then? Thus, your question must be somewhat complex. The level of complexity will depend on the length of the paper or report, the amount of time you have to conduct and process the research, and your existing knowledge of the topic. Your paper should reflect your analysis and interpretation of the best (most current, reliable, relevant) sources you can find, and should present this analysis and interpretation in a clear, easily digestible form. (See also Chapter 5 for information about planning and Chapter 16 for instruction on analysis.)

Your research question should also be one that can be researched. Depending on how much you already know about the topic and how much guidance you're offered by the instructions for a particular paper, you may want to develop a sense of what's available by reading general reference material and looking at the cited sources. This will help you determine whether there's enough good information available for the scope of your project. Stay flexible as you construct your question so that you can revise it according to what you find in an initial survey.

Finally, like all your writing, a research paper or report will have more energy and relevance if you and your readers are genuinely interested in the topic. Even if the general outline of the assignment doesn't catch your interest initially, work hard to find an angle that does.

EXPLORING AN EXAMPLE: WHAT'S FOR DINNER?

Let's look at the general topic of how to buy healthy, environmentally sustainable fish. This might be a fairly narrow and immediate question, such as the following: I'm at the store. Shall I buy the wild-caught or farm-raised salmon? Your research would then focus on data about the particular salmon varieties sold at this store. Which fish are healthier? Which are obtained through environmentally sustainable practices?

Perhaps the question is more general, such as this assignment for a culinary class: What are the advantages and disadvantages of wild-caught versus farm-raised salmon? In a three-page paper due next week, you might focus on identifying the points of comparison (see also Chapter 13), such as differences in nutrition and flavor profiles, and in economic and environmental impact.

Or, your research might have a business perspective. Perhaps your boss asks you to research the best sources of healthy, economical salmon for your restaurant. You have two weeks to find the top five vendors, perform cost analyses, and make recommendations for action.

Finally, your topic might be broader, with more long-term applications: Why do certain types of fish do better than others in a farmed environment? Clearly, this is a topic that requires data from scientific research, which may or may not be available or conclusive.

Whatever the question you construct, you will try to answer it by gathering and evaluating information with care, reading it critically, and interpreting its relevance.

What's for dinner? Wild-caught or farm-raised salmon?

FINDING SOURCES OF INFORMATION

Students sometimes believe that research involves typing a few words into a popular search engine and copying chunks of information from the first Web page that comes up. While a search engine can get you started with some ideas and terminology, it is not necessarily the best source of accurate information. Be prepared to evaluate all Web sites carefully. Furthermore, there are more sophisticated ways to find high-quality sources, for example, through subscription databases that are available through your school or public library. It may be that most sources of accurate information on your topic are only available in print. Finally, your most valuable initial source of information and guidance is a good reference librarian.

Librarians are experts at finding useful resources. Just as you would turn to a dairy farmer to get fresh milk, or to a chef to get a made-from-scratch hollandaise sauce, it is wise to ask a librarian to help you find information. Libraries are vast orchards of books and articles and databases, ripe with facts and ideas. Librarians can show you how to harvest this data. To produce top-notch research, get acquainted with the staff at your school or public library and learn how to find your way around.

Let's look at research in another way. Information sources are like ingredients you've assembled for a dish. You can select prepackaged items, which may or may not be of good quality, or you can choose to shop carefully for the freshest raw ingredients, knowing that they make your final product especially good. Similarly, the choices you make about your information will affect the quality of your research paper.

Once you've chosen a topic, begin your search for information. Of course, the temptation to begin with Google or Yahoo or Wikipedia is irresistible, and you may obtain solid information from such a search, or at least an outline of the major facets of your topic. Your textbook (if you have one) or reference books in the library may offer a more reliable start. You know already that these books are likely to contain accurate information because they were chosen by your instructors or by the librarians. Although they may not contain as much detail as you will eventually need for your paper, they will provide some background information and give you an idea of the vocabulary used in a study of the topic. Your textbook is also likely to include a list of useful books, articles, and *reliable* Web sites.

Suppose you are just beginning a research project on a food-related topic. An excellent place to start is with the reference section of your library, in which you might find general books about food like those listed in Figure 18.1.

Figure 18.1 General Books for Food Research
Compiled by Christine Oppenheimer at the Culinary Institute of America

Davidson, Alan. *The Oxford Companion to Food.* Illus. Soun Vannithone. Oxford: Oxford UP, 1999. Print.

Encyclopedia of Food and Culture. Solon H. Katz, editor in chief. New York: Scribner's, 2003. Print.

Herbst, Sharon Tyler. *The New Food Lover's Companion: Comprehensive Definitions of nearly 6,000 Food, Drink, and Culinary Terms.* 3rd ed. Hauppauge, NY: Barron's Cooking Guide, 2001. Print.

Herbst, Sharon Tyler. *The New Food Lover's Tiptionary: More than 6,000 Food and Drink Tips, Secrets, Shortcuts, and Other Things Cookbooks Never Tell You.* New York: Morrow, 2002. Print.

McGee, Harold. *On Food and Cooking: The Science and Lore of the Kitchen.* New York: Scribner's, 2004. Print.

Montagne, Prosper. *Larousse Gastronomique.* New English ed. New York: Clarkson Potter, 2001. Print.

The Oxford Encyclopedia of Food and Drink in America. Andrew F. Smith, ed. in chief. Oxford; New York: Oxford University Press, 2004. Print.

Webster's New World Dictionary of Culinary Arts. Compiled by Steven Labensky, Gaye G. Ingram, and Sarah R. Labensky. Illus. William E. Ingram. 2nd ed. Saddle River, NJ: Prentice Hall, 2001. Print.

Williams-Sonoma Kitchen Companion: The A to Z of Everyday Cooking, Equipment & Ingredients. Chuck Williams, gen. ed.; text by Mary Goodbody, Carolyn Miller, and Thy Tran. Illus. Alice Harth. Alexandria: VA: Time-Life, 2000. Print.

Glancing at one of these books—perhaps *On Food and Cooking*—we find fourteen pages of books and articles that author Harold McGee used in preparing his own book. McGee lists sources he used throughout the book, sources written both for general and for specialized audiences. He also lists sources for each chapter. For "A Survey of Common Vegetables," McGee lists eight books for the general reader, such as *The Random House Book of Vegetables,* and thirty-five more technical books and articles, such as "Effects of Salts and pH on Heating-Related Softening of Snap Beans" in the *Journal of Food Science.* Each information source can lead you to many more!

As you continue your research, check your library's online catalog for more *specialized* books about your topic. Note the narrower focus of the books listed in Figure 18.2. Like *On Food and Cooking,* these books will lead you to others. Browse through the table of contents and the list of references. Skim a few chapters for evidence that this book might be useful to your research. Don't stop with the first quotable paragraph—there might be riper fruit on the next page.

Your library or school also offers access to certain subscription databases, such as EBSCO's *Hospitality & Tourism Index Full Text* or *Encyclopedia Britannica Online* (see Figure 18.3). An advanced search of these databases can quickly produce reliable information. It's like shopping at a convenient yet quite specialized farm co-op.

Figure 18.2   More Specialized Books for Food Research
Compiled by Christine Crawford-Oppenheimer at the Culinary Institute of America

Bladholm, Linda. *The Asian Grocery Store Demystified.* Los Angeles: Renaissance, 1999. Print.

Claiborne, Craig. *New York Times Food Encyclopedia.* Comp. Joan Whitman. New York: Times, 1985. Print.

Mariani, John F. *The Dictionary of Italian Food and Drink: An A to Z Guide with 2,300 Authentic Definitions and 50 Classic Recipes.* New York: Broadway, 1998. Print.

Mariani, John F. *The Encyclopedia of American Food and Drink.* New York: Lebhar-Friedman, 1999. Print.

McClane, A. J. (Albert Jules). *The Encyclopedia of Fish Cookery.* Photography by Arie de Zanger; designed by Albert Squillace. New York: Holt, Rinehart and Winston, 1977. Print.

Passmore, Jacki. *The Encyclopedia of Asian Food and Cooking.* US ed. New York: Hearst, 1991. Print.

Snodgrass, Mary Ellen. *Encyclopedia of Kitchen History.* New York: Fitzroy Dearborn, 2004. Print.

Solomon, Charmaine. *Charmaine Solomon's Encyclopedia of Asian Food.* With Nina Solon. Boston: Periplus Eds.; North Clarendon, VT: distr. Tuttle, 1998. Print.

Zibart, Eve. *The Ethnic Food Lover's Companion.* Birmingham, AL: Menasha Ridge; Old Saybrook, CT: distr. Globe Pequot, 2001. Print.

Figure 18.3 Selected Online Databases

Encyclopedia Britannica Online

EBSCO Web includes the following indexes:
- EBSCO Animals
- EBSCOhost Español
- Funk & Wagnalls New World Encyclopedia
- General Science Collection
- Hospitality & Tourism Index Full Text
- MasterFile Select: general interest articles and reference works
- Primary Search via Searchasaurus
- TOPIC Search

InfoTrac includes several databases:
- Biography Resource Center
- Business and Company ASAP
- Business and Company Resource Center
- Custom Newspapers
- Expanded Academic ASAP
- Health and Wellness Resource Center and Alternative Health Module
- Health Reference Center Academic
- ¡Informe!
- Junior Edition, K–12
- National Newspaper Index
- Opposing Viewpoints Resource Center
- The Twayne Authors Series

The ingredients are fresh, but you have to belong to the group to buy them. In the case of subscription databases, your school or library does belong, and you are able to access the information through the institution's account.

Although it's easy to find information on the Internet, you may not always get the quality results you need. Subscription databases can help, as can your librarian. See the next section on evaluating your sources.

EVALUATING YOUR SOURCES: BOOKS AND ARTICLES

Not all sources are equally reliable. Just think about the people you know. Whether it's the date of a mutual friend's birthday or the homework due next Monday, some of your friends are probably more likely than others to know the real facts. In doing research for a paper, you should also seek out the most reliable information sources. In the preceding section, we looked at where these can be found: in your textbook, library reference books, and sources listed in those works. If you use other sources of information, be prepared to evaluate them carefully. Ask questions, and look carefully at the answers. For example, if you need information about the homework, ask yourself who in your class is always prepared.

When you evaluate a source of information, begin by asking, **Who is the author? What are his credentials for writing on this topic?** Information is more likely to be accurate if the author has an advanced degree or significant experience in the field, has published other books and articles on this topic, is cited by other experts in the field, or is affiliated with a reputable institution. Who is more likely to have accurate information on healthy eating—the winner of an all-you-can-eat contest at the state fair or a registered dietitian? Whose opinion on a new restaurant seems more valuable—that of an established food writer who publishes regularly in *The New York Times* or a first-time contributor on *Chowhound?* If you were looking for medical advice, would you seek out a doctor who'd been practicing for twenty years or a student pursuing a certificate in medical transcription?

Now, of course, there are going to be exceptions. Maybe that first-time contributor on *Chowhound* is the next James Beard. But where your knowledge of the author is limited, it is wise to take degrees, affiliations, and other publications into account. You can often find information about the author inside the book or on the jacket, or in the article or magazine. You can also search the catalog and databases for additional books and articles published by the author.

Where does the information come from? Consider, for example, the array of magazines lined up by the cashier: Tabloids offer such improbable headlines as "Three-headed Calf Born in Department Store Restroom." Yet would you really look in this type of publication for information about calves or department stores? No. The tabloids are for entertainment, not information.

One step up, perhaps, but also unreliable, are gossip magazines. Packed with photos of celebrities, these magazines are sources of entertainment, though they may also record popular trends in food and dining. For many in the hospitality industry, this type of information might be useful. For example, if a celebrity chef has success with a new dish or a new restaurant, many others around the country might wish to follow his lead. The information is only useful, however, if it is *true.* You would be far more likely to find accurate information on current restaurant trends in a periodical dedicated to the industry, such as *Nation's Restaurant News* or the *Journal of Restaurant and Foodservice Marketing.*

A level above the gossip magazine is the news magazine. While this type of

Many excellent information sources are available only in libraries.

publication is more than just entertainment, its information may be less complete and less accurate than that of a serious, specialized journal. A news magazine or Internet site or even a Tweet can raise awareness of certain medical issues, but it would be wise to consult your physician, or perhaps a medical journal or reputable online site such as www.mayoclinic.org, before beginning or ending a course of treatment. The most reliable journals are published by universities or professional organizations and contain articles by specialists in the field. In general, they do not contain advertisements, and they have titles like the *Journal of the American Medical Association, International Journal of Food Science Technology,* and *Annals of Botany.*

Producing a book costs money, and reputable publishers are very careful to spend money only on solid, useful information. The key word, of course, is "reputable." Just as many magazines are produced only for entertainment, so are many books. As you're researching your topic, look for well-known publishers such as Penguin or Houghton Mifflin. A university press, such as Oxford University Press, is another good source of reliable books because their authors are "screened" for reputation and reliability.

What is reported, and how is it presented? Good information tends to be reported in some depth, supported by facts and citations, and presented in coherent sentences without glaring grammatical errors. A three-sentence teaser in a popular magazine's column on health and wellness will probably not contain the amount of detail you'd need for a research paper on trans fats.

When was it published? Not only the source, but the *date* of the publication is important in determining the accuracy or relevance of the information. If you need to know about a recent change in the Food and Drug Administration (FDA) Model Food Code, an article published two years ago could not help you. If you were looking for current trends in restaurant menus, an article published even last year might be outdated. For many questions, current information is critically important. For other questions, the date does not matter. For example, if you were looking for information on Carême's vertical designs for the banquet table, a book published in 1995 could be just as useful as one published last year.

Why was it written? A critical question in many situations is "Why is he telling me that?" People's motives for telling us something range from an altruistic desire to help or a passion for the subject itself to a need to show off or to deceive and manipulate us. We must try to understand how the author's purpose may affect the quality of his information. Think back to that headline about the calf in the department store. What is the purpose of such a story? Clearly, it is not to inform or to persuade. It is purely entertainment. A news magazine might also want to entertain as well as inform in order to boost sales. It is in competition with other similar magazines and must ask itself "What will sell?" as frequently as "What is accurate and important information?" A scholarly journal, however, is not expecting to make a great deal of money. Rather, it hopes to build its reputation through the publication of important, accurate information. Thus, these journals can be excellent tools for research.

EVALUATING YOUR SOURCES: DIGITAL MEDIA

Evaluating the accuracy of information on the Internet is much more difficult than evaluating the accuracy of print sources. The Internet is like a giant, disorganized store in which all kinds of products of all levels of quality are strewn carelessly about the aisles. There definitely is fresh food, but there's a whole lot of garbage as well. Even worse, there's a lot of garbage pretending to be fresh. And since no one really owns the store, there's no hope of formally separating the fresh from the garbage. You must sift through on your own and assess each item.

Who is the author? What are his credentials? Evaluating the author of an article posted on the Internet can be especially difficult; in fact, it may be impossible. The Web site might be careless in documenting its authorship, or it might even wish to conceal it. If you cannot easily find the name of the person who wrote the article, or the name of the organization that sponsors the Web site, the information may not be legitimate, and it might be wise to avoid it. If you do find the author, try to evaluate his credentials in terms of degrees, work experience, other publications, and affiliations. For example, an author who is affiliated with the National Institutes of Health is more likely to be objective about trans fats than an author who works with a company that sells them!

Where does the information come from? Reputable publishers will check the accuracy of their authors' work. On the Internet, however, there may be no screening whatsoever. Anyone can post information. It's we who must decide which is reliable. One way of evaluating the accuracy or "authority" of a Web site is to look at its domain, the three letters that follow the "dot" and provide some information about the sponsor of the site. Authoritative Web sites generally have one of the following domains:

.edu (sponsored by a college, university, or school)
.gov (sponsored by a nonmilitary government agency)
.org (sponsored by a nonprofit organization)

Other domains exist, such as the popular *.com* (commercial site—think $$$) or the more neutral *.net*. Since anyone can use these domains, however, we need to be careful. Further, a *.com* may be more about profitability than accuracy. In deciding which of two medications to buy, would you take the advice of a drug company or of your physician? While the drug company wants to make a sale, your physician wants to keep you healthy. It makes sense to evaluate a ".com" with particular care for evidence of bias or inaccuracy.

What is reported, and how is it presented? A good source covers the topic with some breadth and depth. Three short lines about the regulations of the FDA regarding trans fat on nutrition labels probably do not contain information relevant to a study of trans fat's effect on human beings. Look for sources that are comprehensive enough to be useful. In addition, look for sources that cite the sources of *their* information.

Reliable sources on the Internet, just like those in print, will cite factual information in footnotes or lists of references. Finally, ask yourself whether the text is well written and the information well documented. Most likely, the care that is taken in presenting the information reflects the value of the information itself.

When was it written? And when was it last updated? Again, this information may be difficult to find on a Web site. If that's the case, consider finding another site. A legitimate sponsor will want the public to know both the source and currency of its information. Check also that links to other Web pages are still working.

Why was it written? It is always important to try and understand *why* someone is giving you certain information. A salesperson wants you to buy the product and perhaps will slant the facts to achieve that purpose. A consumer organization wants you to make a safe, informed choice and will probably be more objective. Be careful, though, that there's no secret commercial sponsorship behind an ostensibly consumer-oriented site. Even an otherwise believable author might be suspect if linked to a commercial sponsor.

ESTABLISHING CREDIBILITY

In professional and academic settings, the quality and credibility of your writing may have significant consequences: A college essay or research paper earns a grade, while a cover letter and résumé hope to land a job. Using accurate and authoritative outside sources can boost your credibility with readers. Using doubtful sources can weaken your credibility.

Your dish is only as good as its ingredients. In the same way, your research is only as good as its information. Take the time to find accurate, objective sources. Visit the library. Talk to the librarians. And most important—don't believe everything you read!

RECIPE FOR REVIEW

FINDING SOURCES OF INFORMATION

1. Once you've chosen a topic, begin your search for information with your textbook or with reference books in the library. Familiarize yourself with the background and vocabulary of the topic.
2. Check your library for books on the topic. These books will also have valuable lists of other references.
3. Talk to the reference librarian about where to find specific information.
4. Search the subscription databases available through your library.
5. Remember that while it's easy to search the Internet for information on a topic, steps one through four above are more likely to yield accurate information!

EVALUATING YOUR SOURCES

1. Who is the author? What are his or her credentials for writing on this topic? What are his or her connections to the product, if any?
2. Where does the information come from? Check out an Internet source with particular care.
3. What is reported, and how is it presented?
4. When was the information published? Is the date relevant to your topic?
5. Why was it written? If to entertain or persuade, is the information and/or author reliable?

CHAPTER EXERCISES

1. List three investigations you have conducted—whether in a kitchen or classroom, a business setting, or your home or library. Then write a paragraph in which you describe one of these investigations in more detail.
2. *Constructing a Research Question.* Imagine you've been assigned to write a 1000-word report on a subject related to healthy eating. Choose a topic that interests you, and construct a specific research question.
3. *What's in Your Library?* Pay a visit to a library—perhaps the one at your school, or a public library. What subscription databases does this library offer? What periodicals are available in print? Choose a few titles from Figures 18.1 or 18.2, and look them up in the library's online catalog. Which ones does the library own? Where are they shelved? What other services does the library provide, such as interlibrary loan or photocopying?
4. *Evaluating the Author.* Evaluate each person below as a source of information on foodborne illness. Which one is *least* likely to be reliable? Why?
   a. a professor of microbiology at a research university
   b. the author of a food safety textbook
   c. the author of three books on food photography
   d. an official at the Department of Health
5. *Choosing the Best Source.* Which of the following would contain the most accurate and current information on the innovative cooking techniques of Thomas Keller, executive chef of the French Laundry? Explain your answer.
   a. a book about promising young chefs published in 1978
   b. an article in *Food and Wine* published in 2011
   c. an article about the French Laundry's menu design published in 2011
   d. a review of Keller's book *The French Laundry* published in 1997

6. *Evaluating Books and Articles.* Find an article about trans fats. Now evaluate its author (whether he has appropriate credentials, what institutions he may be affiliated with), its source (what magazine published the article), coverage (what is reported and how it is presented), its currency (when it was published), and its objectivity (why it was written). Would you use this article for a research paper on trans fats? Explain.

7. *Evaluating Internet Searches.* Search the Internet for information about trans fat. Print the first page of hits. Next, log on to an appropriate subscription database and search for recently published articles in reputable journals. Print the first page of citations. How were the results of each search similar? How were they different?

8. *Evaluating Internet Sources.* Find an article about trans fat on the Internet. Then evaluate its author (whether he has appropriate credentials), its domain (who sponsors the site), coverage (what is reported and how it is presented), currency (when it was written, when last updated), and objectivity (why it was written). Would you use this article for a research paper on trans fats? Explain.

9. *Evaluating Sources in Your Reading.* Evaluate the information sources on the Works Cited page of Travis Becket's research paper in Appendix D.

10. *Evaluating Your Sources.* What was the topic of your last research paper? How did you find information on the topic? In light of the discussion in this chapter, do you think you found the *best* information? Explain.

IDEAS FOR WRITING

1. What do you think of when you hear the term "research paper"? Why? What have you learned about research papers in previous experiences?

2. When you ask a salesperson for advice on which brand or variety to choose, how do you judge the accuracy and objectivity of his response? Include specific examples in your answer.

3. Why is plagiarism a problem? Read one or two articles about plagiarism in school or corporate settings. Then write a response, using specific details from the article(s) to support your discussion.

4. Research the use of "sampling" in popular music. Is this plagiarism? Why or why not?

CHAPTER 19
AN INTRODUCTION TO RESEARCH II—USING AND CITING YOUR SOURCES

After reading this chapter, you should begin to . . .

- take careful notes as you research outside sources;
- avoid cutting and pasting outside material to create a paper; instead, add quotes, paraphrases, and summaries of outside material to supplement but not replace your own writing;
- identify when to cite and when not to cite outside sources;
- cite outside sources appropriately both within the text and in a Works Cited page; and
- use the format required by your instructor or publisher.

Once the *CSI* investigators described in the last chapters have processed a crime scene, they begin to analyze and reflect on the evidence they've gathered. They will draw conclusions based on this evidence and write them up in a report. In some cases the investigators will appear in the courtroom to testify as to the accuracy of their information. Similarly, once you've assembled your sources for a report or research paper, you must read and *think* about the information they provide. Perhaps, like Morgan Spurlock, you will literally *eat* your sources! Finally, you will write up your report or research paper, which should reflect your own interpretation of the information and should draw its basic focus and organization from you—not your sources. Like the crime scene investigators, you will make an independent assessment of the facts and write up your conclusions in your own words.

USING YOUR SOURCES

First, be sure to leave enough time to do the research, that is, to find useful material and to read it carefully. Many problems with plagiarism are caused by procrastination. Students wait until the last minute, then cut and paste paragraphs from hastily retrieved Internet sources. That is the culinary equivalent of opening three or four cans of processed food, arranging the contents on a plate, and leading the customer to believe you spent the day laboring over a hot stove!

Second, as you're doing the research, read carefully (see also Chapter 2), and take notes on the main ideas and interesting details. You can certainly start with a yellow highlighter. However, once you've identified useful passages in your material, it's helpful to write down the main points on a separate sheet of paper or on individual index cards. If you copy the words exactly, enclose them in quotation marks. If you paraphrase or summarize the information—that is, rewrite it entirely in your own words—do not use quotation marks. Even in your notes, it is essential to distinguish between another author's words and your own.

When you take notes, be sure to write the name of the book or article and the name of the author at the top of each page or note card. Include all publishing information as well: the publishing company, city, and date for books; the periodical title, volume, number, and date for articles; and the URL, site sponsor, date posted, and date accessed for Internet sites. Another option is to keep a separate card (or list) that includes the title and publishing information for each source. Whether you quote, paraphrase, or summarize, be sure to write the page number of the original text in your notes.

Next, after you finish reading each chapter or article, it is especially helpful to stop and ask yourself, What did I learn? Without looking back at your notes or the text itself, write down what you discovered. In this way you begin to integrate the new information into your own thinking. Once you've written a brief summary, refer back to the text to check its accuracy and make any necessary corrections. If you add lines of text directly to your notes, however, be certain to enclose them in quotation marks. Any sloppiness in this area could result in a charge of plagiarism.

TAKING NOTES

Whether you use notebook paper or note cards, you must be sure to write down the source's author, title, publishing information, and page number (if applicable). You must also be absolutely certain to distinguish between sentences that you have copied exactly

Some researchers literally *eat* their information sources!

from the source and those that you have paraphrased or summarized. Let's try an example. Suppose, like student Travis Becket, whose research paper is printed in Appendix D, we are interested in environmentally friendly agriculture. Our research might lead to *The Real Green Revolution: Organic and Agroecological Farming in the South* by Nicholas Parrott and Terry Marsden, which contains the following passage on page 39:

> Zaï (or tassa) is a traditional agricultural method used in Burkina Faso to restore arid and crusted areas of fields. The technique involves making seed holes 20–30 cm wide and deep and using the earth to make a raised 'demi-lune' barrier on the downslope side. Compost and/or natural phosphate is placed in each hole and sorghum or millet seeds planted when it rains. This technique improves the organic structure of the soil, helps retain moisture and, through promoting termite activity, increases water filtration into the soil. The crops are planted relatively densely to increase groundcover and prevent water loss through evapotranspiration. Stones removed from the field while digging the holes are often used to make contour bunds to further stabilize the soil and reduce run-off and erosion.

Once we read the paragraph, we stop and think about what it means and about how to record the main ideas and important details. The first step is to copy down all the relevant information about the source. We'll need the authors' names, the title, and the publishing information, which for a book is city, publisher, and year:

Author	Nicholas Parrott and Terry Marsden
Title	*The Real Green Revolution: Organic and Agroecological Farming in the South*
Publishing information	London: Greenpeace Environmental Trust, 2002

Because this book was viewed on the Internet, we will need that information as well:

Medium	Web
Date accessed	October 5, 2005

Finally, we think about the passage and decide what information seems important enough to put on our note cards. We must also decide whether to copy the text exactly, or whether to write a paraphrase or summary of the material.

QUOTING THE ORIGINAL TEXT

Words that are copied directly from the text (**direct quotes**) should be enclosed in quotation marks, even in your notes. You *must* be able to distinguish which words are yours and which belong to the original source. For example, the second sentence looks difficult to paraphrase because of such technical terms as *demi-lune* and *downslope*. Let's copy the sentence exactly onto a note card (Figure 19.1) and enclose it in quotation marks.

Figure 19.1 Taking Notes

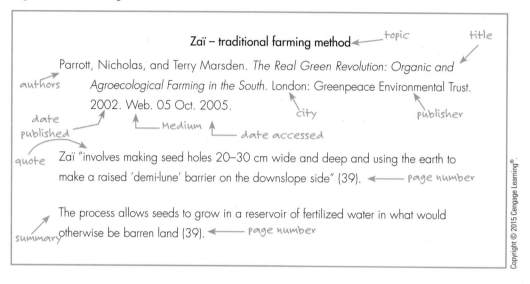

Again, even in your notes, any phrases copied directly from the original passage should be in quotation marks.

Original text   Zaï (or tassa) is a traditional agricultural method used in Burkina Faso to restore arid and crusted areas of fields. The technique involves making seed holes 20–30 cm wide and deep and using the earth to make a raised 'demi-lune' barrier on the downslope side.

Direct quote   Zaï "involves making seed holes 20–30 cm wide and deep and using the earth to make a raised 'demi-lune' barrier on the downslope side" (39).

The number in parentheses following the quote refers to the page on which the passage is found.

Whatever the length of the direct quote, be sure that you have copied words and punctuation exactly and noted the page number(s). Double check the correctness of each quotation before you submit the paper. Any carelessness in your use of sources may look like plagiarism.

WRITING A SUMMARY

A good **summary** captures the main idea of the original in a condensed form, using your own words. A summary does not include material copied directly from the text unless it's placed within quotation marks. The next entry on the note card has been summarized by student writer Travis P. Becket:

Original text	Zaï (or tassa) is a traditional agricultural method used in Burkina Faso to restore arid and crusted areas of fields. . . . Compost and/or natural phosphate is placed in each hole and sorghum or millet seeds planted when it rains.
Summary	The process allows the seeds to grow in a reservoir of fertilized water in what would otherwise be barren land (39).

Exercise 19.1 | Summarizing the Original Text

Write a one-sentence summary of the following passage, also from *The Real Green Revolution*.

Egypt has what is probably the most developed organic sector in North Africa. Initial interest in organic production was triggered as a reaction to increasing health problems experienced by farmers and rural dwellers from pesticide poisoning, and cotton yields remaining constant or declining despite increased use of pesticides. Aerial spraying of cotton is now banned in Egypt and much pest control now done through the use of pheromones, even though systems are not wholly organic.

WRITING A PARAPHRASE

Sometimes neither the summary nor the direct quote is appropriate. We may need more detail than the summary provides, yet we cannot write a coherent paper by simply adding a bunch of quotes together. The solution may be a **paraphrase**, changing the structure and wording of the original text to fit in with our own style and to support our own points more effectively. Remember that a paraphrase translates the exact meaning of the original while using your own vocabulary and sentence structure. Look at the following example:

Original text	Thus this simple and traditional technique is proving of multiple benefit in increasing yields, restoring degraded land and, by generating employment opportunities, helping slow the process of rural/urban migration.
Draft paraphrase	The "simple and traditional" process of Zaï has been proven to restore degraded land, increase crop yields, and simultaneously slow the process of urban migration (39).

Although the phrase "simple and traditional" is correctly enclosed within quotation marks, there are too many other identical or similar words in this draft paraphrase—for example, "is proving" versus "has been proven," "in increasing yields" versus "increase crop yields," and "helping slow the process of rural/urban migration" versus "slow the process of urban migration." Note how the following revised paraphrase changes both the structure of the original sentence and the words themselves:

Revised
paraphrase   As the soil continues to improve through this ancient, environmentally friendly method, both crop production and jobs have expanded while the movement of the population away from the countryside and toward the cities has decelerated (39).

In addition to the structural changes, the wording has been appropriately altered. Where the original reads "this simple and traditional technique," the revised paraphrase reads "this ancient, environmentally friendly method." Where the original says "restoring degraded land," the revision says "as the soil continues to improve." Finally, where the original reads "helping slow the process of rural/urban migration," the revision reads "the movement of the population away from the countryside and toward the cities has decelerated."

QUOTE, PARAPHRASE, AND SUMMARY

Direct Quote
"Whan that April with his showres soote
The droughte of March hath perced to the roote,
And bathed every veine in swich licour,
Of which vertu engendered in the flowr . . .
Thanne longen folk to goon on pilgrimages."
    (Chaucer, "Prologue," lines 1-4, 12)

Paraphrase
When April rains drench the parched earth and wash each root with pure water, from whose strength the flowers grow . . . people feel like taking trips.

Summary
April showers bring May flowers . . . and spring fever.

Work Cited
Chaucer, Geoffrey. "The General Prologue to the Canterbury Tales." *Chaucer's Poetry: An Anthology for the Modern Reader.* Selected and edited by E. T. Donaldson. New York: Ronald Press, 1975. Print.

Let's look at another example:

Original   This technique improves the organic structure of the soil, helps retain moisture and, through promoting termite activity, increases water filtration into the soil.

Paraphrase   As a result of using the Zaï method, more water seeps into and is retained in the earth because of its enhanced composition and proliferating insect population.

Again, notice that both the sentence structure of the paraphrase and the words themselves are different from the original text. The original begins with the main subject, the paraphrase with a pair of phrases. Instead of the original "helps retain moisture," the paraphrase reads "more water seeps into and is retained in the earth."

Exercise 19.2 | Paraphrasing the Original Text

Write a paraphrase of each of the following sentences from Parrott and Marsden. Use your own words and sentence structure, but include the important details. Try to translate the quote's meaning exactly.

1. "The system [Zaï] is labour intensive and best suited to farms with a labour surplus." [note on the British spelling of *labour*]
2. "Initial interest in organic production was triggered as a reaction to increasing health problems experienced by farmers and rural dwellers from pesticide poisoning."

Study your paraphrases carefully, and remember that it is *imperative* that you can distinguish in your notes between a direct quote on one hand and a summary or paraphrase on the other. As a final check before submitting your essay, be sure to compare your quotes, paraphrases, and summaries with the original text.

PROCESSING THE INFORMATION IN YOUR SOURCES

At each stage of your research, try to process new information and connect it to what you already know about your topic. Think about the focus of your paper. Jot down questions, ideas, outlines. Brainstorm. When you ask yourself what a passage from an information source means and how it might relate to what you already know and to what you want to write about, you are using a similar process. This kind of creative reflection helps to make the essay a product of your own thinking, supported but not dominated by other people's words.

As your research progresses, do some freewriting or diagramming of the scope of the paper. Perhaps even do a draft that incorporates the major bits of information, however loosely. But remember—that information should have already been processed, that is, paraphrased or summarized. Do NOT begin a draft by copying chunks of material from outside sources, although you may begin your notes that way. A draft should come straight from you. Then, as you rewrite, you can add quoted or paraphrased material to back up your points. As you do so, be sure to give credit to the authors from whom you've borrowed information.

Once you have a rough draft of the research paper, think about whether it says what you want it to say, just as you would with any other piece of writing. Again, try to avoid writing a research paper by pasting

Like Travis Becket's mother, this woman works hard in her garden.

together chunks of information from outside sources. Instead, blend this information well with your own thoughts and ideas. If you don't mix the batter well enough, you'll end up serving a cake with gobs of flour in it!

In his research paper on environmentally friendly agriculture, Travis Becket begins with a story of his childhood, riding with his mother every Saturday to the farmers' market to sell their fresh herbs and eating up what didn't sell. "I remember wondering if everybody else in America ate as well as I did," he writes in the introduction.

> I wondered this same idea at the University of California Santa Cruz while eating a lunch that, once again, consisted of foods that had been submerged in dirt just a few hours prior. The apprentices who worked in the fields agreed with me about the superior quality of the organic food they had grown. As I saw the way that the apprentices relied on organic foods and how they supported organic farming and eating, a new question arose. "If this is the way that food should be produced in America, is it possible to produce enough for everybody?" For the rest of my time at UCSC, this was the thought in my mind and the question on my lips. If organics is best for the soil and the body, can it be utilized in a way that will feed everybody?

—**Travis P. Becket**, student writer

Travis begins his research with a question that has its roots in his childhood. Like the agriculture it explores, the question itself is organic. While the paper goes on to use many different sources and to explore farming techniques on the other side of the globe, its origin is in the "small arid plot of land just outside of town where [his mother] would slave on her hands and knees bringing up delicate flowers and herbs from the dusty soil." We hear the writer's own voice throughout the paper, strengthened rather than replaced by his outside experts.

INCORPORATING SOURCES INTO YOUR PAPER

As we discussed earlier, you can use outside sources in your writing in three ways: direct quote, paraphrase, and summary. Most information from outside sources will be incorporated in the form of paraphrases or summaries. Your research paper should not be packed full of direct quotes; they are a strong seasoning and should be used sparingly. In general, save direct quotes for material that is especially important to your topic or that is explained particularly well in the original text. There is one exception, however. If you are writing about a literary text—where the text is the subject—you will tend to use many more direct quotes to give readers a "flavor" of the original.

Much of the information you use from outside sources will be paraphrased; that is, you will translate the ideas into your own words, sentence structure, and style. In this way your paper will read more smoothly as a product of your thinking, rather than as an assortment of other people's ideas. It will be a casserole made of fresh ingredients rather than a collection of prepackaged foods arranged on a plate.

WRITING TAG LINES

In order to integrate quotes and paraphrases smoothly into your paper, it is extremely important to introduce them with an appropriate **tag line**. A good server doesn't plop the plate down in front of the customer and stalk away with a toss of the head. Instead, the plate is introduced with a small remark, such as "Here we are" or "Enjoy your dinner," and perhaps a smile. The tag line in a paper often names the **author of the original text**, as in the following example:

> **Nicholas Parrott and Terry Marsden** note that the traditional farming method of Zaï "involves making seed holes 20–30 cm wide and deep and using the earth to make a raised 'demi-lune' barrier on the downslope side" (39).

The tag line may also contain the **title of the original text**, particularly the first time you cite it or if you are citing more than one work by the same author.

> In *The Real Green Revolution: Organic and Agroecological Farming in the South*, Nicholas Parrott and Terry Marsden [the authors] note that the

traditional farming method of Zaï "involves making seed holes 20–30 cm wide and deep and using the earth to make a raised 'demi-lune' barrier on the downslope side" (39).

The tag line may **emphasize the author's credentials:**

Nicholas Parrott and Terry Marsden, **both at Cardiff University,** note that the traditional farming method of Zaï "involves making seed holes 20–30 cm wide and deep and using the earth to make a raised 'demi-lune' barrier on the downslope side" (39).

In the next example, the tag line **suggests the tone** of the quote:

It was Kate Posey, the wistful tour guide at Santa Cruz, who said, "We see things so neatly arranged in grocery stores, sometimes we forget what the plant looks like."

In addition to varying in content, the tag line may also vary in placement. As in the example above, the tag line may precede the quoted or paraphrased material. It may also interrupt it.

"We see things so neatly arranged in grocery stores," **said Kate Posey, the wistful tour guide at Santa Cruz,** "sometimes we forget what the plant looks like."

Or the tag line may follow the quoted or paraphrased material.

"We see things so neatly arranged in grocery stores, sometimes we forget what the plant looks like," **said Kate Posey, the wistful tour guide at Santa Cruz.**

It is also important to incorporate borrowed ideas smoothly into the flow of your *own* thinking. For example, Travis Becket cites Posey within the following passage in a paper on environmentally friendly agriculture:

It is often said that "United we stand, divided we fall." I believe that this old adage holds true for mankind's relationship with the environment. It was Kate Posey, the wistful tour guide at Santa Cruz, who said, "We see things so neatly arranged in grocery stores, sometimes we forget what the plant looks like." She was speaking of the disconnect between mankind and its food, how we as a society often forget that food comes not from a grocery store, but from being submerged in very unappetizing dirt.

—**Travis P. Becket**, student writer

Travis uses the quote to illustrate and emphasize the point he has already made. Quotes must not *substitute* for your own statements and interpretations; instead, they are *added*—like a condiment or garnish—as support, illustration, or proof.

CITING YOUR SOURCES

You must **cite** your sources—that is, tell the reader where you used outside information and where you found it originally (but see What NOT to Cite on page 349). Within the text itself you supply the basic information that will lead the reader to the complete bibliographic entry at the end of your paper. The **format** of these citations is very precise. In this textbook, most of the examples will be given in **MLA style**. Figure 19.7 later in this chapter summarizes the important points of **APA style**. MLA style is generally used for papers in the humanities, such as history, literature, philosophy, and rhetoric and composition. APA style is generally used for the social sciences, including anthropology, economics, political science, psychology, and sociology. Check with your instructor or publisher.

Documentation can be quite a complex process, and this introductory chapter will cover only the basics. For further information, visit the Web sites listed at the end of this chapter or consult one of the several excellent books devoted exclusively to this topic.

USING PARENTHETICAL CITATIONS

A **parenthetical citation** names the outside source you used for particular wording or concepts. Its purpose is to direct the reader to the complete citation on the **Works Cited** page. In MLA format only two bits of information are generally included in the parenthetical citation: **the author's last name and the page number**. (See Figure 19.7 for APA format.)

> "I learned to cook by sight as the colors of the spices turned and then by smell—sweet, earthy, heady, sharp if they are roasting correctly, or the unforgiving acrid smells if they burn" (Bhide 103).

Note that the parentheses lie outside the quotation mark but inside the period. However, if the quote is long enough to be set in a separate, indented paragraph, the parentheses begin one space *after* the period. Quotes should generally be indented if they are longer than four lines (three lines for poetry). See the passage quoted under Taking Notes earlier in this chapter for an example.

If you've used the **author's name in a tag line**, put just the page number in parentheses:

> Monica Bhide explains, "I learned to cook by sight as the colors of the spices turned and then by smell—sweet, earthy, heady, sharp if they are roasting correctly, or the unforgiving acrid smells if they burn" (103).

If you use **more than one source by the same author**, write both the author's name and the title, as well as the page number, in parentheses.

> "I learned to cook by sight as the colors of the spices turned and then by smell—sweet, earthy, heady, sharp if they are roasting correctly, or the unforgiving acrid smells if they burn" (Bhide, "A Question of Taste" 103).

If the source has **two or three authors**, put all the names in the parenthetical citation or in the tag line.

> (Kirszner and Mandell 3)

If the source has **four or more authors**, you may list them all or you may use only the first author's name followed by *et al.,* which means "and others."

> (Alasalvar *et al.* 1411)

If the source **has no author**, use just the title and page number:

> (*Encyclopedia of Food and Culture* 193)

If you're quoting **text that is found in another source**, use the names of both, perhaps by putting the first source in the tag line and the second in parentheses. Study the following example:

> According to Monsanto CEO Robert Shapiro, the end result of these stressors is "loss of topsoil, of salinity of soil as a result of irrigation, and ultimate reliance on petrochemicals" (qtd. in Vasilikiotis).
>
> —**Travis P. Becket**, student writer

If the source **has no page numbers**, as is the case with many Internet sites, you may leave them out or put *n.pag.* for "no pagination." For example, since the article by Christos Vasilikiotis quoted in the last example is from an Internet site without page numbers, none appear in the parenthetical citation. If paragraphs or sections are clearly numbered, you may cite these in parentheses. Consult your instructor, publisher, or librarian for further information.

Although parenthetical citations are most common in research papers, a book like this one may also use a note format, that is, a small number or letter raised slightly above the line of type that refers to a footnote at the bottom of the page or to an end note in the back of the book. Follow the preference of your instructor or publisher.

Exercise 19.4 | Parenthetical Citations

Write a parenthetical citation in MLA format for the following items:

1. A quote from page 96 of Anthony Bourdain's *Kitchen Confidential*
2. A quote from page 96 of Anthony Bourdain's *Kitchen Confidential* in an essay in which you also quote from Anthony Bourdain's *A Cook's Tour*
3. A quote from page 36 of *The Oxford Encyclopedia of Food and Drink in America*
4. A quote from page 20 of *Coffee Basics* by K. Knox and J. S. Huffaker
5. A quote from the Web site of the National Oceanic and Atmospheric Administration (NOAA), *FishWatch*

Exercise 19.5 | More Practice Writing Tag Lines

Write a tag line for each of the sources in Exercise 19.4.

WHAT *NOT* TO CITE

In writing your research paper, you've probably used the following types of information: your own thoughts and experiences, material from outside sources that represents the thoughts and experiences of other writers, and general knowledge, information that everyone shares. You only need to cite the middle type of information, the words and ideas of other writers.

General knowledge includes such information as scientific facts (water boils at 212°F) or historical facts (Barack Obama was the 44th president of the United States). Such information is considered general knowledge even though you yourself may not have known it before. For example, the fact that the boiling point of water is lower (203°F) at mile-high elevations is general knowledge, even though a particular individual may not know it. General knowledge also includes observations or conclusions based on common sense: Burned toast doesn't taste good. If the knowledge is more specialized, such as the precise chemical reaction that occurs when the toast burns, then you must cite the source.

It is not always clear what information falls into the category of general knowledge, that is, what needs to be cited, and what does not. If you read the same information in several different sources, it is possible that it is general knowledge within the subject area. However, it is usually better to err on the side of caution. When in doubt, cite the source of your information.

Exercise 19.6 | To Cite or Not to Cite

Label each of the following items as "Yes" if it needs to be cited or "No" if it is general knowledge and does not need to be cited. Be prepared to explain the reason for your answer.

_____ 1. "Nothing really matters to me" is the concluding line of Queen's "Bohemian
Rhapsody."

_____ 2. The Beatles took the world by storm in the 1960s.

_____ 3. Julia Child was one of the first celebrity chefs in the United States.

_____ 4. Anthony Bourdain had a life-changing job in a restaurant on Cape Cod in 1974.

_____ 5. Anthony Bourdain is the author of *Bone in the Throat* and *Gone Bamboo*.

DEVELOPING THE WORKS CITED PAGE

The Works Cited page (in MLA style) contains an alphabetized list of all the out-side material used or cited in the paper, including publishing information for each one. The purpose of the Works Cited page is not only to acknowledge the outside sources you have used in your paper, but also to give your readers the information they need to find the sources themselves. Readers see the author's name or the source's title in a par-enthetical citation and can find the corresponding entry on the Works Cited page. (APA uses the term References for this page. See Figure 19.7.) Occasionally, as in this textbook, a writer will use a **Works Consulted** page, which includes sources that influenced her thinking, whether or not they were actually cited in the text.

The Works Cited entries are like little "hanging" paragraphs; that is, the first line begins at the left-hand margin, while the subsequent lines are indented. This is the op-posite of a typical paragraph in a text, where the first line is indented and the remaining lines begin at the left-hand margin. In general, the entries for print sources have four parts, each of which ends with a period. Note that *Print* is the medium of publication.

Author. Title. Publishing information. Print.

The citation for a **book with one author** is fairly straightforward:

McGee, Harold. *On Food and Cooking: The Science and Lore of the Kitchen.*
New York: Scribner, 2004. Print.

The same principle apples throughout the many variations described in this section. If the source has **more than one author**, only the name of the first author is inverted. Notice that subsequent editions of the book are added after the title (Figure 19.2).

Figure 19.2 Book Format

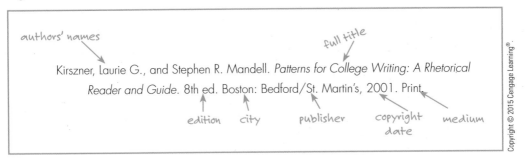

Kirszner, Laurie G., and Stephen R. Mandell. *Patterns for College Writing: A Rhe-*
    torical Reader and Guide. 8th ed. Boston: Bedford/St. Martin's, 2001. Print.

If the source has an **editor instead of an author**, alphabetize the item by title, and add
the editor's name after it:

Encyclopedia of Food and Culture. Ed. Solomon H. Katz. New York: Scribner, 2003.
    Print.

If the source is a **collection of works by various authors**, begin with the author and
title of the work you used in your paper. Then add the information on the collection,
followed by the page numbers of the particular title.

Bhide, Monica. "A Question of Taste." *Best Food Writing 2005.* Ed. Holly Hughes.
    New York: Marlowe, 2005. 102–104. Print.

For a **weekly or monthly magazine**, write the author's name, the title of the article, the
title of the magazine, the date, and the page numbers of the article:

Wemischner, Robert. "Crimson Tide." *Food Arts* Sep. 2004: 87–89. Print.

For a **quarterly magazine**, write the volume number and issue following the title
(Figure 19.3).

Bordelon, Suzanne. "George Pierce Baker's *Principles of Argumentation: 'Com-*
    pletely Logical'?" The Journal of the Conference on College Composition and Commu-
    nication 57:3 (2006): 416–441. Print.

For an **article from a newspaper**, include the section as well as the page number
(Figure 19.3). If the newspaper's title does not name the city in which it is published,
put that information in brackets.

Bowen, Dana. "With City Inspectors in Kitchen, Chefs Can't Cook in a Vacuum."
    New York Times 9 Mar. 2006: A1. Print.

Figure 19.3 Periodical Entries

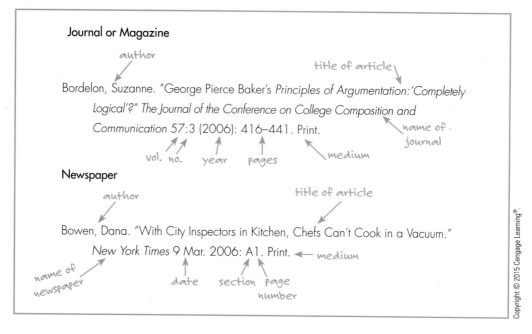

For a **movie or video**, list the title (italicized), director, distributor, year of release, and medium (such as Film or DVD). You may include additional information about the actors or writers before the name of the distributor.

> *Crash.* Written and directed by Paul Haggis. Perf. Don Cheadle, Matt Dillon, Terence Howard, Thandie Newton, Ryan Phillippe. Lion's Gate, 2005. Film.

Electronic sources present some unique issues. Often, it is not clear who the author is, or who has sponsored the site, or even when it was written (Figure 19.4). There may be no page numbers. Further, the site itself may change over time so that it is important to include the date on which you last viewed the material, called the **date of access**, in your notes. Consult an MLA reference work, the MLA's Web site (http://www.mla.org), your instructor, or a librarian if you get stuck.

For a **Web site**, list as much of the following information as you can find:

- author's name
- title of the work (in quotation marks if it is separate from the title of the site; otherwise in italics)
- name of the Web site (if different from the title of the work) in italics
- version or edition
- sponsoring organization

Figure 19.4 Electronic Sources

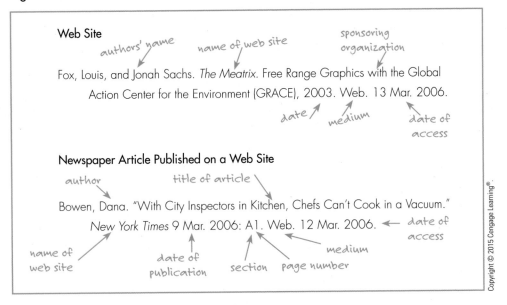

- date of publication (day, month, year, if available)
- medium of publication (Web)
- date of access

For example:

Fox, Louis, and Jonah Sachs. *The Meatrix.* Free Range Graphics with the Global
Action Center for the Environment (GRACE), 2003. Web. 13 Mar. 2006.

If your instructor or publisher requires that you also give the URL, place it within angle
brackets beginning one space after the final period:

Fox, Louis, and Jonah Sachs. *The Meatrix.* Free Range Graphics with the Global
Action Center for the Environment (GRACE), 2003. Web. 13 Mar. 2006.
<http://www.themeatrix.com>.

For an **online magazine**, list as much of the same information as you can.

StarChefs.com: The Magazine for Culinary Insiders. StarChefs. Web. 13 Mar. 2006.

For an **article published or republished online**, add information on the Web site.

Bowen, Dana. "With City Inspectors in Kitchen, Chefs Can't Cook in a Vacuum."
New York Times 9 Mar. 2006: A1. Web. 12 Mar. 2006.

Exercise 19.7 | Creating a Works Cited Page

Using the sources in Exercise 19.4, create a Works Cited page. You will have to look up the full publishing information on the Internet.

Creating a Works Cited page becomes easier as you gain experience. The two keys are to take accurate notes of the author, title, publishing information, and date of access as you consult each source and to follow the format carefully as you prepare each entry. Keeping a "working bibliography" in an electronic file that can be easily edited will save you time later.

FORMATTING A PAPER IN MLA STYLE

In many professional and academic contexts, readers will first begin to judge your credibility by the care you take in adhering to the appropriate format. When submitting a paper in MLA format, follow these guidelines carefully:

- Papers should be typed, double spaced, all the way through in a readable size and font, such as 12-point Times New Roman. One-inch margins are preferable.
- The first line of each paragraph should be indented one-half inch from the left margin (press the Tab key). Leave one space between sentences, unless your instructor or publisher prefers two.
- No cover sheet is needed because the heading on the top left corner of the first page includes the student's name, professor's name, course title, and date (Figure 19.5).
- The title of the paper is centered two lines below the heading. The title should be in ordinary text; it should not be italicized or underlined, enclosed in quotation marks, or typed in bold or capital letters.
- Put page numbers in a header, with the numbers in the right-hand corner, one-half inch from the top of the paper, with your last name one space to the left. *Page* or *p.* is unnecessary.
- Begin the Works Cited page on a separate sheet (Figure 19.6). The heading is centered two spaces above the text, which is also double spaced.

Except for the header, APA format for a research paper or article is quite similar to MLA format. See Figure 19.7.

Figure 19.5 First Page of a Research Paper in MLA Format

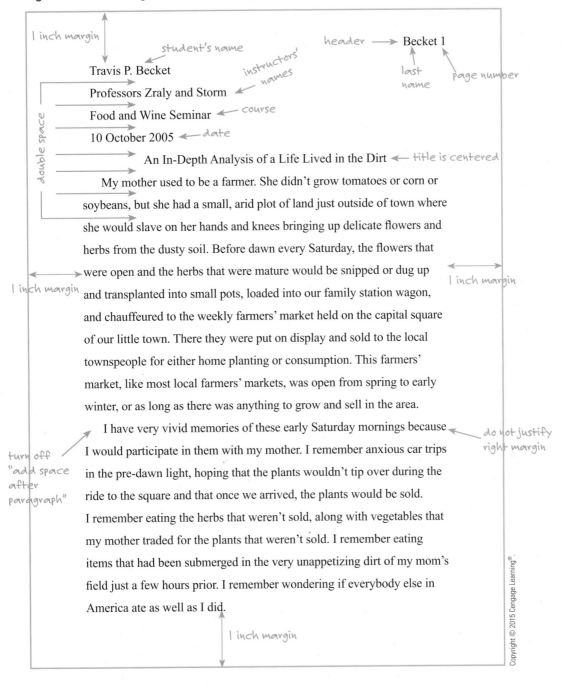

1 inch margin

student's name

instructors' names

header → Becket 1

last name

page number

Travis P. Becket

Professors Zraly and Storm ← instructors' names

Food and Wine Seminar ← course

10 October 2005 ← date

double space

An In-Depth Analysis of a Life Lived in the Dirt ← title is centered

My mother used to be a farmer. She didn't grow tomatoes or corn or soybeans, but she had a small, arid plot of land just outside of town where she would slave on her hands and knees bringing up delicate flowers and herbs from the dusty soil. Before dawn every Saturday, the flowers that were open and the herbs that were mature would be snipped or dug up and transplanted into small pots, loaded into our family station wagon, and chauffeured to the weekly farmers' market held on the capital square of our little town. There they were put on display and sold to the local townspeople for either home planting or consumption. This farmers' market, like most local farmers' markets, was open from spring to early winter, or as long as there was anything to grow and sell in the area.

I have very vivid memories of these early Saturday mornings because I would participate in them with my mother. I remember anxious car trips in the pre-dawn light, hoping that the plants wouldn't tip over during the ride to the square and that once we arrived, the plants would be sold. I remember eating the herbs that weren't sold, along with vegetables that my mother traded for the plants that weren't sold. I remember eating items that had been submerged in the very unappetizing dirt of my mom's field just a few hours prior. I remember wondering if everybody else in America ate as well as I did.

1 inch margin

1 inch margin

do not justify right margin

turn off "add space after paragraph"

1 inch margin

Copyright © 2015 Cengage Learning®

Figure 19.6 Sample Works Cited Page in MLA Format

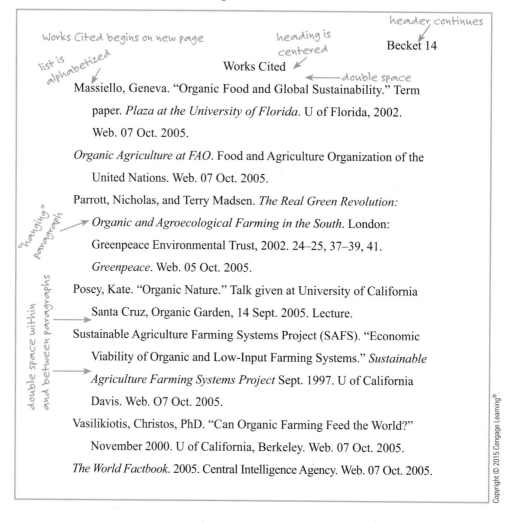

Works Cited begins on new page

list is alphabetized

heading is centered

header continues

Becket 14

Works Cited

double space

Massiello, Geneva. "Organic Food and Global Sustainability." Term

paper. *Plaza at the University of Florida*. U of Florida, 2002.

Web. 07 Oct. 2005.

Organic Agriculture at FAO. Food and Agriculture Organization of the

United Nations. Web. 07 Oct. 2005.

Parrott, Nicholas, and Terry Madsen. *The Real Green Revolution:*

"hanging" paragraph

Organic and Agroecological Farming in the South. London:

Greenpeace Environmental Trust, 2002. 24–25, 37–39, 41.

Greenpeace. Web. 05 Oct. 2005.

Posey, Kate. "Organic Nature." Talk given at University of California

Santa Cruz, Organic Garden, 14 Sept. 2005. Lecture.

double space within and between paragraphs

Sustainable Agriculture Farming Systems Project (SAFS). "Economic

Viability of Organic and Low-Input Farming Systems." *Sustainable*

Agriculture Farming Systems Project Sept. 1997. U of California

Davis. Web. O7 Oct. 2005.

Vasilikiotis, Christos, PhD. "Can Organic Farming Feed the World?"

November 2000. U of California, Berkeley. Web. 07 Oct. 2005.

The World Factbook. 2005. Central Intelligence Agency. Web. 07 Oct. 2005.

RECIPE FOR REVIEW

USING YOUR SOURCES

1. Read and *think* about the information in your sources.
2. Take careful notes. Distinguish quoted material from material that is paraphrased or summarized. Your notes must always include the name and author of the source, as well as the page number and publishing information.
3. Write the paper from scratch; do not cut and paste quotes from your sources.
4. Add **quotes, paraphrases,** and **summaries** of outside sources to support or illustrate your points.

PROCESSING THE INFORMATION IN YOUR SOURCES

1. At each stage of your research, try to process new information and connect it to what you already know about your topic.
2. Try to avoid writing a research paper by pasting together chunks of information from outside sources. Think it through. Use your own words.

INCORPORATING SOURCES INTO YOUR PAPER

1. Most information from outside sources will be incorporated in the form of **summaries** or **paraphrases**. Use **direct quotes** sparingly.
2. Introduce material from outside sources with an appropriate **tag line**.

CITING YOUR SOURCES

1. **Cite** material from outside sources in parentheses in the text.
2. You *must* cite information that you obtained from another source, unless it is general knowledge. Always cite *wording* obtained from another source.
3. List all the outside sources you cited in your paper on the **Works Cited** page.
4. Use the **format** required by your instructor or publisher.

Figure 19.7 Highlights of APA Format

The following examples of APA format highlight some of its key differences from MLA. Compare the sample entries in the right-hand column with those for the same sources in MLA format (pp. 350–353).

A book with one author:
- use just first initial of last name
- follow name with date in parentheses
- capitalize only first word of title/subtitle

McGee, H. (2004). *On food and cooking: The science and lore of the kitchen.* New York, NY: Scribner.

A book with more than one author:
- always put last name first
- put additional data about title in parentheses
- always include both city and state

Kirszner, L.G., & Mandell, S.R. (2001). *Patterns for college writing: A rhetorical reader and guide* (8th ed.). Boston, MA: Bedford/St. Martin's.

A source with editor instead of author:
- follow name with Ed. in parentheses

Katz, S.H. (Ed.). (2003). *Encyclopedia of food and culture.* New York, NY: Scribner.

Source in a collection of works:
- follow source title with In and editor's name
- include page numbers in parentheses
- use p. or pp. before page numbers

Bhide, M. (2005). A question of taste. In H. Hughes (Ed.), *Best food writing 2005* (pp. 102–104). New York, NY: Marlowe & Company.

(continues)

Figure 19.7 Highlights of APA Format (*continued*)

Weekly or monthly magazine:
- follow year of publication with a comma and the name of the month
- do not use p. or pp. before page numbers

Wemischer, R. (2004, September). Crimson tide. *Food Arts*, 87–89.

Newspaper:
- follow year of publication with a comma and the month and day
- use p. or pp. before page numbers

Bowen, D. (2006, March 9). With city inspectors in the kitchen, chefs can't cook in a vacuum. *New York Times*, p. A1.

Film:
- begin entry with producer(s) & director
- put medium in brackets following title
- end entry with country of origin & studio

Grasic, M., Korbelin, J., Nunan, T., and Reimer, A. (Executive Producers), & Haggis, P. (Director). (2005). *Crash* [Motion picture]. USA: Lion's Gate.

Newspaper article published on Web:
- use Retrieved from followed by URL
- do not add punctuation after URL

Bowen, D. (2006, March 9). With city inspectors in the kitchen, chefs can't cook in a vacuum. *The New York Times*. Retrieved from http://www.nytimes.com

Parenthetical citations:
- follow author's last name with comma and year of publication

(Bhide, 2005)

- if page numbers are cited, use p. or pp.

(Bhide, 2005, p. 103)

Notes on formatting a research paper in APA:
- The title of the paper is put in all capital letters and used as a running head.
- The title is also centered on the first page with the author's name and institutional affiliation below it.
- See the APA manual or website for additional information.

HELPFUL WEB SITES

1. For additional help with **MLA style**, visit http://www.mla.org/style.
2. For **APA style**, see http://www.apastyle.org.
3. For **Chicago style**, see http://www.chicagomanualofstyle.org or *The Chicago Manual of Style: The Essential Guide for Writers, Editors, and Publishers*. 15th ed. Chicago: U of Chicago P, 2003.

IDEAS FOR WRITING

1. Explore the Web site *StarChefs.com* (http://www.starchefs.com), and find an article of interest. Summarize the main points of the article in a paragraph. Then write a one-page summary in which you use two direct quotes from the article. Be sure to cite the information parenthetically, as well as in a complete Works Cited entry at the end.

2. Watch "The Meatrix" at http://www.themeatrix.com. Then pick one of the subtopics, such as antibiotics, factory farming, or genetic engineering. Take notes on the information, and develop a summary of the main points.

3. Do further research on one of the topics above or on another of your choice. Consult three reputable sources, using the evaluation techniques discussed in Chapter 16. Take notes on the information, and summarize the main points of each article. Then write a page or two about the topic, incorporating the information you learned as quotes or paraphrases. Use parenthetical citations, and create a Works Cited page.

4. What food-related jobs involve research? Consult at least three information sources as you investigate this question, and incorporate at least two in your answer.

SAVORY · GARLICKY · NUT
FRUITY · GINGERY · LEMONY · CHOCOLA
TART · SALTY · SALTY · TART · JUICY · SAVO
BRINY · BITTER · FRUITY · TART · SUGARY · GINGERY · GA
HONEYED · BITTER · OOMY · GINGERY
CKISH · TANGY

UNIT 3
PRESENTATION

Generic photo credit/grass: © Kutay Tanir

CHAPTER 20
REVIEWING THE PARTS OF SPEECH

After reading this chapter, you should begin to . . .

- identify the nouns in a sentence;
- identify the pronouns in a sentence;
- identify the verb (or verb phrase) in a sentence; and
- identify prepositional phrases.

In the earlier sections of this book, we worked on developing our ideas and on organizing them so that readers can move through them smoothly. In these next chapters, we will focus on editing, a process that requires some understanding of the ingredients and structure of a sentence.

If we didn't have onions, celery, and carrots, it would be difficult to make *mirepoix*. Without meat, lettuce, and bread, we couldn't build the cheeseburger in Figure 20.1. Similarly, sentences are constructed from certain ingredients, the parts of speech. Each of these eight parts of speech correlates to a *role* or *job* to be performed in the sentence.

Two of the most important roles in a sentence are those of the **subject** and **verb**. The role of subject is often played by a noun or pronoun, while the verb's role is always played by a verb.

Figure 20.1   Like this cheeseburger, sentences are constructed from certain ingredients.

© Wallenrock/Shutterstock.com

THE NOUN

As children, we begin to speak by learning the names of people and things that are important in our lives: mama, kitty, juice. A **noun** is the word that names those important things, that names a person, place, thing, or idea. Some nouns refer to categories of persons, places, or things. They are called **common nouns**, and they are not capitalized unless they are used at the beginning of a sentence. *Chef, toque, tomato,* and *preparation* are examples of common nouns. **Proper nouns**, on the other hand, refer to *specific* persons, places, or things, and they are always capitalized. *Julia Child, New York,* and *Cheerios* are examples of proper nouns.

In *The Lord of the Rings*, J.R.R. Tolkien creates a world inhabited by (right to left) wizards, hobbits, elves, dwarves, and men.

In writing class, we are interested in nouns because very often one of them will be the **subject** of a sentence; that is, it will identify or *name* who or what is doing something in the sentence, or who or what is being described by the rest of the sentence. Identifying the subject is important because it can help us find and fix any sentence fragments (Chapter 22), run-on sentences, or comma splices (Chapter 23). It is also important to be able to identify the subject of the sentence in order to make sure that the verb agrees with it (Chapter 24).

A noun can also be used as an **object** of a verb or preposition. It is especially useful to recognize prepositional phrases because neither the subject nor the verb of the sentence can be found inside them. We will look more closely at prepositional phrases later in the chapter.

Exercise 20.1 | Identifying Nouns

Identify the nouns in each of the following sentences. Which noun, if any, is the subject?

1. In *The Lord of the Rings*, J.R.R. Tolkien creates a world inhabited by such creatures as hobbits, elves, wizards, trolls, and orcs, as well as by men.
2. Many of the creatures have unusual, evocative names, for example, Frodo or Galadriel or Gollum.
3. Over the course of the trilogy, the characters cross mountains and rivers, dead marshes, and strangely alive forests.
4. Proud heroes brandish glittering swords and magic rings, while the evil Sauron wields a paralyzing fear.
5. It is a story of courage, strength, and friendship tested by the forces of greed, betrayal, and despair.

THE PRONOUN

Pronouns come in several varieties, summarized in Figure 20.2. **Personal pronouns** can be used in the place of nouns (like an actor's body double), usually to avoid repetition. For example, in the following sentence, the proper noun *Ivan* is repeated so often that it sounds bad:

> As **Ivan** walked into **Ivan's** kitchen, **Ivan** noticed that **Ivan** had left **Ivan's** books on the table.

The sentence is so bogged down with *Ivan*s that we can't even focus on what Ivan has been doing. By substituting appropriate pronouns for *Ivan*, we can produce a sentence that sounds better and makes its point more clearly:

> As Ivan walked into **his** kitchen, **he** noticed that **he** had left **his** books on the table.

The use of the pronouns allows the reader to focus on the other words in the sentence and more easily understand what's happening.

Personal pronouns have three different forms or **cases**, depending on how they are used in a particular sentence (see also Chapter 26): the subjective (*I, we, you, he,*

Figure 20.2 Table of Pronouns

Pronoun Type	Examples
Personal	I, you, he, she, it we, you, they
Possessive	my, mine, your, yours, his, her, hers, its our, ours, your, yours, their, theirs
Relative	who, whom, whose, which, that
Interrogative	what, which, who, whom, whose
Demonstrative	this, these, that, those
Indefinite	each, either, neither one, someone, anyone, no one, everyone something, anything, nothing, everything somebody, anybody, nobody, everybody both, few, several, many all, any, more, most, some, none

she, it, they), the objective (*me, us, him, her, them*), and the possessive (*my, our, your, his, her, its, their*).

Relative pronouns "relate" or refer to a noun or pronoun earlier in the same sentence. Relative pronouns include *who, whom, whose, which, what,* and *that*. Let's look at our friend Ivan again:

> Ivan is a student **who prefers to study late at night**.

Here the relative pronoun *who* refers to the noun *student* and begins the relative clause *who prefers to study late at night*. In fact, *who* is the subject of the clause, which, like other clauses, contains a subject and a verb. Like other subordinate or dependent clauses, a relative clause must be attached to a complete sentence or *independent clause*; it cannot stand alone (see also Chapter 22). Look at the next example:

> We saw the baker **whose recipe for crème brûlée had won first prize**.

Here the relative pronoun *whose* refers to *baker* and begins the relative clause *whose recipe for crème brûlée had won first prize*.

Interrogative pronouns, such as *who, what,* and *which,* are used to ask questions, such as <u>*Who*</u> *is planning to enter the chili competition?* The **demonstrative pronouns**—*this, these, that,* and *those*—direct the reader's attention to particular people or things. For example, <u>*That*</u> *is the best recipe for ratatouille.*

Indefinite pronouns, the largest group, do not refer to a specific person, place, or thing. Often, they suggest an amount. The indefinite pronouns include *all, many, most, some, few, none, one, each, anyone, everybody,* and *nothing*. Look at the following examples:

> **Many** of the most delicious dishes on the table were made with chocolate.

> The lecturer saw that **nobody** was listening.

Exercise 20.2 | Identifying Pronouns

Identify the pronouns in each sentence below. Which pronoun, if any, is the subject?

1. One of the story lines in the movie *Crash* follows a police officer named Ryan and his partner.
2. Officer Ryan, who is stressed by his father's illness, has a hostile encounter with a woman named Christine and her husband.
3. The scene in which Ryan searches her is one of the most uncomfortable in the film.
4. Both of the officers are affected by it, and they dissolve their partnership.
5. Each has a subsequent scene that reverses the audience's assessment of his character.

THE VERB

Like the subject (a role most often played by a noun or pronoun), the **verb** is also an essential ingredient in the sentence. The verb tells what the subject of the sentence is doing, or connects the subject with some more information later in the sentence. Verbs that tell what the subject is *doing* are called **action verbs**. A strong, precise action verb can pull the reader right into the sentence.

The chef **whisked** the eggs for the Greek omelet.

We can almost *hear* the action in the sentence, and research shows that our brains may *feel* the action in the same part of the brain we'd use if we were whisking the eggs ourselves (see Chapter 2).

Exercise 20.3 | Identifying Action Verbs

Identify the action verbs in the following sentences.

1. The professional chef lightly seared the veal shoulder in the skillet.
2. Cordelia slices onions more carefully after she cut her hand last week.
3. Before he put the baking sheet in the oven, Ivan dusted the cookie dough with chopped nuts and powdered sugar.
4. The student read a chapter in the math textbook and wrote the answers to the problems on a sheet of notebook paper.
5. For each of his classes, Javier makes a set of flashcards.

Another kind of verb is the **linking verb**, which connects the subject of a sentence to some additional information later in the sentence. Look at the following example:

The eggs **are** ready to be served.

Here the *eggs* are connected to the information *ready to be served* by the linking verb *are.* Common linking verbs include *is, are, was, were, appear, feel,* and *seem.*

Exercise 20.4 | Identifying Linking Verbs

Identify the linking verbs in the following sentences.

1. This chef is quite knowledgeable about veal.
2. Cordelia was the first student to visit the new restaurant.
3. Fresh out of the oven, the cookies seemed perfect.
4. The students were excited about their next unit in Product Knowledge.
5. Javier's brightly colored flashcards appear to be very useful to him.

A third kind of verb is the **helping verb**, a word (or words) added to the **main verb** to form a **verb phrase**. A phrase is a group of words that acts like a single word. For example, in the sentence "Fernanda has decided to major in baking and pastry arts," the word *has* is a helping verb, *decided* is the main verb, and the verb phrase is *has decided*. Helping verbs are often used to show the **tense** or time of the action (see Chapter 25), as in the following sample sentences:

Sample Sentence	Helping Verb	Verb Tense
The chef is whisking the eggs.	is	present progressive
Yesterday the chef was whisking the eggs.	was	past progressive
The chef had whisked eggs many times before.	had	past perfect
Perhaps the chef will whisk eggs again tomorrow.	will	future

Helping verbs are also used to form the **passive voice**, in which the subject of the sentence *receives* the action of the verb rather than performs it (see also Chapter 25), as in the following sample sentences:

Voice	Verb	Sample Sentence	Explanation
Active	dusted	The baker dusted the cookie dough with chopped nuts and powdered sugar.	*The subject (baker) is* performing *the action of dusting.*
Passive	was dusted	The cookie dough was dusted with chopped nuts and powdered sugar.	*The subject (dough) is* receiving *the action of dusting.*

Helping verbs always come before the main verb in the sentence, though they may sometimes be separated by other words, as in the question "*Did* the baker *dust* the cookie dough with powdered sugar?" Here the verb phrase *did dust* is split by the subject *the baker. Did* is the helping verb. Most of the common helping verbs (Figure 20.3) are used *only* as verbs (with the exceptions of *being, can, will*, and *might*, which may also be used as nouns). Sometimes a verb phrase will contain more than one helping verb, as in the following examples:

should have studied
will be driving
must have been grilled

Figure 20.3 Common Helping Verbs

am	can	had	might	were
are	could	has	must	will
be	did	have	shall	would
been	do	is	should	
being	does	may	was	

Exercise 20.5 | Identifying Helping Verbs

Identify the helping verbs in the following sentences.

1. The terrier has stolen one of Harry's shoes again.
2. He had eaten the other one the day before.
3. Harry should have put his shoes away in the closet.
4. That dog will be stealing shoes every day unless Harry learns to put them away.
5. Harry's shoes must have been almost completely destroyed by now.

Notice the word *almost* in sentence 5. *Almost* is an **adverb**, a word that describes or "modifies" a verb, adjective, or another adverb. Technically, adverbs are not part of the verb. One possible exception is the adverb *not*, which is so much a part of the meaning of the verb that in some languages it becomes part of the verb itself.

Exercise 20.6 | Identifying Verb Phrases

Identify the verb phrases in the following sentences.

1. Geraldo has been invited to play in a special post-season baseball tournament.
2. His family members could not contain their excitement.
3. Geraldo was chosen because of his excellent fielding skills.
4. He had fielded many difficult ground balls during the regular season.
5. The team will be practicing almost every day.

SPOTTING THE TERMINATOR

We've now covered two of the essential ingredients of the sentence, the subject (noun or pronoun) and the verb. While nouns and action verbs tend to be recognized fairly easily, linking and helping verbs seem to fade into the background. They are often small words like *is* that don't appear to carry a particular meaning, certainly not the clear and dramatic meaning of action verbs like *cut* or *burn*. It is therefore important to *memorize* these common verbs and watch out for them as you read a sentence. Otherwise, you may not be able to distinguish between a correct sentence and a fragment.

This inability to distinguish between two similar structures is the type of danger faced by the protagonists in *Terminator 2*. In this film, Arnold Schwarzenegger is a highly functioning robot, the model T100, and he is trying to protect John Connor from another robot, the newer model T1000, called a "terminator" because its sole purpose is to terminate or kill. Now the T1000 is a more sophisticated mechanism and can camouflage itself by becoming part of an inanimate object, or hoodwink its adversaries by assuming a specific human identity. Remember the scene at the mental hospital where John Connor's mother is imprisoned. A mild-looking security guard locks the outside doors and walks back down the corridor. The floor of this corridor is tiled in large black and white squares, a floor we've seen in many buildings. Black and white. Simple, ordinary. These tiles are like words, in fact—black type on a white page. Simple, ordinary. But not every word in a sentence is the same.

Think back to the film. The security guard continues his stroll down the corridor, and the camera scrolls down his uniformed leg to the floor. And suddenly—with a *frisson* of strings—the outline of a face swells up from the tiles. It is the T1000—still covered in black and white squares, but rising up swift and silent, forming an exact replica of the guard, who has been getting himself a cup of coffee from a vending machine, completely oblivious of the danger behind him. Suddenly he wheels around and confronts, open-mouthed, his own self. There is a pause; then the T1000 slowly extends its arm toward the face of its human twin. As the arm begins to lengthen, it turns into a sword

It is the T1000—still covered in black and white squares, but rising up swift and silent behind the guard, who is completely oblivious of the danger.

Copyright © 2015 Cengage Learning®

and finally skewers the hapless guard through the eyeball! Had he noticed the subtle differences in the black and white tiles, he might have been able to avoid this fate.

Similarly, in a sentence, there are some words that are different, words like linking verbs that are so ordinary yet so central to the structure of the sentence that they ought to stand out from the other words just like the face of the T1000 emerges from the tiles. In particular, the words *is, are, has, have, was, were, does,* and *do* are common, ordinary, and crucial. It's useful to memorize them.

THE PREPOSITION

Prepositions are words that show the *position* of one noun (or pronoun) in relation to another, and they are most often found at the beginning of **prepositional phrases**. A prepositional phrase begins with a preposition and ends with a noun or pronoun, which is called the object of the preposition.

As Ivan walked **into his kitchen**, he dropped his books **on the table**.

In this example, *kitchen* is the object of the preposition *into,* while *table* is the object of the preposition *on.* Prepositional phrases may also contain adjectives and/or adverbs, such as *really* and *messy* in the phrase *on the really messy table.* Prepositional phrases may have two or more objects (for example, *between Samuel and Veronica*), and the prepositions themselves may consist of more than one word, such as *according to* or *in addition to.*

Prepositional phrases often answer the question *Where? Where is the knife? In the drawer.* Where are you going? *To the walk-in.* They may also answer the question *When? When did you do your homework? After class.* Not every preposition fits into those two groups, however. The prepositions *with, of, for,* and *to* do not answer the questions *where* or *when,* but they are created in the same way; that is, they begin with a preposition and end with a noun or pronoun, the *object* of the preposition.

with my friends
of the peaches
for the recipe
to the store

Prepositional phrases are helpful to our study of sentence structure because **the subject and verb are never found within them.** Thus the many nouns and pronouns in prepositional phrases can be eliminated from our search for the subject of the sentence. This rule is most useful when the simple subject of the sentence is an indefinite pronoun, like *one,* but the sentence contains distracting juicy nouns like *peaches.*

One **of the peaches** is ripe.

In this example, *One* is the subject of the sentence, while *peaches* is the object of the preposition. If we recognize that *peaches* is part of the prepositional phrase, we may find it easier to identify the tiny pronoun *one* as the subject. If we thought *peaches* was the subject, we might incorrectly write the plural verb *are*. (See Chapter 24 for more on subject–verb agreement.)

Familiarize yourself with the list of prepositions in Figure 20.4. *Of* is perhaps the most useful preposition to know in order to avoid problems with identifying the subject of a sentence: The simple subject of the sentence is not going to follow the preposition *of*. Note that some words used as prepositions can also be used as other parts of speech, for example, *for* (coordinating conjunction) and *until* (subordinating conjunction).

Figure 20.4 Common Prepositions

about	behind	for	out	underneath
above	below	from	outside	unlike
across	beneath	in	over	until
after	beside	inside	past	up
against	between	into	since	upon
along	beyond	like	than	with
among	by	near	through	within
around	despite	of	throughout	without
as	down	off	to	
at	during	on	toward	
before	except	onto	under	

Exercise 20.7 | Recognizing Prepositional Phrases

Copy the following sentences on a separate sheet of paper and place brackets [ ] around the prepositional phrases. If you can, identify the subject as well.

1. *Like Terminator 2*, the story of *The Hunger Games* features a courageous heroine with a young child.
2. At home in District 12, Katniss protects her little sister, Prim, while in the arena she cares for Rue of District 11.
3. One of the most powerful scenes in the story involves Rue and an armful of flowers.
4. Another of the participants in the Games is Peeta, the baker's son.
5. With his instinct for making himself liked, he is very helpful to Katniss.

THE REMAINING PARTS OF SPEECH

Although we noted at the beginning of this chapter that there are eight parts of speech, we have only covered four here: noun, pronoun, verb, and preposition. **Conjunctions** will be discussed at length in Chapter 23, and **adjectives** and **adverbs** in Chapter 27. The eighth part of speech is the **interjection**, something that is thrown into the middle. Interjections add emotion or emphasis, and are often followed by an exclamation point. Look at the following examples:

Wow! That is a great chardonnay!

Hey, watch what you're doing!

Ouch, I didn't realize the pan was hot.

Interjections are not part of the structure of a sentence or connected to any other words. We tend to avoid them in academic writing, unless they're part of a direct quote, as in the following example:

The customer exclaimed, "Wow, what a great chardonnay!"

Now that we've reviewed the basic ingredients of a sentence, the parts of speech, let's look in the next chapter at how they work together.

RECIPE FOR REVIEW

THE NOUN

A **noun** names a person, place, thing, or idea. A **common noun** indicates a general category, while a **proper noun** names a specific item, such as the French Laundry. Nouns can be used as subjects of a sentence and as objects of a preposition.

THE PRONOUN

Pronouns are words that can be used in the place of nouns, usually to avoid repetition, or to identify a general category (everyone) or an amount (*all, one*). See the table of pronouns earlier in this chapter (Figure 20.2).

THE VERB

Every sentence must contain a **verb**. Action verbs tell what the subject of the sentence is doing. Linking verbs connect the subject of a sentence to some additional information and include *is, are, was,* and *were*. Helping verbs are added to the main verb to form a verb phrase. Common helping verbs are listed earlier in this chapter (Figure 20.3).

THE PREPOSITION

Prepositions describe the relationship between nouns through a prepositional phrase, a group of words that starts with a preposition and ends with a noun or pronoun. Examples include *in the kitchen, on the table, after breakfast, with confectioner's sugar.*

CHAPTER QUIZ

DIRECTIONS: In each of the following sentences, identify the underlined word as a noun, pronoun, verb, or preposition.

Example: ___verb___ Television doctors <u>are</u> extremely popular.

_____ 1. In the 1960s, two very popular television <u>doctors</u> were Ben Casey and Dr. Kildare.

_____ 2. Young and handsome, <u>they</u> had a devoted female audience.

_____ 3. Some years later, Dr. Marcus Welby <u>brought</u> a fatherly appeal to his bedside manner.

_____ 4. In the 1990s, the medical drama <u>enjoyed</u> a renewed popularity with the smash hit *ER.*

_____ 5. Unlike the medical dramas <u>of</u> the 1960s that focused on a single doctor, *ER* featured an ensemble cast.

_____ 6. Among the most popular members of *ER*'s medical staff was the smooth and confident Doug Ross, <u>who</u> was played by George Clooney.

_____ 7. The role eventually launched <u>Clooney</u> into an extremely successful career on the big screen.

_____ 8. Another favorite <u>was</u> the young medical student Carter.

_____ 9. During the first episode of the series, both he and the <u>audience</u> were fascinated and intimidated by the fast-paced drama of the emergency room.

_____ 10. Part of the fascination was <u>with</u> Carter's supervisor, the handsome, dedicated, and hypercritical Dr. Benton.

CHAPTER 21
UNDERSTANDING SENTENCE BASICS

After reading this chapter, you should begin to . . .

- identify the subject and predicate of a sentence through understanding sentence patterns;
- identify indefinite pronouns as subjects;
- identify compound subjects and verbs;
- identify verb phrases;
- distinguish between verbs and verbals; and
- identify the subject and verb in sentences with inverted word order.

In Chapter 20, we reviewed the basic ingredients of the sentence, the parts of speech. Now we are going to look at how those ingredients work together to make a sentence, which is one of the writer's most important tools. We will be particularly interested in the ingredients that make up the subject and the verb. This subject–verb pairing tells a miniature story (for example, *pairing tells*) and is the underpinning of every sentence. In this chapter we will work simply on *identifying* the subject and verb; in later chapters we will use this knowledge to check sentences for grammatical correctness.

"PLATING" THE SENTENCE

The **sentence** you write in an essay is like the plate of food you offer to a customer. Both must have certain ingredients before the plate or sentence can be "served." While a traditional plate contains a protein, a starch, and a vegetable, a correct sentence contains a subject, a verb, and a "complete thought," that is, an idea that can stand alone. We might also think of the sentence as a mathematical formula:

subject + verb + stand-alone idea = sentence

The **subject** of the sentence is the person or thing that is performing an action or that is being described by the rest of the sentence. The subject typically consists of one or more nouns or pronouns (or occasionally of phrases behaving like nouns) and may also include descriptive words and phrases. The **verb** tells what the subject is doing (*action verb*) or connects the subject (*linking verb*) to some information in the rest of the sentence, called the **predicate.**

In addition to possessing a subject and verb, a sentence is also said to express a **complete thought** or idea; it can stand alone. We'll discuss this aspect of a sentence in more detail in Chapter 22. But now let's look at the ingredients of the following sentence:

> The chef in the immaculate blue jacket tosses the pizza dough into the air.

The **complete subject** of this sentence is *the chef in the immaculate blue jacket* and the **complete predicate** is *tosses the pizza dough into the air.*

While the complete subject includes all the words that modify or describe the subject, the **simple subject** consists of the noun or pronoun that the sentence can't do without. In this sentence, the simple subject is *chef.* The *jacket* provides an interesting detail, but ultimately it is not essential to the sentence. We also want to iden-

The chef in the immaculate blue jacket tosses the pizza dough into the air.

tify the **simple predicate** of a sentence, the verb. In our example, the verb is *tosses.* The subject and verb are like the *spine* of the sentence, or the *trunk;* other words and phrases form the limbs and branches. Look at the diagram of our same sentence in Figure 21.1.

The spine of this sentence is *chef tosses dough.* Although it does not contain all the information in the sentence, it does state the main point and includes the basic ingredients of simple subject (*chef*) and simple predicate (*tosses*). *Dough* is the direct object of the verb; it's what is being tossed. Note that not every sentence has a direct object. Our main interest in this chapter will be in finding the simple subject and simple predicate (verb) in the sentence, rather than in analyzing all the different parts.

Figure 21.1 Sentence Diagram: "The chef in the immaculate blue jacket tosses the pizza dough into the air."

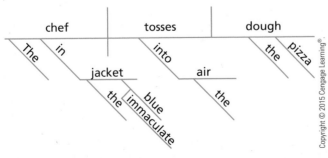

There are a number of reasons that we might want to identify the subject and verb. First, because a complete sentence must contain both of these ingredients, we must be able to identify them in order to recognize and avoid incomplete or fragmented sentences (see Chapter 22). Second, identifying the subject and verb is important in recognizing run-on sentences and comma splices, in which two complete sentences are incorrectly joined together (see Chapter 23). Third, we need to be able to find the subject and the verb in order to check that they agree (see Chapter 24).

UNDERSTANDING COMMON SENTENCE PATTERNS

We can begin looking for the subject and verb by understanding the *pattern* of the sentence, a pattern that is often revealed by the very first word. Like customers at a buffet who stop at the beginning of the line to pick up their trays, we can stop at the beginning of the sentence to "pick up" the pattern.

Perhaps the most common pattern is to begin the sentence with the subject and to follow it with the verb (subject + verb). Many sentences in English begin with the subject or with words that describe the subject. In our earlier example, "The chef in the immaculate blue jacket tosses the pizza dough into the air," the first word of the sentence is *the*. The words *the*, *a*, and *an* are **articles**, words whose purpose is to introduce a noun. If we see one of these words, we know that a noun is coming. Therefore, if one of these words is the first word in a sentence, then the noun that follows it—the first noun

Like customers at a buffet table, we can stop at the beginning
of the sentence to "pick up" the pattern.

in the sentence—is likely to be the subject. Looking back at the example, we notice that the first word is *the,* and the noun that follows is *chef,* the subject of the sentence.

To identify the simple subject of a sentence, stop at the beginning, and look at the first word. If the first word is *the, a,* or *an,* ask yourself *"The* what?" or *"A* what?" The answer to that question will be the subject. Consider the following example:

The large, warm, chocolate chip cookies contain chopped nuts.

Since the first word is *the,* we expect the subject of the sentence to follow shortly: The what? *Cookies.* Note that one or more adjectives may come between the article and the simple subject: *large, warm, chocolate chip.* Here is another example:

A fresh apple makes a healthy and tasty snack.

The subject is a what? *Apple.*

Now, what happens if the first word in the sentence is not an article but an *adverb* or a *preposition?* In the following example, the first word is the adverb *effortlessly.* Since it is not introducing the subject, we will simply put it aside and look at the second word.

Effortlessly, the chef in the immaculate blue jacket tosses the pizza dough into the air.

In this case, the second word is *the,* which does introduce the subject. The what? *Chef.* Now look at the next example:

For hungry children, a fresh apple makes a healthy and tasty snack.

Here the first word is the preposition *for.* We know from Chapter 20 that a preposition is usually the first word in a phrase that ends with a noun or pronoun—so, like *the,* the word *for* is here introducing a noun. However, the noun that follows *for* cannot be the subject of the sentence because it is part of the prepositional phrase. Each word can have only one job. Thus we skip over *children* and look at the next word, *a.* Now we have a recognizable pattern again: The subject is a what? *Apple.*

It is important to begin always with the very first word in the sentence. If we jump right in and choose a juicy-looking noun at random, we may miss an important clue. Read the following sentence, and circle the subject:

At the Frosted Cupcake, the large, warm chocolate chip cookies contain chopped nuts.

Did you want to circle the delicious Frosted Cupcake? It's tempting. But if we look at the very first word, the preposition *at,* we will skip over that prepositional phrase and find the introductory *the.* Then we will ask: The subject is the what? *Cookies.*

The, a, and *an* are useful, but there are other words that are equally helpful in identifying the sentence pattern. If the first word in the sentence is an adjective (*blue, small*), a number used as an adjective (*twenty*), or a possessive pronoun (*my, his, her, your*), then the noun it introduces is most likely the simple subject. Study the following examples:

My birthday is a national holiday. [The subject is my what? *Birthday.*]

Green centerpieces decorated the tables. [The subject is green what? *Centerpieces*.]

Their grandmother ate an exceptionally delicious apple pie. [The subject is their what? *Grandmother*.]

Note that sometimes sentences in this pattern will begin with an adverb or a prepositional phrase:

> **Luckily**, my birthday is a national holiday.
> **In the main dining room**, green centerpieces decorated the tables.

Find the end of the phrase (notice how the comma helps); then "pick up" the pattern. See Figure 21.2.

Once we have identified the subject of the sentence, we ask ourselves, What is the subject doing? For example, what are the centerpieces doing in the earlier example? They're *decorating* the tables; the verb is *decorated*. Very often, however, the subject is not doing something but rather being described in the sentence. In that case, we look

Figure 21.2 Use the "pattern" to find the subject of the sentence.

Introductory Word or Phrase	"Pattern" Word	Subject	Verb
	The	chef	tosses
Effortlessly	the	chef	tosses
	My	birthday	is
Luckily	my	birthday	is
At the Frosted Cupcake	the	(large, warm chocolate chip) cookies	contain
For hungry children	a	(fresh) apple	makes
In the main dining room	green	centerpieces	decorated

Copyright © 2015 Cengage Learning®.

Exercise 21.1 | Finding the Subject and Verb

For each sentence, circle the subject and underline the verb. If it's helpful, cross out any prepositional phrases.

1. The youthful chef in the very tall toque taught a class in Mediterranean cuisine.
2. First, the instructor made a sample risotto.
3. After the demonstration, the students in the class went to their stations.
4. Their enthusiasm about the assignment was contagious.
5. For many of the students, the risotto was the highlight of the day.

for one of the linking verbs, the most common of which are *is, are, was,* and *were.* In the other example, the subject is *birthday,* but there is no action in the sentence. Instead, the verb is tiny little *is* from the face of the T1000.

Sometimes it might be clearer to find the verb in the sentence first. After all, the verb either describes an action (*whisked*) or links the two parts of the sentence (*is, are, was, were*). Further, while the subject of the sentence could be a noun, pronoun, or phrase, the verb is always the verb.

Each word in the sentence has a specific job, and we can use job-related questions to help us find the subject and verb. To find the verb, for example, ask "Which word or phrase refers to an action or links the subject to some additional information?" More whimsically, we might ask if there are any words from the face of the T1000 in the sentence: *is, are, was, were, has, have, does, do.* To find the subject, ask "Who or what is performing the action of the verb, or is being described by the rest of the sentence?" Let's look again at our example:

The chef in the immaculate blue jacket tosses the pizza dough into the air.

Which word refers to an action? *Tosses.* Who or what "tosses the pizza dough into the air"? *Chef.* Let's look at another example:

The new restaurant's menu was a combination of traditional and fusion dishes.

There's no action in this sentence, so we look for a linking verb and find *was.* Then we ask, Who or what "was a combination of traditional and fusion dishes"? *Menu.* Again, note how the subject and verb make little telegram- or headline-style sentences: *chef tosses, menu was.*

INDEFINITE PRONOUNS AS SUBJECTS

Identifying the subject is fairly straightforward when it is a noun or a personal pronoun, but things get more complicated when the subject is an **indefinite pronoun.** While personal pronouns (*I, we, you, he, she, it,* and *they*) refer to definite persons, places, or things, the indefinite pronouns describe general things or identify the number or amount of persons, places, or things. Indefinite pronouns include *one, each, both, all, most, none, many, everyone, something,* and *nobody.* Very often, an indefinite pronoun is the subject of a sentence but does not seem to carry its meaning. Thus the indefinite pronoun may sometimes be difficult to identify as the subject. The secret is to recognize the prepositional phrases in a sentence that might distract you from the simple subject and to memorize the indefinite pronouns so that you will recognize them easily. Let's look at some examples:

One of the peaches is ripe.

Although the sentence seems to be about *peaches,* that word is contained in a prepositional phrase—*of the peaches*—and so cannot be the simple subject. What, then, is ripe? *One.*

One [of the peaches] **is** ripe.

Here's another example:

All of the customers at the table ordered dessert.

Once you bracket off *of the customers* and *at the table,* ask yourself, Who ordered dessert? *All.*

All *[of the customers] [at the table]* <u>ordered</u> dessert.

Exercise 21.2 | Indefinite Pronouns as Subjects

For each sentence, circle the subject and underline the verb. If it's helpful, cross out any prepositional phrases.

1. All of the students took very careful notes on the lecture.
2. Each of them asked the instructor a question about the risotto.
3. Many of the recipes for that class were new to the students.
4. In fact, many students had never tasted goat or rabbit before.
5. One of Sean's favorite dishes was the goat curry.

COMPOUND SUBJECTS AND VERBS

A single sentence may contain more than one subject that shares the same verb; for example, "Forrester and Jamal were both writers." In this sentence, *Forrester and Jamal* is the **compound subject.** Compound subjects may also be connected with *or*; for example, "Blueberries or peaches will make an excellent filling for the cobbler." Sometimes the compound subject may contain modifiers such as adjectives or prepositional phrases.

The fresh blueberries or the peaches in the freezer will make an excellent filling for the cobbler.

For our purposes, ignore the modifiers and identify only the nouns, *blueberries* and *peaches,* which form a compound subject.

Compound Subject: "The fresh blueberries or the peaches in the freezer will make an excellent filling for the cobbler."

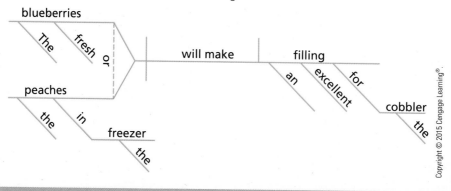

Just as a sentence might have two or more subjects, it may sometimes have two or more verbs that refer to the same subject and are connected by a conjunction such as *and, or,* or *nor.* We need to recognize these **compound verbs** in order to check that all parts agree with the subject and are in the correct tense. To discover any compound subjects or verbs, look carefully at all conjunctions—particularly *and* and *or*—to see what they are connecting. It might be two adjectives (for example, the black *and* white photograph), two prepositions (Did he go up *or* down the stairs?), but it might be two subjects or two verbs: *Jill **stirred and tasted** the soup.*

The sisters liked to pick fresh blueberries in the patch behind the garden.

Compound Verb: "Jill stirred and tasted the soup."

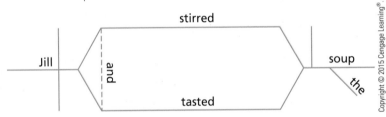

Exercise 21.3 | Compound Subjects and Verbs

Identify the subject(s) and verb(s) in each of the following sentences.

1. As children, Mary and Albert liked to pick fresh blueberries in the patch behind the garden.
2. They and their little sister selected three small tin pails from the cellar and hung them round their necks with baling twine.
3. Then the three children and their dog walked slowly through the blueberry patch, picking the ripe fruit and eating half of it.
4. Later, their mother washed the blueberries and removed their stems.
5. To the children's delight, their mother and father had decided to serve fresh blueberry pie for breakfast.

In the last sentence of Exercise 21.3, the second verb contains an old friend from Chapter 20, the **verb phrase.** *Had* is a helping verb, and *decided* is the main verb. Review the list of helping verbs from Chapter 20 (Figure 20.3), and keep it beside you as you do these exercises. When you see a word that might be a helping verb, look to the right to see if it is followed by a main verb. Conversely, whenever you see a main verb, look to the left to see if it is preceded by one or more helping verbs. In this way, you will become accustomed to identifying verb phrases.

Exercise 21.4 | Identifying Verb Phrases

Identify the verb phrases in the following sentences. Exclude any adverbs.

1. Gregory Peck has starred in a number of well-known films.
2. In *To Kill a Mockingbird*, he was cast as a Southern lawyer, the widower Atticus Finch.
3. His performance in that film is considered one of his best.
4. The actor was required to display both the tenderness of a loving parent and the courage of a social activist.
5. Contemporary audiences are still moved by Peck's courage and compassion.

VERBS VS. VERBALS

Verbals are words that look like verbs but are used in different ways. One example is the **infinitive phrase.** Look at the following sentence:

In five years Janine hopes to manage her own bakery.

Notice the phrase "to manage." Although it begins with the word *to,* it is not a prepositional phrase but an infinitive, that is, the word *to* followed by the base form of the verb (see Chapter 25). The "verb" in an infinitive phrase cannot be the verb in the sentence and might be bracketed off in the same way as a prepositional phrase:

[In five years] Janine hopes [to manage] her own bakery.

Once we've eliminated prepositional and infinitive phrases, we can easily identify the true verb, *hopes.* To find the subject, we ask, Who hopes to manage her own bakery? *Janine.*

[In five years] **Janine** hopes [to manage her own bakery].

Perhaps the most famous infinitive phrase in the English language is "To be or not to be" from Shakespeare's play *Hamlet.* We might modify that quote to read: "To be or not to be—that is *not* the verb."

Note, however, that although an infinitive phrase cannot be the *verb,* it might be the *subject* of a sentence. Consider the old saying "To err is human." The verb is clearly *is.* The word *human* is an adjective describing the subject of the sentence, the infinitive phrase *To err.* Another example is "To roast a turkey is traditional at Thanksgiving." The subject of this sentence is the infinitive phrase *To roast a turkey.*

Another type of verbal is the **gerund**, the base form of the verb plus *–ing,* which is used like a noun. Consider the following example:

Managing her own bakery is Janine's long-term goal.

Although it looks like a verb, here the word *managing* is actually the subject of the sentence. The verb in the sentence is simply *is.* Let's look at another example:

Janine anticipates managing her own bakery in the future.

Again, although *managing* looks like a verb, it is used as a noun, in this case as the direct object of the verb *anticipates.*

Finally, **past participles** and **present participles** look like verbs but are often used in other ways. In fact, a **participle** cannot be the verb in the sentence *unless* it is part of a verb phrase and is preceded by one or more helping verbs. The past participle of regular verbs is formed by adding *–d* or *–ed* to the main verb. The present participle is formed by adding *–ing* to the main verb. The following sentence contains both present and past participles:

Walking into the kitchen, Jeremy grabbed a freshly laundered side towel.

Walking looks like a verb, but it is not preceded by a helping verb and is instead used as an adjective modifying *Jeremy. Laundered* also looks like a verb, but here it is an adjective modifying *towel.* The true verb in this sentence is *grabbed.*

When helping verbs are added to the participles, however, they become verb phrases. Consider the following example:

Jeremy **was walking** through the kitchen, holding a side towel that **had been** freshly **laundered.**

In this sentence, *walking* is preceded by the helping verb *was* and forms the verb phrase *was walking. Laundered* is preceded by the helping verbs *had been* and forms the verb phrase *had been laundered.* (Note that *freshly* is an adverb and not strictly part of the verb phrase.) Look carefully at all words that look like verbs to determine how they are used in a particular sentence.

Exercise 21.5 | Distinguishing Verbs from Verbals

Underline the verbs in the following sentences, being careful to distinguish them from verbals.

1. *Finding Forrester* is an uplifting movie about two very different men.
2. Jamal is a very young man trying to become a better writer.
3. Finding Forrester is the key to Jamal's growth.
4. Inspired by the older man's work, Jamal writes an outstanding story.
5. Audiences still are finding Forrester a likeable and inspiring character.

VARIATIONS IN WORD ORDER

While the subject-first sentence pattern we have been working with is perhaps the most common, there are other patterns as well. In many English sentences, the subject comes before the verb and is often one of the very first words in the sentence. For example, in the sentence "The subject comes before the verb," the subject of the sentence, *subject,* is the second word in the sentence and precedes the verb, *comes.* There are also, however, types of sentences that invert this word order. One type of **inverted sentence** begins with the words *There* or *Here,* as in the following example:

There are several issues in finding the subject and verb in a sentence.

When a sentence begins with *There* or *Here,* cross out that word (which can never be the subject) and bracket off the prepositional phrases in the usual way:

~~There~~ are several issues *[in finding the subject and verb][in a sentence].*

Next, look for the verb to come *before* the subject. In fact, in this example the verb follows immediately after *There.*

~~There~~ <u>are</u> several issues *[in finding the subject and verb][in a sentence].*

Finally, look for the subject to *follow* the verb:

~~There~~ <u>are</u> several **issues** *[in finding the subject and verb][in a sentence].*

The order of subject and verb may also be inverted by an initial prepositional phrase, as in the following example:

In the pantry are several types of flour.

In following our three-step process, we would bracket off *in the pantry* and *of flour,* then identify the linking verb *are* and the simple subject *types.*

[In the pantry] <u>are</u> several **types** *[of flour].*

Questions also change the order of subject and verb. Often the verb is the very first word in a question. Consider the following examples:

Are you in the kitchen?
Is breakfast ready yet?

In the first sentence, the verb *Are* is followed by the subject *you.* In the second, the verb *Is* is followed by the subject *breakfast.*

Some questions begin with a helping verb that is part of a verb phrase rather than with the main verb.

Do you like to snack on fresh fruit?
Have these customers ordered dessert?

In each of these sentences, the verb phrase is split in two by the subject. *Do like* is the verb phrase in the first sentence; *you* is the subject. *Have ordered* is the verb phrase in the second sentence; *customers* is the subject.

A helpful way to begin analyzing a question is to rewrite it as a statement without changing or dropping any words. Thus "Do you like to snack on fresh fruit?" becomes "You do like to snack on fresh fruit." Notice that this brings the two parts of the verb phrase together and puts the subject first, where we most often expect to find it. Once the question is rewritten as a statement, we can bracket off prepositional phrases and find the subject and verb in the usual way:

You <u>do like</u> *[to snack] [on fresh fruit].*

Another type of question begins with a "question word," such as *Why* or *How*. The order of the subject and verb is still likely to be inverted, and the question may still contain a verb phrase. Such question words may be dropped when rewriting the sentence as a statement. For example, "Why is the sky blue?" might be rewritten as "The sky is blue." Or, "How do we make a hollandaise?" might be rewritten as "We do make a hollandaise."

Finally, some types of questions begin with an interrogative pronoun, such as *who*, *what*, or *which*. In these cases, the subject is the pronoun, which tends to come first. Look at these examples:

As his lustful mother and ambitious stepfather watch uneasily, young Hamlet burns to avenge his father's murder.

Who is your favorite actor?
What is the funniest scene in that movie?
Which of the television shows are worth watching?

The subjects of these sentences are *who, what,* and *which,* respectively.

Exercise 21.6 | Identifying the Subject and Verb in Inverted Sentences

Rewrite each of the following sentences on a separate sheet; then cross out *There* or *Here*, bracket off prepositional phrases, underline the verb, and circle the subject in each.

1. Here are the main characters of Shakespeare's *Hamlet*.
2. There is a young Danish prince, sensitive and idealistic.
3. In the cast of characters also are his lustful mother and ambitious stepfather.
4. Have you ever seen the play?
5. Did Daniel Day-Lewis play the role on the London stage?

RECIPE FOR REVIEW

DEFINITIONS

A complete **sentence** has a subject and a verb, and expresses a complete thought or idea. Like pots and pans, sentences are the tools with which we "cook" our ideas. The **simple subject** is a noun or pronoun (or a phrase acting like a noun) that is performing the action of the verb or that is linked to information in the predicate. The **complete subject** includes all the words and phrases that modify the simple subject. The **predicate** is the part of the sentence that is not the subject. It contains the **verb** (or simple predicate), which tells what the subject is doing or links the subject to information in the predicate.

Like pots and pans, sentences are the tools with which we "cook" our ideas.

© Ermess/shutterstock.com

FINDING THE SUBJECT AND THE VERB

1. Use common sentence patterns to identify the subject; then ask what the subject is doing or what word is linking it to the predicate.
2. Another approach is to find the verb first, the word that expresses an action or that links the subject to the predicate (most often, *is, are, was,* or *were*). Then find the subject by asking who or what is performing the action of the verb, or who or what is being described in the predicate.
3. It may be helpful to bracket off prepositional phrases, infinitive phrases, and other words such as adjectives or adverbs that cannot be the subject or the verb.

MORE ABOUT SUBJECTS AND VERBS

1. An **indefinite** pronoun, often followed by a prepositional phrase beginning with *of*, can be the subject of the sentence.
2. A **compound subject** consists of two or more subjects that share the same verb.
3. A **compound verb** consists of two or more verbs that share the same subject.
4. A **verb phrase** consists of one or more helping verbs and a main verb. (See also Chapter 20.)

VERBS VS. VERBALS

Verbals are words that are made from verbs, but don't perform the job of a verb.

1. An **infinitive phrase** is formed with *to* plus the base form of the verb, for example, *to run*. While an infinitive phrase cannot be the verb, it can occasionally be the subject of a sentence: To err is human.
2. A **gerund** is formed with the base form plus *–ing* and is used like a noun. It too can be the subject of a sentence, but not the verb.
3. The **past** and **present participles** look like verbs but are often used in other ways. Unless the participle is immediately preceded by one or more helping verbs, it is not used as a verb.

VARIATIONS IN WORD ORDER

1. When a sentence begins with *there* or *here,* the subject usually follows the verb.
2. In a question, the first word is most likely a verb. The subject follows this initial verb. If the verb is part of a verb phrase, the rest of the phrase follows the subject.

   Are **you** in the kitchen? [verb + **subject**]

   Do **you** like to snack on fresh fruit? [helping verb + **subject** + main verb]

CHAPTER QUIZ

DIRECTIONS: For each sentence, identify the simple grammatical subject and the verb/verb phrase.

1. The scent of the baked goods and coffee caught my senses.

2. There are green centerpieces on every table.

3. The aroma of cloves, nutmeg, and cinnamon tickles one's nose, growing stronger with every step.

4. Was my attention distracted for a moment by the jingling of coffee cups and the sharp clamoring of silverware in the background?

5. The streusel had a very flaky texture and tasted tangy near its fruit-filled center, an equal combination of sweet and sour.

6. The pack of students in their white coats clusters around the bright glass case and its tantalizing, picture-perfect delights.

7. The perfect ingredients in a cup of coffee are extra sugar, extra cream, and a touch of cinnamon.

8. There was a mixture in the air of cloves, nutmeg, fresh-brewed coffee, and cinnamon.

9. The jazz music and dim lighting of the room make for a nice, warm atmosphere.

10. I picked up my cup of coffee and stepped out into the frost-bitten air.

CHAPTER 22
FIXING SENTENCE FRAGMENTS

By the end of this chapter, you should begin to . . .

- identify various types of sentence fragments;
- fix fragments by adding a missing subject or verb;
- fix phrase fragments by combining them with another sentence;
- fix subordinate clause fragments by deleting the subordinating conjunction or by combining them with another sentence; and
- fix relative clause fragments by changing a pronoun or by combining them with another sentence.

Our sentences tell our readers not only about our ideas but also about us. If our sentences contain errors, readers may conclude that we have been careless in proofreading or that we don't know how to fix these errors. Sentence fragments are considered "very serious" errors by both academic and business professionals (see Chapter 29), so let's see what we can do about fixing them.

We have said that a complete sentence requires a subject, a verb, and stand-alone idea. Thus an *incomplete* sentence or **sentence fragment** is missing one or more of those ingredients. It's as if you were served a plate with mashed potatoes and broccoli but no protein, or as if you tried to bake bread without the yeast. To fix the dish—or the sentence—you need to add the missing ingredients.

IDENTIFYING SENTENCE FRAGMENTS

To identify a sentence fragment, ask yourself whether the sentence has a subject and a verb, and—if it does—whether it can stand alone, that is, whether it is an independent or main clause rather than a dependent or subordinate one. Let's look at an example:

The winning contestant in an extraordinarily exciting episode of *Iron Chef*.

To fix a "plate fragment," add the missing protein.

We have a subject, *contestant,* but no verb. What is the contestant *doing?* To fix the sentence, we need to add a verb:

> The winning contestant in an extraordinarily exciting episode of *Iron Chef* **beamed**.

Here's another example:

> Nibbled a small piece of Asiago cheese.

Here we have a verb, *nibbled,* but no subject. *Who* nibbled the cheese? This time, we need to add a subject:

> **The tiny gray mouse** nibbled a small piece of Asiago cheese.

Other fragments may lack *both* a subject and a verb, like the following example:

> Into the frying pan.

We might add the missing ingredients as follows:

> **Geraldine put the butter and onions** into the frying pan.

Finally, there is a type of fragment that contains a subject and verb but nevertheless cannot stand on its own. It's a dependent or subordinate clause, rather than an independent one.

> Although the pork was a bit tough.

This "sentence" has a subject, *pork,* and a verb, *was.* However, it is a sentence fragment because it cannot stand alone. What *about* the pork? We could fix the sentence as follows:

> Although the pork was a bit tough, **it had an excellent flavor.**

The stand-alone idea is not only about missing information, however. For example, the sentence "That's right" is complete even though we don't know what *that* refers to. Sentence completeness is really more about the structure of the sentence than about its content. When a sentence contains a subject, a verb, and a subordinating conjunction such as the word *although*—that is, when it is a subordinate clause—it is structurally incomplete unless it is joined to a main or independent clause. The word *although* is like a coat hanger, and the clause *the pork was a bit tough* hangs from it like a pair of pants. If the coat hanger is physically hooked over a rod in a closet or over your hand, the pants are safe. Similarly, if the subordinate clause is "hooked" to a main clause, such as *it had an excellent flavor*, it forms a complete sentence. But if the coat hanger tries to hover in the air on its own, it will fall to the ground, bringing the pants with it.

Exercise 22.1 | Identifying Sentence Fragments

Read each "sentence" carefully, from the capital letter to the period, and identify it as a complete sentence or a fragment.

_____ 1. Rachel was taking a class in identifying fruits and vegetables.

_____ 2. Learned to recognize twenty varieties of fresh herbs.

_____ 3. The differences between marjoram and oregano particularly subtle.

_____ 4. At the local farmer's market on the outskirts of town.

_____ 5. Although she studied hard for the quiz.

Of course, it's one thing to identify sentence fragments when they're listed separately, as in Exercise 22.1. It is much more difficult to identify them when they are hidden in our essays.

Sentence fragments often appear in our writing because we wrongly place a period in the middle of a thought. The earlier examples might have looked like this in our paper:

Geraldine put the butter and onions. Into the frying pan.

Although the pork was a bit tough. It had an excellent flavor.

Because the two parts are close together (not actually *missing* from the text), it is easy when proofreading to ignore the period and see the two parts as a whole. Therefore, it is very important to read carefully over the final draft of your paper and consider each "sentence" as a unit. Read from the capital letter to the period, and ask yourself whether the sentence contains the three necessary ingredients of a complete sentence. Sometimes it is useful to read the last sentence first, then the next to last, and so on. In that way we do not get caught up in the flow of ideas, and we are more likely to catch errors in grammar and punctuation. It's also helpful to read the sentence aloud. Our voices will naturally drop when we come to the end of an idea that can stand alone. If our voices don't drop but instead stop suddenly, up in the air, so to speak, we may have a sentence fragment.

Exercise 22.2 | Fixing Sentence Fragments

Read each "sentence" carefully, from the capital letter to the period. Fix any sentence fragments by joining them to the sentence before or after.

1. Vincenzo owns a popular Italian restaurant. On New York's lower East Side.
2. After immigrating to the United States. Vincenzo's family finally gathered enough capital to open the restaurant.
3. The restaurant features old family recipes from the south of Italy. Such as Insalata Pantesca.
4. Committed to hiring the best possible staff. The family carefully screens applicants for both front-of-the-house and back-of-the-house positions.
5. Critics from *The New York Times* gave the restaurant a rave review. Citing its authentic cuisine and outstanding service.

MISSING SUBJECTS AND VERBS

A missing subject, somewhat rare in American English, is often rather simple to identify. Remember the plate with the missing protein at the beginning of this chapter? Clearly, if the protein is missing, the plate can be "fixed" by adding it. The same is true of the following sentence:

Served a plate of lamb chops.

The missing subject—*who* served the lamb chops—tends to catch our attention, so this type of sentence fragment is less likely to be missed in editing the final draft. The corrected sentence might read as follows: "**The waiter** served a plate of lamb chops."

Far less clear is the sentence that is missing a verb, particularly a linking verb such as *is* or *are*. Look at the following example:

The plate of slightly rare frenched lamb chops ready to be served.

We seem to have all the information, from a description of what's on the plate to the information that it's ready to be served. What we don't have is the tiny structural essential: the verb. We can fix the sentence by adding one:

The plate of slightly rare frenched lamb chops **is** ready to be served.

Another common type of sentence fragment omits the helping verb, as in the following example:

Semi-sweet chocolate chips stirred into the buttery cookie dough.

We can fix this sentence by adding a helping verb:

> Semi-sweet chocolate chips **were** stirred into the buttery cookie dough.

Finally, both the subject and verb may be missing: "Semi-sweet chocolate chips into the buttery cookie dough." We can fix this sentence by adding the missing ingredients:

> **Daniel mixed** semi-sweet chocolate chips into the buttery cookie dough.

The key to identifying any fragment is to keep in mind our work from Chapter 21 on finding the subject and verb. Remember to distinguish verbs from verbals and to check for missing linking verbs.

This plate doesn't look like a fragment, but what about this sentence?: "The delicious, fresh salad including tomatoes, cucumbers, and feta cheese."

Exercise 22.3 | Fixing Sentences That Are Missing a Subject and/or Verb

Read each "sentence" carefully, from the capital letter to the period. Identify any sentence fragments, and fix them by adding the missing ingredients.

Example: _F_ Wilted, discolored lettuce [is] inappropriate for a salad plate.

1. The delicious, fresh salad including tomatoes, cucumbers, and feta cheese.
2. Some of the salads sprinkled with pine nuts or sugared pecans.
3. Other salads on the menu contained chunks of warm goat cheese.
4. Ordered a salad with a mix of roasted peppers and sun-dried tomatoes.
5. Mixed greens drizzled with raspberry vinaigrette.

SUBORDINATE CLAUSE FRAGMENTS

Remember that a **clause** is a group of words that contains a subject and a verb. An independent clause equals a complete sentence. A dependent or subordinate clause, however, cannot stand alone. Let's look again at an earlier example:

> Although the pork was a bit tough. It had an excellent flavor.

The sentence fragment *Although the pork was a bit tough* is a **subordinate** or **dependent clause**. It cannot stand on its own because it lacks a complete thought or, as we said earlier, an independent structure. Because it contains a **subordinating conjunction** or "coat hanger," it must be attached to a **main or independent clause**, or it will fall. See Figure 22.1 for a list of common subordinating conjunctions.

Figure 22.1 Common Subordinating Conjunctions

after	if	until
although	in order that	when
as	once	whenever
as if	since	where
because	so that	wherever
before	though	whether
even though	unless	while

We remember that the formula for a complete sentence is as follows:

subject + verb + stand-alone idea = complete sentence

The formula for a subordinate clause fragment looks like this:

subordinating conjunction	+	subject	+	verb		=	sentence fragment
Although		*the pork*		*was (a bit tough)*			sentence fragment

Note that a sentence that begins with a *coordinating* conjunction, such as *and, but,* or *yet,* is *not* a fragment. The coordinating conjunction does not affect the structure of the clause in the way that a *subordinating* conjunction does (see Chapter 23 for more details).

Subordinate clause fragments can be corrected in a number of ways. First, they can be fixed by removing the subordinating conjunction, which in our example is the word *Although.* The sentence would become simply this:

The pork was a bit tough.

Subordinate fragments may also be fixed by adding an appropriate main or independent clause to complete the thought:

Although the pork was a bit tough, **the rice pilaf was delicious.**

Perhaps most often in our own writing, however, the subordinate clause fragment lies next to a main clause already, and we have simply neglected to connect the two.

Although the pork was a bit tough. It had an excellent flavor.

Here we must be careful to remove the period, replace it with a comma, and lowercase the *I* in *it.*

Although the pork was a bit tough, it had an excellent flavor.

Remember that these types of fragments are often difficult to recognize because they contain a subject and a verb and because they so often lie next to the independent clause they are meant to "depend" on. Therefore, as you're editing your papers, read only one sentence at a time, from the capital letter to the period, and be especially careful of sentences that begin with one of the common subordinating conjunctions.

Exercise 22.4 | Fixing Subordinate Clause Fragments

Read each "sentence" carefully, from the capital letter to the period. Identify any subordinate clause fragments, and fix them by joining them to a main clause or by removing the subordinating conjunction. Adjust the capitalization as needed.

_____ 1. Mature human brains weigh almost three pounds. Archeological evidence suggests they were bigger five thousand years ago.

_____ 2. While some scientists have compared the brain's texture to toothpaste. Others suggest tofu is a more accurate parallel.

_____ 3. The brain continues to grow until age twenty-five. When the prefrontal cortex reaches maturity.

_____ 4. Because this part of the brain controls risk assessment and decision-making. It may explain some of adolescents' volatile behavior.

_____ 5. According to neuroscientists, male and female brains process pain and stress differently. Although there is no difference in areas like math ability.

RELATIVE CLAUSE FRAGMENTS

Another type of subordinate clause, which becomes a fragment if it is not connected to a main clause, is formed with **relative pronouns**, words that "relate" one part of the sentence to a word or phrase in an earlier part. The relative pronouns include _that, which, whichever, who, whoever, whom,_ and _whomever._ For example, in the sentence "The sled dogs have to be in top condition in order to compete in the Iditarod, which covers over one thousand miles," the relative pronoun _which_ refers to the noun _Iditarod._ Like a subordinating conjunction, the relative pronoun joins a subordinate or dependent clause to an independent one. **Relative clause fragments** have a slightly different formula from the subordinate clause fragments discussed earlier. Sometimes the relative pronoun acts as the subject of its own clause:

relative pronoun as subject + verb = sentence fragment

Look at the following example:

Who won the chili competition.

Who **(relative pronoun)** + won **(verb)**
+ **period** = sentence fragment

Notice that if this clause ended with a question mark instead of a period, *who* would be an interrogative rather than a relative pronoun, and the sentence would be correct. However, since it ends with a period, it is a fragment. This type of relative clause fragment, in which the relative pronoun is both the subordinating conjunction and the subject of the clause, can be fixed in several different ways. First, as with all subordinate clause fragments, a main clause may be added:

I know the students who won the chili competition.

"The sled dogs have to be in top condition in order to compete in the Iditarod."

Diagram of a Relative Clause: "I know the students who won the chili competition."

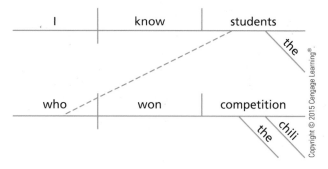

Second, the subordinate clause fragment may lie next to a main clause:

The biggest fans of hot pepper were Carlos and Cecilia. Who won the chili competition.

This fragment may be fixed by removing the period, adding a comma, and making the *W* lower case:

The biggest fans of hot pepper were Carlos and Cecilia, who won the chili competition.

A final option is to replace the relative pronoun with a noun or personal pronoun:

Who won the chili competition. *[incorrect]*
Carlos and Cecilia won the chili competition. *[correct]*
They won the chili competition. *[correct]*

Remember that when a sentence starts with *Who* or *Which* and ends with a question mark, it's okay. However, if such a sentence ends with a period, it's a fragment.

A relative pronoun may also be used as the object of a verb or preposition, as in these sentence fragments:

> Which they put into their award-winning chili.
> In which they entered their famous Red-Hot Chili.

In the first example, *Which* is used as the object of the verb *put*. In the second, *which* is used as the object of the preposition *In*. Like other relative fragments, these two examples can be fixed by joining each to an independent clause, as follows:

> **Carlos and Cecilia bought fresh jalapeño peppers**, which they put into their award-winning chili.
> **Carlos and Cecilia won the competition,** in which they entered their famous Red-Hot Chili.

Look closely at any sentence that begins with *Which* or *In which*.

Finally, a fragment may contain an embedded relative clause attached to a noun. These groups of words rename or describe a noun or pronoun and may look like the following:

> An actor who has won Emmys for both comedic and dramatic roles.

This fragment contains the dependent clause *who has won Emmys for both comedic and dramatic roles,* in which the subject is *who* and the verb is *has won*. It also seems to contain another subject, *actor*. However, there is no verb that pairs with *actor*, and the fragment cannot stand alone. What *about* that actor? To fix this type of fragment, we might delete or change some of the words to make a complete sentence:

> An actor has won Emmys for both comedic and dramatic roles.

Or we might add some words:

> He is an actor who has won Emmys for both comedic and dramatic roles.

In our own writing, such a fragment most likely lies next to a main clause, and, just as we did with the subordinate clause fragments earlier, we need to join the two by removing the period and changing capital letters when necessary.

> **Breaking Bad's** meth-making chemistry teacher is played by Bryan Cranston.
> An actor who has won Emmys for both comedic and dramatic roles.
> *[incorrect]*
> **Breaking Bad's** meth-making chemistry teacher is played by Bryan Cranston, an actor who has won Emmys for both comedic and dramatic roles. *[correct]*

Exercise 22.5 | Relative Clause Fragments

Read each "sentence" carefully, from the capital letter to the period. Identify any relative clause fragments, and fix them by joining each to a main clause or by replacing the relative pronoun. Adjust the capitalization as needed.

_____ 1. The students tasted a variety of chocolates. Which ranged from a light, milky chocolate to a complex, bitter dark chocolate.

_____ 2. Some of the chocolates were made in the United States. Others had been imported from Belgium, Venezuela, and Madagascar.

_____ 3. One of the class favorites was a milk chocolate from France. That held hints of vanilla and caramel.

_____ 4. The 33% cacao in the French chocolate gave it a much richer flavor than that of many popular American chocolates. In which there may be only 11% cacao.

_____ 5. Bacon was the surprise ingredient in a dark chocolate designed by an American chocolatier. A woman who had not only studied in France but traveled widely across Southeast Asia.

RECIPE FOR REVIEW

IDENTIFYING SENTENCE FRAGMENTS

- To be complete, the sentence must contain a subject, a verb, and a stand-alone idea. A **sentence fragment** is missing one or more of these ingredients.
- Read each sentence carefully, from the capital letter to the period, and look for the three essential ingredients. Once you have identified a sentence fragment, then decide whether to correct it by adding or deleting words, or by connecting the fragment to an **independent** or **main clause** before or after it.

SUBORDINATE CLAUSE FRAGMENTS

Subordinate clause fragments begin with a subordinating conjunction ("coat hanger") and are followed by a subject and verb. Because a subordinate clause fragment cannot stand alone, it must be joined to an independent clause, or the subordinating conjunction must be removed.

RELATIVE CLAUSE FRAGMENTS

Relative clause fragments consist of a **relative pronoun** used as the subject or object. A relative clause fragment can be fixed by joining it to the preceding sentence or by changing the relative pronoun to a personal one. Especially confusing are fragments in which a noun is followed by a **dependent** or **subordinate clause** (containing its own subject and verb) but has no verb of its own.

FIXING SENTENCE FRAGMENTS

To check that a sentence is complete, read it aloud to see if it *sounds* unfinished. Pay special attention to sentences that begin with **subordinating conjunctions** ("coat hangers") and **relative pronouns**.
Use the following process to identify sentence fragments.

1. **Is there a subject?**

   If NO, it's a fragment. Add a subject. Then go to step 2.
   If YES, go to step 2.

2. **Is there a verb?**

   If NO, it's a fragment. Add a verb. Then go to step 3.
   If YES, go to step 3.

3. **Does the sentence begin with a coat hanger or a relative pronoun?**

   If NO, the sentence is most likely correct. Move to next sentence.
   If YES, it's a fragment.

    Correct the fragment in ONE of the following ways: (1) dropping the coat hanger, (2) changing the relative pronoun to a personal pronoun, (3) adding a main clause, or (4) joining the fragment to an adjacent sentence.

CHAPTER QUIZ

DIRECTIONS: PART I. Read each "sentence" carefully, from the capital letter to the period. Identify any fragments, and fix them by changing, adding, or deleting words, or by joining them to the sentence before or after. Adjust the capitalization as needed.

_____ 1. *Law & Order* is a crime show franchise that has seen many spin-offs over the years, including the popular *Law & Order: SVU.*

_____ 2. Richard Belzer reprises the role of Detective John Munch, who first appeared in the series *Homicide: Life on the Street.* Which was set in Baltimore.

_____ 3. One of the most popular stars of the show is Mariska Hargitay. Who plays Detective Olivia Benson.

_____ 4. Hargitay speaks a number of other languages in addition to English. Including French, Spanish, and Hungarian.

_____ 5. Hargitay takes her role seriously. And has even founded a charitable organization to help survivors of abuse and assault.

_____ 6. Benson's partner Elliot Stabler, played by Christopher Meloni.

_____ 7. Stabler frequently losing his temper when confronted by the perpetrators of crimes against children.

_____ 8. Although Benson and Stabler have very different personalities. They seem to work well as a team.

_____ 9. In fact, apparently mismatched characters that work well together quite common on television and in the movies.

_____ 10. Written over one hundred years ago. Sir Arthur Conan Doyle's stories about polar opposites Sherlock Holmes and Dr. Watson have been recently re-told in both films and television series.

DIRECTIONS: PART II. Identify the five sentence fragments in the following passage. Then fix them by changing, adding, or deleting words, or by connecting the fragment to the sentence before or after.

"Will the Real Martian Please Stand Up" is an episode of the classic television series *The Twilight Zone.* It's a dark, snowy night, and two state troopers are following up on a call that a UFO has landed in the woods. They find footprints leading from the presumed crash site towards the lights of a diner glimpsed through the trees.

The diner setting seems comfortable, safe, ordinary. A man in a white cap behind the counter serving up cups of coffee. Small tables are scattered casually around the dining area, and a jukebox plays light and cheerful music. Gentle landscape paintings share wall space with special menu items. A bus driver and his passengers enjoy the diner's relaxed mood. But when the troopers enter with news of a bridge that's closed and mysterious footprints in the snow. The music takes on an ominous note. The customers look nervously at each other. Wondering if one of them is an alien. The driver remembers only six passengers on the bus, but there are now seven in the diner.

The atmosphere becomes downright spooky when the lights turn themselves off and on, and the jukebox suddenly plays a new tune. Although no one has touched it. Most unsettling of all, the sugar bowls burst open right in front of the terrified customers. Like the characters in other episodes of *The Twilight Zone*. The diner's inhabitants find the world that looked so ordinary has been turned upside down.

Strange things are happening in this diner from *The Twilight Zone*.

CHAPTER 23
RUN-ON SENTENCES AND COMMA SPLICES

By the end of this chapter, you should begin to . . .

- identify run-on sentences and comma splices;
- separate independent clauses with a period and, if necessary, a capital letter;
- join independent clauses with a coordinating conjunction;
- join independent clauses with a semicolon and, if desired, a conjunctive adverb; and
- join independent clauses with a subordinating conjunction.

In Chapter 22, we looked at sentences that were missing key ingredients, such as a subject, verb, or stand-alone idea. In the case of run-on sentences and comma splices, however, the ingredients are actually doubled (or even tripled). It's as if we had two juicy 10 oz. steaks and two baked potatoes and two servings of green peas all crowded onto a single plate. Or, to use another image, it's as if we have two trains, both traveling in the same direction. But there's a problem—the one behind gets too close and actually *runs on* into the caboose of the first one. Whether it's a bursting stomach or a derailed train, it's a problem. In terms of language, the problem looks like this:

One train stopped the other train kept going.

One train stopped is a complete sentence, and *the other train kept going* is another. When you read the two out loud, you will probably find that your voice drops after *stopped* as

Copyright © 2015 Cengage Learning®.

One train stopped, the other train kept going.

you recognize the completion of a thought, that is, the end of a sentence. On the other hand, you might have been confused and thought that *the other train* was part of the first sentence, as in *One train stopped the other train.* But that would leave the fragment *kept going,* which doesn't make sense.

This is an example of a **run-on sentence**: two independent clauses without an appropriate word or punctuation mark to either join or separate them. We're not thinking of a run-on here as having too many words, but rather as stringing together two or more independent clauses.

run-on sentence = independent clause + independent clause

This kind of run-on sentence can be confusing to readers and is also considered a very serious error by academic and business professionals. As you edit your work, you will want to fix any run-on sentences by assuring that they are correctly separated—

One train stopped. The other train kept going.

—or correctly joined—

One train stopped, and the other kept going.

Closely related to the run-on sentence is the **comma splice**, two independent clauses joined only by a comma.

comma splice = independent clause + comma + independent clause

In Standard American English, a comma is not the appropriate punctuation mark for this situation; the clauses should be separated by a period or joined by a semicolon. It's true that we occasionally see comma splices in published writing. Some writers join short, parallel clauses with a comma, such as the following: Commas are okay, semicolons are better. For most academic and professional audiences, however, you will best meet their expectations by following the rules for writing Standard American English.

Let's imagine the trains again. There between the two powerful trains stands Comma Man,[12] arms outstretched in a desperate attempt to prevent a collision. He is doomed to fail, however, because no matter how many times Comma Man works out at the gym, even if he were to take an illegal steroid cocktail, he will never be strong enough to separate these two trains. What about that plate with the two steaks? Suppose we were to separate the steaks with a few sprigs of parsley—could we serve the plate then? No. We need to get a second plate. There's simply too much food there.

Comma Man will never be strong enough to separate two trains by himself.

IDENTIFYING RUN-ON SENTENCES AND COMMA SPLICES

When you edit your writing, read each "sentence" carefully from the capital letter to the period. A run-on or comma splice will have two independent clauses, two subject–verb pairs.

Joaquin grilled two steaks Dexter added a garnish of mushrooms.

In the first clause, the subject is *Joaquin* and the verb is *grilled*. In the second clause, the subject is *Dexter* and the verb is *added*. The presence of two subject–verb pairs within one "sentence" suggests a run-on or a comma splice. Be careful, however, not to confuse these independent pairs with compound subjects or verbs. All of the following are single, correct, independent sentences. The verbs are underlined; the subjects are in bold.

Joaquin grilled two steaks and added a garnish of mushrooms. [*compound verb*]

Joaquin and **Dexter** grilled two steaks. [*compound subject*]

Joaquin and **Dexter** grilled two steaks and added a garnish of mushrooms. [*compound subject and compound verb*]

Let's go back to the first example: *Joaquin grilled two steaks Dexter added a garnish of mushrooms.* After you locate two clauses or subject–verb pairs in a sentence, look for a subordinating conjunction (or "coat hanger") at the beginning of the sentence or between the two clauses. If one of the clauses is preceded by a subordinating conjunction such as *although, because, after,* or *while,* or by a relative pronoun such as *who, which,* or *that,* the sentence is correct:

> **After** Joaquin grilled two steaks, Dexter added a garnish of mushrooms.
> [*correct*]

> Joaquin grilled two steaks **before** Dexter added a garnish of mushrooms.
> [*correct*]

However, if there are no coat hangers in the sentence, look for the place where the two clauses meet. Perhaps even draw a little box there. If there is nothing in the box—no word like *and,* no semicolon—you have a run-on sentence. If there is just a comma in the box, you have a comma splice (see Figure 23.1 and Recipe for Review).

Figure 23.1 Identifying Run-ons and Comma Splices

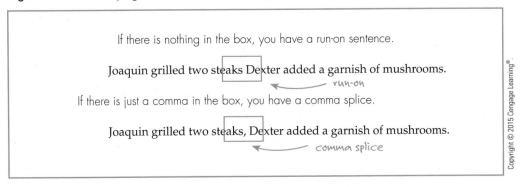

Let's analyze the following examples:

A. Jordan had an unusual job in which he killed and cleaned a ten-pound octopus each day for octopus soup.

Sentence A has two subject–verb pairs: *Jordan had* and *he killed and cleaned.* At the place where they meet, however, there is the relative pronoun *which* (the object of the preposition *in*). This sentence is therefore correct.

B. He picked it up by its large head then he dropped it into boiling water.

Sentence B also has two subject–verb pairs: *he picked* and *he dropped.* At the place where the two clauses meet, we have the word *then,* an adverb rather than a conjunction, and no mark of punctuation. This sentence, therefore, is a run-on.

C. The octopus would make a desperate attempt to escape, it would squirt Jordan with ink and grab the sides of the pot with its tentacles.

Sentence C has two subject–verb pairs: *octopus would make* and *it would squirt and grab.* This is a difficult but extremely common type of comma splice (or run-on) in which the subject of the second clause is a pronoun that refers to the subject of the first clause.

At the point where the two independent clauses meet, there is a comma; therefore this sentence is a comma splice.

D. Finally, Jordan cut open the head and removed the ink bladder, the ink gave the octopus soup its rich black color.

Sentence D has two subject–verb pairs: *Jordan cut and removed* and *ink gave*. Don't be fooled by the compound verb—there are still two subject–verb pairs. At the point where the two independent clauses meet, there is only a comma; therefore this sentence is also a comma splice.

E. Jordan enjoyed his job, however he was very tired at the end of each day's wrestling match with an octopus.

Sentence E has two subject–verb pairs: *Jordan enjoyed* and *he was*. Where the two independent clauses meet, we find a comma and the word *however*. It's tempting to view the sentence as correct. We know the comma can't join the two clauses, but can *however* do it? The answer is no. In this sentence, *however* is used as a conjunctive adverb, rather than as a subordinating conjunction, and adverbs cannot connect two clauses. This sentence is a comma splice. You'll read more about conjunctive adverbs later in the chapter.

Exercise 23.1 | Identifying Run-ons and Comma Splices

Read each "sentence" carefully, and identify it as correct, run-on, or comma splice.

_____ 1. While he was growing up, Dexter's favorite dish was peanut butter and jelly.

_____ 2. He was a picky eater he liked only bland, simple food.

_____ 3. His mother would use plain white sandwich bread, she bought creamy peanut butter and grape jelly.

_____ 4. Dexter was a picky eater as a child, however he grew to like a variety of foods as an adult.

_____ 5. Now one of his favorite foods is steamed clams he also likes clam cakes.

There is a certain simplicity about this chapter. We have two closely related errors, identified in almost exactly the same way, and—almost as simply—four ways to fix them.

1. One train stopped. The other kept going. *[separated with period]*

2. One train stopped, and the other kept going. *[joined with comma and coordinating conjunction]*

3. One train stopped; the other kept going. *[joined with semicolon]*
   One train stopped; however, the other kept going. *[joined with semicolon; conjunctive adverb added]*

4. One train stopped, while the other kept going. *[joined with subordinating conjunction between clauses]*
   While one train stopped, the other kept going. *[joined with subordinating conjunction at the beginning of the first clause]*

FULL STOP: THE PERIOD

One way to fix run-ons and comma splices is to separate them with a **period**. The period indicates the end of a complete thought, the end of a complete sentence. Where the comma is like a waving hand drawing attention to a certain group of words, the period is like the vertical palm of the traffic cop saying "Stop!" It is like a knife slicing through a beef tenderloin.

The correction is made at the same point where we looked for the error, the point where the two sentences meet. If there is nothing there, nothing in that box, then we add a period. If there is a comma at that point, we change it to a period. In both cases, we must then look at the first letter of the next sentence and capitalize it, if necessary. Note that in the second example, *Dexter* is already capitalized because it is a proper noun.

A period slices though a run-on sentence like a knife through raw meat.

> One train stopped. The other train kept going.

> Joaquin grilled two steaks. Dexter added a garnish of mushrooms.

With a period, the hand is no longer waving but firmly signaling a full stop.

Exercise 23.2 | Full Stop

Read each "sentence" carefully, and identify it as correct, run-on, or comma splice. Then fix any errors using a period and, if needed, a capital letter.

_____ 1. Joaquin had worked at the restaurant every Friday night for two years he enjoyed the pressure of the line.

_____ 2. At the restaurant Joaquin especially liked the grill the heat and the danger were exciting to him.

_____ 3. Unlike his friend Dexter, Joaquin had never been a picky eater, his parents encouraged him to try new foods.

_____ 4. Joaquin had always enjoyed steamed clams and calamari, he liked garlic and chili peppers.

_____ 5. Although he enjoyed almost all foods, Joaquin disliked lima beans.

THE FANBOYS

Run-on sentences and comma splices often occur in our writing because there is some relationship between the two ideas they express. Thus, it is often a good idea to keep the sentences connected. One way to do so is to put a **comma** and one of the **coordinating conjunctions** at the point where the two sentences meet, as in the following examples:

One train stopped, **but** the other train kept going.

Joaquin grilled two steaks, **and** Dexter added a garnish of mushrooms.

There are seven coordinating conjunctions: *for, and, nor, but, or, yet, so.* Each one has a somewhat different meaning, and we'll want to use the one that best expresses the relationship between the ideas in the two sentences. *But* and *yet* suggest a contrast or contradiction between the two ideas, as in the first example above. *For* and *so* suggest a cause-and-effect relationship: The steaks weren't done, *so* Joaquin left them on the grill.

These seven coordinating conjunctions, the **FANBOYS**, are words whose job it is to join two (or more) other words, phrases, or clauses. The FANBOYS themselves are the glue that holds the clauses together. Commas are also involved, however. We place a comma before (not after!) the coordinating conjunction when joining two independent clauses. The comma signals the end of one group of words and the beginning of another.

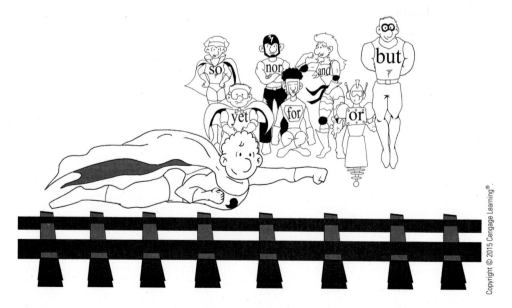

Comma Man & the FANBOYS

Remember Comma Man? He was too weak to prevent the train wreck by himself. However, when he joins up with one of the FANBOYS, they're strong enough to stop the trains and save the day.

compound sentence = independent clause + comma + coordinating conjunction
+ independent clause

Exercise 23.3 | The FANBOYS

Read each "sentence" carefully, and identify it as correct, run-on, or comma splice. Then fix any errors using an appropriate coordinating conjunction and, if needed, a comma.

_____ 1. The air around me was crisp with a slight chill sweet and earthy smells came from the shrubs and flowers.

_____ 2. The café was warm and cozy there were many baked goods on display.

_____ 3. I could hear the bubbling of the espresso machines as they roared and steamed like the trains passing through the valley.

_____ 4. I had a good morning, I'll go with the double espresso and a flaky, buttery croissant.

_____ 5. The iced coffee looked clear, dark, and delicious, it tasted flat and stale.

THE SEMICOLON

Another way to join two sentences or independent clauses correctly is with a **semicolon**. The semicolon is like an equal sign; it tells the reader that on each side is an independent sentence. Yet it also suggests a relationship between the two. English teachers love it when students use the semicolon correctly. However, if they use it incorrectly, their teachers are correspondingly disappointed. By all means, deploy the semicolon appropriately. You could, though, go through your entire life without ever using one.

To join two sentences with a semicolon, insert it at the place where the two clauses meet, just as you would a period. However, note that the first word after the semicolon is *not* capitalized unless it is a proper noun.

One train stopped; the other train kept going. [**the** is not capitalized]

Joaquin grilled two steaks; Dexter added a garnish of mushrooms.
[**Dexter** is always capitalized because it is a proper noun]

If you'd like to continue the train analogy, consider this: We know Comma Man isn't strong enough by himself to separate the two trains, but what would happen if he got into the cab of a semi? See the illustration on p. 532.

Exercise 23.4 | Using a Semicolon

Read each item carefully, and identify it as correct, run-on, or comma splice. Then fix any errors using a semicolon.

_____ 1. Ryan Gosling is an actor who has played a variety of characters from a cold-blooded killer to a devoted lover to a man obsessed with a life-size doll.

_____ 2. Like Justin Timberlake and Christina Aguilera, Gosling sang and danced on the *Mickey Mouse Club* he also appeared in a number of television shows.

_____ 3. In *Remember the Titans* he played a country music fan his roommate taught him to love Motown as well.

_____ 4. His portrayal of the faithful Noah in *The Notebook* made him a star three years later his roles in *Half Nelson* and *Lars and the Real Girl* won him critical acclaim.

_____ 5. In 2011 Gosling wowed audiences with his mysterious yet somehow heroic "driver" on a lighter note he taught comedian Steve Carell how to be a "player" in *Crazy, Stupid, Love.*

THE SEMICOLON PLUS CONJUNCTIVE ADVERB

When we use the semicolon to join two independent clauses, we are suggesting that the ideas are somehow related. We often choose to specify the nature of this relationship by adding an appropriate **conjunctive adverb**, such as *consequently, also, besides, moreover,* or *nevertheless.* As with the coordinating conjunctions, we want to choose an adverb that explains the connection between the two ideas (see Figure 23.2).

Figure 23.2   Selected Conjunctive Adverbs

Conjunctive Adverbs	...and their meanings
also, besides, furthermore, moreover	"and"
however, nevertheless, still	"but" or "yet"
accordingly, consequently, therefore, thus	"because"
also, likewise, similarly	"too"
otherwise	"or else"
finally, meanwhile, still, then	related to time

Copyright © 2015 Cengage Learning®

Look at the following examples:

One train stopped; **however**, the other train kept going.

Joaquin grilled two steaks; **next**, Dexter added a garnish of mushrooms.

© Golden Pixels LLC/Shutterstock.com

"Alicia studied diligently throughout the semester; *consequently*, she received high marks for the course."

The two clauses are actually *joined* by the semicolon. The adverbs describe the relationship between the clauses, but do not connect them. Therefore it is especially important to use the correct punctuation.

In general, when a conjunctive adverb is used, it follows the semicolon and is in turn followed by a comma.

Alicia studied diligently throughout the semester**; consequently**, she received high marks for the course.

However, the conjunctive adverb can be placed in either clause, depending on what it modifies. In fact, it can even be placed in the *middle* of a clause, as in this example:

One of the students in the class, **however**, did not make time to study; she had been focusing on the softball team.

Wherever the conjunctive adverb is placed, it is set off from the rest of the sentence by punctuation on either side.

Exercise 23.5 | Punctuating Sentences with Conjunctive Adverbs

Place a semicolon between the two independent clauses in each of the following sentences. Add commas as needed.

1. Everyone knows that the octopus has eight arms however some people might be surprised to learn of its intelligence.
2. The octopus exhibits several key traits of very smart animals, for example it solves problems.
3. Like dogs, chimpanzees, and humans, the octopus likes to play furthermore it has personality.
4. Scientists can measure whether an individual octopus is passive or shy they can even tell if it's a particularly emotional octopus.
5. An octopus has the ability to change the color and texture of its skin in response to its environment, in addition scientists believe these changes can also be triggered by its emotions.

THE SUBORDINATING CONJUNCTION

The final way we might choose to connect two related sentences is by using an appropriate **subordinating conjunction** or "coat hanger," such as *because, after, although, since, when,* and *while.* These conjunctions may be placed either between the two independent clauses, that is, the same place we've put the other corrections, or at the beginning of the first clause. Study the following examples:

> One train stopped, **while** the other kept going.

> **After** Joaquin grilled two steaks, Dexter added a garnish of mushrooms.

If the subordinating conjunction is placed between the two clauses, a comma is used only when the second clause is a contrast to the first, for example, if it's introduced with *while* or *although.* In general, however, no comma is required after the main clause:

> We ordered a large appetizer **because** we were very hungry.

> We ordered a large appetizer, **although** we weren't very hungry.

However, when the subordinating conjunction is placed at the beginning of the first clause (as in *After* Joaquin grilled the steaks, Dexter added a garnish of mushrooms), a comma should always be placed at the end. The waving hand signals the reader, "Look, here's the beginning of the main clause."

In choosing which subordinating conjunction to use, keep in mind both the word and its placement in the sentence in order to best explain to the reader the relationship between the two clauses. (See the list of subordinating conjunctions in Figure 22.1.) Note that the word *however* can occasionally be used as a subordinating conjunction rather than as a conjunctive adverb, as in the following sentence: *However* you look at it, English is a difficult language.

Exercise 23.6 | Using the Subordinating Conjunction

Read each sentence carefully, and identify it as correct, run-on, or comma splice. Then correct any errors using an appropriate subordinating conjunction and, if needed, additional punctuation.

_____ 1. The storeroom is an important place for students to visit it contains much of the information that they need to judge the quality of fresh ingredients.

_____ 2. Students study pictures of fruits and vegetables in books they can touch and smell the produce in the storeroom.

_____ 3. Sometimes students are surprised by the many unfamiliar kinds of mushrooms, peppers, and salad greens that are available.

_____ 4. Students learn about such varieties as Thai bird chilis and enoki mushrooms, they explore the treasures of the storeroom.

_____ 5. Students take tests that require them to identify specific varieties, they should study in the storeroom.

We've practiced several different ways of joining independent clauses correctly. In your own work, of course, you will choose whatever methods fit your purpose and style. For example, shorter sentences might be connected with a coordinating or subordinating conjunction to create a more fluid and interesting rhythm. Longer sentences, on the other hand, might be more clearly separated with a period. Semicolons give yet a different feel to the sentence, more formal and deliberate. If the relationship between two clauses is unclear or if it needs to be emphasized, use a specific conjunctive adverb.

RECIPE FOR REVIEW

IDENTIFYING RUN-ON SENTENCES AND COMMA SPLICES

To check whether a sentence is a run-on or a comma splice, read from the capital letter at the beginning to the period at the end. Find the subject and verb. Follow these steps:

1. Are there **two separate subject–verb** pairs in the sentence?

   If NO, go on to the next sentence.
   If YES, go to step 2.

2. Is there a **subordinating conjunction** (coat hanger) at the beginning of the sentence or between the clauses?

   If YES, this sentence is correct (but check that there's a comma preceding the coordinating conjunction). Go on to the next sentence.
   If NO, go to step 3.

3. Look at the place where the two clauses meet. Is there a **comma plus a FANBOY** or **a semicolon** at that point?

   If YES, the sentence is correct. Go on to the next sentence.
   If NO, go on to step 4.

4. Look again at the place where the two sentences meet. Draw a small box there.

   If there is nothing in that box, the sentence is a **run-on.**
   If there is a comma in that box, the sentence is a **comma splice.**

FIXING RUN-ON SENTENCES AND COMMA SPLICES

Run-on sentences and **comma splices** can be fixed in one of these four ways:

1. Put a **period** at the place where the two independent clauses meet, and **capitalize** the first letter of the next word.
2. Add a **comma** and a **FANBOY** at the place where the two clauses meet.

3. Put a **semicolon** at the place where the two independent clauses meet, or use a **semicolon**, a **conjunctive adverb,** and a **comma**.

4. Put a **subordinating conjunction** or coat hanger at the place where the two independent clauses meet, *or* put the coat hanger at the beginning of the sentence and add a comma at the end of the first clause.

CHAPTER QUIZ

DIRECTIONS: PART I. Read each item[a] carefully, and identify it as correct, run-on, or comma splice. Then correct the errors in any way you choose.

_____ 1. An important class for culinary students is Food Safety, it offers knowledge that will keep future customers safe.

_____ 2. Much of the information is common sense, especially for those with experience in the industry, some of the details concerning foodborne pathogens require careful study.

_____ 3. Food Safety keeps the customers safe Mathematics keeps the proprietors in business.

_____ 4. Introduction to Gastronomy offers an historical perspective on the industry it features lively discussion of current issues such as organic food, fast food, and slow food.

_____ 5. The composition courses develop students' ability to express themselves in writing, students may use these skills for business proposals, restaurant reviews, and cookbooks.

_____ 6. In one of the restaurant classes, students sit in blue bamboo chairs, the silverware is properly set on each table.

_____ 7. They are told to hold their noses as they taste the mystery food, it has a light, smoky sweet taste.

---

[a] Sentences 6-10 have been adapted from various student essays.

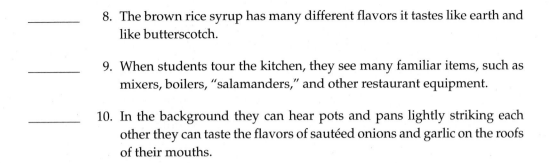

8. The brown rice syrup has many different flavors it tastes like earth and like butterscotch.

9. When students tour the kitchen, they see many familiar items, such as mixers, boilers, "salamanders," and other restaurant equipment.

10. In the background they can hear pots and pans lightly striking each other they can taste the flavors of sautéed onions and garlic on the roofs of their mouths.

DIRECTIONS: PART II. Correct the five sentence errors—a mix of run-ons and comma splices—in the following passage.[b]

Basil and rosemary are aromatic herbs with different scents, flavors, and textures they can be prepared and used in different ways.

Basil is an herb that is predominately used in Italian cuisine. The sweet flavor of the basil and the acidic tomato marry well together. When basil is added to a hot pot of tomato sauce, the aroma intensifies the mixture of sweet and savory is an amazing flavor combination. Basil is a hearty plant with delicate green leaves and white flowers. The leaves are the only thing on the plant that is edible. The best way to prepare the leaves is to tear them right before adding them to a dish, the tearing helps to prevent bruising to the leaf. Another good way to cut basil is to stack several leaves on top of each other, roll them up, and run the knife through. This process is called a chiffonade, which means thin strips of ribbon.

Rosemary is more of a hearty herb it resembles a pine tree but in a smaller version. Unlike that of basil, the taste of rosemary is pungent. It has more of an earthy flavor as opposed to sweet. Potatoes and poultry work well with rosemary because of their bland taste. The rosemary adds a strong boost of flavor to anything bland. The needles

[b] Material was adapted from essay by student writer Amber Ziembiec. The errors were added in order to create this quiz.

are the only edible portion of rosemary, they can be removed from the stem by pulling them down. Once they are removed, I would recommend finely chopping them due to the coarse texture of the leaves. Rosemary is often added to recipes in a sachet and then removed in order to get the flavor of the herb and not the texture. Another way to use rosemary would be to make a bouquet garni, which is a bundle of herbs tied together. This is used when the flavor of the herbs is infused in stocks and sauces.

Both rosemary and basil are easy to work with. The easy tips of preparation help in keeping the herbs fresh and flavorful. Although the two are different, they're both delicious and will enhance any dish over salt any day.

CHAPTER 24
SUBJECT–VERB AGREEMENT

After reading this chapter, you should begin to . . .

- identify the number and person of a noun or pronoun;
- apply the concept of number and person to subject–verb agreement;
- form the present tense of regular and irregular verbs, and the past tense of *to be;*
- make verbs agree with the subject of a sentence when it is a compound subject; an indefinite pronoun; a collective noun, title, or amount; or a singular noun ending in *-s;* and
- make subjects and verbs agree in sentences with inverted word order.

We know that every sentence needs a verb in order to be complete and that strong, specific verbs make our sentences more fluent and descriptive. We should also pay special attention to verbs as we check that our grammar and word usage is correct. In Chapter 22, we looked at sentence fragments and how to fix them, sometimes by adding or altering a verb. In Chapter 23, we used the identification of the subject and verb to fix run-on sentences and comma splices. In this chapter we'll examine how to use verbs correctly in the present tense and how to make them agree with their subjects. Then in Chapter 25 we'll study the principal parts of verbs, the remaining tenses, and the properties of voice and mood.

NUMBER AND PERSON

Both subjects and verbs have something called **number**; that is, the subjects refer either to one item (**singular**) or to more than one (**plural**), and the verb follows suit. For example, the subject of the sentence "The student relaxes in the gazebo" is singular: *student.* In contrast, the subject of the sentence "The students relax in the gazebo" is plural: *students.*Look at the subjects in the following list:

Singular	Plural
I paddle the canoe.	**We** paddle the canoe.
You paddle the canoe.	**You** paddle the canoe.
He paddles the canoe.	**They** paddle the canoe.
The vacationing chef paddles the canoe.	**The vacationing chefs** paddle the canoe.
Lydia paddles the canoe.	**Lydia and Caroline** paddle the canoe.

Subjects also have something called **person. First person** refers to the person who is speaking; it's the person through whose eyes we see the action, like the first-person shooter in a video game. The first-person pronouns are the singular *I* and the plural *we.* **Second person** refers to the person who is spoken to directly, *you.* English now has only one form for both singular and plural in the second person. In the past, however—as Spanish, French, and German, for example, do today—English had a special second-person singular pronoun, *thou.*

Third person refers to the person spoken *about* or seen from outside, like a third-person shooter. Third person includes the singular pronouns *he, she,* and *it,* as well as all singular nouns, such as *chef* and *Lydia.* Third person also includes nouns that refer to places, things, and ideas, such as *city, tomato,* and *friendship.* The third-person plural includes the pronoun *they* and all plural nouns, such as *chefs, cities,* and *tomatoes,* and compound subjects connected with *and,* such as *Lydia and Caroline.* Taken together, number and person create six categories or boxes (see Figure 24.1).

Canoeing in the Adirondack Mountains

Figure 24.1 Singular and Plural Subjects

	Singular	Plural
1st person	I	we
2nd person	you	you
3rd person	he, she, it chef, Lydia city, tomato excellence	they chefs, Lydia and Caroline cities, tomatoes [*no plural form*]

You can see that while the boxes for first and second person have only one word each, subjects in the third person come in many different shapes and sizes.

WHAT IS AGREEMENT?

When we're talking about subjects and verbs, **agreement** means that the form of the verb matches the subject's person and number. For example, the verb *cook* matches the pronoun *you*, but we need *cooks* to agree with *he*. Of course, in order to make the subject and verb "agree" we must first find them, as we did in Chapter 21. Remember, we're looking for the simple grammatical subject. Then we must decide whether the subject is singular or plural and whether it is in the first, second, or third person. That is, we must put the subject into one of the six boxes. Finally, we must choose the verb form that agrees with the subject in terms of number and person. In other words, a verb must be in the same box as its subject (see Figure 24.2).

Figure 24.2 Subject–Verb Agreement

	Singular	Plural
1st person	I *cook*	we *cook*
2nd person	you *cook*	you *cook*
3rd person	he, she, it *cooks* the vacationing chef *cooks* Lydia *cooks* the tomato *cooks*	they *cook* the vacationing chefs *cook* Lydia and Caroline *cook* the tomatoes *cook*

You can see that the form of the verb changes in only one of the boxes, the third-person singular. While the verbs in every other box use the base form *cook*, the verbs in the third-person singular box add an *s*, *cooks*. Note the possibility for confusion here. While most *nouns* form the *plural* by adding *s*, *verbs* form the third person *singular* by adding -*s* or -*es*. Don't make the mistake of thinking that verbs must end in *s* to be plural; in fact, the opposite is true. No plural verbs have an added *s*. Thus in most subject–verb pairs, only one of them can have that *s*. (There are exceptions, but we'll deal with them in a moment.) Look again at this pair of sentences:

The vacationing chef paddles the canoe.

The vacationing chefs paddle the canoe.

Only one gets the *s*, the subject or the verb. To remember which is which, keep in mind that the verb must agree with the subject, not the other way around. So if the subject is singular, the verb gets the *s*.

However, not all nouns form the plural by adding s, for example, *children*. In the sentence "The children relax in the gazebo," neither the subject *children* nor the verb *relax* ends in s. Further, some singular nouns end in s, and not all of them even have a plural form, for example, *news* (see Singular Nouns Ending in s later in this chapter). In the sentence "The news is good," both the subject *news* and the verb *is* end in s.

Subject–verb agreement is a topic filled with such issues and exceptions. One issue is that many dialects of *spoken* English use different rules for subject–verb agreement than formal *written* English does, and that's perfectly okay for speaking or informal writing. For professional or academic writing, however, we should follow the more formal usage. Another issue is that English contains both regular and irregular verbs. While the forms of regular verbs can be predicted, those of irregular verbs must be memorized individually.

VERB FORMS

All verbs have a **base form** or **stem**. To find it, take the infinitive phrase (*to cook* or *to toss*) and remove the *to*. For example, *cook* is the base form of *to cook*, and *toss* is the base form of *to toss*. To put a verb in the **present tense**—that is, to make the verb indicate that its action is occurring right now, in the present—we use either the base form (*cook, toss*) or the base form plus -*s* or -*es* (*cooks, tosses*). For **regular verbs**, like *cook* and *toss*, adding the suffix is straightforward. With **irregular verbs**, however, additional and unpredictable spelling changes occur.

The verbs *have* and *do* both use irregular forms in the third-person singular. We use the base form *have* in most situations: *I have, we have, you have, they have*. For the third-person singular, though, *have* drops the *ve* and adds *s: he has*. The irregular verb *to do* is similar: *I do, we do, you do, they do*. However, in forming the third-person singular, *do* adds the letter *e* along with the suffix -*s* and becomes *does*.

Most irregular is the verb *to be* (see Figure 24.3), which does not even use its base form in the present tense. Instead, it uses the unpredictable forms *am, are*, and *is*. Like regular verbs, irregular verbs have an ending with -*s* and an ending without -*s*, but we

Figure 24.3 The Irregular Verb *to be*

	Singular	Plural
1st person	I *am*	we *are*
2nd person	you *are*	you *are*
3rd person	he, she, it *is* chef *is* Lydia *is* tomato *is*	they *are* chefs *are* Lydia and Caroline *are* tomatoes *are*

will need to memorize the other changes that occur within the word. The verb *to be* also changes form in the past tense (see Figure 24.4).

Figure 24.4 The Past Tense of *to be*

	Singular	Plural
1st person	I *was*	we *were*
2nd person	you *were*	you *were*
3rd person	he, she, it *was* chef *was* Lydia *was* tomato *was*	they *were* chefs *were* Lydia and Caroline *were* tomatoes *were*

VERB PHRASES

As we saw in Chapter 20, many sentences contain verb phrases, that is, two or more words that act like a single word. For example, Samuel *is reading* his textbook, or Veronica *has planned* to visit bakeries in France. In such cases, the first helping verb in the phrase is the one that must agree with the subject. The other parts of the phrase do not change form. Consider the following examples:

Samuel **is reading** his textbook.

Samuel and Veronica **are reading** their textbooks.

The choice is between the singular *is* and the plural *are*. The rest of the verb phrase—*reading*—remains unchanged.

Note that only some of the helping verbs change form: *is/are, was/were, has/have, does/do*. Other helping verbs do not change form, whether they are used with singular or plural subjects: *can, could, did, had, may, might, must, should, will, should*. Compare the following examples:

Singular	Plural
Samuel *could read* the French menu.	Samuel and Veronica *could read* the French menu.
The waiter *must take* the drink order.	The waiters *must take* the drink orders.

MAKING VERBS AGREE

All this time, we've been talking about simply "finding the subject" as if that were the easy part of the job. Yet we remember from Chapter 21 that finding the subject of the sentence can be tricky. Once we find it, we must identify it as singular or plural. Then we make the verb "agree" by choosing the appropriate form.

WHEN SUBJECT AND VERB ARE SEPARATED

Sometimes prepositional phrases or other groups of words can come between the subject and verb and cause confusion. For example, consider the following sentence:

The host in the grey suit and shiny black shoes took the reservations.

In this example, there are three nouns before the verb: *host, suit,* and *shoes.* In looking carefully, we see that *suit* and *shoes* are both objects of the preposition *in* and therefore cannot be the subject. The word *reservations* later in the sentence is the object of the verb *took.* Thus when we ask "Who took the reservations?" the word *host* is the only possible answer and is, in fact, the subject of the sentence.

Similarly, the subject and verb may be separated by an entire clause, as in the following sentence:

The host, who was wearing a grey suit and shiny black shoes, took the reservations.

Here the relative clause *who was wearing a grey suit and shiny black shoes* may be bracketed off—it has its own subject, *who,* and its own verb, *was wearing.* That leaves *host* as the subject of the main clause and the verb *took.*

The **host**, [who was wearing a grey suit and shiny black shoes,] **took** the reservations.

The reason such phrases and clauses can cause confusion is that we instinctively want the verb to agree with the noun nearest to it. We must be aware, though, that the nearest *noun* is not necessarily the simple grammatical *subject* of the sentence.

Exercise 24.1 | When Subject and Verb Are Separated

Read each sentence carefully, identify the simple grammatical subject, and choose the verb that agrees with it.

1. Veronica, who is a student in baking and pastry arts, (plans/plan) to make a chocolate mousse cake for her project.
2. Her friend Samuel, on the other hand, (prefers/prefer) to try a soufflé.
3. The difficulty with soufflés (is/are) the possibility that they will collapse.
4. The purpose of these class projects (was/were) to experiment with a number of different recipes.
5. The students in Chef Vaughn's class (has/have) chosen popular desserts for their class projects.

WHEN THE SUBJECT IS COMPOUND

In Chapter 21 we also talked about **compound subjects**, two or more nouns or pronouns that are connected by *and, or,* or *nor* and share the same verb. When compound subjects are connected by *and*, they are treated as plural:

Samuel and Veronica like to make apple strudel. [no *-s* on *like*]

It's almost like a mathematical equation:

Samuel and Veronica   like [plural form]

1   +   1   =   more than one, or plural

One *tiny* exception is two nouns that are so often used together that they are treated as a unit, for example, *macaroni and cheese* or *rock and roll.* We wouldn't say "Macaroni and cheese *are* my favorite lunch." No, instead we would say "Macaroni and cheese *is* my favorite lunch." These exceptions are rare, however.

Exercise 24.2 | Compound Subjects with *and*

Read each of the following sentences, identify the subject, and choose the verb that agrees with it.

1. Samuel and Veronica (eats/eat) at the restaurant around the corner every Friday night.
2. Rock and roll (plays/play) softly in the background.
3. The salads and steaks (is/are) their favorite items on the menu.
4. The freshness of the greens and the originality of the house vinaigrette (makes/make) ordering the house salad a no-brainer.
5. Meanwhile, the steak and its caramelized onions (is/are) a special favorite of Veronica's.

Compound subjects may also be connected by *or* or *nor,* and here the rule is different. Let's look at the equation:

Samuel or Veronica   likes [singular verb]

1   or   1   =   1

But,

Samuel or his friends   likes or like?

1   or   2   =   ?

To clear up this confusion, a simple rule exists. When a compound subject is connected by *or* or *nor,* the verb agrees with the subject nearest to it. In the first example, *Veronica* is nearer to the verb, so it must take the singular form *likes.* In the second example, *friends* is nearer to the verb, which therefore takes the plural form *like:*

Samuel or his **friends like** to make apple strudel.

If the subjects were reversed, however, it would be a different matter:

His friends or **Samuel likes** to make apple strudel.

Because *Samuel* is closer to the verb, it takes the singular form *likes* (see Figure 24.5). However, in most cases where one subject is singular and the other plural, many writers choose to put the plural subject second, closer to the verb.

Figure 24.5 Agreement with Compound Subjects

Exercise 24.3 | Compound Subjects with *Or*

Read each of the following sentences and identify the subject. Then circle the verb that agrees with it.

1. Chocolate or vanilla (is/are) a possible frosting for this yellow cake.
2. Rainbow sprinkles or chocolate shavings also (looks/look) good on this dessert.
3. One large cake or individual cupcakes (has/have) been successful birthday treats.
4. Ice cream or whipped cream (makes/make) a good addition to any cake.
5. The guests or the birthday child (is/are) likely to complain if no cake at all is served.

WHEN THE SUBJECT IS AN INDEFINITE PRONOUN

Unlike the personal pronouns *he, she,* and *they,* **indefinite pronouns** refer to general rather than specific persons, places, or things and include *one, each, both, none, anything,* and *somebody* (see also Chapters 20 and 21). They are sometimes difficult to identify as the subject simply because they are general words and do not seem to carry the meaning of the sentence in the way that a subject like *the baker* would. But remember that the simple grammatical subject has to do with the *structure* of the sentence rather than with its meaning.

In terms of number, indefinite pronouns can be divided into three categories (see Figure 24.6). The largest group is **singular** and contains such words as *each, one, anything, anyone, anybody, everything, everyone, everybody, something, someone, somebody, nothing, nobody, either,* and *neither.* The very form of these words seems to refer to one "thing," not "things."

Each of the leading actors **is** effective.

One of the supporting actors **has** an especially difficult role.

Everything was ready for the shooting of the last scene.

Nobody was prepared for the film's success.

Neither of the screenwriters **expects** to win an Oscar.

The second group of indefinite pronouns is always **plural**: *both, few, several,* and *many.* These words clearly refer to more than one. *Both* means two, a *few* is

Figure 24.6 Agreement with Indefinite Pronouns

Number	Pronouns	Verbs	Number	Pronouns	Verbs
always singular	each one someone, somebody, something anyone, anybody, anything everyone, everybody, everything no one, nobody, nothing either, neither	is was does has cooks writes	always plural	both few several many	are were do have cook write
still singular, even with a prepositional phrase	each of the leading actors one of the supporting actors either of the directors neither of the screenwriters	is was does has cooks writes	still plural with a prepositional phrase	both of the movies several of the pastries	are were do have cook write

perhaps three, *several* is three to five, and *many* is probably more than five. For example:

Both of the movies **were** nominated for an Academy Award.

Few of the experts **predict** the comedy to win.

Several like the suspenseful and well-acted *Apollo 13.*

Many prefer the moving, fact-based *Philadelphia.*

The final group of indefinite pronouns can be **either singular** or **plural**, depending on their use in a given sentence: *all, any, more, most,* and *some.* To determine whether a pronoun is used as singular or plural, we must look for clues in the sentence or in the surrounding text. One of the most common places for such clues is in a prepositional phrase following the pronoun. Consider the following pair of sentences:

Most of the cake is decorated.

Most of the cakes are decorated.

The grammatical subject in both sentences is the indefinite pronoun *most.* Yet in the first sentence *most* refers to a single *cake* and takes the singular verb *is,* while in the second sentence *most* refers to many *cakes* and takes the plural form *are.* See Figure 24.7.

Figure 24.7 Agreement with Indefinite Pronouns, Singular or Plural

Singular Use	Singular Verb	Plural Use	Plural Verb
All of the bread	is gone.	All of the breads	are gone.
Most of the cake	is decorated.	Most of the cakes	are decorated.
Some of the story	was funny.	Some of the stories	were funny.

Exercise 24.4 | Making Verbs Agree with Indefinite Pronouns

Read each of the following sentences and identify the subject. Then choose the verb that agrees with it.

1. Most of the fans of *The Lord of the Rings,* a trio of novels by J.R.R. Tolkien, (was/were) looking forward to watching the movie.
2. Some of the tickets to the popular film series (was/were) sold in advance.
3. Yet some of the movie version (does/do) not follow the original story.
4. Despite these changes, most of the story (is/are) satisfying to many Tolkien fans.
5. Not all of the fans, however, (appreciates/appreciate) Peter Jackson's interpretation of the well-loved books.

Indefinite Pronouns—Singular or Plural?

Most of the cake *is* decorated.

Most of the cakes *are* decorated.

Copyright © 2015 Cengage Learning®

WHEN THE SUBJECT IS A COLLECTIVE NOUN, TITLE, OR AMOUNT

Collective nouns are words that name a group with several members, such as *audience*, *class*, *flock*, *jury*, and *team*. In American usage, collective nouns are most often treated as singular because the group is thought of as a unit. Even though more than one person is in the audience, for example, we would write "The audience *is* applauding enthusiastically." Study the following examples:

The basketball **team was** ranked number one in the poll.

The **board** of directors **has** decided to approve the budget.

The **flock** of sheep **was** sold at the end of the summer.

Note that in other dialects of English, such as British English, collective nouns are typically plural: The family *are* sitting down to breakfast. However, in American English, collective nouns are most often treated as singular: The family *is* sitting down to breakfast. On the rare occasion when we wish to highlight the individual members of the group, we may use a plural verb.

"The flock of sheep was sold at the end of the summer."

Collective nouns can be quite striking. We all know the *flock* of sheep, the *herd* of horses, even the *school* of fish. But are you familiar with the *flick* of rabbits, the *shiver* of sharks, the *rhumba* of rattlesnakes, or the *murder* of crows? And what about an *eloquence* of lawyers or a *sneer* of butlers?

Like collective nouns, specific **amounts**, whether of money, weight, time, or distance, are considered singular when the amount is treated as a unit. Study the following examples:

Three dollars was too much to pay for that cup of coffee.

Five pounds of sugar **is** needed for this recipe.

Six years seems like a long engagement.

Four miles is a good length for the dog's walk.

As with collective nouns, there are rare occasions when these concepts are considered plural. For example, in the sentence "Three dollars *are* lying on the table," we're thinking of three separate dollar bills.

Fractions and percentages take a singular verb when they refer to a singular item, and they take a plural verb when they refer to a plural item:

Two-thirds of the money was lost in a bad investment. [**money** is singular; **was** is singular]

Two-thirds of the tomatoes were ripe. [**tomatoes** is plural; **were** is plural]

Finally, **titles** of organizations, nations, books, or films always take a singular verb, even when they seem to be plural. For example, the United States is one political entity, although it consists of more than one state.

Simon & Schuster is a well-known publishing company.

The United States was fortunate in its first president.

***The Grapes of Wrath* has** been made into a film.

Exercise 24.5 | Collective Nouns, Titles, and Amounts

Read each of the following sentences, and identify the subject and the verb. If the verb does not agree, write in the correct form.

Example: _was_ The pack of dogs were running wild outside of town.

_____ 1. The men's basketball team at Duke University is often ranked among the top five teams in the nation.

_____ 2. Three-fourths of the birthday money were put into the bank.

_____ 3. The Netherlands are famous for growing magnificent tulips.

_____ 4. The jury were sequestered in a nearby hotel for the duration of the trial.

_____ 5. Ten dollars were too much to pay for that sandwich.

WHEN THE SUBJECT IS A SINGULAR NOUN ENDING IN -S

Some nouns that end in -s are actually singular and take a singular verb, for example, *economics, mathematics, measles, mumps,* and *news.* You don't get sick with a "mump." You don't turn on a "new" at six o'clock. Yet, although they end with -s, *mumps* and *news* both take a singular verb.

The mumps **is** a potentially serious disease for adolescent males.

The news concerning the storm's damage **remains** encouraging.

Mathematics **was** my favorite subject in high school.

Conversely, some other nouns that always end in -s and take a plural verb actually refer to single entities. Examples include *scissors, shears, tweezers, pants,* and *trousers:*

These scissors **seem** dangerously sharp.

The young chef's pants **were** too long.

WHEN THE WORD ORDER IS INVERTED

Finding the subject may be difficult in **inverted sentences**, that is, when the most common word order of subject followed by verb is reversed, as in questions or in sentences that begin with *There* or *Here.* Questions are frequently formed with a verb phrase that is split in two by the subject, making both harder to find.

Does that young man wish to order his dinner now?

One way to tackle such a question is to change it into a statement without dropping or changing any words: That young man does wish to order his dinner now. This change brings the two parts of the verb together—*does wish*—and puts the subject first, which is where we are more accustomed to finding it.

Sentences that begin with *There* or *Here,* even with a prepositional phrase, may also invert the order of subject and verb. Look at the following sentences:

There are many ways to cook chicken.

Here is a delicious recipe for *coq au vin.*

In the kitchen were three hot and tired chicken-loving chefs.

The initial *There* or *Here* will never be the subject, but it alerts us to the change in word order: the verb will come next or shortly thereafter and will be followed by the subject. In the first example, the verb is *are,* followed by the subject *ways.* In the second, the verb is *is,* followed by the subject *recipe.* Occasionally, a prepositional phrase will perform the same function of inverting the word order. The third of our examples begins with the prepositional phrase *In the kitchen,* followed by the verb *were,* and then by the subject *chefs.*

A further complication arises when a sentence with inverted word order begins with a contraction such as *Here's* or *There's. Here's = Here is. There's = There is.* With the verb partly concealed by the apostrophe, we may overlook the fact that it is singular, *is,* and we may therefore overlook a potential error in agreement. Study the following examples:

Here's a fresh scone. [*correct; the singular verb is agrees with scone*]

Here's some fresh scones. [*incorrect; the subject scones requires the plural verb*]

Here are some fresh scones. [*correct; the plural verb are agrees with scones*]

Exercise 24.6 | Inverted Word Order

Read each of the following sentences, and identify the subject and the verb. If the verb does not agree, write in the correct form.

Example: <u>has</u> There have been a series of changes to the menu.

_____ 1. There's few things more delicious than hot chocolate on a cold day.

_____ 2. Fortunately, there are many places you can find that delicious drink.

_____ 3. Do the news ever report special flavors of hot chocolate, such as peppermint or caramel?

_____ 4. Has the different varieties of hot chocolate made it a more popular drink?

_____ 5. Here's more reasons to choose hot chocolate.

RECIPE FOR REVIEW

FINDING THE SUBJECT

As you edit any piece of academic or business writing, you will want to check each sentence for correct **subject–verb agreement. First, find the simple grammatical subject,** keeping in mind the various confusions and exceptions:

1. Be careful of nouns in prepositional phrases or other clauses that look like the subject.
2. Compound subjects connected by *and* are treated as plural.
3. When a compound subject is connected by *or* or *nor*, the verb must agree with the nearest subject.
4. Indefinite pronouns come in three types—the large group that is always singular, the four words that are always plural, and the group that can go either way depending on what the pronoun refers to.
5. Some subjects appear plural but are treated as singular, such as collective nouns, titles, and measured amounts.
6. Watch out for irregular nouns ending in *-s.*
7. Take extra care with inverted word order in questions and in statements that begin with *There* or *Here*.

MAKING THE VERB AGREE

Second, check that the verb agrees with the simple grammatical subject. Singular subjects take verbs that end in *-s* or *-es*. Plural subjects take verbs without the suffix. Remember that only verbs in the present tense change form, with the exception of the past tense of *to be* (*was* and *were*).

CHAPTER QUIZ

DIRECTIONS: PART I. Read each of the following sentences, and identify the subject and verb. If the verb does not agree, write the correct form on the blank.

_____ 1. Each of the kitchens and restaurants has different menus and assignments.

_____ 2. The chefs from each class has to put their orders in to the storeroom three days in advance.

_____ 3. Without the storeroom, the kitchens cannot operate, and neither the chefs nor the students have anything to do.

_____ 4. In the storeroom, the bright colors and earthy scents of the produce create an inviting atmosphere.

_____ 5. Do the school use many different vendors for its food supply?

_____ 6. Some of the walk-ins has an indescribable cold smell.

_____ 7. Freshly picked grapes and a ripe pineapple sits on a small shelf near the door.

_____ 8. Jerusalem artichokes and Daikon radishes are stored in cardboard boxes.

_____ 9. There is sixty to seventy varieties of cheese in the refrigerator.

_____ 10. Like a beating heart, the storeroom pumps out food to all the kitchens at the college.

DIRECTIONS: PART II. Read each sentence in the following passage, and identify the subject and verb. If the verb does not agree, write the corrected sentence on a separate sheet of paper.

In the television series *The Closer,* C.I.A.-trained interrogator Brenda Leigh Johnson takes a new job as head of the Priority Homicide Division of the Los Angeles Police Department. The transition isn't easy, however. Many of the team members resent her taking over from their former boss, Captain Taylor. Others feel that she won't understand the unique environment of L.A. since she's from Atlanta. There's other difficulties as well, such as the demands she makes on her team and her personal relationship with the Chief of Police.

Brenda's first case is that of an unidentified woman who has been found in the home of a successful computer programmer. Captain Taylor and Lieutenant Flynn considers Brenda's presence at the crime scene especially annoying because she proceeds to explain what they've been doing wrong. In addition, the medical examiner resents being summoned to confirm that the seriously decomposed body is, in fact, dead. By the end of her second day on the job, all of the members of Brenda's team has requested transfer to another division.

Turner Network Television/Photofest © Turner Network Television Photographer: Richard Cartwright

In this scene from *The Closer,* the team begins to reevaluate "Miss Atlanta" after observing her interrogation of a suspect.

The hostility begins to abate, however, when the team observes Brenda's interrogation of the victim's innocent-looking secretary. It turns out that the victim is actually the computer programmer, a woman who has been living as a man in order to avoid being arrested on a murder charge in another state. She and the naïve secretary, who believes she is working for a man, has become romantically involved. But when "his" secretary discovers his true identity, she bashes him over the head, then shoot him in the face. Through a combination of cunning and compassion, Brenda elicits a confession from the distraught woman, and her team members begin to reevaluate "Miss Atlanta."

CHAPTER 25
MORE ABOUT VERBS

By the end of this chapter, you should begin to . . .

- identify the principal parts of verbs, particularly irregular verbs;
- use simple, perfect, and progressive tenses appropriately;
- avoid unnecessary shifts in tense;
- use the confusing verb pairs *lie/lay, rise/raise,* and *sit/set* correctly;
- understand active and passive voice, and use passive voice effectively; and
- recognize the subjunctive mood.

In the last chapter, we studied the forms of the present tense and the rules of subject–verb agreement. We're not done with verbs yet, though. Here, we will look at the principal parts or forms of verbs, common problems with verb tense, and the properties of voice and mood.

THE PRINCIPAL PARTS OF VERBS

As we saw in Chapter 24, verbs take different forms in order to show the time an action occurred and to agree with the subject of the sentence in person and number. These forms are built from the verb's **principal parts**: base form, past tense, past participle, and present participle. To find the **base form**, remove *to* from the infinitive; for example, the base form of *to cook* is *cook*. See Figure 25.1 for a summary of the principal parts of **regular verbs**.

Figure 25.1 Principal Parts of Regular Verbs

Verb Form	Formation	Example
infinitive	*to* + base form	*to cook*
present tense	base form (+ *s* in third-person singular)	*cook* *cooks*
past tense	base form + *ed*	*cooked*
present participle	base form + *ing*	*cooking*
past participle	base form + *ed*	*(have) cooked*

Irregular verbs take unpredictable forms. For example, study the frequently used but highly irregular forms of *to be* in Figure 25.2.

Figure 25.2 Principal Parts of the Irregular Verb *to be*

Verb Form	Example
infinitive	*to be*
present tense	*(I) am* *(we, you, they) are* *(he, she, it) is*
past tense	*(I, he, she, it) was* *(we, you, they) were*
present participle	*being*
past participle	*(have) been*

Exercise 25.1 | Using the Verb *to be*

Rewrite the following sentences, inserting the correct form of the verb *to be*.

1. Last week Jonathan and Dolores _____ having dinner at a new restaurant.

2. They had _____ dining at a different restaurant each Friday.

3. Dolores _____ a culinary student and plans to graduate in three months.

4. _____ a culinary student gives Dolores a unique perspective on their restaurant experience.

5. She hopes _____ a restaurant owner herself at some point.

We noted in Chapter 24 that *have* and *do* are also irregular verbs and, like *to be,* they have irregular forms (for example, in the present tense, I *have* but she *has*). Irregular verbs may also form the **past tense** and the **past participle** in unpredictable ways. They may replace the internal vowel(s) of the base form, such as *freeze* changing to *froze;* or they may add a *t,* such as *bend* changing to *bent;* or they may make more sweeping changes in the base form, such as *buy* changing to *bought.* Note that while most verbs use the same form for all persons in the past tense, the verb *to be* is an important exception. However, all verbs form the **present participle** by adding *–ing* to the base form (often dropping the final *e* first).

Figure 25.3 lays out the principal parts of some of the most common irregular verbs. The first column lists the base form, for example, *begin*. The present tense uses the base form, adding *s* for the third-person singular. You might read the base column as *Today we begin*. The second column shows the past tense: *Yesterday we began*. The third column displays the past participle, the form used to build the perfect tenses: *She has begun, We have begun*, or *We had begun*. (The tenses are explained in more detail later in the chapter.)

Remember that in standard written English, the rules for verb forms and for subject–verb agreement may be different from the rules you use when you speak informally. You might *say* "We begun to plan the menu yesterday," but in academic and business writing, it would be better to *write* "We began to plan." As you read through Figure 25.3, mark any verb forms that don't "sound right" to you. These might be the forms that give you trouble in formal writing tasks.

© Evok20/Shutterstock.com

Irregular (*cut*) and Regular (*taste*) Verbs: Today she cuts and tastes watermelon. Yesterday she cut and tasted watermelon. She has cut and tasted watermelon many times before.

Figure 25.3 Selected Irregular Verbs

Base	Past Tense	Past Participle
Today we …	*Yesterday we …*	*We have … before.*
bear	bore	(have) borne
beat	beat	(have) beaten or beat
become	became	(have) become
begin	began	(have) begun
bend	bent	(have) bent
bite	bit	(have) bitten
bleed	bled	(have) bled
blow	blew	(have) blown
break	broke	(have) broken
bring	brought	(have) brought
build	built	(have) built
burn	burned *or* burnt	(have) burned *or* burnt

(continued)

Figure 25.3 Selected Irregular Verbs *(continued)*

Base *Today we ...*	Past Tense *Yesterday we ...*	Past Participle *We have ... before.*
burst	burst	(have) burst
buy	bought	(have) bought
catch	caught	(have) caught
choose	chose	(have) chosen
come	came	(have) come
cost	cost	(have) cost
creep	crept	(have) crept
cut	cut	(have) cut
deal	dealt	(have) dealt
dig	dug	(have) dug
dive	dived *or* dove	(have) dived
do	did	(have) done
draw	drew	(have) drawn
drink	drank	(have) drunk
drive	drove	(have) driven
eat	ate	(have) eaten
fall	fell	(have) fallen
feed	fed	(have) fed
feel	felt	(have) felt
fight	fought	(have) fought
fly	flew	(have) flown
forbid	forbade *or* forbad	(have) forbidden
forget	forgot	(have) forgotten *or* forgot
freeze	froze	(have) frozen
get	got	(have) got *or* gotten
give	gave	(have) given
go	went	(have) gone
grind	ground	(have) ground
grow	grew	(have) grown
hang (a picture)	hung	(have) hung
hang (a person)	hanged	(have) hanged
have	had	(have) had
hear	heard	(have) heard
hide	hid	(have) hidden

(continued)

Figure 25.3 Selected Irregular Verbs *(continued)*

Base	Past Tense	Past Participle
Today we ...	*Yesterday we ...*	*We have ... before.*
hold	held	(have) held
hurt	hurt	(have) hurt
keep	kept	(have) kept
knit	knit *or* knitted	(have) knit *or* knitted
know	knew	(have) known
lay	laid	(have) laid
lead	led	(have) led
leave	left	(have) left
lend	lent	(have) lent
let	let	(have) let
lie	lay	(have) lain
light	lighted *or* lit	(have) lighted *or* lit
lose	lost	(have) lost
make	made	(have) made
mean	meant	(have) meant
meet	met	(have) met
mistake	mistook	(have) mistaken
pay	paid	(have) paid
prove	proved	(have) proven *or* proven
put	put	(have) put
quit	quit	(have) quit *or* quitted
read (pronounced *reed*)	read (pronounced *red*)	(have) read (pronounced *red*)
ride	rode	(have) ridden
ring	rang	(have) rung
rise	rose	(have) risen
run	ran	(have) run
say	said	(have) said
see	saw	(have) seen
sell	sold	(have) sold
send	sent	(have) sent
set	set	(have) set
sew	sewed	(have) sewn *or* sewed
shake	shook	(have) shaken
shine	shone *or* shined	(have) shone *or* shined

(continued)

Figure 25.3 Selected Irregular Verbs *(continued)*

Base	Past Tense	Past Participle
Today we …	*Yesterday we …*	*We have … before.*
shoot	shot	(have) shot
show	showed	(have) shown *or* showed
shut	shut	(have) shut
sing	sang	(have) sung
sink	sank *or* sunk	(have) sunk
sit	sat	(have) sat
sleep	slept	(have) slept
slide	slid	(have) slid
sow	sowed	(have) sown *or* sowed
speak	spoke	(have) spoken
speed	sped *or* speeded	(have) sped *or* speeded
spend	spent	(have) spent
stand	stood	(have) stood
steal	stole	(have) stolen
stick	stuck	(have) stuck
sting	stung	(have) stung
stink	stank *or* stunk	(have) stunk
strike	struck	(have) struck *or* stricken
swear	swore	(have) sworn
swim	swam	(have) swum
swing	swung	(have) swung
take	took	(have) taken
teach	taught	(have) taught
tear	tore	(have) torn
tell	told	(have) told
think	thought	(have) thought
throw	threw	(have) thrown
understand	understood	(have) understood
wake	woke *or* waked	(have) woken/waked/woke
wear	wore	(have) worn
weave	wove *or* weaved	(have) woven *or* weaved
weep	wept	(have) wept
win	won	(have) won
wind	wound	(have) wound
write	wrote	(have) written

Exercise 25.2 | Irregular Verbs

On a separate sheet of paper, write the correct form of the verb in parentheses.

Example: Susan <u>has driven</u> (drive) across the United States several times.

1. Susan's husband Paul has _____ (come) to enjoy these cross-country trips; he _____ (come) on the trip to Bermuda two years ago.

2. Last year they _____ (choose) to travel during the winter; they had _____ (choose) to travel in the summer the year before.

3. Paul's hands _____ (freeze) one night when he had to change a tire, kneeling on the mud that had _____ (freeze) earlier.

4. To warm up, they _____ (go) into a diner where they had _____ (go) two years earlier.

5. Jessica _____ (drink) a cup of hot chocolate flavored with peppermint, a beverage she has _____ (drink) in a number of different restaurants.

VERB TENSES

Verb tense has to do with time—past, present, and future—and whether an action or condition has been completed or is continuing.

THE SIMPLE TENSES

Let's look at a timeline of the **simple tenses**. The present tense is in the middle of the line, the past on the left, and the future on the right.

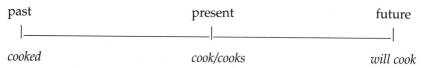

The **present tense** describes an action that is happening or a condition that exists now, in the present. For example, Annabella *cooks* a risotto for dinner, or Annabella's kitchen *is* full of mouthwatering aromas. The present tense also describes an often-repeated action: Annabella *cooks* a risotto every Sunday. When writing about a book or a film, we typically describe the action in the present tense, called the **literary present**: Sam Gamgee *cooks* a pair of rabbits for himself and Frodo in *The Lord of the Rings*. Or, in *To Kill a Mockingbird*, Scout and Jem *are* attacked as they walk home through the woods. It's as if the story happens for the first time each time we read or watch it, or as if it's always happening; therefore, the present tense seems appropriate.

The **past tense** describes an action that occurred in the past or a condition that existed in the past. Regular verbs form the past tense by adding –*ed* or –*d* (*cooked* or *baked*) to the verb base. (See Figure 25.3 for irregular verb forms.) Annabella *cooked* risotto for her grandmother, or Annabella's kitchen *was* full of mouthwatering aromas. The **future tense** is formed with the helping verb *will* plus the base form of the verb and describes an action that is to take place at some time in the future. For example, Annabella *will cook* risotto for her grandmother again next week, or Annabella's kitchen *will be* full of mouthwatering aromas when she cooks on Sunday.

THE PERFECT TENSES

The **perfect tenses** indicate that an action has been completed or that a condition still exists. Because it's finished, an action in a perfect tense precedes an action in the corresponding simple tense. For example, Before I *cooked* the meatloaf yesterday, I *had made* the recipe several times before. Or, I *made* meatloaf for my dinner guests yesterday only after I *had made* it several times for the family. Words like *before* and *after* often suggest a change in tense.

The three simple and three perfect tenses are positioned on the timeline as follows:

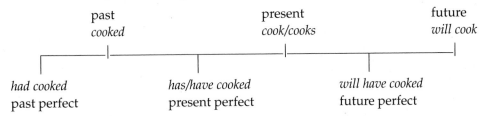

Note that the "perfect" action precedes the "simple" action in each time frame. When two actions occurred in the past but one was completed before the other, we use the **past perfect tense** for the first one. The past perfect is formed with *had* + past participle. For example, Annabella *had cooked* risotto for her grandmother long before she *worked* at the restaurant. Both actions occurred in the past, but one (cooking the risotto) was completed before the other (working at the restaurant). Review the following examples:

Yesterday I bought a steak and mushrooms for dinner. I **had picked** some tomatoes in the garden the day before. [That is, I picked the tomatoes *before* I bought the steak. We need the perfect tense.]

Yesterday I bought a steak and mushrooms for dinner. Then I **picked** some tomatoes in the garden. [That is, I picked the tomatoes in the same time frame as I bought the steak. We do *not* need the perfect tense.]

I saw that there was a long line for the movie. Fortunately I **had** already **bought** tickets. [I bought the tickets *before* I saw the line for the movie. We need the past perfect.]

I saw that there was a long line for the movie. Eventually I **bought** tickets. [I bought the tickets in the same time frame as seeing the line. We do *not* need the past perfect.]

If one action follows another, use the simple past. Use the past perfect only for an action that was completed before the timeline of the other actions described in the simple past. Avoid using the past perfect in place of the simple past; that is, do not add *had* to the verb unless the situation requires the past perfect tense.

The **future perfect tense** is formed with *will have + past participle* and expresses an action or condition that will be completed before another action in the future. For example, Annabella *will have cooked* risotto many times before she begins her new job at the restaurant. Finally, the **present perfect tense** describes an action that occurred or a condition that existed at some indefinite time in the past. For example, Annabella *has cooked* risotto on many occasions. The present perfect may also describe an action or condition that began in the past and continues up until or into the present: Annabella *has begun* to make risotto at work (and may be doing so still).

Exercise 25.3 | Choosing the Appropriate Tense

Choose the correct tense in each pair of verbs in parentheses.

1. Yesterday's basketball game, the last of the season, (was/has been) an exciting one.
2. Joe, who (will be/has been) an inconsistent player for several weeks now, finally began to make good decisions.
3. He stole the ball three times and then (hit/had hit) a series of free throws.
4. Mike made a beautiful pass to Bill, who then unfortunately (missed/will have missed) the shot.
5. Until that point, Bill (had missed/will miss) less than 40% of his shots.

THE PROGRESSIVE TENSES

The six tenses just outlined may also be **progressive** or continuous; that is, they may indicate that the action was, is, or will be continuing. Study the following examples:

- The **past progressive** is formed with *was/were* + present participle: *Vanessa was chopping nuts for the biscotti.* The chopping was a continuous action in the past, but did not move into the present.
- The **present progressive** is formed with *is/are* + present participle: *Vanessa is chopping nuts for the biscotti.* The chopping began earlier and is still going on.
- The **future progressive** is formed with *will be* + present participle: *Vanessa will be chopping nuts for the biscotti.* She hasn't started yet, but the action will continue for an indefinite length of time in the future.

The perfect tenses also have progressive forms:

- The **past perfect progressive** is formed with *had been* + present participle: *Vanessa had been chopping nuts for the biscotti all day.* The action continued for an indefinite period of time in the past, but was completed before another action in the past.

- The **present perfect progressive** is formed with *has/have been* + present participle: *Vanessa **has been chopping** nuts for the biscotti since 10 o'clock this morning.* She began chopping earlier and continues to chop now.
- The **future perfect progressive** is formed with *will have been* + present participle: *By the time we arrive at 11 o'clock, Vanessa **will have been chopping** nuts for one hour.* The action begins in the future, continues for a period of time, and ends before the start of another action in the future.

Certain verbs are rarely used in the progressive, most of which refer to a mental activity rather than to an action in space: *appear, believe, belong, contain, have, hear, know, like, need, see, seem, taste, think, understand,* and *want.* Consider these examples:

Sarah is wanting to bake a perfect angel food cake. *[incorrect]*

Sarah wants to bake a perfect angel food cake. *[correct]*

Exercise 25.4 | Using the Progressive Tenses

Select the appropriate form of the verb in the following sentences.

1. Rosanna (was shopping/is shopping) at the mall all day yesterday.
2. She (was wanting/wanted) to find a special dress for the Valentine's Day party.
3. Her friend Lara also (is needed/needs) a new dress.
4. Lara (will be joining/will have been joining) Rosanna tomorrow for another shopping trip.
5. By tomorrow, Rosanna (was looking/will have been looking) for a dress for two weeks.

AVOIDING UNNECESSARY SHIFTS IN TENSE

One of the most common problems with verb tense is inconsistency, that is, shifting randomly back and forth from the past to the present. Often a story or an essay could be written in either tense. However, once we've made that basic decision, we should generally stay with it and not shift between the two time frames. Study the following example:

Yesterday Mark **went** to the store, where he **bought** a dozen eggs and a gallon of milk. Then he **picks** up a loaf of bread and **took** the items to the checkout line.

Within the flow of these sentences, the present tense *picks* stands out like a cornstalk in a row of cabbages. It's as if *went, bought,* and *took* are on one side of a brick wall and *picks* is on the other. In fact, it can be helpful to think of tenses in relation to this brick wall. For each writing task, make a decision whether to use the past or present tense, that is, whether to choose the left or the right side of the wall. Once you've made that first choice, you must continue to select verbs from the same side of the wall.

Occasionally, though, an event will fall outside the main stream of the story's timeline. Let's go back to Mark and his trip to the store:

> Yesterday Mark **went** to the store. He **bought** a dozen eggs and a gallon of milk. In fact, he **buys** a dozen eggs every week. Then Mark **paid** the cashier.

In this second scenario, the present tense *buys* is correct. The fact that Mark buys a dozen eggs every week is not in the same time sequence as the specific purchases he made yesterday. There's a door in the brick wall, and on occasions like Mark's weekly purchase of a dozen eggs, we have the key to open that door.

Exercise 25.5 | Avoiding Unnecessary Shifts in Tense

Rewrite the following paragraph,* changing verbs when necessary to maintain consistent tense. First put all the verbs in the present tense; then put them all in the past. Which do you prefer? Why?

> You walk into Roth Hall and were able to notice right away that the atmosphere from outside to inside is completely different. The light was soft and very dim. I automatically felt comfortable and warm when I step inside. As we walked further down the hall, it becomes less active and more subtle. I notice the smell of breads and other oven-baked products from the kitchen. The front of the hall didn't really have a smell. The floor was made for walking in any type of shoes that you wanted to. The walls were made of brick and give us a very comfortable feeling.

> * Adapted from an essay by Yolanda Dillard. The errors were added to create this exercise.

CONFUSING VERBS

Lie and *lay* are two words that are often confused with one another. They look and sound like each other and even share the form *lay*. *Lie* means to be in or to assume a prone position, as in *to lie down*. For example, The cloth *lies* smoothly on the table, or The baby *lies* in her crib. *Lie* cannot take a direct object; you can't lie "something." *Lay*, on the other hand, does take a direct object; it means to place or put something somewhere, as in *to lay something down*. For example, The server *lays* the cloth smoothly on the table, or The babysitter *lays* the baby in her crib (*cloth* and *baby* are the direct objects).

Let's look at it this way. In this context, *lay* means *put*. Therefore, if you can't substitute the word *put*, you should most likely use *lie* rather than *lay*. Take the sentence "The bone is laying on the floor." It wouldn't make sense to say "The bone is *putting*

Figure 25.4 *Lay* vs. *Lie*

The dog **lays** the bone on the floor.   The bone **lies** on the floor.

on the floor," so we need *lying* rather than *laying*. See Figure 25.4. The fact that the past tense of *lie* and the present tense of *lay* look the same adds to the potential for misunderstanding. Study Figure 25.5. Most errors in the use of *lie* and *lay* occur when forms of *lay* are used with the meaning of *lie*. Note that while *lie*'s past tense is identical to *lay*'s present tense, no form of *lie* ends in –*d*. Do not use *laid* unless something is being put down: I *laid* the book on the table.

Another pair of confusing verbs is *rise* and *raise*. *Rise* is used for items that move up on their own, like the sun; *rise* doesn't take an object. For example, The sun *rises* every morning. *Raise*, on the other hand, is used with direct objects and means to bring or put up. The cadet *raises* the flag every morning. Study the forms and examples in Figure 25.6.

Figure 25.5 *Lie* and *Lay*

	to lie *(down)*	to lay *(something down)*
present tense	*lie/lies* The cloth *lies* smoothly on the table.	*lay/lays* The server *lays* the cloth smoothly on the table.
past tense	*lay* The cloth *lay* on the table yesterday.	*laid* The server *laid* the cloth on the table yesterday.
past participle	*lain* The cloth *has lain* smoothly on the table many times.	*laid* The server *has laid* the cloth smoothly on the table many times.
present participle	*lying* The cloth *is lying* smoothly on the table.	*laying* The server *was laying* the cloth smoothly on the table.

Figure 25.6 *Rise and Raise*

	to rise *(up on its own)*	to raise *(something up)*
present tense	*rise/rises* The internal temperature *rises* as the chicken cooks.	*raise/raises* You *raise* the temperature of the chicken by cooking it.
past tense	*rose* The internal temperature *rose* as the chicken cooked.	*raised* You *raised* the temperature of the chicken by cooking it.
past participle	*risen* The internal temperature *has risen* as the chicken cooked.	*raised* You *have raised* the temperature of the chicken by cooking it.
present participle	*rising* The internal temperature *is rising* as the chicken cooks.	*raising* You *are raising* the internal temperature of the chicken by cooking it.

A third pair of bewildering verbs is *sit* and *set*. *Sit* means to assume a seated position and does not take an object. (There's an exception when *sit* is used in the sense of *seat*, to cause someone to assume a seated position, for example, sit yourself down, or the theatre sits five hundred people.) For example, The students *sit* at narrow desks. In contrast, *set* means to put or place something somewhere; that is, it takes a direct object. For example, The students *set* their books down on their desks. Note that *set* has only one form for the present tense, past tense, and past participle. Use *set* only with the meaning to set something down. Otherwise, use *sit* or *sat*. See Figure 25.7.

Figure 25.7 *Sit and Set*

	to sit *(on something)*	to set *(something down)*
present tense	*sit/sits* Every day the diners *sit* at the wooden table.	*set/sets* Every day the servers *set* the table for dinner.
past tense	*sat* Yesterday the diners *sat* at the wooden table.	*set* Yesterday the servers *set* the table for dinner.
past participle	*sat* The diners *have sat* at the wooden table many times before.	*set* The servers *have set* the table for dinner many times before.
present participle	*sitting* The diners *are sitting* at the wooden table.	*setting* The servers *are setting* the table for dinner.

Note that *set* can also mean to harden or solidify, as in Let the Jell-O *set* in the refrigerator overnight. In this context, *set* does not take a direct object.

Exercise 25.6 | Choosing the Correct Verb

Choose the correct verb in each of the following sentences.

1. The terrier circled his bed three times and (lay/laid) down on the soft flannel.
2. After bustling about the dining room all evening, the server (sat/set) down and drank a glass of water.
3. The temperature typically (rises/raises) after the morning fog disappears.
4. The secret to the movie's success (lies/lays) in its exotic locations and thrilling action sequences.
5. When she (lay/laid) out the good china, she accidentally broke a plate.

ACTIVE AND PASSIVE VOICE

The concept of **voice** has to do with who or what is *performing* the action of the verb and who or what is *receiving* the action. In the **active voice**, the subject of the sentence is active; that is, the subject is performing the action of the verb.

> The chef **whisked** the eggs for the Greek omelet. [The subject, *chef*, is actively doing the whisking.]

In the **passive voice**, the subject of the sentence is *receiving* the action.

> The eggs **were whisked** for the Greek omelet. [The subject, *eggs*, is passively receiving the whisking.]

Look at Figure 25.8. Here the focus is on the eggs, not the person whisking them: The eggs *were whisked*. If we wished to include the information that the chef performed the action, we could say The eggs were whisked *by the chef*, but the focus is still on the eggs.

Verbs in the passive voice use a form of *to be* plus an appropriate participle. For the

Figure 25.8 *"The eggs were whisked for the Greek omelet."*

© Marina Dyakonova/Shutterstock.com

Figure 25.9 The Simple Tenses

Verb/Tense	Active Voice	Passive Voice	Forming the Passive Voice
whisk/present	*whisk/whisks* The chef *whisks* the eggs.	*is/are whisked* The eggs *are whisked* by the chef.	present tense of *to be* + past participle of *whisk*
whisk/past	*whisked* The chef *whisked* the eggs.	*was/were whisked* The eggs *were whisked* by the chef.	past tense of *to be* + past participle of *whisk*
whisk/future	*will whisk* The chef *will whisk* the eggs.	*will be whisked* The eggs *will be whisked* by the chef.	future tense of *to be* + past participle of *whisk*

Copyright © 2015 Cengage Learning®

simple tenses—present, past, and future—the passive voice employs the past participle. See Figure 25.9. For the perfect tenses, the passive voice employs a form *to have*, the past participle of *to be* (that is, *been*), and the past participle of the main verb. See Figure 25.10. For the progressive tenses, the passive voice employs a form of *to be*, the present participle of *to be* (that is, *being*), and the past participle of the main verb. See Figure 25.11.

In general, the active voice cuts out unnecessary words and adds life to your writing. Look at the difference between these two sentences:

PASSIVE: The baguettes were taken out of the oven by Katie.

ACTIVE: Katie took the baguettes out of the oven.

While it isn't incorrect to use the passive voice, we want to be sure the passive is nicely balanced with the active. Long strings of passive sentences can drain the energy from your writing.

Figure 25.10 The Perfect Tenses

Verb/Tense	Active Voice	Passive Voice	Forming the Passive Voice
whisk/present perfect	*has/have whisked* The chef *has whisked* the eggs.	*has/have been whisked* The eggs *have been whisked* by the chef.	present tense of *to have* + *been* + past participle of *whisk*
whisk/past perfect	*had whisked* The chef *had whisked* the eggs.	*had been whisked* The eggs *had been whisked* by the chef.	past tense of *to have* + *been* + past participle of *whisk*
whisk/future perfect	*will have whisked* The chef *will have whisked* the eggs.	*will have been whisked* The eggs *will have been whisked* by the chef.	future tense of *to have* + *been* + past participle of *whisk*

Copyright © 2015 Cengage Learning®

Figure 25.11 The Progressive Tenses

Verb/Tense	Active Voice	Passive Voice	Forming the Passive Voice
whisk/present progressive	*is/are whisking* The chef *is whisking* the eggs.	*is/are being whisked* The eggs *are being whisked* by the chef.	present tense of *to be* + *being* + past participle of *whisk*
whisk/past progressive	*was/were whisking* The chef *was whisking* the eggs.	*was/were being whisked* The eggs *were being whisked* by the chef.	past tense of *to be* + *being* + past participle of *whisk*
whisk/future progressive	*will be whisking* The chef *will be whisking* the eggs.	*will be whisked* The eggs *will be whisked* by the chef.	future tense of *to be* + *being* + past participle of *whisk*

*In the passive voice, the simple future is more commonly used than a future progressive form.

There are some occasions, however, when the passive voice is preferred. For example, you may wish to highlight the recipient of the action or you may not know who or what performed the action, as in these examples:

> The delighted customer was offered a choice between two complimentary desserts. [The emphasis is on the recipient of the action; we don't care who made the offer.]

> The expensive laptop was stolen from his car. [We don't know who performed the action.]

Sometimes we know who performed the action, but we'd like to avoid naming the person. For example, "A mistake was made in the Accounting Department." By avoiding a specific accusation, the passive here softens the blow, perhaps allowing the reader to understand and accept the information more readily.

Exercise 25.7 | The Passive Voice

Each of the following sentences uses the passive voice. Rewrite each one in the active voice. Then explain which you prefer, and why.

1. The delicate wine glass was broken by the inexperienced server.
2. A three-point shot was made at the buzzer by the phenomenal freshman.
3. The lead guitar in Pink Floyd is played by David Gilmour.
4. A copy of the keys will be made by each new tenant.
5. An essay about the perils of drunk driving was written by the man convicted three times of driving while intoxicated.

THE SUBJUNCTIVE MOOD

We probably don't think of grammar as having any emotion—yet it does have moods! The **indicative mood** reflects an ordinary, everyday mood; verbs in the indicative mood tell or ask without suggesting any hidden meaning. The large majority of our sentences are in the indicative mood. Second, the **imperative mood** is used to give orders or commands, for example, "Sharpen your knife" or "Add the egg whites now." Note that the subject of a command is understood to be *you*. You are the one to add the egg whites. The imperative mood occurs frequently in spoken English and is used extensively in a most familiar publication—the cookbook.

Finally, there is the **subjunctive mood**, which is used mostly in formal situations to talk about a wish or to make a statement that is not factual. The subjunctive is typically used with *were* and *be*. Study the difference between these two sentences:

> If the bell *rings* before we finish the story, we will finish it tomorrow. [*rings* is in the indicative mood; it is possible for the bell to ring]

> If the bell *were to ring* now, it would interrupt the test. [*were to ring* is in the subjunctive mood; the bell is unlikely to ring]

This form of the subjective mood uses *were* in all cases, singular or plural: I were (not *was*), you were, he/she/it were (not *was*), we were, you were, they were.

> If I *were* you, I wouldn't stir that sauce so vigorously. [Use the subjunctive mood because I am *not* you.]

Another form of the subjunctive uses *be* instead of the regular verb forms: I be, you be, he/she/it be, we be, you be, they be. *Be* is used in certain formal structures, for example, in clauses following words such as *advise, ask, recommend, request,* and *suggest.*

> Jack's supervisor recommended that he *be given* another chance.

> Jill advises that the bell *be rung* ten minutes before closing.

Exercise 25.8 | The Subjunctive Mood

Read each sentence carefully. If the underlined verb in the sentence is correct, write the letter C on the line. If the subjunctive mood is required, write the appropriate form (*be* or *were*) on the line.

_____ 1. The doctor recommended that the x-ray <u>was</u> repeated.

_____ 2. If it <u>rains,</u> Grandma will take down the clothes that are hanging out to dry.

_____ 3. If I <u>was</u> you, I would take those cookies out of the oven.

_____ 4. Jane would be thrilled if Bingley <u>was</u> to propose to her.

_____ 5. Jane's mother suggested that Bingley <u>be</u> invited to dinner.

RECIPE FOR REVIEW

VERB FORMS

1. Regular verbs use predictable forms for their tenses and participles (Figure 25.1).
2. Irregular verb forms are unpredictable and must be memorized (Figures 25.2 and 25.3).

CHOOSING THE APPROPRIATE TENSE

1. Use the **past tense** for action that happened or a condition that existed in the past.
2. Use the **present tense** for action that is happening now or is often repeated, as well as to describe the action in a book or film.
3. Use the **future** for action that is to take place in the future.
4. Use the **past perfect** when one action in the past was completed before another.
5. Use the **present perfect** for an action that occurred or a condition that existed at some indefinite time in the past.
6. Use the **future perfect** for an action that will be completed before another time in the future.

Tense	Example
past	Annabella **cooked** risotto for her grandmother last week.
present	Annabella **cooks** a risotto every Sunday.
future	Annabella **will cook** risotto for her grandmother again next week.
past perfect	Annabella **had cooked** risotto for her grandmother long before she worked at the restaurant.
present perfect	Annabella **has cooked** risotto on many occasions.
future perfect	Annabella **will have cooked** risotto many times before she begins her new job at the restaurant.

USING THE PROGRESSIVE TENSES

Each of the six tenses has a **progressive** form, which indicates that the action is continuing. The past, present, and future construct the progressive with a form of *to be* plus the present participle (*—ing*). The perfect tenses form the progressive with a form of *to have* plus the present participle.

AVOIDING UNNECESSARY SHIFTS IN TENSE

If you begin a story in the past tense, keep your verbs in the past. Similarly, if you begin a story in the present tense, keep your verbs in the present. Remember the brick wall. However, if a single action takes place out of the flow of events, choose the appropriate tense for that exception.

CONFUSING VERBS

Study the confusing verb pairs in Figures 25.4 and 25.5 (*lie* and *lay*), 25.6 (*rise* and *raise*), and 25.7 (*sit* and *set*).

ACTIVE AND PASSIVE VOICE

Do not allow long strings of **passive** sentences to creep into your writing. The **active voice** is often clearer and livelier.

THE SUBJUNCTIVE MOOD

Use the **subjunctive** form *were* to talk about a wish or make a statement that is not factual. Use *be* in clauses following *advise, ask, recommend, request, suggest.*

CHAPTER QUIZ

DIRECTIONS: PART I. Choose the correct verb in each pair of parentheses.

1. The charm of the movie *Star Trek* (lies/lays) in the liveliness and vulnerability of its characters.

2. Young Jim Kirk (had drank/had drunk) too much and started a fight at the bar.

3. Young Uhura also (had went/had gone) to the bar, where she met Kirk for the first time.

4. Young Spock had to (chose/choose) between a career on Vulcan or with the Federation.

5. When we went to the movies last night, we (see/saw) a double feature.

6. George likes to watch science fiction blockbusters while Catherine (prefers/preferred) quirky independent films.

7. Both the cat and the dog (are lying/are laying) on the sofa.

8. If I (was/were) a cat, I would hiss at the dog.

9. *Homicide: Life on the Street*, an Emmy-winning crime drama from the 1990s, had a gritty feel that (rang/rung) true with viewers.

10. In the first season, rookie Tim Bayliss requested that he (was/be) assigned to the case of a 12-year-old girl named Adena Watson.

DIRECTIONS: PART II. Read the following passage, and change the five verbs in the present tense to the past.

In a later season of *Homicide,* Bayliss and his partner Frank Pembleton were assigned to a unique murder case in which the "victim" was still alive. John Lange was on his way to work via the subway when he is pushed onto the tracks. Lange was wedged between the train and the platform, and his spinal cord was severely damaged. The paramedics on the scene tell Pembleton and Bayliss that Lange would bleed to death as soon as he was moved. The emotionally distant Pembleton responds to the dying man's questions and fears. Meanwhile, Bayliss concentrated on a witness who was behaving oddly. The man was mentally ill and intentionally pushed Lange off the platform. During this time Detectives Lewis and Falsone are trying to find Lange's girlfriend, without success. As the medics prepared to move Lange, Pembleton kneels by his side. Things went badly. When the detectives emerged from the subway, they watched helplessly as the ambulance drove away.

CHAPTER 26
PRONOUNS AND POINT OF VIEW

By the end of this chapter, you should begin to . . .

- use the subjective, objective, and possessive cases appropriately;
- ensure that pronouns agree with their antecedents;
- maintain clear pronoun reference;
- use reflexive and intensive pronouns appropriately; and
- maintain appropriate and consistent point of view.

Pronouns are words that can substitute for nouns, often to avoid awkward repetition. For example, the following sentence sounds silly because *Lee* is repeated so often: "After *Lee* received *Lee's* instructions from *Lee's* sous chef, *Lee* transferred the noodles with *Lee's* tongs." The sentence is so bogged down with *Lee's* that we don't even know what Lee has been doing. By substituting appropriate pronouns for *Lee*, we can produce a sentence that sounds better and makes its point more clearly: "After Lee received *his* instructions from *his* sous chef, *he* transferred the noodles with *his* tongs."

"After Lee received his instructions from his sous chef, he transferred the noodles with his tongs."

© erwinova/Shutterstock.com

Although we can easily see the advantages of using pronouns, we should be careful to use them correctly in terms of case, agreement, reference, and point of view.

Let's keep this between you and **I**. *[incorrect case]*

Everyone was happy to receive **their** desserts. *[lack of agreement]*

Mike told Jack that **he** was lazy. *[unclear reference]*

Students will learn to make various emulsions; **you** might have trouble with hollandaise sauce. *[unnecessary shift in point of view]*

When you're editing a final draft, give the pronouns some extra attention.

USING PRONOUN CASES

In many languages, such as Spanish, French, and Italian, words change form to indicate the different jobs they perform in a sentence. English has lost many of these changes and relies more on word order, but these forms do remain to some degree in **case,** the name given to the different jobs (and corresponding forms) of nouns and pronouns. We'll look at the subjective, objective, and possessive cases, summarized in Figure 26.1.

Figure 26.1 Pronoun Cases

Cases of Singular Pronouns

Person	Subjective	Objective	Possessive
1st	I	me	my/mine
2nd	you	you	your/yours
3rd	he	him	his/his
	she	her	her/hers
	it	it	its/___

Cases of Plural Pronouns

Person	Subjective	Objective	Possessive
1st	we	us	our/ours
2nd	you	you	your/yours
3rd	they	them	their/theirs

THE SUBJECTIVE CASE

The **subjective case** is used for the subject of a sentence. In the sentence "He is intrigued by the concept of fusion cuisine," the subject *He* is in the subjective case. When pronouns stand alone like this, we tend to use them correctly in both informal conversation and formal writing. However, we sometimes use pronouns differently when they are part of a group of words connected by *and* or *or*. Here informal usage may conflict with the rules of standard written English. You may hear a sentence such as the following:

Me and her are planning to go to the movies this weekend. *[incorrect]*

Yet you wouldn't say "*Me* is planning to go to the movies" or "*Her* is planning to go to the movies." In formal usage, both pronouns should be in the subjective case. "*She* is planning to go to the movies" and "*I* am planning to go to the movies" both sound right. Keep the pronouns in the same case as you combine them:

She and I are planning to go to the movies this weekend. *[correct]*

Similarly, the subjective case is used with subjects of dependent clauses.

Harry is thrilled because **he** [not *him*] and his brother are vacationing in
Hawaii this year.

In this sentence, *he and his brother* is the compound subject of the dependent clause *because he and his brother are vacationing in Hawaii this year.* We would not say "*Him* is vacationing in Hawaii." Again, look at each pronoun separately to determine if it should be in the subjective case.

Finally, the subjective case is used with a pronoun that follows a linking verb, such as *is, are, was,* or *were*. Yet in casual conversation we might very well use the objective case, for example, *me* instead of *I*.

It's me. *[informal]*

It is I. *[formal]*

Linking verbs do not have objects, so the objective form *me* (described in the next section) is technically incorrect and would give a poor impression in academic and business writing, where we are expected to follow the rules for standard written English.

It was **I** [not *me*] who suggested the new menu item.

It was **they** [not *them*] who asked for a quote on the catering job.

THE OBJECTIVE CASE

The **objective case** is used with the objects of verbs (both direct and indirect) and prepositions. The **direct object** of a verb receives the action; it answers the question "Who or what received the action of the verb?" For example, in the sentence "Derek Jeter threw him the ball," *ball* is the direct object of the verb *threw. Him* is the **indirect object**, answering the question "To *whom* did Jeter throw the ball?"

If we consider each pronoun separately, we will most likely *hear* the correct case. Would you ever say "Loretta served I coffee"? No, that doesn't sound right. "Loretta served *me* coffee." But what if two people were served? You might *say* informally "Loretta served Harry and I coffee." However, once you check the pronoun by itself,

This time the coffee wasn't too sweet for Harry and me.

you'll *write* "Loretta served Harry and me coffee." We should also look carefully at the pronouns that follow prepositions. We would never *say* "The coffee was too sweet for I," but we *might* say "The coffee was too sweet for Harry and I." But if it's too sweet for *me,* then it's too sweet for *Harry and me.*

Let's look at some more examples. We wouldn't say "Pass the salt to *I*"; therefore, we shouldn't write "Pass the salt to *Tim and I.*"

Culinary school was the best choice for Alison and **me** [not *I*].

Keep this information between you and **me** [not *I*].

We'll probably hear *I* used incorrectly, especially in *between you and I,* even when speakers are trying to sound polished and professional. Because this rule is often misunderstood, we need to think carefully as we're editing our formal writing.

Finally, the objective case is used for both the subject and object of an infinitive. For example:

Catherine asked **him** to serve the first course.

Him is the subject of the infinitive *to serve,* as well as the object of the verb *asked.* In the next sentence, the pronoun is the *object* of the infinitive *to serve* and so is in the objective case, *her.*

Catherine asked Peter to serve **her**.

Finally, you might have a sentence with two pronouns, one the subject and one the objective of an infinitive phrase: "Catherine asked *him* to serve *her.*"

CHOOSING THE CORRECT CASE

Choosing the correct pronoun case is made more difficult because we often use one case in informal speech and another in formal writing. The choice is especially confusing when a pronoun and a noun are used together. In the two examples that follow, check the case of the pronoun by mentally crossing out the noun.

Us students often need to work on the weekends. [incorrect; you wouldn't say "*Us* need to work."]

We students often need to work on the weekends. [correct; think "*We* need to work."]

Sometimes it's difficult for **we students** to make time to study. [incorrect; you wouldn't say "It's difficult for *we* to make time."]

Sometimes it's difficult for **us students** to make time to study. [correct; think "It's difficult for *us*."]

A choice is also required after *than* and *as*. Choose the subjective or objective case depending on your meaning, and check the usage by completing the clause. For example:

Jeannette likes chocolate better **than I.**

Jeannette likes chocolate better **than I** *[like chocolate].*

In other words, I don't like chocolate as much as Jeannette likes chocolate.

Jeannette likes chocolate better **than me.**

Jeannette likes chocolate better **than** *[she likes]* **me.**

In other words, Jeannette doesn't like me as much as she likes chocolate. Study the next examples, which use *as* instead of *than*.

Jeannette does not like anchovies **as much as I** *[like anchovies].*

Jeannette does not like anchovies **as much as** *[she likes]* **me.**

Exercise 26.1 | Choosing the Correct Case

Identify the correct pronoun in each sentence.

1. (She/her) and Janine worked at a bakery café.
2. Bob gave Janine and (she/her) a monkey Danish.
3. He asked (she/her) to tell (he/him) if it tasted good.
4. Between you and (I/me), the Danish was a bit too sweet.
5. Janine likes sugar more than (I/me) do.

THE CASE OF THE POSSESSIVE

The **possessive case** has two functions. The first is to modify nouns, for example, *my* brother or *their* opinions. The possessive here works like an adjective and is sometimes called a **possessive adjective** or a determiner. We rarely have difficulty with the possessive, except in terms of pronoun–antecedent agreement, described in the next section, or when the possessive modifies a word that acts like a noun, such as a gerund (a verb plus –*ing*, such as *keeping*). Study the following examples:

Paul was pleased by **their** neatness. [*their* modifies the noun *neatness*]

Paul was pleased by **their** keeping the walk-in neat. [*their* modifies the gerund *keeping*]

In these sentences, *keeping* is a gerund used as a noun and is modified by the possessive form *their*. Remember that a verb plus –*ing* may also be a present participle used as an adjective, as in the following sentence:

The police caught **him** climbing out the window.

Here the phrase *climbing out the window* modifies the pronoun *him*, which is the object of the verb *caught*.

In some situations, you may choose either the objective case to emphasize the pronoun or you may choose the possessive case to emphasize the gerund (verb plus –*ing*). The following example emphasizes the pronoun:

The police observed **him** climbing.

The police were looking at *him*; we don't know whether or not the *climbing* was important. In the next example, however, the police are focused on the *climbing* itself (Figure 26.2):

The police observed **his** climbing.

Figure 26.2   Using the Objective and Possessive Cases

The police observed him climbing.

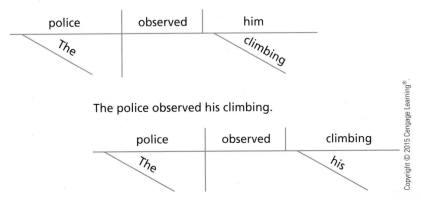

The second use of the possessive is to replace a noun phrase. For example, we might say "The book is my book," but we are more likely to say "The book is mine." In this second sentence, *mine* substitutes for the phrase *my book*. We can also use the **possessive pronoun** in the subject position. In answer to the question "Is your dry cleaning ready?" we might reply, "Mine is ready." Most pronouns have different forms that correspond with these different uses. Study the following chart:

Number & Person	Pronoun	Possessive Adjective	Possessive Pronoun
1st person singular	*my/mine*	That is my book.	That book is mine.
2nd person singular	*you/yours*	What is your problem?	The problem is yours.
3rd person singular masculine	*his/his*	Is that his desk?	The desk is his. *[same form for both]*
feminine	*her/hers*	Is that her pen?	The pen is hers.
neutral	*its/___*	The knife lost its edge.	_____ *[not in use]*
1st person plural	*our/ours*	This is our restaurant.	The restaurant is ours.
2nd person plural	*your/yours*	Your dinner is ready.	Yours is ready.
3rd person plural	*their/theirs*	It is their responsibility.	Theirs is the responsibility.

PRONOUN–ANTECEDENT AGREEMENT

Like subjects and verbs, pronouns and their antecedents must agree. **Antecedent** means "something that comes before," that is, the word a pronoun refers to. For example, in the following sentence, *Aunt Frances* is the antecedent while *her* is the pronoun that agrees with it.

Aunt Frances traveled a great deal to visit her nieces and nephews.

Pronoun–antecedent agreement means that pronouns must agree with their antecedents in person, number, and (in the third person) gender. *Aunt Frances* is a third-person, singular feminine noun; *her* is the third-person, singular feminine pronoun. They agree. Note that *her* is also in the correct case, the possessive, to modify the *nieces and nephews*.

As we edit our writing and check that each pronoun agrees with its antecedent, the first rule is about number: use a singular pronoun if its antecedent is a singular noun or pronoun; use a plural pronoun if its antecedent is a plural noun or pronoun. We also need to use pronouns in the same person as the antecedent: first, second, or third.

I opened my menu. [I *and* my *are both first-person singular*]

We opened our menus. [We *and* our *are both first-person plural*]

Note that *you* takes the same form in both singular and plural contexts. Like French and Spanish still do, English once had a separate singular form, *thou*, which was used for family and friends, while *you* was used for groups and for individuals of higher social status. *You* has generally referred to both numbers since the seventeenth century, except in certain dialects and within certain religious groups.

We're familiar with number and person from our work with subject–verb agreement. In the third-person singular, a third category appears: **gender**. Follow these guidelines:

- Use a **feminine pronoun** (*she, her, hers*) when the antecedent is feminine (*Mrs. Perez, Joyce, girl*).
- Use a **masculine pronoun** (*he, him, his*) when the antecedent is masculine (*Uncle John, Edward, boy*).
- Use a **neutral pronoun** (*it, its*) when the antecedent has no gender (*book, case, rose*).

If the antecedent is a plural noun or pronoun (*girls, boys, books*), use a plural pronoun (*they, them, their, theirs*). Study Figure 26.3 and the following examples:

Figure 26.3 Pronoun–Antecedent Agreement

Person	Singular Antecedents	Singular Pronouns That Agree	Plural Antecedents	Plural Pronouns That Agree
1st	*I*	*I, me, my*	*we*	*we, us, our*
2nd	*you**	*you, your*	*you**	*you,* your*
3rd/masculine	*he* *Sergio*	*he, him, his*	*they* *Sergio and Jeannette*	*they, them, their*
3rd/feminine	*she,* *Jeannette*	*she, her, hers*	*students* *chefs*	
3rd/neutral	*it* *dog* *tomato*	*it, its*	*dogs* *tomatoes*	

* Note that *you* is both singular and plural in number, and both subjective and objective in case.

Mrs. Perez is an excellent cook; **she** sometimes shares **her** recipes with friends.

I asked **Uncle John** about **his** trip to Costa Rica when we visited **him** at Thanksgiving.

Don't judge a **book** by **its** cover.

Do you know the **Johnsons**? **They** moved into **their** new house across the street last week.

When the gender of a pronoun's antecedent is clear, we easily use pronouns that agree. However, as with subject–verb agreement, difficulties can arise when the antecedent is an indefinite pronoun, such as *everyone* or *anybody*. In casual speech, these words are sometimes assigned a plural pronoun; for example, "Everyone is ready for *their* quiz tomorrow." However, in formal English these words are always singular and take both singular verbs and singular pronouns. But then we have to ask about the gender. If *everyone* refers only to males or only to females, our choice is clear. But what if it's a mixed group, or what if we don't know who's in the group? In the past, writers used *he* to refer to a mixed or unknown group. Now we try to avoid such **sexist language**, that is, expressions that inappropriately specify one gender when both should be included. Thus we don't want to use simply *his* (see also Chapter 9); instead we might rewrite the sentence as follows:

Everyone is ready for **his or her** quiz tomorrow.

The sentence is correct; however, if many repetitions are required, writing *his or her* may become awkward and wordy. In a longer work like this textbook, we can alternate between *he* in one chapter and *she* in the next, or, in general, we can rewrite sentences so that they sidestep the agreement issue completely, as in the following examples:

Everyone is ready for tomorrow's quiz. *[eliminate possessive pronouns]*

The students are ready for their quiz tomorrow. *[use plural nouns and pronouns]*

The same questions arise when the antecedent is a singular **generic noun**, that is, when it names a typical member of a group; for example, "The average server in this restaurant wears a nametag on their uniform." *Server* is singular, so *their* is incorrect. However, since *server* could be male or female, we don't want to use just one pronoun. To avoid sexist language while maintaining agreement in number, we could substitute *his or her* for *their,* or we could rewrite the sentence more smoothly using the plural, as in the following sentences:

The average server in this restaurant wears a nametag on his or her uniform.

The servers in this restaurant usually wear nametags on their uniforms.

Like agreement between subjects and verbs, agreement between pronouns and antecedents has rules about conjunctions. Though often ignored in informal speaking and writing, these rules generally apply in academic and business writing. First, when antecedents are joined by *and,* they require a plural pronoun (as well as a plural verb).

The pear and banana are ripening in **their** skins. *[pear + banana = their]*

Second, when antecedents are joined by *or* or *nor*, the pronoun should agree with the nearer one.

The pear or the banana is ripening in **its** skin. *[its agrees with* banana*]*

The pear or the bananas are ripening in **their** skins. *[their agrees with* bananas*]*

Note that sentences will be smoother if the plural antecedent follows the singular. "The bananas or pear is ripening in its skin" sounds awkward.

Exercise 26.2 | Pronoun–Antecedent Agreement

On a separate sheet of paper, write the appropriate pronoun for each blank.

1. The students in the class opened _____ textbooks.
2. Each chef sharpened _____ knife.
3. Anybody would appreciate such an addition to _____ income.
4. Everyone occasionally makes mistakes with _____ pronoun use.
5. Matthew or Robert likes sugar in _____ coffee.

CLEAR PRONOUN REFERENCE

Sometimes we run into trouble when we are not clear about what each pronoun refers to. Look at the following sentence:

Mike told Jack that **he** was lazy.

Does *he* refer to *Mike* or *Jack?* That is, is Mike himself lazy? Or does Mike think Jack is lazy? This unclear **pronoun reference** can be corrected by adding a reflexive pronoun (*himself*) or repeating the appropriate noun.

Mike told Jack that **he himself** was lazy.

Mike told Jack that **Jack** was lazy.

Another problem in pronoun reference arises when we use *you, it,* or *they* without referring to specific persons or things. *You* is acceptable only when we intend to address the reader directly, as in a letter or a recipe.

You should baste the turkey frequently to keep it moist.

So who's the lazy one—Mike or Jack?

In most formal writing, avoid *you* altogether, for example, by using the passive voice.

> Basting the turkey frequently will keep it moist.

Any time you use *it* or *they*, be sure you know what it's referring to and that it's necessary. For example, the sentence "In the movie *it* shows how the penguins try to protect their eggs from the bitter Antarctic cold" might be rewritten more clearly as follows:

> **The movie shows** how the penguins try to protect their eggs from the bitter Antarctic cold.

In addition, avoid using *they* when you don't really know who *they* are.

> After a snowfall, **they** work quickly to clear the roads for the school buses.

If you know who *they* are, use the specific noun.

> After a snowfall, **the town** works quickly to clear the roads for the school buses.

If you don't know who *they* are, rewrite the sentence in the passive voice.

> After a snowfall, **the roads are quickly cleared** for the school buses.

Finally, use specific words instead of the pronouns *it, that, this,* or *which* to refer to whole sentences or concepts.

> The episode of *NYPD Blue* in which Bobby Simone died was particularly heart-wrenching. **This** helps explain why some viewers prefer the relatively impersonal *Law & Order.*

What does *This* refer to? The reader has to stop and think. We can make our meaning clearer by replacing the weak *this* with a specific noun phrase.

> **The emotional stress of that episode** helps explain why some viewers prefer the relatively impersonal *Law & Order.*

Exercise 26.3 | Clear Pronoun Reference

Rewrite each of the following sentences to correct unclear pronoun reference.

1. Cecilia and her mother thought that *she* needed a vacation.
2. George told his friends that *they* had tickets for the Duke game.
3. The movie *Vertigo* was suspenseful, and *you* were on the edge of your seat.
4. In the movie *it* showed the hero dangling from a gutter six stories above the ground.
5. The gutter scene was traumatic for the hero, who is afterwards afraid of heights. Later, *this* prevents him from following the girl up the tower stairs.

REFLEXIVE AND INTENSIVE PRONOUNS

Reflexive pronouns are formed by adding *–self* to the personal pronouns (Figure 26.4) and are used when the subject of the sentence is also the object.

> Andrew told **himself** to work more quickly.

Intensive pronouns, which have the same forms as reflexive pronouns, are used to add emphasis to their antecedents.

> The executive chef **himself** made the rounds of the dining room.

Figure 26.4 Reflexive and Intensive Pronouns

Person	Singular	Plural
1st	myself	ourselves
2nd	yourself	yourselves
3rd	himself, herself, itself	themselves

Copyright © 2015 Cengage Learning®.

Be sure to use the standard forms of these pronouns: *himself,* not *hisself; themselves,* not *theirselves.* In addition, avoid using *myself* or *ourselves* as the subject of a sentence.

> Janet and **myself** enjoyed the fresh Greek salad with oodles of feta cheese. [*incorrect;* we wouldn't say "*Myself* enjoyed the fresh Greek salad"]

> Janet and **I** enjoyed the fresh Greek salad with oodles of feta cheese. [*correct;* think "*I* enjoyed the salad"]

> The Ortegas and **ourselves** had a late dinner at Bistro Urbano. [*incorrect;* we wouldn't say "*Ourselves* had a late dinner"]

> **We** and the Ortegas had a late dinner at Bistro Urbano. [*correct*]

POINT OF VIEW

Point of view, the narrator's position with regard to the story, is established partly through the choice of pronouns, for example, *I, we, you, he/she, they,* and *one.* Use the **first person,** *I* and *we,* for writing that emphasizes your personal experience, including letters and essays.

> I believe I am an excellent candidate for the position.

> When I was ten years old, my life changed in a single instant.

Of course, other pronouns, such as *he* or *they,* might appear in the writing, but the perspective is the first person. Think about the first-person shooter in a video game. You *see* others in the game, but you look through the eyes of the first-person shooter just as you look through your own eyes.

> I wanted to play a video game with them. [*first-person point of view*]

Use the **second person,** *you,* for directions and recipes.

> Next, mix the dry ingredients in a separate bowl. [*the subject of this command is understood to be* you]

In other contexts, the pronoun *you* may seem too informal. Of course, *you* will also appear in a letter, but the letter is usually written from a first-person point of view.

> Dear Mr. Jones, I look forward to working with you.

Use the **third person**—*he* or *she, they,* or *one*—in certain narratives or in very formal academic or professional writing. In these situations, you will probably not use I, we, or *you* at all.

He realized that his dream of attending culinary school was now within reach.

Many students struggle to balance their school work with a paying job.

Follow the guidelines of your instructor or publisher.

Once you've established the appropriate point of view in a piece of writing, be careful not to confuse the reader by shifting unnecessarily to another point of view, for example, from *I* to *you*. Study the following sentences:

I visited an aquarium in Boston that had a colony of penguins. **You** could see the young ones learning to swim. *[shift from first to second person]*

I visited an aquarium in Boston that had a colony of penguins. **I** could see the young ones learning to swim. *[both sentences now in the first person]*

Audiences clap enthusiastically when the penguin parents are reunited with their chicks. **You** often feel emotional when nature films involve family groups. *[shift from third to second person]*

Audiences clap enthusiastically when the penguin parents are reunited with their chicks. **Viewers** often feel emotional when nature films involve family groups. *[both sentences now in third person]*

Like shifts in verb tense, shifts in point of view are distracting and confusing to the reader. Try to stay with the same point of view throughout each essay.

Downtown Chicago from a Bird's Point of View

© EugeneF/shutterstock.com

Exercise 26.4 | Maintaining Consistent Point of View

Correct any unnecessary shifts in point of view in the following passage,* avoiding the second person altogether.

Food competitions are time-demanding and stressful, but try being the team captain looking over four other students and having to deal with the teachers and judges. First I picked the students that I wanted to be on the team; then you put them in a place they would succeed in. After two long days of brainstorming, you finally came to agreement on the menu. If we forgot to pack anything, it will throw you off completely.

Now we get to the meat of the competition: the cooking. I started to work on the salad as Sarah, my assistant, started on the appetizer. This is when things began to go wrong: there was too much liquid in the polenta. Luckily, I found some cheese from another group, and you thickened the polenta with it.

*Adapted from an essay by Joey Jacobsen. Errors were added to create this exercise.

RECIPE FOR REVIEW

USING PRONOUN CASE

1. Study the case forms in Figure 26.1.
2. Use the **subjective case** for the subjects of independent and dependent clauses, and with subject complements (for example, It is *I* at the door).
3. Use the **objective case** for the direct and indirect objects of verbs, the objects of prepositions, and the subjects and objects of infinitives.
4. Use the **possessive case** to modify nouns and gerunds (words made from verbs that act like nouns).

ENSURING PRONOUN–ANTECEDENT AGREEMENT

1. Pronouns must agree with their **antecedents** in **person**, **number**, and **gender**.
2. Avoid *they, them,* and *their* with singular indefinite pronouns such as *everyone* and with singular generic nouns such as *the typical student*.
3. Use a plural pronoun with two or more antecedents joined by *and*. When antecedents are joined by *or* or *nor,* the pronoun should agree with the nearer antecedent.

MAINTAINING CLEAR PRONOUN REFERENCE

1. Repeat the antecedent or use a reflexive pronoun to avoid unclear **pronoun reference**.
2. Avoid using *it, they,* or *you* without a clear, specific antecedent.
3. Avoid using *it, that, this,* or *which* to refer to a whole sentence or concept.

USING REFLEXIVE AND INTENSIVE PRONOUNS

1. Study the reflexive and intensive forms in Figure 26.3.
2. Use **reflexive pronouns** when the subject of the sentence is also the object.
3. Use **intensive pronouns** to add emphasis to their antecedents.
4. Avoid using *myself* as the subject of a sentence.

APPROPRIATE AND CONSISTENT POINT OF VIEW

1. In formal essays, avoid addressing the reader directly with *you.*
2. Use point of view consistently; for example, avoid shifting from *they* to *you* to *one.*

CHAPTER QUIZ

DIRECTIONS: Rewrite the following sentences on a separate sheet of paper, correcting any pronouns that are used incorrectly.

> Example: You and me need to talk.
> Correction: You and **I** need to talk.

1. Beth thought that her and her husband would enjoy a bottle of chardonnay on their picnic.

2. Let's keep that information between you and I.

3. Us students don't always get enough sleep.

4. Everyone needs to have his day of rest.

5. The typical *Law & Order* attorney speaks passionately on their client's behalf.

6. The orange or the tangerine has a sticker on their peel.

7. Penelope and Audrey thought she should apply to culinary school.

8. Jim made toast with butter, but it was too cold.

9. Karen and myself saw the movie three times.

10. When the characters collided on the football field, people in the theater laughed so hard you cried.

CHAPTER 27
ADJECTIVES, ADVERBS, AND OTHER MODIFIERS

By the end of this chapter, you should begin to . . .

- use adjectives and adverbs appropriately;
- use positive, comparative, and superlative forms correctly; and
- avoid misplaced and dangling modifiers.

A **modifier** describes, explains, or limits another word in some way. Modifiers can be single words like adjectives and adverbs, or they can be groups of words like phrases or clauses. Both the form and the placement of modifiers are important in making our points clear to the reader and in demonstrating our knowledge of standard written English.

USING ADJECTIVES AND ADVERBS

Adverbs are generally recognizable by their *–ly* ending and are used to modify verbs, adjectives, and other adverbs.

> The water in the saucepan boiled rapidly. [The adverb *rapidly* modifies the verb *boiled.*]

> The water in the saucepan was at a very rapid boil. [The adverb *very* modifies the adjective *rapid.*]

> The water was boiling very rapidly. [The adverb *very* modifies the adverb *rapidly.*]

Most **adjectives**, on the other hand, do not end in *–ly* and are used to modify nouns, sometimes following a linking verb.

> The rapid boil stopped once the saucepan was removed from the flame. [The adjective *rapid* modifies the noun *boil.*]

> The saucepan was still hot, though. [The adjective *hot* follows the linking verb *was,* but modifies the noun *saucepan.*]

Figure 27.1 Adjectives and Adverbs with Identical Forms

Adjective	Adverb
The Olympic athlete was *fast*. Compare: The Olympic athlete was *quick*.	The Olympic athlete ran *fast*. Compare: The Olympic athlete ran *quickly*.
We studied for the hard test.	We studied hard for the test.
Late papers will not be accepted.	Don't hand your paper in late.
The road was wide and straight.	Drive straight after the second light.

However, problems arise when adjectives and adverbs have unexpected forms or are used in place of one another.

While most adverbs end in *–ly*, some do not, such as *fast, hard, late,* and *straight*. In fact, these adverbs have the same form as their adjective counterparts (Figure 27.1). *Friendly* and *lively*, however, do not have adverb forms. They must be used in a phrase such as "in a friendly way" or "in a lively manner."

WELL AND GOOD

Well can be used both as an adjective and as an adverb. As an adjective, it means healthy, as in a Get Well card. *Well* is also the adverb form of the adjective *good*. Sometimes confusion ensues because the two words are often used one way in casual speech and another way in formal written English. While *well* can be used as either an adjective or an adverb, *good* is used only as an adjective. It must modify a noun, even if it follows the verb. In that case, the verb will be a linking verb. Remember that linking verbs include *to be* and *to seem*, as well as some meanings of *to feel, to smell,* and *to taste*. In general, if a verb can be replaced with *is* or *are*, it is a linking verb.

I thought the movie was good. [correct; *good* modifies the noun *movie*]

The sauce tastes good. [correct; *good* modifies the noun *sauce*]

The sauce tastes good.

In the first example, the adjective *good* correctly modifies the noun *movie*, although it follows the linking verb *was*. It was a *good movie*. Similarly, in the second example, the adjective *good* correctly modifies the noun *sauce*. It's a *good sauce*. (Like the other verbs of the "senses"—*smells, feels, sounds, looks*—the verb *tastes* is sometimes used as a linking verb.) But see what happens when we try to make *good* modify a verb:

Tony cooks good. [incorrect; *good* cannot modify a verb]

In this sentence, the word *good* is used incorrectly to modify the verb *cooks* and should be changed to its adverb form, *well*.

Tony cooks well. [correct]

Use an adverb to modify a verb.

To modify the verb *cooks*, choose an adverb rather than an adjective.

Tony cooks   well   .

= adverb (*well, efficiently*)

= adjective (*good, efficient*)

Some other pairs of adjective/adverb forms that create confusion are *bad/badly, real/really,* and *slow/slowly*. In the first sentence that follows, an adjective (*real*) is used informally in place of an adverb.

The risotto was real tasty. [informal; *real* is an adjective and so cannot modify another adjective, *tasty*]

The adverb form must be used to modify an adjective, as in the next sentence:

The risotto was really tasty. [correct; the adverb *really* modifies the adjective *tasty*]

Study the following pairs of correct sentences:

The performance is going badly. [The adverb *badly* modifies the verb *is going.*]

The moldy cheese tastes bad. [The adjective *bad* follows the linking verb and modifies *cheese.*]

The first date went well. [The adverb *well* modifies the verb *went.*]

The first date was good. [The adjective *good* follows the linking verb and modifies *date.*]

Use an adverb to modify an adjective.

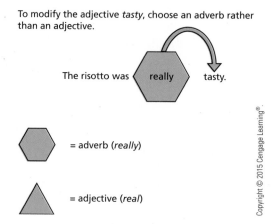

To modify the adjective *tasty*, choose an adverb rather than an adjective.

The risotto was < really > tasty.

⬡ = adverb (*really*)

▲ = adjective (*real*)

Slow is sometimes used as an adverb in the common expressions "drive slow" or "go slow." To be strictly correct, however, use the formal adverb *slowly*.

The bus was traveling slowly through the busy city streets.

Beware of similar confusions with the adjective/adverb pairs *awful/awfully, poor/poorly, quick/quickly,* and *quiet/quietly.* Remember to use an adjective to modify a noun and an adverb to modify a verb, adjective, or another adverb. Once you decide whether you need an adjective or adverb, be sure to use the correct form.

Exercise 27.1 | Using Adjectives and Adverbs

Rewrite each of the following sentences, correcting any errors in the use of adjectives and adverbs.

  Example: Seth wrote *poor* with his left hand.
  Rewrite: Seth wrote *poorly* with his left hand.

1. The strange-looking drink nevertheless tasted good.

2. Tom told Maria that she danced good.

3. Leo was real careful not to spill a drop as he poured the coffee.

4. The stage set was so detailed and colorful that it looked real.

5. Jerry reminded his classmates to beat the egg whites real good.

COMPARATIVE AND SUPERLATIVE FORMS

Adjectives and adverbs have three forms. The first is the **positive**, a form that describes a noun without comparing it to another one. In our preceding discussion, all the adjectives and adverbs were in the positive form. The second is the **comparative**, which is formed by adding the suffix *–er* or the word *more*. The comparative is used to judge *two* items against each other. The third is the **superlative**, which is formed by adding the suffix *–est* or the word *most*. The superlative is used to compare *more than two* items. Study the three adjective forms in these examples:

Trey is happy. [positive]

Bennett is happier than Trey. [comparative]

Trish is the happiest of all. [superlative]

Trey's cake is delicious. [positive]

Bennett's cake is more delicious than Trey's. [comparative]

Trish's cake is the most delicious of all. [superlative]

Adverbs form the comparative and superlative in a similar way:

Trey works fast. [positive]

Bennett works faster. [comparative adds *–er*]

Trish works the fastest of all. [superlative adds *–est*]

Trey washes plates quickly. [positive]

Bennett washes plates more quickly. [comparative adds *more*]

Trish washes plates the most quickly of all. [superlative adds *most*]

Note that when *quick* is used as an adjective, it takes the suffixes *–er* and *–est* in its comparative and superlative forms.

Bennett is a *quicker* dishwasher, but Trish is the *quickest*.

Unfortunately, it is not always possible to predict which adjectives and adverbs will add a suffix to form the comparative and superlative and which will add the words *more* and *most*. The majority of one-syllable adjectives and adverbs add a suffix, *-er* or

Trey is quick, Bennett is quicker, but Trish is the quickest.

quick   quicker   quickest

–est. Those with two syllables use the suffixes or the words *more* or *most.* Adjectives and adverbs with more than two syllables typically use the words *more* and *most,* rather than the sufficxes. Check a dictionary to be sure.

In addition to these two common variations, some adjectives and adverbs have irregular forms (Figure 27.2).

Figure 27.2 Irregular Comparative and Superlative Forms

Positive	Comparative	Superlative
bad (adjective)	worse	worst
badly (adverb)	worse	worst
good (adjective)	better	best
well (adverb)	better	best
little (adjective)	littler	littlest
little (adverb)	less	least
many (adjective with number)	more	most
much (adjective with amount)	more	most

Finally, note that only one form of the comparative and superlative may be used. The first of the following sentences is incorrect:

Bennett is *more friendlier* than Trey. [incorrect; do not use both *more* and the suffix *–er*]

Bennett is *friendlier* than Trey. [correct]

Bennett is *more friendly* than Trey. [correct]

Exercise 27.2 | Using Comparatives and Superlatives

On a sheet of paper, write the appropriate form of the adjective or adverb specified in parentheses.

Example: The chef searched for the _____ (*good*/superlative) recipe.
Rewrite: The chef searched for the <u>best</u> recipe.

1. Alyssa needed _____ (*many*/comparative) jalapeño peppers for the chili sauce.

2. This restaurant has the _____ (*large*/superlative) selection of wines in the city.

3. I have rarely seen a _____ (*funny*/comparative) movie than *Tootsie.*

4. Dan diced the onions _____ (*efficiently*/comparative) than Tom did.

5. While everyone felt badly about the abandoned dog, Cindy seemed to feel _____ (*badly*/superlative).

MISPLACED MODIFIERS

The role of a modifier is to describe or explain one of the words in a sentence. A **misplaced modifier** is so far away from the word it describes that the reader may be confused. Look at this sentence:

> The goal was to make tall sugar sculptures *of the contest*. [The modifier *of the contest* is misplaced.]

This sentence is confusing because it seems as if *of the contest* is describing the *tall sugar sculptures*. It's as if the hollandaise sauce intended for the asparagus were put on the dinner roll instead. The meal looks better when the sauce is in the right place, and the sentence is clearer when the phrase is placed next to the noun it truly modifies, *goal*.

> The goal *of the contest* was to make tall sugar sculptures. [correct]

Such errors in placement are not uncommon, and they can be difficult to spot in our own writing. We know what we mean. Our goal in editing is to be sure our readers will also know what we mean.

Be particularly careful with words such as *almost, even, just,* and *only*. They must be placed right next to the words they modify in order to avoid confusion. Consider the following sentence:

> Javier only eats dark chocolate. [He doesn't eat any other food?!]

Since the word *only* modifies *chocolate*, not *eats*, it should be placed next to it.

> Javier eats only dark chocolate. [He doesn't eat any other kind of chocolate.]

Exercise 27.3 | Correcting Misplaced Modifiers

Rewrite the following sentences to correct the misplaced modifiers.

> Example: The goal was to make tall sugar sculptures *of the contest*. [misplaced modifier]
>
> Rewrite: The goal *of the contest* was to make tall sugar sculptures. [correct]

1. *Pastry Daredevils* documented a competition in sugar sculptures, a series on the Food Channel.

2. One of the competitors almost tried to make a sculpture nine feet in height.

3. The sculptures reflected the chefs' imaginative interpretations of a fairy tale airbrushed with food coloring.

4. The *Meilleur Ouvrier de France* (M.O.F.) walked quickly over the obstacle course considered a top craftsman in France.

5. The winner created a six-foot sculpture who received a check for ten thousand dollars.

Here is another example:

Javier only eats dessert when he has a cup of coffee.

Only does not modify *eats*. Instead, it modifies the clause *when he has a cup of coffee* and should be placed next to it.

Javier eats dessert only when he has a cup of coffee.

DANGLING MODIFIERS

A **dangling modifier** is usually a phrase at the beginning of the sentence that does not truly modify the noun or pronoun that follows it. Without that connection, the modifier is said to "dangle." Look at this example:

After waiting for over an hour, their table was finally ready.

Who has been waiting for over an hour? The reader expects the phrase *after waiting for over an hour* to modify the nearest noun. Logically, though, the *table* hasn't been waiting: *they* have. Yet the word *they* does not even appear in the sentence. It's like being served a salad with a side of butter. The butter doesn't "modify" the salad. To correct the "dangle," we might rewrite the sentence in a couple of different ways.

After waiting for over an hour, they were finally seated at their table.

Who was waiting? *They* were. When we change the subject of the sentence to *they*, the phrase *after waiting for over an hour* modifies it, and the sentence makes sense. We've put a dinner roll on the table.

After they had waited for over an hour, their table was finally ready.

In this second rewrite we changed the dangling participial phrase into a solid dependent clause. The butter has been replaced by oil and vinegar.

Sugar sculptures and pastries must be transported with care!

Exercise 27.4 | Correcting Dangling Modifiers

Rewrite the following sentences to correct the dangling modifiers.

> Example: After practicing for a year, her name was entered in the sugar sculpture competition. [Who was practicing? Not *her name*.]
>
> Rewrite: After practicing for a year, she entered the sugar sculpture competition. [*She* was practicing, not *her name*.]

1. Required to use certain methods of preparing the sugar, the sculptures also reflected the competitors' imaginations.
2. Avoiding specific fairy tales, her sculpture looked like a French harlequin.
3. Using a blow torch, the sculptures were melted and molded into the proper shapes.
4. While balancing the sculptures carefully, they were carried over an "obstacle course" to see if they would break.
5. Focused on keeping the sugar sculptures upright, her foot tripped on the steps.

RECIPE FOR REVIEW

USING ADJECTIVES AND ADVERBS

1. **Adverbs** are generally recognizable by their –*ly* endings; they modify verbs, adjectives, and other adverbs.
2. Most **adjectives**, on the other hand, do not end in –*ly*; they modify nouns, sometimes following a linking verb. For example, the peaches are ripe.
3. Use *good* only as an adjective: The meal was *good*, but the meal was cooked *well*.
4. Use the **positive form** when no comparison is intended. Use the **comparative form** (-*er* or *more*) of adjectives and adverbs to compare *two* items. Use the **superlative form** (–*est* or *most*) to compare *more than two* items. Study the irregular forms of the comparative and superlative in Figure 27.2.
5. Do not use both forms of the comparative (–*er* and *more*) or both forms of the superlative (–*est* and *most*) to modify a single word. Study these examples:

    Leroy was more friendlier than Alan. [incorrect]

    Leroy was friendlier than Alan, or Leroy was more friendly than Alan. [correct]

MISPLACED MODIFIERS

Ensure that adjectives and adverbs—whether they are words or phrases—are placed right next to the words they modify.

> The goal was to make tall sugar sculptures of **the contest**. [The prepositional phrase *of the contest* modifies *goal* and should be placed right next to it.]
>
> The goal **of the contest** was to make tall sugar sculptures. [*correct*]

DANGLING MODIFIERS

Ensure that modifiers refer to a specific word in the sentence; don't let them dangle.

> After waiting for over an hour, their table was finally ready. [*Who* has been waiting for over an hour?]
>
> After waiting for over an hour, they were finally seated at their table. [*correct*]

CHAPTER QUIZ

DIRECTIONS: Rewrite each of the following sentences, correcting the modifiers.

1. On their trip to Hawaii, Christine noticed that her boyfriend surfed good.

2. She also noticed that the fresh pineapples tasted real good.

3. Christine walked quick downstairs every night for a piña colada.

4. Rhoda liked the fresh pineapple who was another friend on the trip.

5. She only ate pineapple slices, however.

6. Rhoda could surf more better than Christine's boyfriend.

7. After spending a week on the beach, her tan was the deeper of the three friends'.

8. Watching her friends in the water, it would have been fun to surf, too.

9. Sunburned from the day before, her hat provided some welcome shade.

10. Nevertheless, she felt even badder the next day.

CHAPTER 28
MAINTAINING PARALLELISM

By the end of this chapter, you should begin to . . .

- identify and correct items in a series that are not parallel in structure;
- identify and correct items in a comparison that are not parallel in structure;
- correct the parallelism in items joined by *both/and, either/or, neither/nor,* or *not only/but also;* and
- add words when necessary to complete a parallel structure.

You may remember having studied parallel lines in high school. The lines run along into infinity, always the same distance apart. It's important to maintain that **parallelism** in real-life situations such as train tracks. If one track went off in a different direction, the train might jump the rails! Parallelism is also important in the culinary world. A restaurant wouldn't use different patterns of china and silver on the same table because the place settings wouldn't be *parallel.*

Maintaining parallelism (also called parallel structure and parallel construction) is about meeting the reader's expectations, making your meaning clear, and creating smooth and pleasing rhythms in your sentences. If the *ideas* in a sentence are somehow equivalent, the *structure* that expresses them should be similar: that is parallelism. For example, notice the parallel structure of the second, third, and fourth sentences in the following passage:

> When one lists the responsibilities of a chef, they usually do not include addressing food-related issues or politics at all. They would of course, include serving quality food that is safe. They would include providing an enjoyable setting to experience the food. They would include making a meal at their establishment satisfying and valuable.
>
> —**Payson S. Cushman**, student writer

After the first sentence, which states what a chef's responsibilities do *not* include, the passage adds three parallel sentences that outline what these responsibilities *do* include. Each sentence begins with *They would include* followed by a gerund.

They would include + **serving** + quality food that is safe.

They would include + **providing** + an enjoyable setting to experience the food.

They would include + **making** + a meal at their establishment satisfying and valuable.

Parallel structures are often used to add emphasis. The repetition of the same structure— "they would include"—builds to the final important phrase "satisfying and valuable."

MAINTAINING PARALLELISM IN A SERIES

When we have two or more equivalent items in a series, we want to be sure they are constructed using the same forms or parts of speech, for example, all nouns or all adjectives. Consider this example:

The steak was thick, juicy, and **it had a good flavor**. *[NOT parallel]*

Suppose a triangle represents an adjective and a rectangle represents a clause. Note how the sentence in Figure 28.1 does not have a parallel structure. Instead, we have a series of three comments on the steak in two different grammatical forms: two adjectives and one clause.

Figure 28.1 Faulty Parallel Structure: The steak was thick, juicy, and it had a good flavor.

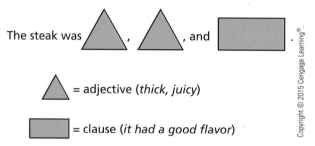

To correct the problem, we need to put all three comments in the same form, for example, by changing the clause to an adjective—

The steak was thick, juicy, and **flavorful**. *[parallel]*

—that is, by changing the rectangle to a triangle (see Figure 28.2).

Figure 28.2 Corrected Parallel Structure: The steak was thick, juicy, and flavorful.

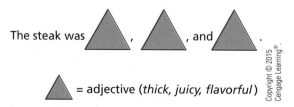

In the next example, the three objects of the preposition *for* are not parallel in structure. The first and second are ordinary nouns, but the third is a verbal.

> Dr. House is known for his biting sarcasm, his intensely blue eyes, and **making clever deductions** about a patient's illness. *[NOT parallel]*

In the second sentence, all three objects are ordinary nouns (*sarcasm, eyes, deductions*), and the structure *is* parallel:

> Dr. House is known for his biting sarcasm, his intensely blue eyes, and **his clever deductions** about a patient's illness. *[parallel]*

Phrases should also be in the same form. In the following sentence, however, the first phrase is a gerund (verb + *ing*), while the second is an infinitive (*to* + verb).

> The large tiger cat loved **sleeping** on pillows and **to annoy** the dog.
> *[NOT parallel]*

To correct the parallelism, you must either begin both phrases with a gerund or begin both with an infinitive. It doesn't matter which structure you choose as long as both phrases use the same form.

> The large tiger cat loved **sleeping** on pillows and **annoying** the dog.
> *[gerunds]*

> The large tiger cat loved **to sleep** on pillows and **to annoy** the dog.
> *[infinitives]*

Exercise 28.1 | Maintaining Parallelism in a Series

Rewrite the following sentences, correcting the parallelism.

1. *Wedding Crashers* is a movie about two friends who like to crash weddings and eating finger foods.
2. Owen Wilson plays John, with Jeremy played by Vince Vaughn.
3. The film's humor comes from its witty dialogue and how it often approaches the content from a politically incorrect viewpoint.
4. Vince Vaughn is an especially delightful "straight man," who delivers his lines with dexterity and his 6'5" frame is surprisingly agile.
5. The supporting cast is marvelous, from Christopher Walken's crazed-looking but supportive father of the bride and Isla Fisher plays his spoiled but charming daughter.

"Wedding Crashers"
Owen Wilson (left)
and Vince Vaughn

New Line Cinema/Photofest

MAINTAINING PARALLELISM IN A COMPARISON

You're probably familiar with the expression "You can't compare apples and oranges." We *can*, however, compare Red Delicious *apples* and Granny Smith *apples*. Thus when we compare or contrast two ideas—for example, with the words *as* and *than*—we must use the same species of fruit, that is, the same grammatical structure. When we don't, we get a sentence like the following:

Is it more important to **serve** healthy food than **keeping up** with food fashions? *[NOT parallel]*

The first phrase is an infinitive, *to serve*, while the second is a gerund, *keeping*. To maintain parallelism, put both in the same form. Just as we can compare two apples, we can compare two infinitives (*to serve, to keep*), or two gerunds (*serving, keeping*):

Is it more important **to serve** healthy food than **to keep up** with food fashion? *[parallel]*

Is **serving** healthy food more important than **keeping up** with food fashion? *[parallel]*

Let's look at another example:

Eddy likes **basketball** as much as **grilling** a steak. *[NOT parallel]*

Here a noun is paired incorrectly with a verbal. Instead, a noun should be paired with another noun or a verbal with another verbal.

Eddy likes **playing** basketball as much as **grilling** a steak. *[parallel]*

See also Chapter 26 for information on using pronouns with *than* and *as*.

Eddy likes playing basketball as much as grilling a steak.

Exercise 28.2 | Maintaining Parallelism in a Comparison

Rewrite the following sentences, correcting any problems with parallel structure.

1. Did you enjoy Vince Vaughn's dancing as much as how he made balloon animals?
2. Owen Wilson's character was initially more romantic than the way his friend was.
3. During the touch football session on the lawn, Wilson was more interested in flirting with another of Walken's daughter's than he wanted to play the game.
4. Is Vince Vaughn's slapstick humor during the game as funny as he has a deadpan expression?
5. Walken's scowling son Todd, hunched over his painter's palette, is more appealing than his daughter has a manic fiancé.

MAINTAINING PARALLELISM WITH BOTH/AND, EITHER/OR, NEITHER/NOR, AND NOT ONLY/BUT ALSO

When ideas are joined with the conjunctions *both/and, either/or, neither/nor,* and *not only/but also,* they must be expressed using the same forms or structures. For example:

Not only was the food delicious, but we also got good service. *[NOT parallel]*

The sentence could be rewritten as follows:

> Not only was the food delicious, but the service was also good. *[parallel]*

We received two things: *food* and *service*. Let's look at another example:

> Brenda Leigh Johnson is both smart and has a lot of courage. *[NOT parallel]*

The sentence might be rewritten with two adjectives (*smart, courageous*) or two nouns (*intelligence, courage*).

> Brenda Leigh Johnson is both smart and courageous. *[parallel]*
>
> Brenda Leigh Johnson has both intelligence and courage. *[parallel]*

Place the initial word of the pair (*both, either, neither,* or *not only*) carefully so that the two structures that follow are identical. For example, in this sentence, the word *either* should immediately precede the word *Russian*:

> The actress either was of Russian or Ukrainian descent. *[poor placement]*
>
> The actress was of either Russian or Ukrainian descent. *[clearer placement]*

Exercise 28.3 | Maintaining Parallelism with *both/and*

Rewrite each of the following sentences, correcting the parallel structure.

1. Police chief Brenda Leigh Johnson is both an astute interrogator and she is also poor at housekeeping.
2. Her subordinates not only admire her but also they think she's a bit odd.
3. Her relationship with her boss is complicated not only because they were once dating but also he left her for another woman.
4. Sergeant Gabriel was the first officer at her new job who began either to like her and he respects her now, too.
5. Unable to find her way around Los Angeles, Chief Johnson needs him both as moral support and she needs a guide so she doesn't get lost.

COMPLETING PARALLEL STRUCTURES

Sometimes we have the beginnings of parallel structure between two elements or between items in a series, but we lack certain words that would make the structure completely parallel. Study the following example:

> Edoardo liked the fresh herbs at the farmers' market better than the store.

Because the second item in this sentence is incomplete, the sentence seems to be comparing *herbs* and *store*. Did he like the herbs better than the store? Or did he like the herbs at one place better than he liked the herbs at another place? By adding a pronoun and a preposition, we make the second item complete and the meaning clear:

> Edoardo liked the fresh herbs at the farmers' market better than **those at** the store.

In this revised sentence, we are clearly comparing the two locations for the fresh herbs, the *market* and the *store*. Here's another example:

> Before taking the job, SooJin met with the manager and sous chef.

In this sentence, it is not clear whether SooJin met with one person or two. Add the article *the* to clarify that the manager and the sous chef are two separate people:

> Before taking the job, SooJin met with the manager and **the** sous chef.

Finally, with a series of clauses that begin with *that*, it is often clearer to repeat *that* in each clause. Look at this sentence:

> She told me that she wanted to see a comedy, Tracy wanted to see an action film, and George wanted to stay home.

As written, this sentence could be a comma splice with the second independent clause beginning at *Tracy*. Note how the addition of *that* makes the structure clear.

> She told me that she wanted to see a comedy, **that** Tracy wanted to see an action film, and **that** George wanted to stay home.

Exercise 28.4 | Completing Parallel Structures

Rewrite the following sentences, adding the appropriate words to complete the parallel elements.

1. In the classic 1980s comedy *Tootsie*, Dustin Hoffman had more trouble finding acting work as a man than a woman.
2. His agent told him that he was too much of a perfectionist, he argued too often with directors, and no one in New York would work with him.
3. Hoffman's character found that he became both a better person and actor when he dressed as a woman.
4. He liked himself better as Dorothy than Michael.
5. His friends at home liked him more than at work.

RECIPE FOR REVIEW

MAINTAINING PARALLELISM IN A SERIES

In writing, **parallelism** means that if the *ideas* in a sentence are somehow equivalent, the *structure* that expresses them should also be similar. Put two or more equivalent items in a series in the same form or part of speech, for example, all nouns or all adjectives, all gerunds or all infinitives.

> The steak was thick, juicy, and it had a good flavor. *[NOTparallel]*
>
> The steak was thick, juicy, and flavorful. *[parallel]*

MAINTAINING PARALLELISM IN A COMPARISON

In a comparison using *as* or *than,* put equivalent items in the same form or part of speech, for example, both nouns, both adjectives, or both infinitives.

> Julius doesn't like basketball as much as grilling a steak. *[NOT parallel]*
>
> Julius doesn't like playing basketball as much as grilling a steak. *[parallel]*

MAINTAINING PARALLELISM WITH *BOTH/AND*, ETC.

When ideas are joined with the conjunctions *both/and, either/or, neither/nor,* or *not only/but also,* put them in the same form.

> Brenda Leigh Johnson is both smart and has a lot of courage. *[NOT parallel]*
>
> Brenda Leigh Johnson is both smart and courageous. *[parallel]*
>
> Brenda Leigh Johnson has both intelligence and courage. *[parallel]*

COMPLETING PARALLEL STRUCTURES

Add words where necessary to complete a parallel structure.

> Edoardo liked the fresh herbs at the farmers' market better than the store. *[incomplete]*
>
> Edoardo liked the fresh herbs at the farmers' market better than *those at* the store. *[complete]*

DIRECTIONS: Rewrite each of the following sentences, correcting any errors in parallel structure.

1. In *Crash*, Shaniqua dislikes Officer Ryan because he is disrespectful, manipulative, and he's in an irritable mood.

2. Jean realizes that she likes talking to her maid more than her friend Carol.

3. Officer Hanson is not only upset with his partner's racism but also he feels that his boss is being unfair.

4. Anthony is kinder to the illegal immigrants in the back of the van than Jean and Rick.

5. Among the various characters, Daniel the locksmith is one who both maintains his dignity in the face of prejudice and he also encourages others to rediscover their self-respect.

CHAPTER 29
EDITING AND PROOFREADING THE FINAL DRAFT

By the end of this chapter, you should begin to . . .

- recognize the importance of proofreading in a business or professional setting;
- use editing and proofreading strategies effectively;
- take advantage of spell check and other spelling aids;
- use basic rules to improve your spelling; and
- recognize commonly misused words.

Once the final draft of your essay, letter, email, or résumé is complete and polished in terms of content, organization, and style, you must then **edit** the grammar and usage (Chapters 22–28). Finally, you must **proofread** the writing carefully one or more times before submitting or mailing it. Almost inevitably, so-called typographical errors in spelling and punctuation (Chapters 29–31) will occur in anything we write. These are errors that we would be able to recognize and fix if we could read our own work carefully and objectively. Although these errors don't seem to be connected with the *content* of the writing, they may actually have a powerful—and negative—effect on the reader, in the way that a cracked plate might diminish our delight in a beautiful lobster or a slice of chocolate cake. **Proofreading** is like the final wiping of the plate just before you serve it to the customer. It shows that you understand and respect the customers' expectations, that you take pride in your employer and in your own work.

WHY BOTHER WITH PROOFREADING?

Now as much as we might all appreciate the importance of a clean plate at a restaurant, it may be harder to believe that sentence fragments, misplaced apostrophes, and usage errors could really affect the way we're viewed outside of the English classroom. Yet research has shown that employers *do* judge us by our grammar and spelling.

For example, in "Ethos and Error: How Business People React to Errors," Larry Beason reports on his study of fourteen business professionals' reactions to proofreading errors:

> Some students perceive errors to be minor concerns and teachers who think otherwise to be "picky" (i.e., inconsequential). In some ways, these students are right. As a composition teacher, I might be annoyed or momentarily confused by error. . . . [However, i]n the nonacademic workforce, errors can affect people and events in larger ways. (51)

Beason's findings echo my experience of teaching in a culinary college. The chef faculty, most of whom come directly from the hospitality industry, complain bitterly to me about the bad writing of some of our students. When they show me a particular paper, the problems are almost always due to lack of proofreading. The chefs are quite irritated by these errors, which are most often in spelling and punctuation, and sometimes they are frustrated by sentence fragments or lack of sentence clarity. Grammar can be quite an emotional topic!

Proofreading is like the final wiping of the plate just before you serve it to the customer.

It's also a political one. Using "good" English can be seen as a mark of status. Using "bad" English, on the other hand, may make writers appear ignorant or uneducated. John C. Bean discusses this effect in *Engaging Ideas: The Professor's Guide to Integrating Writing, Critical Thinking, and Active Learning in the Classroom*:

> The sentence *He brung it*, though grammatical, is produced in a nonstandard dialect of English. Those who speak this dialect probably do so because it is the dialect of their parents and peers. Unfortunately for their success in college and professional life, their parents and peers do not speak the prestige dialect of our culture—a sociological and political issue, not an issue of intelligence or verbal skill. (71)

Two points are essential here. First, the way people write and speak does *not* mean anything about their intelligence, abilities, and value as human beings. Second, the way people speak and write *can* affect the way they are viewed as professionals, and that can have important consequences. Proofreading is about *ethos*, about the trustworthy, fair-minded, and knowledgeable character that writers try to establish with their readers.

Copyright © 2015 Cengage Learning®

(See also Chapter 16.) For business professionals, meticulous proofreading suggests that you are or would be a careful, dependable, thoughtful employee.

Research has also shown that some types of errors are viewed as worse than others by business professionals. Some of the errors have to do with "status," such as nonstandard verb forms. Others are relatively free of "status," but are nevertheless considered very serious or serious errors. Study the following lists, adapted from Maxine Hairston's "Not All Errors Are Equal: Nonacademic Readers in the Professions Respond to Lapses in Usage":

Status-Marking Errors

Type of Error	Example
Nonstandard verb forms in past tense or past participle	*brung* instead of *brought, had went* instead of *had gone*
Lack of subject–verb agreement	*we was* instead of *we were, he don't* instead of *he doesn't*
Double negatives	*There isn't no bread on the table* instead of *There's no bread* or *There isn't any bread*
Objective pronoun as subject	*Him and Janet were the last ones hired* instead of *He and Janet were the last ones hired*

Very Serious Errors

Type of Error	Example
Sentence fragments	*Everyone talking about the new policy* instead of *Everyone is talking about the new policy*
Run-on sentences	*The broccoli was tender the butter was melted* instead of *The broccoli was tender, and the butter was melted*
Proper nouns not capitalized	*The restaurant was on fifth avenue* instead of *Fifth Avenue*
Subject–verb agreement errors (not status marking)	*One of the apples are ripe* instead of *One of the apples is ripe*
Usage error: *of* instead of *have*	*Would of* instead of *would have*
Insertion of comma between the verb and its complement	*They decided, to visit the zoo* instead of *They decided to visit the zoo*
Lack of parallelism	*The steak was juicy, tender, and had a good flavor* instead of *The steak was thick, juicy, and flavorful*
Faulty adverb forms	*more saltier* instead of *more salty* or *saltier*
Use of transitive *set* for intransitive *sit*	*The plates set on the table* instead of *The plates sit on the table*

Serious Errors

Type of Error	Example
Dangling modifiers	*After waiting for over an hour, their table was finally ready* instead of *After they waited for over an hour, their table was finally ready* or *After waiting for over an hour, they were finally seated*
I as object pronoun	*Between you and I* instead of *Between you and me*
Lack of commas to set off interrupters such as *however*	*The answer however was incorrect* instead of *The answer, however, was incorrect*
Lack of commas in series	*The steak was thick juicy and flavorful* instead of *The steak was thick, juicy, and flavorful*
Tense switching	*He goes to the store and bought milk* instead of *goes* and *buys,* or *went* and *bought*

Source: Maxine Hairston's "Not All Errors Are Created Equal" in College English 43.8 (1981): 794–806.

Editing and proofreading are not just extra work that your English teacher assigns to torment you. They are skills you will need in the workplace as well as in school, skills that contribute to the overall impression you make as a thoughtful and reliable professional.

Exercise 29.1 | Proofreading Practice

Read through the following passage at least three times, looking for status-marking, very serious, and serious errors. Correct any errors you find. (NOTE: There are ten errors, only three of which were caught by the software's spelling and grammar check.)

Filled with indignation, Hary heads for his favorite diner to get a cup of coffee he's looking down ad his newspaper as he enters the diner and doesnt notice the uneasy expressions on the faces of the waitress the cook and some of the customers—though us in the audience see them. As he remains absorb in the paper. The waitress, loretta, puts the coffee cup on the counter and begins to pour in sugar from the glass jar. She pours and she pours, all the time glancing nervously up at Harry and then around the diner. On an on she pours, while the audience begins to chuckle and Harry remains oblivious.

STRATEGIES FOR PROOFREADING

Proofreading requires a clear and focused mindset that has little in common with the creative energy flowing through earlier phases of the writing process. Instead of the big picture, we must concentrate on the little details. We must be careful to look at each word as it is written. If we go too quickly, we tend to "read" what we *think* we wrote or what we *intended* to write, and we can miss what is actually on the page.

Proofreading requires a clear and focused mindset.

First, **find the right time and place for proofreading**. If you can, avoid proofreading immediately after writing. Try to let some time pass, ideally at least twenty-four hours. If you are a "morning person," it might be most effective to proofread in the morning. If you are a night owl, however, there might be another time of day when your brain is best suited to careful, detail-oriented work. Some people find that listening to music helps them concentrate, while others need absolute quiet.

Next, if you've written the paper on a computer, **run spell check and then print out a hard copy** for proofreading. While some editing can be done right on the screen in the earlier stages of writing, the final proofreading is best done with pencil and paper.

Then, find some way of slowing your reading down so that you **focus on only one word or sentence at a time**. You might follow along with a finger as you read, or you might cover your paper with a separate sheet (perhaps of a different color) and move this cover sheet slowly down your paper to reveal one line of text at a time. Especially when checking spelling, some writers read their sentences (even their entire texts) backwards in order to focus on the surface details. Start with the last sentence (or the last word in the sentence); then move to the sentence before it, then the sentence before that. The idea is to separate the meaning of the passage from its grammar, spelling, and punctuation.

Read your paper out loud. Reading aloud—or having someone else read the paper aloud to you—can help you find all kinds of errors. If someone else is reading, though, be sure you are also able to look at the paper or at another copy of it. Punctuation is not usually read aloud, but as you *hear* the sentences, you may *see* punctuation errors. Listen for sentence fragments and unclear phrasing. Notice any hesitation in your voice or the other reader's voice: it might signal a problem with a word or sentence. You might also read the text aloud to an audience. The pressure of a listener may help you hear the paper in a new way, and that can help with revising content and organization, as well as with proofreading grammar and mechanics.

It can be helpful to **read through the paper several times, looking for different types of errors** with each read-through. You may want to read once to check sentence completeness and sentence boundaries. Look at each sentence individually, from the capital letter (there should be one!) to the period. Listen for any problems with agreement or clarity. In another read-through, perhaps circle each punctuation mark. To check spelling, it can be effective to read the essay *backwards*. Having someone else check the essay is also useful. In any case, you would be wise to proofread it yourself at least twice and perhaps a third time before sending or submitting it.

Of course, you should **always use spell check, if it's available, but realize it won't catch everything**. Pay attention to the endings of words, for example, adding *–d* or *–ed* to some verbs in the past tense. Double check the spelling of proper nouns and of little words such as *on, or, of; it, if, is, in;* and *an, and, any*. Double check any numbers and charts. Look at headings, headers and footers, notes, and Works Cited pages. If you introduce a numbered list of steps, for example, or of items within a category, check that the numbers match. Be sure that you meet any special formatting instructions, such as font type and size.

Finally, think about what mistakes *you* are likely to make, and **create your own proofreading checklist**. Figure 29.1 lists the major types of errors and indicates which

Figure 29.1 Proofreading Checklist

Check ☑	Proofreading Checklist	For More Information
☐	Check that each sentence is complete.	Chapter 22
☐	Eliminate run-on sentences and comma splices.	Chapter 23
☐	Check that each verb agrees with its subject.	Chapter 24
☐	Check that verb forms are correct.	Chapters 24–25
☐	Check that verb tense is appropriate and consistent.	Chapter 25
☐	Check that pronouns are used correctly in terms of case, agreement, reference, and point of view.	Chapter 26
☐	Check that modifiers are used correctly.	Chapter 27
	Correct any errors in parallel structure.	Chapter 28
☐	Check that each sentence begins with a capital letter and ends with the appropriate punctuation mark.	Chapter 30
☐	Check overall use of capital letters and apostrophes.	Chapter 30
☐	Check internal punctuation: commas, colons, and semicolons.	Chapter 31
☐	Use spell check; then check your personal list of commonly misspelled words.	Chapter 29
☐	Check that commonly misused words are used correctly.	Appendix B

chapter in this book explains how to fix them. Exercise 29.2 asks you to create your own proofreading checklist. Keep track of teachers' comments and corrections. Do a read-through that is specifically focused on your personal checklist. If you know you have trouble with certain words, use the search feature of your word-processing program to find them. Then double check the spelling and usage.

Exercise 29.2 | Your Personal Proofreading Checklist

Fill in the following chart with the five most "serious" and/or frequent errors you tend to make. When you're proofreading your work, read it through multiple times, looking for one type of error with each read.

Type of Error	Example
1.	
2.	
3.	
4.	
5.	

IMPROVING YOUR SPELLING

The purpose of spelling, like that of punctuation, is to make sure the reader knows what you mean; that's the bottom line. However, spelling also reveals how much care you have taken with your writing and how well you understand the expectations of a particular audience. You certainly don't want bad spelling to show up in important business contexts, as it did in this restaurant review:

> Many of the Italian ingredients and cooking terms—arugula, bruschetta, mascarpone, carbonara—are misspelled on the menu.[13]

Poor spelling may seem relatively unimportant to a restaurant's success, but the reviewer adds that the restaurant's "casual approach to service can be off-putting," and her overall assessment is negative. A misspelled word is like a dirty water glass—it makes a bad impression. On the other hand, good spelling makes a good impression.

Spelling also has benefits in terms of reading and writing.[14] Good spelling isn't just about memorizing the look of a word—though that's important—but about understanding where words come from and how different forms are constructed. This deeper knowledge of spelling helps readers remember learned words more easily and figure out the meaning of new words, both of which improve reading comprehension. Good spelling also helps with the complexity of the writing process. We have to pay attention to many things when we write, from grammar, spelling, and punctuation—sometimes handwriting as well—to content, organization, sentence structure, and word choice. If we don't have to struggle with basic spelling, we have more brain power available for the other elements of communication.

But what can you do if you have trouble with spelling? First of all, don't feel too bad! It doesn't mean you can't *think* or *write*. Shakespeare spelled the same word three different ways on a single page, and he is one of the most admired authors in the English language. Second, you don't have to do it alone. Many professional writers don't spell well, but they have editors to support them, while students may visit an on-campus tutoring center. Another piece of good news is that the spelling of English words is not as random as it might seem. About 80% follow particular rules, some of which are covered in the next section, and these rules may be learned. Your instructor can help you get started or advise you about any special needs. Or you may want to explore some of the many books and websites about spelling practice. In the meantime, try these suggestions:

- **Always use spell check** before submitting a paper or sending an email. Although it won't catch all your typos, it's an excellent way to catch many of them. Furthermore, it makes a bad impression if you *don't* use it. Your readers can often tell if you haven't used spell check (if you typed *deffanittly*, for example), and they may assume you don't care much about your work. However, spell check works best for writers who already spell fairly well.
- **BUT remember that spell check can't do everything**. Spell check works by matching the spelling of each word in your document against its own "dictionary." Yet this dictionary does not contain all the words or names you may use and so cannot check their spelling. If spell check does not recognize a word, it might be that the word is incorrectly spelled (and the letters are so far off that spell check cannot suggest an alternative) or it might be that the word is correct but not in spell check's dictionary. In that case, you may want to *add* the word to the dictionary so that spell check will recognize it in the future. Be careful to get the spelling right when you do!
- **AND remember that spell check cannot tell you whether words have been *used* correctly**. For example, it cannot tell you that *chose* is incorrect in the infinitive phrase *to choose*. Spell check doesn't realize that *dinning* is not the correct spelling of *dining*. Does that mean you shouldn't use spell check? No, of course not. *Always* run your writing (including email) through spell check before proofreading it or giving it to anyone else to read.
- **What about the dictionary?** Sometimes we've been told to check spelling in a dictionary. The difficulty there is that if you have no idea how to spell a word, you don't know where to look. If the word begins with the *s* sound, for example, will you look under *s* or *c*, or even *p*? *Scenery, certain,* and *psychology* all begin with the same sound but not with the same letters. However, the dictionary *is* extremely important in helping you choose between synonyms (*resolute* or *obstinate*, for example) and in confirming that spell check has suggested or

auto-corrected the right word. *Definite* and *defiant* are both spelled correctly, but only *you* can tell which word you mean.

- **Check the spelling of commonly misused words.** (See Appendix B for details.)
- **Improve your accuracy by studying basic spelling rules.** (See the next section.)
- **Keep a list of words that you often misspell.** Another helpful practice is to keep a list of the words that you yourself often misspell. You can use this list in two ways. First, you can memorize the correct spellings of the words on your list. Second, you can look for these words as you proofread your writing, and then use the list to check whether they are spelled correctly. If you find that you are misspelling words because you're confusing the meaning, write the definition as well as the spelling on your list. In addition, refer to the appendices of this book (as well as other books or online sources) for lists of commonly misspelled words, selected culinary terms, and commonly misused words.
- **Check culinary terms carefully.** Since the culinary world uses words from many different languages, spelling can be especially complicated. We must move smoothly from French (*hors d'oeuvre, niçoise*) to Italian (*focaccia, prosciutto*) to Spanish (*paella, tortilla*). We must also spell words from languages that use a different alphabet (*challah, Szechuan*). And, of course, we must spell all kinds of English words, such as *cocoa, doughnut, leek,* and *Worcestershire sauce.*

Exercise 29.3 | Tracking Misspelled Words

Start a list of words that you've misspelled in your essays. Look over the selected culinary terms in Appendix A, and add to your list any whose spelling you are unsure of.

Exercise 29.4 | Commonly Misspelled Words

Identify the correctly spelled word in each pair.

1. definate	definite
2. succeed	suceed
3. writing	writting
4. occurence	occurrence
5. disappointment	dissappointment
6. extremely	extreemly
7. schedual	schedule
8. probably	probaly
9. accessible	accessable
10. recieve	receive

Exercise 29.5 | Identifying Misspelled Culinary Terms

Identify the correctly spelled word in each pair.

1.	restaurant	restaraunt
2.	vegtable	vegetable
3.	tomatos	tomatoes
4.	license	licence
5.	dining	dinning
6.	guacemole	guacamole
7.	thyme	time
8.	aperitif	apperitif
9.	cinamon	cinnamon
10.	vinagrette	vinaigrette

SPELLING RULES

No one disputes that English is a difficult language to spell. It has borrowed words from different languages and gone through various stages of pronunciation and spelling, and the end result is often confusing. However, there are certain rules that govern spelling, and it is useful to know them. Do you remember the rhyme "*i* before *e*, except after *c*, and when sounded like *a*, as in *neighbor* and *weigh*"? Thus we write *ei* in *receive* and *ceiling* because of the *c*, but *ie* in *believe* (see Figure 29.2). But of course there are also exceptions, such as *seize, either, weird, leisure,* and *neither.*

Figure 29.2 Spelling with *ie* and *ei*

Spelling Rule	Examples	Exception
Use *ie* (not *ei*) for the *e* sound	brief, niece, retrieve	either *and* neither (though there is some regional variation in pronunciation of these two words), leisure, seize, weird
BUT after *c* use *ei* for the *e* sound	ceiling, deceive, receive	
Use *ei* when the sound is not *e*, and especially when it is *a*	neighbor, weigh, height	friend, mischief

Another type of confusion concerns words that end with the sound "seed." There are three different spellings: *–cede, –ceed,* and *–sede* (see Figure 29.3).

Figure 29.3 Words with *–cede*, *–ceed*, and *–sede*

Suffix	Example
–cede (several words)	concede, intercede precede, recede
–ceed (three words)	exceed, proceed, succeed
–sede (one word)	supersede

When a **prefix** is added to the beginning of a word, the original spelling does not change; we simply add the two parts together. For example, *con + junction = conjunction*, and *mis + spell = misspell*. However, the prefix *all–* drops one *l*, as in *already, altogether,* and *always*. A number of rules govern the spelling of a word when a **suffix** is added to the end (see Figure 29.4).

Figure 29.4 Spelling Rules for Suffixes

Spelling Rule	Examples
Add *–s* to form the plural of regular nouns, BUT add *–es* if the noun ends in *s, ss, sh, ch,* or *x*	apples, pears, cartons BUT grasses, peaches, boxes
Do not change the spelling when you add *–ly* or *–ness*, EXCEPT if the word ends in *y,* change *y* to *i,* and then add the suffix	stubborn + ness = stubbornness EXCEPT happy + ness = happiness
Drop the final *e* if the suffix begins with a vowel	dine + ing = dining hope + ing = hoping
Keep the final *e* if the suffix begins with a consonant	hope + ful = hopeful EXCEPT argue + ment = argument
If the word ends in a consonant + *y,* change *y* to *i,* unless the suffix begins with *i*	hurry + ed = hurried hurry + ing = hurrying
Change *f* to *v* for plurals	knife/knives, life/lives, wife/wives
Double the final consonant before the suffix if the word ends in one vowel plus one consonant and is accented on the last syllable	run + ing = running occur + ed = occurred BUT cancel + ed = canceled (because the last syllable is not accented)
The suffix *–ful* always has one *l*	hopeful, beautiful, plentiful

COMMONLY MISUSED WORDS

Salt and sugar look very much alike, though salt granules are generally larger. However, the two have quite different tastes and chemical properties. What would happen if you mixed up the quantities in a cookie dough recipe and added a cup and a half of *salt* instead of sugar? Ugh! Similarly, English contains a number of words that resemble one another but have different spellings and meanings. Would you offer your customers a *desert* menu? Should you *except* or *accept* the produce delivery? Does it make sense to eat *diner* in a *dinner?*

Prepare for your next proofreading task by skimming through Appendix B and identifying any word pairs that you find confusing. Read and study the explanations. Perhaps make up your own personal mnemonic device to remember the difference between them. (For example, *dessert*—the food not the sand—has two *s*'s because it's "so sweet.") Then, when you proofread a paper, pay special attention to these words.

Dessert—it's so sweet.

Exercise 29.6 | Commonly Misused Words

Read through Appendix B: Commonly Misused Words, and write down five pairs of words that look confusing or that you know have confused you in the past. Study the explanations and examples. Then, for each word, write a sentence that illustrates its correct usage.

Exercise 29.7 | Using the Right Words

For each of the following sentences, choose the correct word from the pair in parentheses.

1. The knife had a speck of tomato sauce on _____ blade. (its/it's)

2. "_____ important to work with a sharp knife," said the chef-instructor. (Its/It's)

3. We had already driven _____ the restaurant before we saw the sign. (passed/past)

4. We _____ the restaurant before we saw the sign. (passed/past)

5. "_____ ready to bake cookies?" asked George. (Whose/Who's)

6. "I am," said Derek. "_____ recipe are we going to use?" (Whose/Who's)

7. "We will use _____ recipe, Derek." (your/you're)

8. "_____ going to need lots of brown sugar, then." (Your/You're)

9. The customers at the local Italian restaurant look at _____ menus. (their/there/they're)

10. _____ are four kinds of homemade pasta available. (Their/There/They're)

RECIPE FOR REVIEW

A BAKER'S DOZEN PROOFREADING STRATEGIES

1. Find the right time and place for proofreading.
2. Run spell check and then print out a hard copy.
3. Focus on only one word or sentence at a time.
4. Read your paper out loud.
5. Read through the paper several times, looking for different types of errors.
6. Always use spell check, if it's available, but realize it won't catch everything.
7. Pay attention to the endings of words, for example, adding *–d* or *–ed* to some verbs in the past tense.
8. Double check the spelling of proper nouns and of little words such as *on, or, of; it, if, is, in;* and *an, and, any.*
9. Double check any numbers and charts.
10. Look at headings, headers and footers, notes, and Works Cited pages.
11. If you introduce a numbered list of steps or of items within a category, check that the numbers match.
12. Be sure that you meet any special formatting instructions, such as font type and size.
13. Create—and use—your own proofreading checklist.

IMPROVING YOUR SPELLING

1. Use spell check on every piece of writing.
2. Use a dictionary to check the spelling and definition of words highlighted by spell check.
3. Add words and names to spell check as needed.
4. Learn spelling rules.
5. Keep a list of words that you sometimes misspell, and check for them in each piece of writing. Add new words to the spell-check feature on your computer.
6. Refer to published lists of commonly misspelled words, culinary terms, and commonly misused words (such as those in the appendices of this book).
7. Look at your essays and note which of the commonly misused words in Appendix B you tend to use or misuse. Then add them to your personal proofreading checklist and review them carefully whenever you proofread your writing.

CHAPTER QUIZ

DIRECTIONS: PART I. SPELLING. One word is misspelled in each of the following sentences. Write the correct spelling on a separate sheet of paper.

_____ 1. The customers were pleased with the hotel accomodations.

_____ 2. It was necessary to chose smoking or non-smoking rooms, of course.

_____ 3. Latter, they went to the hotel's three-star restaurant.

_____ 4. The dinning room was beautifully decorated with red velvet curtains and gold picture frames.

_____ 5. The soup du jur was butternut squash with apple slices and sour cream.

_____ 6. No one was dissappointed with its creamy texture and rich autumn flavors!

_____ 7. The next course followed imediately, a salad of impossibly fresh mixed greens.

_____ 8. There were also hot roles and butter, as well as large Calamata olives.

_____ 9. By the time the main course arrived, the dinners were not even hungry.

_____ 10. After a last sip of wine, everyone headed threw the doors toward the elevators.

DIRECTIONS: PART II. COMMONLY MISUSED WORDS. Fill in the blank in each sentence with the appropriate word in parentheses.

11. The customers were unable to _____ between the lemon meringue pie and the apricot flan. (choose/chose)

12. The daily special was served with a _____ cup of coffee or tea. (complementary/complimentary)

13. "Which of the _____ looks good to you?" asked Marianne. (deserts/desserts)

14. "What's for _____?" asked Joey. (diner/dinner)

15. Many Americans resolve to _____ weight after the winter holidays. (loose/lose)

16. Andrew and _____ shared a delicious mushroom risotto. (I/myself)

17. "May I have a _____ of that New York cheesecake?" (peace/piece)

18. _____ excited about trying the vodka a la penne. (Their/There/They're)

19. No one is fonder of chicken lo mein _____ Vinnie is. (than/then)

20. You _____ may enjoy Vinnie's favorite someday. (to/too/two)

21. Is this the pistachio pudding cake _____ you were talking about this morning? (that/which)

22. Is Rachel the one _____ intends to make the cake this afternoon? (who/which)

23. Rachel learned the recipe from Will, _____ had learned it from his mother. (that/who)

24. Anna saw a girl _____ she had known in kindergarten. (who/whom)

25. John saw a girl _____ was dancing with her father. (who/whom)

CHAPTER 30
PUNCTUATION I—
END MARKS, CAPITALIZATION, APOSTROPHES, ABBREVIATIONS, NUMERALS, ITALICS, UNDERLINING, AND QUOTATION MARKS

By the end of this chapter, you should begin to . . .

- use end marks appropriately;
- use capitalization appropriately;
- use apostrophes correctly for possessives, contractions, and certain plurals;
- use abbreviations and numerals according to the appropriate style guide;
- use italics and underlining appropriately, for example, for certain titles; and
- use quotation marks correctly, for example, for certain titles and direct speech.

Punctuation marks, such as those that come at the end of a sentence, provide visual, nonverbal guides to the structures and meanings of written language. They function like road signs, directing the reader's movement through the text. With capital letters at the beginning of the sentence and appropriate marks at the end, punctuation frames our ideas, just as an elegant table setting frames the culinary delicacies from the kitchen.

Just as the rules for setting the table may vary between restaurants, the rules governing the use of punctuation, capitalization, and abbreviation, for example, may vary between style guides. In general, we're following the **MLA style** guide in this chapter and the next. Any differences between the MLA and **APA style** guides about a particular rule will be noted. Otherwise, assume that the guides agree.

END MARKS

End marks are those punctuation marks that indicate the end of a sentence, the end of a thought. They're like stop signs that tell us we've reached the end of a city block. They also tell us something about the *kind* of sentence, whether it is a statement, a question, or an exclamation. Generally speaking, leave one space between sentences, as well as between words.

1. A statement, like this one, is followed by a **period**.

    Punctuation is an important part of clear writing.

    If the sentence ends with a period that is part of an abbreviation, do not add a second period.

    The appointment is for tomorrow at 10:00 a.m.

2. A question is followed by a **question mark**.

    What is the most common type of punctuation?

3. However, an **indirect question** would be followed by a period rather than a question mark.

    The students asked what the most common type of punctuation is.

4. An **exclamation point** is used to convey strong emotion or to emphasize a command. Use it sparingly in formal writing.

    What a delicious dessert!

    Don't touch that pan!

Exercise 30.1 | End Marks

Punctuate the following paragraph with the appropriate end marks.

Clint Eastwood's career has taken some interesting turns in the last decade From *Unforgiven* to *Mystic River,* he has revisited the genres of the cowboy movie and the police thriller that were his bread and butter twenty and thirty years before He has also, as a director, coaxed some superb acting from his stars Sean Penn's emotional portrayal of a vengeful father in *Mystic River* was recognized with an Oscar Do you remember the scene outside the park gates when Penn realizes his daughter has been murdered What a brilliant performance

---

CAPITALIZATION

Like end marks, **capitalization** reinforces the structure of the sentence, in this case by marking its beginning. Capital letters are also used for proper nouns, titles, and some abbreviations and acronyms.

Just as in this sentence, the first word of every English sentence begins with a capital letter. The capital letter that begins the sentence and the period or question mark that ends it indicate the completion of a thought or stand-alone idea.

1. Capitalize the **first word of a sentence**.

    > The movie was released in December, just in time to be considered for the Academy Awards.

2. **Capitalize the first word of a statement or a question** that forms part of a sentence, whether or not it is set off by quotation marks.

    > We asked ourselves, What are the differences between the cuisines of Greece and those of other Mediterranean countries?

    > The food safety instructor says, "Wash your hands for twenty seconds in the hottest water you can tolerate."

3. **Do *not* capitalize the first word of a quoted *phrase*,** unless that word would be capitalized for another reason.

    > Dominique paid close attention to the instructions regarding washing hands "in the hottest water you can tolerate."

4. **Capitalize the first word of an independent clause that follows a colon. Do *not* capitalize the first word that follows a semicolon,** unless that word would be capitalized for another reason.

    > Captain Ahab is obsessed with the idea of killing the white whale that took off his leg; his story is told in the novel *Moby-Dick*. [Do not capitalize *his*.]

    > The narrator of the story is a young man called Ishmael; Queequeg, a cannibal from the South Seas, is his friend. [Capitalize the proper noun *Queequeg*.]

Captain Ahab (left) is obsessed with the idea of killing the white whale, Moby-Dick. Queequeg stands behind him.

Exercise 30.2 | Capitalization and End Marks

Correct the capitalization and add appropriate end marks as you rewrite the following sentences.

1. one of my favorite restaurants is chez marcel
2. the newspapers say it offers "The best french cuisine outside of paris"
3. as we arrive, the hostess exclaims, "welcome to chez marcel"
4. my friends want to try something new; They order escargot
5. i ask myself, how daring do i feel tonight

In addition to marking the beginning of a sentence, capitalization points out the difference between a general category and a specific individual or example. It is the difference between a *professor* and *Professor Fromm*, between a *restaurant* and *The Cheesecake Factory*, between a *movie* and *The Hobbit*.

5. **Capitalize proper nouns,** which include the following:

- The names of specific persons and animals, such as *John Hancock, Sojourner Truth*, and *Seabiscuit*; also capitalize their titles when these precede the name, as in *Professor Malik, Dr. Garcia*, and *Chef Marcus Samuelsson*, and when the title is used in place of the name, such as *Senator, Coach*, or *Chef.*
- Words showing family relationships when used with the person's name or when used in place of the person's name, such as *Aunt Debbie* or *Dad*; do not capitalize these titles when they are preceded by a possessive, such as *my aunt Debbie* or *my father*.
- The names of religions, races, and nationalities, or adjectives derived from these names, such as *Islam, Judaism, Hispanic, Caucasian, Brazilian, Thai.*
- The names of specific places, including specific cities, states, countries, and continents, such as *Seoul, Alaska, Mexico*, and *Australia*; specific islands, mountains, oceans, lakes, and rivers, such as *Ellis Island, Mount Kilimanjaro, the Indian Ocean, Lake Michigan*, and *the Yangtze River*; and specific streets, such as *Fifth Avenue, Mulberry Street*, and *Sunset Boulevard.*
- The days of the week, months, and special dates—but not the seasons—such as *Monday, July, Valentine's Day*, and *summer.*
- The names of other specific things—ships, planes, awards, etc.—such as *the Titanic, Air Force One*, and an *Academy Award.* (Note that in an ordinary sentence, the names of the ship *Titanic* and the plane *Air Force One* would be italicized, while an Academy Award would not.)
- The names of specific brands, but not the common nouns that may follow: *Cheerios, Sprite, Heinz ketchup, Dodge minivan.*

6. **Capitalize the titles of specific organizations, events, and historical periods**, such as *the League of Women Voters, the Boston Tea Party,* and *the Colonial Era.*

7. **Capitalize the first word and other important words in the titles** of books, newspapers, stories, poems, movies, and other works of art, such as *Joy of Cooking, The Washington Post,* "A Rose for Emily," "Sailing to Byzantium," *Men in Black,* and the *Mona Lisa.*

   - For both MLA and APA, capitalize nouns, pronouns, verbs, adjectives, and adverbs. Do **not** capitalize articles (*a, an, the*), prepositions (*from, to, of*), or coordinating conjunctions (*and, but*) within the title.
   - For MLA, capitalize subordinating conjunctions (*although, as, because, if, while*).
   - For APA, capitalize all words of more than three letters (for example, *From* would be capitalized in a title in APA style but not in MLA style). Note that the APA rules for capitalizing words in titles are different depending on whether the title appears in the body of the text or in the list of references.

8. **Capitalize words formed from proper nouns**, for example, *the English language, Roman numerals.*

9. **Always capitalize the pronoun *I*.** The other pronouns are not capitalized, unless they begin a sentence or are part of a title.

Exercise 30.3 | Capitalization of Proper Nouns

Rewrite the following phrases, correcting the capitalization where necessary. Some items are already correct.

    Example: New York city
    Correct: New York City

1. mexico city
2. mr. kim
3. professor Lauria
4. aunt Winifred
5. my cousin Tony
6. a vietnamese dish
7. a place in the country
8. a park avenue address
9. new year's eve
10. on tuesday night
11. rice krispies
12. the Middle ages
13. the bill of rights
14. *the Lord of the rings*
15. a Mediterranean diet

APOSTROPHES

Apostrophes have two major roles: to form the possessive of nouns and to make **contractions**, which are combinations of two words in which some letters are omitted. Apostrophes are also used to form the plural of letters of the alphabet.

APOSTROPHES WITH POSSESSIVE FORMS

1. In general, **form the possessive of a singular noun by adding an apostrophe plus the letter s.** For example, instead of writing *the story of the chef*, we could write *the chef's story;* instead of *the reputation of Chicago for deep-dish pizza*, we could write *Chicago's reputation for deep-dish pizza.* **The rule applies also to singular nouns that already end in s;** we still add an apostrophe plus s to form the possessive: *the bus's route, Henry James's novel.*

2. **For most plural nouns and all plural proper nouns, add just an apostrophe to form the possessive:** *the girls' team, the Andersons' restaurant.* **For nouns with irregular plural forms, add an apostrophe plus s:** *the children's team, the men's team.*

3. **Be careful to distinguish between the simple plural, the singular possessive, and the plural possessive.** They sound the same, but the apostrophe changes the meaning.

   > The chefs = more than one chef
   > The chef's = belonging to one chef
   > The chefs' = belonging to more than one chef

   > The chefs were unpacking their mystery baskets.   *[plural]*
   > The first chef's basket contained an assortment of mushrooms.
   > *[singular possessive]*
   > The competition judged the chefs' creativity.   *[plural possessive]*

4. **Do *not* use apostrophes for possessive pronouns,** such as *ours, yours, hers, its,* and *theirs.* Be careful not to confuse the possessive *its* with the contraction *it's.* To form the possessive of singular indefinite pronouns, however, add an apostrophe plus s: *someone's glove, nobody's fool.*

5. **To form the possessive of hyphenated words, add an apostrophe plus s to the last word:** *brother-in-law's car.* (Note that the plural of hyphenated words is formed differently: *brothers-in-law.*) The plural possessive of hyphenated words contains two s's: *brothers-in-law's cars.* The names of organizations also form the possessive by adding apostrophe s to the last word: *Johnson & Johnson's, Simon & Schuster's.*

6. When **an item is owned in common,** the possessive is formed by adding apostrophe s to the last name: *Jack and Jill's rhyme, Bill and Ted's Excellent Adventure.* **When ownership is not shared,** each name forms the possessive with apostrophe s: *Anna's and Carla's hats.* Each woman has her own hat.

The chef's mystery basket contained an assortment of mushrooms.

APOSTROPHES WITH CONTRACTIONS

Another use of the apostrophe is to indicate that one or more letters have been left out, as in the following contractions:

I'm = I am

isn't = is not

hasn't = has not

haven't = have not

you're = you are

he's = he is

they're = they are

didn't = did not

For formal business and academic writing, you will most likely avoid contractions. Check with your employer or instructor. If you do use them, however, be sure to use them correctly.

APOSTROPHES WITH PLURALS

Finally, the apostrophe may be used to form the plurals of letters of the alphabet.

Dot your *i*'s and cross your *t*'s.

When Debbie was a little girl, she made hearts over her *i*'s.

The rules concerning apostrophes continue to evolve. For example, dates used to require an apostrophe (*the 1980's*); now they do not (*the 1980s*). Follow the guidelines of your instructor or publisher.

Exercise 30.4 | Apostrophes

In the following sentences, add or delete apostrophes where necessary.

1. Mariano Riveras one of the most beloved Yankees players'.
2. He is one of the Yankees core four, a group thats been playing together for 15 years'.
3. Another of that groups members is Andy Pettitte, who's success in the postseason is legendary.
4. Theres a third member, shortstop Derek Jeter, whose known as Mr. November because of his excellent postseason play.
5. The fourth member of the core four is Jorge Posada; its clear that he has a catchers broad perspective on the game.

Perhaps someday this young slugger will face a big league closer like Mariano Rivera.

© Andrea Leone/Shutterstock.com

ABBREVIATIONS

You're probably quite familiar with the **abbreviations** used in recipes (*lb, oz, tsp*) and cell phone texts (*u, LOL, TTYL*). In your academic and business writing, however, you will use abbreviations only occasionally. In general, do not replace a word with an abbreviation in the text of your paper, unless it is generally acceptable. For example, do not use an ampersand (&) or plus sign (+) for "and" or the letter *u* for "you."

> We ordered the macaroni & cheese. *[informal]*

> We ordered the macaroni and cheese. *[preferred]*

Personal titles are an exception to this rule. Titles such as *Mrs.* and *Dr.* are typically written as abbreviations when used before a name: *Mrs. Robinson, Dr. Seuss*. When they are

Figure 30.1   Acceptable Abbreviations

	Examples	Meaning
Titles	Mr., Mrs., Ms. Dr., St.	man, married woman, woman doctor, saint
Expressions of Time	a.m. p.m.	before noon after noon
Academic Degrees	AOS AAS AA/AS BA/BS MA/MS PhD MD	Associate of Occupational Studies Associate of Applied Studies Associate of Arts/Associate of Science Bachelor of Arts/Bachelor of Science Master of Arts/Master of Science Doctor of Philosophy Doctor of Medicine
Acronyms	FDA HACCP MLA APA	Food and Drug Administration Hazard Analysis Critical Control Point Modern Language Association American Psychological Association

not used with a name, however, such titles are spelled out, for example, *Is there a doctor in the house?* Other exceptions are listed in Figure 30.1.

In the texts of business letters and of papers in MLA format, avoid all but the standard abbreviations in Figure 30.1. The APA permits abbreviations that appear as words in *Merriam-Webster's Collegiate Dictionary* (2005; see the APA *Publication Manual* for abbreviations specific to psychology). The abbreviations for Latin expressions and other words listed in Figure 30.2 may be used within parentheses, tables, and Works Cited pages. See Chapter 19 for additional abbreviations used in citations.

Figure 30.2   Abbreviations within Parentheses, Tables, and Works Cited Pages

	Examples	Meaning
Latin Expressions	etc. i.e. e.g.	and so on that is for example
Names of States and Countries	GA, IL, OR USA Arg.	Georgia, Illinois, Oregon United States of America Argentina
Expressions of Time	Feb. Mon. hr.	February Monday hour

Note carefully which abbreviations have periods (*Dr.*) and which don't (*MD*). Consult the appropriate style guide (MLA or APA, for example) when necessary.

If you plan to use a less familiar abbreviation or **acronym**, spell it out the first time, followed by the abbreviation in parentheses; then abbreviate the term consistently throughout the paper. Do not alternate between spelling out the term and abbreviating it.

> According to the Food and Drug Administration (FDA). . . .
>
> The FDA also said. . . .

Explain abbreviations and acronyms unless you are certain your audience will understand them. For example, HACCP could be used without explanation in a letter to the Department of Health, but it's probably best to begin with "Hazard Analysis Critical Control Point (HACCP)" in an essay for English.

NUMERALS

As with abbreviations, there are rules for deciding whether to use numerals or words to represent numbers. Rules about numbers vary from style to style. The MLA suggests spelling out numbers that can be written as one or two words. Thus, *fifty* and *ninety-eight* would be spelled out, while *150* and *125th* would be represented by numerals.

> The new restaurant did 150 covers per night.
>
> The owner bought fifty new chairs.
>
> We got off the train at 125th Street.
>
> Bonnie scored in the ninety-eighth percentile on the math test.

In contrast, the APA prefers to use words for numbers less than 10 and numerals for numbers 10 and over.

> The owner bought fifty new chairs. *[MLA]*
>
> The owner bought 50 new chairs. *[APA]*

Both MLA and APA styles agree on the following points:

- **Do not begin a sentence with a numeral.**

  > 150 covers were expected on a Friday night. *[incorrect]*
  >
  > One hundred fifty covers were expected on a Friday night. *[correct]*
  >
  > We expect 150 covers on a Friday night. *[correct]*

- Except at the beginning of a sentence, **numerals should be used in dates, addresses, and page numbers, and with symbols or abbreviations.**

  December 7, 1941

  1600 Pennsylvania Avenue

  See pages 5–7.

  $29.99; 3 tsp; 65 mph; 11:30 a.m.

In MLA format, *consistency* is important. If the rules require a numeral for one of the numbers in a sentence or paragraph, use numerals for all the numbers in that category.

  There were only three croissants and 100 munchkins on the table. *[inconsistent]*

  There were only 3 croissants and 100 munchkins on the table. *[consistent]*

  There were only three croissants and one hundred munchkins on the table. *[consistent]*

Exercise 30.5 | Abbreviations and Numerals

Rewrite the following sentences, spelling out the abbreviations and numerals where necessary. Abbreviate any words from Figure 30.1.

1. I went to the Dr.'s office yesterday & got 3 Rx for the flu.
2. Did you know that mister León has a B.P.S. in cul. arts?
3. 2 oz. of cheese won't be enough; we need at least four.
4. Have you been to that new restaurant on Second Ave.?
5. 100 years ago there were no televisions, computers, cell phones, etc.

ITALICS AND UNDERLINING

Italics and **underlining** are generally used in the same way, but italics are used for typed papers and underlining for handwritten work.

1. **Use italics for the titles of books, periodicals, movies, television series, works of art, and ships.** However, chapters in a book, articles in a periodical, and episodes in a television series are enclosed in quotation marks. Look at the following examples, as well as Figure 30.3.

   "Chowder," a chapter in Melville's *Moby-Dick*, is an early example of food writing.

   Brian and Patrick's favorite episode of *The Office* was "Dwight's Speech."

Figure 30.3 Italics vs. Quotation Marks

Use italics* for the titles of ...	Use quotation marks* for the titles of ...
• books and plays	• chapters in a book
• periodicals (magazines and newspapers)	• articles in a periodical
• movies	• short stories
• television series	• episodes in a television series
• works of art, such as paintings	• essays
• long musical works, such as operas	• speeches
• CDs and record albums	• poems
• ships and spacecraft	• songs
• websites and online databases	• page or article on a website
• reports and brochures	

*The *MLA Handbook* lists a number of exceptions to these guidelines, titles that are capitalized but not italicized or enclosed in quotes. These include names of buildings (the Eiffel Tower), organizations (the Modern Language Association), political texts (Declaration of Independence), religious texts (Bible, Koran, Talmud), and books within such texts (Genesis, Acts).

If the title of one italicized work contains the title of another that would also be italicized, both MLA and APA prefer that the second work appear in plain type (reverse italicization) rather than quotation marks.

> Ulysses *Annotated: Notes for James Joyce's* Ulysses [*Ulysses* would normally be italicized]

2. **Use italics when referring to a letter or word and when using words in a foreign language.**

> British writers spell words like *colour* and *honour* with an extra *u.*
>
> The cooks prepared their *mise en place.*

Be sure to add all marks from the original language. If the word has been naturalized into English, do not use italics. Check with a dictionary if you are uncertain.

3. **Italics can be used to add emphasis** to a sentence or to certain words or phrases in a sentence. In informal or conversational writing, italics can help convey the rhythm of speech. In formal writing, however, try to highlight important points through the structure of the sentence rather than through italics.

> Please be sure that in future orders, the lettuce is *not* wilted.
>
> Please send only the very freshest heads of lettuce.

Exercise 30.6 | Italics and Underlining

Rewrite the following sentences, underlining words and phrases where necessary.

1. Have you read The Lord of the Rings or just seen the movie?
2. The King's Speech won the Academy Award for Best Picture.
3. Alex enjoyed that recent article in Food and Wine.
4. Large ensemble casts have been popular on television with such series as Boardwalk Empire and Modern Family.
5. The students in beginning French quickly learned to say bonjour.

QUOTATION MARKS

Quotation marks are used chiefly for certain titles and for reporting another writer or speaker's actual words.

1. **Use double quotation marks to set off the titles of songs, poems, short stories, individual episodes in a television series, articles, and chapters**. Note that the titles of books, magazines, and movies are underlined or italicized (see Figure 30.3), although many newspapers put movie titles in quotation marks rather than italics.

   "Happy Birthday" is one of the world's most popular songs.

   Edgar Allan Poe's poem "The Raven" has been memorized by generations of schoolchildren.

   "Chowder" is the title of a chapter in Herman Melville's nineteenth-century novel *Moby-Dick*.

   Poe also wrote short stories, such as "The Tell-Tale Heart."

   Note that the period in the last example falls *inside* the end quote.

2. Use quotation marks to **set off words and phrases that might be unfamiliar** to the reader, such as slang expressions.

   Joanie told Angela to "bring it."

   Use quotation marks only the first time the word appears. If the expression or phrase is commonly used, it does not require quotation marks.

   Angela advised her friend to let sleeping dogs lie.

   Quotation marks are sometimes used informally to suggest irony. Use italics rather than quotations marks to refer to a word or letter.

3. **Use quotation marks for material that is quoted directly from another text.** See Chapter 19 for more details.

4. **Use quotation marks to set off direct speech**, that is, when you use the words exactly as they are spoken or written. Put the quotation marks before the first and after the last word. Don't forget the final set of quotation marks.

> Angela said, "I read *Moby-Dick* in college."

Quotation marks are *not* used to mark **indirect speech**, which does not quote the exact words spoken.

> Angela said that she had read *Moby-Dick* in college.

> [She actually said, "I read *Moby-Dick* in college."]

Use a comma, a question mark, or an exclamation point after a direct quote and before the ending quotation mark.

> "Did you like *Moby-Dick*?" asked Jennifer.

In Edgar Allan Poe's famous poem, the raven sits on a sculpture of Greek goddess Pallas Athena and utters one word: "Nevermore."

Do not use more than one punctuation mark at the end of a quote.

> "Yes, I did!," replied Angela. [*incorrect*]
>
> "Yes, I did!" replied Angela. [*correct*]
>
> "Yes, I did," replied Angela. [*correct*]

When a sentence in the quote is interrupted, do not capitalize the next word.

> "When we go out to dinner on Friday nights," said Jamal, "we like to try new restaurants." [The *we* after the comma is not capitalized.]

Use single quotation marks to set off one quoted phrase within another.

> "Sometimes the waiters sing 'Happy Birthday,'" said Jamal.

While commas and periods fall within quotation marks, semicolons and colons fall outside. Question marks and exclamation points belong inside if the quote itself is a question or an exclamation; otherwise they too go outside.

> Diane asked, "Do you like to sing along?"
>
> Did the other customers sing "Happy Birthday"?

If you are quoting a conversation, begin a new paragraph with each change of speaker, as in the following examples:

> "What's your favorite television show?" asked Cheryl.
>
> "I'm torn between *Scandal* and *The Good Wife*," Sandra replied. "What about you?"
>
> "I love *House of Lies*."

In American English, single quotation marks are used only for a quote within a quote.

> Samantha said, "I thought 'The Lottery' was well written, but I found 'Those Who Walk Away from Omelas' was more interesting."

Exercise 30.7 | Using Quotation Marks

Rewrite the following sentences, adding quotation marks where appropriate.

1. A classic Motown hit of the 1960s was I Want You Back by the youthful Jackson Five.
2. One of Ernest Hemingway's most famous short stories is Hills Like White Elephants.
3. I read an article in *Food and Wine* called Grilled in Japan.
4. Have you ever been to a Japanese restaurant? they asked.
5. Yes, she replied. I'm a big fan of sashimi.

RECIPE FOR REVIEW

END MARKS

End marks, such as periods, question marks, and exclamation points, are used to indicate the end of a sentence and to show whether the sentence makes a statement, asks a question, or receives special emphasis.

CAPITALIZATION

Capital letters are used to mark the beginning of a sentence, a direct quote, or a statement that forms part of a sentence. Do *not* capitalize the word that follows a semicolon, unless that word would be capitalized for another reason. Capital letters are also used to indicate a proper noun, that is, the name of a specific person, place, or thing.

APOSTROPHES

Use **apostrophes** for the following forms:
- Possessives: *the student's schedule, the students' schedules*
- Contractions: *isn't, they're*
- Plurals of letters: *x's* and *y's*

ABBREVIATIONS

Avoid **abbreviations** in your academic writing, except for those described in Figures 30.1 and 30.2.

NUMERALS

Follow MLA or APA guidelines on when to use **numerals** and when to spell out numbers.

ITALICS AND UNDERLINING

Use **italics** in typed papers and **underlining** in handwritten work for the following:
- Titles of books, magazines, movies, and CDs (see Figure 30.1)
- Letters or words referred to as letters or words
- Words in a foreign language
- Emphasis

QUOTATION MARKS

Use **quotation marks** for the following:
- Titles of songs, poems, short stories, and articles (see Figure 30.1)
- Slang or unfamiliar words and phrases
- Direct quotes in a literary analysis or research paper
- Direct speech

CHAPTER QUIZ

DIRECTIONS: PART I. Rewrite the following passage, correcting the capitalization and adding appropriate end marks, apostrophes, and quotation marks.

alex and his friend milo often talked about music alex was a big fan of green day and especially liked such political songs as american idiot his friends taste was a bit different

weird al yankovich is a genius alex youve got to admit it milo frequently remarked

yes hes funny alex would reply but whats he doing to wake people up

what about Canadian idiot milo suggested now theres a song with a political message

sometimes i think youre the idiot milo exclaimed alex

DIRECTIONS: PART II. Correct the punctuation in the following sentences. Sentences may have more than one error.

1. 2 servers + a line cook were still needed at the new restaurant on Park Ave.

2. Doctor Casey had already made a reservation for 5 for Thurs. night.

3. 1 of Jeremy's favorite dishes is liver & onions.

4. Mister Jones often ordered 2 helpings of mac & cheese when he ate lunch at the local diner.

5. 100 people attended the gallery opening on Oct. third.

6. Amber saw Pirates of the Caribbean in the theater 3 times.

7. Ben checked the walk-in and found 5 bags of carrots, 12 heads of lettuce, and two boxes of cremini mushrooms.

8. After reading Kitchen Confidential, the culinary students applied at 3 or 4 restaurants on Cape Cod.

9. In winters bone, the young heroine teaches her 2 younger siblings how to skin a squirrel.

10. Chapter V of moby-dick is called breakfast.

CHAPTER 31
PUNCTUATION II—
COMMAS, COLONS, SEMICOLONS, PARENTHESES, BRACKETS, HYPHENS, DASHES, AND SLASHES

By the end of this chapter, you should begin to . . .

- use commas appropriately to separate clauses, phrases, and words;
- use commas in numbers, dates, addresses, etc.;
- use colons appropriately, and avoid using colons after *for example,* etc.;
- use semicolons appropriately between two independent clauses, etc.;
- use parentheses, brackets, hyphens, dashes, and slashes appropriately.

Like other punctuation marks, the ones in this chapter direct the reader's attention to meaningful groups of words. They are like the hands of a traffic cop telling cars to stop or go, turn right or left. They are like the hands of a waiter guiding the customer through a meal, from pointing out the table and offering the menu to serving the dishes and sweeping up the crumbs.

THE COMMA

The **comma** is one of the most misused punctuation marks; in fact, it is often overused. There are certain occasions when commas must be used in standard written English, and there are occasions when they must not be used. There are also times when the comma *may* be used to add emphasis or to make the meaning clearer. We're sometimes told to place a comma wherever we pause in reading the sentence, and that works well as we're writing a rough draft. However, once we're proofreading the final copy, that

The comma is like a hand giving a short wave to the reader as if to say, okay, here's where the next clause begins.

advice may not always be useful. Rather, it makes sense to consult a list of rules and to use commas only when these rules apply. When in doubt, leave commas out.

1. **Add a comma before the coordinating conjunction that joins two independent clauses.**

    One train stopped, but the other kept going.

    Joaquin grilled two steaks, and Dexter added a garnish of mushrooms.

    In these two examples, the comma is like a hand giving a short wave to the reader as if to say, okay, here's where the next clause begins.

2. **Add a comma after an introductory subordinate clause.** Remember, a subordinate clause is a group of words that contains a subject, a verb, and a subordinating conjunction ("coat hanger").

    While one train stopped, the other kept going.

    After Joaquin grilled two steaks, Dexter added a garnish of mushrooms.

    Again, the comma is like a hand drawing the reader's eye to the subject of the main clause, Dexter.

Exercise 31.1 | Coordinate and Subordinate Clauses

Rewrite the following sentences, adding commas where necessary.

1. When Emma first meets Frank Churchill she thinks he is very handsome and well-mannered.
2. As she gets to know him better she does not completely trust him.
3. Frank is not perfect yet Emma would like him to marry her best friend, Harriet.
4. While Emma is busy matchmaking she fails to notice that both Frank and Harriet are in love with other people.
5. She doesn't realize that Frank is in love with Jane Fairfax and she also doesn't realize that she herself is in love with Mr. Knightley.

3. **If a subordinate clause follows the main clause, add a comma if the clause is nonrestrictive**, that is, if it could be omitted without altering the fundamental meaning of the sentence.

> Nonrestrictive: The Boston fans greatly admired David Ortiz, who had hit several home runs during the season.
>
> We came home early, although the party was not over.
>
> I went to the new restaurant, which we learned later had received good reviews.

The comma is omitted when the subordinate clause is **restrictive**, that is, when it limits the meaning of a word in the main clause or is otherwise essential to the meaning of the sentence. Note that a subordinate clause that begins with the pronoun *that* is always restrictive; therefore it is not preceded by a comma.

> Restrictive: The crowd cheered for the player who hit the home run.
>
> We came home early because we were tired.
>
> I went to the new restaurant that everyone was talking about.

4. **Add a comma after an introductory word or phrase.**
   The purpose of punctuation is to map out the meaning of the sentence so that the reader is able to follow it clearly. Since the main clause and its subject are especially important to the meaning of a sentence, commas are often used after an introductory word or phrase as an indication that these are going to be *followed* by this main clause.

> First, the server asked for their drink orders.
>
> After ordering their drinks, the customers opened the menus.

Use *two* commas—like two hands holding a tray—to enclose a word or phrase that interrupts the sentence.

Many writers place a comma after four or more introductory words, or after two or more prepositional phrases. Note that if the introductory word or phrase is short and the meaning is clear, the comma may be omitted.

> Yesterday we went to a new restaurant downtown.
>
> In the window there was a photograph of the award-winning chef.

5. **Add commas on both ends of words, phrases, or clauses that interrupt the sentence.** Use *two* commas—like two hands holding a tray—unless the phrase begins or ends the sentence.

> Dr. House, **however**, is not always popular with his coworkers.
>
> **However**, Dr. House is not always popular with his coworkers.
>
> Dr. House is not always popular with his coworkers, **however**.

In the second and third examples, the capital letter and the period, respectively, act as the other "hand" that helps the comma hold the tray.

Appositives, which are words or phrases that sit next to a noun and rename it, are usually separated from the rest of the sentence with commas, unless they are very short or unless they restrict the meaning of the noun.

> The new show, a hospital drama, premiered on Tuesday night. [commas set off *a hospital drama*, which renames *show*]
>
> My aunt Sally loves the show. [*Sally* restricts the meaning; it's not my aunt *Betty*. Therefore no comma is used.]

Words or phrases used in **direct address** are also separated from the rest of the sentence by commas.

> I am sorry, Dr. House, but your license has been suspended.

Exercise 31.2 | Using Commas with Interrupters

Rewrite the following sentences, adding commas where necessary.

1. Another popular medical series this one with a large ensemble cast is *Grey's Anatomy.*
2. Meredith Grey from whom the series derives its name is an intern at a hospital.
3. She initially shares a house with two other interns Izzy and George.
4. The interns' supervisor Dr. Bailey runs a tight ship.
5. In addition the show is enlivened by the many romantic entanglements.

6. **Add commas between three or more items in a** series. Both MLA and APA style guides prefer that a comma precede *and*.

> The apple was green, round, and juicy.

Note that if you use a conjunction between each item, you do not need commas.

> The apple was green and round and juicy.

You may choose to add commas where they are not required, however, as in the example that follows, if each item is rather long and the sentence would be clearer with punctuation.

> The fruit salad consisted of Granny Smith apples bought from the grocery store and used with their bright green skins intact, and blueberries and raspberries picked that morning at a local farm, and walnut pieces that were left over from holiday baking.

When you have a series of adjectives describing a noun, insert a comma between those that modify the noun directly:

> The café was painted a bright, cheerful color.

Both *bright* and *cheerful* describe *color,* and the sentence might have been written as follows:

> The café was painted a bright and cheerful color.

When adjectives modifying the same noun could be joined by *and (bright and cheerful color),* they are separated by commas if *and* is removed *(bright, cheerful color).* In the next example, however, *bright* is now an adverb modifying *yellow* and is not separated from it by a comma.

> The café was painted a bright yellow color.

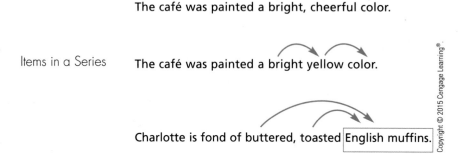

The café was painted a bright, cheerful color.

Items in a Series

The café was painted a bright yellow color.

Charlotte is fond of buttered, toasted English muffins.

We wouldn't write *a bright and yellow color;* thus, we do not place a comma after *bright.* Finally, do not add a comma between an adjective and a noun if the adjective limits or qualifies the meaning of the noun. For example, there is no comma between *toasted* and *English* in the following sentence because the adjective *English* limits the muffins to a certain variety. They're not *corn* muffins, but *English* muffins.

> Charlotte is fond of buttered, toasted English muffins. *[correct]*
>
> Charlotte is fond of buttered, toasted, English muffins. *[incorrect]*

One common qualifier is the season of the year. In the following sentence, we wouldn't speak of the mild *and* summer evening; therefore, there is no comma between the two adjectives.

> The children watched the fireflies throughout the mild summer evening. *[correct]*
>
> The children watched the fireflies throughout the mild, summer evening. *[incorrect]*

Exercise 31.3 | Commas with Items in a Series

Rewrite the following sentences, adding commas where necessary.

1. The two business partners bought a small attractive restaurant on a side street.
2. The newly opened café had fresh seasonal vegetables on the menu.
3. The customers especially enjoyed the varied tender salad greens.
4. Another popular item was the thick nutritious vegetable soup.
5. For dessert many customers ordered the very rich chocolate cake.

7. **Add a comma to mark the thousandth place in numbers larger than four digits,** such as 150,000 or 23,671. The comma is optional in four-digit numbers, but be consistent. If you're using other numbers that must have a comma, add a comma to the four-digit numbers as well.

> Marlene made 1,129 phone calls at work last month. [*correct*]
>
> Marlene made 1129 phone calls at work last month. [*correct*]
>
> At that rate, she will have made 13548 calls by the end of the year. [*incorrect*]
>
> At that rate, she will have made 13,458 by the end of the year. [*correct*]

Do *not* add commas to telephone numbers, years, or zip codes.

8. **Add a comma between elements of a date,**

> Julia Child was born on August 15, 1912.

and add a comma after the date if the sentence continues, as in this example:

> Julia Child was born on August 15, 1912, and was an influential figure in the American culinary world.

However, do not add commas when the date is given in inverted order—day, month, year—as in the following example: 15 August 1912. Do *not* use a comma when you write just the month and day or just the month and year.

> Julia Child was born on August 15.
>
> Julia Child was born in August 1912.

9. **Add a comma between elements of an address, except between the state and the zip code.** Use a comma after the address if the sentence continues.

> The President of the United States lives at 1600 Pennsylvania Avenue, Washington, D.C. 20500.

10. **Add a comma between a name and abbreviations** such as *MD* or *Jr.* Use a comma after the abbreviation if the sentence continues.

> Sanjay Gupta, MD, wrote a book called *Monday Mornings*, which was turned into a television show.

11. **Add a comma after the greeting of a personal letter and after the closing of all letters.** Note that the greeting of a *business* letter is followed by a colon.

> Dear John,
>
> Sincerely yours,
>
> *BUT*
>
> Dear Superintendent Yang:

Commas are often added where they don't belong. Observe the following rules:

- Don't put a comma between the subject and the verb of a sentence.
- Don't put a comma between a verb and its object.
- If a pair of commas is needed to separate an interrupter from the rest of the sentence, don't skip one.
- Don't use a comma to separate two independent clauses.
- Don't use a comma unless you have a specific purpose in mind.

Finally, let's look at the one rule most people remember: put a comma wherever you pause in the sentence. It's true a comma will make the reader pause briefly (though not as long as a semicolon or period). However, if you use a comma for this reason, be sure it's not breaking any of the rules in this section at the same time.

THE COLON

Colons are like a pair of eyes tipped over, like the emoticon :) without the smile. They mean "look at this."

1. **Use a colon to introduce a list or a quotation.**

    Dexter dislikes all vegetables except the following: broccoli, carrots, and corn.

    Perhaps one of the most well-known sentences in the English language comes from *Hamlet:* "To be or not to be, that is the question."

2. **Colons may be used between independent clauses**, if the first clause is explained or summarized by the second. In APA format, the first word after the colon is always capitalized. In MLA format, the first word is capitalized only if it states a rule or principle.

    Dexter applies this same selectivity to ice cream flavors: he prefers pure chocolate or vanilla, with an occasional scoop of cookies and cream to add texture. [MLA]

    Dexter applies this same selectivity to ice cream flavors: He prefers pure chocolate or vanilla, with an occasional scoop of cookies and cream to add texture. [APA]

3. **Use a colon in the greeting of a business letter.**

    Dear Sales Associate:

4. **Use a colon in expressions of time.**

    Dinner was served at 7:00 p.m.

5. **Use a colon in certain parts of bibliographic citations.** (See Chapter 19 for additional details on bibliographic citations.) Study the following examples:

> Boston: Bedford/St. Martin's [colon between city and publisher/MLA]
>
> Boston, MA: Bedford/St. Martin's [colon between state and publisher/APA]
>
> *Food and Wine* 18:63-65 [colon between volume and page numbers/ MLA only]
>
> *Food and Wine,* 18, 63-35 [comma between title, volume, and page numbers/APA only]

Some style manuals require a colon between biblical chapter and verse; the Modern Language Association prefers a period. Follow the preference of your instructor or publisher.

6. **Do not use a colon after the expressions** *for example, including,* **and** *such as;* **between a verb and the rest of the sentence; or between a preposition and its object.**

> Dexter enjoys many types of potatoes, such as: mashed, baked, and fried. [*incorrect*]
>
> Dexter enjoys many types of potatoes, such as mashed, baked, and fried. [*correct*]
>
> Dexter's favorite vegetables are: broccoli, carrots, and corn. [*incorrect*]
>
> Dexter's favorite vegetables are broccoli, carrots, and corn. [*correct*]
>
> Dexter's mother made his favorite meal of: lasagna and garlic bread. [*incorrect*]
>
> Dexter's mother made his favorite meal of lasagna and garlic bread. [*correct*]

Exercise 31.4 | Using the Colon

Add or delete a colon where necessary in the following sentences.

1. Each episode of *Law & Order* follows a specific sequence the discovery of the body, the police investigation, and the jury trial.
2. Over the years, several different actresses have played Jack McCoy's assistant, for example: Jill Hennessey, Carey Lowell, and Angie Harmon.
3. Detective Briscoe's partner has also been played by different actors, including: Benjamin Bratt and Jesse L. Martin.
4. Jennifer is a huge fan of the show she has at least ten seasons on DVD.
5. Did you watch the episode last night at 1000 p.m.?

A "Semi" Colon

THE SEMICOLON

The **semicolon** is somewhere between a comma and a period. It's as if our friend Comma Man got into a semi to increase his strength. Like a comma, the semicolon is part of a single sentence. Like a period, the semicolon can handle two independent clauses. While we take a pause at a comma, we take a longer one at a semicolon, and an even longer one at a period.

1. **Use a semicolon to join two independent clauses** that are very closely related in meaning. (See also Chapter 23.)

    > Raw eggs may contain a dangerous bacterium called *Salmonella;* they should always be stored at cool temperatures.

    A **conjunctive adverb**, such as *consequently* or *however,* may be used to describe the relationship between two clauses.

    > Raw eggs may contain a dangerous bacterium called *Salmonella;* consequently, they should always be stored at cool temperatures.

    Such conjunctive adverbs are typically followed by a comma, particularly when they interrupt the sentence, as in the previous example.

2. **Use semicolons instead of commas to separate independent clauses that are joined by a coordinating conjunction and already contain a number of commas.**

    > On the following day, dressed in clean chef whites, the new students learned to prepare vegetable stock, beef stock, and chicken stock; and their instructor, who was fair but strict, was pleased with their progress.

3. **Semicolons may be used instead of commas to separate items in a series when these already contain a number of commas.**

> *Mystic River* is the story of three friends: Sean Devine, a quiet child, now a state trooper and the only one of the three to go to college; Jimmy Markham, the leader of the group, a small-time crook who went straight after serving two years in prison; and Dave Boyle, perhaps the central figure, the boy who was kidnapped, the man who couldn't escape.

See Exercises 23.4 and 23.5 for practice in using semicolons.

PARENTHESES

Parentheses are used to set off words and phrases that explain or refer to something within the main sentence. The parentheses indicate that this information is less important and that the structure and meaning of the sentence are not affected. Look at these examples:

> The Food and Drug Administration (FDA) does not regulate the sale of dietary supplements.

> Parentheses may be used like commas to set off explanatory information (see Chapter 31).

Parentheses are like "stage whispers" or "asides" in a play. The actor turns from the other cast members and speaks directly to the audience, often in an exaggerated whisper. While the stage whisper is intended to be heard, and sometimes contains such information as explanations of the actor's motives or of elements in the story, it is not

Universal/Photofest

Jamie Foxx (at the piano) won an Oscar for his portrayal of Ray Charles in 2004's *Ray*.

part of the regular dialogue. Think about Romeo in the garden, listening raptly to Juliet's outpouring of desire. In an aside to the audience he wonders, "Shall I hear more, or shall I speak at this?"

Punctuation marks generally fall outside the parentheses, unless they are part of the phrase inside the parentheses. Consider the following examples:

> After Barrett saw *Ray* (the biography of Ray Charles), he bought the soundtrack.

> After Barrett saw *Ray* (What a great movie!), he bought the soundtrack.

BRACKETS

Brackets are used within quotations to set off words, phrases, or explanations that were not in the original text.

> "After I saw *Ray* [the biography of Ray Charles]," said Barrett, "I bought the soundtrack."

Brackets are also used to set off explanatory words and phrases within parentheses.

Exercise 31.5 | Parentheses and Brackets

Rewrite the following sentences, adding parentheses or brackets where necessary.

1. The students developed a Hazard Analysis Critical Control Point HACCP plan for the restaurant in their case study.
2. "My mom's the chef at Bistro Urbano a trendy downtown restaurant," the boy bragged to his friends.
3. Commas are also important in setting off words and phrases from the rest of the sentence see Chapter 28.
4. *American Idol* a reality series drew more viewers than the Olympic Games that night.
5. The company's new CEO Chief Executive Officer made it a policy to visit each department once a week.

HYPHENS

Hyphens are the short lines used within single words to form **compound numbers**, such as *thirty-three* or *ninety-one,* and with the prefixes *all–, ex–,* and *self–,* for example, *ex-boyfriend* and *self-esteem.* Hyphens are also used with **compound adjectives**, that is, adjectives that are modified by an adverb and directly precede a noun.

> The servers appreciated the well-behaved children. *[hyphen required]*

However, no hyphen is required if the adverb ends in *–ly.*

The servers appreciated the surprisingly polite children. [no hyphen]

Note that in APA style, you would use an en dash, which is slightly longer than a hyphen, to join compound adjectives of equal weight. For example, use a hyphen for *well-behaved children* in the previous sentence, but use an en dash for *Atlanta–Tampa flight.* See Figure 31.1.

When writing by hand, use hyphens to break words at the end of a line in order to maintain an orderly margin. However, when using a word processor, turn off the auto-hyphenation feature. Set the margin to align left and press the Enter key only at the conclusion of the paragraphs; the computer will "wrap" the text automatically at the end of each line.

Figure 31.1 Using Hyphens and Dashes

	hyphen -	en dash –	minus sign –	em dash —
MLA	to form compound numbers or adjectives	*N/A*	*N/A*	to set off a thought that interrupts the sentence
APA	to form compound numbers or adjectives (but see *en dash*); to indicate a negative number	to form compound adjectives when words are of equal weight	use a hyphen if minus sign not available	to set off a thought that interrupts the sentence

Copyright © 2015 Cengage Learning®.

DASHES

Dashes—like commas—are used between words and phrases to set off a thought that interrupts the rest of the sentence. Also called em dashes, they can add a lively, conversational tone to the text but should be used sparingly in very formal academic or business writing.

The new bakery—the one around the corner—featured an assortment of muffins.

Dashes may also be used like a colon to introduce additional material or to explain or rename a word or phrase in the sentence.

In a single year, Jamie Foxx was nominated for two Oscars for two separate films—*Ray* and *Collateral.*

SLASHES

In formal writing contexts, **slashes** have some very specific uses: when citing URLs, quoting lines of poetry, offering paired alternatives, and writing certain abbreviations. See Figure 31.2.

Figure 31.2 When to Use a Slash

Use of Slash	Example
In URLs	http://www.imdb.com
Between lines of poetry quoted within a paragraph	"'Twas brillig, and the slithy toves / Did gyre and gimble in the wabe"
Between paired alternatives	We are expecting a yes/no answer. He/she should send a résumé by email.
In certain abbreviations	HIV/AIDS AFL/CIO
In fractions or division	He ate 2/3 of the apple.
In dates written with numerals only	11/7/12

RECIPE FOR REVIEW

COMMAS (THE HELPING HANDS)

Add a comma in the following situations:

1. Before a coordinating conjunction that joins two independent clauses
2. After an introductory subordinate clause
3. Before a nonrestrictive clause or phrase
4. After an introductory word or a phrase
5. On both sides of words, phrases, or clauses that interrupt the sentence, including words or phrases used in direct address
6. Between three or more items in a series
7. To mark the thousandth place in numbers *larger* than four digits (the comma is optional in four-digit numbers)
8. Between elements of a date and after the date if the sentence continues
9. Between elements of an address, except between the state and the zip code, and after the address if the sentence continues

10. Between a name and abbreviations such as *MD* or *Jr.* and after the abbreviation if the sentence continues
11. After the greeting of a personal letter and after the closing of all letters (note that the greeting of a *business* letter is followed by a colon)

COLONS (A PAIR OF EYES)

Add a colon in the following situations:

1. Introducing a list or quotation
2. Between related independent clauses
3. Following the greeting in a business letter
4. In expressions of time
5. Between certain parts of bibliographic citations
6. Do *not* use a colon in these situations:
   - After the expressions *for example, including,* and *such as*
   - Between a verb and the rest of the sentence
   - Between a preposition and its object

SEMICOLONS (COMMA MAN IN A SEMI)

Add a semicolon in the following situations:

1. Between two independent clauses
2. Between two independent clauses that contain several commas and are joined by a coordinating conjunction
3. Between items in a series when these already contain a number of commas

PARENTHESES

1. Use parentheses to set off information that explains or refers to something within the sentence.
2. In general, place punctuation marks outside the parentheses.

BRACKETS

1. Use brackets within quotation marks to set off words, phrases, or explanations that were not in the original text.
2. Use brackets to set off explanatory words and phrases within parentheses.

HYPHENS

1. Use hyphens to form compound numbers and with the prefixes *all–, ex–,* and *self–*.
2. Use hyphens with compound adjectives before a noun, for example, *a well-known recipe.*

3. Use hyphens to break words at the end of a line in a handwritten text (but turn this feature off on a word processor).
4. See Figure 31.1.

DASHES

1. Use dashes to set off a thought that interrupts the rest of the sentence.
2. Use dashes to introduce additional material or to explain or rename a word or phrase in the sentence.

SLASHES

1. Use slashes when citing URLs, quoting lines of poetry, noting paired alternatives, indicating division, and representing dates and certain abbreviations.
2. See Figure 31.2.

CHAPTER QUIZ

DIRECTIONS: Rewrite the following sentences,* adding or deleting commas, colons, and semicolons as necessary. Assume all other punctuation is correct. Some sentences have more than one error.

1. While some characters in *Mystic River* are timid and reserved others are intense and fearless.

2. My personal favorite is, Jimmy Markham played by Sean Penn.

3. Jimmy is a loving compassionate family man but he is forced to backpedal into a life that had been forgotten a life in organized crime.

4. Markham captained a crew that included the Savage brothers and "Just Ray" Harris, it landed him directly in federal prison.

5. These painful years molded the character into what the film depicts; a powerful rugged leader, who commands loyalty.

6. However with the birth of his eldest daughter the elements of love compromise and family are created as well.

*Sentences adapted from an essay by student writer Adam McGlone. Errors were introduced to create this quiz.

7. As the film continues to unfold Jimmy Markham rises to a climactic implosion and his wrath is felt by all.

8. Jimmy's sight once transparent and clear is now opaque with rage and vengeance.

9. In the end the teachings of Katie's birth are ironically in vain Markham is forced to honor his slain daughter, by dishonorable means and actions.

10. His past is now the present and the dragon's slumber is permanently disturbed.

APPENDIX A
SPELLING OF SELECTED CULINARY TERMS

A

a la carte
aioli
alcohol
al dente
amandine
ambrosia
anchovy
anglaise
antipasto
aperitif
appetizer
artichoke
arugula
asparagus
aspic
au gratin
au jus
au lait
avocado

B

bain marie
baklava
balsamic
banana
barbecue
baste
béarnaise
béchamel
benedict
beurre blanc
beverage
biscotti
biscuit
bisque
bleu (cheese)
blintz

bok choy
bologna
bordelaise
borscht
bouillabaisse
bouillon
bouquet garni
bourbon
braise
breakfast
brie (cheese)
brioche
broccoli
broccoli rabe
brochette
brunoise
bruschetta
Brussels sprouts
buffet
bulgur
bundt
burrito
business

C

cacciatore
Caesar
café
cafeteria
caffeine
Cajun
calamari
calcium
calorie
calzone
Canadian (bacon)
canapé
cannelloni

cantaloupe
caper
cappuccino
carambola
caramel
caraway
carbonara
cardamom
carob
carpaccio
carrot
casserole
cassoulet
casual
catsup
cauliflower
caviar
cayenne
celery
cèpes
cereal
ceviche
challah
chalupas
champagne
charcuterie
chardonnay
charlotte
chateaubriand
chef
chervil
chestnut
chicory
chiffonade
chili con carne
chipotle
chocolate

cholesterol
chorizo
chow mein
chowder
chutney
cilantro
cinnamon
cocoa
coconut
colander
coleslaw
collard greens
complement
complimentary
compote
condiment
consommé
coq au vin
cordon bleu
coriander
coulis
couscous
crème brûlée
crème caramel
crêpe
cremini, crimini
croissant
croquette
crouton
crudités
crystallized
cucumber
cuisine
cumin
curry
custard
customer

D
Daikon
daily
daiquiri
decadent
demi-glace

demitasse
dessert
Dijon
diner
dining
dinner
dolmades, dolmas
dough
doughnut
duxelle

E
employee
emulsify
enchilada
endive
enoki
entrée
escargot
escarole
excellent

F
fagioli
Fahrenheit
fajita
falafel
fennel
feta
fettuccine
filet, fillet
fines herbes
Florentine
foccaccia
fondue
formaggio
french (fries)
fricassée
frisée
fromage

G
ganache
garde manger
gastronomy

gazpacho
gelatin
gelato
ghee
giblets
gluten
gnocchi
Gorgonzola
goulash
gourmet
granola
gratinée
gratuity
Gruyère
guacamole
gumbo
gyro

H
halibut
haricot verts
haute cuisine
herring
hollandaise[15]
hors d'oeuvre
hummus
hygiene

J
jaggery
jalapeño
jambalaya
jardinière
Jarlsberg
Jerusalem artichoke
jicama
jigger
juice
julienne

K
Kahlúa
Kaiser
kale
kasha

kebab, kabob
kedgeree
kernel (of corn)
ketchup
kielbasa, kielbasy
kitchen
kiwi
knead
knife, knives
kohlrabi
kosher
kumquat

L

lasagna
leek
lentil
license
linguine
liqueur
liquor
loin
lox

M

mâche
Madeira
mahi mahi
maitre d'hotel
manager
marinade
marinara
marinate
marsala
marzipan
mascarpone
mayonnaise
measure
medallion
Mediterranean
menu
meringue
mesclun
minestrone

mirepoix
mise en place
miso
mocha
morel
mousse
mousseline
mozzarella
mussel

N

nachos
niçoise
nutrition
nutritious

O

omelet
oregano
orzo
ouzo

P

paella
palate
pallet
parfait
parmesan
pasteurized
pâté de foie gras
persillade
pesto
petit four
pico de gallo
pierogi
pilaf
pimiento, pimento
polenta
pomegranate
porcini
portabella
potage
potato
potatoes
poultry

primavera
prix fixe
prosciutto
protein
Provençal
provolone
purée

Q

quahog
quesadilla
quiche
quinoa

R

radicchio
ragout
raisin
ramekin
raspberry
ratatouille
ravioli
receipt
recipe
rémoulade
restaurant
restaurateur
rhubarb
ricotta
rigatoni
risotto
roll
Roquefort
rotini
roulade
roux

S

sachet
saffron
sake
salmon
salsa
salsify
sambuca

sandwich
sashimi
sauerbraten
sausage
sauté
scallion
scallops
scampi
semolina
sesame
shallot
sherbet
shiitake
shish kebab
sommelier
sorbet
soufflé
soup du jour
sous chef
spaetzle
spaghetti
spatula
special
spinach
streusel
strudel
sushi
swordfish
Szechuan, Sichuan

T

Tabasco
tamale

tandoori
tapas
tapenade
tarragon
tartar sauce
temperature
tempura
teriyaki
terrine
Thai
thermometer
thyme
tiramisu
tofu
tomato
tomatoes
tortellini
tortilla
tostada
tournedos
tuile
turmeric

U

udon (noodles)
utensil

V

vanilla
variety
vegetable
velouté
venison

vermicelli
vichyssoise
Vidalia
vinaigrette
vinegar
vintage
virgin (olive oil)
vodka

W

Waldorf
wasabi
weight
whisk
whiskey
wok
wonton
Worcestershire sauce

Y

yeast
yogurt

Z

zabaglione
zinfandel
ziti
zucchini

APPENDIX B
COMMONLY MISUSED WORDS

accept, except

- *Accept* is a verb that means "to receive," as in "The restaurant manager *accepted* the delivery of the fresh produce."

- When *except* is used as a verb, it means "to exclude." For example, "The manager *excepted* the lettuce from her receipt of the fresh produce delivery." As a preposition, *except* means "excluding," as in "The manager accepted all of the produce *except* the lettuce."

affect, effect

- *Affect* is most often used as a verb that means "to influence the outcome," as in "The poor spelling *affected* the grade on his essay." Less frequently, *affect* may be used as a noun to mean an emotional state, as in "The doctor noted that the patient's *affect* was good."

- *Effect* is most often used as a noun that means "consequence" or "result." For example, "The most likely *effect* of his improved study habits is a change in his grades." When used as a verb, *effect* means "to cause or achieve," as in "His improved study habits *effected* a change in his grades."

alumni, alumnae

- *Alumni* is a plural form that means "male graduates of a school" or "both male and female graduates of a school." For example, "The college's *alumni* give generously to the scholarship fund." *Alumnus* is the singular form and may refer to both male and female graduates.

- *Alumnae* is also a plural form, but it refers exclusively to *female* graduates. *Alumna* is the singular form and refers only to female graduates.

amount, number

- Use the word *amount* for the quantity of a noncount noun, a quantity considered a unit. "The caterer required a large *amount* of dough for dinner rolls."

- Use the word *number* for the quantity of a count noun, a quantity considered as several discrete items. "The caterer required a large *number* of dinner rolls."

because

- The use of the construction "the reason is because" is common but *informal*. "For example, we might *say*, "The reason he likes this restaurant is *because* it has good service."

- In more *formal* situations, "the reason is that" is preferred. "The reason he likes this restaurant is *that* it has good service."

- A more concise wording is the following: "He likes the restaurant because it has good service."

being as, being that

- The phrases "being as" and "being that" may be used in conversation, but they are too informal and wordy for academic writing. "Being that I was hungry, I fixed myself a sandwich."

- The *preferred* usage is "since" or "because": "*Since* I was hungry, I fixed myself a sandwich."

beside, besides

- *Beside* is a preposition that means "next to" to someone or something. For example, "The server laid the spoon *beside* the knife."

- *Besides* is an adverb that means "also" or "furthermore": "*Besides* setting the tables for lunch, the server wiped off the menus."

between, among

- *Between* is used in formal English when considering two items, even when they are part of a larger group. "How can I choose *between* coffee and espresso?" Note that—like all prepositions—*between* takes the objective case. It's always "between you and *me*," not "between you and *I*."

- *Among* is used with a group. "There was agreement *among* us that this was the funniest movie we'd ever seen."

brake, break

- *Brake* refers to the part of the car (think of the central *a* in both words) that stops the wheels. For example, "Dolores used the *brake* as she approached the intersection."

- *Break* refers to the action of splitting something into two or more pieces: "Dolores used to *break* the eggs into their own bowl before combining them with the rest of the ingredients."

capital, capitol

- *Capital* can be used as a noun to mean "assets" or "resources" or to mean the first city. "The Johnsons invested a good deal of *capital* in the new restaurant," or "Springfield is the *capital* of Illinois." As an adjective, *capital* often means "punishable by death," as in "Murder is a *capital* crime."

- *Capitol* refers to the building that houses the legislature. "The senators headed for *Capitol* Hill to vote on the energy bill."

choose, chose

- The difference between these two is time (and pronunciation): *Choose* and *chooses* are in the present tense; *chose* is the irregular past-tense form.

- Present tense: "The Dietrichs often *choose* an Italian restaurant for special occasions."

- Past tense: "On Halloween, however, they *chose* to eat at a Japanese restaurant."

- Infinitive: *Choose* is used with the *infinitive* form: "It was difficult to *choose* between the two desserts."

cite, sight, site

- *Cite* means "to quote or refer to": "The food critic often *cited* the works of M.F.K. Fisher."

- *Sight* means "vision" or "view": "The customers were fascinated by the *sight* of the roasted suckling pig."

- *Site* means "place" or "location": "The entrepreneur studied possible *sites* for the new restaurant."

cloths, clothes

- *Cloth* describes fabric in general or a useful item such a dishcloth or tablecloth. "Cooks often keep a clean *cloth* tucked into their aprons." (Keep that extra *e* tucked out of sight.)

- *Clothes* refers to items that people wear: "Fortunately they had brought dry *clothes* to change into after their visit to the water park."

complement, compliment

- As a verb, *complement* means to balance or match, particularly in the hospitality industry. "The wine was chosen to *complement* the main course." As a noun, *complement* means quota or amount. "The new restaurant did not yet have a full *complement* of wait staff."

- In contrast, the verb *compliment* means "to flatter or praise": "The baking instructor *complimented* the student on her marzipan." As a noun, *compliment* means "flattery" or "praise": "My *compliments* to the chef!"

complementary, complimentary

- *Complementary* means "matching" or "balanced": "The couple's personalities were *complementary*."

- *Complimentary* means either "approving" or "free": "The hotel guests were *complimentary* about the *complimentary* Continental breakfast."

conscience, conscious

- A *conscience* is what tells us when we're doing wrong: "My conscience is clear," we say, or "My conscience is bothering me."

- We're *conscious* when we're awake and aware: "The patient opened his eyes; he was conscious" or "I was conscious of a smoky smell coming from the kitchen."

could, can

- This pair of helping verbs adds the idea of ability or permission to the main verb: "Todd *can* paint well." *Could* is the past tense of *can*: "Todd *could* paint well as a child."

- *Could* also adds an element of doubt or uncertainty to the main verb and can be used in the subjunctive mood: "If Todd were to try singing, though, I'm not sure he *could* do it."

- Do not use *could* to mean simply "was able to." The simple past tense is clear and appropriate.

  > After I *could* arrive at our apartment, I felt relief to see her face. [incorrect]
  > After I *arrived* at our apartment, I felt relief to see her face. [correct]

could have, could of

Do not use *of* in expressions such as *could of, would of,* or *should of*; the correct usage is *could have, would have,* or *should have*. "The customers *could have* paid by cash or credit card."

course, coarse

- The definitions of these two words are clear; however, a misspelling can create a problem for the reader. *Coarse* is an adjective meaning "rough" or "untreated": "The sea salt had a *coarse* texture."

- *Course*, on the other hand, refers to a path, direction, academic class, or part of a meal: "The main *course* at the wedding reception was served under the tent."

desert, dessert

A *desert* is full of sand—it's dry and uncomfortable. A *dessert* is full of sugar—it's rich and fabulous! The difference between them is the extra *s*. Think of it this way—Dessert. So sweet.

> Travelers in the dry and sandy *desert* often long for a cool and refreshing *dessert*.

Desert can also be used as a verb mean "to abandon": "The boys *deserted* their playmates when they were called in for dessert."

diner, dinner

The clue here is in the pronunciation of the two words. With a single *n, diner,* the *i* is long, and the word refers to a person who is eating or to a type of restaurant. With a double *n, dinner,* the *i* is short and refers to a meal.

- *Diner* with a long *i* refers to a person who is eating ("The *diners* at the new restaurant were enthusiastic about their meal") or to a type of restaurant ("We ate at many different *diners* on our cross-country trip").

- *Dinner* with a short *i* refers to the meal. "The *dinners* at the new restaurant were enjoyed by all the customers."

few, little

- *Few* is used with count nouns, that is, with individual items. "There were *few* diners in the restaurants after 10 p.m."

- *Little* is used with noncount nouns, that is, with amounts rather than countable items. "There was *little* light in the restaurant after it closed."

fewer, less

- *Fewer* is used with count nouns (see also *few/little*): "There were *fewer* diners in the restaurant on Monday than on Thursday."

- *Less* is used with noncount nouns (see also *few/little*): "There was *less* trouble with the seating chart when Maria was working."

has got, have got

Rather than writing *has got* or *have got*, write simply *has* or *have:* "That ugly sofa *has* to go" or "They *have* too much time on their hands."

have, of

Do not use *of* in expressions such as *could of, would of,* or *should of*; the correct usage is *could have, would have,* or *should have.* "The customers *could have* paid by cash or credit card."

in, into

- In formal English, *in* refers to a static location: "The lion stalked regally back and forth *in* its cage."

- *Into* refers to movement from one location to another: "The children skipped merrily *into* the zoo to visit the lions."

its, it's

These two words sound the same—that is, they are *homonyms*—but they are spelled differently and have completely different meanings. Try to understand the difference and use the two words correctly.

- *Its*—like the possessive forms of other pronouns (*hers, ours, yours*) and *unlike* the possessive forms of nouns—does not use an apostrophe. For example, "She noticed that the risotto had begun to burn in *its* pan."

- *It's* uses the apostrophe to indicate that this word is a contraction; in other words, some letters are missing. *It's* is a shorter or contracted way to write *it is*. For example, "*It's* easy to burn risotto if you are not careful."

lead, led

- *Lead* is the correct spelling of the metallic element pronounced "led," as well as of the present tense of the verb "to lead": "The negative effects of kryptonite on Superman could be blocked by *lead*."

- *Led* is the correct spelling for the past tense of the verb "to lead": "Superman *led* the way into the dark tunnel."

leave, let

- *Leave* means "to go away" or "to abandon": "*Leave* your collection of shot glasses behind when you spend a month in the mountains." The expression "*Leave* me alone" means "go away."

- *Let* means "to allow": "*Let* the customers finish their main course before you offer them the dessert menu." The expression "*Let* me alone" means "stop bothering me."

like, as

- While *like* is a preposition and must be followed by a noun, *as* is typically a subordinating conjunction. "Keri uses her knife *like* a professional" or "Keri uses her knife *as* a professional does."

- In formal English, do not use *like* for *as if* or *as though*. "He looks *like* he would be interesting to talk to" is informal. The better choice would be "He looks *as though* he would be interesting to talk to."

loose, lose

- *Loose* is most often an adjective that means "relaxed, free, or baggy": "The *loose*-fitting pants allowed the chefs to move freely about the kitchen."

- *Lose* is a verb that means to misplace, elude, or be defeated: "The vegetables will *lose* a good deal of their nutritional value if they are boiled too long."

myself

Do not use the reflexive pronoun *myself* in place of *I* or *me*. Write "my friends and I," not "my friends and *myself*." See Chapter 26: Pronouns and Point of View.

of, off

Watch your spelling here.

- *Of* indicates possession: "The top *of* the table was scarred by knife cuts."
- *Off* indicates location: "The knife fell *off* the table." Note that in formal English we do not use *of* with *off*:

  The knife fell *off of* the table. [*informal*]
  The knife fell *off* the table. [*formal*]

palate, palette, pallet

- *Palate* refers to the roof of the mouth and can also mean "taste" or "appreciation": "This sommelier has an excellent *palate*."
- *Palette* refers to the range of colors used by a painter, or to the board on which these colors are mixed: "The artist added a fresh tube of red paint to her *palette*."
- *Pallet* means the large, stackable wooden tray used in storage: "We unloaded a few *pallets* of lettuce this morning."

passed, past

- *Passed* is the past tense of the verb "to pass": "Despite the double yellow line, Brendan *passed* the slowly moving car in front of him."
- *Past* is a preposition meaning "beyond": "Brendan drove *past* the car in front of him."
- *Past* is a noun referring to an earlier period of time or an adjective that means "historical" or "earlier."

  In the *past*, refreshments had been served at these tournaments. [*noun*]
  Refreshments had always been served at *past* tournaments. [*adjective*]

peace, piece

- *Peace* is the opposite of war; note that they both contain the letter *a*: "Make *peace*, not war."
- *Piece* is the spelling for a serving of pie; note that *pie* is a part of *piece*: "I'd like a *piece* of that cherry pie, please."

personal, personnel

- *Personal* means "individual" or "private": "The chief executive officer made a *personal* decision to retire early."
- *Personnel* refers to employees: "*Personnel* decisions are handled by the human resources department."

principal, principle

- The noun *principal* means "head" or "leader," or perhaps a sum of money. "The *principal* of the high school declared a snow day." You might remember the spelling by thinking of the high school principal as your *pal*.
- The noun *principle* means "rule" or "belief": "The class studied the *principles* of English grammar." Note that both *principle* and *rule* end in *–le*.

shall, will

In most cases, *shall* and *will* are interchangeable. However, *shall* may be used in a more formal or elevated context or to make a suggestion. "Shall we go to the zoo tomorrow?" Occasionally, *will* suggests special determination: "I will go to the zoo tomorrow."

should have, should of

Do not use *of* in expressions such as *could of*, *would of*, or *should of*; the correct usage is *could have*, *would have*, or *should have*. "The customers *should have* paid by cash or credit card."

stationary, stationery

- *Stationary* means "motionless" or "in one place"; note the repeated *a*, like the letter *a* in *place*. "The crane was *stationary* over the weekend."

- *Stationery* means "writing paper"; think of the *-er* in *paper*. "Matilda is fond of lavender-colored *stationery*."

than, then

- *Than* is a conjunction used with comparisons; note the *a*'s in *than* and *compare*. "This chili is much hotter *than* that one."

- *Then* is an adverb having to do with time; note the *e*'s in *then* and *time*. "I'll taste the chili; *then* I'll have a glass of milk."

there, their, they're

These three words are often confused with one another. Try to remember the difference with associations such as the following:

- *There* has to do with place, even with pointing. It contains the word "here," which also relates to place. "The knife is *there* on the table."

- *Their* is the possessive form of the pronoun *they*; it refers to a person, not a place. Furthermore, it contains the word "heir," which also refers to a person. "The knife is on *their* table."

- *They're* is completely different because it's spelled with an apostrophe. It's a contraction, like *it's*, meaning that some letters are missing. *They're* is shorthand for *they are*. For example, "Chef Trotter owns many knives; *they're* on the table."

threw, through, thru

- *Threw* is the past tense of the verb "to throw": "Carlotta *threw* the ball to third base and got the runner out."

- *Through* is the preposition that means "from one end to the other" or "because of": "Carlotta walked *through* the dining room, collecting the bottles of ketchup left on the tables."

- *Thru* is an abbreviated spelling of *through* and should be avoided in formal writing.

to, too, two

- *To* is a preposition: "Carol went *to* the store."

- *Too* means "also"; think of too many *o*'s. "Casey went to the store, *too*."

- *Two* is the number. "*Two* other friends went to the store with Casey."

vain, vane, vein

- *Vain* means "conceited" or "useless": "The Olympic gold medalist was sometimes accused of being *vain*" or "The student tried in *vain* to fix his broken hollandaise sauce."

- *Vane* refers to the object on the top of the barn, often a rooster or an arrow, that indicates the direction of the wind: "The weather *vane* was rusty but effective."

- *Vein* is the tube that carries blood back into the heart: "The students removed the *veins* from the prawns." Or we could talk about a *vein* of precious metal or minerals running through a rock.

weather, whether

- *Weather* is the rain, sleet, or snow reported on the news: "The bad *weather* discouraged many people from attending the outdoor concert."

- *Whether* is a subordinating conjunction that means "if": "The producers don't know *whether* their concert will be successful."

where, were, we're

- *Where* is a relative pronoun that may sometimes be used like a subordinating conjunction.

  Where are you going? [*pronoun*]
  David told his mother *where* he was going. [*conjunction*]

- *Were* is the past tense of the verb "to be": "David and Diana *were* going to the concert."

- *We're* is the contraction for "we are": "*We're* going to the concert."

who, which, that

- *Who* refers to people only, *which* to animals and things only, and *that* to either people or things.

    These are the students *who* have scored above 90 on the quiz.
    These are the quizzes, *which* happen to be printed on yellow paper.
    These are the quizzes *that* the students took yesterday.

- *Who* may begin a restrictive or nonrestrictive clause (see also Chapter 31):

    These are the students *who* have scored above 90 on the quiz. [*restrictive*]
    These students, *who* scored above 90 on the quiz, are already studying for their final exam. [*nonrestrictive*]

- *Which* may begin only a nonrestrictive clause:

    These are the quizzes, which happen to be printed on yellow paper.

- *That* may only begin a restrictive clause. Do not use a comma in this case (see Chapter 31).

    These are the quizzes, *that* the students took yesterday. [*incorrect use of comma with restrictive clause*]
    These are the quizzes *that* the students took yesterday. [*correct*]

who, whom

- Use *who* whenever the subjective case is required: "I know who you are."

- Use *whom* when the objective case is required: "I know whom you are with." [*Whom is the object of the preposition with.*]

whose, who's

- *Whose* is the possessive form, as in the sentence "The hostess is speaking with the server *whose* customers have finished their appetizers."

- *Who's* is a contraction of *who* and *is*. For example, "The hostess is speaking with the server *who's* getting ready to go home."

woman, women

One letter here changes both the meaning and the pronunciation of the word that refers to 51% of the population! Just like the words *man* and *men*, the word with *a* is singular, and the word with *e* is plural. "The *woman* [*one woman*] at the front of the line bought tickets for the three *women* behind her."

would have, would of

Do not use *of* in expressions such as *could of, would of,* or *should of*; the correct usage is *could have, would have,* or *should have*. "The customers *would have* paid by cash or credit card."

your, you're

- *Your* is the possessive form; it means "belonging to you." For example, "*Your* pastries are delicious."

- *You're* is a contraction; it means "you are." For example, "*You're* fortunate to live near this pastry shop."

APPENDIX C
TYPES OF WRITING

Just as there are different types of restaurants, bakeshops, and service, there are many different types of writing that we'll likely encounter as we move through various academic and professional settings. This appendix offers an overview of these types of writing and their different purposes and expectations.

ACADEMIC WRITING

Various types of writing are assigned in school settings, from fairly informal journals and response papers to high-pressure essay tests, formal essays, and research papers. In order to be successful (that is, learn the most and get the best grades), it is important to understand what each type of writing is asking you to do.

Journals

Journals are assigned in many courses. In a biology course, the journal may be a record of your observations, say of an egg in an incubator or the growth of a bean sprout. In a developmental psychology course, journal entries might ask you to record and analyze childhood memories. Literature courses may assign journal entries in which you respond to readings. Journal instructions will vary on whether paragraphing, grammar, and mechanics will count, and on whether there's a minimum and/or maximum length to each entry. In general, however, instructors who assign journal entries are looking for thoughtful responses rather than a perfect presentation. Read the directions carefully.

In a composition or literature class, journal entries may be part of the initial phase of writing an essay. In the relative freedom of the journal, which is often written in a kind of stream-of-consciousness mode, you are able to explore an idea in a number of different ways before you have to think about introductions and comma splices.

Writing for me is an escape; it is something that allows me to truly express myself in the purest way. There is no immediate judgment there is no room for others to interject, it is all about me. It is also nice to be heard, if not verbally than at least in writing, writing gives me a medium to express my ideas fully without having to be interrupted with questions or comments. This has led me to develop my thinking to deeper levels, go beyond the superficial banter of everyday life and dive into its complexities.

Reading likewise provides escape for me. Reading gives me a chance to hear what others think about things. Issues that I might not think twice about have entire books written about them, and being able to explore the thinking of another always seems to reveal something about me; do I agree or disagree with them, are there parallels in my life to the life of this person? All of these questions are raised when reading something.

Just as I feel that I give a part of myself to my writing, so I also think that when we read something moving we take a part of the person and we grow as a result.

—**Lindsay Fitzgerald**, student writer

For an example of a journal entry about a specific literary text, see Alicia Lacey's thoughts on the poem "cutting greens" by Lucille Clifton in Chapter 17, p. 305.

Response or Reaction Papers

Response or **reaction papers** may be assigned in courses in all disciplines. In a history class you might be asked to read and respond to a news article about a recent violation of the First Amendment, while in marketing class the assignment might be to assess the effectiveness of the latest set of Super Bowl advertisements. Response papers are more formal in shape and requirements than a journal entry, but they share the goal of encouraging students to write thoughtfully about a particular reading or topic, and they may be less rigid than an essay in terms of their structure and the use of standard grammar and mechanics. However, your instructor will have his or her own expectations, and it is essential that you understand what these are.

Read the directions carefully, and be sure to ask questions if you don't understand them. The instructions may include information on length (by the page or the word, usually) and format (for example, typed, handwritten, cover page or no cover page). Often the instructions on format include a particular font and size (for example, Times New Roman, 12 point). Most likely you will be quoting from the text or texts you are responding to, so be sure you know how your instructor would like you to cite the sources (MLA or APA format, for example). As with all academic writing, be prepared to do several drafts.

Preparing to write a response paper first requires a careful reading of the text or texts (see Chapter 2 for a fuller discussion of reading; see Chapter 17 for information about **close reading**). Your first task is to understand clearly what the author is saying. You may have existing knowledge and opinions on the topic, but it's important to separate those from the author's points. Take notes on main ideas and on questions you might raise in class or research on your own.

Essay Tests

Essay tests are common across all academic disciplines and call for a very different approach than journals and response papers do. Essay tests are generally focused on answering a question or solving a problem, and are designed to test your knowledge on a particular topic and/or your ability to apply principles to a new problem. An essay test is like a mystery basket. You've been working on individual ingredients and methods, and now the time has come to cook something with them under pressure.

Preparing for an essay test starts with keeping up with the homework and classwork throughout the course. Take time each week to review key concepts and readings. Keep track of the small details as well, perhaps with a set of flashcards. The more thoroughly you've prepared overall, the more ideas and examples you'll be able to draw on for the essay test. Although many students don't like the pressure of an exam, an essay test can sometimes feel like a valuable opportunity to show what's been important to *you* about the course.

One of the biggest challenges in an essay test is to understand exactly what the question is asking. To use a culinary example, if the instructions ask you to poach the salmon, it would be a bad idea to grill it! Read the directions carefully. Although it's tempting to jump right in and start writing, taking a minute to check that you understand the instructions can help you follow them accurately. Sometimes a question will have several parts to it; be sure to answer all of them. Look for special instructions, such as "include examples" or "refer to the First Amendment." Be sure that you know the meaning of each word in the question, including such common instructions such as *discuss, compare,* and *analyze* (see Figure C.1).

Figure C.1   Instructions for Essay Tests

Instruction	What it's asking you to do
analyze	break down the topic into parts: what are they? how do they work together?
compare *compare and contrast*	look for both similarities and differences
contrast	look for differences
define	explain the meaning, often by using examples
describe	provide details about the appearance, sound, flavor, etc.
discuss	provide information/details about an idea, event, or object
evaluate	judge the quality or effectiveness
explain	tell *why* or *how*
explore	look at various aspects of the topic, without necessarily evaluating them
identify	list and describe
illustrate	give examples/details/stories related to topic
trace	describe the sequence of events or outline the development

In an essay test, clear, complete, and correct content is usually more important than style. This is not the time to struggle with writing a clever introduction. Get to the point, and make it clear. Often you'll use the language of the question in your introduction. The following sample student introduction responds to this prompt: *Read Amit Majmudar's "Twin Gluttons" and analyze its tone or attitude about the struggle between life and death.*

   They say the one thing guaranteed in life is death. Amit Majmudar seems to have a firm grip on that frightening reality. It is, however, the different ways that he expresses that grip that truly help those that read his poems understand as well. As in "Rites to Allay the Dead," in "Twin Gluttons" Majmudar shows death as a crafty weasel always gathering what it wants, but he then shows Life as a gluttonous slob that consumes all it can in order to maintain its life before Death consumes it.

He seems to hold a very ominous tone about the struggles between life and death, while still being able to maintain a "disappointed father" point of view.

—**Brianna Bowering**, student writer

Note how the writer used the essay prompt's language: "tone" and "struggle between life and death."

Another important aspect of essay tests is managing your time, whether the test takes place entirely in class or whether it's a take-home. There may be a time or length limit—consider that in your planning. An in-class essay test will probably have a time limit. You should try to plan your time in such a way as to cover all parts of the question. If time is left, you can go back and edit or expand the answer.

Instructors will vary in how much conventional grammar and spelling counts as part of the grade. Read your instructions carefully. The more these things count, the more time you should leave to edit and proofread. In a composition or literature class, it is more likely that grammar and spelling will be a significant part of the grade. Pay close attention to the specifics, and allot your time in proportion to the grade value. That is, if grammar is worth 10% or 15%, while spelling is worth 5%, spend twice as much time checking your grammar.

Essay

The word **essay** comes from a French word meaning "to try." An essay "tries" to explain an idea, often in a personal voice and using personal anecdotes. When you're preparing an academic essay, as with the essay tests discussed earlier, it is important to read the instructions carefully and understand precisely what you are being asked to do with any particular assignment. Be sure you understand the meaning of the verbs in the directions (see Figure C.1), and be sure to answer all parts of the question. Essays are usually assigned over a period of time (two to four weeks, perhaps) so that you have time to explore the idea fully and to get assistance with all stages of composition. Because of this time frame, essays are often expected to be carefully edited and proofread. In a composition or literature course, the use of grammar and mechanics may comprise a significant part of the grade. For other instructors, though, the development of ideas may be important. As always, be sure to understand the particular requirements of an assignment.

Research Papers and Reports

While essays rely heavily on the author's own voice and personality, **research papers and reports** are more strictly informational. Because they are intended to communicate information that has been gathered and digested beforehand, there usually isn't that sense of personal exploration that is present in many essays. The style of a research paper or report is generally more formal, although instructors' expectations will vary. Some, for example, expressly forbid the use of the first person (*I, we*), while others allow it. Check with your instructor.

Research papers rely heavily on outside sources. Finding and evaluating this material is the first task (see Chapter 18), requiring the skilled use of search engines, evaluation of the accuracy of the resulting sources, thoughtful reading of the sources, and careful note-taking on both content and citation information. In writing up the results of the research, you must incorporate and cite this material correctly (see Chapter 19).

PROFESSIONAL WRITING

Although you probably won't receive a "grade" on your professional writing, you will be judged by it—by its content, grammar, and overall appearance. A positive judgment might result in a job offer or a continued business relationship with your reader. A negative judgment might mean the loss of business. (See Chapter 29.) Types of professional writing include business letters and emails, résumés, and reports.

The language of a business letter or résumé, like that of an essay, should be clear and accurate. It is also important to remember that all types of written communication, whether paper or digital, can be subpoenaed by a court of law and used in evidence. Be sure that the information in all your letters, emails, and reports is accurate and appropriate.

Business Letters

While some business communication can be done by phone or by email, much is done by letter. Letters are often the first contact you have with a new business opportunity, for example, a cover letter applying for a new position or the initial letter in a negotiation for a catering job. Therefore it's important that you communicate clearly and make a good impression.

Part of that good impression is following the expected format. A business letter is usually typed on 8½-by-11-inch paper in a professional font like Times New Roman or sometimes Arial. The letter has five parts: the heading, address, salutation, body, and closing. The **heading** contains the name and address of your business and the date of the letter. Do not abbreviate the name of the month. If you use **letterhead** stationery on which the heading is already printed, simply add the date. Next, the **address** gives the name and often the **title** of the person and/or business that you are writing to. Be sure to demonstrate your professionalism and attention to detail by spelling the names and titles accurately!

The **salutation** or greeting should be flush with the left margin and two lines below the address. If you know the name of a particular person, use it, such as "Dear Mr. Mitchell" or "Dear Chef Waters." If you don't know the name of a specific person, you may address the company generally ("Dear First National Bank") or a job title within the company ("Dear Manager," "Dear Sales Associate").

The **body** of a letter starts two lines below the salutation. In general, each paragraph is single spaced, with double spacing between paragraphs. As with essays, the first paragraph or introduction of a letter should indicate the subject or purpose of the letter and catch the reader's attention. Particularly when the recipient doesn't know you personally, as in a job application, the first paragraph has to do something to ensure he or she reads the whole letter. Unlike essays, however, business letters typically address the readers directly (*you*) and strive to make their points very briefly. If an idea or proposal requires fuller development, it would more likely be included in an attached report.

Most business letters are no longer than one page. If you must use a second page, however, be sure to choose plain paper of the same quality as the first page. Type a heading on the second page that includes the name of the recipient, the date, and the page number. There should be at least two lines of text on the second page.

The **closing** begins two lines below the body of the letter. Close a formal letter with "Sincerely yours" or "Yours truly." If you know the recipient of the letter personally, you may use "Best wishes" or "Regards." Four lines below, type your name and your title, if appropriate. You will sign the letter above your name. Sign your full name, unless you are on a first-name basis with the recipient of the letter. Business letters may also have additional notes following the closing and the signature that indicate that material has been enclosed with the letter or that copies of the letter have been sent to other people.

Best regards,

Julia Fernandez

Julia Fernandez
Director of Sales and Marketing

Enclosure

cc: Anna Vitelli, Vice President
Sales and Marketing

Most business letters follow one of two formats on the page. With letterhead stationery, writers tend to use the **block format**, in which every line begins at the left-hand margin (Figure C.2). On plain paper, you may use a ***modified* block format**, in which the heading and closing begin at (or slightly to the right of) the center line, while all other lines are flush with the left-hand margin. Some writers also indent the first line of each paragraph when using a modified block format (Figure C.3). In any case, the letter should be centered on the page and should make an attractive picture, like a beautifully plated dish. The envelope should also be typed, and the name, title, and address should match those inside the letter.

In addition to following the expected format, you can make a good professional impression through clear language, vocabulary appropriate to the line of business, standard grammar, correct spelling, and general neatness. Be friendly and courteous, but maintain a professional distance. Don't assume you're going to be best friends with the recipient of your letter. As in all your formal writing, avoid clichés, slang, and sexist language.

Digital Communication

Email is a quick and convenient way to keep in touch with friends and family, and in this context you can feel pretty free to write as you would like. However, when you're using email in a business setting, you should take care to present yourself and your company professionally. Just as in a business letter, your tone in a work-related email should be professional, and your writing should be clear and concise.

In order to maintain a professional tone, be sure to include both a salutation and a closing, even within your own organization. In a formal email to outside recipients, both the salutation and closing should be similar to those in a business letter: "Dear Mr. Mitchell" or "Best regards." Within your own company, however, the salutation may be less formal, for example, "Good morning, Ms. Grey" or "Hi Marjorie." Similarly, the closing need not be as formal as "Yours truly"; it might be as simply as "Best, Jane Doe" or "Thanks, John." Unless the recipient is a close personal friend, however, always include both a salutation and a closing.

Some companies ask their employees to use a **signature block**, that is, to sign emails with their full name and title, department, company, street address, telephone and fax numbers, and website, if applicable. Sometimes the business logo is included. Signature blocks may be programmed to conclude every email but are especially appropriate when the recipients are outside the company. Look at the following example:

Gerald Abernathy, Executive Chef
Bistro Urbano
67 Main Street
Urbanville, NY 19901
(999)555-7721
www.bistrourbano.com

The subject line of an email should—obviously—indicate what the communication is about. The body of the email message should contain a brief introduction that includes the subject and purpose of the communication, a concise explanation of the specifics, and a conclusion that indicates what action is desired. If a fuller account of the details is necessary, attach it in a separate file. Workers may receive hundreds of email messages per day. Respect their time; keep your emails brief and to the point. In general, make only *one* point per email. If your communication is more complex, use separate emails or a written report, or schedule a face-to-face meeting.

Another aspect of professionalism is following the rules of standard written English for grammar and spelling. Use complete, correct sentences. Check the spelling of every email document. Avoid informal abbreviations such as *IMHO* (in my humble opinion) or *PMFJI* (pardon me for jumping in). In addition to the informality, the expressions themselves are too stale and worn for any professional correspondence. It is also wise to avoid *emoticons*, the "faces" created with punctuation marks such as :) for a smile or :(for a frown, unless you are writing to someone you know well.

Additional and compelling reasons to be professional in your email correspondence concern their lack of privacy. Email messages are often stored indefinitely by organizations, may be read by supervisors, and can be subpoenaed by a court of law. Therefore, resist the temptation to bash the boss electronically or to shoot an angry email to a colleague. Be smart, and take a moment to think. If you wouldn't put it in a business letter, don't put it in a business email.

A final word about business email: your readers will notice unclear, unprofessional, or misspelled messages. They don't have to be English teachers to identify a sloppy email, just as they don't need to be gourmet chefs to recognize a cracked plate! Proofread every email carefully before you send it.

Social Media

Social media—such as tweets, blogs, and social networking sites—may not have specific writing requirements, but they can potentially have a significant impact on your academic and professional lives. On the one hand, these media help friends and colleagues communicate quickly and easily, as well as find new friends and business associates. Many businesses also use social media as a way of engaging and communicating with their customers. Your experience and skills with social media may very well be attractive to potential employers. On the other hand, both students and professionals sometimes overestimate the degree of privacy in these media. Colleges and potential employers have been known to make admissions and hiring decisions based on what they find on Facebook. Consider applying any available privacy settings on the sites you use, and remember that material sometimes remains accessible on the Web long after the party is over!

Résumés

A **résumé** is a summary of your qualifications for a job, both in terms of training and of experience. Depending on what a potential employer prefers, you will mail a paper copy or email an electronic copy of your résumé. Sometimes large organizations ask you to submit your résumé and cover letter online. If the employer's preference is not clear, ask. You may occasionally submit a paper copy of your résumé in person at the place of business or at a career fair.

In whatever format they're submitted, résumés generally contain certain types of information in a typical order. The heading should clearly state your name and address, as well as ways to contact you, such as your telephone number and email address. The rest of the résumé should be tailored specifically to the job for which you are applying. The next sections typically describe your education and work experience, followed by any other relevant skills or activities. At the end of the résumé you often list the names and addresses of references or note that you have such references available.

However, a résumé is not simply a list of schools you've attended and jobs you've had. Once you identify a job you'd like to apply for, review your training and experience and decide which aspects are most closely aligned with the job requirements. Sometimes your education will be the most important factor (Figure C.4); at other times it will be your work history (Figure C.5). Unpaid work can also be important. For example, if you were applying for a job as a restaurant manager, your ten years of "volunteering" in your family's establishment would be significant. On the other hand, don't include information that is not relevant to the particular job you're applying for. The fact that you used to be a rocket scientist will probably not get you hired as a pastry chef.

Like a menu, a résumé will probably be studied for only two or three minutes, especially when there are many applicants for a position. Therefore, ensure that the important information is visible and concise. In addition to your contact information, employers need to know the types of establishments you've worked in and the specific tasks and responsibilities you've performed. Begin these descriptions with active verbs like *supervised* or *created*. Avoid full sentences that begin with *I* or *My responsibilities were*.

Your résumé should be printed on high-quality paper and should be free of typographical errors. This document represents you in a competition. If it appears sloppy or is difficult to follow, your potential employers may not even take the time to read it. On the other hand, try to make your résumé stand out in a positive way with a decorative line, an appealing color, or an unusual (but legible and professional) font. Show intelligence and creativity in designing this "menu" for potential employers.

An important point about your résumé is *accuracy*. Do not misrepresent or inflate your achievements. If you haven't received the degree yet, don't mislead your prospective employer into thinking you have. If you were a line cook at your previous job, don't say you were the sous chef. Even if you were to be hired, this false information could get you fired immediately.

Finally, résumés are typically accompanied by a **cover letter** (Figure C.3) in which you introduce yourself to the prospective employer and specify the job for which you are applying. Never send a résumé without a cover letter! The cover letter should be clear and specific. Are you applying for a

Figure C.2 Business Letter in Block Format

Bistro Urbano
67 Main Street
Urbanville, NY 19901

February 27, 2012

Andrea Palmer
The Coffee Company
123 East Market Street
Urbanville, NY 19901

Dear Ms. Palmer:

It was a pleasure to speak with you on the phone last week. We are very interested in trying out the two new coffee varieties you spoke of, the Mocha Madness and Vanilla Vice.

Please send three pounds of each, and bill our account.

We look forward to expanding our business with you.

Sincerely yours,

Gerald Abernathy, Executive Chef

Figure C.3   Sample Cover Letter in Modified Block Format

123 Orchard Lane
Urbanville, NY 19901

March 11, 2012

Paola Allende, Executive Chef
Café Conquistador
85 Wisteria Lane
Suburbia, WA 99999

Dear Chef Allende:

    I am relocating to the Seattle area and would like to apply for the position of sous chef at Café Conquistador advertised in *The Seattle Times.*

    My wife's brother lives in Seattle and has told me of your innovative establishment. I am particularly intrigued by the many South American dishes on your menu since my mother is from Peru and our family restaurant includes several items from her native country. Further, this cuisine is a specialty of the restaurant where I am currently working as a sous chef.

    I will be in Seattle next week and hope to visit your restaurant at that time. I will telephone you on Monday morning to inquire about scheduling an interview. A copy of my résumé is enclosed with this letter.

    You can reach me on my cell phone at 555-555-1221 or via email at limajones@gmail.com. I look forward to meeting you soon.

Sincerely yours,

David Jones

Enclosure

Figure C.4 Sample Résumé Featuring Education

Anjelica Garcia-Jones
123 Orchard Lane, Urbanville, NY 19901
cell phone: (999)555-1222
email: agarciajones@gmail.com

CAREER OBJECTIVE: To obtain a supervisory position at arestaurant where I can utilize my professional degrees, front of house management experience, and wines expertise.

EDUCATION

Smithfield Culinary College, Marketville, NY

Bachelor of Arts in Hospitality Management   June 2005
- Future Leader in the Industry Award, 2005
- Dean's List, junior and senior years
- Member, Sommelier Society

Urban Business School, Urbanville, NY

Bachelor of Arts in Business Administration   June 2001
- Graduated with honors
- Member, Student Council, senior year
- Junior year abroad, Lima Business School, Peru
- Most Promising Freshman Scholarship, 1997–1998

WORK EXPERIENCE

Dining Room Manager & Sommelier

Bistro Urbano, Urbanville, NY   6/05–present
- Supervised front of house operations
- Developed new systems of scheduling and evaluating wait staff
- Expanded wine list to include South American vintages

Bookkeeper

Bistro Urbano, Urbanville, NY   7/01–8/03

RELEVANT SKILLS AND INTERESTS

Fluent in Spanish
Member, Women Chefs & Restaurateurs

Figure C.5 Sample Résumé Featuring Experience

David Jones
123 Orchard Lane, Urbanville, NY 19901
cell phone: (999)555-1221
email: limajones@gmail.com

WORK EXPERIENCE

Sous Chef

Bistro Urbano, Urbanville, NY   5/01–present
- Supervised staff of 8 at small urban café
- Managed purchasing and inventory
- Developed daily lunch special in South American cuisine

Sous Chef

Downtown Diner, Urbanville, NY   6/98–5/01
- Worked sauté and grill stations at busy city diner
- 150 lunch covers daily
- Promoted to sous chef in 2001

Tournant

The Four Seasons, Chicago, IL   4/97–8/97
- Rotated through each station as an intern
- Trained my replacement at this four-star/five-diamond restaurant

Cook

Jones Bar & Grill, Urbanville, NY   6/92–8/96
- Line cook in family-owned restaurant serving American and
  South American dishes

EDUCATION

Smithfield Culinary College, Marketville, NY

Associate of Occupational Studies in Culinary Arts   May 1998

PROFESSIONAL SKILLS AND MEMBERSHIPS

Fluent in Spanish

Member of the American Culinary Federation and
  National Restaurant Association

particular job? Are you interested in future opportunities? Like a news article, the cover letter should begin with the important W's: tell *who* you are, *why* you are writing, *what* position you're applying for.

The role of the cover letter is to make the reader look at your résumé and consider you for an interview. Do some research on the employer, and use that information in your cover letter. For example, you might say something like "I became particularly interested in your establishment when I learned of the opening of your Asian-themed snack bar." Use the cover letter to highlight the most important and interesting information about you that is *relevant* to this specific job, particularly the information that reflects the requirements of the position. If an advertised job requires fluency in Spanish, for example, and you are fluent in Spanish, be sure to put that fact in the cover letter.

In organizing a cover letter, look closely at the job description or the advertisement. The order in which the qualifications and/or duties are listed may be a clue as to their relative importance; that is, the most important may be listed first. You may then wish to put your letter in that same order, highlighting which of the qualifications you possess and which duties you have had experience with.

The résumé and cover letter are important pieces of *persuasive* writing (see Chapter 16). Think about who your readers are and what they need to know about you.

FOOD WRITING

Restaurant Reviews

Restaurant reviews are a popular feature in any newspaper or magazine, whether in print or online. They tend to be more informal in style than academic papers or business letters and reports. However, you should keep in mind the same priorities of identifying the purpose, audience, and scope of the assignment. Tell the story of your particular experience at the restaurant, adding details on its background and history, if relevant. Give a balanced account of the service, décor, and dishes. Use specific, vivid sensory details to "paint a picture" for the reader. (See Chapters 9 and 12.) Depending on where you intend to submit or post the review, you may need to use a particular format or font.

The connections between restaurant reviews and social media are evolving in interesting ways. In "Everyone's a Critic," the first few paragraphs of which are printed here, Ike DeLorenzo researches the impact of the "new bookends" of dining out.

> Restaurant dining has new bookends. The experience often begins and ends with the Web. Before you go out, you find a good place to eat; after you dine, you post a review. Millions of diners are now civilian critics, letting Chowhound, Yelp, City-search, and others in on their recent meals.
>
> The domain of criticism was once the preserve of magazines and newspapers. This year has seen a flurry of activity for restaurant review sites, and for some new approaches to public critiques. Two big players—the biggest actually—want in on the action. Last week, Facebook began mailing door stickers to restaurants asking diners to "like" (there's no "dislike") and comment about restaurants with Facebook pages. Google recently launched Google Place Pages, also with door stickers, which allow diners with smartphones to point the camera at a bar code and

instantly display a comments page. All of this is enough to make restaurateurs worry about every single diner.

In the same way that travelers use various websites to find evaluations of hotels, diners are now turning to online food sites for advice on where to eat. As staggeringly fast as participation in food and restaurant websites has grown, so has the attention being paid to amateur critics. Comments and ratings from any one diner may, of course, be biased or even false. Many Internet pundits believe in something called "the wisdom of the crowd." The theory is that with many people commenting, you eventually get to the truth about a restaurant. As the public posts about the food, the service, the ambience, the béarnaise, the baguettes, a fuller and more accurate picture is supposed to evolve. The amateurs are not going away, which restaurateurs once might have hoped, and they are making chefs nervous.

The article raises important questions about the accuracy and ethics of such review sites as Yelp. Know your audience—and your Internet host! Read the full text of the article in Chapter 7's *A Taste for Reading*.

Food Blogs

Food blogs are also extremely popular, though perhaps few of them lead to a best-selling book and film the way *Julie & Julia* did! As with all types of writing, fresh ideas and vivid, specific language make for good reading. The following is part of an entry from a blog called *Snackish*.

"How To Eat a Stroopwafel"
Stroopwafels are my all-time favorite cookie, but they can be devilishly difficult to find. I suppose scarcity has a way of making the heart grow fonder, but when I do amass a stockpile of them my fondness doesn't fade the way it does halfway into a box of Girl Scout cookies. What makes this the perfect cookie is the combination of textures. Stroopwafels consist of two buttery waffle wafers sandwiching a thin, faintly gooey layer of syrup. They're sweet, but not too sweet, crisp, yet deliciously crumbly.

—**Sara Bogush**, *Snackish—Food and Photography in New York City*

Menus

Menus, and the research that goes into developing them, are an important part of a restaurant's success. The design and quality of the menu should reinforce the "brand identity" of the restaurant, the unique nature of the dining experience at this particular establishment, and this in turn can influence the customers' likelihood of returning. Routine analysis of each menu item's performance allows management to identify items that are not turning a profit and should be deleted. Such analysis also identifies promising menu items that should be moved to a more prominent location on the page. With its multi-purpose ends to inform, entertain, and persuade, the menu is a complex document requiring a number of different skills.

Menu pricing, for example, demands an understanding of recipe costing, seasonality, and psychology, as well as an analysis of competitors. Costing out every written recipe is the best way to ensure that you don't lose money needlessly—and with the average lifespan of a restaurant now well under one year, every dollar you can save will be important. Then look around at your competitors. What are they charging for an appetizer of quesadillas? Be sure to factor in the relative portion size and quality of the dish as well. Pay attention to the seasonal changes in the quality and cost of your ingredients.

The psychology of menu pricing is especially intriguing, as again you attempt to understand your audience and use the most persuasive prices. For example, be sure to take into account that customers have certain expectations regarding pricing. They would be quite surprised if a humble dish of roast turkey with mashed potatoes and gravy cost more than a ten-ounce filet mignon! In addition, retailers everywhere know that $8.95 looks less expensive than $9.00. Finally, although in many menus the prices are set off in their own column or in a special typeface, consider whether prices that simply follow the menu description might keep your customers focused on the food rather than on their finances. Although you may not want the customers to focus on the cost, you yourself should regularly analyze the profit history of each menu item and consider deleting those that perform poorly.

The menu's presentation is also important, as it in many ways embodies the particular dining experience you're offering. Like the experience itself, the menu should be entertaining. It should be attractive and reflect the same theme as the restaurant's décor and cuisine. It would be silly, for example, to use an inexpensive, informal menu design at a trendy, upscale bistro. Yet that inexpensive, informal menu might be just right for a small diner. Photographs of food items can be very persuasive. You do want to be certain, however, that your staff can routinely produce items as perfect in appearance as the glossy images on the menu; if not, customers may send the dish back to the kitchen. Another popular visual tool is a little icon beside particular menu items, like a heart that indicates "heart-friendly" dishes low in fat and sodium.

Some menu designers recommend using three colors: one for general categories such as Pasta or Dessert, a second for the majority of the menu descriptions, and a third to highlight one or two items in each category. Type font styles and sizes can be used in the same way. In addition, pay attention to where individual items are placed. Those at the top of any category and those on the right-hand page tend to attract the most attention. Menu inserts and table tents are also effective in directing customers' notice to particular items. Be sure to use all of the available space, without crowding, of course. The "sundries" you list on the back page might add a nice chunk to the check. Organize the menu into logical categories. Customers typically spend only three minutes reading it; be sure they can find what they are looking for, as well as the items you particularly want them to find.

In terms of the menu's text, use everything you know about writing to create vivid, tempting descriptions of each item. Be clear about the nature of your restaurant and the kinds of customers you hope to attract; then write content that will appeal to your particular audience. Avoid using culinary jargon or foreign words, unless you translate them. Most customers would rather not order an item at all than feel foolish asking you what it is. You should make each dish sound appealing, although you may want to spend more time on the especially profitable ones. Be concise, and especially try to avoid such wordy clichés as "accompanied by," "served with," and "atop a bed of." Focus on specific nouns, sensory adjectives, and active verbs.

Finally, proofread your menu very, very carefully for spelling and grammar. The care with which you create the menu should reflect the same care with which you create the meal.

For information on writing instructions, such as **recipes**, see Chapter 14.

APPENDIX D
ANNOTATED RESEARCH PAPER

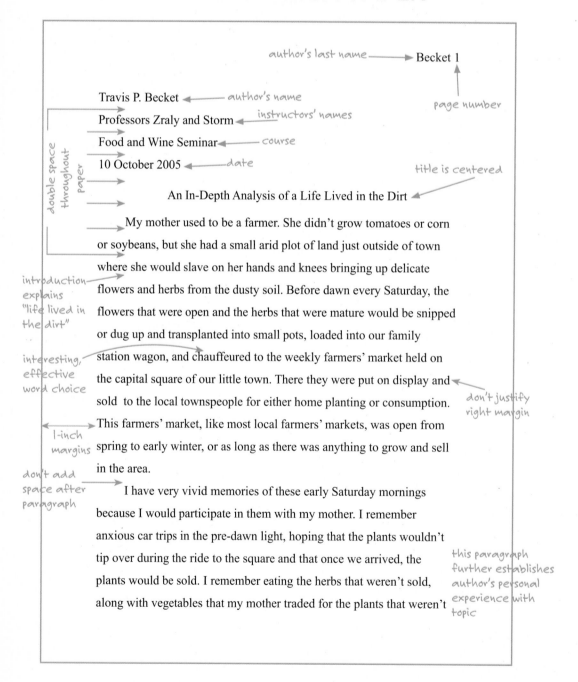

author's last name → Becket 1

page number

Travis P. Becket ← author's name

Professors Zraly and Storm ← instructors' names

Food and Wine Seminar ← course

10 October 2005 ← date

title is centered

An In-Depth Analysis of a Life Lived in the Dirt ← title is centered

double space throughout paper

My mother used to be a farmer. She didn't grow tomatoes or corn or soybeans, but she had a small arid plot of land just outside of town where she would slave on her hands and knees bringing up delicate flowers and herbs from the dusty soil. Before dawn every Saturday, the flowers that were open and the herbs that were mature would be snipped or dug up and transplanted into small pots, loaded into our family station wagon, and chauffeured to the weekly farmers' market held on the capital square of our little town. There they were put on display and sold to the local townspeople for either home planting or consumption. This farmers' market, like most local farmers' markets, was open from spring to early winter, or as long as there was anything to grow and sell in the area.

introduction explains "life lived in the dirt"

interesting, effective word choice

don't justify right margin

1-inch margins

don't add space after paragraph

I have very vivid memories of these early Saturday mornings because I would participate in them with my mother. I remember anxious car trips in the pre-dawn light, hoping that the plants wouldn't tip over during the ride to the square and that once we arrived, the plants would be sold. I remember eating the herbs that weren't sold, along with vegetables that my mother traded for the plants that weren't

this paragraph further establishes author's personal experience with topic sold. I remember eating items that had been submerged in the very unappetizing dirt of my mom's field just a few hours prior. I remember wondering if everybody else in America ate as well as I did.

I wondered this same idea last month at the University of California at Santa Cruz while eating a lunch that, once again, consisted of foods that had been submerged in dirt just a few hours prior. The apprentices who worked the fields agreed with me about the superior quality of the organic food they had grown. As I saw the way that the apprentices relied on organic foods and how they supported organic farming and eating, a new question arose. "If this is the way that food should be produced in America, is it possible to produce enough for everybody?" For the rest of my time at UCSC, this was the thought in my mind and the question on my lips. If organics is best for the soil and the body, can it be utilized at a level that will feed everybody?

After many questions and much research I have come to the conclusion that there are parts of the world that benefit environmentally and socially from environmentally friendly (EFA) systems. America is not currently in a place where large-scale EFA systems can be supported economically, but with the proper growth and advancement in knowledge and technology, combined with the ultimate futility of conventional agricultural practices, organic and sustainable agriculture can and should be the nation's predominant agricultural system.

Let it be said that an EFA system, such as organics, sustainable and biodynamic farming, is defined generally as one that "relies on ecosystem management rather than external agricultural inputs" for the growth, protection, and overall success of the crops (*Organic Agriculture*). An example would be instead of using a pesticide to kill a natural insect predator of a crop, a different crop is grown near the primary crop, attracting a different insect that feeds off of the predator insect. All of the plants are indigenous, as well as the insects they bring, and the ecosystem is not affected negatively. In contrast, a conventional agricultural system is one that relies on "off-farm inputs" such as pesticides, herbicides, and other agro-chemicals for the success of the crop, with the main focus being on the success of the crop and not the ecosystem as a whole. In the earlier example, the farmers would spray pesticides on the crops in order to kill the insect pest *(Organic Agriculture)*.

even short phrases are sometimes quoted

no page number available for this web site

period follows parenthesis

In general, the areas of the world that are currently best suited for EFA systems are underdeveloped or poor regions, or small self-sustained communities. This is because EFA systems tend to rely on the natural resources that are currently available, as opposed to expensive inputs such as chemicals and machinery.

where EFA systems are currently successful

Burkina Faso is in an area of sub-Saharan Africa where desertification and soil erosion is a major problem, stealing millions of hectares of arable land every year. Desertification is the spread of desert-like conditions to areas that were once arable, caused by overgrazing of livestock, improper irrigation, and planting too many crops in one area *(World Factbook)*. A traditional method of sustainable farming was rediscovered in the area, and now the traditional method of "Zaï" is being applied to these damaged lands. According to Nicholas Parrott and Terry Marsden of Cardiff University, since this process was started in 1990, the food supply has become less vulnerable as the process of desertification is in reverse and the land is producing more (38). Zaï "involves making seed holes 20-30 cm wide and deep and using the earth to make a raised 'demi-lune' barrier on the downslope side. Compost and/or natural phosphate is placed in each hole and

first example

tag line

a direct quote is an exact copy of the original text's words and punctuation sorghum or millet seeds planted when it rains" (Parrott and Marsden 39). The process allows the seeds to grow in a reservoir of fertilized water in what would otherwise be barren land. As a result of using the Zaï method, more water seeps into and is retained in the earth because of its enhanced composition and proliferating insect population. To prevent the earth from wearing away, rocks are saved to build retaining walls around the fields (Parrott and Marsden 39).

a paraphrase restates information in your own words

both authors and the page number appear in the parenthetical citation

This form of EFA has had innumerable positive effects on the environment of Burkina Faso. Since the early 1990s, the return of over 100,000 hectares to arable condition has improved crop production by 35%. Further, production has stabilized between dry and wet years (Parrott and Marsden 39).

effective transition

There have also been many social benefits in Burkina Faso because of Zaï. Like other organic farming methods, it requires manpower and thus has increased employment for men who might otherwise have moved from these rural areas to find jobs in the larger cities. This combined with the greater yield on crops and the increased return on sales has strengthened the food security for the people; they now have more reliable food sources year-round. Neighboring nations such as Niger, which was once known for abuse of agrochemicals, have adopted this traditional farming method and met with the same success, restoring 5,800 hectares of degraded land in recent years (Parrott and Marsden 39).

Zaï has strong cultural importance as well. As the soil continues to improve through this ancient, environmentally friendly method, both crop production and jobs have expanded while the movement of the population away from the countryside and toward the cities has decelerated (Parrott and Madsen 39). The use of Zaï has helped

borrowed material is documented in each paragraph, even when the source is identical to validate the importance of local knowledge and culture. Knowing that they relied on traditional practices and "indigenous knowledge" to succeed where technology was failing, the citizens of Burkina Faso now have the self-confidence to address other environmental and social issues; as a nation they can be more self-reliant. Because of these events Burkino Faso was the first African country to host the International Federation of Organic Agricultural Movements (IFOAM) International Scientific Conference, where it was stated that "organic agriculture in developing countries is not a luxury but a precondition for attaining food security" (qtd. in Parrott and Marsden 38).

documenting an indirect source

Another account of a beneficial agricultural transfer from conventional farming to EFA comes from The Maikaal Bio-Cotton Project, in Madhya Pradesh, India. Cotton is a crop that is especially prone to insect infestation, and the typical method of defense is the application of bountiful amounts of pesticides and insecticides. This was how farmers in Madhya Pradesh dealt with the whitefly pest, despite the evident health damage it was causing the ecosystem and the workers. Despite repeated applications of pesticides, the whitefly problem did not relent, as the fly had developed pesticide resistance to the specific pesticide used on the plants. The solution for most farmers was either to switch to a new pesticide or to a new cash crop. Many chose the latter due to "declining returns and toxicity problems" (Parrott and Marsden 24).

transition to second example

Rather than completely shut down, in 1992 several cotton farmers joined together with their local spinning mill to start India's first certified organic agriculture project. One technique used was to determine a natural insect predator of the whitefly, and then to grow plants that attracted this natural predator to close proximity to the cotton.

explanation of EFA project

The natural predators consume the whitefly, reducing the insect problem. Other techniques such as crop-rotation with wheat, soybeans and chili, mating pattern disruption of the whitefly, and organic compost-spreading have been implemented. In seven years, the project has grown from several farms' worth of land to almost 1,000 farmers and over 15,000 acres of land. The project now uses many other biodynamic techniques that have been developed by organic chemists that work for the project (Parrott and Marsden 24-5).

results of project

As a whole, the farms involved in the project report a 20% higher yield of organic cotton, soybeans, wheat, and chili than other farms in the area that are not participating. The higher yield means higher income as well due to the crops' certified organic status. Composting has resulted in soil that retains moisture more efficiently and has cut down the amount of weeds that grow around the crops. In addition, "labour requirements are substantially reduced and production costs for organic cotton are 30–40% of those for conventional production" (Parrott and Marsden 25).

effective transition

One final benefit of the Maikaal Bio-Cotton Project was that it opened India up to the relatively new organic cotton export market, where the majority of the demand came from industrialized nations like the USA. Since the cotton was certified organic, it carried a much higher price tag than conventional cotton and the farmers received a larger payment (Parrott and Marsden 25).

By these two accounts I have strived to show that an organic or sustainable agriculture system can have manifold benefits on ecosystems that are unbalanced or altogether destroyed, and on the economy and culture of the region in which they are grown. Obviously different growing regions present different environmental and social challenges, but the essence of EFA is that it strengthens the relationship

discussion of first two examples

a lecture is also cited

between the ecosystem and the economy. The economy of a region that practices EFA inherently relies on the overall stability and health of the ecosystem, and as the ecosystem detoxifies itself and returns to a more balanced state, it naturally produces a higher yield of more resilient crops, which then catch a higher market price (Posey).

What about America and other industrialized nations that already have a strong conventional farming system built on efficiency and maximum output? In the short run, there is very little chance that organic agriculture can sustain the demand needed to feed everybody. The problem does not lie in whether or not an EFA system can produce the needed volume of food on the same amount of land that is currently being farmed conventionally, but in that the logistics of distribution make it economically unfeasible (*Organic Agriculture*).

application to other nations

The reason the price of organic food is often so much higher in stores is because EFA farms operate on much smaller scales of output, but they still pay the same price for storage and transportation that conventional farmers do. In some cases distribution costs are higher for organics, since by law they must still be segregated from conventional foods during transportation and holding. This increases the price of the food substantially, but since organic foods are still relatively limited in terms of supply, the demand raises the price even higher. Large farming organizations in America offset the incredibly high price of storing and shipping crops with the large volumes of crops that they handle. This is called economies of scale (*Organic Agriculture*).

explanation of barriers to EFA in the United States

Currently the most economically successful organic systems in America are small self-sustained communities, similar to the one I grew up in. This is because labor and transportation costs are virtually nonexistent due to the incredible small volume of production. The costs for labor, handling, and distribution stay within the economy, and they achieve efficiency because oftentimes the transportation costs are no more than paying for gas in the family station wagon (Posey). Also, entities that sell less than $5,000 a year or less in organic food do not have to be certified "Organic" by the USDA. This "flying beneath the radar" allows these local farmers to dramatically reduce their initial overheads (Massiello).

this is a term paper published on the Internet

Although it is not economically feasible currently, a sustainable system of agriculture very well may be necessary for the continual production of food in this country. As the population of the nation and world grow, more stress is put on conventional forms for higher yields of crops. This stress often comes in the form of chemical fertilizers and other agrochemicals. According to Biotechnology giant Monsanto CEO Robert Shapiro, the end result of these stressors along with conventional farming methods is "loss of topsoil, of salinity of soil as a result of irrigation, and ultimate reliance on petrochemicals" (qtd. in Vasilikiotis). Shapiro has also stated that "the commercial industrial technologies that are used in agriculture today to feed the world . . . are not inherently sustainable. They have not worked well to promote either self-sufficiency or food security in developing countries." Feeding the world with a continual reliable food source "is out of the question with current agricultural practice" (qtd. in Vasilikiotis). In the long run, conventional agricultural systems that are reliant on agrochemicals produce weak soil, weak plants, and the need for more agrochemicals to sustain yields.

this paragraph stresses the value of EFA and the risks of conventional practices

tag line

ellipsis indicates part of original text omitted

Shapiro was quoted in another source

transition to third example, this one in the United States

One last research project worth mentioning comes from the University of California–Davis, called the Sustainable Agriculture Farming Systems Project (SAFS). This eight-year project was conducted during the 1990s to compare "conventional farming systems with alternative production systems that promote sustainable agriculture"

(Vasilikiotis). It measured the yields of two-year and four-year conventional farming systems, organic systems, and low-input systems. The crops grown were tomatoes, corn, safflower, and beans (SAFS).

abbreviation saves space

At the end of eight years, the conventional, organic, and low-input systems all had generally comparable yields. The yields of the organic system were lower for the first three years, but once the soil was detoxified of the agrochemicals used in previous years, the yields increased to the same level as those of the conventional system, and then ultimately surpassed the conventional system by the last years of the reports (the study is still active). All throughout this test period the nitrogen, organic carbon, and nutrient content levels of the organic and low-input systems increased, while the nutrient content levels in the conventional system decreased (Vasilikiotis).

results of the study

What this study shows is that although the costs to raise the organic crops were higher, they returned a higher yield than the conventional two- and four-year systems. There was also a visible increase in the soil quality as compared to the conventional system, and when the organic crops were sold at a premium price, there was a significantly higher gross return over the conventional system (SAFS). For the future of our nation's food source, we should be looking towards organics, sustainable agriculture, and other EFA systems. Despite the initial cost of production, they offer what appears to be the only viable option for reliably feeding all the people in the nation. In the event that society realizes its need for a self-sustainable agriculture system, organics could fill the total production level that would be left by conventional farming. If the nation were dedicated enough to invest in large-scale EFA production systems, economies of scale could be reached in terms of the volume of crops that would be transported at one time. In volume, shipping and distribution

discussion of the results

suggested course of action

overcoming barriers to EFA in the United States

could be cost-effective. This would dramatically reduce the market price for organic foods, making them a practical option.

paper is beginning to wind down

The current place in our world for organic, sustainable, and biodynamic agriculture is very uncertain. It has been proven that they are successful in areas of the world that suffer from environmental pollution or degradation, and where conventional farming practices are no longer an option due to pests developing immunities to agrochemicals. EFA

summary of EFA benefits

systems restore life to the land, and can increase the economical stability of poor regions by creating new jobs, increasing income levels, and helping to assure food security. Unfortunately, due to the prices of

summary of barriers

production and distribution compared to the volume being distributed, EFA systems are too expensive for American farmers and consumers to support on a large scale. Thus, the maximum benefit of many organic systems goes to the local community. Organics and other EFA systems must be taken seriously when it comes to long-term food production. They have proven to produce high yields and long-term stability.

It is often said that "United we stand, divided we fall." I believe that this old adage holds true for humanity's relationship with the environment.

conclusion emphasizes and expands topic's significance

tag line

It was Kate Posey, the wistful tour guide at Santa Cruz, who said, "We see things so neatly arranged in grocery stores, sometimes we forget what the plant looks like." She was speaking of the disconnect between human

quotes add interest and credibility but don't replace author's words

beings and their food, how we as a society often forget that food comes not from a grocery store, but from being submerged in very unappetizing

conclusion looks back to introduction and author's childhood

dirt. It is the connection with the dirt that makes us appreciate the taste of the food, and understand our place in the ecosystem. Organics brings society, economy, and ecology back into a state of interdependence and strength. But just as with soil quality, it will take a few years to detoxify

final statement of main idea

the society and economy and to reach maximum yield.

Works Cited

Massiello, Geneva. "Organic Food and Global Sustainability." Term paper. *Plaza at the University of Florida*. U of Florida, 2002. Web. 7 Oct. 2005.

Organic Agriculture at FAO. Food and Agriculture Organization of the United Nations. Web. 7 Oct. 2005.

Parrott, Nicholas, and Terry Madsen. *The Real Green Revolution: Organic and Agroecological Farming in the South*. London: Greenpeace Environmental Trust, 2002. *Greenpeace*. Web. 5 Oct. 2005.

Posey, Kate. "Organic Nature." Talk given at University of California Santa Cruz, Organic Garden, 14 Sept. 2005. Lecture.

Sustainable Agriculture Farming Systems Project (SAFS). "Economic Viability of Organic and Low-Input Farming Systems." *Sustainable Agriculture Farming Systems Project* Sept. 1997. U of California Davis. Web. 7 Oct. 2005.

Vasilikiotis, Christos, PhD. "Can Organic Farming 'Feed the World'?" November 2000. U of California, Berkeley. Web. 7 Oct. 2005. <http://www.cnr.berkeley.edu/~christos/articles/cv_organic_ farming.html>.

The World Factbook. Central Intelligence Agency. 2005. Web. 7 Oct. 2005.

GLOSSARY OF TERMS

abbreviation—a punctuation mark (') used to form contractions and possessives

access, date of—see *date of access*

acronym—a "word" constructed of the first letters of the words in a phrase or title, for example, HACCP (Hazard Analysis Critical Control Point)

action verb—a verb that tells what the subject of a sentence is doing; see also *verb*

active voice—verb form used when the subject of the sentence is performing the action of the verb; compare *passive voice*

address—in a letter, the name of the person and/or business that you are writing to

adjective—a word that describes or modifies a noun

adverb—a word that describes or modifies a verb, adjective, or another adverb; see also *conjunctive adverb*

agreement—when one word in a sentence changes form to match or "agree with" another word, for example, *subject–verb agreement* and *pronoun–antecedent agreement*

allusion—a reference to or description of a person, place, event, or work of art or literature

alternating format—in a compare and contrast essay, a type of organization in which you focus on the first characteristic of the two items, then the second characteristic, and so on; also called *point-by-point format*

analogy—a comparison of the similarities between two items, often to explain an unfamiliar concept using a more familiar one; *metaphors* and *similes* are analogies

analysis—breaking down a topic or an idea into its component parts and examining how it's put together in order to learn something about the whole

antecedent—a word, phrase, or clause for which a pronoun is substituted; see *pronoun–antecedent agreement*

APA style—format for documentation used by the American Psychological Association (APA)

apostrophe—the raised "comma" (') that is used to form possessives and contractions

appositive—a word or phrase that sits next to a noun and renames it

argument—a series of connected statements or claims that are supported by evidence and used to prove a point; sometimes used interchangeably with *claim*

articles—the words *a, an,* and *the,* which specify whether a noun refers to a specific or general person, place, or thing; *a* and *an* are *indefinite articles; the* is a *definite article*

audience—those who receive a communication, for example, through reading an essay, listening to a speech, or watching a movie

auxiliary verb—see *helping verb*

base form—with verbs, the word that follows *to* in an infinitive phrase (for example, the base form *cook* is part of the infinitive phrase *to cook*); also called the *stem*

block format—(1) in a compare and contrast essay, a type of organization in which you write all about the first item, then all about the second; (2) in a letter, a format in which every line begins at the left-hand margin

body—(1) the middle section of an essay, containing specific information that develops the main idea of the piece; (2) the content of a letter

brackets—a type of punctuation mark used in pairs [ ], often within quotes to indicate inserted material

brainstorm—to generate ideas and information through freewriting, making lists or charts, talking to others, or doing research or experiments

capitalization—using capitals or uppercase for the initial letter of a sentence or proper noun

case—(1) the name given to different forms of nouns and pronouns: the *subjective case* is used for the subject of a sentence (*Ivan* or *he*), the *objective case* for a direct or indirect object and with prepositions (*Ivan* or *him*), and the *possessive case* for modifiers (*Ivan's* or *his*); (2) one of two types of letters, *uppercase* (or capital letters) and *lowercase*

causal chain—a sequence in which one event is the cause of another, which in turn causes another, and so on

causation—see *cause and effect*

cause and effect—a way of developing ideas by analyzing the causes and/or effects of an event or condition. An *immediate cause* occurs a short time before the event; a *remote cause* is farther away in time. A *main cause* is the most important or powerful cause; a *contributing cause* is a less important or powerful cause.

central idea—the main point you want to make, the claim you want to prove in an essay; sometimes called the *thesis* or *thesis statement*

character—a person in a literary work; sometimes *characters* are animals or mythological creatures

characterization—methods used by an author (such as speech, action, description, and narration) to portray a character's personality

Chicago style—a documentation format laid out in *The Chicago Manual of Style*

chronological order—an organizational plan that follows the sequence of events

citation—(1) quoting from an outside source to add authority to your work; (2) a source cited in your work; see also *parenthetical citation*

cite—to quote and document an outside source in your work

claim—a statement supported by evidence that forms part of a larger *argument*

classification—organizing a topic into different kinds or categories

clause—a group of words that contains a subject and a verb; clauses may be *independent* or *main* and stand

alone as a complete sentence; or they may be *dependent, subordinate,* or *relative* and unable to stand alone

cliché—a phrase that has been used so often that it has lost both precision and interest, for example, *hungry as a horse*

close reading—a focused and thorough study of a text

closing—the line that ends a letter, for example, *Sincerely yours,* plus your name and title

"coat hanger"—in this textbook, a subordinating conjunction

collective noun—a word that names a group with several members, such as *team*; in American usage, collective nouns are usually treated as singular; see also *noun*

colon—the punctuation that looks like two periods, one above the other (:), used to introduce a list or connect independent clauses

comma—a punctuation mark (,), used to separate parts of sentences

comma splice—a sentence error in which two independent clauses are joined by a comma only

common noun—a noun that refers to a category rather than a specific individual, place, or thing, for example, *city* rather than *Chicago*; see also *noun* and *proper noun*

communication—any of several ways of sharing information, feelings, and ideas; communication may use words (*verbal*) or not (*nonverbal*). *Speech* and *writing* are examples of nonverbal communication.

compare and contrast—to develop an idea by looking for similarities and differences

comparative form—the form of an adjective or adverb created by adding the suffix *–er* or the word *more* and used to judge two items against each other

comparison—see *compare and contrast*

complete predicate—see *predicate*

complete subject—see *subject*

complete thought—one of the three elements of a sentence, in addition to the subject and verb, and not to be confused with context or information. A complete thought suggests an independent *structure*; that is, the sentence can stand alone.

complex sentence—two clauses joined by a subordinating conjunction

compound adjectives—adjectives that contain more than one word, such as *cage-free* or *well-behaved*

compound number—a number spelled with two words connected by a hyphen, such as *twenty-one*

compound sentence—a sentence that contains two or more simple sentences joined by a coordinating conjunction, semicolon, or colon

compound subject—two or more subjects that share the same verb

compound verb—two or more verbs that share the same subject

compound-complex sentence—a sentence that contains a series of connected dependent and independent clauses

conclusion—the end of an essay, which may summarize its main points, state or restate the main idea, resolve the problem, and provide the reader with a sense of closure

conjunction—a word that joins two or more words, phrases, or clauses. The *coordinating conjunctions* (the so-called *FANBOYS: for, and, nor, but, or, yet, so*) join equal elements; *subordinating conjunctions* (such as *because, although, while*) join a dependent to an independent clause.

conjunctive adverb—a word or phrase that modifies an entire clause and suggests how its idea is connected to that of another word or clause; for example, *however* or *then*

connotation—the feelings or associations that make a word seem positive or negative, or simply neutral; compare *denotation*

context—the time and place, as well as the audience, purpose, and subject of a communication; see also *kairos*

contraction—a combination of two words in which missing letters are indicated by an *apostrophe*

coordinating conjunction—a conjunction that joins equal elements; see also *conjunction* and *FANBOYS*

count nouns—generally refer to concrete things and can be counted; compare *noncount nouns*

cover letter—a type of business letter in which you introduce yourself to the prospective employer and specify the job for which you are applying; usually accompanied by a résumé

critical analysis essay—analysis of a literary or other artistic "text" that looks at how specific features or elements work to create certain effects

cut and paste—(1) editing functions on the word processor; (2) to physically separate and tape together sentences and paragraphs from a handwritten or printed essay

dangling modifier—an error in which a *modifier*, often an initial participial phrase, does not actually refer to a specific word in the sentence

dash—a punctuation mark (in MLA format, the em dash —) used variously like a comma, semicolon, or colon; see also *em dash, en dash,* and *hyphen*

date of access—in the list of works cited, the *date of access* is the day, month, and year on which you last viewed an electronic source

definite article—*the*; see also *article*

definition—an explanation of what an item looks like or what it is made of, where you can find it, what it does, what it's used for; see also *extended definition, denotation,* and *connotation*

demonstrative pronoun—a word (*this, these, that, those*) that directs the reader's attention to particular nouns or pronouns

denotation—the basic definition of a word; compare *connotation*

dependent clause—a group of words that contains a subject and verb but cannot stand alone as a complete sentence; also called a *subordinate clause*

description—writing that "paints a picture," often using sensory details

direct address—using the name or title of the person you are writing or speaking to, for example, "Yes, Chef"

direct object—the *direct object* of a verb receives the action of the verb; compare *indirect object*

direct quote—an exact copy of the words and punctuation of the original text; compare *paraphrase*

draft—(1) to write or compose; (2) a piece of writing, often the *first* or *rough draft*, or a *revised* or *final draft*

edit—to correct or revise the grammar, word usage, and punctuation of a text

edition—a specific version or printing of a book; second and later editions should be specified when documenting a source

editor—one who collects various essays or poems into a book and/or prepares a manuscript

em dash—these long dashes—like commas—are used between words and phrases to set off a thought that interrupts the rest of the sentence

emphatic order—organizational plan that corresponds to the importance of the ideas or the emphasis you want to give them

en dash—shorter than the em dash (—), the en dash (–) is used in APA format to join a compound adjective where the words are of equal weight

end marks—punctuation marks that indicate the end of a complete sentence, including the *period, question mark,* and *exclamation point*

essay—a series of paragraphs or sections that develops a single main idea; see also *personal essay*

ethos—the character of a speaker or writer; persuasive strategies that show the reader you are knowledgeable, fair-minded, and trustworthy

euphemism—a watered-down term used supposedly to spare the reader's feelings when uncomfortable things like death or sex must be discussed

example—an event, story, fact, or other specific information that is used to illustrate, explain, or prove a general point; see also *extended example*

exclamation point—punctuation mark (!) at the end of sentence used to add emphasis or emotion

exemplification—the process of developing an idea through examples

extended definition—writing in which several paragraphs or an entire paper is focused on defining a complex term such as *success, marriage,* or *tortillas*

extended example—writing in which several paragraphs or an entire paper develops a single example; see also *example*

FANBOYS—a common acronym for the seven coordinating conjunctions: *for, and, nor, but, or, yet,* and *so*

feminine pronouns—a group of third-person singular pronouns that refer to females: *she, her, hers*

figurative language—a group of methods by which you compare one item with another to create pictures or explore ideas; a *figure of speech* refers to a single method

figure of speech—a method of comparing items to create pictures or explore ideas, for example, *metaphor* or *personification*

first person—*I* (singular), *we* (plural)

flashback—in a narrative, a scene that takes place before the current time

format—the style or rules governing the layout of a paper and the documentation of sources

fragment or **sentence fragment**—an incomplete sentence, one that is missing a subject, a verb, and/or an independent structure or "complete thought" so that it cannot stand alone

freewriting—a method of brainstorming that allows writers' ideas to flow freely, without editing

future perfect tense—see *perfect tenses*

future tense—formed with *will* + the base verb, it describes an action or condition that is expected but has yet to occur

gender—a characteristic of third-person singular pronouns, which may be *masculine (he, him, his), feminine (she, her, hers),* or *neutral (it, its)*

generic noun—a noun that names the typical member of a group, such as *the average student*

genre—a type or category of literature, music, etc., for example, *detective story* or *romantic comedy*

gerund—the base form of the verb + *–ing*, for example, *cooking* or *baking*; used as a noun

heading—(1) in an essay in MLA format, your name, the instructor's name, the course title, and the date in the upper left-hand corner; (2) in a letter, your name and address and the date

helping verb—in a verb phrase, one or more words that indicate the mood, tense, or voice of the main verb; also called *auxiliary verb*

hyphen—the short line used (-) within a word to connect compound numbers or adjectives

image—word or words that refer to one or more of the five senses

imagery—the collection of images in a single work; sometimes used for *figurative language*

imperative mood—a sentence in this mood is a command, such as *Please sit down*; see also *mood*

in medias res—some stories start "in the middle of things" instead of at the beginning

indefinite article—*a* and *an*; see also *article*

indefinite pronoun—a pronoun that refers to a general rather than a specific person, place, or thing (*everyone*); often, it suggests an amount (*some*)

independent clause—a group of words that contains a subject and a verb and that can stand alone; also called *main clause*

indicative mood—a sentence in this mood is a simple statement or question; see also *mood*

indirect object—the person or thing *to* which or *for* which the action is performed; compare *direct object*

indirect question—contains the content but not the exact words, for example, *He asked me what the homework was.* The exact words would be enclosed in quotation marks, as in *"What is the homework?" he asked.*

indirect speech—contains the content but not the exact words of a conversation, for example, *She mentioned that she has a sister.* The exact words would be enclosed in quotation marks, as in *"I have a sister," she said.*

infinitive—*to* + base form of verb, such as *to cook, to write,* or *to be*; *infinitives* may function like nouns

infinitive phrase—see *infinitive*

informative writing—intends to communicate information

instructions—directions on how to do something; a recipe

intensive pronouns—formed by adding *–self* to the personal pronouns and used to add emphasis

interjection—an exclamatory word such as *Hey!* that can be added to or deleted from a sentence without changing the sentence's structure

interrogative pronoun—a pronoun such as *who* or *what* used to ask a question

introduction—the beginning of an essay; an introduction should catch the reader's attention and generally states the topic of the paper

inverted sentence—a sentence in which the verb precedes the subject

irony—the use of words or other techniques to convey a meaning opposite to the obvious or literal one. In *dramatic irony,* the audience knows something the character does not; in *verbal irony,* the effect of the words is the opposite of their literal meaning.

irregular verbs—verbs that change form in unpredictable ways; compare *regular verbs*

italics—a slanted style of print (*print*) used for the titles of books, periodicals, movies, television series, works of art, and ships; for words in a foreign language; and when referring to a letter or word

jargon—the technical vocabulary specific to particular jobs, professions, or specialties

kairos—the context, or time and place, of a particular piece of writing

letterhead—a type of stationery on which the individual's or company's name, address, and/or logo are printed

linking verb—a word that "links" or joins the subject to the rest of the sentence; linking verbs include forms of *to be, to appear,* and *to seem*

literary present—the use of the present tense in discussing a literary work

logos—in persuasive writing, a strategy that uses reasoning and evidence, such as facts, statistics, and examples

lowercase—refers to small letters; compare *uppercase*

main clause—a group of words that contains a subject and a verb and that can stand alone or form part of a compound or complex sentence; also called *independent clause*

masculine pronouns—a group of third-person singular pronouns that refer to males: *he, him, his*

metaphor—a figure of speech in which one thing is said to *be* another; for example, "The kitchen was a cardboard box inferno."

misplaced modifier—a word or phrase that is out of position relative to the word it describes

MLA style—format for documentation used by the Modern Language Association (MLA)

modified block format—in a letter, a format in which the heading and closing begin at (or slightly to the right of) the center line, while all other lines are flush with the left-hand margin

modifier—a word, phrase, or clause that describes, explains, or limits another word, phrase, or clause; *adjectives* and *adverbs* are modifiers; see also *dangling modifier* and *misplaced modifier*

mood—a property of verbs including the *indicative mood*, which tells or asks without suggesting any hidden meaning; the *imperative mood*, which is used to give orders or commands; and the *subjunctive mood*, which is used mostly in formal situations to talk about a wish or to make a statement that is not factual

narration—the process of telling a story

narrator—the character who is telling the story; the narrator can be participating in the events or stand outside the story itself

neutral or **gender-neutral pronouns**—third-person singular pronouns that don't specific a gender: *it, its*; note that all third-person plural pronouns are gender-neutral: *they, their, theirs*

noncount nouns—include things that cannot be counted and do not have a plural form; see *count nouns*

nonrestrictive clause—compare *restrictive clause*

nonverbal communication—communication without words; compare *verbal communication*

noun—a word that names something—a person, place, thing, or idea; a *common noun* may refer to categories of persons, places, and things; a *proper noun* refers to a specific person, place, or thing and is always capitalized; a *generic noun* names the typical member of a group; see also *collective noun*

noun fragment—a group of words that renames or describes a noun but does not form a complete sentence

number—a property of subjects and verbs, which are either *singular* (one) or *plural* (more than one)

object—the *object of a preposition* is the noun or pronoun that follows the preposition to form a prepositional phrase; the *direct object* of a verb receives the action of the verb; the person or thing *to* which or *for* which the action is performed is the *indirect object*

objective case—a noun or pronoun form used for the objects of verbs or prepositions; see *case*

outline—to put the main (and supporting) ideas in order; some writers create an outline before beginning a rough draft; others make an outline *after* completing a rough draft and use it to guide the revision process

paragraph—a group of sentences that develops a single main idea

paraphrase—to restate or translate the original text into your own words without quotation marks

parallelism—when equivalent ideas are expressed in equivalent grammatical forms

parentheses—a punctuation mark ( ) used to set off words and phrases that explain or refer to something within the main sentence.

parenthetical citation—information enclosed in parentheses within the text about a source you've used in your work participle—a form of the verb used as an adjective; the *present participle* adds *–ing* to the base form; the past participle of regular verbs adds *–d* or *–ed*

passive voice—verb form used when the subject of the sentence is *receiving* that action of the verb; compare *active voice*

past participle—see *participle*

past perfect tense—see *perfect tenses*

past tense—describes an action that occurred in the past or a condition that existed in the past; regular verbs add *-d* or *-ed* to form the past tense; see also *tense*

pathos—a strategy in speaking or writing intended to invoke pity or courage or hope, which in turn moves the reader to agreement and possibly action

perfect tenses—the *past perfect* indicates that one action in the past was completed before another; the *present perfect* indicates an action that occurred or a condition that existed at some indefinite time in the past; the *future perfect* describes an action that will be completed before another time in the future; see also *tense*

period—a punctuation mark (.) that indicates the end of a sentence

periodical—a magazine, journal, or newspaper published at regular intervals

person—a characteristic of pronouns; see *first person, second person, third person*

personal essay—a piece of writing in which the author tries to explain an idea from his or her personal perspective; often characterized by a more intimate tone and less formal organization than academic essays

personal pronoun—a word that refers to a specific person, place, thing, or idea, for example, *I, we, you, he, she, it, they*

personification—a figure of speech that attaches human thoughts and feelings to inanimate objects

persuasive writing—writing that seeks to compel a response from the audience, whether it is sympathy, agreement, or action; see also Aristotle's persuasive strategies: *logos, ethos, pathos,* and *kairos*

phrase—a group of words that functions like a single word

plot—the sequence or arrangement of events in a story

plural—more than one, as in the *plural form* of a noun

point-by-point format—see *alternating format*

point of view—the narrator's position with regard to the story, generally first person (*I*) or third person (*they*)

positive form—the form of an adjective or adverb that describes a noun without comparing it to another one

possessive adjective—the form of the possessive that modifies a noun: *my, our, your, his, her, its, their*

possessive case—a noun form that indicates possession, usually by adding *'s*; see *case*

possessive pronoun—the form of the possessive that replaces a phrase (That book is *mine,* that is, *my book*): *mine, ours, yours, his, hers, theirs*; note that *it* is not used in this way

predicate—the part of the sentence that is not the subject; the *simple predicate* is the verb

prefix—a word or syllable attached to the beginning of a word to make a new word

preposition—a word that shows the "position" of one noun in relation to another

prepositional phrase—a group of words that begins with a preposition and ends with a noun or pronoun

present participle—see *participle*

present perfect tense—see *perfect tenses*

present tense—describes an action that is happening now, in the present; see also *tense*

principal parts—see *verb*

process—an activity performed in a certain sequence of steps with the necessary equipment and ingredients; see also *process analysis, process narrative,* and *instructions*

process analysis—an explanation of how a process is performed; a type of organization according to the sequence of steps in a process

process narrative—the story of how a process was performed

progressive tenses—indicate that an action was (*past progressive*), is (*present progressive*), or will be (*future progressive*) continuing

pronoun—word used in place of a noun or to indicate an amount; see also *personal pronoun, possessive pronoun, relative pronoun, reflexive pronoun, demonstrative pronoun, interrogative pronoun*

pronoun reference—a pronoun should refer clearly to a particular noun or nouns

pronoun-antecedent agreement—pronouns must agree with their antecedents in person, number, and gender

proofread—to read a piece of writing in order to find and correct errors in spelling and punctuation

proofreading—the final check of a piece of writing for spelling and punctuation errors

propaganda—written or spoken material that seeks to compel a response from the audience through manipulation rather than through open debate

proper noun—a noun that refers to a specific person, place, or thing and is always capitalized, for example, *Chicago* or *Uncle John*; see also *noun*

punctuation marks—provide visual, nonverbal guides to the structure and meaning of a sentence; see Chapters 29–31

purpose—the reason for communication, for example, to inform, entertain, and/or persuade

quarterly—a periodical published four times per year

question mark—punctuation mark (?) at the end of a sentence to indicate a question; see also *indirect question*

quotation marks—used to set off speech and the titles of songs, poems, short stories, individual episodes in a television series, articles, and chapters

recipe format (vs. essay format)—Recipes are different in that they usually begin immediately with a list of ingredients. The steps themselves may be listed or appear in small "paragraphs," but they are not in essay format. The steps are written in the imperative mood (that is, as commands).

reflexive pronouns—formed by adding *–self* to the personal pronouns and used when the subject of the sentence is also the object

refutation—an outline of some of the arguments *on the opposite side* and explanation of why these arguments are unreasonable, unethical, or otherwise less persuasive than your arguments

regular verbs—follow the same general rules as they change form, for example, add *–ed* to form the past tense; compare *irregular verbs*

relative clause—a type of dependent clause containing a relative pronoun that connects or "relates" to a noun or pronoun in an earlier part of the sentence

relative clause fragment—a sentence fragment containing a relative pronoun (*who, which, that*)

relative pronoun—a word that "relates" to another noun and connects it to a dependent or relative clause; relative pronouns include *who, which*, and *that*

research—gathering information or evidence in order to answer a question

restrictive clause—a clause that limits the meaning of a word or is otherwise essential to the meaning of a sentence; a *nonrestrictive* clause is *not* essential to the meaning of a word or sentence

résumé—a summary of your qualifications for a job, both in terms of training and of experience

revision—the process of reevaluating and rewriting a piece of writing; literally *re-seeing*

rhetorical modes—ways of developing an idea and/or organizing an essay; rhetorical modes include narration, description, exemplification, compare and contrast, process analysis, and cause and effect

rhyme—similarity or identity of sound between words, particularly at the end of lines of poetry

rough draft—the first version of an essay, also called the first draft

run-on sentence—two independent clauses joined without an appropriate conjunction and/or punctuation

salutation—the greeting in a letter, such as *Dear John*

second person—*you* (singular and plural)

semicolon—a punctuation mark that looks like a comma with a period on top (;), often used to join related independent clauses

sensory details—information that comes from the five senses (sight, smell, taste, touch, hearing)

sentence—a group of words that contains a subject, a verb, and a "complete thought," that is, an idea that can stand alone; see also *simple sentence, compound sentence, complex sentence,* and *compound-complex sentence*

sentence fragment or fragment—an incomplete sentence, one that is missing a subject, a verb, and/or an independent structure or "complete thought" so that it cannot stand alone

setting—where and when a story takes place

sexist language—expressions that inappropriately specify one gender when both should be included, for example, *he* used to mean "people in general"

signature block—conclusion of an email that may include sender's full name and title, department, company, street address, telephone and fax numbers, website, and business logo

simile—a figure of speech in which one thing is said to be *like* another; contains the words *like* or *as*

simple predicate—see *predicate*

simple sentence—a sentence that contains only one subject–verb pair or independent clause

simple subject—see *subject*

simple tenses—the *past, present,* and *future tenses* of verbs

singular—one, as in the *singular form* of a noun

slang—words or phrases that have become popular within a certain group of people but may not be recognized by a general audience

slash—a punctuation mark (/) used when citing URLs, quoting lines of poetry, offering paired alternatives, and writing certain abbreviations

spatial order—an organizational plan that follows the physical layout

speaking—a form of verbal communication

specific details—examples, descriptions, or factual information that develops, explains, or illustrates an idea

speech—a type of *verbal communication*

stanza—a group of lines in a poem, very much like a paragraph

stem—see *base form*

story—a story answers the question *What happened?* and includes characters, setting, and plot. Stories are often enriched with vivid descriptive details, a complex problem for the characters, suspense, and surprising twists and turns in the plot.

subject—the word or group of words that is performing the action of the sentence or that is being described by the rest of the sentence; the *simple subject* consists of one or more nouns or pronouns (or phrases acting like nouns); the *complete subject* includes all the words that modify or describe the subject

subject–verb agreement—verbs must agree with their subjects in number and person

subjective case—see *case*

subjunctive mood—used mostly in formal situations to talk about a wish or make a statement that is not factual; see also *mood*

subordinate clause—a group of words that contains a subject and verb but cannot stand alone as a complete sentence; also called a *dependent clause*

subordinate clause fragment—a type of incomplete sentence that consists of a subordinating conjunction plus a subject and verb

suffix—a word or syllble attached to the end of a word to make a new word

summary—a condensed statement of a text's main idea(s) and key supporting points

superlative form—the form of an adjective or adverb created by adding the suffix *–est* or the word *most* and used to compare *more than two* items

symbol—a thing that represents or stands for something else; for example, a dove may symbolize peace

symbolism—the use of symbols in a text

tag line—a phrase that introduces outside material, often by naming the author and/or title of the source

tense—a characteristic of verbs that indicates the time that an action was performed or that a condition existed; see also *past tense, present tense, future tense, simple tenses, perfect tenses,* and *progressive tenses*

text—(1) a book or written work; (2) the original wording of a source; (3) more broadly, any artistic work, including films and paintings

textual evidence—includes quotes, summaries, details, and descriptions from and of the "text," details that can be independently verified by the reader

thesis or **thesis statement**—a sentence that summarizes the central idea of an essay; the topic of the paper plus the point the author hopes to make about that topic

third person—*he, she, it* (singular); *they* (plural)

title—(1) the name of a piece of writing, such as an essay, story, poem, or book; (2) a name that describes a person's job or rank, such as *Dr., Chef,* or *Assistant Manager*

topic sentence—the main idea of a paragraph

transition or **transitional expression**—a word or phrase that shows the connection between ideas; transitions can move the reader from one part of a sentence to the next, from one sentence to the next, or from one paragraph to the next

uppercase—refers to capital letters; compare *lowercase*

URL—an acronym for *Uniform Resource Locator* or Internet address

verb—an essential ingredient of a sentence, it is a word or phrase that tells what the subject of the sentence is doing or connects the subject with some information later in the sentence; *regular verbs* follow the same general rules as they change form, while *irregular verbs* have different forms that must be memorized; the *principal parts* of a verb include the infinitive or base form, the past tense, and the past and present participles; see also *action verb, helping verb, linking verb,* and *verb phrase*

verb phrase—a main verb preceded by one or more helping verbs

verbal—a word that is made from and thus resembles a verb but is used in a different way, for example, as a noun (see *gerund* and *infinitive phrase*) or adjective (see *participle*)

verbal communication—see *communication*

voice—(1) used of a writer, the combination of features—including the attitude toward the topic, the choice of details that develop the topic, the choice of vocabulary, and the rhythm of the sentences—that creates a distinctive flavor; (2) a characteristic of verbs; in the *active voice*, the subject of the sentence is performing the action of the verb, while in the *passive voice*, the subject of the sentence is *receiving* that action

Works Cited page—a list in MLA style of all the sources cited in your paper

Works Consulted page—a list of sources read for the purpose of writing the paper, not all of which are necessarily *cited*

writing—a type of verbal communication

NOTES

1. For example, see Peter Elbow's *Writing with Power: Techniques for Mastering the Writing Process* and *Writing without Teachers*.

2. For example, see Annie Murphy Paul, "Your Brain on Fiction."

3. For a fuller discussion of the dual nature of an essay's "shape," see Peter Elbow's "The Music of Form: Rethinking Organization in Writing."

4. "American Diner Slang," written and researched by BH, ed. Bernadette Lynn, *h2g2* (19 Mar. 2003), British Broadcasting Company.

5. For example, see "Jargon Buster: Winter Sports" for the terms in the first sentence; "Wine Terms" for the fourth; and "Glossary of Internet & Web Jargon" for the fifth.

6. For example, see Annie Murphy Paul, "Your Brain on Fiction."

7. Alan Dundes, "Seeing Is Believing" in *Interpreting Folklore*. See also Barb Stuckey, *Taste: Surprising Stories and Science about Why Food Tastes Good* (New York: Atria, 2012), pp. 103–106, for a discussion of sight's role in flavor.

8. Adapted from a classroom activity conducted by David Bourns at Oakwood School, Poughkeepsie, New York, 1971.

9. For example, see Ann C. Noble, "The Wine Aroma Wheel."

10. See Frank H. Messerti, MD, "Chocolate Consumption, Cognitive Function, and Nobel Laureates"; Ashutosh Jogalekar, "Chocolate Consumption and Nobel Prizes: A Bizarre Juxtaposition If There Ever Was One"; and Ted Bunn, "Does Chocolate Cause Nobel Prizes?"

11. For example, see Peter Elbow, *Writing without Teachers*, and Alfred E. Guy, Jr., "Process Writing: Reflections and the Arts of Writing and Teaching," as well as other essays in Teresa Vilardi and Mary Chang, eds., *Writing-Based Teaching: Essential Practices and Enduring Questions*.

12. Thanks to Sharon Zraly for introducing me to Comma Man.

13. Elizabeth Dye, "Straight Out of Brooklyn."

14. For example, see Moats; Jones; and the extensive reference list in Hayward and Phillips.

15. This text follows *The New Food Lover's Companion: Comprehensive Definitions of Nearly 6,000 Food, Drink, and Culinary Terms* by Sharon Tyler Herbst in spelling *hollandaise* with a small *h*. However, many writers and chefs spell *Hollandaise* with a capital *H*.

WORKS CONSULTED

About a Boy. Dir. Chris Weitz and Paul Weitz. Perf. Hugh Grant, Nicholas Hoult, and Toni Collette. Based on the novel by Nick Hornby. Universal, 2002. Film.

Allen, Richard. "Camera Movement in *Vertigo.*" *The Alfred Hitchcock Scholars/MacGuffin webpage.* 12 Jan. 2006. Web. 8 Mar. 2006.

Alred, Gerald J., Charles T. Brusaw, and Walter E. Oliu. *The Business Writer's Handbook.* 6th ed. Boston: Bedford/St. Martin's, 2000. Print.

"American Diner Slang." Written and researched by BH. Ed. Bernadette Lynn. *h2g2* 19 Mar. 2003. BBC. Web. 24 Jan. 2006.

The American Heritage Book of English Usage. Houghton Mifflin, 1996. *Bartleby.com: Great Books Online.* Web. 14 Nov. 2005.

American Psychological Association. *Publication Manual of the American Psychological Association.* 6th ed. Washington, DC: American Psychological Association, 2010. Print.

"American Slang." *h2g2* 28 Jul. 1999. BBC. Web. 24 Jan. 2006.

Apollo 13. Dir. Ron Howard. Perf. Tom Hanks, Bill Paxton, Kevin Bacon, Gary Sinise, Ed Harris, and Kathleen Quinlan. Universal, 1995. Film.

Bantick, Christopher. "Spelling Sux, OK?" *The Age.* 8 Dec. 2003. Web. 13 Dec. 2005.

Bauman, M. Garrett. Ideas and Details: *A Guide to College Writing.* 5 Ed. Boston: Heinle, 2004. Web. 8 Mar. 2006.

Bays, Jeff. "Hitchcock: Basic Film Techniques." *Borgus.com.* January 2006. Print.

Beach, Richard, Deborah Appleman, Susan Hynds, and Jeffrey Wilhelm. *Teaching Literature.* 2004. Web. 25 Feb. 2012.

Bean, John C. "Dealing with Issues of Grammar and Correctness." *Engaging Ideas: The Professor's Guide to Integrating Writing, Critical Thinking, and Active Learning in the Classroom.* 2nd ed. San Francisco: Wiley, 2011. 66–86. Print.

Beason, Larry. "Ethos and Error: How Business People React to Errors." *College Composition and Communication* 53:1 (Sep. 2001): 33–64. Print.

Beckson, Karl, and Arthur Ganz. *A Reader's Guide to Literary Terms: A Dictionary.* New York: Farrar, Straus and Giroux, 1960. Print.

Bhide, Monica. "A Question of Taste: It's Not Easy Accepting Who Gets to Lick the Spoon." *The Washington Post* 21 February 2005: C10. Reprinted in *Best Food Writing 2005.* Ed. Holly Hughes. New York: Marlowe, 2005. 102–104. Print.

Big Night. Dir. Stanley Tucci and Campbell Scott. Perf. Stanley Tucci, Tony Shalhoub, and Isabella Rossellini. Samuel Goldwyn Company, 1996. Film.

Bourns, David. Adapted from a classroom activity conducted at Oakwood School, Poughkeepsie, New York, 1971. Lecture.

Brians, Paul. *Common Errors in English Usage.* Home page. Washington State University. Web. 13 Dec. 2005.

Bunn, Ted. "Does Chocolate Cause Nobel Prizes?" *Ted Bunn's Blog.* University of Richmond Campus Unit Blogs. 11 Jan. 2013. Web. 27 Jul. 2013.

Bureau of Labor Statistics. "Chefs, Cooks, and Food Preparation Workers." *Occupational Outlook Handbook, 2006-2007 Edition.* 20 Dec. 2005. The U.S. Department of Labor. Web. 3 Mar. 2006.

"California Fungi—*Cantharellus cibarius.*" *MykoWeb.* The Fungi of California, 1996–2008. Web. 22 Apr. 2013.

Casagrande, June. *It Was the Best of Sentences, It Was the Worst of Sentences: A Writer's Guide to Crafting Killer Sentences.* Berkeley: Ten Speed Press, 2010. Print.

The Chicago Manual of Style. 15th ed. Chicago: University of Chicago Press, 2003. Print.

Child, Julia. "Julia Child Quotes." *Brainyquote*. BookRags
Media Network. 2001–2013. Web. 23 Jul. 2013.

———. "Julia Child—Quotes." *Goodreads*. 2013. Web. 23
Jul. 2013.

———. "Top 20 Julia Child Quotes." *Matchbook: Field Guide
to a Charmed Life*. 15 Apr. 2013. Web. 23 Jul. 2013.

Chocolat. Dir. Lasse Hallström. Perf. Juliette Binoche,
Johnny Depp, Alfred Molina, Lena Olin, Judi Dench.
Miramax, 2000. Film.

Christ, Henry I., and J. C. Tressler. *Heath Handbook of
English*. Boston: D. C. Heath, 1961. Print.

Clines, Raymond H., and Elizabeth R. Cobb. *Research
Writing Simplified: A Documentation Guide*. 3rd ed.
Addison Wesley Longman, 2000. Print.

The College Board. "Resume-Writing 101: Get Your
Resume in Shape for Jobs and Internships." 2006.
CollegeBoard.com. Web. 21 Feb. 2006.

Collins, Suzanne. *The Hunger Games*. New York: Scholastic
Press, 2008. Print.

"A Cost of Corporate Jargon?" The Public Relations Society
of America *Strategist*, Spring 2003: 3. Qtd. in Douglas
J. Swanson. Home page. University of Wisconsin–
LaCrosse. Web. 18 Feb. 2003.

Crash. Written and directed by Paul Haggis. Perf. Don
Cheadle, Matt Dillon, Ryan Phillippe, Sandra Bullock,
Terrence Howard, and Thandie Newton. Lionsgate,
2005. Film.

"Culinary Terms." *Lowfat Lifestyle*. 2002. Web. 13 Dec. 2005.

"A Cup of Joe." *h2g2* 10 Oct. 2003. BBC. Web. 24 Jan. 2006.

The Cutting Edge: The Magic of Movie Editing. Written by
Mark Jonathan Harris. Dir. Wendy Apple. Narrated
by Kathy Bates. Starz! Encore Entertainment,
2004. Film.

Dartmouth Writing Program. Dartmouth College. 2004.
Web. 10 Nov. 2012.

Delwiche, Aaron. "Introduction: Why Think about
Propaganda?" *Propaganda Critic* 29 Sep. 2002.
Web. 16 Feb. 2006.

"Drinking Age ProCon.org." *ProCon.org*. 15 Jul. 2013. Web.
18 Jul. 2013.

Dundes, Alan. "Seeing Is Believing." *Interpreting Folklore*.
Bloomington: Indiana University Press, 1980. 86–92.
Print.

Dye, Elizabeth. "Straight Out of Brooklyn." *Willamette
Week Online* 16 June 2004. Web. 14 Dec. 2005.

Elbow, Peter. "The Music of Form: Rethinking
Organization in Writing." *College Composition and
Communication* 57.4 (2006): 620–666. Print.

———. *Writing with Power: Techniques for Mastering the
Writing Process*. New York: Oxford University Press,
1981. Print.

———. *Writing without Teachers*. New York: Oxford
University Press, 1973, 1998. Print.

Eldred, Tony. "Let's Make It Hard for People to Buy Stuff."
Eldred Hospitality Management Specialists 2006. Web. 24
Jan. 2006.

Elmore, Sam. "A Blank Page." *Get the News.net*. 1994. Web.
16 Nov. 2005.

Finding Forrester. Dir. Gus van Sant. Perf. Sean Connery,
Rob Brown, and F. Murray Abraham. Written by Mike
Rich. Columbia Pictures, 2000. Film.

Fisher, M. F. K. Foreword. *The Art of Eating*. Hoboken:
Wiley, 2004. 353. Print.

———. "Love and Death Among the Molluscs." *The Art of
Eating*. Hoboken: Wiley, 2004. 125–8. Print.

Foote, Jon. "Jargon." *E-mail Humor*. Planet Footey. 2002.
Web. 24 Jan. 2006.

Friedman, Steven Morgan. "Incomprehensible Business
Jargon." *WestEgg.com*. Web. 10 Mar. 2006.

Germano, William. "Passive Is Spoken Here." *The Chronicle
of Higher Education* 22 Apr. 2005: B20. Print.

Gibaldi, Joseph. *MLA Handbook for Writers of Research
Papers*. 6th ed. New York: Modern Language
Association, 2003. Print.

The Girl with the Dragon Tattoo. Dir. David Fincher. Based
on the novel by Stieg Larsson. Perf. Rooney Mara,
Daniel Craig, and Christopher Plummer. Columbia
Pictures, 2011. Film.

"Glossary of Internet & Web Jargon." *UC Berkeley—Teaching
Library Internet Workshops*. University of California at
Berkeley. Web. 10 Mar. 2006.

"Grammar Guide." *GrammarStation.com*. 2002. Web. 18 Nov. 2005.

Grandin, Temple. "How Does Visual Thinking Work in the Mind of a Person with Autism? A Personal Account." *Phil. Trans. R. Soc. B* 364 (2009): 1437–1442. *Dr. Temple Grandin's Web Page*. Web. 26 Apr. 2013.

Greenbaum, Sidney, and Randolph Quirk. *A Student's Grammar of the English Language*. Longman Group UK Limited, 1990. Print.

Guide to Grammar and Writing. Capital Community College Foundation. Web. 26 Mar. 2013. <http://www.grammar.ccc.commnet.edu/grammar>.

Guy, Alfred E., Jr. "Process Writing: Reflection and the Arts of Writing and Teaching." *Writing-Based Teaching: Essential Practices and Enduring Questions*. Ed. Teresa Vilardi and Mary Chang. Albany: State University of New York Press, 2009. 53–70. Print.

Hacker, Diana. *The Bedford Handbook*. 6th ed. Instructor's Annotated Edition. Boston: Bedford/St. Martin's, 2002. Print.

Hairston, Maxine. "Not All Errors Are Created Equal: Nonacademic Readers in the Professions Respond to Lapses in Usage." *College English* 43.8 (Dec. 1981): 794–806. Print.

Hall, Donald. "Four Kinds of Reading." *Thinking in Writing*. 2nd ed. Ed. Donald McQuade and Robert Atwan. New York: Knopf, 1983. 163–166. Print.

Hayward, Denyse V., and Linda M. Phillips. "The Relationship between Spelling and Reading Ability." *Encyclopedia of Language and Literacy Development*. 20 Sep 2012. Web. 21 Jul. 2013.

Heinrichs, Jay. *Thank You for Arguing: What Aristotle, Lincoln, and Homer Simpson Can Teach Us about the Art of Persuasion*. New York: Three Rivers Press, 2007. Print.

Herbst, Sharon Tyler. *The New Food Lover's Companion: Comprehensive Definitions of Nearly 6,000 Food, Drink, and Culinary Terms*. Hauppauge, NY: Barron's Cooking Guide, 2001. Print.

Hooker, Richard J. *The Book of Chowder*. Boston: The Harvard Common Press, 1978. Print.

Hult, Christine A. *Researching and Writing across the Curriculum*. Needham Heights, MA: Boston: Allyn & Bacon, 1996. Print.

The Hunger Games. Screenplay by Gary Ross and Suzanne Collins. Based on the book by Suzanne Collins. Perf. Jennifer Lawrence, Josh Hutcherson, and Woody Harrelson. Lionsgate, 2012. Film.

Iyer, Pico. "In Praise of the Humble Comma." *TIME Magazine* 24 Jun. 2001. Web. 5 Apr. 2012.

Jacob, Dianne. *Will Write for Food*. New York: Marlowe, 2005. Print.

"Jargon Buster: Winter Sports." *Virgin.net*. Web. 19 Feb. 2006.

"Job Search: Cover Letters." *Career Services @ Virginia Tech*. Virginia Tech. 14 Feb. 2006. Web. 21 Feb. 2006.

"Job Search: Resumes and Vitae." *Career Services @ Virginia Tech*. Virginia Tech. 26 Jan. 2005. Web. 21 Feb. 2006.

Jogalekar, Ashutosh. "Chocolate Consumption and Nobel Prizes: A Bizarre Juxtaposition If There Ever Was One." *The Curious Wavefunction: Scientific American Blog Network* 12 Nov. 2012. Web. 25 May 2013.

Jones, Judith. "1 Tsp. of Prose, Recipes to Taste." *New York Times* 8 Dec. 2004. Reprinted in *Best Food Writing 2005*. Ed. Holly Hughes. New York: Marlowe & Company, 2005. 86–89. Print.

Jones, Susan. "The Importance of Spelling." *Spelling City*. Web. 21 Jul. 2013.

Kelly, William J., and Deborah L. Lawton. *Odyssey: A Guide to Better Writing*. 2nd ed. Boston: Allyn & Bacon, 2000. Print.

Kemmer, Suzanne. "Modern Usage of English: Medical Jargon." Home page. Rice University. 2003. Web. 10 Mar. 2006.

Kennedy, X. J., and Dana Gioia. *Backpack Literature: An Introduction to Fiction, Poetry, Drama, and Writing*. 4th ed. Boston: Pearson, 2010. Print.

Kennedy, X. J., Dorothy M. Kennedy, and Jane E. Aaron. *The Bedford Reader*. 11th ed. Boston: Bedford/St. Martin's, 2012. Print.

Kimball, Cornell. "A Study of Some of the Most Commonly Misspelled Words." David Barnsdale. Web. 13 Dec. 2005 <http://www.barnsdle.demon.co.uk/spell/error.html>.

Kirszner, Laurie G., and Stephen R. Mandell. *Patterns in College Writing: A Rhetorical Reader and Guide*. 7th ed. New York: St. Martin's Press, 1998. Print.

Kliff, Sarah. "No, Congress Did Not Declare Pizza a Vegetable." *The Washington Post* 12 Nov. 2011. Web. 9 Apr. 2012.

Liebman, Bonnie. "Designed to Sell." *Nutrition Action Healthletter* (Oct. 2006): 8–9. Print.

List, Carla. *An Introduction to Information Research*. Dubuque, Iowa: Kendall/Hunt, 1998. Print.

Lockley, JoLynne. "Resume Tips for Culinary Professionals." *CookingSchools.com*. Web. 21 Feb. 2006.

Lopate, Phillip. Introduction. *The Art of the Personal Essay: An Anthology from the Classical Era to the Present*. Ed. Phillip Lopate. New York: Anchor Books, 1995. xxiii–liv. Print.

Lunsford, Andrea A., John J. Ruszkiewicz, and Keith Walters. *Everything's an Argument/with Readings*. 5th ed. Boston: Bedford, 2010. Print.

Maddox, Garry. "How Experts Get Movie Titles Wrong." *The Sydney Morning Herald Blogs: Entertainment*. 12 Oct. 2005. *The Sydney Morning Herald*. Web. 22 Jan. 2006.

McAdams, Mindy. "A Spelling Test." 21 Nov. 1995. Home Page. Sentex Communication Corps. Web. 13 Dec. 2005.

McGee, Harold. *On Food and Cooking: The Science and Lore of the Kitchen*. 1984. New York: Collier Books, 1988. Print.

———. *On Food and Cooking: The Science and Lore of the Kitchen*. Rev. ed. New York: Scribner, 2004. Print.

McWhorter, John. "Talking with Your Fingers." *The New York Times* 23 Apr. 2012. Web. 26 Apr. 2012.

Melville, Herman. *Moby-Dick or, The Whale*. 1851.

Memento. Dir. Christopher Nolan. Perf. Guy Pearce, Carrie-Anne Moss, and Joe Pantoliano. Newmarket Entertainment, 2001. Film.

Messerti, Frank H., MD. "Chocolate Consumption, Cognitive Function, and Nobel Laureates." *New England Journal of Medicine* 367 (18 Oct. 2012):1562–4. Web. 25 May 2013.

Meyer, Danny. *Setting the Table: The Transforming Power of Hospitality in Business*. New York: HarperCollins, 2006. Print.

Milne, A. A. "A Word for Autumn." *Not That It Matters*. 1920.

Miss Congeniality. Perf. Sandra Bullock, Michael Caine, Candice Bergen, Benjamin Bratt, and William Shatner. Dir. Donald Petrie. Warner Brothers, 2000. Film.

Missouri Department of Conservation. "Safe Mushroom Hunting." *The Weather Channel*. Web. 22 Apr. 2013.

Moats, Louisa C. "How Spelling Supports Reading and Why It Is More Predictable Than You May Think." *American Educator* Winter 2005/2006: 12–43. Print.

Modern Language Association. *MLA Handbook for Writers of Research Papers*. 7th ed. New York: Modern Language Association of America, 2009. Print.

Murray, Donald H. "The Maker's Eye: Revising Your Own Manuscripts." 1973. Reprinted in *Language Awareness: Readings for College Writers*. Ed. Paul Escholz, Alfred Rosa, and Virginia Clark. 8th ed. Boston: Bedford/St. Martin's, 2000. 161–5. Print.

Mystic River. Dir. Clint Eastwood. Perf. Sean Penn, Tim Robbins, Kevin Bacon, Marcia Gay Harden, and Laura Linney. Screenplay by Brian Helgeland. Based on the novel by Dennis Lehane. Warner Brothers, 2003. Film.

Noble, Ann C. *The Wine Aroma Wheel*. Web. 13 Aug. 2006.

OWL Online Writing Lab. Online Writing Lab at Purdue University. 2004. Web. 5 Feb. 2012.

Parker, Jackie. "The Music of Language." *Academic Exchange*. January 5, 2012. Web. 5 Apr. 2012.

Paul, Annie Murphy. "Your Brain on Fiction." *The New York Times Sunday Review* 17 Mar. 2012. Web. 26 Apr. 2012.

Peha, Steve. *Teaching That Makes Sense*. 2003. Teaching That Makes Sense, Inc. Web. 10 May 2006.

Pink, Daniel H. *A Whole New Mind: Moving from the Information Age to the Conceptual Age*. New York: Riverhead, 2005. Print.

Pinker, Steven. "Chasing the Jargon Jitters." *TIME Magazine* 13 Nov. 1995. Web. 24 Jan. 2006.

<http://pinker.wjh.harvard.edu/articles/media/1995_11_13_time.html>.

Pollan, Michael. *The Omnivore's Dilemma*. New York: Penguin, 2006. Print.

Powell, John. *How Music Works: The Science and Psychology of Beautiful Sounds, from Beethoven to the Beatles and Beyond*. New York: Little, Brown, 2010. Print.

Pulp Fiction. Written and directed by Quentin Tarantino. Perf. John Travolta, Samuel L. Jackson, Uma Thurman, Harvey Keitel, and Tim Roth. Miramax, 1994. Film.

Rader, Walter. *Online Slang Dictionary*. Home page. University of California at Berkeley. 2003. Web. 24 Jan. 2006.

"Resumes." *StarChefs Job Finder*. StarChefs: The Magazine for Culinary Insiders, 2005. Web. 21 Feb. 2006.

A River Runs Through It. Dir. Robert Redford. Story by Norman McLean. Perf. Craig Sheffer, Brad Pitt, and Tom Skerrit. Columbia Pictures, 1992.

Rombauer, Irma S., and Marion Rombauer Becker. *Joy of Cooking*. Indianapolis: Bobbs-Merrill, 1975. Print.

Rubino, Robert. "Let's Stop the Sports/War Jargon Swap." *Northern California ACES: A Chapter of the American Copy Editors Society*. 3 Nov. 2003. Web. 19 Feb. 2006.

Saving Private Ryan. Dir. Steven Spielberg. Perf. Tom Hanks, Matt Damon, Edward Burns, and Tom Sizemore. DreamWorks SKG, 1998. Film.

Savoie, Sean. "The Cadence of Great Writing." *Reflexive English Language Training*. 2002. Web. 26 Apr. 2012.

Schrobsdorff, Susanna. "Attack of the Weasel Words." *Newsweek*. 13 Jul. 2005. *MSNBC.com*. Web. 18 Feb. 2006.

The Shipping News. Dir. Lasse Hallström. Based on the novel by E. Annie Proulx. Perf. Kevin Spacey, Judi Dench, Julianne Moore, Cate Blanchett, and Pete Postlethwaite. Miramax, 2001. Film.

Simmons, Robin L. *Grammar Bytes! Grammar Instruction with Attitude*. Web. 3 Aug. 2005. <http://www.chompchomp.com/terms/relativeclause.htm>.

Stand and Deliver. Written by Ramón Menéndez and Tom Musca. Dir Ramón Menéndez. Perf. Edward James Olmos and Lou Diamond Phillips. Warner Bros., 1998. Film.

Stone Writing Center @ Del Mar College. Del Mar College. Web. 21 Feb. 2006.

Straker, David. *Changing Minds*. 2002–2013. Web. 13 Apr. 2012.

Straus, Jane. *The Blue Book of Grammar and Punctuation*. 8th ed. 2004. Pub. Jane Straus. Web. 18 Nov. 2005.

Strunk, William, Jr. "Words Often Misspelled." *The Elements of Style*. 1918. *Bartleby.com: Great Books Online*. Web. 13 Dec. 2005.

Stuckey, Barb. *Taste: Surprising Stories and Science about Why Food Tastes Good*. New York: Atria, 2012. 106–108. Print.

Sudden Impact. Dir. Clint Eastwood. Perf. Clint Eastwood and Sondra Locke. Warner Brothers, 1983. Film.

Super Size Me. Dir. Morgan Spurlock. Showtime Independent Films, 2004. Film.

"Talk the Talk." *iVillage: The Website for Women*. NBC Universal. Web. 18 Feb. 2006.

Temple Grandin. Based on Temple Grandin's books *Emergence: Labeled Autistic* and *Thinking in Pictures*. Perf. Claire Danes, Julia Ormond, and David Strathairn. Home Box Office (HBO), 2010. Film.

Terkel, Studs. "Interview with Lane Tech High School Students," Parts 1–3. *Studs Terkel: Conversations with America*. Radio broadcast. Chicago Historical Society. 2002. Web. 11 Mar 2006.

Terminator 2: Judgment Day. Dir. James Cameron. Perf. Arnold Schwarzenegger, Linda Hamilton, and Robert Patrick. TriStar Pictures, 1991. Film.

Tortilla Soup. Perf. Hector Elizondo, Elizabeth Peña, and Raquel Welch. Based on *Eat Drink Man Woman*. Samuel Goldwyn Company, 2001. Film.

Truss, Lynne. *Eats, Shoots & Leaves*. New York: Gotham Books, 2003. Print.

The University of West Florida Writing Lab. The University of West Florida. 2003. Web. 18 Nov. 2005.

Vilardi, Teresa, and Mary Chang, eds. *Writing-Based Teaching: Essential Practices and Enduring Questions*. Albany: State University of New York Press, 2009. Print.

Vowell, Sarah. "Shooting Dad." *Take the Cannoli: Stories from the New World*. New York: Simon & Schuster, 2000. 15–24. Print.

Walston, John. *BuzzWhack.com*. Web. 18 Feb. 2006.

Warriner, John E. *English Composition and Grammar*. Benchmark ed. Orlando: Harcourt Brace Jovanovich, 1988. Print.

Warriner, John E., and Francis Griffith. *English Grammar and Composition*. Rev. ed. New York: Harcourt, Brace & World, 1965. Print.

Wartman, Kristin. "Pizza Is a Vegetable? Congress Defies Logic, Betrays Our Children." *The Huffington Post*. 18 Nov. 2011. Web. 9 Apr. 2012.

Watson, Don. *WeaselWords.com.au*. Web. 18 Feb. 2006.

"Wine Terms." *Tasting Wine*. Web. 19 Feb. 2006.

The Wizard of Oz. Dir. Victor Fleming. Perf. Judy Garland, Frank Morgan, and Ray Bolger. Metro Goldwyn Mayer, 1939. Film.

The Writing Center. University of North Carolina at Chapel Hill. 2010–2013. Web. 9 Apr. 2012.

"Writing Your Resume." *Okanaga College*. Cooperative Education, Graduate and Student Employment Center, Okanaga College. Web. 21 Feb. 2006.

Yarber, Mary Laine, and Robert E. *Reviewing Basic Grammar: A Guide to Writing Sentences and Paragraphs*. 5th ed. New York: Longman, 2001. Print.

YourDictionary.com. "100 Most Often Misspelled Words in English." YourDictionary.com. 2005. Web. 13 Dec. 2005.

INDEX